THE SERIAL KILLER FILES

Also by Harold Schechter

Nonfiction

Deviant: The Shocking True Story of Ed Gein, the Original "Psycho"

Deranged: The Shocking True Story of America's Most Fiendish Killer

Fiend: The Shocking True Story of America's Youngest Serial Killer

Fatal: The Poisonous Life of a Female Serial Killer

Bestial: The Savage Trail of a True American Monster

The A to Z Encyclopedia of Serial Killers (with David Everitt)

The Devil's Gentleman: Privilege, Poison, and the Trial that Ushered in the Twentieth Century

Depraved: The Shocking True Story of America's First Serial Killer

True Crime: An American Anthology

The Whole Death Catalog

Killer Colt: Murder, Disgrace, and the Making of an American Legend

Fiction

Outcry

Nevermore

The Hum Bug

The Mask of Red Death

The Tell-Tale Corpse

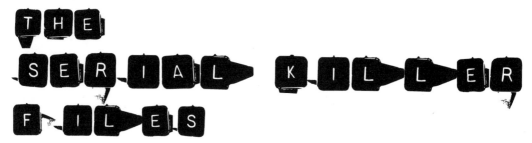

THE SERIAL KILLER FILES

The Who, What, Where, How, and Why of the World's Most Terrifying Murderers

Harold Schechter

Ballantine Books • New York

A Ballantine Book

Published by The Random House Publishing Group

www.ballantinebooks.com

Book design by Meryl Sussman Levavi/Digitext

Library of Congress Cataloging-in-Publication Data

Schechter, Harold
The serial killer files : the who, what, where, how, and why of the world's most terrifying murderers / Harold Schechter.—1st ed.
p. cm.
Includes bibliographical references and index.
ISBN 0-345-46566-0 (pbk.)
1. Serial murders—History. 2. Serial murderers. I. Title.

HV6505.S34 2004
364.152'3—dc22
2003062982

Manufactured in the United States of America

First Edition: January 2004

10 9

for

Joe and Whitney

CONTENTS

INTRODUCTION

There are people who genuinely believe that serial killers are a strictly contemporary phenomenon, a symptom of something horribly amiss in the moral fabric of modern American society. The public's intense fascination with sensational crime (demonstrated so dramatically in the fall of 2002, when the airwaves were filled with twenty-four/seven coverage of the so-called Beltway Sniper rampage in the Washington, DC area) has likewise been viewed as depressing proof of our supposed cultural decline.

Since the purpose of this book is to provide the most accurate information about the subject of serial killers, let's begin by considering a pair of images that should help correct these common misconceptions.

The first, at the top of the following page, shows a child-snatcher who has just decapitated a little victim after assaulting her in the woods. The picture comes from a nineteenth-century publication called the *Illustrated Police News* of London. Like today's supermarket tabloids, this weekly periodical ran stories about all sorts of bizarre phenomena, from ghostly visitations to encounters with sea serpents. Its real speciality, however, was grisly true crime—real-life accounts of atrocious murders, accompanied by graphic illustrations. Largely because of its emphasis on gore, the *Illustrated Police News* had the highest circulation of any publication in Victorian England.

The second image, below, is by the famous Mexican artist, José Guadalupe Posada (1852–1913). It shows a homicidal maniac named Francisco Guerrero, the "slitter of women's throats," committing an atrocity upon an unnamed victim in 1887. This illustration was one of thousands Posada produced for mass reproduction in the form of "broadsides"—one-page ac-

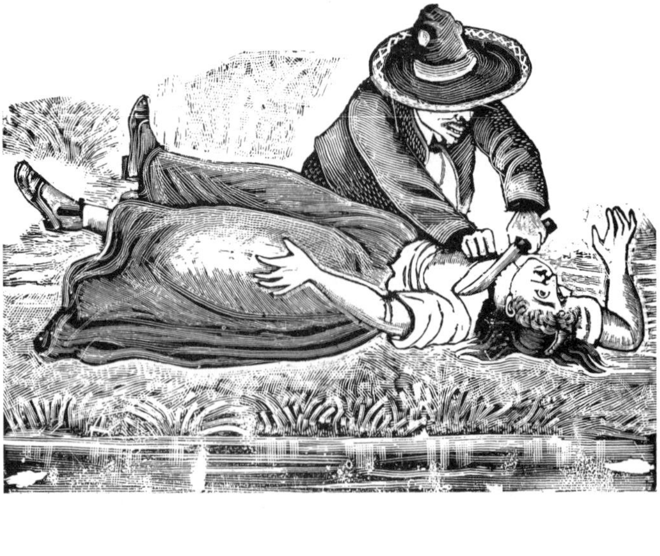

counts of sensational news events, the vast bulk of which dealt with shockingly violent crimes.

Though Posada has long been recognized as a significant artist, neither his illustration nor the anonymous one from the *Illustrated Police News* was meant to be great art. They were created strictly for commercial purposes: to sell papers by appealing to the public's taste for gruesome horror. Certainly, they weren't supposed to be educational in any way. Nevertheless, there are several lessons we can draw from them:

Serial killers have always existed. They just weren't called serial killers in the old days. Back when these two pictures were first published, for example, newspapers often described such criminals in supernatural terms: "murder fiends" or "bloodthirsty monsters" or "devils in human shape."

In addition to the legendary ones that everyone has heard about, like Jack the Ripper (an exact contemporary of the two long-forgotten murderers in these illustrations), there are many serial killers who, for whatever reason, never achieve lasting notoriety. Lots of them, however, commit crimes every bit as hideous as those perpetrated by more infamous killers.

Serial murderers aren't limited to the United States. They can be found in England, in Mexico—in fact, all around the world.

There's nothing new about the interest in serial murder. People have always been fascinated by it. They want every last grisly detail, preferably with accompanying pictures. Nowadays we have twenty-four-hour news channels to satisfy that need. A hundred years ago, when cheap, mass-produced printing was state-of-the-art, there were illustrated tabloids. Only the technology has changed. The public's appetite for sensational true-crime stories has remained exactly the same.

This final point offers further food for thought. Given how deeply unsettling the subject of serial murder is, it's legitimate to wonder *why* it has always possessed such popular appeal. Why do so many people want to see pictures, hear stories, and read books (like this one) about such morbid matters?

One clue to this mystery is suggested by the great nineteenth-century American poet Emily Dickinson. Though the popular image of the "Belle of Amherst" is of a prim Victorian spinster, Dickinson was, in fact, a tough-minded person with a taste for newspaper sensationalism (in one of her letters, she confesses her fondness for stories about fatal train wrecks and factory accidents where "gentlemen get their heads cut off quite informally"). One of Dickinson's most memorable poems, "One need not be a Chamber—to be Haunted," deals with the fact that everyone, even the most law-abiding person, possesses a hidden side that is fascinated with the forbidden. One stanza from the poem goes:

> Ourself behind ourself concealed—
> Should startle most—
> Assassin hid in our Apartment
> Be Horror's least.

Dickinson is referring to the part of the human personality that psychologists call "the shadow": the brutish Mr. Hyde that lurks beneath the proper veneer of our civilized selves and that loves to dream about all kinds of taboo experiences.

Of course, to say that all of us have a shadow side that revels in lawless fantasies does not mean that everyone is a potential serial killer. There is a world of difference between thought and action, between dreaming and doing. Indeed, one of the distinguishing characteristics of serial killers is precisely their willingness to step over that line and turn their twisted fantasies into nightmarish reality. Plato made this point several thousand years ago when he wrote: "The virtuous man is content to dream what the wicked man really does."

The doings of those supremely wicked people we call serial killers—and the dark dreams they inspire in the rest of us—are the subject of this book.

WHAT IT MEANS

ORIGIN OF THE TERM

One reason people tend to think that serial murder is a frighteningly new phenomenon is that, until about twenty years ago, no one ever heard of such a thing. For most of the twentieth century, the news media never referred to serial killers. But that isn't because homicidal psychos didn't exist in the past.

Indeed, one of the most infamous American serial killers of all time, Albert Fish, committed his atrocities around the time of the Great Depression. After his arrest, his unspeakable crimes were covered extensively by the newspapers. Nowhere, however, is Fish described as a serial killer. The reason is simple. The phrase hadn't been invented yet. Back then, the type of crime we now define as serial murder was simply lumped together under the general rubric of "mass murder."

Credit for coining the phrase "serial killer" is commonly given to former FBI Special Agent Robert Ressler, one of the founding members of the Bureau's elite Behavioral Science Unit (aka the "Mind Hunters" or the "Psyche Squad"). Along with his colleague John Douglas, Ressler served as a model for the character Jack Crawford in Thomas Harris's Hannibal Lecter trilogy.

In his 1992 memoir, *Whoever Fights Monsters,* Ressler writes that, in the

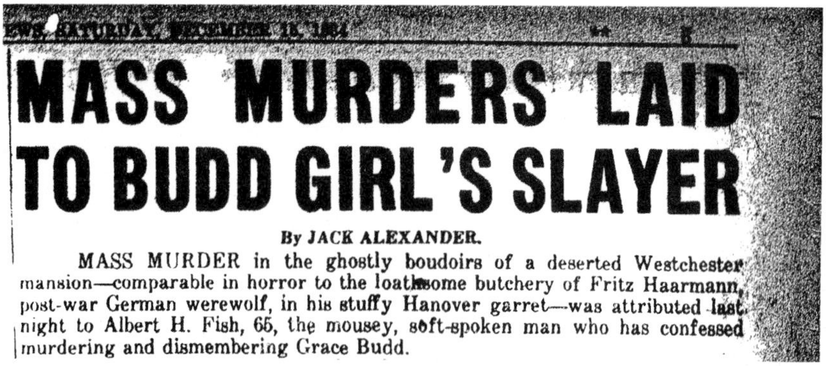

MASS MURDERS LAID TO BUDD GIRL'S SLAYER

By JACK ALEXANDER.

MASS MURDER in the ghostly boudoirs of a deserted Westchester mansion—comparable in horror to the loathsome butchery of Fritz Haarmann, post-war German werewolf, in his stuffy Hanover garret—was attributed last night to Albert H. Fish, 65, the mousey, soft-spoken man who has confessed murdering and dismembering Grace Budd.

early 1970s, while attending a weeklong conference at the British police academy, he heard a fellow participant refer to "crimes in series," meaning "a series of rapes, burglaries, arsons, or murders." Ressler was so impressed by the phrase that, upon returning to Quantico, he began to use the term "serial killer" in his own lectures to describe "the killing of those who do one murder, then another and another in a fairly repetitive way."

In thinking up the term, Ressler also says he had in mind the movie-matinee adventure serials of his boyhood: *Spy Smasher, Flash Gordon, The Masked Marvel,* etc. Like a child looking forward to the latest installment of his favorite cliffhanger, the serial killer can't wait to commit his next atrocity.

That is Ressler's version of how he came to invent the phrase that has now become such a vital part of our language. There is just one problem with the story. There is documented proof that the expression "serial murderer" existed at least a dozen years before Ressler supposedly invented it.

According to Jesse Sheidlower, editor of the major new revision of the *Oxford English Dictionary,* the term can be traced as far back as 1961, where it appears in a citation from *Merriam-Webster's Third New International Dictionary.* The quote, which is attributed to the German critic Siegfried Kracauer, is:

> [He] denies that he is the pursued serial murderer.
>
> —first documented use of the term "serial murderer," as it appears in *Merriam-Webster's 1961 Third New International Dictionary*

By the mid-1960s, the term "serial murderer" had become common enough, at least overseas, that it was used repeatedly in the 1966 book *The Meaning of Murder* by the British writer John Brophy.

> Jack the Ripper, still unidentified and still the most famous of all serial murderers, was not altogether true to type. The typical serial murderer kills once too often and gets caught.
>
> —from *The Meaning of Murder* (New York: Thomas Y. Crowell, 1966), p. 189

It's possible that, during his visit to England (where Brophy's book was originally published), Ressler picked up the term, perhaps subliminally. To give credit where it is due, it was evidently Ressler who altered the phrase from "serial *murderer*" to the slightly more punchy "serial *killer.*"

In any event, if he can't really be credited with coining the expression, Ressler certainly helped introduce it into American culture. Surprisingly, it did not enter into common usage until quite recently. The earliest published example of the phrase "serial killer" that the editors of the *Oxford English Dictionary* have been able to come up with is only twenty years old. It comes from the article "Leading the Hunt in Atlanta's Murders" by M. A. Farber, published in the May 3, 1981, issue of the *New York Times Magazine.*

Here, reprinted for the first time, is the passage containing the first known published use of the term "serial killer":

> Someone, raising a question that trails Brown from forum to forum, asks about race and the murders. Some Atlantans fear racial violence if a "serial" killer is discovered to be white.

DEFINITIONS

Since the term "serial killer" was invented to describe a specific type of criminal, you'd think the definition would be clear-cut. However, confusion surrounds the term. Even the experts can't agree.

Let's start with the official FBI definition:

> Three or more separate events in three or more separate locations with an emotional cooling-off period between homicides.
>
> —FBI *Crime Classification Manual* (1992)

This definition stresses three elements:

1. *Quantity.* There have to be at least three murders.
2. *Place.* The murders have to occur at different locations.
3. *Time.* There has to be a "cooling-off period"—an interval between the murders that can last anywhere from several hours to several years.

The last two characteristics are meant to differentiate serial killing from *mass murder,* in which a suicidal, rage-filled individual slaughters a bunch of people at once: a disgruntled employee, for example, who shows up at his office with an automatic weapon and blows away a half dozen coworkers before turning the gun on himself.

There are several problems with the FBI definition. In one respect, it's much too *broad,* since it can be applied to homicidal types who aren't serial killers: professional hit men, for example, or Western outlaws like William "Billy the Kid" Bonney, who is said to have gunned down twenty-one men before he reached the age of twenty-one. "Mad bombers" like Ted Kaczynski also meet the FBI's criteria. But none of these types match the common conception of a serial killer.

In another respect, the FBI definition is overly *narrow,* since it specifies that a serial killer has to commit his crimes "in three or more separate locations." To be sure, some serial killers range far and wide in their search for prey. Ted Bundy, for example, murdered women in several different states. Others, however, prefer to do their dirty work in one place. John Wayne Gacy, for example, turned the basement of his suburban split-level into a private torture chamber and even disposed of his victims' remains at home, stashing them in the crawl space until he ran out of room.

The main defect in the FBI definition, however, is what's missing from it—namely, any sense of the specific *nature* of the crimes. When Siegfried Kracauer first used the term "serial murderer," he was discussing the character played by Peter Lorre in Fritz Lang's classic movie, *M:* a repulsive, moon-faced pervert who preys on little girls. A few years later, John Brophy used it to describe killers like Jack the Ripper and Earle Leonard Nelson, the infamous "Gorilla Murderer" of the 1920s who strangled and raped several dozen women across the United States and up into Canada. And when Robert Ressler and his colleagues in the Behavioral Science Unit adopted the term in the 1970s, they applied it to homicidal psychopaths like Ted Bundy, John Wayne Gacy, and Edmund Kemper. In all these cases, there was one common thread: a strong component of depraved sexuality.

Recognizing this fact, some experts stress the sexual motivations behind serial murder, defining it as the act of ultraviolent deviants, who get twisted pleasure from inflicting extreme harm on their victims and who will keep on committing their atrocities until they are stopped.

Of course, there are criminals who match this profile but who can't be considered serial killers for one simple reason: they are caught after committing a single homicide. An example is James Lawson, described in the book *The Evil That Men Do* by Stephen Michaud and former FBI Special Agent Roy Hazelwood (another member of the FBI's original Mind Hunter team).

A convicted rapist, Lawson was sent to a California state mental institution, where he struck up a friendship with a fellow inmate, James Odom. The two men began sharing their fantasies of rape and murder, encouraging each other's sickest impulses and forming a bond based on their mutual depravity. No sooner were they released than they decided to put their dreams into action. Abducting a twenty-five-year-old female convenience store clerk, they drove her to an isolated location. First Odom raped her in the backseat while Lawson watched.

Then Lawson went to work on her with his knife.

> I wanted to cut her body so she would not look like a person, and destroy her so she would not exist. I began to cut on her body. I remember cutting her breasts off. After this, all I remember is that I kept cutting on her body.
>
> —James Lawson

Fortunately, the two men were traced and arrested in short order. However, Lawson's case raises an interesting question. There's no doubt that he had the mentality of a serial killer; his confession makes that brutally clear. How many women would he have had to butcher before qualifying for that label? "Three or more," according to the FBI definition. But that number seems arbitrary. Let's suppose that, over the span of several weeks, the police in a small California town had found the remains of *two* female victims, killed and mutilated in the same way. Wouldn't they be justified in suspecting that a serial killer was on the loose?

These flaws in the FBI definition are rectified in another, more flexible one formulated by the National Institutes of Justice, which many authorities regard as a more accurate description:

> A series of two or more murders, committed as separate events, usually, but not always, by one offender acting alone. The crimes may occur over a period of time ranging from hours to years. Quite often the motive is psychological, and the offender's behavior and the physical evidence observed at the crime scenes will reflect sadistic, sexual overtones.
>
> —National Institutes of Justice

CATEGORIES OF CARNAGE: SERIAL/MASS/SPREE

Though people sometimes confuse the terms and use them interchangeably, there are important differences between serial murder and the other major types of multiple homicide, *mass murder* and *spree killing*.

For the most part, serial murder is a sex crime, a fact that accounts for its distinctive features. The classic pattern of serial murder is a grotesque travesty of normal sexual functioning.

Most people who haven't had sex for a while begin to crave it more and more. They daydream about it. In vulgar terms, they grow increasingly horny. If unattached, they eventually seek out a willing partner. Once they've gratified their sexual urges, the need subsides for a certain period of time.

In a parallel way, the serial killer spends his time fantasizing about dominance, torture, and murder. In effect, he grows horny for blood. When his twisted desires get too strong to resist, he goes prowling for unwitting prey. His excitement reaches a climax with the suffering and death of the victim. Afterward, he experiences a "cooling-off" period. (This is somewhat of a misnomer since it is during this lull between crimes that the killer's bloodlust begins to build again. It would be more accurate to describe it as a "cooling-off/heating-up" period.) During this time, he may make use of "trophies" he has taken from a murder scene to relive the crime in his mind, savoring the memory of his victim's suffering.

In short, their unspeakable acts are a source of supreme pleasure to serial killers, who achieve the highest pitch of arousal—even to the point of orgasm—by inflicting savage harm on other human beings. Because doing terrible things feels so good to them, serial killers try not to get caught, so they can keep on enjoying their atrocities for as long as possible.

Mass Murder

Apart from the fact that they both involve multiple homicides, mass murder and serial killing have almost nothing in common.

Whereas the serial killer is often described as a predator, the mass murderer is stereotypically defined as a "human time bomb." Though there have been a number of female mass murderers, the great preponderance are male. In general, the mass murderer is someone whose life has come unraveled—who has been thrown out by his wife or fired from his job or suffered some other humiliating blow that pushes him over the edge. Filled with an annihilating rage at everything he blames for his failure, he explodes in a burst of devastating violence that wipes out everyone within range (a phenomenon that has entered slang as "going postal," a sardonic tribute to the number of US Postal Service workers who seem to have perpetrated such acts).

If serial murder is, in essence, a sex crime, mass murder is almost always a suicidal one. In blind, apocalyptic fury, the mass murderer has decided to go out with a bang and take as many people with him as possible. Typically, once the bloodbath is over, the mass murderer will either end his own life or provoke a fatal shoot-out with the police ("suicide by cop," as it is called).

> Someday before I kill myself, I'll bring some people down with me.
>
> —Sylvia Seegrist, mass murderer

Since his intention is to blow away as many people as possible, the mass murderer almost always uses firearms. This is in marked contrast to most serial killers, who (with notable exceptions like David "Son of Sam" Berkowitz and Zodiac) prefer the sadistic "hands-on" thrill of stabbing, strangling, mauling, and mutilating.

A key element of mass murder is that, by definition, it occurs in a single location. Indeed, it is this factor, as much as anything else, that amounts for the devastating nature of the crime. The mass murderer is someone who—like a suicide bomber—detonates without warning in a restaurant, a playground, a schoolroom, an office, or even (as in the 1999 case of Larry Gene Ashbrook) a church, turning a safe, familiar setting into the scene of a corpse-strewn massacre.

Though mass murderers don't exert the same morbid fascination as serial killers—largely because their crimes are less sensationally gruesome and sexually perverted—they often run up substantial body counts. Charles Whitman, for example—the Texas Tower sniper who, on August 1, 1966, barricaded himself on the observation deck overlooking the University of Texas campus and began picking off people below—killed fourteen victims in the course of his massacre. And even this grim total was surpassed by the case of James Huberty, one of the worst mass-murder episodes of modern times.

James Huberty and the McDonald's Massacre

CASE STUDY

The site was significant: a suburban McDonald's restaurant. This all-American symbol of happy family life and material satisfaction represented everything that James Oliver Huberty had struggled so hard—and failed so miserably—to achieve.

His life had been difficult from the start. His mother, a religious zealot, became a missionary and abandoned her family when James was only seven. Raised by his father, he grew up lonely and resentful, a boy whose sole companion was his dog and whose only interest was guns.

His earliest ambition, to work in a funeral home, didn't pan out. Though he received a license from the Pittsburgh Institute of Mortuary Science, he lacked the personal skills necessary for a successful mortician. "He was a good embalmer, but just didn't relate to people," was one professional assessment.

Still, he managed to prosper for a while. In 1965—at the age of twenty-three—he married his girlfriend, Etna. A few years later, they moved into a comfortable house in Massillon, Ohio. By the early seventies, Huberty was the father of two, with a good, steady job as a welder at a utility plant in nearby Canton. His family was the center of his existence. Outside of Etna and the girls, he had no social contacts. He bickered constantly with his neighbors and spent much of his spare time reading gun magazines and survivalist literature. On the whole, however, Huberty's life during this period was as stable and content as it would ever be.

The bottom fell out in the early 1980s, when hard times hit the area. The plant closed, Huberty lost his job, and—as Etna later put it—"his life came crashing in around him." After nearly six months of unemployment, he landed another job, but was soon laid off again. He started to talk of suicide—and worse.

According to an acquaintance, it was around this time that Huberty began voicing scary thoughts. "He said he had nothing to live for, no job or anything. He said that if this was the end of his making his living for his family, he was going to take everyone with him."

In late 1983, in a desperate hunt for a better life, the forty-one-year-old Huberty moved his family to San Ysidro, California, a suburb of San Diego just north of the Mexican border. He found work as a security guard, but the job didn't last. His family was forced to move again and again, each time to a slightly shabbier apartment. Huberty grew increasingly paranoid, venting his bitterness at the world. On Wednesday, July 18, 1984, after a morning trip to Traffic Court to pay a ticket, Huberty reached the end of the line. "Society had its chance," he said to his wife. In their bedroom a few hours later, he dressed in camouflage pants and a black T-shirt. His wife asked where he was going.

"Hunting humans," he said.

Not long afterward, he showed up at the local McDonald's with a semiautomatic rifle, a 9-mm pistol, a twelve-gauge shotgun, and a canvas bag full of ammo. Almost immediately, he opened fire. Seventy-five minutes later, twenty-one people were dead, many of them children, and another nineteen wounded. The massacre didn't stop until a SWAT team sniper fired a .308-caliber into James Huberty's dark heart.

Spree Killing

With one key exception, spree and mass murder are more or less identical phenomena.

Like the mass murderer, the spree killer is someone who has become so profoundly alienated and embittered that he no longer feels connected to human society. His life has amounted to nothing, and his murderous rampage is his way of bringing his intolerable existence to an explosive end. Most spree killers prefer death to surrender; others allow themselves to be captured, knowing that they will be executed or locked away forever. One way or another, their lives are over.

Two major motives fuel the spree killer's final, hate-filled act: revenge against the world and a desire to show that—all evidence to the contrary—he is a person to be reckoned with. Tormented by his failure to achieve those things that seem to come so easily to others—satisfying work, loving relationships—he will prove that he is special in at least one regard: in his power to wreak havoc.

Like the mass murderer, the spree killer sometimes targets specific victims: the boss who fired him, the professor who flunked him, the bully who made his high school years a living hell. But the randomness with which he mows down everyone unlucky enough to cross his path shows that his rage is really directed against society itself.

The defining difference between the spree killer and the mass murderer has to do with *motion.* Whereas the mass murderer slaughters in one place, the spree killer moves from site to site, killing as he goes. In that sense, spree killing might best be described as *mobile mass murder.*

In 1949, for example, a crazed ex-GI named Howard Unruh stunned the nation when he strode through his quiet New Jersey neighborhood and methodically gunned down everyone in his path.

Howard Unruh, the Retaliator

CASE STUDY

The first major spree killer of the post–World War II era, Howard Barton Unruh fit the classic profile of his kind. In the fall of 1949, he was a twenty-eight-year-old misfit, living alone with his mother in a shabby three-room apartment in East Camden, New Jersey. His empty, aimless existence couldn't have been drearier. He had no job, no friends, no prospects for the future. A closeted gay in an intensely homophobic era, he led a sordid secret life, traveling to Philadelphia several times a week for loveless sex with anonymous pickups. Otherwise, he spent much of his time playing with his toy trains or practicing pistol-shooting in a makeshift target range in his basement.

HOWARD UNRUH

(Novelty trading card courtesy of Roger Worsham)

Just a few years earlier, he had felt like *somebody.* That was in the army, where he had distinguished himself during the war as a gunner in the 342d Armored Field Artillery. Now back home, he was a nothing: an utter failure. He had tried college, enrolling in Temple University's School of Pharmacology under the GI Bill, but he had dropped out after only three months.

He became convinced that his neighbors were talking behind his back, viewing him with contempt for living off his frail, aging mother. He began to keep a diary, listing grievances against his neighbors and making little cryptic notations beside their names: "Ret.W.T.S." or "D.N.D.R."

The abbreviations stood for "Retaliate When Time Suitable" and "Do Not Delay Retaliation."

On Tuesday, September 6, 1949, the day of retaliation arrived.

Rising promptly at 8:00 A.M., Howard washed, shaved, and dressed in his best tropical-worsted suit, white shirt, and bow tie. He went into the kitchen for his breakfast, prepared as always by his doting mother, who noticed that Howard seemed strangely distracted. After polishing off fried eggs and Post Toasties, he went down to the basement, returning with a length of heavy lead pipe. Summoning his mother into the living room, he raised the pipe threateningly, as if to brain her.

"What do you want to do that for, Howard?" Mrs. Unruh stammered. Backing toward the door, she flung it open and fled the house in terror.

Howard stood for a moment. Then, shaking off his daze, he went to his bedroom, got his 9-mm Luger pistol with two loaded clips and thirty-three loose cartridges, and hit the streets.

His first stop was Pilcharik's shoe shop. The owner, John Pilcharik, was kneeling by his bench, nailing a sole onto a shoe when Unruh entered at 9:20 A.M. Unruh strode directly up to Pilcharik and, without a word, shot the cobbler in the face, then fired again into his head. He then turned and headed next door to Clark Hoover's barbershop.

Hoover was busily trimming the hair of a six-year-old boy named Orris Smith. "I've got something for you, Clarkie," Unruh said as he stepped to the chair and shot both the barber and the little boy. As the child's mother, who was seated nearby, shrieked and ran toward her dying boy, Unruh nonchalantly headed out.

Over the next ten minutes, he calmly made his way through the neighborhood, shooting victims as he went: both specific targets of his paranoid hatred and random passersby unfortunate enough to find themselves in his way. When he ran out of ammunition—less than fifteen minutes after firing his first shot into the face of Joe Pilcharik—thirteen people lay dead or dying, and another three were badly wounded.

Returning to his apartment, Unruh flopped down on his bed. Moments later, about sixty heavily armed officers surrounded the house. A ferocious gun battle ensued, ending when Unruh was driven from his room by tear gas.

As Unruh was being handcuffed, the officer asked: "What's the matter with you? You some kind of psycho?"

"I'm no psycho," Unruh indignantly said. "I have a good mind."

The state disagreed. Unruh was permanently confined to a maximum security psychiatric hospital for the criminally insane.

While Howard Unruh turned his neighborhood into a corpse-littered battleground during thirteen horrifying minutes, some spree killers cover far more territory, conducting their rampage by car over the span of days or even weeks. That was the case in late 1957, when a pair of teen hoodlums—James Dean wannabe Charles Starkweather and his underage sweetheart Caril Ann Fugate—sped across Nebraska, killing ten people over twenty-six days. In the spring of 1997, Andrew Cunanan slaughtered four men as he made his way in a succession of stolen vehicles from Minneapolis to Miami Beach in search of his ultimate target, the celebrated Italian fashion designer Gianni Versace. And in the fall of 2002, John Muhammed and his teenage protégé, Lee Malvo, allegedly terrorized Virginia, Maryland, and Washington, DC, from a blue Chevy Caprice, after first committing a pair of shootings down in Montgomery, Alabama. For a variety of reasons—the interval between shootings, the taunting messages to the police, the sinister calling card left at one crime scene—many experts assumed that a serial killer was on the loose while the sniper shootings were taking place. Once the alleged perpetrators were caught, however, it became clear that Muhammed fit the definition of a spree killer: a man with a miserably failed personal and professional life, venting his rage in a murderous vendetta against the world.

A Better Term?

Since mass and spree murder are essentially two manifestations of the same psychological phenomenon, a new term has recently been proposed that covers both kinds of crime. In a series of articles published shortly before the first anniversary of the Columbine massacre, *The New York Times* refers to figures like Dylan Klebold, Charles Whitman, and others as *rampage killers*—a highly expressive phrase that pinpoints the essential difference between these types of offenders and serial killers.

Recommended Reading

Graham Chester. *Berserk!: Motiveless Random Massacres* (1993)
Art Crockett. *Spree Killers* (1994)
Brian Lane and Wilfred Gregg. *The Encyclopedia of Mass Murder* (1994)
New York Times, "Rampage Killers," April 9–12, 2000
Pan Pantziarka. *Lone Wolf: True Stories of Spree Killers* (2000)
Ronald Tobias. *They Shoot to Kill* (1981)

PSYCHOPATH VS. PSYCHOTIC

When the arresting officer asked Howard Unruh if he was "some kind of psycho," he was using a common slang term nowadays most commonly associated with the title of Alfred Hitchcock's classic slasher film. But the policeman's question is more complicated than it may seem. There are two very different types of "psychos": *psychopaths* and *psychotics.* Most serial killers fall into the first category, though some belong to the latter.

Psychopaths: The Mask of Sanity

> Serial killers have a dead conscience. No morals, no scruples, no conscience.
>
> —Richard "Night Stalker" Ramirez

Technically, psychopaths aren't legally insane. They know the difference between right and wrong. They are rational, often highly intelligent people. Some are capable of great charm. Indeed, the scariest thing about them is that they seem so normal.

Their pleasant personalities, however, are just a show. Underneath their "masks of sanity"—to use the famous phrase coined by psychologist Hervey Cleckley—they are profoundly disturbed individuals.

The most striking feature of the psychopathic personality is his utter lack of empathy. He is incapable of love, incapable of caring, incapable of feeling sorry for anyone but himself. Other people are simply objects to be exploited and manipulated for his own profit and pleasure.

As criminologist Edward Glover puts it his book *The Roots of Crime,* psychopaths are "outstandingly selfish, egotistical, and deceitful." Nothing matters to them but their own needs. At their worst, they have monstrous dreams of torture, rape, and murder that they pursue without the slightest compunction. Such extreme criminal psychopaths are devious, cold-blooded predators who hide their evil hearts behind bland, plausible facades.

Because they feel no guilt or remorse, psychopaths are able to maintain an uncanny cool in situations that would cause a normal person to break into a cold sweat. For example, when one of Jeffrey Dahmer's handcuffed and bleeding victims managed to escape and run out into the street, Dahmer calmly talked the police into returning the young man to his custody. He then led him back to his hellish lair and slaughtered him.

Melville on Psychopaths

Though the term "psychopath" wasn't coined until 1891 by a German psychologist named Koch, the kind of personality it describes has always existed. The great American novelist Herman Melville not only recognized this fact but created a powerful portrait of a criminal psychopath in his final masterpiece, *Billy Budd.*

One of Melville's major themes is the lurking evil concealed behind benign appearances. In *Billy Budd,* this theme is embodied in the character John Claggart, a seemingly friendly man who is wicked to the core.

At one point in the novella, the author pauses to contemplate the source of Claggart's villainy. Living in a pre-Freudian age, Melville does not use the clinical language of modern-day psychology in accounting for the character's behavior, relying instead on such old-fashioned phrases as "natural depravity" and "the mania of an evil nature." But his description of the master-at-arms's malevolent personality makes it clear that Claggart is a classic instance of what we now call a criminal psychopath:

> Though the man's even temper and discreet bearing would seem to intimate a mind peculiarly subject to the law of reason, not the less in heart he would seem to riot in complete exemption from that law, having apparently little to do with reason further than to employ it as an ambidexter implement for effecting the irrational. That is to say: Toward the accomplishment of an aim which in wantonness of atrocity would seem to partake of the insane, he will direct a cool judgment sagacious and sound. These men are madmen, and of the most dangerous sort, for their lunacy is not continuous, but occasional, evoked by some special object.

In this passage, Melville pinpoints the essence of the psychopath: a person who commits the most unspeakable atrocities with cool, rational judgment.

"MORAL INSANITY"

During Melville's lifetime, psychiatrists both here and in Europe were grappling with the same problem as *Billy Budd:* how to explain the psychology of criminals who are rational and even intelligent, but who take pleasure in committing murders that are so hideously savage as to seem, by definition, insane. The term they came up with was "moral insanity."

In the early 1870s, for example, a twelve-year-old boy named Jesse Harding Pomeroy attacked and tortured a series of younger boys in Boston. After less than seventeen months at a reformatory he was released, only to commit a pair of hideous mutilation murders on a little boy and girl. Under arrest, the "Boy Fiend" (as the newspapers dubbed him) was examined by various psychiatrists who found that he had "sharp wits" and "a good memory," had "no delusions whatsoever," possessed "a knowledge of right and wrong in the abstract," and had an above-normal "intellectual capacity."

At the same time, he "was unquestionably defective on the moral side to a degree which was plainly much more pronounced than in the criminal. The unusual, atrocious, and cruel nature of his criminal acts, his pursuit of crime for crime's sake only, his utter insensibility to suffering, and his gratification in torturing victims for the same reason that a cat does a mouse before killing it" all plainly indicated that his "motives and conduct were far different from those of the ordinary malefactor."

In short, the experts concluded that though Pomeroy was intellectually unimpaired, he was *morally* insane—or, as they variously described him, a "moral degenerate," a "moral defective," or a "moral imbecile." Though these terms don't sound particularly scientific (or politically correct), they are exactly what we mean nowadays by a psychopath.

> These patients have good memory and understanding, ability to reason and contrive, much cleverness and cunning, and a general appearance of rationality, coexistent with very deficient control, absence of moral sense and human sentiments and feelings, perverted and brutal instincts, and propensities for criminal acts of various kinds which may be perpetrated deliberately and cleverly planned, yet committed with little or no motive and regardless of the consequences to themselves and others.
>
> —nineteenth-century definition of "moral insanity"

Psychotics: The Living Nightmare

Psychosis is defined as a severe mental disorder characterized by some degree of personality disintegration. Psychotics live in a nightmarish world of their own. They suffer from hallucinations and delusions—hear voices, see visions, are possessed by bizarre beliefs. They have lost touch with reality. Unlike psychopaths—who appear to be normal, rational people even while leading grotesque secret lives—psychotics match the common conception of insanity. The main forms of psychosis are schizophrenia and paranoia.

For the most part, serial killers aren't psychotic. There have been some notable exceptions, however—like the paranoid schizophrenic Herbert Mullin.

CASE STUDY

Herbert Mullin and the Die Song

For the first twenty-two years of his life, Herbert Mullin showed no signs of the raging psychosis that would eventually take possession of his mind and result in the brutal deaths of thirteen random victims.

Born in Salinas, California, in April 1947, he seemed to a have a normal childhood. He belonged to the Boy Scouts, played Little League baseball, built a tree house with friends.

Years later, he remembered his childhood differently, insisting that his parents had deliberately tried to ruin his life by sending telepathic messages to his schoolmates, threatening to kill them in the afterlife if they played with him. By the time he made this wild accusation, Mullin was already far gone in madness.

From first grade until his sophomore year of high school he attended Catholic parochial school, then—after his family moved to Santa Cruz—transferred to San Lorenzo Valley High, where he found a girlfriend and formed a close attachment to a buddy named Dean.

After Dean's death in a car crash, Mullin first manifested bizarre symptoms, creating a kind of shrine to his friend in his bedroom and staring at it for hours on end. Around this time, Mullin was also introduced to marijuana. It is difficult to know how much significance to attach to either event, however. After all, many people have had similar experiences—losing loved ones in tragic accidents, experimenting with drugs—without turning into deranged psycho-killers.

The first indication that something was seriously wrong with Mullin occurred at a family gathering for his parents' twenty-ninth anniversary in March 1969. Over dinner, Mullin robotically imitated every word and gesture of his brother-in-law, Al. His behavior was so bizarre that he was finally convinced to check himself into a state mental hospital, where he was diagnosed as suffering from a "schizophrenic reaction."

Though the psychiatrists judged that his mental condition was deteriorating and the "prognosis was poor," they had no power to keep him in custody. After six weeks, Mullin left.

For the next few years, he drifted, working at a succession of menial jobs—dishwasher, gas station attendant, truck driver for Goodwill Industries. For a while he lived in Hawaii. He was in and out of mental hospitals. He began to hear voices commanding him to shave his head and burn his penis with a lighted cigarette. He obeyed both orders. Doctors, recognizing that he was in the grip of extreme paranoid schizophrenia, warned that his condition was "grave." They had no idea of just how dangerous Herbert Mullin was becoming.

By October 1972, the voices were telling him to kill. He became convinced that he had been chosen by Albert Einstein to go out and murder people as a way of preventing a cataclysmic earthquake. He described his mission as "singing the die song." He explained it to a psychiatrist:

> You see, the thing is, people get together, say, in the White House. People like to sing the die song, you know, people like to sing the die song. If I am president of my class when I graduate from high school, I can tell two, possibly three young male *Homo sapiens* to die. I can sing that song to them and they'll have to kill themselves or be killed—an automobile accident, a knifing, a gunshot wound. You ask me why this is? And I say, well they have to do that in order to protect the ground from an earthquake, because all of the other people in the community had been dying all year long, and my class, we have to chip in so to speak to the darkness, we have to die also. And people would rather sing the die song than murder.

On October 13, 1972—not long after a voice in his head barked, "Why won't you give me anything? Go kill someone! Move!"—Mullin clubbed a fifty-five-year-old drifter to death with a baseball bat on a highway shoulder in the Santa Cruz Mountains. Less than two weeks later, he picked up a twenty-four-year-old hitchhiker, stabbed her to death with a hunting knife, then dragged her corpse into some bushes and disemboweled her. Eight days later, he entered the confessional of St. Mary's Church in Los Gatos and stabbed the priest to death.

In the midst of this hideous campaign, Mullin tried to enlist in the Marines. He impressed the recruiting officer as a "highly intelligent and motivated young man [who] most likely will be . . . a credit to the corps." Ultimately, however, he was turned down. Ten days after applying, Mullin massacred five people—including two brothers, ages four and nine—in a remote area of the Santa Cruz Mountains. Not long afterward, while hiking in a state park, he came upon four teenage boys in a makeshift cabin and shot them all in the head while they begged for their lives. His final victim was a seventy-two-year-old man, shot while working in his yard. Mullin's car was spotted speeding away from the murder scene, and he was quickly picked up.

In spite of overwhelming evidence of his extravagant mental derangement, the jury deemed Mullin "sane by legal standards" and found him guilty of eight counts of second-degree murder and two counts of first. On September 18, 1973, he was sentenced to life imprisonment. He will be eligible for parole in 2020, at the age of seventy-three.

BEYOND MADNESS

Because serial killers commit such appalling acts, some experts feel that these criminals can't be placed in any of the usual clinical categories of mental disorder. To them, serial killers exist in a class by themselves, somewhere beyond the outer limits of comprehensible human behavior.

In his book *The Meaning of Murder,* for example, John Brophy writes: "Such men are monsters, who live not merely beyond the unmapped frontiers of sanity but beyond the frontiers of madness as madness is conceivable to most people."

Like Brophy—who reverts to the ancient term "monsters" to describe serial killers—some experts have recently abandoned psychological jargon altogether and have gone back to the age-old notion of *evil* to describe such beings. At a meeting of the American Psychiatric Association in May 2001, forensic psychiatrist Michael Welner of the New York University School of Medicine defined evil as "an intent to cause emotional trauma, to terrorize or target the helpless, to prolong suffering and to derive satisfaction from it all."

That pretty much sums up the behavior of serial killers.

Recommended Reading

Hervey Cleckley, *The Mask of Sanity* (1976)
Edward Glover, *The Roots of Crime* (1960)
Donald Lunde, *Murder and Madness* (1975)

WHO THEY ARE

Apart from the obvious characteristics—sick minds, twisted desires, a compulsion to kill again and again—it's hard to generalize about serial killers. According to writer Stephen Michaud, the only safe thing you can say about them "is that an inexplicably large percentage are named Wayne or Ricky Lee."

Michaud, one assumes, is at least half-joking. (Actually, there don't seem to be that many Ricky Lees among the world's serial killers.) But his larger point is well-taken. There are so many exceptions to every rule that talking about the typical traits of serial killers is surprisingly tricky.

For example, it's usually said that most serial killers are white. That's certainly true in the United States, where the majority of the population is Caucasian. But it's clearly not the case in, say, South Africa, which has a startlingly high number of serial killers, almost all of them black. Even in our own country, there have been plenty of African-American serial killers.

It's also part of the received wisdom of criminology that serial killers are almost always male. Again, that's true—but only if you define "serial murder" as a very specific type of crime, namely, savagely violent sexual homicide of the kind epitomized by Jack the Ripper. That particular brand of mutilation sex-murder is, in fact, only perpetrated by men. (As culture critic Camille Paglia puts it, "There are no female Jack the Rippers.") But under the broader definitions formulated by the FBI and National Institutes of Justice, a considerable number of females qualify as serial killers.

Still, if we limit ourselves to the United States and to those psychopathic sex-killers first associated with the term "serial murder" back in the 1970s and 1980s—Gacy, Bundy, Kemper, Ramirez, and the rest of that unholy crew—there are certain general statements that hold true.

The sort of serial killer most people think of when they hear that term is a white male between the ages of twenty-five and thirty-five. He is not psychotic but rather psychopathic, suffering from what is often referred to nowadays as "Antisocial Personality Disorder." He is most probably an extreme loner—a socially maladjusted misfit with few, if any, meaningful relationships. Cut off from the world of normal human connections, he indulges in particularly vivid, highly perverse fantasies of torture, domination, and murder. At some point, he crosses a line and acts out these fantasies on actual victims. Depending on his sexual orientation—that is to say, whether he is a gay or a heterosexual serial killer—his victims will either be male or female.

Though profoundly disturbed in his emotional and psychological makeup, he is not intellectually deficient. On the contrary, he has an above-average intelligence, combined with a criminal cunning that allows him to escape detection long enough to perpetrate a series of atrocities.

TEN TRAITS OF SERIAL KILLERS

At the tenth triennial meeting of the International Association of Forensic Sciences held at Oxford, England, in September 1984, Robert Ressler and John Douglas of the FBI's Behavioral Science Unit, along with Professors Ann W. Burgess and Ralph D'Agostino, delivered a seminal paper on serial murder, based on a study of thirty-six jailed offenders, including Edmund Kemper and Herbert Mullin. In their presentation, they listed the following traits as the "general characteristics" of these killers:

1. Most are single white males.
2. They tend to be smart, with a mean IQ of "bright normal."
3. Despite their intelligence, they do poorly in school, have spotty employment records, and generally end up as unskilled workers.
4. They come from deeply troubled families. Typically, they have been abandoned at an early age by their fathers and grow up in broken homes dominated by their mothers.
5. There is a long history of psychiatric problems, criminal behavior, and alcoholism in their families.
6. As children, they suffer significant abuse—sometimes psychological, sometimes physical, often sexual. Such brutal mistreatment instills them with profound feelings of humiliation and helplessness.

7. Because of their resentment toward their distant, absent, or abusive fathers, they have a great deal of trouble with male authority figures. Because they were dominated by their mothers, they have a powerful hostility toward women.
8. They manifest psychiatric problems at an early age and often spend time in institutions as children.
9. Because of their extreme social isolation and a general hatred of the world and everyone in it (including themselves), they often feel suicidal as teenagers.
10. They display a precocious and abiding interest in deviant sexuality and are obsessed with fetishism, voyeurism, and violent pornography.

It is important to remember, however, that these traits were extrapolated from a small sample of thirty-six sadistic lust-murderers, all men and most of them white. There are many other serial killers who possess different characteristics.

Edmund Kemper, Epitome of Evil

CASE STUDY

A psychopathic killer who embodies most of the traits in the FBI's pioneering paper on serial murder—and, indeed, who served as one of the interview subjects for that famous study—is Edmund Kemper III, aka the "Coed Killer."

Kemper's upbringing in a broken home was a nightmare of unrelenting emotional abuse. A hulking boy who grew up to be a six-foot-nine-inch, three-hundred-pound behemoth, he was the target of unremitting ridicule from his mother. She constantly belittled both his physical appearance and "weirdo" personality.

Growing up in that toxic atmosphere of rejection and humiliation, he developed an intense sense of self-loathing along with an equally virulent hatred of his hectoring mother, which would eventually be projected onto all of womanhood.

He began to show signs of extreme psychological disturbance in grade school. While other boys played at being Superman or Davy Crockett, little Edmund pretended he was being executed in the gas chamber. Once, when someone found out about his crush on his second grade teacher and teasingly asked why he didn't kiss her, Edmund replied, "If I kiss her, I'd have to kill her first"—an early expression of his growing belief that the only women he could count on not to reject him were dead ones.

As is common with serial killers, Kemper's sadism manifested itself at a shockingly early age. At first, he contented himself with dismembering his sister's dolls. Before long, however, he was torturing house pets. He decapitated one family cat with a machete and buried another alive. By his early teens, he would indulge in masturbatory reveries of slaughtering everyone in town and having sex with their corpses.

In the winter of 1963, the fifteen-year-old Kemper was shipped off to live with his paternal grandparents on their ranch in North Fork, California. The following August, while his grandma Maude sat at the kitchen table, Edmund shot her in the head with a .22 rifle before stabbing her repeatedly and dragging her corpse into her bedroom. When his grandfather returned from running errands a short time later, Edmund shot him to death as he walked through the door. He then notified his mother and sat down to wait for the police. When questioned about his motives, Kemper shrugged, "I just wondered how it would feel to shoot Grandma." The murder of his grandpa was, he said, an act of mercy: a way to spare the old man the pain of discovering what had happened to his wife.

Diagnosed as a paranoid schizophrenic, Kemper—not yet sixteen—was committed to Atascadero State Hospital, where he appears to have spent much of his time raptly listening to the fond reminiscences of the various serial rapists he met on his ward. His fantasies became even more dominated by scenarios of sexual violence. Concealing his seething inner life from his therapists, he assumed a mask of docility and newfound religious conviction and was paroled after only five years. In a stunning display of institutional obtuseness, the parole board—against the express advice of Kemper's doctors and his own wishes—discharged him into the care of his mother.

Kemper received no counseling or psychiatric treatment of any kind after his discharge. In September 1972, he *was* examined by a panel of state psychiatrists appointed to determine his mental state. Satisfied with his responses, they deemed him fully rehabilitated and sealed his juvenile record. Following the interview, Kemper headed for the Santa Cruz Mountains in his car. Inside its trunk was the head of a fifteen-year-old hitchhiker he had killed, raped, and dismembered the day before.

Her name was Aiko Koo, and she was the third victim of the "rehabilitated" Kemper. His first two were eighteen-year-old roommates from Fresno State College, Mary Ann Pesce and Anita Luchessa. Kemper had picked them up the preceding May, driven them to a secluded stretch of road, stabbed them to death, then stuffed their bodies in his trunk and drove them home. Smuggling the corpses into his bedroom, he amused himself with his "trophies," snapping Polaroid photos, dissecting the bodies, having sex with the viscera. Eventually, he bagged the remains and disposed of them, burying their bodies in the mountains and tossing their heads into a ravine.

Six young women would meet the same fate. Living out the necrophiliac fantasies he had entertained since childhood, Kemper took particular pleasure in raping the corpses and especially in sodomizing the decapitated heads. On at least two occasions, he indulged in cannibalism, slicing flesh from the legs of his victims and consuming it in a macaroni casserole. He also kept teeth, hair, and patches of skin as grisly trophies.

Psychiatrists would later speculate that all of these poor women were surrogates for the real object of Kemper's hatred: his mother. That his frenzy climaxed with a horrendous act of matricide tends to confirm this theory. On the day before Easter 1973, Kemper crept into his mother's bedroom at sunrise with a knife and hammer, smashed in her skull, slit her throat, cut off her head, and raped her decapitated corpse. In one of the more symbolically resonant acts in the annals of criminal depravity, he jammed her larynx down the garbage disposal—which promptly spat it back out into his face. "That seemed appropriate," Kemper would later tell the police, "as much as she'd bitched and screamed and yelled at me over so many years." He also propped her head on the mantel and used it as a dartboard. Later that day, he invited her best friend over for dinner. When she arrived, he strangled her with a scarf, took her corpse to bed, and spent the night molesting the body.

The following morning, Easter Sunday, he fled eastward, driving nonstop to Pueblo, Colorado, where—realizing he had nowhere to run—he put in a call to the police back home. At first, no one at the precinct believed his confession. As is common with serial killers, Kemper was a police buff who had befriended many members of the Santa Cruz department. Eventually, however, he persuaded them, then patiently waited at the phone booth for the authorities to arrive and place him under arrest.

He offered a full and sickeningly detailed confession. At his trial, he was judged to be legally sane and convicted of eight counts of murder. When the judge asked him what punishment he felt was suitable for his crimes, Kemper replied—not unreasonably—"Death by torture." He was sentenced to life in prison, where he remains as of this writing.

WARNING SIGNS

Psychoanalysis is based on the belief that you can explain an adult's troubled behavior by tracing the causes back to his childhood experiences. But as Freud himself admitted, it's impossible to do the opposite: i.e., look at a young child's experiences and predict exactly how he'll behave as a grown-up.

This certainly holds true in the case of serial killers. If you look at the life of, say, Peter Kürten—who grew up in a household where incest was rife and who was tutored from an early age in the joys of animal torture and bestiality—it seems inevitable that he ended up becoming a sadistic lust-murderer. On the other hand, if you take a different child who has been subjected to a disturbed, even degenerate, upbringing, you can't say for sure that he will turn out to be a homicidal psychopath.

Still, in attempting to locate the root causes of serial murder, researchers have identified three major warning signs that are often found in the backgrounds of these criminals. These three behavioral red flags—often referred to as the psychopathological *triad*—are *enuresis* (bed-wetting), *pyromania* (fire-starting), and *precocious sadism* (generally in the form of animal torture).

1. *Bed-Wetting.* There's nothing unusual or alarming about bed-wetting in itself; it's a common phenomenon among little children. When the problem persists into puberty, however, it may well be a sign of significant

and even dangerous emotional disturbance. According to the findings of the FBI's Behavioral Science Unit, fully 60 percent of sex-murderers were still suffering from this condition as adolescents—like the African-American serial killer Alton Coleman, who wet his pants so often that he was saddled with the taunting nickname "Pissy."

2. *Fire-Starting.* Given their lust for destruction, it's no surprise that, among their other twisted pleasures, many serial killers love to set fires, a practice they often begin at an early age. Some of the most notorious serial killers of modern times were juvenile arsonists. Ottis Toole, for example—Henry Lee Lucas's loathsome accomplice—began torching vacant houses when he was six years old. Carl Panzram—arguably the most unrepentant killer in the annals of American crime—took positive pride in the havoc he could wreak with a matchstick, boasting in his jailhouse memoirs that, at the tender age of twelve, he caused $100,000 worth of damage by burning down a building at reform school. Carlton Gary firebombed a grocery store while still in his teens. And David Berkowitz—who ultimately confessed to more than fourteen hundred acts of arson—was so obsessed with fires as a little boy that his schoolmates nicknamed him "Pyro."

   Firebombing stores and incinerating buildings is, of course, an intensely pathological expression of anger and aggression. But it's more than sheer malice that underlies the incendiary crimes of serial killers. According to specialists in the psychology of perversion, there is always an erotic motive at the root of pyromania. "There is but one instinct which generates the impulse to incendiarism," writes Wilhelm Stekel in his classic work on aberrant behavior. "That is the sexual instinct, and arson clearly shows its connecting points with sex."

   True, there are often "secondary motives" behind a pyromaniac's acts—revenge, for example, like Panzram's desire to get back at his tormentors. But above all (as Stekel writes), "the incendiary is sexually excited by the flames; he likes to watch them burn." Anyone who doubts this has only to read Flora Schreiber's writings about the New Jersey serial killer Joseph Kallinger, who was thrown into orgasmic raptures by the mere thought of the fires he had caused.

   In short, serial murderers who enjoy starting fires do so for the same reason that they love to torture and kill. It turns them on.

Oh, what ecstasy setting fires brings to my body! What power I feel at the thought of fire . . . Oh, what a pleasure, what a heavenly pleasure! I see the flames and no longer is a fire just a daydream. It is the reality of heaven on earth! I love the excitement of the power fire gives me . . . The mental image is greater than sex!

—Joseph Kallinger

---

3. *Animal Torture.* Juvenile sadism directed at lower life-forms is nothing new. There have always been children and adolescents (usually male) who enjoy hurting small creatures. Certainly Shakespeare knew about such things. In *King Lear,* he writes about "wanton boys" who pull the wings off of flies for "sport." And in Mark Twain's *Adventures of Huckleberry Finn,* the hero finds himself in a one-horse town where a bunch of young loafers are amusing themselves by tying a tin pan to the tail of a stray dog and watching him "run himself to death."

As disturbing as such behavior is, however, it pales beside the kinds of cruelties perpetrated by budding serial killers. As an adolescent, Peter Kürten took pleasure from performing intercourse with various animals while simultaneously stabbing them or slitting their throats. At ten, Edmund Kemper buried his family cat alive in the backyard. Afterward, he dug up the carcass, brought it back to his bedroom, cut off the head, and stuck it on a spindle. Three years later, after his mother brought a new cat into the house, Kemper sliced off the top of its skull with a machete, then held its foreleg while it showered him with blood.

Besides collecting roadkill, little Jeffrey Dahmer liked to nail live frogs to trees, cut open goldfish to see how their innards worked, and perform impromptu surgery on stray dogs and cats. Dennis Nilsen—the so-called British Jeffrey Dahmer—once hanged a cat just to see how long it would take to die. Albert DeSalvo enjoyed trapping house pets in wooden crates and shooting them with a bow and arrow, while Carroll Cole (aka the "Barfly Strangler") got a kick out of choking the family dog unconscious.

Other violent psychopaths have disemboweled their pets, burned them alive, fed them ground glass, and cut off their paws.

According to ASPCA therapist Dr. Stephanie LaFarge, "anyone who hurts animals has the potential to move on to people." Of course, most boys who commit minor acts of childhood sadism outgrow such behavior and look back with shame at the time they blew up an anthill with a cherry bomb or dismembered a daddy longlegs. By contrast, the cruelties perpetrated by incipient serial killers grow more extreme over time, until they are targeting not stray animals and house pets but other human beings.

For them animal torture isn't a stage. It's a rehearsal.

I found a dog and cut it open just to see what the insides looked like, and for some reason I thought it would be a fun prank to stick the head on a stake and set it out in the woods.

—Jeffrey Dahmer

These two scenes from William Hogarth's *The Four Stages of Cruelty* (1751) depict the transition from animal cruelty to sex murder. In the first, a London street urchin named Tom Nero tortures a dog. In the second, the grown-up Tom has just been apprehended after slitting the throat of his pregnant lover.

HOW SMART ARE SERIAL KILLERS?

There's a simple explanation for the fact that so many serial killers have above-average IQs. Generally speaking, it requires a certain degree of intelligence to get away with repeated acts of homicide. There are plenty of sex criminals who have committed atrocious acts of mutilation-murder. Fortu-

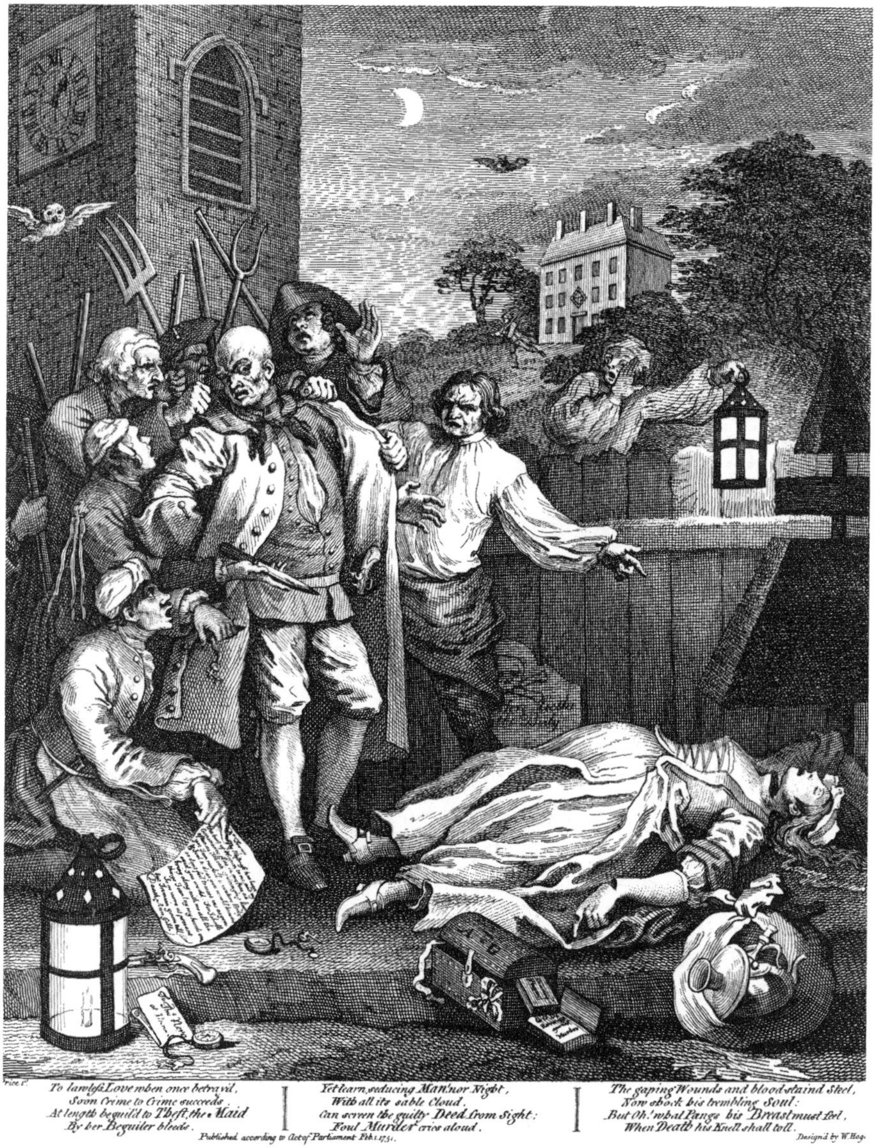

nately, most of them are so sloppy or stupid that they are caught right away and so never have a chance to become serial offenders. "I've seen many murderers who might well have gone on to become serial killers," criminal psychiatrist Dorothy Otnow Lewis testified, "if they'd had the wits not to get arrested."

Still, there's a tendency to exaggerate the mental capacities of serial killers, particularly since they are so often portrayed in the media as intellectual prodigies *à la* Hannibal Lecter—a psychopath so staggeringly erudite that he commits murder to the strains of Mozart and knows Dante by heart in the original Italian. Lecter, however, is a purely mythic creation. He is a reflection not of the way serial killers really *are* but of how they like to think of themselves. In their pathological narcissism—their profoundly misguided sense of their own superiority—serial killers like to imagine that they are criminal masterminds who can outwit the world. Serial killers with genius-level IQs, however, are almost nonexistent. Some, in fact, are profoundly stupid, relying on low criminal cunning rather than brains to elude the law. Ottis Toole, for example—Henry Lee Lucas's accomplice and the psycho believed responsible for the abduction and murder of little Adam Walsh—had an IQ of 75. Others are profoundly psychotic, lost in their own bizarre worlds of paranoid delusion.

Even the brightest serial killers are a lot less intelligent than they think. John George Haigh, the infamous British "Acid Bath Murderer" of the 1940s, was a highly intelligent and cultivated man. For all his sophistication, however, he mistakenly believed that the Latin phrase *corpus delecti*—the legal term for the body of evidence indicating that a crime has occurred—referred to the actual cadaver of a homicide victim. This erroneous belief that a person could not be indicted for murder if no corpse was found eventually led to his undoing.

Ted Bundy was a law student and rising young figure in the Washington State Republican party. Insisting on serving as his own defense lawyer during his murder trial, he turned the proceedings into a travesty and proved the adage that a man who defends himself has a fool for a client.

Gay serial killer Randy Kraft had an IQ of 129 and made big bucks as a computer consultant. Still, he got himself arrested while driving drunk with a strangled corpse on the passenger seat.

And when Gary Heidnik—a financial whiz who made a fortune on the stock market—was arrested for keeping chained and tortured "sex slaves" in the basement of his Philadelphia home, the best defense he could come up with at the time of his arraignment was that the women were already there when he moved into the house.

MALE AND FEMALE

In October 2002, Aileen Wuornos—the Florida hooker who shot seven male motorists in the span of a year—was executed for her crimes. From the time of her arrest, she was widely touted in the media as "America's first female serial killer." Catchy as that label was, it was completely inaccurate. There have been dozens of female serial killers in our country's history.

The phrase "female serial killer" conjures up images of a distaff Jack the Ripper: a lone woman psychopath, coolly stalking and snaring her victims, then butchering and mutilating them in a sex-crazed frenzy. In fact, there *are* no women who fit that particular model (at least not outside of overheated Hollywood fantasies like *Basic Instinct*). When police discover a corpse with its throat slit, its torso cut open, its viscera removed, and its genitals excised, they are justified in making one basic assumption: the perpetrator was a man.

That doesn't mean that there's no such thing as a female serial killer. It just means men and women commit serial murder in different ways.

The sort of atrocities perpetrated by male serial killers—the kind involving rape, mutilation, dismemberment—seem to be a function of particular masculine traits. More specifically, there are unmistakable parallels between this kind of violence—phallic-aggressive, penetrative, rapacious, and (insofar as it commonly gratifies itself upon the bodies of strangers), undiscriminating—and the typical pattern of male sexual behavior. For this reason, it is possible to see sadistic mutilation-murder as a grotesque distortion (or "pathological intensification," in the words of Dr. Richard von Krafft-Ebing) of normal male sexuality.

But if this intensely savage type of serial murder is exclusive to men—a monstrous expression of male sexuality—what, then, is the equivalent *female* form? Clearly, it must reflect female sexuality. Generally speaking, female serial killers differ from their male counterparts in roughly the same way that the sexual responses and behavior of women typically differ from those of men.

A useful analogy here is pornography. It is a truth universally acknowledged that—while men are aroused by extremely raw depictions of abrupt, anonymous, anatomically explicit sex—women in general prefer their pornography to involve at least a suggestion of emotional intimacy and leisurely romance. Whether these differences in taste are a function of biology or culture is an open question. The indisputable fact is that the differences are real.

An analogous distinction holds true for serial killers. Female psychopaths are no less depraved than their male counterparts. As a rule, however, brutal penetration is not what turns them on. Their excitement comes—not from violating the bodies of strangers with phallic objects—but from a grotesque, sadistic travesty of intimacy and love: from spooning poisoned medicine into the mouth of a trusting patient, for example, or smothering a sleeping child in its bed. In short, from tenderly turning a friend, family member, or dependent into a corpse—from nurturing them to death. (What made Aileen Wuornos unusual was that she was a rare, though by no means unique, example of a woman who killed her victims in the assaultive, phallic style of male serial stalkers like David "Son of Sam" Berkowitz.)

The majority of female serial killers throughout history have relied on poison to dispatch their victims. For most people, there is a quaint *Arsenic and Old Lace* quality associated with such crimes, as though disposing of a few people by feeding them arsenic-laced oatmeal were a rather genteel form of murder. The truth is that, compared to the lingering agonies suffered by the average poisoning victim, the deaths meted out by male serial killers like Jack the Ripper, "Son of Sam," or the Boston Strangler—the swift executions by knife blade, bullet, or garrote—seem positively humane. Female poisoners, in other words, differ from the popular stereotype of the dotty old maid getting rid of a burdensome houseguest with a little nip of lethal hot cocoa. Many are terrifying sadists who derive intense perverted pleasure from the sufferings of their victims.

There is no doubt that male serial sex-murder tends to be more lurid—more spectacularly violent—than the female variety. Whether it is more *evil* is another matter. After all, which is worse: to dismember a streetwalker after slitting her throat, or to cuddle in bed with a close friend you've just poisoned, and to climax repeatedly as you feel the body beside you subside into death?

CASE STUDY

Jane Toppan, the Jolly Psychopath

Like so many other serial killers, Jane Toppan was the product of a severely unstable upbringing. Her real name was Honora Kelley. She was born in Boston in 1857, the child of a poor Irish couple. Her mother died when Honora was a baby, leaving her in the dubious care of her father, Peter, a chronic drunk prone to violent outbursts and so wildly eccentric that his neighborhood nickname was "Kelley the Crack" (as in "crackpot").

In 1863, Kelley—eager to be free of his family burdens—deposited Honora and her older sister Delia in the Boston Female Asylum, an institution for orphaned and other desperately needy girls. He never saw his children again.

Jane Toppan

Less than two years later, Honora was "placed out"—signed over as a full-time, live-in servant—to Mrs. Abner Toppan, a middle-aged widow from Lowell, Massachusetts. Though never formally adopted, she was given the name Jane Toppan. Her position in the household was always equivocal. On the one hand, she was treated as a member of the family. On the other, she was never allowed to forget her lowly origins or her place as a menial. Within the community, her dark Irish looks branded her a permanent outsider. After a childhood of abuse, rejection, and abandonment, she grew up in a constant state of humiliation. It was the perfect recipe for the making of a psychopath.

At no point in her life did Jane appear criminally deranged. On the contrary, she struck most acquaintances as a lively, outgoing person—"Jolly Jane," they called her. Like others of her ilk, however, she had a hidden self that was hopelessly diseased. She was a lifelong liar and gossip, spreading malicious rumors about people she envied. She was also—like many prospective serial killers—a secret pyromaniac, who derived intense erotic pleasure from starting fires. Beneath her amiable exterior existed a poisonous well of malevolence, a deep, implacable longing to do harm.

She found the perfect outlet for her dark desires in nursing. Enrolling in the training school of Cambridge Hospital, she impressed many of the doctors with her competence and pleasing personality. Secretly, however, she was experimenting on her patients, administering various poisons to them late at night when no one else was around. Eventually, she settled on a lethal combination of atropine and morphine as the most satisfactory method. Exactly how many victims she killed during those years is unclear, though the number was at least a dozen. As she later confessed, she became addicted to murder. Making people die gave her a "voluptuous delight." Her pleasure was even more intense when she climbed into bed with her victims and held their bodies tight while they suffered their final convulsions.

Eventually, she hired herself out as a private nurse. Her professional skill and personal charm made her a favorite among some of the most respectable families in Cambridge. No one knows for certain how many patients died as a result of her care during this ten-year period of her life, though estimates range as high as a hundred. Among them were her best friend, Myra Conners, and her foster sister, Elizabeth.

As with other psychopaths in the grip of a murderous compulsion, her killings escalated in frequency. Her undoing came in the summer of 1901 while vacationing in a Cape Cod cottage owned by an old friend, Alden Davis. Within a six-week span, Jane murdered Davis, his wife, and two married daughters. The shocking obliteration of the entire family aroused suspicion, and Jane was soon arrested.

In custody, she stunned some of Boston's leading psychiatrists by admitting that her murders were motivated by "an irresistible sexual impulse." She got a powerful erotic charge from holding her poisoned victims in her arms while they died. This need had grown increasingly powerful over the past year, and during the preceding summer she "had let herself go."

She was diagnosed as "morally insane"—the Victorian term for a criminal psychopath—and sentenced to spend the rest of her life in a mental asylum. No sooner had her brief trial ended than she shocked the nation by confessing to thirty-one murders.

She spent the remaining thirty-six years of her life in a state mental hospital, dying at age eighty-four in 1938. According to legend, she would occasionally beckon to one of the nurses, and, with a conspiratorial smile, say:

"Get the morphine, dearie, and we'll go out into the ward. You and I will have a lot of fun seeing them die."

Angels of Death

Jane Toppan falls into a common category of female serial killer, the psychopathic nurse who, instead of serving as an "Angel of Mercy," acts as an "Angel of Death." The annals of crime are filled with such homicidal health-care workers.

Anna Marie Hahn

Typical of the breed was Anna Marie Hahn, a German émigré who settled in Cincinnati and took up a career as a live-in nurse, tending strictly to lonely old men with large bank accounts. After getting her hands on their cash, she would dispatch them with various lethal potions, arsenic-spiked beer being a favorite. (One prospective victim became suspicious when some houseflies dropped dead after sampling the mug of brew Nurse Hahn had just served him.) Between 1932 and 1937, she poisoned an indeterminate number of elderly clients, possibly as many as fifteen. Arrested in 1937, she was convicted of first-degree murder and—on December 7, 1938—became the first woman to die in Ohio's electric chair.

Genene Jones

A more recent—and even more prolific—"Angel of Death" was Genene Jones. Originally a beautician, she switched to vocational nursing in 1977 to pursue her lifelong dream of caring for critically ill children. Unfortunately, this dream was motivated not by any healthy desire to help others but by a psychopathic need to prove that she was a "miracle worker" who could rescue tiny patients from the brink of death.

In 1981, after four years of work at various hospitals in and around San Antonio, Texas, she accepted a position at the Bexar County Medical Center. Not long afterward, administrators began to notice an alarming increase in the deaths of little patients. An investigation was quickly launched and suspicion quickly focused on Nurse Jones. Like other compulsive killers who continue to commit their horrors even while under official scrutiny, Nurse Jones kept right on going.

Resigning from Bexar in March 1982, she joined the staff of the Kerr County clinic. Almost immediately, Kerr found itself plagued with a rash of inexplicable medical emergencies involving young children, who were seized with violent respiratory attacks while undergoing routine checkups. Once again, the link between these events and Genene Jones was impossible to ignore, particularly when an incriminating bottle of muscle relaxant turned up in her possession.

Eventually, a jury took just three hours to convict her of first-degree murder. She was sentenced to ninety-nine years in prison. Her motives sprang from the depraved narcissism characteristic of psychopaths. To prove herself a heroine, she would inject her victims with medications that precipitated respiratory failure or cardiac arrest, then rush to their rescue. Sometimes, she did, in fact, manage to save them, but all too often they succumbed. She is thought to be responsible for the deaths of as many as forty-six babies and young children.

> These women take great delight in their secret hidden power. In watching the suffering and slow death of her victims, she receives the utmost stimulation. . . . She strives for the will to power which is characteristic of her sadistic nature and obtains this through the anguish and suffering of her victims.
>
> —J. Paul de River, *The Sexual Criminal*

Black Widows

Since serial killers seem almost supernaturally evil, they are often given the kinds of lurid nicknames accorded to comic book supervillains. Just as homicidal nurses are known as "Angels of Death," another common type of female psycho-killer is known as the "Black Widow."

Named after the poisonous female spider that devours its own mate, this criminological category refers to women who murder a whole string of husbands—along with anyone else they perceive as an obstacle to their own happiness, such as burdensome children, interfering in-laws, inconvenient acquaintances, and the like. In their book, *Murder Most Rare,* Michael and C. L. Kelleher identify the essential traits that make this kind of serial killer particularly deadly:

> The Black Widow is typically intelligent, manipulative, highly organized, and patient; she plans her activities with great care. Her crimes are usually carried out over a relatively long period of time, and she is rarely suspected of murder until the victim count has become significant or the number of deaths among her relatives and acquaintances can no longer be considered coincidental. In many cases, the Black Widow begins to murder relatively late in life (often after the age of thirty) and therefore brings a good deal of maturity and patience to the planning and commission of her crimes. She relies on her ability to win the confidence and trust of her victims as a precursor to any attack. For this reason, she is seldom viewed as a suspect, even after she has committed several murders. . . . The average Black Widow will claim between six and thirteen victims during her active period, which generally ranges from ten to fifteen years.

Nannie Doss

One of the more notorious Black Widows of recent times was the pudgy, bespectacled Nannie Doss, dubbed the "Giggling Granny" because of her habit of chortling in amusement while discussing her crimes. The product of a harsh and abusive upbringing, Doss was a lifelong addict of true romance magazines, seeking refuge from the unpleasant realities of her existence in sugar-coated fantasies of undying love. Unfortunately, the men she met and married—generally through classified lonely hearts ads—were anything but Prince Charmings. Most were philandering alcoholics. When each new mate proved less than ideal, Nannie dispatched him with a generous dose of rat poison, mixed into whiskey or coffee or stewed prunes. Between 1929 and 1953, she murdered four husbands. She might have added to that tally if the doctor who treated her final husband hadn't grown sufficiently suspicious to order an autopsy, which turned up enough arsenic in the victim's body to have killed eighteen men.

Under arrest, she indignantly denied that she murdered for profit—and, in fact, the money she realized from her husbands' savings account and life insurance policies was barely enough to cover their funeral expenses. Her motive, she claimed, was love. "I was searching for the perfect mate, the real romance of life," she told interrogators. Of course, that didn't explain why she also poisoned two children, a grandchild, two sisters, and her mother.

In 1955, Doss was sentenced to life in prison, where she died of leukemia ten years later after writing her memoirs for *Life* magazine.

> My late husband sure did like prunes. I fixed a whole box and he ate them all.
>
> —Nannie Doss

Marie Besnard

An exact contemporary of the "Giggling Granny" was the French Black Widow, Marie Besnard, known in her country as the "Queen of Poisoners." Born in 1896 in Loudon, France, she received strict religious training at a local convent—an education that didn't prevent her from acquiring an apparently well-deserved reputation for sexual promiscuity as an adolescent.

In 1920, at the age of twenty-three, she wed an older cousin, Auguste Antigny. The marriage ended abruptly seven years later when her husband died of what the doctors called "fluid in the lungs"—the first in a long string of medical misdiagnoses that would be made on Marie's murder victims.

In 1929, she married her second husband, Leon Besnard. Over the course of the next twenty years, Leon's family would be eliminated, one by one, in a series of shockingly unexpected deaths that came to be known locally as the "Besnard curse." The first to die were two great-aunts. Then Leon's father, mother, sister, two spinster cousins, and finally Leon himself. During this time, Marie also knocked off her own father, mother, and an elderly couple she had befriended. Her victims' deaths were attributed to everything from strokes to bizarre accidents. Two of her victims died, she claimed, when they had mistakenly eaten from a bowl of lye, thinking it was a special dessert.

That the police accepted such far-fetched explanations suggests that the investigation into the "Besnard curse" was led by Inspector Clouseau. After the thirteenth suspicious death, authorities decided to perform an autopsy on Leon Besnard, whose body was found to be full of arsenic. More exhumations followed, all with the same result.

Arrested in 1950, Marie first confessed, then recanted and hired the best lawyers money could buy. Her legal dream team did its job. She was brought to trial three times: in 1952, 1954, and 1961. The first two proceedings ended in mistrials, the third with her acquittal. In France, her case is considered to be the "perfect crime."

Deadlier Than the Male

"The female of the species is more deadly than the male," wrote Rudyard Kipling. Anyone who doubts that female psychopaths can be as lethal as any man should consider the following cases:

Marie de Brinvilliers (1630–1676)

The spoiled, sexually promiscuous daughter of a prominent Parisian family, Marie murdered her father, two brothers, and as many as fifty other victims with a poison that she secretly tested on unwary patients at a Parisian pauper hospital. In July 1676, she was publicly beheaded for her crimes in front of Notre Dame Cathedral.

Anna Zanzwiger (1760–1811)

Born in Nuremburg, Germany, Anna grew to be a profoundly unattractive woman, and was said to resemble a toad. In her forties—after a life of hardship and disappointment, including a miserable marriage to an abusive alcoholic that ended when he drank himself to death—she hired herself out as a housemaid to a succession of well-to-do men, hoping that one would become so dependent on her domestic skills that he would marry her. Unfortunately, each of her prospective mates was either already married or engaged. Zanzwiger attempted to solve this problem by murdering the women with arsenic. She also killed one of her employers for spite and poisoned the food of at least a dozen other people—including an infant to whom she gave a teething biscuit dipped in arsenic-laced milk. By the time of her arrest in 1811, the act of poisoning had grown to be an uncontrollable passion. She was beheaded in July of the same year. Her body was then lashed to a wagon wheel and displayed in public.

> It is perhaps better for the community that I should die, as it would be impossible for me to stop poisoning people.
>
> —Anna Zanzwiger, at her sentencing

The execution of Marie de Brinvilliers

Gesina Gottfried (1798–1828)

A native of Bremen, Germany, the beautiful, blond Gesina was a classic psychopath, who experienced supreme ecstasy from watching people die and was, by her own admission, "born without a conscience." During a ten-year span, she poisoned sixteen people, including her three husbands, her two young sons, her parents, a brother, an old friend, and the wife and five children of an employer named Rumf. Arrested in March 1828, after Rumf grew suspicious, she displayed not the slightest trace of remorse. On the contrary, she boasted of her crimes. "I was born without conscience," she declared, "which allowed me to live without fear." Convicted of six counts of murder, she was beheaded in 1828.

Hélène Jegado (c. 1803–1851)

During her thirty-year career as a a domestic servant in villages throughout Brittany, France, Jegado murdered as many as twenty-seven people with no motive other than the sheer pleasure of killing. Wielding arsenic as her weapon, she poisoned men, women, and children. Arrested after killing off another servant in the household of a university professor, she staunchly maintained her innocence, denying all responsibility for the long string of corpses she had left in her wake. Wherever she went, she tearfully insisted, people just happened to die. The evidence against her, however, was overwhelming. She was guillotined in 1851.

Mary Ann Cotton (1832–1873)

One of the most prolific serial killers in English history, Mary murdered an estimated twenty-three people in a twelve-year period. Among her victims were her three husbands, ten children, five stepchildren, a sister-in-law, and an unwanted suitor. Most of the deaths were attributed to "gastric fever" until an autopsy on her seven-year-old stepson revealed enough arsenic in his stomach to have killed three men. She was hanged on March 24, 1873, and quickly immortalized in a popular children's rhyme.

Mary Ann Cotton

> Mary Ann Cotton
> She'd dead and she's rotten
> She lies in her bed
> With her eyes wide oppen
> Sing, sing, oh, what can I sing
> Mary Ann Cotton is tied up with a string.
> Where, where? Up in the air.
> Sellin' black puddens a penny a pair.
>
> —Nineteenth-century British nursery rhyme

Sarah Jane Robinson (1839–1905)

A frighteningly remorseless psychopath who felt no qualms about subjecting her nearest relations to agonizing deaths, the Irish-born Sarah Jane Tennent emigrated to America after being orphaned at the age of fourteen. Her lethal career began around 1880, when she poisoned her husband, three of her eight children (including her infant twin sons) and the elderly landlord to whom she owed fifty dollars in back rent. Her homicidal mania reached a pitch during an eighteen-month period that began in February 1885, when—partly for mercenary reasons, partly out of sheer depravity—she murdered her sister, her brother-in-law, her one-year-old niece, her six-year-old nephew, her own twenty-five-year-old daughter and twenty-three-year-old son. Arrested in August 1886, she became known in the press as America's worst "poison fiend." After one mistrial, she was condemned to hang, though her sentence was later commuted to life in prison. She spent the remainder of her life in a narrow cell decorated with engraved newspaper portraits of her victims.

Marti Enriqueta (?–1912)

This self-styled witch kidnapped, sexually abused, and ritualistically butchered small children in Barcelona, Spain, in the early years of the twentieth century. She apparently cannibalized her victims, then boiled the leftovers for use as an ingredient in the "love potions" that she sold to local peasants. She was arrested and executed in 1912 after a young victim named Angelita—who had been forced to eat human flesh while in captivity—escaped from Enriqueta's lair and alerted the police.

Julia Fazekas (c. 1865–1929)

A midwife in the remote Hungarian village of Nagyrev, Fazekas not only delivered babies but also performed illegal abortions and supplied poison to any woman wishing to rid herself of an unwanted husband, troublesome child, aging parent, or wealthy uncle. Ordering flypaper in bulk, she would boil off the arsenic coating and render it into powder, which she sold to her clients for $8 to $40 a dose, depending on what they could afford. For two decades following the end of World War I, countless local women—who would come to be known as "the angel-makers of Nagyrev"—availed themselves of her lethal services. When the police finally caught on and came to arrest her, Fazekas committed suicide with one of her own potions. Eventually—in a case that gained worldwide notoriety—thirty-four peasant women, ranging in age from forty-four to seventy-one, were put on trial for murdering relatives with Fazekas's poison. Eighteen were convicted, eight executed, the rest acquitted.

Dorothea Puente (1929–)

Born in Mexico, Puente was abandoned as an infant and raised in an orphanage. Over the next forty years, she married four times and gave birth to a daughter whom she immediately put up for adoption. In 1983, at the age of fifty-three, she was sent to prison for drugging old men and stealing their money. Released in 1985, she rented a run-down house in Sacramento, California, and opened a rooming house for elderly persons on fixed incomes. Over the next two years, more than a dozen of her boarders disappeared. In November 1988—investigating neighborhood complaints about the stench emanating from Puente's property—police found the first of seven corpses on her premises. Puente took flight, though she was eventually arrested in Los Angeles. She was charged with nine counts of murder, although authorities believed her victims totaled twenty-five. After a marathon six-month trial, she was convicted and sentenced to life imprisonment without the possibility of parole.

Aileen Wuornos (1956–2002)

Commonly, if mistakenly, called "America's first woman serial killer," Wuornos had the kind of upbringing that is almost guaranteed to produce a psychopathic criminal. Her father was a habitual pedophile who eventually hanged himself after being arrested for molesting a seven-year-old girl. At six months of age, Aileen was abandoned by her mother and left in the care of her grandparents. Her violent, alcoholic grandfather constantly threatened to kill her. He threw her out of the house when Aileen gave birth to an illegitimate child after being raped. She was fourteen years old. From then on, she became a drifter, selling her body for drinks, drugs, and food. At twenty, she married a seventy-year-old man, a union that lasted all of a month. Two years later, she attempted suicide by shooting herself in the stomach. Upon recuperating, she robbed a convenience store and spent slightly more than a year in prison. Her rage against the world—and particularly against men—reached a lethal pitch in late 1989, when she shot to death a male motorist who had picked her up at a Florida truck stop and driven her to a remote wooded area for sex. Six more nearly identical murders followed over the next year. Eventually, Wuornos was arrested in a biker bar. She claimed self-defense for all seven murders. At her 1992 trial, her lesbian lover turned state's evidence and testified against her. Wuornos was convicted and sentenced to death. Ten years later, in October 2002, the sentence was finally carried out.

Recommended Reading:

Ann Jones, *Women Who Kill* (1996)
Michael and C. L. Kelleher, *Murder Most Rare: The Female Serial Killer* (1998)
Terry Manners, *Deadlier Than the Male: Stories of Female Serial Killers* (1995)
Michael Newton, *Bad Girls Do It! An Encyclopedia of Female Murderers* (1993)
Patricia Pearson, *When She Was Bad* (1997)
Kerry Segrave, *Women Serial and Mass Murderers: A Worldwide Reference* (1990)

BLACK AND WHITE

Though the great majority of American serial killers are white, there is no racial or ethnic basis for this fact. That is to say, there's nothing "white" or "black" or, for that matter, Asian or Hispanic or anything else about serial murder. Serial murder is a *human* phenomenon found throughout history and in virtually every culture, with the possible exception of the Inuits.

(Actually, one serial killer, William Tahl, *was* an Eskimo by birth, but he committed his homicides in Texas and California, earning a spot on the FBI's "Most Wanted" list in 1965.)

The preponderance of white serial killers in our own country is simply a matter of demographics. In point of fact, as the *New York Times* reported in an article on October 28, 2002, "black serial killers occur in roughly equal—or even slightly greater—proportion to the number of blacks in the population." According to recent studies, between 13 and 22 percent of United States serial killers are African-American.

Why, then, are people so surprised to learn that a fair number of serial killers are black men? Unfortunately, the most likely explanation has to do with lingering racial prejudice.

Serial murderers generally kill within their race. White serial killers tend to prey on white victims; blacks on black. And the sad fact is that the white majority is not especially interested in crimes involving minority victims. As a result, these cases get relatively little media coverage. This is true, not just of serial murder but of other horrific crimes as well. When the pretty blond Mormon girl, Elizabeth Smart, was abducted from her home in Salt Lake City in June 2002, for example, her picture ended up on the cover of *Newsweek*. By contrast, when a four-year-old African-American girl, Dannariah Finley of Orange, Texas, was abducted from home and slain just one month later, the newspapers barely reported the story.

Indeed, some white serial killers have deliberately exploited this sorry circumstance in order to avoid detection. Jeffrey Dahmer, for example, preyed mostly on African-American and Asian young men, apparently in the belief that the police would pay less attention to the disappearance of minority victims. And in the 1920s, the hideously deranged child-killer/cannibal Albert Fish snatched an untold number of black children from the streets of inner-city ghettos for the same reason.

In short, one reason that most Americans haven't heard much about black serial killers is that, throughout the decades, the police have been lax in pursuing them and the media uninterested in reporting on them—so long, that is, as the victims were also black.

Jarvis Catoe

It is significant that one of the most notorious African-American serial killers of the mid–twentieth century, Jarvis Catoe, only got caught after he began to target white women. In March 1941, a twenty-five-year-old newlywed named Rose Abramowitz approached Catoe, who was loitering outside her Washington, DC apartment building. Abramowitz hired him to wax the linoleum floor of her kitchen. Once inside her home, Catoe strangled and raped her, then made off with twenty dollars. A few months later, twenty-three-year-old Elizabeth Strieff got into his car during a rainstorm, mistaking it for a taxi.

Driving her to a nearby garage, Catoe raped and strangled her, then dumped her nude body in another garage a short distance away. His final victim, also Caucasian, was a twenty-six-year-old Bronx waitress named Evelyn Anderson. A watch belonging to Anderson was recovered from a New York City pawnshop and traced back to Catoe. In custody, he confessed to having strangled ten women with his bare hands and raped at least four others during the preceding three years. The majority of his victims had been—as the newspapers put it—"Negro women," a fact that undoubtedly accounted for the initially lethargic response of the police in pursuing the culprit. Convicted of the Abramowitz murder, Catoe was sentenced to death and electrocuted on January 13, 1943.

Henry Louis Wallace

In restricting himself to victims of his own race, another African-American psychopath—Henry Louis Wallace—was more typical of serial killers in general, though he deviated from the usual pattern in another regard. Whereas most male serial killers prey on strangers, Wallace murdered a string of acquaintances. Between September 1992 and March 1994, the crack-addicted Wallace raped and strangled nine young black women in and around Charlotte, North Carolina, all people who knew and trusted him. Some were employees at the Taco Bell he managed. Several worked with his girlfriend. One was his girlfriend's roommate. Others knew his sister. As with many serial killers, the pace of Wallace's crimes escalated over time. His first six murders occurred over a twenty-month span; his final three within seventy-two hours. Finally arrested in January 1994, he promptly confessed to all nine killings and was sentenced to death. Because they were slow to acknowledge a link among Wallace's earliest murders, the Charlotte police were accused of racism: of failing to take the case seriously because the victims were black.

Carlton Gary

Carlton Gary, another notorious black serial killer, had particular tastes when it came to victims. He only killed outside his race, limiting himself to female Caucasians. He also liked his women old.

Abandoned by his father and shuttled from pillar to post throughout his hardscrabble childhood, Gary accumulated a long rap sheet for robbery, arson, and drug dealing while still in his teens. His combination of exceptional intelligence, glib charm, and psychopathic cunning made him especially dangerous. At one point in his life, he was even dating a female deputy sheriff while pushing drugs and committing serial murder on the side. Arrested in May 1970, as a suspect in the rape-murder of an eighty-five-year-old Albany, New York, woman, Gary managed to pin the blame on an acquaintance. Eventually after several stints behind bars on lesser charges, he escaped from prison and made his way back to his native city, Columbus, Georgia. Between September 1977 and April 1978, that city was rocked by a string of murders committed by a shadowy intruder dubbed the "Stocking Strangler." His victims were seven white women, the youngest fifty-nine, the oldest just shy of ninety. After embarking on a string of restaurant holdups, Gary was arrested for armed robbery in 1978 and sentenced to twenty years in jail. Four years later, however, he escaped. He wasn't nabbed for good until May 1984. Charged with three of the "Stocking Strangler" murders, he was convicted on all counts and sentenced to die in Georgia's electric chair.

Other African-American serial killers include:

Coral Watts. Diagnosed as a paranoid schizophrenic, Watts began dreaming of killing women in his childhood. When a psychiatrist asked if these dreams disturbed him, Watts replied: "No, I feel better after I have one." He first assaulted a woman when he was fifteen years old. When asked about his motives, he shrugged, "I felt like beating her up." He began to make his homicidal dreams a reality in 1980 when he terrorized Ann Arbor, Michigan, as the "Sunday Morning Slasher." Falling under suspicion, he relocated to Houston, where he killed an indeterminate number of women, perhaps as many as forty. Finally arrested in 1982, he struck a controversial deal with the prosecutor's office, confessing to thirteen murders in exchange for a burglary conviction and sixty-year sentence. Despite a public outcry, he is slated to be paroled in 2006 at the age of fifty-eight.

She was evil. I could see it in her eyes.

—Coral Watts, explaining his reasons for killing one of his thirteen admitted victims

Alton Coleman. During a fifty-three-day period in the summer of 1984, Coleman, along with his female accomplice Debra Brown, murdered eight people in five Midwestern states, beginning with seven-year-old Tamika Turks of Gary, Indiana. After raping the little girl, Coleman jumped up and down on her chest until her rib cage fractured and punctured her vital organs. His other victims, all black, ranged in age from fifteen to seventy-seven. Some were strangled, some stabbed, others bludgeoned or shot. Besides serial murder, Coleman committed at least seven rapes during this period, as well as three kidnappings and fourteen armed robberies. Arrested in July 1984, he was tried and convicted in three different states: Ohio, Illinois, and Indiana. He managed to delay his execution until April 26, 2002, when—after devouring a last meal of filet mignon, fried chicken, corn bread, biscuits with brown gravy, french fries, broccoli with cheese, salad, onion rings, collard greens, sweet potato pie with whipped cream, and butter pecan ice cream—he was put to death by lethal injection. Relatives of his many victims watched on closed-circuit TV.

Celeophus Prince, Jr. Unlike most serial killers, Prince preyed exclusively on victims outside his own race. Between January and September 1990, he brutally murdered six women in the San Diego community of Clairemont, stabbing one of them more than fifty times and leaving bloody circles smeared on his victims' breasts as a "signature." His MO involved following unsuspecting women to their homes, then breaking in and butchering them with a kitchen knife. Like Alton Coleman—whose victims included an Ohio woman and her ten-year-old daughter—Prince murdered a mother and daughter, then bragged about the double killing to a friend and took to wearing the dead woman's wedding ring on a chain around his neck. Dubbed the "Clairemont Killer" during his nine-month reign of terror, he was the object of the largest police manhunt in the history of San Diego. Arrested in September 1991, he was eventually convicted of six counts of first-degree murder, twenty counts of burglary, and one count of rape. He remains on San Quentin's death row, awaiting execution.

Wayne Williams and the Atlanta Child Murders

CASE STUDY

More than twenty years after the accused perpetrator was found guilty and sentenced to life imprisonment, questions continue to surround the case of the so-called Atlanta Child Murders. The story began in July 1979, when a woman scavenging the roadside for empties stumbled on the corpses of two African-American boys, one shot dead with a .22-caliber pistol, the other asphyxiated. Over the next two years, twenty-seven more victims would be added to the official list of homicides connected to the killer. During that fearful time, the case would spark panic and outrage in Atlanta's black community, generate nationwide media attention (including an article in the *New York Times Magazine* that would feature the earliest documented use of the term "serial killer"), and bring help from the highest reaches of the government, up to and including the president himself. And not even the arrest and conviction of the prime suspect put an end to the controversy.

Right from the start, the killings posed an enormous problem for law enforcement agents. There was no consistency—no identifiable *signature*—in terms of the killer's MO. Most of the victims were strangled, but some were shot, others stabbed or bludgeoned to death. And though most of the victims were males, a few were young girls. On March 4, 1980, for example, twelve-year-old Angel Lenair left her house to play after completing her homework and never returned. Six days later, her body was found lashed to a tree, an electrical cord tied around her neck and someone else's panties stuffed down her throat.

As his reign of terror continued, moreover, the killer began to prey on older

(Bill Lignante—ABC News)

Wayne Williams

victims: twenty-year-old Larry Rogers, twenty-one-year-old Eddie Duncan, twenty-three-year-old Michael McIntosh, twenty-seven-year-old Nathaniel Cater.

By the spring of 1980, the city's African-American community was in an uproar over the failure of the police to stop the killings. Rumors swirled that the Ku Klux Klan was on a campaign to annihilate the black youth of Atlanta, while Roy Innis of the Congress of Racial Equality went public with a theory that the murders were the work of a Satanic cult. Dozens of bounty hunters—drawn by the prospect of a hundred-thousand-dollar reward—descended on the city. Celebrities from Burt Reynolds to Muhammad Ali offered financial assistance while President Reagan pledged federal funds to help track down the killer. A special task force—including thirty-five FBI agents—interviewed 20,000 people in person and another 150,000 over the phone.

The case began to break in the early-morning hours of May 22, 1981, when officers on stakeout at a bridge over the Chattahoochee River heard a loud splash and halted the car that was crossing the span. Its driver was a twenty-three-year-old African-American named Wayne Williams.

There was certainly nothing in Williams's background that matched the typical profile of a serial killer. The son of schoolteacher parents, he grew up in a stable and loving household where he was encouraged to cultivate his talents. A radio enthusiast who dreamed of making it big in the music business, he showed a great deal of early promise. By the time he was sixteen, he was broadcasting music from a radio station he had set up in the basement of his home. Besides electronics, he had a keen interest in photography and became highly skilled with a camera.

Still, there were definite signs that all was not right with the enterprising young Williams. Despite his intelligence and ambition, he couldn't make it through college, dropping out of Georgia State after just one year. His dream of discovering the next Stevie Wonder came to nothing, and he gained a reputation as a blowhard and liar—the kind of person who claims to have important contacts and is always making big promises that never pan out. An extreme loner, he had no real social relationships and continued to live with his parents into his twenties. He also began displaying some troubling behavioral traits, including a fondness for impersonating police officers (a common tendency among serial killers), as well as a morbid interest in accident scenes—the grislier the better. Monitoring police transmissions on his shortwave, he rushed to the sites of car wrecks or fires or even plane crashes, shooting photographs and videos, then peddling them to the local media.

After being stopped on the bridge, Williams was questioned and let go. Two days later, however, a corpse was fished out of the river, and he was brought into the station for another grilling. Afterward—playing to the media—he staged an at-home news conference, loudly proclaiming his innocence and offering various alibis that subsequently proved to be full of holes. While the police put him under round-the-clock surveillance, forensic specialists worked frantically to link him to the crimes.

When FBI scientists were finally able to match fibers and dog hairs found on several of the victims to Williams's car mats, home carpeting, and bedspread, police moved in and arrested him on June 21, 1981.

At his nine-week trial, the prosecution portrayed Williams as a violent homosexual filled with racial self-loathing who harbored a virulent contempt for black youths. Witnesses were produced who testified to having seen Williams in the company of several victims. Toward the end of the trial, the defense put Williams on the stand, but the tactic backfired when he was goaded into a display of uncontrolled anger, denouncing the prosecutor as a "fool" and lashing out at various government agents. In the end—despite his impassioned protestations of innocence—he was convicted of two counts of murder and given a life sentence for each.

Even today, many people believe that Williams was railroaded: that the circumstantial evidence on which he was convicted was flimsy at best and possibly manufactured by the government; that key information that might have aided his case was suppressed; that Williams received inadequate representation.

One fact, however, suggests that the cops got the right man after all: once Wayne Williams was arrested, the Atlanta Child Murders stopped.

YOUNG AND OLD

"Killer kids" who commit mass murder have become an all-too-common feature of contemporary American society. During the late 1990s there seemed to be a veritable epidemic of them: sixteen-year-old Luke Woodham of Pearl, Mississippi, who killed three schoolmates and wounded seven after knifing to death his own mother; fourteen-year-old Michael Carneal of West Paducah, Kentucky, who gunned down three fellow students and wounded five others at an early-morning prayer meeting; fifteen-year-old Kip Kinkel of Springfield, Oregon, who murdered his parents, then shot twenty-four students, killing two; Andrew Golden and Mitchell Johnson—ages eleven and thirteen—who set off a fire alarm at school to draw their classmates outside, then opened fire, killing four students and a teacher. And, of course, the Columbine killers: seventeen-year-old Dylan Klebold and eighteen-year-old Eric Harris, whose April 1999 massacre in Littleton, Colorado left a dozen students and a teacher dead and twenty-three other people wounded.

By contrast, serial murder perpetrated by minors is an exceptionally rare phenomenon. The most infamous case in American history is that of Jesse Harding Pomeroy, the Boston "Boy Fiend," whose criminal career began

Jesse Pomeroy

when he was twelve. During a nine-month reign of terror that began in December 1871, Pomeroy lured a string of smaller boys to remote locations in Chelsea and South Boston, then bound, beat, and tortured them. Arrested and shipped to reform school, he was released after less than seventeen months; whereupon he promptly committed a pair of appalling mutilation-murders on a ten-year-old girl and a four-year-old boy. Pomeroy was only fourteen when he was tried, convicted, and sentenced to death. A controversy immediately erupted over the morality of executing a minor, and his sentence was ultimately commuted to life. He lived until 1932, having spent just over forty years of his nearly sixty-year incarceration in solitary confinement—the second-longest such stretch in US penal history.

Though Pomeroy began torturing children when he was twelve, he didn't graduate to homicide until he was fourteen—which makes Craig Price of Warwick, Rhode Island, the youngest serial killer in US history. During the late 1980s, at the age of thirteen, the black youth—who had been "peeping" on a neighborhood woman named Rebecca Spencer—broke into her house and killed her with a kitchen knife. Two years later, he stabbed to death another local woman, Joan Heaton, and her two daughters, ages eight and ten. Dubbed the "Slasher of Warwick," he was arrested when a detective noticed a large cut on his hand. Freely confessing to the murders, he was sent to the state prison in Cranston and is scheduled for parole in 2019.

CASE STUDY

Mary Bell, the British Bad Seed

The savage murder of a pair of preschoolers by a psychopathic killer who exults in the atrocities is appalling enough. But when that killer turns out to be a child, too—and, even more shockingly, an eleven-year-old girl with a heart-shaped face and big blue eyes—the crime is guaranteed to set off an explosion of horror, outrage, and stunned disbelief. This is precisely what happened in the summer of 1968, when Britain was rocked by the case of Mary Bell, arguably the most notorious juvenile psycho-killer of the twentieth century.

Because of her youth and angelic appearance, Mary has sometimes been described as the British Bad Seed—a reference to the 1956 movie about a pretty, pigtailed schoolgirl whose picture-perfect exterior conceals the heart of a psychopathic monster. The comparison is only partially valid. The fictional "Bad Seed" was raised in a loving, stable household by a devoted Mommy and Daddy. Her evil was innate. Mary Bell, by contrast, was *made* into a monster. Raised by a viciously depraved young prostitute, the little girl was allegedly subjected to unimaginable abuse, held down by her mother while strange men sexually brutalized her. In light of the soul-deforming horrors she suffered from her earliest years, it is little wonder that Mary Bell herself became a cold-blooded predator.

During her nightmarish childhood, she manifested the classic symptoms that experts see as a predictor of serial murder: cruelty to animals, abnormally prolonged bed-wetting, and vandalism (though not, as is often the case, pyromania). That she cannot technically be classified as a serial killer—at least according to the FBI's definition—is only because her victim count fell one short of the minimum. However, there is little doubt that Bell would have continued taking lives had she been able to.

Her violent attacks on other children began during the second week of May 1968, when, within twenty-four hours, she and her best friend Norma assaulted four little acquaintances in Scottswood, a dreary, economically depressed industrial community in northern England. Ten days later, on May 25, the body of three-year-old Martin Brown was found in a derelict house, blood and saliva bubbling from his mouth. It was Mary who excitedly ran to tell the boy's aunt, Rita Finley. In the succeeding days, Mary and Norma showed up repeatedly at Mrs. Finley's house to plague her with tormenting questions: "Do you miss Martin?" "Do you cry for him?" Finally—unable to stand it any longer—the grieving woman threw the grinning children out of her house and told them never to return.

Portrait of Mary Bell by Joe Coleman

Two days after the discovery of Martin's body, the local nursery was vandalized by intruders, who left the place a wreck. Amid the debris, police found four taunting notes written in a childish hand, including one that read:

we did
murder
Martain
brown
Fuckof
you Bastard

Two months passed. On Wednesday, July 31, another three-year-old Scottswood boy, Brian Howe, went missing. When his worried older sister Pat went looking for him, she ran into Mary Bell and Norma, who eagerly offered to help search for the toddler. Mary led the girl to a stretch of industrial waste ground where local children liked to play and where Brian's corpse was later discovered between two concrete blocks. The little boy had been strangled and sexually mutilated with a broken pair of scissors that lay nearby. The letter "M" had been carved into his naked belly with razor.

Before long, investigators focused their suspicions on Mary and Norma. At Brian's funeral on August 7, Chief Inspector James Dobson kept his eye on Mary Bell. "I watched her as she stood in front of the Howes' house while the coffin was brought out," he would later explain. "That was when I knew I couldn't risk another day. She stood there laughing, laughing and rubbing her hands. I thought, My God, I've got to bring her in or she'll do another one."

Brought to the police station for questioning, Mary and Norma accused each other of the murder of Brian Howe. The two girls were brought to trial in December. After nine days, Norma was acquitted, while Mary—labeled a cunning, remorseless psychopath by experts—was sentenced to "detention for life."

Her later life has been marked by periodic controversy and public uproar. At first, she was placed in a reform school, where—within two years—she accused a housemaster of sexual assault. Later, she was transferred to a prison, where she declared herself a lesbian and paraded around with a rolled-up stocking stuffed in the crotch of her pants. In 1977, she was transferred to a less secure facility, from which she promptly escaped. Though she was quickly captured again, she was at large long enough to lose her virginity to a young man who later sold his story to the tabloids. Shortly before her parole in 1980, she was moved to a halfway house, where she promptly managed to get pregnant by a married man. She aborted that pregnancy, but became a mother in 1984 after her release from jail. She eventually settled in a small town but was driven out by angry residents when they discovered her true identity. The quiet, anonymous life she finally managed to construct for herself and her child was shattered in 1998 with the publication of Gitta Sereny's *Cries Unheard,* which ignited a firestorm when the author disclosed that she had paid the onetime child-murderer for her participation.

Overaged serial killers are just as rare as juvenile ones. Albert Fish—arguably the most perverted figure in the annals of American crime—was a genuine geriatric monster. In 1928, the gaunt, grandfatherly-looking Fish lured a twelve-year-old girl to an abandoned house in Westchester, New York, then strangled her, butchered her body, and carried away several pounds of her flesh, which he proceeded to make into a stew and consume in a state of extreme sexual excitation over the course of a week. He was finally captured after sending an unspeakable letter to the little girl's mother, in which he gloatingly described every atrocity he had perpetrated on the child. He was electrocuted in 1936 at the age of sixty-five, becoming the oldest man ever put to death in Sing Sing.

Recommended Reading:

Jonathan Kellerman, *Savage Spawn: Reflections on Violent Children* (1999)
D. Lassiter, *Killer Kids* (1998)
Cliff Linedecker, *Killer Kids* (1993)

STRAIGHT AND GAY

The vast majority of sadistic lust-murderers are heterosexual men, venting their virulent hatred of women on prostitutes, coed hitchhikers, and other female victims of opportunity. Gays, however, aren't exempt from this psychopathology. Some of the most infamous serial killers of recent times have been homosexual men: John Wayne Gacy, Jeffrey Dahmer, Dean Corll, Dennis Nilsen.

Though gays constitute only a small minority of serial killers—about 5 percent, according to the most informed estimates—they are even more prone to "overkill" than their straight counterparts, indulging in the most horrific extremes of torture, mutilation, and dismemberment. They are also among the most prolific of serial killers. The sheer promiscuity of their crimes is a kind of grotesque mirror of the untrammeled sexual lifestyle embraced by so many gay men in the pre-AIDS era of the 1970s.

Why homosexual serial killers as a group should be especially sadistic is an interesting question, though one element is surely the prevailing homophobia of American society, which causes many gay men to grow up with a deep-seated sense of self-hatred, a violent homophobia of their own. When these feelings are combined with the psychopathology of a serial killer, the results can be particularly appalling.

Randy Kraft

Though less notorious than some of his psychopathic peers, Randy Kraft—aka the "Scorecard Killer"—committed atrocities every bit as horrendous as those of John Wayne Gacy or Dean Corll. And his victim count allegedly surpassed those of both.

An exceptionally bright man who grew up in ultraconservative Orange County, California, Kraft embraced right-wing politics in his teens, joining the ROTC and demonstrating in favor of the Vietnam War. As the sixties progressed, however, he did an about-face, growing his hair long and switching political allegiances to the left. He also "came out" as a gay man. It was during the freewheeling 1970s that he embarked on his sinister secret life. While working by day as a highly paid computer consultant, he spent his nights cruising for male pickups, who would, with terrifying regularity, end up as hideously violated corpses.

Between October 1971 and his arrest twelve years later, Kraft murdered an estimated sixty-seven young men, ranging in age from thirteen to thirty. The victims—whose corpses were generally dumped beside California freeways—had typically been subjected to unspeakable tortures. Some were castrated; others had swizzle sticks or other pencil-sized objects shoved up their penises; still others had been sodomized with everything from toothbrushes to tree branches. At least one had his eyes burned with a cigarette lighter. Many had their nipples gnawed off.

Early on the morning of May 14, 1983, Kraft was pulled over for drunk driving by two California Highway Patrol officers, who were startled to discover a strangled young man in the passenger seat. Searching Kraft's vehicle, they found, stashed under a floormat, forty-seven Polaroids of naked young men who appeared to be either dead or unconscious. Inside the trunk was an attaché case containing a coded list that turned out to be Kraft's meticulously recorded "scorecard" of murder victims. After a long-delayed and protracted trial, he was convicted of sixteen counts of murder and now awaits execution in San Quentin prison.

Kraft made the news again in 1993, when he filed a 60-million-dollar lawsuit against the author of a book about his case, claiming that the writer had unfairly portrayed him as a "sick, twisted man" and ruined his "prospects for future employment." Apparently the judge did not feel that the condemned serial killer's job prospects were as bright as Kraft did. His suit was dismissed.

> There's nothing wrong with him, other than he likes killing for sexual satisfaction.
>
> —Prosecutor Bryan Brown on Randy Kraft

William Bonin

During the very same period that Randy Kraft was racking up his appalling body count, another gay serial killer, William Bonin, was at large in Southern California.

Bonin endured the kind of nightmarish childhood so often found in the case histories of serial killers. His father was a brutal drunk who once gambled away the family home, routinely beat his wife and children, then died from cirrhosis of the liver when Bonin was a little boy. His mother—who spent most of her time playing Bingo—totally neglected her sons, frequently leaving them in the care of her father, a known pedophile who had sexually abused his own children while they were growing up.

At eight years old, Bonin was arrested for stealing license plates and sent to a reformatory. There, he was sexually molested by other juvenile inmates, as well as by at least one adult counselor. From that point on, according to one authority, he developed "an unstinting, often schizophrenic, interest in pedophilia." Released from detention, he returned to his Connecticut home, where he promptly began molesting his younger brothers and other neighborhood children.

Joining the Air Force, Bonin served as an aerial gunner in Vietnam, won a good conduct medal, and was given an honorable discharge. Unbeknownst to his superiors, his tour of duty included two incidents in which he had sexually assaulted other men at gunpoint.

Returning to the States, he moved to Southern California and almost immediately plunged into his life of depravity. In 1969, he was arrested after sodomizing five underage boys. Deemed a "mentally disordered sex offender," he was sent to Atascadero State Hospital, where he spent the next five years. Sixteen months after his release in 1974, he was arrested again for raping a fourteen-year-old boy at gunpoint. For that offense, he spent three more years behind bars. He got out in 1978, but in less than a year was arrested again, this time for assaulting a seventeen-year-old hitchhiker. Through a bureaucratic screwup, however, Bonin was almost immediately set free.

"No one's ever going to testify again," he vowed to the friend who drove him home from jail. "This is never going to happen to me again."

Making good on that threat, Bonin made sure that none of his next nearly two dozen victims lived to identify their attacker. Cruising the highways in his drab green Chevy van—sometimes alone, often with an accomplice—he would pick up a teenage hitchhiker, drive to a remote spot, sodomize and kill the boy, then dump the body along the freeway. Generally, the victims were strangled with their own T-shirts, which were wrapped around their necks and twisted, tourniquet-like, with a tire iron. Sometimes, they were subjected to other tortures as well: ice picks jammed into their ears, acid poured down their throats, coat hangers thrust up their rectums. Between August 1979 and

June 1980, twenty-one young men died at the hands of the sadistic fiend whom the press dubbed the "Freeway Killer."

The end of his horrific career came when one of his accomplices was busted for another crime and, as part of a plea deal, pointed the finger at Bonin, who was immediately placed under round-the-clock surveillance. Within twenty-four hours, police arrested him for sodomizing a fifteen-year-old boy. Bonin eventually confessed to twenty-one murders and was given the death sentence. During the next seventeen years, while he tried every legal maneuver to have his sentence overturned, he painted, read, wrote letters to the families of his victims, and played bridge with other serial killers, including Randy Kraft. He was finally put to death by lethal injection on February 23, 1996.

> I'd still be killing. I couldn't stop killing. It got easier each time.
>
> —William Bonin after his arrest, when asked by a reporter what he would do if he were still at large

Larry Eyler

Two years after the capture of Southern California's "Freeway Killer," a homicidal sadist with a strikingly similar MO sent shock waves through gay communities across the Midwest. Dubbed the "Highway Murderer," his real name was Larry Eyler. For nearly two years, he cruised the interstates of Illinois, Indiana, Wisconsin, and Kentucky, stopping at small-town pubs, red-light districts, gay bars, and even the occasional upscale, residential neighborhood. Night after night, he hunted for prey—male, generally white and young, and desperate for something: cash, company, or just a ride. Between late 1982 and mid-1984—while local police, state troopers, and FBI agents crossed signals, missed evidence, and botched investigations—Eyler had his unspeakable way with nearly two dozen victims, dumped their mutilated corpses just off the open highways, then kept driving.

He first struck in the fall of 1982, savaging two young men and discarding their remains in Indiana and Illinois. Two more bodies were found in December. In his murderous frenzy, the killer slashed his victims' throats and bellies, leaving their entrails hanging out. He had also left a bizarre, ritualistic "signature": in several cases, white tube socks, not belonging to the victims, were found on their feet.

Throughout the spring of 1983, more trussed and butchered bodies turned up in the neighboring states. Despite calls for action from the gay communities of Chicago and Indianapolis, police were slow to acknowledge that a homosexual lust-killer was on the loose. It was not until May 1983—when the "Highway Murderer" had already claimed ten victims—that a task force was organized to investigate the crimes. The nameless executioner was profiled as a violently self-loathing gay whose atrocities were a way of striking out at the homosexuality he hated and feared in himself.

It wasn't long before thirty-one-year-old Eyler was identified as a prime suspect by a young man named Mark Henry, who, several years earlier, had been handcuffed at knifepoint by Eyler after accepting a ride in his pickup truck, then stabbed when he tried to escape. Several months after police received this tip, Eyler was arrested when an Indiana State Trooper spotted him emerging from the woods with a partially bound young man. A search of Eyler's pickup truck turned up a batch of incriminating evidence: surgical tape, nylon rope, and a hunting knife stained with what proved to be human blood. However—in one of those legal decisions that drive strict law-and-order types crazy—the search was ruled illegal and Eyler set free.

Like other serial killers who believe, in their overweening arrogance, that they can outwit the law forever, Eyler—knowing full well that he was under surveillance—continued to kill. He wasn't stopped for good until August 21, 1984, when the janitor of a Chicago apartment building discovered the body parts of a dismembered male in several gray plastic trash bags and Eyler was fingered as the person who had dumped them there.

Convicted and sentenced to death, Eyler tried to bargain with authorities. In exchange for a lesser punishment, he confessed to several unsolved murders and also named another man—Robert Little, a fifty-three-year-old library science professor at Indiana University—as an accomplice in one of the mutilation-killings. Little was ultimately tried and acquitted. Eyler died of AIDS in March 1996, having confessed to twenty-one murders.

William MacDonald, the Sydney Mutilator

CASE STUDY

In 1926, Allen Ginsberg was born in Newark, New Jersey. He would grow up to be a major cultural force in 1960s America, a pioneer of gay liberation who celebrated his homosexuality and wrote some of the most influential poetry of the late twentieth century.

Two years earlier, another boy with the same name was born in Liverpool, England. He, too, would end up in the history books—though not as a poet and certainly not as an icon of sexual tolerance. A tormented gay who hated and feared his own sexual orientation, this other Allen Ginsberg would turn out to be one of the most ghastly murderers in recent history, a lust-killer so savagely violent that he came to be known as "the Mutilator."

In later life, he would blame his troubles, rather conveniently, on an incident that occurred in 1943, when—during a stint in the army—he was raped in an air-raid shelter by a fellow soldier. The problem with this story—besides the fact that there is no proof of its truth—is that Ginsberg had already been diagnosed as a schizophrenic long before it supposedly happened.

Discharged from the army in 1947, he soon found himself committed to a mental asylum in Scotland, where he spent six nightmarish months crammed inside a freezing cell with gibbering madmen and subjected to a daily regimen of shock treatments. Shortly after he emerged from this bedlam, he left Great

Britain, emigrating first to Canada, then to Australia, where he dropped his birth name and took on the identity that would gain lasting infamy in the annals of crime: William MacDonald.

In 1960, the thirty-six-year-old MacDonald, living in Brisbane, committed his first murder when he picked up a fifty-five-year-old alcoholic named Amos Hurst. Accompanying Hurst to a sleazy hotel, MacDonald strangled him as they sat together on a bed drinking beer.

The experience was powerfully stimulating for MacDonald and left with him a craving for more. At the start of 1961, he moved to Sydney. By day, he worked in the post office as a letter sorter, while at night he prowled parks and public toilets, looking for homosexual pickups.

Six months after arriving in Sydney, he was overcome with the urge to kill. Carrying a bag containing a long-bladed knife and a lightweight plastic raincoat, he lured a forty-one-year-old homeless man named Alfred Reginald Greenfield to a deserted swimming pool and plied him with beer until Greenfield passed out. Then—after donning the raincoat—MacDonald killed the unconscious derelict with dozens of stab wounds to the face and neck, severing his jugular. He then stripped Greenfield naked from the waist down and sliced off his genitals, which he took away with him and threw into the harbor.

After another six-month hiatus—or "cooling-off period," in the jargon of criminology—MacDonald's blood hunger again reached an overwhelming pitch. In November 1961, he butchered another forty-one-year-old male pickup named Ernest Cobbin, slashing the latter's throat as he sat on a public toilet, then castrating him and carrying away the grisly trophy in a plastic bag, which he later tossed into Sydney Harbor.

A nearly identical atrocity followed in March 1962. By then, a massive manhunt was under way for the maniac known as the "Mutilator." Shortly afterward, having been evicted by his landlord and sacked from his job, MacDonald moved to a suburb of Sydney. He took on a new name—Alan Brennan—and opened a sandwich shop. He perpetrated his final horror that November, when he brought a forty-two-year-old derelict, James Hackett, back to his shop. Rendering him stuporous with drink, he butchered and mutilated him. Afterward, he hid the corpse in the basement and—in a panic—fled the city for Brisbane.

When the badly decomposed corpse was discovered more than a month later, it was mistakenly identified as that of the shop owner, Alan Brennan. The cause of death was given as accidental electrocution. Had MacDonald stayed away, he would have remained free to kill again. Instead, for unexplained reasons, he returned to Sydney, where he soon bumped into an acquaintance named John McCarthy, who was understandably startled to see the supposedly deceased Brennan walking around on the streets. When MacDonald turned and fled, McCarthy notified the press. It wasn't long before a leading newspaper ran the story under the headline, "THE CASE OF THE WALKING CORPSE." Exhuming the remains of "Brennan," authorities now determined that the dead man was really James Hackett and that he had been stabbed to death and sexually mutilated. They became convinced that the real Brennan was the notorious "Mutilator." Before long, MacDonald was arrested in Melbourne and brought back to Sydney. At his 1963 trial, he was found guilty of four counts of murder and given life in prison, where he passes his days reading literary classics and listening to Chopin, Liszt, and Gilbert and Sullivan.

BLOODTHIRSTY "BI"S

While most sadistic lust-murderers prefer victims of either their own or the opposite sex, a few can be classified as bisexual. The extravagantly perverted Albert Fish, for example, derived as much twisted pleasure from raping and castrating young boys as he did from torturing and cannibalizing little girls. Thirty years earlier, in the late 1890s, an equally depraved monster roamed the French countryside, preying on victims of both sexes. He has long been forgotten, though his crimes were even more appalling than those of his contemporary, Jack the Ripper. His name was Joseph Vacher.

In contrast to certain psychopaths whose pleasant looks belie their depraved minds—Ted Bundy, for example, or Jeffrey Dahmer—Vacher's physical appearance was as repulsive as his soul. One side of his face was paralyzed, his right eye exuded a steady flow of pus, his lips were contorted and scarred. These deformities were the result of a self-inflicted wound sustained at twenty-four when—after shooting a woman who had spurned him—he turned the pistol on himself and fired into his own head. His appearance was sufficiently disquieting to cause people to flinch when they saw him. Vacher, in the self-pitying way of most psychopaths, would later claim that he had been driven to commit his hideous crimes because the world was so very mean to him—a dubious assertion since his sadistic tendencies had manifested themselves long before the failed suicide attempt that made his features so revolting.

Born in 1869, he took great pleasure in torturing animals as a child and showed the kind of precocious interest in sex typical of future serial killers. At school, he enjoyed introducing his little playmates to mutual masturbation. In his late adolescence, he joined a monastery but was promptly expelled for encouraging the same practice, along with sodomy, among the novice monks.

After a stint in the army—during which he terrorized his fellow soldiers with unprovoked outbursts of near-homicidal rage—the incident occurred that left him disfigured for life. Rebuffed by a young woman he proposed to, he shot her three times, then turned the gun on himself. The young woman survived, as did Vacher, who was committed to an insane asylum and treated for "persecution mania." Incredibly, he was declared cured after less than a year and discharged in April 1894.

One month later, he embarked on one of the most hideous sprees in the annals of serial murder. Armed with knives, scissors, and a cleaver, he took up the life of a tramp and roamed the countryside, searching for victims to butcher.

The list of his atrocities is as follows:

March 20, 1894. Vacher strangles a twenty-one-year-old woman, cuts her throat, stomps on her abdomen, rips flesh from her breasts, and rapes her corpse.

November 10, 1894. He murders and mutilates a thirteen-year-old girl.

May 18, 1895. He murders and mutilates a seventeen-year-old girl.

August 24, 1895. He strangles a fifty-eight-year-old widow and rapes the corpse.

August 28, 1895. He murders a sixteen-year-old girl, rips open her abdomen, and tears out the entrails.

August 31, 1895. He strangles, castrates, and anally sodomizes the corpse of a seventeen-year-old shepherd boy.

September 29, 1895. He murders and castrates a fifteen-year-old boy.

September 10, 1896. He murders a nineteen-year-old newlywed woman, then rapes the corpse.

Joseph Vacher attacks a victim

October 1, 1896. He murders a fourteen-year-old shepherdess, tears out her vulva, and carries it away with him.

May 27, 1897. He murders a fourteen-year-old boy, anally sodomizes the body, then throws it down a well.

June 18, 1897. He murders a thirteen-year-old shepherd boy and sodomizes the corpse.

In August, 1897, Vacher was finally arrested after attacking a young woman named Marie-Eugenie Plantier, who was collecting pinecones in the woods. Her screams brought her husband and sons running. Overpowered, Vacher was taken into custody and charged with offending public decency. Before long, police realized that they had the notorious "Ripper" on their hands. After offering a written, sickeningly detailed confession to all eleven murders, he was brought to trial in 1898. He offered every conceivable excuse for his outrages, from temporary insanity to an uncontrollable impulse induced by a childhood case of rabies. The judge was unpersuaded. Convicted, Vacher was guillotined on December 31, 1898.

PARTNERS IN CRIMES

In the popular imagination, the stereotypical serial killer is a lone wolf: a solitary psycho who holes up in his lair, brooding on his sick, sadistic fantasies until, driven by an overwhelming compulsion, he emerges to go prowling for a victim. And in fact there are quite a few serial killers who fit this pattern. But many do not. A surprising number of them—anywhere from 10 to 28 percent, according to the best estimates—go hunting in pairs.

Lake and Ng

Team killers, as they are now generally called, have perpetrated some of the most heinous crimes of modern times. In the early 1980s, a self-styled survivalist named Leonard Lake—whose keenest desire was to abduct women and keep them as sex slaves—joined forces with a sadistically simpatico Asian named Charles Ng. Together—in a specially designed and equipped concrete bunker constructed on a piece of wooded property in the remote Sierra Nevada foothills of northern California—they lived out their depraved fantasies, raping, torturing, and killing a string of captives while videotaping the atrocities. Their unspeakable activities came to an end in June 1985, when a hardware store clerk spotted Ng stashing a stolen bench vise in the trunk of Lake's car. By the time the cops arrived, Ng had fled. A check of Lake's car revealed that it belonged to someone else. The police also found a silenced pistol in the trunk. Brought to the station house for questioning, Lake—realizing that the jig was up—plucked two hidden cyanide tablets from the lapel of his shirt and swallowed them. He went into a coma and died four days later.

A subsequent search of Lake's isolated premises turned up a blood-soaked bed fitted with restraints, blood-caked power tools, homemade pornographic videos showing the two men debasing their captives, handwritten diaries detailing these outrages, and—buried around the property—an appalling cache of human remains, including the bodies of seven men, three women, two babies. There were also forty-five pounds of human bone fragments, suggesting that up to twenty-five people had met death at the hands of the psychopathic pair.

An arrest warrant for twelve murders was issued for Ng. He was ultimately arrested in Canada for shooting a security guard during a store theft. After years of legal wrangling, he was finally extradited and brought back to the US, though he managed to delay his trial until October 1998—thirteen long years after his capture. After an eight-month trial, he was found guilty of the murder of six men, three women, and two baby boys. He was sentenced to death.

> God meant women for cooking, cleaning house, and sex. When they are not in use, they should be locked up.
>
> —Leonard Lake

Bittaker and Norris

California was also the hunting ground for Lawrence Bittaker and Roy Norris, a pair of quintessential psychopaths who bonded in prison, where they dreamed up a monstrous plan to kidnap, torture, and kill teenage girls while recording the crimes on tape. No sooner were they released than Bittaker purchased a used GMC cargo van that they christened "Murder Mack." After a few dry runs in which they scouted locations, they put their hideous scheme into action on June 24, 1979, snatching a sixteen-year-old girl who was on her way home from church. They drove her to an abandoned mountain road, then raped her before garroting her with a wire coat hanger. Over the next few months, they abducted and murdered five more girls, ranging in age from thirteen to eighteen. The victims were raped, mutilated, bludgeoned, tortured with ice picks driven into their ears, slashed, and strangled. Meanwhile, their agonized cries and terrified pleas were recorded on tape, while Norris chanted: "Keep it up, girl! Keep it up! Scream till I say stop!"

They were finally captured after Norris boasted of his crimes to a friend, who notified the police. Cutting a deal with the authorities, Norris testified against Bittaker, who was ultimately found guilty of five counts of first-degree murder and sentenced to death. Norris received a sentence of forty-five years to life and will be eligible for parole in 2010. Bittaker has passed his time on death row filing nuisance suits against the state prison system (including one that claimed that he had been made to suffer cruel and unusual punishment from being served a broken cookie on his lunch tray) and enjoying daily bridge games with other condemned serial killers.

Corll and Henley

A particularly horrific case of team killing came to light on August 8, 1973. Early that morning, police in the Houston suburb of Pasadena received an urgent phone call from seventeen-year-old Elmer Wayne Henley, summoning them to the apartment of an older man named Dean Corll. When the cops arrived, they found Corll's naked body on a bedroom floor with six bullets in him. It was clear at a glance that bizarre things had been going on in the room. Plastic sheeting covered the carpet, as though to protect it from blood. Sinister-seeming items—a bayonet, an enormous dildo, a roll of duct tape, a jar of Vaseline, and a bunch of thin glass pipettes—lay scattered on the floor. Most alarming of all was the large wooden torture board equipped with restraints.

(Novelty trading card courtesy of Roger Worsham)

Henley—who was there with two other teenagers, a boy named Tim Kerley and a girl named Rhonda—poured out his lurid story. Corll—whose job at his family's confectionery business had earned him the nickname the "Candyman"—was a thirty-four-year-old gay who liked to party with much younger males. Henley was a friend of his. The previous night, Wayne had invited Tim and Rhonda to Corll's house for a glue-sniffing party. Eventually, all three teenagers passed out. When Wayne awoke, he found himself bound to the torture board. Corll—infuriated that Wayne had brought along a girl—was brandishing a gun and threatening to kill him. Frantically, the boy pleaded for his life, promising that he would rape Rhonda while Corll "took care" of Tim. When Corll finally relented and loosened Henley's bonds, the latter managed to get his hands on the gun and kill the older man.

But there was more and worse to come. Henley confessed that, for several years, Corll had paid him and another young man, David Brooks, to procure young male victims. The boys—most in their teens, though one as young as nine—had been invited to Corll's home for drug and booze parties. There, they had been overpowered by the much older, powerfully built "Candyman," bound to his board, and subjected to hideous tortures. Some had been castrated, some had the catheter-sized pipettes shoved into their urethras and crushed, at least one had his penis chewed off. Eventually, they had been murdered and their bodies disposed of in various locations, including a boat shed several miles south of Houston.

At first Henley maintained that he had merely supplied Corll with victims—some of them, appallingly enough, his own friends and neighbors.

Eventually, he admitted that he had been an active participant in the orgiastic torture-slayings.

Twenty-seven moldering bodies were eventually recovered, seventeen interred in the boat shed. Convicted of one count of murder, David Brooks was sentenced to life. Henley, convicted of murder in the deaths of six boys, received six consecutive ninety-nine-year sentences.

The Lives and Lies of Henry Lee Lucas and Ottis Toole

Separately and together, the lives of Henry Lee Lucas and his sometime partner-in-atrocity are so unspeakably depraved that they seem like the most lurid, over-the-top horror fiction. And, in fact, it has become difficult to tell exactly how much of the story is true and how much is pure, malevolent make-believe. Long regarded as America's most prolific serial killer with a victim count numbering in the hundreds, Lucas eventually recanted his confessions, claiming that he was innocent of virtually every murder he had admitted to. He became the sole condemned prisoner in Texas whose death sentence was commuted by then-governor George W. Bush. Still, there's no doubt that Lucas and Toole were an unusually loathsome pair of reprobates, responsible for any number of heinous crimes.

(Novelty trading card courtesy of Roger Worsham)

By all accounts, Lucas's childhood was sheer Southern Gothic nightmare. Born in August 1936, he grew up dirt-poor in a two-room log cabin in the backwoods of Virginia with eight siblings, a moonshiner father who lost both legs after falling down drunk in front of an oncoming freight train, and a viciously depraved prostitute mother named Viola who entertained her tricks at home. According to Henry, Viola forced him to watch when she had sex with her customers, made him dress in girl's clothes when he went off to school, killed his favorite pets as a form of punishment, and once beat him so severely on the head with a chunk of wood that he went into a twenty-four-hour coma.

By the time he was thirteen, Henry had been inducted into the joys of animal torture and bestiality by one of his mother's johns. He took particular pleasure in trapping various creatures, slitting their throats, then having sex with the dead bodies. His first alleged human victim, killed in 1951, was a seventeen-year-old girl. When she fought off his attempted rape, he strangled her and buried her corpse in the woods.

In 1954, the eighteen-year-old Lucas received a six-year prison term for burglary. He was released in September 1959. Six months later, during a drunken argument with his mother, he stabbed her in the neck. She died forty-eight hours later. Receiving a term of twenty to forty years for second-degree murder, he was soon transferred to a state hospital for the criminally insane and paroled after only ten years. Eighteen months later, he was back in prison for molesting two teenage girls. He was released in August 1975, and began to drift around the country, reputedly killing victims as the spirit moved him. In late 1976, he crossed paths with Ottis Toole.

A snaggle-toothed degenerate with Neanderthal features and a subnormal IQ, Toole had a childhood reportedly as nightmarish as Lucas's. According to the standard accounts, he was abandoned by his drunkard father, subjected to the religious ravings of his fanatical mother, and sexually abused by a sister. His grandmother, an alleged Satanist who concocted charms from human body parts, supposedly forced him to accompany her on her periodic forays to local graveyards, where she dug up her ingredients. By the time he was six, Toole was a confirmed arsonist, torching neighborhood houses because, as he later explained, "I just hated to see them standing there."

The cretinous, bisexual Toole allegedly committed his first murder in 1961, when he was fourteen. While hitchhiking, he was picked up by a traveling salesman who drove him to a remote spot for sex. Afterward, according to his account, Toole jumped behind the steering wheel and deliberately ran over the older man with his own car. By 1974, he had hit the open road in an old pickup truck, drifting from place to place.

By the time he met Lucas in a Jacksonville, Florida, soup kitchen in 1976, there is some evidence that Toole was already a serial killer who had murdered four victims in a six-month span. Recognizing each other as depraved soul mates, Lucas and Toole hooked up for the next six and a half years. The exact nature and number of the enormities they may or may not have perpetrated during his period remains murky. Presumably, they spent a considerable amount of their spare time, raping, killing, and mutilating countless victims, as well as indulging in acts of necrophilia and cannibalism. Also during this period Lucas became smitten with Toole's underage niece, Becky Powell—who would ultimately become yet another slain and dismembered victim.

Lucas was picked up on a weapons charge in June 1983. A few days later, apparently stricken with an uncharacteristic attack of remorse, he summoned his jailer and began to spew out a staggering confession. He had stabbed an eighty-two-year-old woman named Kate Rich, had sex with her corpse, then lugged it home, cut it to pieces, and burned it in a woodstove. And she was just one of dozens—no, scores—of his victims. Over the next eighteen months—as investigators from various states tried to clear up unsolved murder cases—the tally kept growing. Lucas claimed that he had killed women in twenty-seven states with nylon rope, a phone cord, guns of every caliber, knives, vases, a hammer, a roofer's ax, a two-by-four. Traveling under heavy guard—dining on decent food and staying in pleasant motels—he led detectives to supposed crime scenes all over the country. By the time he finished, he had admitted to six hundred murders.

In the meantime, Ottis Toole had been convicted on an arson charge and sentenced to twenty years in prison. Implicated by Lucas, Toole added his own litany of confessions, claiming, among other things, that he and Henry had been involved with a Satanic cult called "The Hand of Death" that sacrificed children and practiced ritual cannibalism. He also claimed to be the unknown deviant who had snatched, murdered, and decapitated Adam Walsh, son of the future host of *America's Most Wanted*—an admission he later retracted. There are many, however, including John Walsh, who remain convinced that Toole was in fact the perpetrator of that unspeakable deed.

Henry, too, ultimately recanted, proclaiming that his countless confessions were a hoax. He had never killed anyone, he insisted, apart from his mother. He had simply been toying with the police, making them look like fools while they shepherded him around the country, treating him to steak dinners and milk shakes.

Eventually, Lucas was convicted of eleven counts of murder. He received the death sentence, however, for only one of them—the killing of an unidentified female hitchhiker nicknamed "Orange Socks" (after the sole item of clothing she was wearing when her corpse was discovered in a culvert off a Texas freeway in 1979). Ironically, compelling evidence surfaced after Henry's trial indicating that he couldn't possibly have committed the "Orange Socks" murder. (Among other things, work records showed that he was in Florida on the day she was killed.) Lucas, it seemed, was going to be executed for a crime he didn't commit. Given the number of homicides he *was* responsible for (anywhere from three to fifteen, according to the best estimates), most people couldn't work up much sympathy for his plight. Four days before he was to die by lethal injection, however, Governor Bush commuted his sentence. Lucas—who had grown obese on prison fare—died of a heart attack in March 2001. Toole had predeceased him by five years, dying in prison in September 1996 of liver failure, evidently accelerated by AIDS.

FOLIE À DEUX

Coined in 1877 by two French psychologists named Lasèque and Fabret, the term *folie à deux* has been translated in various ways: "insanity in pairs," "double insanity," "reciprocal insanity," "collective insanity." In its original meaning, it refers to a rare psychological phenomenon in which two or more closely associated people—often, though not always, family members—share the same psychotic delusion. In a well-known case reported in the 1930s, for example, two middle-aged sisters became convinced that they were being blackmailed by a popular radio personality who was sending coded threats to them in the songs he performed on the air.

Nowadays, the term is most often used to describe something slightly different—not a shared paranoid fantasy but a pernicious bond between two people who bring out the worst in each other, egging each other on to engage in criminal acts that neither person, individually, would have the courage to commit on his own. In most such cases of *folie à deux,* there is one dominant personality who takes the lead in instigating and planning the crimes and one subordinate member who serves as an eager accomplice. In this sense, the term might best be translated—as psychologist Horace B. English half-humorously suggests—as "gruesome twosome." There have also been rare cases involving mutually toxic trios or even foursomes (what might be called *folie à trois* or *folie à quatre*).

Not all criminal pairs who fall under the spell of a *folie à deux* are serial murderers. Leopold and Loeb, for example—the college-age "thrill killers" of the 1920s who murdered a fourteen-year-old acquaintance to prove that they could commit the perfect crime—were clearly in the grip of a *folie à deux.* So were Pauline Parker and Juliet Hulme, the adolescent New Zealand girls who bludgeoned Pauline's mother to death in 1954 (and whose sensational case was the basis for Peter Jackson's 1994 film, *Heavenly Creatures*).

The *folie à deux* phenomenon has also been a factor in the cases of other notorious murderers, such as the two sociopathic spree killers who gained notoriety as the "Beltway Snipers" in the fall of 2002, and the teenage mass murderers, Dylan Klebold and Eric Harris, of Columbine infamy.

It should be said that not all psychopaths who team up to commit serial murder are examples of a *folie à deux.* Individually, for example, Henry Lee Lucas and Ottis Toole were already serial killers before they joined forces. Strictly speaking, the term only applies to two or more people who, however criminally inclined, would never have taken the plunge into full-blown serial homicide had they not been emboldened by an enthusiastic partner. Lake-Ng and Bittaker-Norris are classic examples.

Bianchi and Buono

Another pair who conform to the same depraved pattern were Angelo Buono and Kenneth Bianchi: the so-called Hillside Stranglers. Born in 1951 to an alcoholic prostitute who gave him up at birth, Bianchi—like a surprising number of serial killers—was adopted as an infant. By his early childhood, he was already manifesting psychopathic symptoms. He was a compulsive liar and chronic underachiever who erupted into violent tantrums at the slightest frustration. He dreamed (again, like many serial killers) of becoming a policeman, but when his application to the local sheriff's department was rejected, he drifted into security work. This position allowed him to indulge his taste for petty thievery, which also got him fired from a succession of jobs.

In 1976, he moved from Rochester, New York, to Los Angeles and quickly teamed up with his cousin, Angelo Buono—a sadistic pimp with a long history of violence toward women. Though Buono had been guilty of outrageous brutality (allegedly, he once sodomized his wife in front of their

(Novelty trading card courtesy of Roger Worsham)

children after she refused to have sex with him), he—like Bianchi—had never been known to commit murder. Together, however, they made a monstrous combination. In the fall of 1977, they embarked on one of the most appalling serial murder sprees of modern times.

Posing as police officers, the two lured unsuspecting females into their car, then abducted them and drove them to Buono's suburban home. Afterward, the victims' naked, savaged bodies would be disposed of, often on wooded hillsides around the city.

The first to die was a Hollywood hooker named Yolanda Washington. Two weeks later, on Halloween, the corpse of a fifteen-year-old runaway was dumped on a Glendale lawn. Over the next few months—while the city went into a panic—eight more bodies would be found. The victims ranged in age from twelve to twenty-eight. All had been sexually violated (sometimes with objects like soda bottles), strangled, and tortured in various ways: injected with cleaning solution or burned with an electric cord or asphyxiated with slow, almost voluptuous, cruelty.

The killings stopped abruptly in February 1978. One year after the last of the Los Angeles murders, a pair of young women were raped and murdered in Bellingham, Washington. Suspicion quickly alighted on a young man who had moved to Bellingham within the past year and worked as a security guard: Kenneth Bianchi.

Linked by solid evidence to both the Bellingham rape-murders and several of the "Hillside" killings, Bianchi almost succeeded in convincing authorities that he was a victim of multiple personality disorder, and that the crimes had been carried out by an evil alter ego named "Steve." When this ruse was exposed by a psychiatric expert, Bianchi agreed to plead guilty and testify against his cousin in order to avoid execution. Both men received life sentences. Bianchi is spending his in Walla Walla prison in Washington. On September 21, 2002, the sixty-seven-year-old Buono was found dead in his cell in Calipatria State Prison, apparently the victim of a heart attack.

The Chicago Rippers

Ever since the late 1960s, America has been awash with rumors about devil-worshiping cultists who engage in unspeakable orgies of torture, rape, and human sacrifice. In almost every instance, these stories turn out to be false—the overheated imaginings of people who have watched *Rosemary's Baby* and *The Omen* one too many times. On rare occasions, however, several psychopaths will band together and garb their perverted practices in the trappings of Satanic ritual. This is precisely what happened in Chicago during the early 1980s with a crew of young deviants who became known as the "Chicago Rippers" and exemplify a case of *folie à deux* involving more than two participants.

The accused ringleader of this degenerate gang was Robin Gecht, a lanky twenty-eight-year-old electrician whose deeply troubled background included accusations of molesting his sister. He also once did work for the city's most infamous contractor, John Wayne Gacy. Along with his accomplices—brothers Thomas and Andrew Kokoraleis and Edward Spreitzer, all in their early twenties—Gecht is believed to have abducted and killed as many as eighteen women in as many months, beginning in May 1981. Some were hookers, others middle-class singles or housewives (including the wife of a former Chicago Cubs pitching ace). All the women were raped, tortured, and subjected to hideous mutilations. Specifically, the killers would use a wire garrote to slice off the breasts of their victims. These grisly trophies were then taken back to Gecht's attic bedroom, which had been converted into a Satanic chapel. There, the depraved foursome would perform an unholy communion, eating portions of amputated breast before consigning it to a "relic box."

The case was finally broken when one of his savaged victims survived and provided police with information that led them to Gecht and his cohorts. Under questioning, Tom Kokoraleis spilled his guts. The Chicago Rippers quickly turned on each other.

Gecht has consistently maintained that, like Charles Manson, he never killed anyone: his followers did. He was put on trial for attempted murder and rape and is currently serving 120 years in Illinois. Andrew Kokoraleis was executed by lethal injection in 1999. His brother, Tom, was luckier. He won a reversal of a murder conviction on a legal technicality and received a reduced sentence of seventy years. Edward Spreitzer was condemned to death in 1986, but his sentence was subsequently commuted to life by Governor George Ryan.

KILLER COUPLES

It's appalling enough to think of male buddies hitting the highways to commit serial homicide, like some kind of depraved parody of Dean Moriarty and Sal Paradise in Jack Kerouac's *On the Road.* But there's another type of psychopathic team that seems, if anything, even more unbelievably sick: the killer couple, the husband-wife or boyfriend-girlfriend who engage in sadistic lust-murder as a way to spice up their sex life. While the male partner is almost always the dominant figure in such depraved duos, the woman is generally an active participant, not merely abetting her monstrous mate but getting her own twisted pleasure from their joint atrocities.

The Gallegos

That was certainly the case with Gerald and Charlene Gallego, who enjoyed serial murder the way other couples savor a weekend getaway at a romantic country inn. The son of a skid row prostitute and a violent career criminal whose life ended in Mississippi's gas chamber, Gallego, born in 1946, carried on the family sociopathic tradition. He racked up more than two dozen arrests by the time he was thirty for various felonies, including incest and rape. Possessed of a sleazy charm, he was catnip to a certain kind of woman and was married and divorced seven times by the age of thirty-two. In September 1977, he finally met the woman of his depraved dreams.

The spoiled only child of a prosperous California couple, Charlene Williams was a violin prodigy, a certified genius with an IQ of 160. She was also a profoundly troubled young woman who flunked out of junior college after one semester, had two brief, disastrous marriages in her early twenties, and was heavily into drugs and kinky sex. She and Gallego moved in together one week after meeting at a Sacramento poker club. "I thought he was a very nice, clean-cut fellow," she would say of her wildly degenerate lover.

Their sex life was predictably sordid, Gerald bringing home a teenage runaway for threesomes, Charlene indulging herself with an occasional lesbian lover. Impotent when it came to anything approaching normal sex, Gerald required increasingly perverse pleasures to achieve arousal. Exactly who first thought up the idea of supplying him with "disposable sex slaves" is unclear. What is indisputable is that, beginning in September 1978, the homicidal couple embarked on a monstrous scheme.

Their MO was the same from the start. Driving Gallego's van, they would troll for victims in likely places: county fairgrounds, parking lots of malls, shopping centers, and taverns. While Gerald lurked inside the parked vehicle with pistol at the ready, Charlene would approach the prospective victims—generally, though not always, pairs of teenage girls—and lure them back to the van, usually with an offer of free drugs. Once in the clutches of the depraved duo, the victims would be driven to a remote location, sexually assaulted by both husband and wife, then slaughtered and dumped. Altogether, the Gallegos murdered ten victims, ranging in age from thirteen to thirty-four, all but one of them female.

They were arrested in November 1980, when a witness noted their license plate during their abduction of a young couple who had just left a fraternity dance. Eventually, Charlene struck a deal with prosecutors, agreeing to testify against her husband for a sentence of just under seventeen years. Sentenced to death in 1983, Gerald managed to delay execution through various legal maneuvers but came to a deservedly nasty end anyway, when—in July 2002 at the age of fifty-four—he died of rectal cancer.

Bernardo-Homolka

The sheer level of sexual degeneracy displayed by killer couples staggers belief. Golden-boy Paul Bernardo and his pretty blond wife Karla Homolka were another prime example of the breed. The Ken and Barbie of serial killers, the young Canadian couple presented a picture-perfect image to the world. Beneath their wholesome exterior, however, lurked two of the most depraved personalities imaginable.

Raised, like so many serial killers, in a severely dysfunctional household (his father was a pedophiliac Peeping Tom who molested his own daughter, his mother a grotesquely obese depressive who immured herself in the basement), Bernardo grew up to be a classic psychopath: a man of superficial charm and apparent normality who harbored profoundly malevolent impulses and lacked anything resembling a conscience. While the world assumed he was a successful accountant, he was actually making his money as a small-time smuggler, running cigarettes across the border in cars with stolen license plates. The women he dated soon found themselves not with the sensitive young man they imagined, but in the hands of a vicious sadist who liked to beat and degrade them and whose favorite sexual activity was anal rape.

Karla Homolka, as devoid of moral faculties as her lover boy, turned out to be the perfect mate for Paul, eagerly satisfying—and encouraging—his most depraved desires. He liked to videotape her while she fondled herself and talked of how much fun it would be to procure thirteen-year-old virgins for him to rape. When Paul expressed a wish to deflower her little sister, Tammy, Karla was only too happy to assist, stealing some animal sedative called halothane from the veterinary clinic where she worked. On December 23, 1990—after a happy pre-Christmas dinner in the Homolka home—Paul plied the fifteen-year-old with Halcion-laced drinks. Once she was out cold, he raped her while Karla held a halothane-soaked rag over her little sister's face to make sure she stayed unconscious. Unfortunately, she threw up, choking to death on her vomit.

Tammy Homolka was the first to die at the hands of the hideously perverted pair. Between June 1991 and April 1992, Bernardo and Homolka snatched three more teenage girls. The victims would be subjected to a range of degradations and torments, Karla and Paul taking turns having sex with their captives while the other videotaped the outrages. In the end, the girls would be murdered, and their bodies—sometimes dismembered, sometimes left intact—dumped in a lake or ditch.

While these horrendous killings were going on, Paul—with Karla's encouragement—was conducting a separate career as a serial rapist in Scarborough, Canada. Eventually—when he began beating Karla—she turned on him. Already under suspicion as the "Scarborough Rapist," Bernardo was arrested and ultimately charged with two counts of first-degree murder, two counts of aggravated assault, two counts of forcible rape, two counts of kidnapping, and one count of performing an indignity on a human body. In exchange for her full cooperation, Karla received a lenient sentence. Bernardo, convicted on all counts, was sent to prison for life.

> We had this sexual fantasy, see, so we just carried it out. I mean, like it was easy and fun and we really enjoyed it, so why shouldn't we do it?
>
> —Charlene Gallego, explaining why she and her husband abducted, raped, and murdered ten people

The Wests

Outside the pages of the Marquis de Sade, it would be hard to find human beings as obscenely evil as the British psycho-couple, Fred and Rose West. Like Karla Homolka—who sacrificed her own sister to her partner's sadistic lusts—the Wests had no qualms about preying on their nearest kin. Incest was just one of the countless perversions they delighted in. Arguably, the Wests were even more monstrous than their Canadian counterparts since their victims included several of their own children.

Born in 1941, the simian-looking Fred West was reportedly the product of a household in which incest was rife. By the time he was twenty, he was a habitual thief and convicted child molester who had impregnated a thirteen-year-old girl ("Doesn't everyone do it?" he said in his defense when confronted with this crime).

In 1962, he married a troubled teen and part-time prostitute, Catherine "Rena" Costello, who was carrying another man's baby. Shortly afterward, she gave birth to a girl, Charmaine. With Fred—who enjoyed impregnating his women almost as much as he liked watching them have sex with other men—she quickly conceived again. Their daughter, Anna Marie, was born in 1962.

For a while, Fred drove an ice-cream truck—a job that offered ample opportunity to prey on little girls. Later, he found work in a slaughterhouse, an experience he would later put to appalling uses.

In 1967, fed up with her husband's perverse sexual demands, Rena moved out. No sooner was she gone than Fred took up with a teenage mistress named Anna McFall and quickly got her pregnant. When she began to pressure him into marriage, Fred killed and dismembered her, keeping her fingers and toes as souvenirs—a grotesque ritualistic "signature" he would repeat on future occasions.

After briefly moving back in with Fred, Rena abandoned him for good, leaving him to raise their children, Anna Marie and Charmaine, whom Fred was routinely molesting. Finally, in 1969—when Fred was twenty-eight—he met the woman who would become his partner in the unspeakable for the remainder of his abhorrent life.

Rosemary Letts was sixteen at the time, the daughter of a schizophrenic father and depressive mother who had undergone shock treatments while pregnant with her. Rose grew up a sexually debauched, foul-mouthed loner who liked to climb into bed with her younger brother and fondle him.

Within a year of moving in with Fred, she gave birth to a daughter, Heather. Shortly afterward—apparently in a fit of pique—she killed Fred's stepchild, Charmaine. Fred disposed of the girl's body in his preferred manner, saving fingers and toes for his ghastly collection. Fred's daughter by Rena, Anna Marie, was subjected to repeated sexual torture by her father and his new wife—Rose holding the eight-year-old down while Fred raped her. When Rena showed up looking for her children, she was murdered and disposed of the usual way: her body dismembered, fingers and toes removed.

For the next two decades, the Wests led an outwardly respectable life while pursuing a secret existence of unimaginable depravity. Rose worked out of their home as a prostitute, advertising herself in swinger magazines. Frequently pregnant, she gave birth to seven more children, some by Fred, others by clients. Not content with their criminally kinky sex life (among countless other horrors, Fred liked to bring friends home and watch them have sex with his underage daughter, Anna Marie), the Wests turned to sadistic serial murder for the ultimate thrill. At least nine young women—ranging in age from fifteen to twenty-one—were lured to their home or snatched from the streets. Once in captivity, they were subjected to protracted sexual torture (sometimes lasting as long as a week) before being killed, dismembered, and buried in the cellar. When the cellar got too crowded, the Wests turned it into a nursery bedroom for their brood and began to plant new corpses in their rear garden.

The final victim to be interred in their backyard was their own seventeen-year-old daughter.

In August 1992, alerted by accusations of child abuse, the police showed up at the Wests' home and arrested Fred and Rose for the rape of a minor. Taken into government care, the children revealed that their parents had kept them in line with a chilling threat. If they didn't behave, they were told, they would end up "under the patio, like Heather." Excavating the backyard, investigators quickly turned up human remains. They then turned their attention to the cellar, which yielded its ghastly trove. On New Year's Day, 1995, having confessed to twelve murders, Fred West hanged himself in his jail cell with a bedsheet. Eight months later, Rose went on trial. She was ultimately sentenced to life imprisonment on ten counts of murder.

Brady-Hindley

Thirty years before the Wests' atrocities came to light, another British killer couple, Ian Brady and Myra Hindley—aka the "Moors Murderers"—earned everlasting infamy as the most heinous criminals of their day.

The illegitimate child of a Glasgow waitress who turned him over to another couple to be raised, Brady displayed classic psychopathic symptoms from early childhood. Though exceptionally bright, he did poorly in school, was subject to frequent violent tantrums, and indulged in extreme cruelty to animals—stoning dogs, decapitating rabbits, and, on one occasion, burying a cat alive. He got into trouble with the law from an early age and did prison time in his late teens.

(Novelty trading cards courtesy of Roger Worsham)

In 1961, while working as a stock clerk, the twenty-one-year-old Brady met Myra Hindley, an eighteen-year-old peroxide blond typist desperate for relief from the crushing boredom of her life. Falling under Brady's toxic spell, she submitted avidly to his pornographic fantasies, posing in Nazi/dominatrix regalia and lapping up Brady's half-baked Sadean "philosophy."

Encouraged by his lover's slavish devotion, Brady felt increasingly impelled to explore the outer limits of human depravity. Between November 1963 and December 1964, the monstrous couple abducted, raped, and murdered four children, then buried their remains on the moors. Generally, it was Hindley who lured the victims to their doom. Exactly how much she participated in the actual killings remains a matter of dispute, though Brady clearly took the more active role. Their final murder was, in many ways, the most appalling. After snatching ten-year-old Lesley Ann Downey from a local fair, they brought her back to Hindley's house, bound and stripped her, forced her to pose for pornographic pictures, then—before killing her—tape-recorded her heartrending pleas for mercy.

In October 1965, Brady picked up a gay seventeen-year-old named Edward Evans, brought him back to Hindley's house, and split his skull open with an ax in full view of a witness, Myra's brother-in-law, Dave Smith. Sickened by the crime, Smith reported it to the police. After arresting Brady and Hindley, police searched Myra's home and came upon a claim check tucked into a prayer book. This led them to a locker in the local train station. Inside the locker, they found two suitcases containing a cache of incriminating evidence, including the tape recording of little Lesley Downey's torture. When the tape was subsequently played at the trial of the monstrous couple, people throughout the courtroom—not only jury members and spectators but hardened police officers as well—openly wept. Only Brady and Hindley appeared unmoved.

In May 1966, both of the "Moors Murderers" were sentenced to life in prison. In the succeeding decades, the public's loathing for the two remained undiminished. When a portrait of Hindley—painted in a kind of pointillist style from child-sized handprints—was exhibited at a 1998 art show in London, it sparked nationwide outrage. On November 15, 2002, Myra died of respiratory failure at the age of sixty. Brady remains behind bars.

> He is cruel and selfish, and I love him.
>
> —Myra Hindley, writing about Ian Brady in her diary

Clark-Bundy

It is hard to know what early influences turned Douglas Clark into a monster. Though frequently uprooted in his younger years—his father, a navy lieutenant commander, was constantly moving the family from one international post to another—Clark enjoyed a privileged upbringing, living in the kind of colonial luxury that a handsome American salary can bring in places like the Marshall Islands and India. He was waited on by servants and attended elite private schools. It was the sort of life that has produced other intensely self-centered individuals who grow up with a keen sense of entitlement and a concern for nothing but their own pleasures. In Clark's case, it produced something infinitely worse—a sexually predatory psychopath. His nasty adolescent pranks (secretly recording his girlfriends during sex, for example, then playing the tapes for his buddies' amusement) were just a warm-up for some of the most unspeakable atrocities in the annals of American serial murder.

The forces that warped Carol Bundy are easier to discern. Though—in her typically deluded way—she would later recall her childhood in idealized terms as a warm and happy time, she was actually subjected to horrific abuse by both her parents. Her mother's idea of discipline was to inflict savage beatings with a belt and tell the little girl that no one loved her or wanted her around the house. On the night his wife died, Carol's alcoholic father announced to his two underage daughters—thirteen-year-old Carol and her eleven-year-old sister, Vicky—that it was now their responsibility to take their mother's place in his bed. For the next year, until he remarried, he took turns molesting both girls.

At seventeen, Carol married a fifty-six-year-old man to get away from her father (who hanged himself a few years later). When her new husband tried to force her into prostitution, she left him for another man, who promptly began to beat her. In 1979, she fled with her children to a home for battered women, then settled in an apartment in Van Nuys, California, where she quickly entered into an obsessive affair with the married building manager, John Murray. When he eventually brushed her off, Carol was shattered. Three months later, she met Douglas Clark.

By then, Clark had a long history of sexually exploiting desperate women. In Carol Bundy—an overweight, severely myopic thirty-seven-year-old whose lifetime of abuse had robbed her of every shred of self-esteem and who was pathologically needy for anything resembling affection—he found a perfect match: a woman who might almost be described as his soul mate, though there is little in Douglas Clark's subsequent actions to suggest that he possessed a human soul.

In thrall to her new lover, Carol quickly became his eager slave. When she wasn't busy with her nursing job at the Valley Medical Center, she was helping him enact increasingly depraved sexual fantasies. She began by snapping pictures of him while he had sex with various pickups—one of them a child no older than eleven. Having his girlfriend photograph his pedophiliac encounters, however, wasn't kinky enough for Clark, who had begun to indulge in elaborate daydreams of murder, mutilation, and necrophilia. In June 1980, he picked up a pair of teenage runaways, forced them to perform oral sex on him at gunpoint, then killed them both with bullets to the head. Afterward, he sodomized the corpses before dumping them down a highway embankment. Then he went home to share the story of his outrage with Carol.

It wasn't long before the ever-submissive Carol was actively participating in Clark's enormities. Sometimes, she accompanied him when he went cruising the seedy Sunset Strip for young hookers. He would lure them into his car, then shoot them in the head while they went down on him. Other times—in an obscene travesty of the loving housewife fixing a nice brown-bag lunch for her hubby to take to work—she would prepare a "kill bag" for Clark (containing knives, paper towels, liquid cleanser, plastic bags, and rubber gloves), then see him off on his nighttime prowl.

Her complicity in Clark's atrocities reached a pitch of perversity when Clark brought home the decapitated head of twenty-year-old streetwalker Exxie Wilson. Throwing herself into the unspeakable spirit of her lover's "games," Bundy applied cosmetics to the head and gave it a pretty hairdo, after which Clark took it into the bathroom for some necrophiliac fellatio. "We had a lot of fun with her," Bundy later told police. "I made her up like Barbie."

However devoted to her depraved lover, Bundy still carried a torch for John Murray. She occasionally met him for furtive sexual encounters, during one of which she revealed to him that her new lover, Doug Clark, was the "Sunset Slayer" whose crimes were all over the newspapers. A few days later—regretting her indiscretion—she arranged to meet Murray again, then stabbed him to death, cut off his head, and brought it home in a plastic bag for future disposal.

Shortly afterward, the unrelenting horror of her life became too much for Bundy. Breaking down at her workplace, she began to sob, "I can't take it anymore. I'm supposed to save lives, not take them." Before long, she and Clark were under arrest. Eventually, Bundy was sentenced to two consecutive terms of twenty-seven and twenty-five years to life. Clark received the death penalty and is still on death row, twenty years after his conviction.

The Birnies

Like other monstrous couples, Australians David and Catherine Birnie were two unspeakably codependent perverts who used rape, torture, and murder to spice up their sex life. As is typical in such cases, the man was the prime instigator, while his female partner was a slavish—if enthusiastic—accomplice, who threw herself into their joint atrocities as a way of pleasing her man.

A scrawny ne'er-do-well who grew up in various government institutions and was in trouble with the law throughout his adolescence, David Birnie met his future partner-in-crime when they were both children. In their late teens, they teamed up to commit a series of robberies that eventually landed both of them in jail. Catherine, released after a six-month stint, went to work as a live-in domestic servant. She fell in love with her employer's son and ended up marrying him. As their relationship deteriorated in succeeding years, however, she pined for David Birnie. In 1985, she abandoned her husband and five children, moved back in with Birnie, and took his last name without bothering with the formality of a marriage. Before long, their mutually toxic relationship led them to explore new extremes of depravity.

Like other killer couples, the Birnies were heavily into deviant sex. As their craving for ever-kinkier experiences accelerated, Birnie began to talk openly about his fantasies of abduction and rape. They first acted on these degenerate desires in October 1986, when they lured a twenty-two-year-old coed to their ramshackle house on the outskirts of Perth, bound and gagged her at knifepoint, and chained her to a bed. Birnie raped her repeatedly in front of Catherine. Then the depraved duo drove the victim to a wilderness area, where she was garroted with a nylon cord and buried in a shallow grave.

Three more nearly identical atrocities followed. The last of these crimes was so appalling that even Catherine was shaken by it. The victim—a twenty-one-year-old girl abducted from a bus stop—was taken into a forest, raped, stabbed repeatedly, then placed in a shallow grave. As Birnie began covering her up with dirt, she sat bolt upright. Grabbing an ax, Birnie smashed her on the skull. When this tremendous blow didn't kill her, Birnie was forced to split her head in two.

They brought another victim home for sexual abuse and murder just five days later. Catherine—unnerved by the sheer horror of the previous incident—left the sixteen-year-old girl unbound and alone in the bedroom while Birnie was away at work. The captive managed to escape and gave the police complete details about the identity of her tormentors.

Under arrest, Birnie and his common-law wife soon confessed to all four torture-killings and led police to the buried remains. At their 1987 trial, they each pleaded guilty to four counts of murder and were given the maximum sentence of life in prison.

THE FAMILY THAT SLAYS TOGETHER

Some team killers are connected, not just by a sick psychological bond—a shared, mutually inciting interest in torture and murder—but by actual ties of kinship. The Hillside Stranglers, for example, were cousins. So, too, were a pair of bloodthirsty psychopaths who terrorized the American frontier more than two centuries ago.

The Harps

Their names were William and Joshua Harpe. Though often referred to as siblings, they were actually first cousins—the children of two Scottish brothers who emigrated from their homeland to North Carolina sometime around 1760.

As young men during the Revolutionary War, the younger Harpes picked the wrong side, fighting alongside the British. Their motives had less to do with politics than with the opportunities for rape, pillage, and murder that the conflict afforded them. After taking part in a losing battle in South Carolina, the brutish pair deserted the Redcoats and fled to the wilderness. Before long, they had abducted a couple of women and carried them off to Tennessee, settling down around Chattanooga. Over the next few years, they raided farms and robbed unwary travelers. They are also reputed to have killed at least four of their own offspring: unwanted babies born to their captive women.

Sometime around 1794, the two killer cousins dropped the final "e" from their family name and changed their Christian names to Micajah and Wiley. Along the frontier, however, they would come to be known simply as Big Harp and Little Harp—names that would strike fear into the backwoods residents. In 1798, the Harps embarked on what many criminal historians regard as the first serial murder spree in American history. Over a nine-month period, they roamed from Tennessee to Virginia to Kentucky to Illinois, slaughtering an estimated forty victims at a time when the entire population of the country was less than six million.

Some of their murders were especially atrocious. On one occasion, they stripped a man naked, tied him to a horse, then blindfolded the animal and ran it off a cliff. On another, Big Harp picked up his own four-month-old daughter by the ankle and bashed her brains out against a tree because he was worried that the crying infant might alert a posse to his whereabouts. The Harps were also fond of slitting open their victims and filling their bellies with stones before sinking the corpses in a river.

Eventually, Big Harp was shot and seriously wounded by a pursuing posse near present-day Dixon, Kentucky. One of the posse members, Moses Stegall—whose wife and child had been murdered by the Harps—decapitated the still-living outlaw with a hunting knife, impaled the head on a tree, and left it there to rot. To this day, the spot is known as Harp's Head.

Little Harp escaped, changed his name to Sutton, and took up with a band of Mississippi river pirates. In 1804, however, after being recognized in Greenville, Mississippi, he was arrested, convicted, and hanged. As with his brother, his head was cut off and displayed on a stake as a warning to other outlaws.

The Kallingers

Other team killers have been even more closely related to each other than the Harp cousins. In the early 1970s, for example, a Philadelphia shoemaker named Joseph Kallinger enlisted his own son as an accomplice in a series of horrendous crimes.

Born in 1936, Kallinger was abandoned in his infancy and adopted at eighteen months by a sadistic Austrian couple who subjected him to savage floggings, beat him with a hammer, and convinced him that his penis had been permanently stunted by a hernia operation he was forced to undergo at age six. Two years later, he was gang-raped at knifepoint by a bunch of older boys.

Unsurprisingly, he grew up violently disturbed. As an adolescent, he liked to masturbate while clutching a knife and stabbing at pornographic pictures. He was a lifelong pyromaniac who set fires for both pleasure and profit, torching homes for insurance money as well as for the ecstatic sense of power derived from seeing buildings go up in flames.

Briefly committed on two occasions to mental hospitals, he was diagnosed as a schizophrenic sadist with intense hostility toward women. For the most part, however, he managed to pass himself off as normal. Marrying twice, fathering seven children, he opened a shoe repair shop in the Kensington district of Philadelphia. To the outside world, he appeared to be a respectable, self-employed member of the community.

At home, his sadistic violence was never far below the surface. His children were its primary targets. In early 1972, three of them filed abuse charges against him, including his thirteen-year-old daughter, Mary Jo—who claimed that, as punishment for some minor infraction, her father had once branded her thigh with the blade of a red-hot spatula. Kallinger was convicted, but released on probation after just a few months behind bars.

By 1974, his psychosis was in full bloom. Among other symptoms, he began to hear voices—issued by an invisible floating head named "Charlie"—commanding him to murder and castrate young boys. When he asked his thirteen-year-old son Michael for help in this deranged mission, the boy readily agreed. On July 7, 1974, they lured a young Puerto Rican boy into an abandoned factory, stripped him, gagged him with his socks, and sliced off his penis.

The next victim was Kallinger's twelve-year-old son, Joey. Kallinger drowned him in a stagnant pool in the cellar of an abandoned rug factory while Michael watched.

Beginning in November 1974, Kallinger and his son went on a wide-ranging rape and robbery spree, invading homes in New Jersey, Pennsylvania, and Maryland, assaulting the female residents and making off with money and jewelry. Their nine-month crime wave culminated in a horrific episode, when—after gaining entrance to a house in Leonia, New Jersey, and trussing up eight people at gunpoint—Kallinger slit the throat of a twenty-one-year-old woman when she refused to bite off the penis of a male victim. Two weeks later, he and his son were arrested.

Michael—deemed by the courts to have been under his father's nefarious influence—was released into foster care after a stint in reform school. Kallinger was sentenced to life. In prison, he underwent a progressive mental breakdown, proclaiming himself God, declaring his desire to slaughter every person on earth. He also developed an obsessive fascination with his own feces, which he liked to eat from the toilet, smear on his skin, and mail to pen pals. He died of a seizure on March 26, 1996, at the age of fifty-nine.

The Pandys

Another serial sex-killer who enlisted his own child—in this case his daughter—to participate in his atrocities was Belgian pastor Andras Pandy. A stout, bespectacled man with a perpetual half smile and a goofy Prince Valiant hairdo, the middle-aged clergyman looked like the last person on earth capable of homicidal depravity. Underneath his innocuous facade, he was a psychopath of monstrous proportions.

A refugee from Hungary, Pandy settled in Brussels in 1956 and became a respected pastor and founder of a humanitarian organization, presumably set up to provide foster care for children orphaned during the Romanian revolution that toppled the Ceaucescu dictatorship. At home, however, he was a vicious sexual predator. He began raping his daughter Agnes when she was thirteen. Psychologically enslaved to her degenerate dad, Agnes was forced to assist him in a series of horrendous crimes. Between 1986 and 1992, they murdered an indeterminate number of victims, bludgeoning some with a sledgehammer, shooting others, then hacking up the bodies and dissolving the dismembered pieces in a vat of Cleanest—a store-bought drain opener with a high acid content. Six of the victims were Pandy's own family members—his first and second wives, several children and stepchildren. Others were apparently orphans recruited through his "charitable" organization, along with women he lured into his clutches through "lonely hearts" ads in a Hungarian newspaper.

In 1997, Agnes—by then pushing forty—confessed to police. Searching Pandy's home, investigators turned up ghastly evidence of his atrocities—human bones and teeth in the basement, chunks of human flesh in his freezer. Arrested in 1997, the "Pastor Diabolique"—as he was dubbed by the local press—finally went on trial in February 2002, and received a life sentence for six counts of murder. For assisting her monstrous father, Agnes was given a sentence of twenty-one years.

It was my task to take out the organs while Pandy was cutting up the remains. I just used a kitchen knife. You have to exercise strength. It's not that easy.

—Agnes Pandy, explaining how she had eviscerated one of her own stepsisters

---

The Beanes

Among the more sensational crimes of the blood-soaked 1960s were the appalling murders perpetrated by the so-called Manson family. Of course, the wild-eyed bunch who carried out this slaughter weren't really relatives; just a band of psychopathic pseudohippies under the sway of their deranged messiah. But there *have* been a few cases in which entire families have collaborated in serial murder.

One legendary killer clan was the barbarous tribe headed by a fifteenth-century outlaw, Sawney Beane. Born during the reign of James IV of Scotland, the bloodthirsty Beane and his common-law wife fled from civilized society and found refuge in a cave on the Galloway coast, where they proceeded to spawn a family that—through years of incestuous breeding—eventually grew to four dozen members. The main component of their diet was human flesh. Preying on unwary travelers, the feral clan not only robbed but cannibalized their victims, "butchering them in their den, then salting and pickling the meat for future consumption," as historian Michael Anglo writes.

According to legend, hundreds of people ended up as provender for the man-eating Beanes. Their hideout was finally discovered when some travelers spotted several members of the monstrous family feasting on the flesh of a freshly killed husband and wife who had been ambushed on the way home from a fair. Led by the Scots king himself, a small army rounded up the entire clan, who were condemned to a punishment commensurate with their crimes.

"The sex organs of the men were cut off and cast into a fire, and their hands and legs severed from their bodies," historian Anglo explains. "They were left to bleed to death while the females were forced to watch. Finally, cursing and swearing, the women were thrown into fires and slowly burned to death."

MARRIED WITH CHILDREN

Though female psychos like Karla Homolka, Charlene Gallego, and Rosemary West were active accomplices in their husbands' depravities, not every woman married to a sadistic sex-murderer participates in his atrocities. Indeed some of these wives aren't even aware that their mates are serial killers.

Undoubtedly a certain amount of denial is at work in such cases. When Herb Baumeister's wife, Julie, asked him about the half-buried human skeleton that their son had stumbled across in their wooded backyard, Herb hastily explained that it was just an old, discarded lab specimen inherited from his physician father. Unlikely as this story was, Julie chose to believe it. Mostly, however, the fact that certain serial killers are able to fool their own families is testimony to one of the most chilling traits of these psychopaths: their ability to pass themselves off as normal, to conceal their monstrous secret identities from the rest of the world, even from those who share their homes.

Peter Kürten, for example, was married to a perfectly respectable woman who never had an inkling that her spouse was the infamous "Monster of Düsseldorf," responsible for butchering twenty-nine victims in 1929. Nor did the wife of the Russian maniac Andrei Chikatilo ever guess that she was wed to a creature who not only slaughtered more than fifty victims but perpetrated unspeakable acts of torture, mutilation, and cannibalism on their bodies. Peter Sutcliffe—aka the "Yorkshire Ripper"—maintained his facade as a happily married family man while conducting a savage five-year murder spree that claimed the lives of thirteen women.

To be sure, some wives of serial killers come to realize that their husbands are seriously disturbed. John Wayne Gacy's first wife, for example, divorced him after it became clear that he was an inveterate molester of boys. His second marriage ended for similar reasons. And in 1944, the wife of serial prostitute killer Steve Wilson left her husband because of his penchant for sneaking up on her while she was naked and and slicing her buttocks with a razor blade—his idea of an affectionate gesture.

Even in such cases, however, the women never guess the full scope of their husbands' depravity. Of course, the crimes committed by a creature like Gacy are so inconceivable that it's easy to see why his wife wouldn't suspect. After all, it's one thing to leave your husband because he prefers to have sex with teenage boys. The thought that he might also be torturing them to death before stashing their corpses in the crawl space would simply not occur to most people.

Some women married to serial killers do eventually discover what kind of monsters they're living with. Unfortunately for most, this realization comes too late. Like the wife of British sex-slayer John Reginald Christie—who ended up buried beneath the floorboards of her own dining room—these poor women are doomed to learn the dreadful truth the hard way.

CASE STUDY

Herb Baumeister, Family Man

Situated twenty miles from the state capital, Westfield, Indiana, is an exclusive bedroom community of million-dollar estates, so safe and sheltered that locals refer to it as "the golden ghetto." But in the summer of 1996, residents of that exclusive enclave were stunned to discover that a monster had been living in their midst.

His name was Herb Baumeister. Like John Wayne Gacy—another gay Midwestern sex-killer who maintained a facade of suburban propriety—Baumeister was regarded as a pillar of the community, a successful, self-made businessman who generously gave to charities and was well liked by his neighbors. What the world didn't know was that—again, like Gacy—Baumeister led a depraved double life. He made secret forays into the gay hangouts of Indianapolis, where he would pick up young men who would never again be seen alive.

His victims—at least eleven, though possibly many more—would be lured back to his sprawling Tudor-style home. There, they would be strangled during sex, their corpses disposed of in the woods behind the house.

What made these crimes seem even more shocking was that, for at least three years, Baumeister had committed them not merely within the tranquil confines of Westfield but right under the noses of his own family. How, people wondered, could someone with a wife and three children get away with such atrocities?

Psychopathic cunning had something to do with it. So did denial, especially on the part of Herb's wife, Julie. In 1994, when she confronted her husband about a half-buried human skeleton that their son had stumbled upon in the wooded backyard, Herb gave her a cock-and-bull story: the skeleton, he claimed, was just an old anatomical specimen he had inherited from his physician father and had decided to discard. Julie chose to believe him. Eventually, however, even she was forced to face up to the dreadful truth.

Born in 1947, Baumeister showed no signs of mental disturbance until high school. Then his increasingly erratic behavior caused his father to take him for mental evaluations. Though diagnosed as a schizophrenic, there is no record that he received any treatment. After flunking out of college, he drifted from job to job, though his bizarre outbursts—which included urinating on his boss's desk—made it impossible for him to remain gainfully employed.

After marrying in 1971, he and his wife opened a string of flourishing thrift shops in Indianapolis. Eventually, they were able to afford an estate in Westfield: a four-bedroom house with an indoor pool and riding stable on eighteen acres of wooded property. To all outward appearances, they were living the American Dream. The reality, of course, was a nightmare that no one knew a thing about—apart, that is, from Herb and the young men who fell into his clutches.

During the frequent overnight trips taken by Julie and the kids—often to visit Herb's widowed mother at her lakeside condominium—Baumeister traveled to the gay bars of the city, trolling for victims. When young men began disappearing in early 1993, the gay community was quick to take note. Articles appeared in a local gay newspaper. The police were notified. But—as is often the case when gay victims are involved—authorities were slow to take action.

It was not until November 1995 that—thanks to the efforts of a private investigator, hired by the mother of one of the missing men—Baumeister was identified as a suspect. Another eight months would pass before members of the sheriff's department searched his property. By then, Baumeister's life had unraveled: his business had foundered, his long-suffering wife had filed for divorce, and he himself had absconded in his 1989 Buick. Searching the wooded property behind the house, investigators eventually turned up thousands of human bone fragments: jawbones, thighbones, fingers, ribs, vertebrae, all stripped clean by animals and the elements, some partly burned. Experts estimated that, altogether, the skeletal fragments constituted the remains of eleven young men.

By the time the digging was over, Baumeister himself was dead. Fleeing to Canada, he committed suicide in an Ontario park on the evening of July 3, 1996, shooting himself in the head with a .357 Magnum after eating a peanut butter sandwich. The note he left made no mention of his atrocities, attributing his act to personal and family matters: his failed business and broken marriage.

Recommended Reading:

James Alan Fox and James Levin. *Overkill: Mass Murder and Serial Killing Exposed* (1996)
Eric W. Hickey, *Serial Murderers and Their Victims* (1991)
David Lester, *Serial Killers: The Insatiable Passion* (1995)
Michael Newton, *Serial Slaughter* (1992)
Joel Norris, *Serial Killers* (1988)

BLUEBEARDS

One of the most famous of all fairy tales, "Bluebeard" was originally recorded by the French writer Charles Perrault in his classic collection, *Contes du temps passé* (*Tales of Past Times*), more commonly known in English as *Mother Goose's Tales.* The story concerns a fabulously rich gentleman. Despite the creepy coloration of his facial hair—which causes young women to flee at the sight of him—he woos and wins a beautiful maiden and brings her home to one of his country estates. Called away on an extended business trip, he gives his new bride the keys to the castle, telling her that she is free to open any door except the small one at the end of the ground-floor gallery.

No sooner is he out the door, of course, than—overcome with curiosity—his young bride heads for the forbidden room. Opening the door with trembling hands, she steps inside. At first, she can see nothing clearly because the window curtains are drawn. As her eyes become adjusted to the dimness, she is greeted by a fearful sight:

"The floor was all covered over with clotted blood, on which lay the bodies of several dead women ranged against the walls," Perrault writes. "These were all the wives whom Bluebeard had married and murdered, one after another."

When her husband returns home and discovers his new bride's disobedience, he pulls out his cutlass and gets ready to add her to the collection of butchered ex-wives in his storage room. At the last minute, however, she is rescued by the timely arrival of her brothers.

In criminology, the name of this legendary lady killer is applied to a specific type of psychopath: the man who marries and knocks off a succession of women. (In this sense, the Bluebeard killer is the male counterpart of the female "Black Widow.")

Two things distinguish the Bluebeard type from other kinds of serial killers who prey on female victims. First, while psychos of the Ted Bundy/Edmund Kemper/Hillside Strangler variety target random strangers, the Bluebeard's victims are his own wives or girlfriends. Second, while most serial killers are driven primarily by sexual sadism, the Bluebeard—though clearly deriving satisfaction from his atrocities—is also motivated by profit.

Here are some examples of infamous twentieth-century "Bluebeards":

Henri Landru

His spiky beard wasn't blue, but in many other respects Henri Landru bore a striking similarity to his fairy-tale prototype. Though distinctly unattractive, the bald, bushy-browed, middle-aged Frenchman had no trouble attracting the opposite sex. Of course, his victims were especially vulnerable: women who had been widowed in the devastation of World War I and were desperate for male companionship. Landru was a practiced con artist who had already served seven prison sentences for fraud before he turned his hand to serial murder.

He made the lethal transition when he was in his forties. His usual MO was to place a matrimonial ad in the newspaper, describing himself as a well-off widower with two children and a warm, affectionate nature. When a sufficiently wealthy prospect nibbled at this bait, the charming Landru would sweep her off her feet and whisk her away to a rented villa outside Paris. After she had signed over all her worldly possessions to him, the woman would never be seen or heard from again.

Exactly how Landru killed his victims has never been determined, though their remains were evidently disposed of in a large stove purchased for that specific purpose. Ten women died at his hands. All were middle-aged widows, except one. This was a poor nineteen-year-old servant girl Landru picked up at a train station. That she met the same fate as his other victims reinforces the belief that—like all Bluebeard killers—Landru was not motivated solely by greed but also by sadism.

He was finally caught after one of his victims—a rich widow named Madame Buisson—vanished. Her relatives immediately grew suspicious, though they were unable to track Landru down since he was using a pseudonym. On April 11, 1919, Buisson's sister happened to spot Landru escorting an attractive young woman into a Paris china shop. She alerted the police, who confronted him the next day. In his pocket, they found a little black book, containing notes on all his victims. In November 1921, two and a half years after his arrest, he was convicted, despite steadfast proclamations of innocence. On February 23, 1922, the "French Bluebeard" was guillotined.

George Joseph Smith

Born in 1872, this British Bluebeard became infamous as the "Brides in the Bath Murderer" for his sinister MO. A small-time crook and charming con artist, Smith initially limited himself to scamming gullible spinsters out of their life savings by luring them into bigamous marriages. (He was legally wed throughout his adult life to his first wife, who left him without ever obtaining a divorce.) The moment Smith had his hands on his new bride's money, he would disappear. Usually telling her that he was going out on an errand—to pick up a newspaper or buy a pack of cigarettes—he would never return. On one occasion, he brought his newlywed wife to the National Gallery of Art and, after viewing some paintings, excused himself to go to the bathroom. She never saw him—or her life savings—again.

Smith progressed from swindle to murder in 1912. After getting his fourth "wife," Bessie Mundy, to make out a will leaving him property worth £2,500, he rented a house and had a new zinc-and-enamel bath installed. Shortly afterward, Bessie was found drowned in the tub.

Smith made it appear that, at the time of this tragic "accident," he had gone out to buy fish for their dinner. In reality, of course, he had not sneaked outside until the dreadful deed was done. Crime writer John Brophy vividly describes the method Smith employed:

> With honeymoon playfulness he would enter the room where his bride was already in the bath, admire her naked beauty, bend over her fondly, and, still murmuring endearments, hold her feet. Suddenly, he would tug her feet upwards, thus jerking her head at the end of the bath, below the water, so that in a few moments she would be drowned with no bruises on the body or other signs of assault and resistance.

The next woman to die in this fashion was a nurse named Alice Burnham. After marrying her in November 1913, Smith insured her life for £500. She drowned in the bathtub shortly thereafter, while Smith was ostensibly out of the house buying eggs.

Smith's final murder victim was Margaret Lofty. After marrying her in December 1914, he got her to make out a new will, naming him as beneficiary. Shortly thereafter, the honeymoon pair moved into rented rooms in Highgate. The very next day, while Smith was supposedly out purchasing tomatoes, his new bride drowned in the tub.

The end came for Smith when the father of his second victim, Alice Burnham, read a newspaper account of Margaret Lofty's death. That two of Smith's brides had died in identical "accidents" within days of their weddings struck Mr. Burnham as highly suspicious. He quickly shared his suspicions with the police, who launched an investigation. Eventually, Smith was arrested and put on trial. Despite protestations of his innocence, the jury needed only twenty-three minutes to convict him. He was executed on August 13, 1915.

Johann Hoch

A native of Germany, Johann Schmidt came to America in 1887 at the age of twenty-five, abandoning a wife and three children. In 1895, under the name Huff, he bigamously married a well-off widow named Martha Steinbucher. Four months later, she fell ill with a devastating intestinal ailment. As she writhed in agony, she told her physician that she had been poisoned, but—attributing the remark to delirium—he paid her no heed. She died the next day. Immediately afterward, her husband sold her property for $4,000 and disappeared.

Huff's second murder victim was Caroline Hoch of Wheeling, West Virginia, who was hit with a violent illness shortly after their wedding. On a visit to the stricken woman, her minister surprised Huff in the act of giving his wife some white powder—presumably medicine. The next day, Caroline was dead. Huff immediately sold the house, claimed his wife's insurance policy, then faked his own suicide and disappeared.

Now calling himself Hoch, the killer made his way to Chicago. Along the way he preyed on an indeterminate number of women, murdering some, merely fleecing and abandoning others. For a while he worked in the Chicago stockyards, an occupation that would ultimately earn him his homicidal nickname: the "Stockyard Bluebeard."

In December 1904, Hoch placed a matrimonial ad in a German newspaper and, soon afterward, received a reply from forty-six-year-old widow Marie Walcker, who owned a small candy store. They were married a short time later. A week after the wedding, Marie was stricken with excruciating abdominal pains, a violent thirst, and a tingling in her extremities that felt, she said, like ants crawling over her flesh—all classic symptoms of arsenic poisoning. Her physician, however, diagnosed the problem as nephritis. She died two weeks later. No sooner had Marie exhaled her last, agonized breath than Hoch proposed to her sister, Julia, who had come to tend her dying sibling. Three days later, Hoch and Julia were married. Hoch soon disappeared with all of Julia's money.

Notifying the police, Julia learned that Hoch was already under suspicion for swindle and murder. Caroline Hoch's body had previously been exhumed, but examiners were unable to determine if there was poison in her stomach because Hoch had taken the precaution of eviscerating the corpse and dumping the organs in the river. Authorities had better luck with the body of Marie Walcker. A postmortem examination turned up lethal traces of arsenic in her viscera.

Police immediately distributed the fugitive's photograph. Hoch—who had fled to New York City—was arrested when his landlady recognized his picture in the papers. When police searched him, they found a fountain pen on his possession. Instead of ink, the reservoir contained 58 grains of a powdered substance that turned out to be arsenic. He was convicted of the murder of Marie Walcker and hanged on February 23, 1906. The number of his victims is unknown; estimates range from six to twenty-four.

Herman Drenth, aka Harry Powers

A classic case of a Bluebeard killer who murdered both for pleasure and profit was Herman Drenth. Born in the Netherlands in 1892, he emigrated to America, where he changed his name to Harry Powers. In 1927, he settled in Clarksburg, West Virginia, where he sold Electrolux vacuum cleaners door-to-door and helped operate a small grocery store. In addition to these activities, the pudgy, middle-aged Powers also led a sinister secret life.

Through various matrimonial bureaus, Powers—using the pseudonym "Cornelius Pierson"—would correspond with lonely women, describing himself as a wealthy widower whose busy work life as a civil engineer did not leave him time to pursue marriage by more conventional means. In his letter, he promised to give his wife "everything within reason that money can buy," but above all his "true love and absolute devotion." Those women who fell for his beguiling words, however, ended up losing all their worldly possessions—and, in many cases, their lives.

Exactly how many widows and spinsters were lured into Powers's clutches is unknown. He himself ultimately suggested that he had slain as many as fifty. There is no doubt, however, about the last five people he killed.

In 1931, he won the heart of a forty-three-year-old widow named Asta Eichler and brought her, along with her three young children, from their home in Park Ridge, Illinois, to a remote cabin he had built in Quiet Dell, a rural hamlet about five miles outside Clarksburg. No one ever heard from the Eichlers again. Shortly afterward, a fifty-one-year-old divorcee, Dorothy Lemke of North Uxbridge, Massachusetts, also disappeared after going off with her new mail-order husband, Cornelius Pierson.

When Mrs. Eichler's friends and relatives became alarmed, an investigation was launched that eventually led back to Powers. He was arrested and jailed in August 1931. In the meantime—thanks partly to some neighbors who had complained of the stench emanating from the property—police had turned their attention to his Quiet Dell hideaway. There in a drainage ditch running from the cellar, they turned up the rotting remains of the two women and five children.

Drenth was subjected to a particularly brutal third degree. He was severely beaten, his left arm was broken, and boiled eggs were pressed under his armpits. Eventually, he confessed to everything.

He had turned the cabin cellar into a torture chamber, subjecting his captives to a horrifying ordeal. The three Eichler children—nine-year-old Annabel, twelve-year-old Harry, and fourteen-year-old Greta—had been locked in a cage, starved, and forced to watch their mother being hanged from a ceiling beam. When Harry tried to struggle free to save his mother, Powers crushed his skull with a hammer. The other children were strangled to death, as was Dorothy Lemke.

When word of Powers's confession spread through Clarksburg, a mob of approximately five thousand men tried to break into the jail to lynch him. It took a troop of state police armed with tear gas canisters to disperse them. Powers was tried and convicted in December 1931, and hanged three months later at Moundsville State Penitentiary.

> Beat any cathouse I was ever in.
>
> —Harry Powers describing the pleasure he got from watching victims die

Gilles de Rais, alias Bluebeard

CASE STUDY

One of the most enigmatic figures in the history of true crime, Gilles de Rais, is remembered both as a great hero and as the most infamous of villains. An aristocrat from the province of Brittany in northwestern France, he was an honored military leader in the epic struggle to drive out the English during the second half of the Hundred Years' War. He served as the chief lieutenant for none other than Joan of Arc. Some say his mind was unhinged by Joan's execution in 1431. Or perhaps there had been a streak of madness and cruelty in him since childhood. Whatever the explanation, he eventually went to his death convicted of raping, torturing, and murdering over a hundred children.

Not everyone is convinced of his guilt. Some chroniclers have argued that de Rais was innocent, that he was framed by a fellow aristocrat. In the end, though, popular culture cast its own verdict: de Rais was considered the inspiration for the legend of Bluebeard, the most famous of fairy-tale serial killers.

Born in 1404, Gilles was descended from a family of knights and began his career as a soldier at the age of sixteen. He met Joan of Arc at the court of French king Charles VII nine years later when the teenage girl originally convinced the monarch that God had sent her on a divine mission to save France from the English. Gilles fought alongside Joan when she broke the English siege of Orleans and continued to serve under her in subsequent battles, including her defeat at Paris, where she was captured.

By this time, de Rais had been given the title of Marshal of France in recognition of his wartime service. But his military career was coming to an end. After Joan's capture, he returned to his family's castle in Brittany, where he held the position of baron. At this point, his life began to take a bizarre and gruesome turn.

According to the official version of the case, he immersed himself in alchemy as a way to replace the fortune that he was squandering. Soon, he intensified these efforts by indulging in conjuring and Satanism. These pastimes were all part of a larger descent into madness, which, beginning in 1432, included child murder.

Gilles's servants would provide him with victims, either through abduction or enticement. The children were of both sexes, though most were boys. Gilles sodomized his victims, killed them either through strangulation or decapitation, disemboweled them and masturbated on their entrails. This reign of horror went on for eight years. When de Rais was finally arrested in 1440, the authorities found the dismembered remains of fifty bodies in one of the castle's towers. All told, his victims numbered 140. Or so the records of de Rais' trial tell us.

The person who pressed charges against de Rais was the Duke of Brittany. One theory has it that the duke framed Gilles because he coveted the war hero's lands. Another possibility is that de Rais was indeed guilty, and that the duke might have let him get away with his crimes—the victims were only commoners, after all—if not for the land issue. Whatever the motivation behind de Rais' arrest, his trial left little doubt about his guilt at the time.

There were, in fact, two trials: one for heresy, focusing on de Rais' alleged involvement in black magic, and the other for the murders. On October 25, 1440, Gilles was excommunicated. The next day he was hanged above a roaring fire.

In disguised form, de Rais' horrible legacy lived on in folktales about Bluebeard, best known in the Charles Perrault version of the story written over 250 years after the bloody baron's death. In Perrault's story, Bluebeard's newlywed enters a forbidden chamber in her new husband's castle to discover the dismembered corpses of his previous wives, an abattoir reminiscent of de Rais' tower filled with the remains of his mangled victims. One question, though: How did de Rais, the serial child torturer and murderer, become transformed into a wife killer? According to Leonard Wolf's biography of de Rais, the originators of the Bluebeard tales turned the villain into a killer of adults in order to make the memory of de Rais' hideous crimes easier to absorb. But this, like other aspects of de Rais' life, is open to debate. Some scholars even dispute that de Rais was an inspiration for the Bluebeard legend. They claim that the true source was another folktale revolving around a character named Conomor, who was a sixth-century aristocrat, a wife-killer and, like de Rais, a resident of Brittany.

You who are present -- you, above all, whose children I have slain -- I am your brother in Christ. By Our Lord's Passion, I implore you, pray for me, forgive me with all your hearts the evil I have done you, as you yourselves hope for God's mercy and pardon.
The Theatrical Execution of Gilles De Rais

The Execution of Gilles de Rais by Michael Rose

WORK AND PLAY

According to the FBI, a serial killer is anyone who murders three or more victims with a significant interval of time between each homicide. Under that definition, a mob "enforcer" would qualify. One reason that such professional assassins aren't regarded as serial killers, however, is precisely because they *are* professionals. Murder is their business (as indicated by the name of the most famous gang of hit men in the history of organized crime: "Murder, Inc").

Serial killers, by contrast, don't perpetrate atrocities for a living. They do it for pleasure. Murder isn't their job: it's their passion.

When they aren't indulging in sadistic daydreams or clandestinely carrying out their sickest fantasies, serial killers, by and large, lead drearily ordinary lives. To be sure, the long-ago past affords several instances of illustrious individuals who engaged in monstrous behavior: Gilles de Rais; Elizabeth Bathory, the Hungarian "Blood Countess" who bathed in the gore of her victims; Vlad the Impaler, the Transylvanian prince who served as the model for Dracula. In modern times, however, it is impossible to find a single example of a famous, highly accomplished person who turned out to be a serial killer. (This is one reason why all the theories that claim to prove that Jack the Ripper was a member of the royal family or a celebrated artist seem so dubious.)

By and large, serial killers are, in their everyday lives, total nonentities, toiling at unskilled, if not menial, jobs: truck driver, janitor, garbageman. Some are full-time criminals: petty crooks and con artists who are in and out of jail throughout their adult lives. Despite their often superior intelligence, their profoundly antisocial personalities make it difficult for them to achieve anything professionally. True, some serial killers have been relatively successful. John Wayne Gacy, for example, built a thriving business as a home contractor. More typical, however, was Jeffrey Dahmer—a bright young man with a good education who couldn't hold down a job more challenging than that of assembly-line worker at a Milwaukee chocolate factory.

Of course, some serial killers deliberately seek out work that serves their twisted interests. A classic case is the monstrous Albert Fish, who preyed on countless young children in the early decades of the twentieth century. From the time he was seventeen, Fish worked as a painter. The psychiatrist who examined him, Dr. Fredric Wertham, explained the diabolical rationale for Fish's choice of profession:

> He worked in many different institutions. He worked in Y.M.C.A.s, he worked in homes for the tubercular, he worked in any kind of home where there were children, where he thought he could get children. In all these places, he made his headquarters the basement or cellar. And he had the habit of wearing a painter's overalls over his nude body, which gave him two advantages. First of all, he was nude in a moment. And secondly, he would be seen only in his painter's clothes, and if they [a witness or a surviving victim] later met him on the streets or in his other clothes, they wouldn't recognize him.

Other serial killers make use of their jobs to snare potential victims. Harvey Carignan—the so-called Want-Ad Killer—lured young woman to their deaths by advertising for employees at the Seattle gas station he managed.

While not specifically conducive to their criminal pursuits, some jobs held by serial killers are consistent with their morbid psychologies. Peter Sutcliffe, the "Yorkshire Ripper," for example, found employment in a mortuary, while his unspeakable countryman Frederick West worked for a while in a slaughterhouse. And there is something creepily apt about the business run by the Kansas City, Missouri, lust-killer, Bob Berdella: a suburban curio shop called "Bob's Bizarre Bazaar" that specialized in human-tooth earrings, plaster-of-Paris skulls, and other macabre *tchotchkes.*

On the other hand, some serial killers have worked at jobs so wildly at variance with their own malevolent natures as to border on the grotesque. A particularly striking case was that of the Houston sex-killer Dean Corll. A cross between Willy Wonka and the Marquis de Sade, Corll worked at his mother's candy factory. Beloved by neighborhood children for freely handing out samples of pecan sweets, they called him the "Candyman."

There have also been been clergymen serial killers (such as the Belgian lust-killer, Andras Pandy); dentist serial killers (like Glennon Engleman of St. Louis, who bumped off seven people over twenty-two years); and serial killers who have picked up extra money by babysitting for their neighbors (like Wisconsin ghoul Ed Gein).

UNCIVIL SERVANTS

It has become part of popular lore that certain kinds of government workers are particularly prone to mass murder; a perception reflected in the phrase "going postal." Whether mailmen account for a disproportionately high percentage of "rampage killers" is open to question. It is certainly true, however, that a number of highly infamous serial killers have worked as civil servants.

David Berkowitz, for example, worked at a post office by day, sorting letters at a branch in the Bronx. At night, he would transform into "Son of Sam," the phantom shooter who preyed on young women in the bicentennial summer of 1976. Another American psycho who relied on firearms to dispatch his victims was the serial sniper Thomas Dillon, who worked for more than twenty years as an employee of the Canton, Ohio, Water Department.

At roughly the same time that David Berkowitz was terrorizing Gotham, Dennis Nilsen—aka the "British Jeffrey Dahmer"—was earning his own place in the annals of horrific crime. As an employee of the British Manpower Service Commission, Nilsen spent his days helping out-of-work youths find jobs. After hours, however, he showed how much he cared for young men by luring them to his flat, murdering them, and keeping their corpses around for companionship until they became unbearably rank. At that point, he dismembered the bodies and flushed them down the toilet.

Peter Manuel, the Man Who Talked Too Much

CASE STUDY

Twenty years before the crimes of Dennis Nilsen were revealed to a stunned and sickened world, another civil servant was moonlighting as a serial murderer. His name was Peter Manuel.

Born to British parents in Manhattan in 1927, Manuel and his family returned to their homeland when he was five. From an early age, he was in trouble with the law. At twelve, he was arrested for burglarizing a bicycle shop and received a year's probation. Just five weeks later, he was back before the judge for housebreaking. This time, he was sent to reform school. Over the next few years, he escaped and was returned eleven times.

In 1942, he assaulted the wife of a school employee. This time, Manuel was hit with a term at Borstal, the prison for juvenile offenders. Released in 1944, he went to live with his parents, who had since moved to Scotland.

(Novelty trading card courtesy of Roger Worsham)

A compulsive criminal, Manuel soon reverted to burglary. Arrested again in February 1946, after breaking into a house, he was released on bail. Within the next two weeks, he sexually attacked three women. The first two managed to fend him off; the third—a married woman recuperating from a hospital stay—was too weak to resist. After beating her into submission, he dragged her to a railway embankment and raped her. Within days, Manuel was identified as the culprit. Brought to trial, he received an eight-year prison sentence and was shipped off to prison.

Upon his release in 1953, he returned to Glasgow and landed a civil service job with the city Gas Board through the influence of his father—a member of the District Council. It wasn't long before Manuel was back to his old sociopathic ways. Arrested for attempted rape in 1955, he managed to convince the jury that his victim had voluntarily submitted. He walked free of that charge.

One year later, he graduated to murder.

The first to die at his hands was nineteen-year-old Ann Knielands. Manuel killed her with an iron bar, wielding the implement with such savage force that her skull was shattered into fifteen pieces. As a known sex offender who had been working at a building site not far from where the corpse was found, Manuel was questioned by police. He claimed to have been at home at the time of the killing, an alibi confirmed by his father, who knew it was untrue.

Two months later, in March 1956, Manuel was arrested for attempted burglary and released on bail. On the night of September 17, he broke into the house of a family named Watt and found three women inside: Marion Watt, her sixteen-year old daughter, Vivienne, and Mrs. Watt's sister, Margaret Brown. He shot them all in the head at close range. Arrested on suspicion of murder, Manuel was released for lack of proof.

His next victim was a taxi driver name Sidney Dunn, killed with gratuitous cruelty and for no apparent reason other than sheer bloodlust. Manuel shot him in the head and slashed his throat for good measure in early December 1957. Less than three weeks later, on December 28, he raped and killed Isabelle Cooke.

Manuel's final outrage was the massacre of another family: forty-five-year-old Peter Smart, his wife, and ten-year-old son. As in the Watt incident, all three victims were shot at close range in the head during a housebreaking.

When currency stolen from the Smart home was traced to Manuel, police searched his house and turned up other incriminating evidence. Taken into custody, he soon began confessing so effusively that the press quickly dubbed him "The Man Who Talked Too Much." It became clear to observers that, though six of Manuel's nine victims had been killed in the course of burglaries, theft wasn't his main motivation. Sadism was. As his biographer John Bingham put it, "Manuel did kill for pleasure. He liked killing. The act of killing thrilled him."

At his trial, he tried to recant his confession, but the tactic failed. He was convicted on seven counts of murder and hanged on July 11, 1958.

KILLER COPS

Before becoming a member of the English Civil Service, Dennis Nilsen served as a rookie police officer in London. He resigned after one year, apparently because of the contradictions in his life: lawman by day, abject prowler of homosexual pubs after dark.

That one of the most notorious psychopaths of modern times would seek employment as a constable might seem a grim irony. In fact, it is surprisingly common for serial killers to be drawn to police work. In his best-selling memoir *Mindhunter,* famed FBI profiler John Douglas explains the psychology behind this phenomenon:

> The desire to work with the police was another interesting revelation, which was to come up over and over again in our serial killer studies. The three most common motives of serial rapists and murderers turn out to be domination, manipulation, and control. When you consider that most of these guys are angry, ineffectual losers who feel they've been given the shaft by life, and that most of them have experienced some sort of physical or emotional abuse . . . it isn't surprising that one of their main fantasy occupations is police officer.
>
> A policeman represents power and public respect. When called upon to do so, he is authorized to hurt bad people for the common good. In our research, we discovered that, while few police officers go bad and commit violent crimes, frequently serial offenders had failed in their efforts to join police departments and had taken jobs in related fields, such as security guard or night watchman.

Even when they aren't interested in joining the force themselves, serial killers often go out of their way to develop friendly relationships with local lawmen. Douglas writes that infamous "Coed Killer," Edmund Kemper, used to "frequent bars and restaurants known to be police hangouts and strike up conversations. This made him feel like an insider, gave him the vicarious thrill of a policeman's power. But also, once the Coed Killer was on the rampage, he had a direct line into the progress of the investigation, allowing him to anticipate their next move." The same thing was true of appalling cannibal killer Arthur Shawcross, who, as Douglas writes, "hung around [police hangouts] and enthusiastically pumped them for information."

Sometimes, serial killers play at being policemen for the most sinister reasons. Kenneth Bianchi, half of the "Hillside Strangler" team, was a security guard who had tried and failed to join the sheriff's department. Later, he and his degenerate cousin, Angelo Buono, lured unwary young women into their car by flashing badges and pretending to be cops.

CASE STUDY

Gerard Schaefer, Maniac Cop

Gerard Schaefer may not have been the world's sickest serial killer, but he was inarguably the author of the sickest piece of literature ever to emerge from the cesspit of a psychopathic mind. In 1990, while serving a life sentence for murder, he published a collection of violently pornographic stories called *Killer Fiction,* insisting that it was sheer fantasy, though at other times he strongly intimated that the contents were, in fact, chronicles of his actual crimes. In either case, the stories offer unparalleled insight into the unspeakable workings of a mind filled with most virulent hatred of women. The title of one section speaks volumes: "Whores: What to Do About Them." To Schaefer, all women were whores; his idea of "what to do about them" involved subjecting them to the most hideous tortures imaginable. In a typical passage, he gleefully describes the murder of a "Junior League society bitch" his protagonist picks up on spring break:

> I watched her eyes drop to the shaft of steel buried in her belly, just above the crest of her pubic triangle. She watched my hand as I pulled the blade up and across, neatly gutting her. She stared with wide-eyed fascination as the ropy coils of her own intestines slid out of her belly and hung to her knees. Her eyes were filled with disbelief. Her terror must have blocked off the pain. I angled the cutting edge up under her rib cage [sic] and lanced it into her heart. The green eyes rolled back in her head, becoming white marbles. . . . I was heartened. It was a satisfying and skillful kill.

The author of this obscenity—and the perpetrator of an unknown number of unspeakably sadistic crimes—was born in Wisconsin in 1946. By the time he was twelve, he was a confirmed fetishist who enjoyed masturbating while wearing women's panties. He had also discovered the joys of masochistic bondage, inventing games in which he tied himself to a tree and struggled to get free. "I'd get sexually excited and do something to hurt myself," he later explained.

When Schaefer was fourteen, his family moved to Florida. In high school, he had a reputation as a weirdo loner, spending his spare time shooting harmless creatures in the Everglades or peeping through the bedroom windows of neighborhood girls. His earliest goal was to become a priest, but—after being rejected by a local seminary—he renounced his faith. Enrolling in a community college, he found himself possessed by increasingly intense homicidal fantasies involving appealing young women, who were instantly classified in his warped mind as "whores." At this point, however, his murderous impulses were still vented strictly on animals, though he had worked his way up from songbirds and land crabs to cattle. He particularly enjoyed beheading cows with a machete, then raping the carcasses.

Schaefer now aimed his sights on a teaching career. During his brief stint as a student teacher in 1969, a number of females vanished from the vicinity of Schaefer's residence. Their bodies would never be recovered, though police would eventually find some of their teeth, along with other evidence connecting them to Schaefer, among his stash of souvenirs.

After being dismissed from his teaching job, Schaefer landed a job with a small-town police department in Wilton Manors, Florida. He was fired after six months, apparently for using the department's computer to dig up personal information about local women. In spite of this blot on his record, he managed to get himself hired a few months later by the Martin County Sheriff's Department. This time he lasted only a month.

On July 21, 1972—twenty-two days after joining the department—Schaefer picked up two teenage female hitchhikers, drove them to a swamp, then gagged and handcuffed them at gunpoint. Arranging nooses around their necks, he tied the ropes to a tree branch and made the terrified girls stand on the slippery roots, so that if they lost their balance and fell, they would hang. Then, he left them alone.

When Schaefer returned a few hours later, he expected to find two dangling corpses. Instead, the girls were gone, having managed to escape.

Telephoning his boss, Schaefer sheepishly admitted that he had made a boo-boo. "You're going to be mad at me," he said. He described what he had done to the two girls, though he swore that he was only trying to scare them out of the hitchhiking habit for their own good. Still, he admitted that he had possibly "overdone" it.

He was fired on the spot, charged with false imprisonment and assault, then released on a fifteen-thousand-dollar bond.

That September, while Schaefer was awaiting trial, two Fort Lauderdale teens, Georgia Jessup and Susan Place, were picked up at the latter's home by an older man. "Jerry Shepherd" had promised to drive them to a beach. The two girls were never seen alive again.

Two months later, in November 1972, Schaefer came up for trial on his assault charges. Berating him as a "thoughtless fool," the judge sentenced him to a year behind bars with three year's probation.

While Schaefer was doing his time in jail, the skeletal remains of Susan Place and Georgia Jessup were found in the same swampy area where Schaefer had taken the two hitchhikers. Forensic analysis indicated that the victims had been "tied to a tree and butchered." Thanks to Susan's mother—who had jotted down the license plate number of the man who had picked up the girls a few months earlier—Schaefer was soon identified as the prime suspect. A search of his house turned up a trove of evidence connecting him not only to the two butchered girls but to a staggering number of other local women, some as young as thirteen, who had gone missing over the years.

Eventually Schaefer received two concurrent life sentences for the murders of Susan Place and Georgia Jessup. His true body count, however, was clearly far higher. He himself admitted to more than a hundred murders. With a sadistic smirk characteristic of his ilk, he claimed that he couldn't be sure of the exact number. "One whore drowned in her own vomit while watching me disembowel her girlfriend," he wrote in a letter. "Does that count as a valid kill? Did the pregnant ones count as two kills? It gets confusing."

Schaeffer's life came to a deservedly nasty end in December 1995, when another inmate slashed his throat and stabbed him in both eyes, ostensibly for taking the last cup of hot water from a dispenser on their cellblock.

MEDICAL MONSTERS

In a famous scene from the 1993 thriller *Malice,* Alec Baldwin, playing a prominent surgeon undergoing legal questioning, says, "You ask me if I have a God complex? Let me tell you something: I *am* God."

The crimes of serial killers are motivated by a monstrous lust for both pleasure and power. To compensate for profound, deep-seated feelings of humiliation and worthlessness rooted in their childhoods, these psychopaths develop a pernicious need to prove their omnipotence. Gaining total control over a helpless human being and dispensing death at their whim makes them feel like God. As "Coed Killer" Edmund Kemper put in explaining the perverse gratification he derived from his atrocities, "I was making life-and-death decisions . . . playing God in their lives."

This urge to "play God" has led a number of serial killers to seek careers in medicine. Another motive, of course, is that doctors have access to a steady supply of prospective victims: vulnerable, trusting people who, because they are ill to begin with, can be killed off without arousing too much suspicion.

Among the most infamous medical monsters on record are:

Thomas Neill Cream

Born in Glasgow in 1850, this Victorian serial murderer emigrated to Canada when he was thirteen, at which point he was already displaying criminal propensities. He earned a medical degree from McGill University in 1874 and was soon misusing his newly acquired surgical skills by performing illegal abortions, killing an unknown number of women in the process. In 1881, having moved to Chicago, he poisoned his mistress's elderly husband by lacing the old man's epilepsy medication with strychnine. Convicted of murder, he was sentenced to life in Joliet prison. He ended up doing only ten years.

Upon his release, he sailed for England and embarked on a career as a serial killer of prostitutes, slipping strychnine to five London streetwalkers before his arrest in 1892 at his home on Lambeth Palace Road. Sentenced to hang, the so-called "Lambeth Poisoner" ensured his immortality with his astonishing last words. As he stood on the gallows, hood over his head, he cried out, "I am Jack the—". Just then, the trapdoor crashed open, drowning out the final word. Though Cream certainly shared some traits with his legendary contemporary—most prominently a murderous rage against prostitutes—there is good reason to doubt his final claim, since he was languishing in jail in Joliet at the time of the Ripper killings.

(from the *Illustrated Police News of London*)

The Case of Dr. Thomas Neill Cream

Marcel Petiot

In twentieth-century Europe, the social chaos created by the two world wars afforded prime opportunities for homicidal maniacs to ply their monstrous trade. This was particularly true in Weimar Germany, which produced some of the most monstrous lust-murderers of modern times, most notably Fritz Haarmann and Peter Kürten. It was also the case in France during World War II, when one of that country's worst serial killers took ghastly advantage of the horrors around him.

Born in 1897, Marcel Petiot, like most psychopaths, had a history of criminal behavior extending from his youth, when he got into trouble for stealing money from schoolmates. In succeeding years, he was involved in drug-trafficking, arrested for shoplifting, and convicted of theft while serving as the mayor of his native town, Villaneuve.

Despite his criminal record and a stint in a mental asylum, Petiot earned a medical degree. In 1933, he moved to Paris, where he continued to be involved in shady activities even while building a successful practice. It was after the Nazi occupation of France that he hit on the insidious scheme that would earn him everlasting infamy.

Posing as a Resistance member, Petiot let it be known that he could smuggle wealthy Jews out of France for a hefty fee. When his desperate "clients" showed up at his house bearing their most precious possessions, they received an injection, supposedly an immunization shot against unnamed "foreign diseases." In reality, it was strychnine. Petiot then placed them in a specially constructed death chamber equipped with a peephole, through which he could view their final agonies. He would then dispose of the corpses in his personal crematorium.

His atrocities came to light in 1944 when firemen showed up at his house to investigate reports of a black, fetid cloud of smoke emanating from his chimney. They discovered human limbs in his furnace and the mutilated corpses of twenty-seven people stacked like firewood in the basement. Petiot stuck to his story that he was a member of the Resistance. The corpses, he claimed, were those of Nazi soldiers, killed by the Resistance and turned over to him for disposal. In the end, however, he failed to convince the jury that tried him. In March 1946, he was sent to the guillotine for the murder of twenty-six victims, though the actual total may have been far higher—perhaps as many as 150.

Michael Swango

Swango's father was a Marine colonel who enforced strict military discipline on the rare occasions he was at home. Michael grew up without much feeling for his martinet dad, though he did come to appreciate the old man a little more after the latter's death, when he discovered a scrapbook kept by Colonel

Swango containing newspaper clippings of car crashes, violent crimes, and other disasters. "I guess he wasn't such a bad guy after all," said Michael, himself a lifelong aficionado of gruesome news.

His extreme interest in everything from savage sex crimes to Nazi atrocities was only one of young Michael's peculiarities. During the 1960s, while his peers wore love beads and marched against the Vietnam War, Swango worked hard to turn himself into Rambo, painting his car military green, sporting fatigues, and dropping to the floor to do a hundred push-ups at the slightest provocation. Eventually, he joined the Marine Corps, remaining for just one tour of duty. In 1979, after receiving an honorable discharge, he enrolled in Southern Illinois University Medical School. There, he quickly gained a reputation for weird behavior. Though exceptionally bright, he demonstrated bizarre lapses in knowledge. On one occasion, he was unable to locate the patient's heart in a chest X-ray, and his dissection of a cadaver in anatomy class was so bungled that the mangled specimen became a schoolwide joke. Excited by the sight of car wrecks and other accidents—the gorier the better—he spent more time working as a volunteer ambulance attendant than going to classes. As a result, he was almost denied his diploma.

Despite his poor performance, he was offered an internship at the Ohio State University Medical Center, where patients on the road to recovery suddenly began dying of heart failure whenever young Dr. Swango was making his nightly rounds. Eventually, he fell under suspicion of the nursing staff, who reported their concerns to hospital administrators. Eager to avoid a scandal—and potentially ruinous lawsuits—the officials conducted a shockingly cursory investigation that exonerated Swango of any crime. This was the first of many instances in which the medical establishment turned a "blind eye" (to use the title of James Stewart's powerful 1999 book on the case) to the nefarious doings of the psychopathic Swango, allowing him to go on satisfying his sadistic needs for an unconscionably long period of time.

Leaving Ohio under a cloud of suspicion, Swango returned to Illinois, where he joined an ambulance corps. He raised eyebrows among coworkers with his gleeful appreciation of hideous accidents. Before long, he was amusing himself by doctoring the snacks of his fellow paramedics with an arsenic-based ant poison. Caught red-handed, he was arrested, convicted on seven counts of aggravated battery, and given a five-year sentence.

Released on good behavior after only two years, he moved to Virginia and—while supporting himself as a lab technician—began sending out résumés, trying to get back into medical practice. Astonishingly, he was offered a residency at the University of South Dakota, whose director accepted at face value Swango's explanation for his jail time (according to Swango, he had gotten into a barroom brawl and ended up becoming the fall guy, though others were really to blame).

Swango didn't last long at his new position. In an act of hubris characteristic of psychopaths, he applied for membership in the American Medical

Association, which turned up the truth about his battery charge during a background check and conveyed the information to his new employers, who quickly let Swango go.

Undaunted, the ever-resourceful Swango next managed to land a job at Veterans Administration hospital on Long Island, New York, where—true to psychopathic form—he began killing off recuperating patients. This time, when the facts about Swango's background came to light, the Justice Department finally stepped in.

Realizing that the Feds were on his tail, Swango fled the country and headed for South Africa, where he landed a job in a remote Lutheran hospital. The shocking rash of sudden, unexplained deaths that occurred whenever "Dr. Mike" was on his rounds, however, aroused the suspicions of the hospital staff, and Swango was soon on the lam again. After hiding out in Zimbabwe and Europe for a year, he returned to the United States but was arrested as soon as he stepped off the plane. The deadly doctor—who may have been responsible for as many as sixty murders and who confessed in his diary that nothing turned him on more than "the sweet, husky, close smell of indoor homicide"—was convicted of killing three patients and sentenced to life without parole.

> I controlled other people's lives, whether they lived or died. I had that power to control. After I didn't get caught for the first fifteen, I thought it was my right. I appointed myself judge, prosecutor and jury. So I played God.
>
> —Homicidal health-care worker Donald Harvey, accounting for his fifty-two murders

CASE STUDY

Harold Shipman, England's Doctor Death

Those who have looked into the background of Dr. Harold Shipman for the sources of his psychopathology have come up short. Yes, he was known to have been unusually attached to his mother and deeply traumatized by witnessing her slow death from cancer when he was in his teens. According to some psychiatrists, the sight of the family physician administering morphine injections to ease her final agonies left an indelible mark on his psyche, one that drove him, in later life, to re-create that traumatic scene again and again. Still, this explanation—like every theory offered by the experts—is a clear case of grasping at straws. It is likely that we will never know how or why this much-beloved family physician became England's—and possibly the world's—most prolific serial killer.

Aside from being a loner who struck certain teachers as "a bit strange," there was nothing apparently abnormal about the adolescent Shipman. It was not until he got his medical degree and joined a practice in the north England town of Todmorden that he showed signs of psychological trouble. After suffering a series of blackouts, Shipman told his colleagues that he was an epileptic—an explanation that they accepted until it was discovered that he had been forging prescriptions for a morphinelike painkiller called pethidine and injecting himself with the drug on a regular basis. Arrested for forgery and stealing drugs, Shipman was hit with a sizable fine and forced out of the practice. After kicking his habit in rehab, however, he was soon back on the job, finding work with another medical practice.

In 1992, he broke from the group and set himself up in private practice in the town of Hyde. His warm bedside manner and the time and care he lavished on his patients made the bespectacled, gray-bearded physician a local favorite, especially among the elderly female population. No one noticed—at least at first—just how rapidly those old women began to die off.

Shipman's MO was always the same. He would pay an unexpected afternoon house call on a fairly healthy patient, kill her with an injection of the painkiller diamorphine, then hurry away. Later—often summoned by a frantic call from a relative who had discovered the corpse—he would return and sign the death certificate, attributing the unexpected death to natural causes.

It was not until 1997 that someone—a woman named Debbie Bramboffe, the daughter of the local undertaker—realized that something sinister was going on. Struck by the unusually high death rate among Dr. Shipman's elderly female patients—and by the bizarre fact that their bodies were invariably found fully dressed and seated in their favorite easy chairs or resting on a settee—Mrs. Bramboffe shared her suspicions with another local physician, Dr. Susan Booth. Before long, an investigation was under way.

Aware that authorities had begun to examine the death certificates of his patients, Shipman still could not stop killing. Indeed, by then, his homicidal mania had grown so extreme that he was sometimes murdering patients at the rate of one a day.

The underlying psychological causes that finally led to his arrest are a matter of debate. Some attribute his undoing to arrogance and a growing sense of invincibility, others to an unconscious wish to get caught. What is beyond dispute is that, in June 1998, Shipman killed Mrs. Kathleen Grundy—an unusually fit octogenarian and the former mayor of Hyde—then crudely forged a will in her name that left him her entire fortune of nearly £400,000. As soon as Mrs. Grundy's daughter set eyes on the document, she saw it was a fake and contacted the police, who already had Shipman in their sights. Before long, Mrs. Grundy's body was exhumed and autopsied. When lethal amounts of morphine were discovered, Shipman was arrested.

At first, the townspeople of Hyde refused to accept that their neighbor and trusted physician could be guilty of murder. Shopkeepers hung posters in their store windows that read, "We don't believe it." They were forced to face the truth, however, when Shipman was convicted of fifteen murders in January 2000. Nothing, however, could have prepared them for the ultimate shock—the revelation, after a prolonged investigation by the British government, that the number of suspicious deaths connected to Shipman totaled at least 297 and possibly as many as 345.

What drove him to do it? At his trial, the prosecuting attorney, Richard Henriques, gave the only possible answer: "He was exercising the ultimate power of controlling life and death, and repeated the act so often he must have found the drama of taking life to his taste."

In short, Dr. Harold Shipman killed several hundred human beings for the simple reason that he liked it.

NICKNAMES

Our tendency to mythicize serial killers—to see them not as predatory criminals, but as creatures of superhuman evil—is reinforced by the media's habit of tagging them with lurid nicknames. This sensationalistic ploy (designed to sell papers by exploiting our primitive, childlike fascination with monsters) began with the first celebrity psycho of the modern era—"Jack the Ripper"—and continues to this day. (When a card featuring the Grim Reaper was found at one crime scene during the 2002 shooting rampage in the Washington, DC, area, the unknown perpetrator was immediately dubbed the "Tarot Card Killer.")

Here is a list of notorious serial killers and their tabloid-style monikers:

Richard Angelo, "Angel of Death"
Martha Beck and Raymond Fernandez, "Lonely Hearts Killers"
David Berkowitz, "Son of Sam"
Kenneth Bianchi and Angelo Buono, "Hillside Stranglers"
William Bonin, "Freeway Killer"
Ian Brady and Myra Hindley, "Moors Murderers"
Harvey Louis Carignan, "Want-Ad Killer"
David Carpenter, "Trailside Killer"
Richard Chase, "Vampire of Sacramento"
Andrei Chikatilo, "Mad Beast"
Reg Christie, "Monster of Rillington Place"
Douglas Clark, "Sunset Slayer"
Carroll Cole, "Barfly Strangler"
Dean Corll, "Candyman"
Jeffrey Dahmer, "Milwaukee Cannibal"
Theo Durrant, "Demon of the Belfry"
Albert Fish, "Moon Maniac"
John Wayne Gacy, "Killer Clown"
Carlton Gary, "Stocking Strangler"
Ed Gein, "Plainfield Ghoul"
John Wayne Glover, "Granny Killer"

Vaughn Greenwood, "Skid Row Slasher"
Belle Gunness, "Lady Bluebeard"
Fritz Haarmann, "Vampire of Hanover"
John George Haigh, "Acid Bath Killer"
William Heirens, "Lipstick Killer"
Gary Heidnik, "Sex-Slave Killer"
Dr. H. H. Holmes, "Chicago Bluebeard"
Keith Jesperson, "Happy Face Killer"
Edmund Kemper, "Coed Killer"
Paul John Knowles, "Casanova Killer"
Peter Kürten, "Monster of Düsseldorf"
Pedro Lopez, "Monster of the Andes"
Richard Macek, "Mad Biter"
William MacDonald, "Sydney Mutilator"
Earle Leonard Nelson, "Gorilla Murderer"
Thierry Paulin, "Monster of Montmartre"
Jesse Pomeroy, "Boy Fiend"
Heinrich Pommerencke, "Beast of the Black Forest"
Richard Ramirez, "Night Stalker"
Melvin Rees, "Sex Beast"
Angel Maturino Resendez, "Railway Killer"
Danny Rolling, "Gainesville Ripper"
Charles Schmid, "Pied Piper of Tucson"
Lucian Staniak, "Red Spider"
Peter Sutcliffe, "Yorkshire Ripper"
Coral Eugene Watts, "Sunday Morning Slasher"
Randall Woodfield, "I-5 Killer"

Some serial killers have never been caught and are known only by their tabloid monikers (or what might be called their *psychonyms*). The best known of these—besides Jack the Ripper—are: the Ax Man of New Orleans, the Mad Butcher of Kingsbury Run, the Monster of Florence, and Zodiac.

Richard Ramirez, the Night Stalker

CASE STUDY

Richard Ramirez—the twenty-five-year-old man who held Los Angeles in the grip of fear during the hot summer of 1985—had some heartfelt words for the court that sentenced him to death: "You maggots make me sick. You don't understand me. I am beyond good and evil. I will be avenged. Lucifer dwells in us all." Like all psychopaths, he felt not the slightest twinge of remorse for the horrors he had visited upon the city. As he left the courtroom he shrugged off the well-deserved punishment that awaited him: "Big deal. Death always went with the territory. I'll see you in Disneyland."

Born into a poor Mexican-descended family in El Paso, Texas, Ramirez was an average student until he reached high school, when things went from bad to worse. As a motel worker he was caught breaking into a woman's room and grabbing her as she exited the shower. The woman's husband caught and beat him up, but the couple did not press charges. Ramirez moved to LA and acquired a rap sheet for drug and driving violations.

(Button pin courtesy of Roger Worsham)

Richard "The Night Stalker" Ramirez

In the spring of 1985, he began to roam the neighborhoods of suburban LA in stolen cars, looking for homes to vandalize—and people to destroy. Later, when the LA police intensified their manhunt, he drove up to San Francisco for prey. Usually high on coke or speed, he slipped into darkened houses where sleeping couples lay, killing the husband first, then raping and savaging the woman. Once he carved out the eyes of a female victim and took them away as trophies.

From June 1984 until his capture over a year later, it seemed to the terrified residents of Los Angeles that a demon was on the loose. The press dubbed him the "Night Stalker." No one felt safe. The shadowy fiend did not focus on any particular age group or sex or race. He raped women in their eighties; he tortured young mothers in front of their children. He would help himself to a snack while his victims bled to death before his eyes and leave Satanic pentagrams on their bodies or the walls of their homes.

As his crimes escalated, Ramirez—like many serial killers—developed a sense of omnipotence. He believed that he was being protected by Satan.

He was wrong.

In August 1985, he attacked a couple—shooting the man in the head and raping the woman—then fled in their car. After recovering the stolen vehicle, police lifted a fingerprint and were able to match it to Ramirez's rap sheet. His mug shot was immediately broadcast on local TV. A few days later, during an attempted carjacking in East LA, he was recognized by passersby, pounced on, and nearly beaten to death. Only the timely arrival of the police saved him from the enraged mob.

His fourteen-month trial was a media sensation. The unrepentant Ramirez mugged for reporters, flashing a pentagram he had drawn on his palm, making devil's horns with his fingers, and chanting, "Evil . . . Evil . . . Evil. . . ." Hordes of groupies flocked to the proceedings, showering him with fan letters and love notes. When one young woman was asked about her fascination with the notorious psycho-killer, she replied: "When I look at him, I see a real handsome guy who just messed up his life because he never had anyone to guide him." Ramirez later married one of his female admirers.

He was ultimately convicted of thirteen murders, though he later confessed to more. "I've killed twenty people, man," he told a fellow inmate. "I love all that blood." He currently resides on death row in San Quentin.

SERIAL KILLERS INTERNATIONAL

There's little doubt that America is the world's leading producer of serial killers, though any true measurement has to take into account the sheer size of our population. The FBI estimates that there are between thirty and fifty serial killers at large in our country at any given time. That might seem like a shockingly high number, but in a nation of more than 280,000,000 people, it's a minuscule percentage.

England, for example, may be afflicted with only a few serial killers a year, but its population is less than a fifth of ours. Indeed, in a study of serial murder between the years 1962 and 1982, the crime expert Colin Wilson lists eighteen cases in the US and eleven in Great Britain. According to that finding, the incidence of serial murderers for that twenty-year period turns out to be significantly *higher* in Britain—18 per 100,000, compared to 8.3 for the United States. Recent British serial killers, moreover, include not only some of the most depraved murderers of modern times—like Fred and Rosemary West—but also the single most prolific: Dr. Harold Shipman, responsible for as many as four hundred murders.

Still, there are definite cultural factors in America that are conducive to serial murder. The fragmented, highly dysfunctional families that are a fertile breeding ground for criminal psychopaths. The rootlessness and anonymity of American life, which make it possible for serial killers to keep on the move or live in a community without attracting notice. The large number of "targets of opportunity"—teenage runaways, inner-city prostitutes, etc. And, of course, the unusually high level of violence in general, which has always been a feature of our society.

It's important to recognize, however, that serial murder is not limited to any one nation. It's a universal phenomenon, one that has existed throughout history and in every part of the globe. Indeed, a comprehensive survey of international serial killers would require a book of its own. For a sense of just how widespread the phenomenon is, here is a sampling of serial killers from other lands.

Ramiro Artieda

Though this Bolivian psychopath gained infamy in the late 1930s for the serial strangling of seven young women, he began his homicidal career by killing his own brother, Luis, to gain control of the family estate. Unfortunately for future victims, the police were unable to gather sufficient evidence to convict him, and Artieda was allowed to go free.

Jilted by his eighteen-year-old fiancée—who evidently had qualms about marrying an accused fratricide—Artieda left for the United States, where he studied acting. No sooner had he returned to Bolivia than a string of eighteen-year-old women—who all bore a striking physical resemblance to Artieda's former girlfriend—began to die, each strangled by a dark-haired stranger posing in a different role. One was lured to her death by a "film-company executive," another by a "visiting professor," another by a "traveling salesman," yet another by a "monk." After a final, failed murder attempt in May 1939, Artieda was identified by an intended victim and arrested.

Under interrogation, he admitted to strangling seven women, presumably as a way of taking revenge on the female sex after being spurned by his fiancée. He also confessed to the murder of Luis. He was executed by a firing squad on July 3, 1939.

Wayne Clifford Boden

Viewers of Michael Moore's Academy Award-winning documentary, *Bowling for Columbine,* may be forgiven for thinking of Canada as an idyllic land where violent crime is so rare that its citizens go to sleep with their front doors unlocked. Thirty years ago, however, Montreal was the scene of a series of murders as gruesome as any in the bad old USA.

The horrors began in July 1968, when the naked corpse of a twenty-one-year-old schoolteacher named Norma Vaillancourt was found in her Montreal apartment. The victim had been raped and strangled, and her breasts savaged by bite wounds. Just over one year later, the killer struck again, raping and strangling another petite young brunette, then shredding her breasts with his teeth.

It wasn't until his third atrocity that police finally got a lead. In November 1969, twenty-year-old Marielle Archambault met the same grisly fate as the previous victims. Searching her apartment, investigators found a crumpled snapshot of a nice-looking young man. Marie's coworkers at a downtown jewelry shop were able to identify him as a guy named "Bill" who had stopped by the store to chat with her on the day of her murder.

Two months later, the "Vampire Rapist"—as the newspapers were by then calling him—struck again, raping and strangling twenty-four-year-old Jean Way, then subjecting her corpse to his trademark mutilation.

With the police hot on his trail, the phantom killer decamped for Calgary twenty-three hundred miles away, where he murdered his final victim, a young schoolteacher named Elizabeth Porteous, in May 1971. Interviewing Porteous's friends, police learned that she had been dating a man named "Bill," who drove a blue Mercedes. Spotting a car matching that description parked just a block away from the victim's apartment, police set up a stakeout and apprehended the owner as he approached the vehicle.

He turned out to be twenty-three-year-old Wayne Clifford Boden. His cuff link had been found in the shredded remnants of Elizabeth Porteous's dress as her body was being transported to the medical examiner's lab. Boden admitted that he had gone out with her on the night of her murder, but he insisted that she had been alive when he left her. At his trial, however, a forensic odontologist established beyond doubt that the bite marks on the victim's breasts could only have been made by Boden. Convicted and sentenced to life imprisonment for the Calgary murder, he was subsequently tried again in Montreal and given an additional three life sentences.

Luis Alfredo Garavito

Americans like to think they have the biggest and best of everything. We take perverse pride in having produced the worst serial killers of modern times: Ted Bundy, John Wayne Gacy, Jeffrey Dahmer, et al. The truth is, however, that the enormities of even our most monstrous psycho-killers pale before those of the Colombian lust-murderer Luis Alfredo Garavito. The fact that his name is virtually unknown on these shores is clearly a function of cultural chauvinism: Americans just aren't especially interested in psychopathic foreigners. Certainly the sheer magnitude of his crimes makes him a serious candidate for the title of "Worst Serial Sex-Killer of the Twentieth Century."

Born in 1957 in the coffee-growing area of Pereira, Garavito—the youngest of seven children—was subjected to regular, brutal beatings by his alcoholic father and raped by two adult male neighbors. He grew up to be an alcoholic, as well as a depressive with suicidal tendencies. After just five years of schooling, he dropped out of school and, at sixteen, became a drifter, finding occasional work as a store clerk and street vendor of religious articles.

During a seven-year span that began in 1992, Garavito murdered no fewer than 140 boys between the ages of eight and sixteen. He killed them in more than fifty cities across Colombia, as well as in Ecuador. Posing in various benign guises—a teacher, a priest, a social worker, a representative of a charitable organization—glib, smooth-talking Garavito would win the confidence of his victims, often by buying them soft drinks or giving them small sums of money. Then he would invite them on a long walk into the countryside. When the boys began to grow tired, Garavito pounced. He would tie them up with nylon line, rape them, mutilate them, then slit their throats or behead them.

That these enormities went undetected for years was a function of Colombia's dire conditions. His victims were poor, often homeless, street children: the displaced products of a country in the throes of social disintegration. For the most part, no one even noticed that they were missing. It wasn't until twenty-seven skeletons were found in a ravine in the western province of Pereira that authorities launched an investigation. Eventually—after nearly ninety more skeletons were uncovered—the police were led to Garavito, already in jail awaiting trial for the slaying of an eleven-year-old boy in the city of Tunja. During a marathon grilling, Garavito confessed to 140 murders, each of which he had painstakingly recorded in a notebook. Colombia having no death penalty, he was sentenced to fifty-two years for the Tunja murder—a shockingly mild punishment in light of his unparalleled enormities.

Saeed Hanaei

For more than two years, an Iranian serial killer—nicknamed the "Spider" because of his sinister skill at luring victims into his web—killed at least sixteen prostitutes in the holy city of Mashad. The women were all strangled with their head scarves, then swaddled head to toe in their black chadors and dumped on the streets. Far from causing outrage, however, these horrific crimes were actually applauded by many hard-line supporters of the fundamentalist regime, who viewed the unknown serial killer as a righteous crusader against corruption.

Eventually, a thirty-nine-year-old construction worker, Saeed Hanaei, was arrested for the crimes. According to his confession, he had embarked on his murderous mission after his own wife was mistaken for a prostitute by a cabdriver. Blaming the large number of prostitutes in the city for this humiliating episode, Hanaei had decided to kill as many of them as he could as a "religious obligation." Hanaei was utterly remorseless, declaring that killing the women was no harder than "breaking open a melon."

At first, some hard-liners rallied to his defense, arguing that he was simply trying to clean up the country. They fell silent, though, when he revealed that he had had sex with most of his victims before strangling them. He was hanged in the prison compound in Teheran on the morning of April 18, 2002.

> They were worthless as cockroaches to me. Toward the end, I could not sleep at night if I had not killed one of them that day.
>
> —Saeed Hanaei

Javed Iqbal

In 1999, a thirty-seven-year-old, independently wealthy Pakistani named Javed Iqbal was brutally beaten by a pair of young servant boys. When he reported the crime to the police, they not only brushed off his charges but accused him of sodomy. At that moment, Iqbal decided to take a dreadful revenge against "the world I hated." He vowed to murder exactly one hundred children.

During the next six months, he made good on this hideous pledge. Enticing young teens—most of them beggars and runaways—to his small apartment in Lahore, he fed them, took their snapshots, and offered them a bed. Once they were asleep, he asphyxiated them with cyanide. Later, he dissolved their bodies in a vat of acid and dumped the residue down an alleyway sewer. Iqbal not only saved their clothing and shoes but kept a meticulous record of his victims, recording their names, ages, the dates of their deaths, and even the cost of disposing of them (roughly $2.40 per victim, including the cost of the acid). As soon as he reached his goal, he turned himself in.

Convicted in March 2000, he was given a sentence commensurate with the monstrosity of his crimes. He was to be strangled in front of the parents of his victims, then cut into a hundred pieces and dissolved in acid. He appealed the sentence but was then found dead in his cell, an apparent suicide, in October 2001.

> I could have killed five hundred, this was not a problem. But the pledge I had taken was one hundred children, and I did not want to violate this. My mother had cried for me. I wanted one hundred mothers to cry for their children.
>
> —Javed Iqbal

Muhammad Adam Omar Ishaak

In the early 1980s, the University of Sana opened Yemen's first medical school, producing physicians who, in succeeding years, would serve throughout the country and across the Arab world. Among its graduates were Yemen's first women doctors. The reputation of this proud institution was badly tarnished in the summer of 2000, however, when one of its employees—a forty-eight-year-old morgue attendant named Muhammad Adam Omar Ishaak—turned out to be a deranged sex-killer whose victims included two of the school's own female students. An emigrant from the Sudan who had arrived in Yemen on a wave of impoverished African job-seekers, Ishaak—or the "Sana Ripper," as he was dubbed—confessed to raping, killing, and dismembering his victims, before soaking their remains in acid and dumping them in the morgue drains.

From the start, however, a great deal of controversy surrounded Ishaak, who kept altering his story. At first, he claimed to have butchered more than fifty women as a transient worker in a half dozen Arab countries. Later, he lowered the number to sixteen victims, all of them from Yemen, insisting that he had never worked anywhere else except his native Sudan, where he had been a gravedigger. His story changed again, however, when one of his supposed victims—a twenty-one-year-old woman whose mutilation-murder he had described in grisly detail—turned up alive. In the end, he admitted to only two murders, those of a twenty-four-year-old Iraqi medical student and a twenty-three-year-old Yemeni, both female, whose body parts were found in the morgue drains.

Though some observers clung to the belief that Ishaak was a scapegoat, set up by powerful figures seeking to cover up a sex-and-murder scandal at an exclusive Sana brothel, Ishaak was sentenced to death. He was publicly executed outside the gates of the medical school in August 2001—shot through the heart and head after receiving eighty lashes with a whip of knotted leather.

The "Kobe School Killer"

In the spring and summer of 1997, Japan was riveted by a hideous crime. On Tuesday morning, May 27, several passersby spotted what looked like a manikin's head resting in front of the gate to a junior high school in the port city of Kobe. Upon closer examination, it proved not to be a fake but—much to the horror of witnesses—the decapitated head of a mentally retarded eleven-year-old boy named Jun Hase who had been missing for several days. Stuffed inside the mouth was a note that read: "Well, let's begin a game. Can you stop me, police? I desperately want to see people die. I think it's fun to kill people. A bloody judgment is needed for my years of great bitterness." A rash of other crimes had lately occurred in the vicinity. Just a half mile from the school gate, a ten-year-old girl had been bludgeoned to death with a steel pipe in March, and a nine-year-old girl seriously stabbed the same day. Before that, two other elementary school girls had been attacked by a hammer-wielding assailant, though both escaped serious injury. And then there were the animals: two dead kittens—one with its paws cut off—left in front of the school, along with a decapitated pigeon.

Realizing that a serial killer was on the loose, the police began looking for a man in his thirties who had been seen in the company of little Jun shortly before the boy's disappearance. In early June, the killer sent several sinister letters to a local newspaper, declaring that murder brought him a sense of inner peace and threatening to kill "three vegetables a week"—by which he apparently meant children.

Given the degree of the killer's psychopathology, it should have come as a tremendous relief when he was finally caught at the end of June. But in fact, his arrest precipitated a nationwide spasm of anguished soul-searching. The killer turned out to be a fourteen-year-old boy, reportedly from a nice, middle-class home. Though Japanese law forbade the release of his name, certain facts about him emerged. Like most serial killers, he began manifesting sociopathic symptoms at an early age. He loved to play with hunting knives in elementary school and enjoyed torturing animals, on one occasion lining up frogs on the street and running over them with his bicycle. He maintained a detailed diary of his crimes and engaged in bizarre rituals. After luring Jun Hase to a wooded hill, he had strangled the boy, removed his head with a saw, taken it home in a plastic bag, and washed it in a purification ceremony before leaving it at the school gate.

Under Japanese law, the "Kobe School Killer" cannot be jailed because of his youth. One way or another, he is expected to be back on the streets by the time he is eighteen.

> I can relieve myself of hatred and feel at peace only when I'm killing someone. I can ease my own pain only when I see others in pain.
>
> —from a note sent by the "Kobe School Killer"

Pedro Lopez

The man who would grow up to become the notorious "Monster of the Andes" had the sort of childhood almost guaranteed to produce a criminal psychopath. Born in rural Colombia in 1949, Lopez—one of thirteen children of a penniless prostitute—was raised in utter squalor. At eight, he was kicked out of his home after his mother caught him fondling one of his own little sisters. Out on the streets, he quickly fell victim to a middle-aged pedophile who—promising him food and shelter—lured him to an abandoned building and raped him.

Making his way to Bogotá, he subsisted on whatever he could beg, pilfer, or scavenge. He was briefly taken under the wing of a sympathetic American couple who enrolled him in a school for orphans. This relatively normal interlude in his life ended abruptly when he stole some money from the school (allegedly after being molested by one of the male teachers) and ran away.

By his midadolescence, Lopez had turned to car theft, a vocation that landed him in jail when he was eighteen. Two days after he started his seven-year sentence, he was gang-raped by a quartet of older inmates. Not long afterward, Lopez killed all four of his attackers with a homemade shiv. Deemed an act of self-defense, the killings earned him only an additional two years.

Released in 1978, Lopez embarked on a nomadic career of sadistic lust-murder that would earn him international infamy as possibly the most prolific serial killer of all time. Traveling widely through Peru, he raped and strangled scores of young girls, many snatched from Indian tribes. Once, after being caught during the abduction of a nine-year-old Ayachucos child, he was beaten, tortured, and nearly buried alive. Only the timely intervention of an American missionary saved him.

Deported from the country, Lopez resumed his homicidal ways in Colombia and Ecuador. He was finally caught in April 1980, while attempting to lure a twelve-year-old girl from an Ecuadorian marketplace. In custody, Lopez was initially silent, though he finally opened up to his "cellmate"—actually a priest in prison garb, planted there by the authorities. Confronted with the horrifying admissions he had made to the disguised priest, Lopez broke down and offered a full confession that would have seemed flatly incredible if subsequent developments hadn't supported its truth.

In the two years between his release from prison and his capture, Lopez claimed to have murdered at least a hundred girls in Ecuador, the same number in Colombia, and "many more" in Peru. He would scout village markets for the most innocent-looking children he could find, then—having decided on a victim—lure her away with small trinkets. Once he had her in his power, he would strangle the girl while raping her, prolonging his pleasure as long as he could while he watched the life drain from her eyes. "It took the girls five to fifteen minutes to die," he told interrogators. "I would spend a long time with them, making sure they were dead. I would use a mirror to check whether they were still breathing. Sometimes, I had to kill them all over again."

Initially skeptical over his staggering claims, police became convinced when Lopez led them to a secluded area where they dug up the remains of fifty-three female victims, ages eight to twelve. Charged with 110 counts of murder, Lopez was convicted in 1980 and sentenced to the maximum under Ecuadorian law: life imprisonment.

> I am the man of the century. No one will ever forget me.
>
> —Pedro Lopez

Archibald McCafferty

As a slayer of three, Archie "Mad Dog" McCafferty may not have been one of Australia's worst serial murderers in purely quantitative terms. But he was certainly one of the most viciously deranged.

McCafferty was actually a citizen of Scotland who emigrated to Australia with his parents at the age of ten. Like the madman he would most often be compared to—Charles Manson—he spent his adolescence in and out of various institutions. By the age of twenty-four, he had racked up nearly three dozen convictions for everything from housebreaking and burglary to car theft and assault. One of the few crimes he hadn't been arrested for was murder. Not that he wasn't prone to violence. Until his midtwenties, however, his sadism was vented largely on small animals—puppies, cats, chickens—which he liked to strangle for fun.

In 1972, he married a young woman named Janice, who soon became pregnant. To give the devil his due, McCafferty seemed to recognize how frighteningly unstable he was and checked himself into psychiatric hospitals on several occasions, usually after he got drunk or stoned on angel dust and subjected his young wife to a savage beating. What finally pushed him over the edge into raging homicidal mania was the accidental death of his infant son, Craig. In March 1973, the baby smothered when Janice brought him into her bed and rolled over on him in her sleep.

A short time later, McCafferty—whose body was covered with hundreds of tattoos—added a new one, the number 7, inscribed on the web between thumb and forefinger of his right hand. Its significance would soon be made terrifyingly clear. In his spiraling madness, McCafferty had decided to murder seven people to "avenge" his son's death.

Six months later, McCafferty put his insane scheme into motion. Janice had fled back to her family, and Archie was now living with a suicidal young woman named Carol Howes. Residing with them was an emotionally unbalanced teenager, Julie Todd, whom they had befriended at a psychiatric clinic. This unholy threesome became the core of a gang that also included three other teenagers, a trio of seventeen-year-old boys McCafferty had met at his favorite tattoo parlor.

The first to die was an inebriated fifty-year-old news seller named George Anson. He was jumped by the gang, dragged to a side street, then stabbed seven times by McCafferty. By that point, McCafferty was deeply delusional. He had become convinced that the seven homicides he was planning to commit would bring his dead son back to life.

Victim number two was a forty-two-year-old miner named Ronald Cox, abducted at gunpoint after stopping to give a lift to two of McCafferty's teen accomplices. Driven to the cemetery where McCafferty's son was buried, Cox was made to lie facedown in the mud and shot in the back of the head. The following morning, the gang killed another well-meaning stranger, Evangelos Kollias, who had stopped to give two of the teenagers a lift.

After shooting Kollias in the head and dumping his body, McCafferty drove toward Blacktown, where his wife, Janice, had taken refuge at the home of her mother. He planned to kill both women, along with the mother's live-in boyfriend. Fortunately for the intended victims, McCafferty's car ran out of gas along the way. He decided to defer their executions. Shortly afterward, one of his gang members, a boy named Rick Webster, having become convinced that he had been targeted for death by McCafferty, turned him in to the police.

At the 1974 trial of the "Australian Charles Manson" (as the press dubbed him), psychiatrists offered conflicting testimony as to McCafferty's mental state. All agreed, however, that the twenty-five-year-old was a remorseless killer who posed a permanent threat to the community. McCafferty concurred with this opinion, stating that "if given the chance, I will kill again, for the simple reason that I have to kill seven people, and I have only killed three, which means I have four to go."

Hit with three life sentences, McCafferty spent the next twenty-three years in some of Australia's toughest prisons, where he gained a reputation as a particularly dangerous and incorrigible inmate. Despite his life sentences—supplemented with additional time for various offenses he committed while in jail (including manslaughter and drug-peddling)—he was paroled in 1993. Much to the delight of Australians—and the dismay of the Scots—he was deported to his homeland, where he declared that he was a "changed person." He remarried and fathered a child.

Sixteen months later, he was put on two years' probation after threatening to kill some cops.

> You and the rest of your family can go and get fucked because anyone who has anything to do with me is going to die of a bad death.
>
> —Archie McCafferty in a note to his wife

The "Monster of Florence"

One of the most gruesome—and perplexing—of modern murder mysteries, the series of crimes perpetrated by the so-called Monster of Florence has earned renewed notoriety in recent years as the case that inspired Thomas Harris to set his novel *Hannibal* in Dante's native city.

The case began in August 1968, when an adulterous couple was shot to death while parked in a cemetery, where they'd gone for some quick, furtive sex. The double murder appeared to be solved when the woman's cuckolded husband was arrested and convicted. But he was ultimately proved to be innocent, since he was still languishing in prison six years later when the killer struck again.

In September 1974, another couple—this time a pair of teenage lovers—was shot repeatedly while making out in their car. The girl was then dragged outside and stabbed nearly a hundred times in a frenzy of bloodlust. Afterward, the killer arranged her nude body in a spread-eagle position and thrust a vine branch up her mutilated vagina.

The pattern was established: double murders committed on moonless nights by a sexually sadistic "lovers' lane" maniac.

Seven years later, in June 1981, an off-duty policeman on a walk in the Florentine countryside happened upon the phantom-killer's next pair of victims. A thirty-year-old man was slumped behind the wheel of his car. He had been shot repeatedly and his throat had also been slashed. Sprawled at the bottom of a steep bank a few yards away was the savaged body of the man's twenty-one-year-old lover, whose vagina had been removed with a razor-sharp implement.

More horrors followed. In October 1981, another young couple who had parked for a romantic interlude at a scenic overlook just north of Florence was slaughtered by the maniac, who—once again—absconded with the woman's excised vulva. The following June, a couple was slain while making love in their car, though this time—apparently spooked by passing traffic—the killer fled without committing his usual mutilations.

In September 1983, two teenage boys were executed while sleeping in their parked camper nineteen miles south of Florence. This was a departure for the killer, who had so far focused on heterosexual couples, and police theorized that he might have mistaken one of the youths—who sported shoulder-length blond hair—for a girl.

In any case, he returned to his usual MO ten months later, when he slaughtered two young lovers who had parked just north of Florence. This time, he not only cut out the girl's genitals but removed her left breast. He repeated this atrocity the following September when he slaughtered a French couple in a campsite just outside Florence. Several days after their bodies were found, an assistant in the public prosecutor's office received a chunk of the woman's amputated breast in the mail.

During the next eight years, a hundred thousand people were questioned. More than two decades after the first killings, the case finally appeared to be solved when a suspect was arrested in January 1993. He was seventy-one-year-old Pietro Pacciani, a semiliterate farmhand and amateur taxidermist who had served time in the 1950s for a particularly grisly murder. After catching his fiancée in the embrace of a traveling salesman, he had stabbed and stomped the man to death, then raped the corpse. Pacciani had also done a stint in prison in the late 1980s for beating his wife and sexually molesting his two daughters. His 1994 arrest was a nationwide media sensation. Despite a paucity of hard evidence—and his own protestations of innocence—he was convicted of seven double murders. Two years later, however, his conviction was overturned on appeal. By then, police had come to believe that Pacciani was the ringleader of a small gang of killers, who had committed the murders for ritualistic purposes. In the end, three of his alleged confederates were put on trial. One was acquitted, two convicted of participating in five of the double slayings. Pacciani himself died, presumably of natural causes, before he could be retried, making it unlikely that the "Monster of Florence" mystery would ever be definitively resolved.

Arnfinn Nesset

A balding, bespectacled nursing home administrator, Nesset looked about as dangerous as Mr. Rogers. And yet he has entered the criminal-history books as Norway's most prolific serial killer, convicted of twenty-two murders and suspected of as many as 138.

When elderly, infirm patients at the Orkdal Valley Nursing Home began dying at rapid pace in the late 1970s, no one paid much attention until journalists received a tip that the director, Arnfinn Nesset, had been stocking up on curacit, a derivative of the notoriously lethal muscle relaxant, curare. Brought in for questioning, Nesset first insisted that he had purchased the drug to kill a pack of wild dogs that had been prowling around the premises. Abruptly, however, he changed his story and began confessing to a homicidal compulsion that had been going on for almost twenty years.

At first he admitted to twenty-seven killings. Before long, the number had grown to forty-six. Then sixty-two. But even that staggering sum was probably conservative. "I've killed so many, I'm unable to remember them all," he said. He had been doing away with elderly patients since he became a nursing home worker in 1962. Some of his homicides, he claimed, were mercy killings. Mostly, however, he murdered for the sheer sadistic joy of it.

Shortly before his trial was set to open, Nesset suddenly recanted and pleaded innocent. His lawyers tried to convince the jury that he was mentally unbalanced, a pathologically deluded individual who believed he was a "demigod" with the power of life and death over the elderly. The ploy didn't work. In March 1983, Nesset was convicted of twenty-two counts of murder and given the maximum sentence under Norwegian law: twenty-one years behind bars.

Anatoly Onoprienko

A Ukrainian psychopath who wreaked such devastation that newspapers dubbed him the "Terminator," Onoprienko was dumped in an orphanage as a child by his widowered father—an act that instilled the abandoned boy with a lifelong rage against normal, stable families. A late-blooming serial killer, he did not commit his first homicide until 1989. At the age of thirty, he and a confederate shot and killed an entire family—two adults and eight children—in the course of a robbery. Over the next seven years, he made up for lost time, conducting an ever-escalating rampage of slaughter that left more than fifty men, women, and children dead.

Just a few months after his first killings, Onoprienko—approaching a parked car with the intention of stealing it—discovered a family sleeping inside and shot all five occupants, including a five-year-old boy. He then burned their bodies.

Several years elapsed before he struck again. In December 1995, he broke into the home of a family named Zaichenko and murdered all four members—father, mother, and two young sons—with a sawed-off double-barrel shotgun. Nine days later, he slaughtered another family of four, torched their home, then killed a witness while fleeing the scene.

His reign of terror had begun in earnest.

Increasingly possessed by the need to murder random victims, Onoprienko killed seven more people in three separate incidents over a two-day span in early January 1996. Some victims were shot as they sat in parked or stalled cars, others were pedestrians, and one was a policeman on patrol.

Between mid-January and his arrest in April, Onoprienko broke into six more homes, slaughtering families wholesale with axes, guns, and hammers. By then, the largest manhunt in Ukraine was under way for the phantom killer. The village of Bratkovichi—where several of his worst massacres had taken place—was under the protection of a National Guard Unit equipped with rocket launchers and armored vehicles.

The end came in April 1996. Onoprienko was staying at the home of a cousin, who—after stumbling upon a hidden cache of weapons—kicked Anatoly out of his house and notified the police. Tracking Onoprienko to his girlfriend's apartment, the police found a mountain of evidence tying him to the spate of unsolved murders.

In custody, Onoprienko confessed to fifty-two homicides, offering various explanations for his atrocities. At different times, he insisted that he was under the control of God, Satan, and space aliens; he also claimed that he had killed out of sheer boredom. Despite evidence that he was a paranoid schizophrenic, he was judged competent to stand trial and was convicted and sentenced to death in April 1999.

> I would be sitting, bored, with nothing to do . . . So I would get in the car or catch a train and go out to kill.
>
> —Anatoly Onoprienko

Jose Antonio Rodriguez Vega

A pervert whose sexual pathology combined elements of necrophilia and gerontophila (erotic attraction to the elderly), Rodriguez Vega conducted a two-year reign of terror in the Spanish coastal town of Santander. Following his 1986 release from prison on a rape charge, he began talking his way into the homes of solitary old women under the pretext of performing minor household repairs. Once alone with his victims, he would strangle and rape them (in that order), then set about expunging every sign of his presence.

He did such a thorough job of cleaning up after himself—neatly tucking the bodies into bed and removing all traces of incriminating evidence—that most of the deaths were chalked up to natural causes. Only after his arrest—when police found the cache of "trophies" he had removed from his victims' homes—did the full extent of his crimes become known: sixteen murders in all, earning him a place in the criminal record books as the most prolific serial killer in recent Spanish history.

During his 1991 trial, the sadistic Rodriguez Vega seemed to revel in the grief he had caused his victims' families. He was sentenced to 440 years in prison, though—given the leniency of the Spanish penal system—there is every likelihood he will end up serving no more than twenty.

Morris Sithole

Between January and October 1995, more than three dozen young black women fell victim to a serial killer in the vicinities of Johannesburg and Pretoria. Because the crimes occurred in three suburbs—Atteridgeville, Boksburg, and Cleveland—they were dubbed the "ABC Murders." All the victims had been raped, then strangled with their purse straps or articles of clothing. At least a dozen of the corpses were found in a field strewn with a bizarre assortment of objects: knives, mirrors, crosses, burned Bibles, even dead birds impaled with pins like voodoo dolls. Stymied in their efforts to find the killer, South African authorities brought in ex–FBI agent Robert Ressler—a founding member of the bureau's pioneering team of "Mind Hunters"—who predicted that the case would eventually be solved and came up with the following profile: "a black male, twenty-five to thirty-five, an eye-catching dresser with a fancy car who charms his victims into entering his car willingly."

In early October, a Capetown newspaper received an anonymous telephone call from the killer, in which he described the murders as an act of revenge. He claimed to have been imprisoned in the past on a false accusation of rape. Having been subjected to unrelieved "torture" for the fourteen years behind bars, he had decided to inflict suffering on all womanhood. "I force a woman to go where I want," he said, "and when I go there I tell them, 'Do you know what? I was hurt, so I'm doing it now.' Then I kill them."

As a result of the call, police soon identified a suspect: a surprisingly soft-spoken ex-convict named Morris Sithole. In October 1995, after a nationwide manhunt, the thirty-one-year-old Sithole was tracked to a Johannesburg slum. Wielding a hatchet, he wounded one of the arresting officers before he himself was shot and taken into custody. In a series of taped jailhouse confessions, he smoked and munched on an apple while casually describing the terrified last moments of his victims. He freely admitted that he hated women and felt that he was teaching them "a very good lesson" by murdering them. Tried in 1997, he was convicted of thirty-eight murders, making him South Africa's most prolific serial killer. Prohibited from imposing the death penalty, the judge gave him the maximum sentence: 2,410 years.

Lucian Staniak

Communist Poland's answer to Jack the Ripper, Lucian Staniak committed a string of sadistic sex-murders over the span of three years, most timed to coincide with public celebrations.

The first hint of the horrors to come was a letter sent to a Warsaw newspaper on the eve of a national holiday. "There is no happiness without tears, no life without death," read the note, which was written with red ink in a spidery scrawl. "Beware! I am going to make you cry." The next day, the naked, disemboweled corpse of a seventeen-year-old schoolgirl was found in a park in the city of Olsztyn. The morning after this appalling discovery, another blood-colored note was sent to a newspaper editor: "I picked a juicy flower in Olsztyn and I shall do it again somewhere else, for there is no holiday without a funeral."

Six months would pass before the killer made good on his threat. In January 1965, he waylaid a sixteen-year-old girl on her way home from a student parade, raped her, garroted her with a wire, then hid her corpse in a factory basement.

His next atrocity took place on November 1—All Saints' Day—when he attacked a young woman at a freight terminal, immobilizing her with chloroform before raping her and savaging her lower body with a screwdriver.

Her mutilated corpse was found the next day inside a wooden packing crate, a six-inch metal spike protruding from her vagina. The following day, he sent the newspapers another letter written in red: "Only tears of sorrow can wash out the stain of shame; only pangs of suffering can blot out the fires of lust."

Exactly six months later, on May 1—Labor Day in Poland—a seventeen-year-old girl was raped and disemboweled in a suburb of Warsaw. In a hideous gesture reminiscent of Jack the Ripper's atrocities, the killer left the victim's entrails draped across her thighs.

By that point, a major manhunt was under way for the madman whose sinister, crimson-hued notes had earned him the nickname the "Red Spider." Various clues led the police to deduce that the killer resided in the city of Katowice.

Their big break came on Christmas Eve, 1966, when the hideously mangled body of seventeen-year-old Janina Kozielska was found aboard a train. Before fleeing, the killer had slipped one of his trademark notes through the slot of the mail car: "I have done it again."

Police quickly established that, two years earlier, Janina's fourteen-year-old sister had met the same awful fate—a fact that suggested that the girls were acquainted with the killer. Before long, detectives had also discovered that both sisters were models at the Art Lover's Club in Cracow—an intriguing lead, since police analysts had already determined that the red ink used by the killer was actually thinned-down artist's paint.

Checking the roster of the club, investigators zeroed in on twenty-six-year-old Lucian Staniak, the only member who lived in Katowice. Their suspicions were strengthened when they broke into his locker and discovered a red-painted picture of a disemboweled woman with flowers sprouting from her gaping belly.

On January 31, 1967, detectives tracked down and arrested Staniak, though not before he killed his final victim, an eighteen-year-old art student raped and butchered at a train station. Though he confessed to twenty murders, he was ultimately convicted of six and committed to a lunatic asylum for life.

Li Wenxian

Information about serial murder in hard-line Communist societies is difficult to come by, since—according to official party propaganda—such heinous crime is strictly a product of decadent Western capitalism and could not possibly exist in a people's republic. And indeed, the world might never have heard about the monster known as the "Guangzhou Ripper" if the hideously violated corpse of a young woman had not floated ashore in the then-British colony of Hong Kong in March 1992. The victim's body had been slit from throat to groin and her fingers sliced off. When authorities determined that the body had drifted in from the mainland, the outside world learned the truth that the Red Chinese government had been at pains to conceal: a vicious lust-murderer was at large in their worker's paradise.

The savaged corpse that washed up in Hong Kong that March was actually the Ripper's seventh known victim. The first—a young woman missing her genitals—had turned up in the province of Guangzhou in February 1991. Over the next six months, five more young women met identically gruesome deaths—raped, murdered, mutilated, then dismembered, stuffed into burlap rice bags, and dumped on rubbish heaps.

Partly because of their reluctance to admit that a serial killer could possibly be at large in their country (the same willful blindness that hampered the hunt for the Russian "Mad Beast," Andrei Chikatilo), the Chinese police were slow to resolve the case. Six more women came to grisly ends over the next four years. The break finally came in November 1996, when a woman survived the Ripper's savage assault and identified her attacker as a construction worker named Li Wenxian, a onetime farmer who had migrated to Guangzhou in 1991, just prior to the start of the Ripper slayings. In custody, Wenxian confessed to all thirteen murders, exposing another discomfiting fact that clashed with the utopian mythology of the Communist state—that prostitution, as well as serial homicide, existed in China. A classic "harlot slayer," Wenxian had vowed revenge against all prostitutes after one of them—so he claimed—had cheated him of money shortly after his arrival in Guangzhou. Convicted of murder and rape, he was sentenced to death in December 1996.

Who Is Killing the Women of Juarez?

Since August 1993, a killing spree of unprecedented proportions has drawn worldwide media attention to the Mexican city of Juarez, just across the border from El Paso, Texas. Though exact figures are hard to determine, sources most familiar with the case estimate that well over three hundred young women have been savagely murdered in the past decade.

The victims tend to be slender, dark-haired young women between the ages of fourteen and sixteen who have disappeared on their way to or from work at the foreign-owned sweatshop factories known as *maquiladoras.* Their bodies, often horribly mutilated, have turned up in the desert or alongside the roads leading to the squatter camps ringing the city. Though many have apparently died at the hands of pimps, drug dealers, jealous husbands, and brutal boyfriends, at least one-third of the victims—as many as ninety in the past decade—are believed to have been raped, maimed, and slaughtered by one or more serial killers.

The first "official" victim in the case was a young woman named Alva Chavira Farel, found beaten, raped, and strangled in January 1993. By mid-September 1995, more than forty brutalized corpses had turned up, some with their right breasts severed and their left nipples bitten off—the grisly "signature" of the homicidal madman the press had dubbed the "Juarez Ripper" or *el Depredator Psicópata.*

A supposed solution to the case occurred in October 1995, with the arrest of an Egyptian-born chemist, Abdel Latif Sharif, a man with a long history of brutal assaults on women in the United States. After serving time on a rape charge in Florida, he relocated to Mexico, where he was taken into custody on suspicion of murder in October 1995 and allegedly confessed to five of the Juarez killings. At his trial in March 1999, he received a thirty-year sentence.

Following Sharif's arrest, Mexican police triumphantly proclaimed that the case was closed. Unfortunately, the corpses soon began piling up again—this time, at an even faster rate.

More suspects were arrested, including ten members of a gang called *Los Rebeldes* ("The Rebels"), accused of receiving a large sum of cash from Sharif to commit atrocities that would make it appear as if the "Juarez Ripper" were still at large, thereby exonerating Sharif. Despite the imprisonment of these latest perpetrators, however, there was no letup in the atrocities.

In the ensuing years, the grim pattern has continued: suspects are arrested, the police trumpet the solution of the case, then more butchered corpses turn up. Theories about the identity of the killer or killers abound. Candidates have ranged from a gang of homicidal bus drivers known as *Los Choferes* ("The Chauffeurs") to the so-called Railway Killer, Angel Maturino Resendez, to Satanists, drug cartels, and members of the Juarez police force.

One persistent rumor, reported in the May 2, 2003, edition of the *New York Daily News,* is that "roving gangs kidnapped the women to harvest their organs and sell them on the black market to wealthy people needing transplants—possibly in the United States." Most experts, however, scoff at this notion. A much likelier solution, as FBI Special Agent Art Werge has said, is that the culprits are not international organ traffickers or devil-worshiping cultists but garden-variety psychopaths, "acting out sexual fantasies that are violent that they simply get a kick out of."

A HISTORY OF SERIAL MURDER

SERIAL MURDER: OLD AS SIN

There's a common belief that serial murder is a modern phenomenon which started, according to certain self-proclaimed experts, with the crimes of Jack the Ripper. Not to put too fine a point upon it, this is utter nonsense. The harsh fact is that we belong to a violent species; the kinds of outrages committed by serial killers have been an aspect of human society at all times in all places. As the Bible says, "There is no new thing under the sun"—and that applies to sadistic murder as much as to anything else.

Indeed, recent scientific evidence suggests that a taste for savage cruelty is encoded in our DNA, an evolutionary inheritance from our earliest primate ancestors. In his book *Demonic Males,* Harvard anthropologist Richard Wrangham demonstrates that chimpanzees (who are "genetically closer to us than they are even to gorillas") routinely commit acts of torture and mayhem as appalling as anything recorded in *Psychopathia Sexualis.* Not only do they prey upon vulnerable members of their own species, but their assaults "are marked by a gratuitous cruelty—tearing off pieces of skin, for example, twisting limbs until they break, or drinking a victim's blood—reminiscent of acts that among humans are regarded as unspeakable crimes during peace time and atrocities during war."

That human beings have always indulged in extraordinarily barbaric behavior is made clear in everything from ancient Greek myths (like the story of Atreus, who butchered his brother's sons and baked them in a cannibal pie) to the recorded deeds of medieval knights, who—far from being the chivalrous paragons of popular stereotype—were brutish warriors who felt free to pillage, rape, and (when they got drunk enough on mead) indulge in mass slaughter, sometimes of helpless women. Anyone who claims that there was no such thing as mutilation sex crime in centuries past clearly hasn't read Shakespeare's *Titus Andronicus,* in which a young woman is gang-raped, then has her tongue cut out and hands chopped off to prevent her from identifying her assailants.

Given all the shocking evidence that lust-murder has always been a component of human behavior, how is it that people have come to believe that serial killers are unique to modern times?

There are several answers. First, a man who committed repeated acts of appalling mutilation-murder on innocent victims wasn't necessarily regarded as a criminal in past ages. Throughout the millennia when bloody warfare was a routine feature of people's lives, a psychopathic killer who enjoyed inflicting savage harm on others could join the army, butcher men, women, and children to his heart's content—and earn a promotion for it. Francisco Goya's famous series of engravings, *Disasters of War*—with its horrific images of rape, castration, and dismemberment—makes it appallingly clear that combat has always afforded an opportunity for uniformed sadists to gratify their bloodlust. This has been true even in recent times. One American soldier, for example, described a sight he witnessed in Vietnam. After shooting a peasant woman to death, one member of his squad "went over there, ripped her clothes off, and took a knife and cut from her vagina all the way up, just about to her breast and pulled her organs out, completely out of her cavity, and threw them out. Then he stooped and knelt over and commenced to peel every bit of skin off her body and left her there as a sign for something or other."

Indeed, depending on who his victims were, a homicidal maniac wouldn't necessarily have to bother becoming a soldier. Anyone could get away with serial murder, as long as he was preying on people who "didn't matter." If a peasant girl in twelfth-century Europe was attacked, raped, and murdered while walking through the forest, no one in authority would notice or care. Even today, certain serial killers deliberately target despised or disenfranchised members of the population—prostitutes, say, or poor ghetto children—knowing that authorities are far less likely to take such crimes seriously.

In our own country, just a little over a century ago, a psycho-killer could travel west and butcher all the Native Americans he wanted to with impunity. Anyone who doubts this sorry truth is referred to Cormac McCarthy's *Blood*

One of the many atrocities portrayed in Goya's *Disasters of War* (1863)

Meridian, a fact-based novel about a troop of white scalp-hunters who commit atrocities that would make Jack the Ripper blanch but who are rewarded for their actions because their victims are Indians. Larry McMurtry's *Lonesome Dove* trilogy also contains vivid portraits of frontier psychopaths, like Mox Mox the "Manburner" and pretty-boy sniper, Joey Garza—fictional creations who reflect the violent realities of the lawless West. Back in those days, such remorseless killers were called "bad men" or "desperadoes," but if they existed today they would be defined as serial killers.

Another reason why people assume that serial killers have only come into existence in modern times is that, back in the preindustrial days, there was no such thing as the press. There are no newspaper records of, say, fourteenth-century serial killers, not because human beings didn't commit hideous sex crimes back then, but because there were no newspapers. It's significant that Jack the Ripper's crimes coincided with the rise of mass literacy and the appearance of the first cheap tabloid-type papers, like the *Illustrated Police News* of London. Jack the Ripper was not the first serial sex-killer, not by a long shot. But he was the first celebrity psycho made internationally famous by the media.

Besides the clergy, the aristocracy were the only literate members of the population back in the Middle Ages, and they were only interested in reading about their own kind. It's no surprise, therefore, that the homicidal monsters whose names have come down to us from the distant past tend to be aristocrats themselves: Gilles de Rais, for example, or Vlad the Impaler. But again, that doesn't mean that there weren't plenty of degenerate killers among the "lower orders" as well. It just means that bloodthirsty peasants who preyed on their own class rarely made it into the official chronicles, which tended to stick to the doings of the high and mighty.

As David Lester points out in his book *Serial Killers: The Insatiable Passion,* "Record keeping was highly unreliable in times past and crime detection was very rudimentary (the authorities would have had great difficulty in identifying a serial killer's work), and so the true incidence of serial murder in premodern times is unknown."

Recommended Reading

David Lester, *Serial Killers: The Insatiable Passion* (1995)
Richard Wrangham and Dale Peterson, *Demonic Males: Apes and the Origins of Human Violence* (1996)

GRIM FAIRY TALES

Because the literacy rate among the peasants of premodern Europe was basically zero, there are few written records of early serial killers. Evidence exists, however, that such monsters walked among them.

That evidence is in the form of fairy tales. Nowadays we think of fairy tales as a charming variety of kiddie lit, but originally they were oral stories intended for adults. And though they are full of magic and enchantment, they are also, as many scholars have pointed out, historical documents, reflecting social realities of the time. The extremely gruesome content of many of these tales makes it clear that their audience was quite familiar with the kind of homicidal maniacs we now call serial killers.

In "The Robber Bridegroom," for example—one of the tales recorded by the Brothers Grimm—the heroine sneaks into her boyfriend's home and watches in horror as he and some buddies bring home a young woman, get her drunk on wine, then kill her, chop her up in pieces, and devour her body. And in another Grimm story, "Fitcher's Feathered Bird," an overly curious young woman discovers that her new husband is a serial ax-murderer when she enters a forbidden room and finds "a great bloody basin" filled with "human beings, dead and hewn to pieces." When her husband returns home and realizes that his wife has discovered the terrible truth about him, he wastes no time in getting rid of her: "He threw her down, dragged her along by her hair, cut her head off on the block, and hewed her in pieces so that the blood ran on the ground. Then he threw her into the basin with the rest."

Perhaps the most famous fairy tale reflecting early fears of serial killers is "Little Red Riding Hood." Many scholars believe that ancient superstitions about werewolves stem, at least partly, from real-life cases of medieval

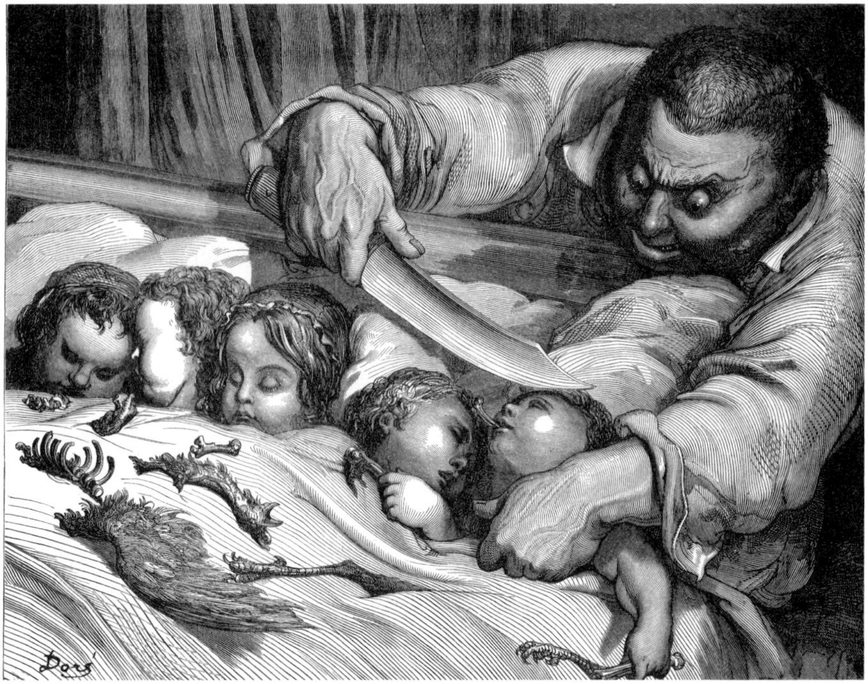

An ogre cuts the throats of seven sleeping children in this Gustav Doré illustration of the fairy tale "Hop o' My Thumb"

mutilation-murderers who killed with such bestial ferocity that they were thought to be actual wolf-men, or *lycanthropes.* The two most famous of these were Peter Stubbe and Gilles Garnier.

> Serial murder may, in fact, be a much older phenomenon than we realize. The stories and legends that have filtered down about werewolves and vampires may have been a way of explaining outrages so hideous that no-one [sic] in the small and close-knit towns of Europe and early America could comprehend the perversities we now take for granted. Monsters had to be supernatural creatures.
>
> —John Douglas, *Mindhunter*

For us, the werewolf is a character in old horror movies, some tormented guy played by Lon Chaney, Jr., who gets hairy and vicious in the light of the full moon. But Europeans in the sixteenth century had different ideas. Werewolves constituted a vexing issue of criminal justice and public policy. When officials at the time discovered that some crazed criminal was on a murderous rampage, not only killing but tearing apart his victims, they didn't regard him as someone driven by twisted psychological impulses. They characterized him as someone who had welcomed the power of Satan and had literally turned into a monster.

In December 1573, the regional parliament in Franche-Comte in eastern France issued a proclamation outlining the most effective and proper ways to catch, convict, and punish werewolves. The authorities were responding to the recent shocking case in nearby Dole of Gilles Garnier, the most notorious of French lycanthropes. Sixteen years later, German concerns about werewolves in their midst came to a head in the trial of a man named Peter Stubbe. Together, these two cases give us some idea of the ferocity of these so-called demons, the serial killers of their day, as well as the brutality of the authorities' response.

The alleged werewolves came to their savage criminal careers from different directions. Garnier was known as a hermit—today he would be called a loner—who gave up his solitary life to take a wife and start a family. He soon found, though, that he was unable to live up to his role as a provider. Supposedly, he made his deal with the devil out of desperation. Not so with Stubbe. The way contemporary chroniclers tell it, he was born bad and practiced black magic and indulged in cruelty from an early age. Once the two men made their pacts with Satan, the distinctions between them blurred. Both became addicted to murder and cannibalism, both preferred to prey upon children.

A lycanthrope makes off with a baby

Supposedly turning into a wolf when he applied an enchanted ointment, Garnier murdered four children. Stubbe was said to accomplish his transformation thanks to a magical belt. He killed thirteen kids, along with one man and two women. In his monster incarnation, Stubbe reportedly had "eyes great and large, which in the night sparkled like brands of fire; a mouth great and wide, with most sharp and cruel teeth; a huge body and mighty paws." It's easy to understand why people in those days thought that Stubbe or other similar killers took such a nightmarish form. Their crimes seemed to be the work of infernal creatures.

Garnier would strangle his young victims, then rip them apart and feast upon the flesh of their legs, arms, and belly. In one case, he tore off the leg of a boy. In another case, he tore off a chunk of a girl's flesh and took it home to his wife so that she could cook it for dinner.

The attacks by Stubbe along the Rhine River in Westphalia might have been even more ferocious. Like Garnier, he consumed parts of his victims and was particularly fond of eating "hearts panting hot and raw." Once he was reputed to have eaten an entire victim without leaving a trace. Although he often roamed the countryside looking to waylay strangers, he would also target his own family. He raped both his sister and his daughter before turning them into his accomplices, and he murdered his son and devoured his brain.

When the authorities finally tracked down these psychos, they made it clear that they planned to make graphic examples of them. After his trial,

(Lambeth Palace Library)

The crimes, trial, and torture of the "werewolf," Peter Stubbe, from a 1590 pamphlet

Garnier was turned over to Dole's Master Executioner of High Justice, who burned the alleged werewolf alive. Officers of the law in the German town of Bedburg went several steps further when dealing with Stubbe. First they put him on the rack and tortured a confession out of him. Then, after the formality of a trial, they strapped him to a wheel, tore away chunks of his flesh with red-hot pincers, crushed his limbs with the head of an ax, decapitated him, and burned what was left of his body. The gruesome procedure was not only an act of revenge but also intended as a deterrent. To underscore the message for any other aspiring werewolves in the vicinity, the authorities tied the torture wheel to a pole and left Stubbe's head impaled on the pole's tip.

While these cases show that horrendous serial murder is nothing new, they also demonstrate that media fascination with this sort of crime is also old news. Immediately following the executions of both werewolves, the professional printers, empowered by the new media innovation of movable type, cranked out pamphlets recounting all the grisly details of each case. Included in the Stubbe booklet was the sixteenth-century equivalent of a comic strip depicting his crimes and capture and, in the final four panels, showing the excruciating details of his punishment.

Recommended Reading

David Everitt, *Human Monsters* (1993)
Catherine Orenstein, *Little Red Riding Hood Uncloaked* (2002)

SERIAL SLAUGHTER THROUGH THE AGES

According to Thomas Carlyle, "history is but the biography of great men." Of course, he wasn't thinking about *criminal* history when he made that remark. Far from being the biography of great men, the history of serial murder is largely the chronicle of psychopathic creeps—misfits, losers, and utter nonentities—whose only claim to fame is a capacity for spectacularly sick acts of violence.

Of course, there have been some exceptions—individuals who would have made it into the history books even if they hadn't been among the most depraved killers who ever lived. This was particularly true in the distant past, when a number of notorious psycho-killers were members of the high aristocracy, and sometimes of the royalty itself.

Ancient Rome

In an age when watching an arena full of helpless human beings get torn to pieces by wild animals was regarded as an enjoyable pastime, it required something very special to stand out as a particularly degenerate individual.

The behavior of certain ancient emperors, however, was so grotesquely depraved that it was shocking even by the sadistic standards of pagan Rome. Though Tiberius, Justinian, and Caligula all engaged in unspeakable perversions, the worst of them all was arguably Nero.

Like most psychopaths, Nero began to act on his sadistic propensities at an early age. As an adolescent (according to the Roman historian, Suetonius) he liked to disguise himself in a cap and prowl the streets at night "in search of mischief. One of his favorite games was to attack men on their way home from dinner, stab them if they offered resistance, and then drop their bodies down the sewer."

His "games" became increasingly baroque. Later in life, he liked to pretend he was one of the ravenous beasts of the Coliseum. Dressing himself in the skin of a wild animal, he would leap from a den and "attack the private parts of men and women who stood bound to stakes," biting and ripping off their genitals in a state of savage ecstasy.

Among his countless other atrocities, he once castrated a boy named Sporus, dressed him up as a bride, and married him in a mock ceremony; turned a bunch of captive Christians into human torches and used them to light up a garden party; and tore out the womb of his own mother Agrippina, so that he could see where he had come from.

Agrippina herself once employed the services of a female poisoner named Locusta who—according to crime maven Michael Newton—"takes the honors as the first publicly identified practitioner of serial murder." Eager to rid herself of her husband, the emperor Claudius, Agrippina hired Locusta for the job, which the latter carried out successfully with a tempting dish of poisoned mushrooms. Later, she was also called upon to eliminate Claudius's son, Britannicus. Eventually, she paid for her crimes (which reportedly included the murder of at least five other victims) in a manner that was typical of the extravagant depravities of Nero's Rome. As Newton describes it, "she was publicly raped by a specially trained giraffe, after which she was torn apart by wild animals."

The Premodern Age

Even in our own age of twenty-four/seven news coverage, most serial murder cases are barely reported by the media (it's a safe bet that, unless you're a hard-core crime junkie, you've never heard of Todd Reed, a devoted father and part-time poet arrested for the murder of three Portland prostitutes in May 2000; or Tommy Lynn Sells, a drifter who, following his arrest by Texas authorities in January of that same year, confessed to ten killings in six states). So it's impossible to say how many serial sex-murders were committed five hundred years ago, when newspapers didn't exist and crimes among the peasantry went largely unrecorded (unless they were spectacularly gruesome, like those of Peter Stubbe and Gilles Garnier).

The most infamous figures of premodern Europe were highborn sadists like Gilles de Rais, the original Bluebeard, who was executed in 1440 for the torture-murder of 140 children (though estimates of his victims range as high as 300). Perhaps even more appalling—at least if all the legends are to be believed—was the Hungarian "Blood Countess," Erzebet (or Elizabeth) Bathory. Born in 1560 into one of Hungary's most ancient families, the beautiful Erzebet grew up in the same spooky area inhabited by the fictional Count Dracula, at the foot of the Carpathian Mountains. While still in her teens, she was reputedly initiated into the pleasures of torture, devil-worship, and sexual perversion by assorted family members. Her monstrous nature came into full blossom after she married an aristocratic warrior, Count Nazady, and moved into his castle, which was equipped with a well-stocked torture dungeon.

Between her marriage in 1575 and her arrest more than thirty years later, Bathory was responsible for a staggering number of murders—perhaps as many as 650. Most of her victims were peasant girls. Lured to the grim castle by the promise of employment—or sometimes abducted outright—the young women were subjected to unspeakable torments for the delectation of the degenerate countess, who was driven into a sexual frenzy by their agonies. She was especially fond of ripping out chunks of their flesh with a custom-made pincers, though she also made frequent use of whips, scissors, needles, red-hot branding irons, spike-lined cages, and her own teeth. According to legend, she was also in the habit of butchering her virginal captives, filling a tub with their blood, and bathing in the gore as a way of preserving her youth.

Eventually, having exhausted the supply of nubile peasant girls from the surrounding countryside, Bathory began to prey on the daughters of minor nobility, a practice that finally aroused the authorities and led to her arrest in 1610. During her trial, she was accused, among countless other atrocities, of cutting off parts of her victims' bodies and making them eat their own flesh. Condemned to a living entombment in a bricked-up chamber in her castle, she died of apparent starvation in 1614.

For several centuries, the name of another notorious woman of the distant past, Lucretia Borgia, was synonymous with female serial murder. A member of the most powerful family of the Italian Renaissance, Lucretia was infamous for her sexual excesses (which supposedly included incest with her father, the pope) as well as her habit of getting rid of enemies with a poisoned powder she dispensed from a sinister ring. Indeed, throughout the Victorian era, every time a new female poisoner like Lydia Sherman appeared, she was immediately branded a latter-day "Borgia." There seems to be a growing consensus among historians, however, that tales about Lucretia's crimes were merely rumors spread by her political enemies and that she was, in fact, a model of virtue who never engaged in sexual misconduct or killed anyone at all.

CASE STUDY

Vlad the Impaler

Yes, there once was a real-life Dracula. But no, he did not bite the necks of young, voluptuous women and drain them of their blood. Still, he was more than horrendous enough to qualify as a monster—if, that is, fifteenth-century accounts can be believed.

Vlad the Impaler

His name was Vlad III, and he was prince of the Romanian principality of Wallachia, just south of the fictional Dracula's Transylvania home. His father was known as Dracul, Romanian for dragon. Vlad's own moniker of Dracula meant son of Dracul. Not a true serial killer, Vlad was reputed to be a deranged autocrat who vanquished his enemies, both real and imagined, with unspeakable sadism. His Dracula moniker might be better known today, but in the fifteenth century he had another nickname—Vlad Tepes, meaning Vlad the Impaler, in honor of his favorite torturous pastime. It is this bloodthirsty reputation that impressed Bram Stoker enough to use Vlad as the basis for his now legendary creature of the night.

Some historians, though, claim that all this might be a bum rap.

They assert that the accounts of Vlad's atrocities were exaggerated and that he was, in fact, a great Romanian hero, a defender of his homeland against foreign aggression. They insist that Vlad's actions must be placed in the proper historical context, a period when his country needed a strong, if somewhat stern, leader.

Vlad took the Wallachian throne in 1456 when his country was hard-pressed by the Ottoman Turks surging up from the south. At the same time, Romanian principalities had to maintain a volatile alliance with the Hungarians to the north. According to author Kurt W. Treplow, Vlad Dracula "lived in a moment of great importance for the future of the Romanian people," and his defiance in the face of Ottoman conquerors kept "alive the spirit of independence" among his countrymen.

While Vlad's defenders focused on his political and military accomplishments, his enemies preferred to dwell on exactly how he went about defying the Turks and other adversaries. How much these detractors have embellished Vlad's dark side is difficult to say. What we do know is that the accounts of Dracula's savagery are hair-raising.

When it came to his torture method of choice, Vlad the Impaler was supposed to have been unnervingly creative. Using his victims' weight as they slid down a greased, pointed pole, he would sometimes impale them through the mouth, other times through the anus or the heart or navel. Depending on his whim of the moment, blinding, burning, or scalping might also be a part of the hideous process. Often this type of execution was reserved for enemies in war. In 1461, while retreating from relentless Ottoman troops, he was known to have left a veritable forest of impaled Turks in his wake. His attitude toward Saxons apparently wasn't much better. On April 2, 1459, in the Transylvanian town of Brasov he ordered the impalement of thousands of Saxons, the stakes arranged around a table where he calmly ate his dinner amidst the carnage.

Other targets of Vlad's were the boyars, the Romanian aristocrats, who may have been involved in the assassination of Vlad's father. Once, the story goes, he invited many of them to his castle for a lavish banquet, then burned them all alive in the dining hall.

His sadism could also be directed at specific individuals for violating his deeply felt, if insanely strict, sense of morality. For the crime of adultery (when committed by women) he would skin the culprit alive and carve out her genitalia. Once he was supposed to have been shocked to see that a peasant woman had fashioned her husband's shirt far too short. He had a red-hot poker thrust up her vagina and out through her mouth. In what he must have considered a magnanimous gesture, he then presented the widowered peasant with a new wife. Vlad also "roasted children of mothers and they had to eat their children themselves," according to a 1462 pamphlet on Dracula's life.

The pamphlet was published by Germans, who were enemies of Vlad and probably had valid reasons for hating him. This hatred could very well have inspired the pamphlet's author to magnify or even invent atrocities. True or not, this version of Vlad's life, one of the first best sellers produced by the Gutenberg press, spawned his monstrous reputation that has endured through the centuries.

More recent historians have discredited the original Dracula pamphlet as a hatchet job, but even if you accept the idea that Vlad was a notable leader according to the standards of his time, the chances are that he indulged in a certain amount of barbarism. After all, the rules of warfare and capital punishment were a lot less fussy in the fifteenth century. Perhaps he was truly vicious but no worse than other warrior-aristocrats of his day.

Vlad enjoys his favorite form of torture

The Seventeenth Century

By the 1600s, cheaply printed pamphlets and single-sheet "broadsides" made news stories available to the English masses, who—like ordinary people everywhere—were primarily interested in freakish accidents, bizarre occurrences, and sensational crimes—the gorier the better. Many of these early publications have survived; their contents make it clear that there's nothing new about serial murder.

In a fascinating study published in the magazine *History Today,* Professor Bernard Capp of the University of Warwick summarizes some of the notorious seventeenth-century murder cases that he managed to dig up during his researches. There was, for example, the 1675 case of "the bloody innkeeper" who ran a cheap lodging house in Gloucester, catering largely to commercial travelers. After a few years, the owner and his wife had made enough from their business to move into a larger house. The inn was purchased by a blacksmith, who set about converting the place into a smithy. As he was digging up the backyard to lay foundations for his shop, the new owner was horrified to discover the decomposing corpses of seven fully clothed men, one with a rusty knife still embedded in his chest. History does not record what happened to the homicidal innkeeper and his wife, though—from what we know about English justice in the 1600s—it seems safe to assume that they came to very unpleasant ends.

So did another killer couple of the era, Thomas Sherwood (aka "Country Tom") and his distaff accomplice Elizabeth Evans (aka "Canterbury Bess"). For several years, the two plied their murderous trade in London. Bess would pick up a tipsy fellow at a playhouse or tavern and lure him to a remote spot, where Tom would be waiting in ambush. The victim would be murdered and stripped of his belongings, including every scrap of his clothing. At least five men met their deaths at the hands of this infamous pair, who ended their lives on the Newgate gallows.

Ordinary people who had lived apparently respectable lives for years were suddenly revealed to be homicidal maniacs. In 1671, a man named Thomas Lancaster secretly administered arsenic to his wife, her father, her three sisters, her aunt, a cousin, and a young female servant, killing them in succession. "For good measure," Capp writes, "he poisoned some neighbors, too."

Then, as now, "angels of death"—male and female caregivers with a psychopathic urge to murder their charges—were not uncommon. At an almshouse in Coventry, eight inmates were poisoned with ratsbane in 1619 by a man named John Johnson, who committed suicide when he fell under suspicion for the crimes. There were also "Black Widow" killers like Elizabeth Ridgway, who poisoned both her husband and former suitor, as well as her mother and a former servant.

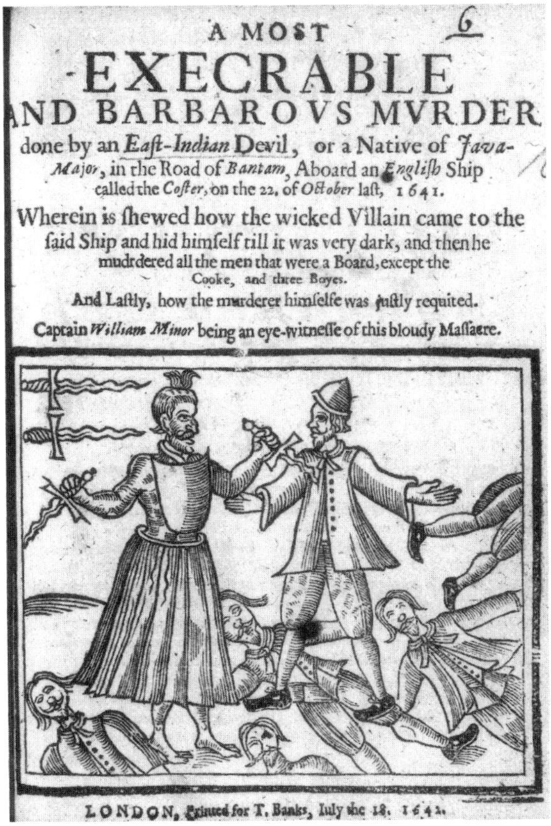
A MOST
EXECRABLE
AND BARBAROVS MVRDER
done by an *Eaſt-Indian* Devil, or a Native of *Java-Major*, in the Road of *Bantam*, Aboard an *Engliſh* Ship called the *Coſter*, on the 22. of *October* laſt, 1641.
Wherein is ſhewed how the wicked Villain came to the ſaid Ship and hid himſelf till it was very dark, and then he mudrdered all the men that were a Board, except the Cooke, and three Boyes.
And Laſtly, how the murderer himſelfe was juſtly requited.
Captain *William Minor* being an eye-witneſſe of this bloudy Maſſacre.
LONDON, Printed for T. Banks, July the 18. 1642.

(British Library)

An "East-Indian Devil" slaughters the crew of an English ship, as portrayed in a 1642 engraving

All of these and other cases uncovered by Professor Capp illustrate his point: human nature has remained more or less unchanged throughout the ages, and "multiple murders and serial killings were probably no rarer in seventeenth-century England than today."

Recommended Reading

Bernard Capp, "Serial Killers in 17th-century England," *History Today* (March 1996)

The Eighteenth Century

One of the most notorious serial killers of the 1700s may never have existed. This was Sweeney Todd, the so-called "Demon Barber of Fleet Street." According to crime writer Martin Fido, Todd was a completely fictitious character invented by Victorian writers of cheap "blood-and-thunder" fiction. Peter

Haining, on the other hand—another British author who frequently writes about horror and crime—not only claims that Sweeney was real but describes him as "the greatest mass murderer in English history."

According to Haining's "definitive biography" of this legendary monster, Sweeney Todd was born in the London slums in October 1756, the child of poor silk weavers who abandoned him when he was twelve. Apprenticing himself to a cutler, young Sweeney became adept at handling and sharpening razors. Two years later, he was accused of petty theft and thrown into Newgate Prison, where he ended up becoming the assistant of a barber named Plummer.

Upon his release in 1775, the nineteen-year-old Sweeney—a sullen, coarse-featured young man with a bitter grudge against the world—became an itinerant barber before leasing a shop on Fleet Street. There, over the next twenty-five years, he would perpetrate more than 160 grisly murders.

The diabolical device he employed to dispatch his unwary customers was a cunningly designed "revolving chair." When activated by a hidden bolt, the chair flipped backward, pitching the victim through a trapdoor into the cellar. Those who weren't killed outright by the fall had their throats slit by the fiendish barber. Afterward, their bodies were butchered and made into meat pies by Margery Lovett, owner of a neighborhood bakeshop.

Eventually, according to Haining, both Todd and his female accomplice were arrested. Mrs. Lovett reportedly committed suicide in prison. Todd was tried, convicted, and hanged on January 25, 1802.

There is no question about the authenticity of another eighteenth-century serial killer, though her real name has long been forgotten, along with the biographical details of her early life. In the annals of crime, she is known by her

Sweeney Todd dismembers a female victim

nickname, "La Tofania," and—if the accounts of her crimes are even halfway accurate—she stands as one of the most prolific murderers in history.

Tofania's homicidal career actually began in the late 1600s, when—using a specially brewed, arsenic-based potion that came to be called "*aqua tofania*" after its creator—she murdered a close male relation (possibly her first husband, though the records are a bit fuzzy on this score) in Naples, Italy. Soon, this enterprising female psychopath—who was reportedly motivated as much by a sadistic hatred of men as by greed—had made poison her business, peddling her concoction to aristocratic women eager to rid themselves of odious mates or tiresome lovers.

By 1719, the death rate among seemingly robust Neapolitan noblemen had reached such a point that the viceroy himself launched an investigation. The sixty-six-year-old Tofania—rumored to be the leader of a militant, man-hating sisterhood—was quickly identified as the prime suspect. Alerted by friends, she took refuge in a convent, until the viceroy—enraged by rumors that her followers had poisoned the city wells—sent a troop of soldiers into the sanctuary and had her arrested. Under torture, she confessed to six hundred murders. She was tried, convicted, and killed by strangulation in 1723.

Recommended Reading

Michael Newton, *Bad Girls Do It!* (1993)
Peter Haining, *Sweeney Todd: The Real Story of the Demon Barber of Fleet Street* (1993)

The Nineteenth Century

Though Jack the Ripper is far and away the most famous psycho-killer of the Victorian Era, there were plenty of other nineteenth-century serial murderers. Some were a lot more deadly than "Saucy Jack."

Even before Victoria ascended to the throne, Britain was rocked by one of the most sensational crime cases of the century—that of William Burke and William Hare. British laws at the time placed severe restrictions on human dissections, making it exceptionally difficult for doctors and medical students to obtain specimens for anatomical study. As a result, aspiring surgeons and their teachers were often forced to turn to grave robbers—or "Resurrection Men," as they were called—to supply them with raw material.

The names of Burke and Hare became associated with this ghoulish breed of entrepreneurship: the loathsome body snatcher who would sneak into a graveyard at night, dig up a freshly buried corpse and sell it for a few pounds to an anatomy school. However, these two came to their macabre profession by another route. In 1827, Hare and his common-law wife were running a squalid boardinghouse in the Edinburgh slums when an elderly lodger died, owing them four pounds. To cover the debt, Hare hit upon the idea of selling the old man's corpse to an anatomist. With the help of his friend Burke, he conveyed the cadaver to a medical school run by a celebrated surgeon, Dr. Robert Knox, who paid them £7.10s—an enormous sum to two poor Irish immigrants who normally made a pittance as laborers.

Impressed with the monetary potential of dead bodies, but disinclined to engage in the difficult, dirty, and dangerous business of grave-robbing, Burke and Hare opted for an easier method of obtaining marketable corpses: they would produce their own. Not long afterward, when another of Hare's lodgers fell ill, the men eased him into a coma by feeding him whiskey, then suffocated him by pinching his nose and sealing his mouth. This time, they got £10 from Dr. Knox. Another ailing inmate of Hare's hostelry soon met the same end.

Having exhausted the supply of sick lodgers at Hare's boardinghouse, the two began preying on neighborhood beggars, local prostitutes, and other street people. Luring them to Hare's place with the promise of liquor and food, they would suddenly pounce upon the unwary victims and suffocate them. Fifteen people—twelve women, two handicapped boys, and an old man—were murdered this way before the two killers were caught.

To save his own skin, Hare turned King's evidence. In January 1829, Burke was hanged before a cheering crowd of twenty-five thousand spectators and his body publicly dissected. His name would enter the English language, the verb "to burke" meaning to murder someone for the purpose of dissection.

Hare's lodging house wasn't the only hostelry-from-hell in the nineteenth century. In our own country, a family nicknamed the "Bloody Benders" ran a roadside inn in Kansas where, as one writer has put it, "horror rather than hospitality was the rule."

The Bender family consisted of the sixty-year-old patriarch, John (generally referred to simply as "Old Man Bender" in historical accounts), his wife, known only as "Ma"—just forty-two years old but with the cold-eyed, wizened looks of a hag—a hulking dim-witted twenty-seven-year-old son, John, Jr., and a daughter named Kate, a young woman in her early twenties who, by default, was considered the brains of the operation. Though Kate has gone down in legend as a red-haired temptress, she appears to have been a ruddy-faced, mannish-looking female who held seances under the name "Professor Miss Katie Bender" and claimed to be a faith healer.

Sometime around 1870, the Bender family arrived in Labette County, Kansas, and built a home along a lonely stretch of road a few miles south of the railway town of Cherryvale. The dwelling was little more than a one-room log box, sixteen by twenty feet in size. The interior was divided in half by a canvas curtain. One side served as the family's living quarters. The other was turned into a rudimentary inn, where a traveler could get a hot meal or drink or a bed for the night. Some visitors, however, got much more than they bargained for.

(Kansas State Historical Society)

The Bender shanty

The Benders, it turned out, were really running a frontier murder-and-robbery operation. When a prosperous-looking traveler showed up, he would be ushered into the dining area and seated at the table with his back to the canvas divider. While Kate beguiled him with some dinnertime conversation, her father or brother would be lurking on the other side of the curtain with a sledgehammer at the ready. When the unsuspecting guest leaned his head back against the curtain, the hammer would come crashing down, shattering the back of his skull. The body would then be dragged into the bedroom, where it would be robbed, stripped, and dumped through a trapdoor into the cellar. There, his throat would be slit for good measure. Later, the body would be taken out and buried in the pasture.

The dreadful truth about the Benders came to light in the spring of 1873 when a physician named William York left Fort Scott on horseback for his home in Independence and never showed up. Retracing his route, a posse led by York's brother eventually happened on the Bender place. The Benders denied all knowledge of the missing Dr. York. A few days later, however—fearing that they were under suspicion—they pulled up stakes and fled. When word got around that the Benders had absconded, the posse returned to the farm and made a horrific discovery. In the pasture were seven shallow graves containing the corpses of eight human beings. Seven were grown men (including Dr. York). One was an eighteen-month-old girl, who had been traveling with her father. The Benders hadn't bothered to brain her. They had simply tossed her into the pit with her father's mangled corpse and buried her alive.

Angry posses scoured the prairies for the fugitives. To this day, no one can say for certain what became of the Benders. In her memoirs, however, Laura Ingalls Wilder of *Little House on the Prairie* fame writes that her father was one of the men who went out in search of the Benders. Though he never spoke about the experience, she deduced, from the grim expression on his face when he returned from the manhunt, that the posse had in fact caught up with the four Benders and dispensed well-deserved frontier justice.

At the same time that the Bloody Benders were running their lethal roadhouse in Kansas, Boston was being terrorized by the depredations of a juvenile psychopath named Jesse Harding Pomeroy. The crimes of the Boston "Boy Fiend" (as the newspapers dubbed him) began in late 1871, when the sadistic twelve-year-old lured a string of children to various remote locations, where they were stripped, flogged, and tortured with knives and sewing needles. Arrested in late 1872, he was sent to a reformatory but managed to win a discharge after only eighteen months. Just six weeks after his release—while working in a shop run by his mother—he killed a ten-year-old girl and hid her body in the cellar. Five weeks later, he lured a four-year-old boy to a lonely stretch of marshland and savaged his body with a penknife, slashing his throat, stabbing his eyes, and nearly severing his genitals. Arrested in April 1873, the fourteen-year-old Pomeroy was convicted and sentenced to death—a judgment that ignited a bitter two-year controversy over the morality of hanging a minor. The sentence was ultimately commuted to life in solitary confinement, a punishment that many people felt was even harsher than death.

Even while the argument over Pomeroy's death sentence was raging, Boston was stunned by another serial murder case. On May 23, 1875, a pretty five-year-old girl named Mabel Young, who had just attended Sunday school at the Warren Avenue Baptist Church, was lured into the belfry by the twenty-four-year-old sexton, Thomas Piper. He promised to show her his pet pigeons. Once he had her alone in the tower, Piper broke her head open with a cricket bat brought to church that morning for precisely that purpose. When the little girl's body was discovered, suspicion immediately alighted on Piper. He was already a suspect in another brutal murder, that of a young female servant named Bridget Landregan, whose skull had been crushed with a makeshift club during an attempted rape two years earlier. First proclaiming his innocence, Piper finally confessed not only to the killings of Mabel Young and Bridget Landregan but to two other unsolved homicides: the December 1873 rape-murder of a young woman named Sullivan, who had been savagely bludgeoned with a club, and a nearly identical assault seven months later on a young prostitute named Mary Tynam. The "Belfry Murderer"—as Piper came to be called—went to the gallows on May 26, 1876.

"WITH MY KNIFE I CUT HER THROAT."

(Rare Books Division, New York Public Library, Astor, Lenox, and Tilden Foundations)

Jesse Pomeroy kills 10-year-old Katie Curran in this illustration from an 1875 crime pamphlet

Twenty years later and on the opposite side of the continent, another belfry murder would send shock waves through America. On the morning of April 13, 1895, several San Francisco women arrived at the Emmanuel Baptist Church on Bartlett Street to decorate it for Easter. Spotting a strange, reddish brown trail leading to a closed-off storage closet, they opened the door and recoiled in horror at the sight of a horribly violated corpse. The victim was twenty-one-year-old Minnie Williams. Her clothes had been ripped off and her underwear shoved down her throat with a stick. She had been slashed to death with a silver table knife—her wrists severed, her breasts cut to ribbons. The broken-off blade of the murder weapon still protruded from her chest. A subsequent autopsy revealed that she had been raped after death.

The following day—Easter Sunday—policemen searching the church for more evidence made another horrifying discovery: the nude and bloated body of eighteen-year-old Blanche Lamont, who had vanished ten days earlier. Her killer had strangled her with his bare hands, then, as in the case of Minnie Williams, committed necrophiliac rape.

A suspect was quickly identified and taken into custody: Theodore Durrant, a handsome and charming young medical student, who still lived at home with his parents and served as assistant superintendent of the church Sunday school. His three-week trial in September 1895 was a nationwide sensation and drew dozens of swooning, female groupies, one of whom—

Theodore Durrant carries a victim to the belfry

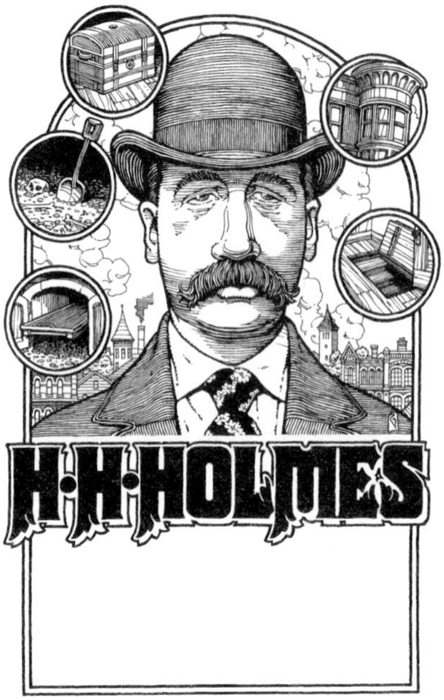

Dr. H. H. Holmes by Rick Geary

dubbed the "Sweet-Pea Girl" by the press—brought the handsome young psycho-killer a daily bouquet of the flowers. Despite his protestations of innocence, the jury took just five minutes to convict Durrant, who was hanged, after several postponements, on January 7, 1898. Such was the public's antipathy toward the so-called Demon of the Belfry, even after his death, that his parents had a hard time finding someplace to dispose of his body, and finally had to transport it to Los Angeles for cremation.

Horrific as Durrant's crimes were, they were easily surpassed by the most infamous medical monster of his day, Herman Mudgett, aka Dr. H. H. Holmes, one of the most prolific serial killers in American history. Though he confessed to twenty-seven murders of men, women, and children, Holmes is suspected of many more—possibly several hundred. Most were committed in the notorious "Horror Castle" he erected in a suburb of Chicago during the time of the great 1893 World's Fair.

At around the same time that Holmes was overseeing the construction of his nightmarish building, another homicidal physician, Dr. Thomas Neill Cream, was busily poisoning a string of prostitutes in London. Besides medical training and a taste for serial murder, Cream shared something else with H. H. Holmes. Before moving to London, Cream had committed murder in Chicago—a crime for which he had received a life sentence, though (unaccountably) he was released after only ten years.

As a poisoner of five prostitutes, Cream wasn't nearly as lethal as female contemporaries like Sarah Jane Robinson, who killed eleven known victims, including her husband, sister, and five children. Dr. Cream won everlasting notoriety, however, with his dying claim—cut short when he plunged through the trapdoor of the gallows—that he was Jack the Ripper.

Recommended Reading

Thomas S. Duke, *Celebrated Criminal Cases of America* (1910)
Martin Fido, *The Chronicle of Crime* (1993)
Carl Sifrakis, *The Encyclopedia of American Crime* (1982)
Colin Wilson, *The Mammoth Book of True Crime 2* (1980)

The Whitechapel Horrors

Jack the Ripper holds a special place in true-crime history for two reasons. First, the infamous butcher of London's East End ushered in the modern age of serial lust-murder. And second, he spawned a spate of books and documentaries, a veritable genre unto itself that has supplied a seemingly endless string of theories purporting to solve this grisly, unsolved case.

Even though many so-called Ripperologists have claimed to have identified England's most notorious murderer, the bare facts of the case tell us virtually nothing about who the Ripper actually was. What we do know is that he went about his work with unbridled savagery and instigated a citywide panic, qualities that would characterize all of the most celebrated serial murder cases that would follow.

The murders occurred between August and November of 1888. According to most accounts, there were five victims in all. All were prostitutes, as would be the case with so many future serial killers. The first victim, Mary Anne Nichols, was found with both her throat and abdomen slashed. As ghastly as this killing might have seemed at the time, it was mild compared to what would happen to the Ripper's other victims. On September 8, the killer nearly decapitated Ann Chapman, then carved open her stomach and yanked out her intestines. At the end of the month, he murdered two women in one night. It seems the Ripper was interrupted and had to flee while in the middle of mutilating Elizabeth Stride, but he took his time with Catherine Eddowes, cutting off pieces of her face, disemboweling her, and making off with her kidney. His final victim was Mary Kelly, killed on November 9. In the process of carving her from head to toe, he removed her nose and the skin covering her forehead, pulled out her entrails, nearly amputated one of her arms, and skinned her thighs.

Most of the information we have about the Ripper—negligible as it is—comes from a series of letters he wrote to a news agency and a local vigilance committee. The most famous of these, signed "From Hell," revealed that his crazed appetites were not confined to murder and mutilation. The letter writer enclosed half of Eddowes's kidney and described how he had fried and eaten the other half.

The murders ended with the Mary Kelly atrocity. After that, the Ripper seemed to disappear without a trace.

Quickly, theories emerged about who the mystery killer really was. Some believed he was a doctor, in particular a man named Dr. Stanley. The idea was that only a man with surgical skill could have taken apart the victims with such precision, though it's a little hard to understand how someone could confuse the ravaged remains of Mary Kelly with the work of a gifted surgeon. A butcher could have done as well. Which brings us to another theory, that the Ripper was actually a *shochet,* a Jewish ritual slaughterman. Other people disputed the very idea that the Ripper was a man, saying that the killer might have been a deranged midwife, a Jill the Ripper. Perhaps the most fanciful theory proposed that the murders were the work of an agent of the Russian tsar's secret police as part of an effort to make the English police look ineffectual.

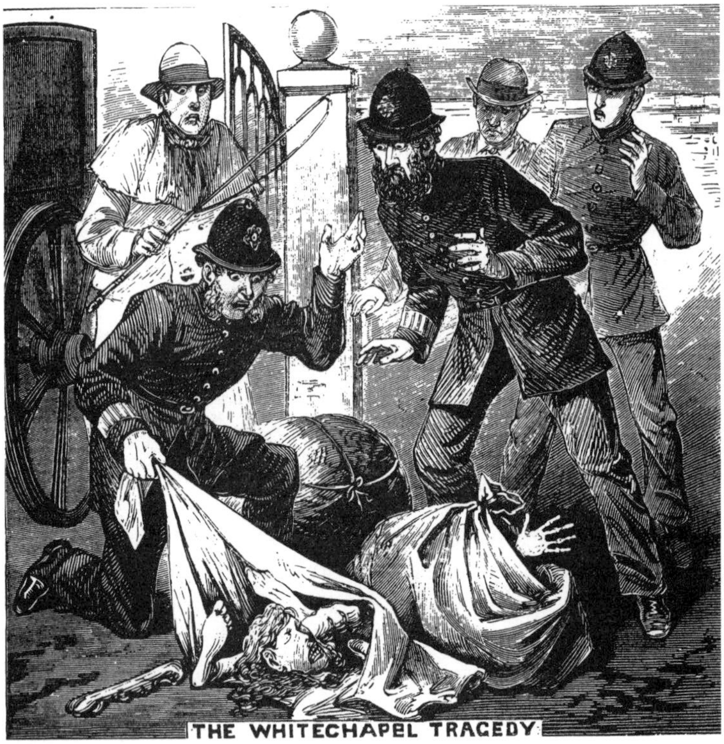

The Whitechapel Horrors

A general rule of thumb in murder investigations is that the chances of finding the culprit diminish after the first couple of weeks; by that time, the thinking goes, the killer's trail starts to go cold. Undaunted by this piece of conventional police wisdom, authors continued to assert that they have discovered the definitive solution to the Ripper case over a hundred years after the final murder.

A book in the 1970s pointed the finger at Queen Victoria's grandson, Edward, the Duke of Clarence. In 1993, Hyperion published *The Diary of Jack the Ripper,* the alleged journal of the killer, a Liverpool cotton merchant named James Maybrick. The authenticity of the diary was discredited by a prominent document expert. The most recent exposé came in 2002 under the hopefully definitive title of *Portrait of a Killer: Jack the Ripper, Case Closed.* In this highly controversial work, crime novelist Patricia Cornwell implicates a post-impressionist painter named Walter Sickert. Sickert's name had come up before in other Ripper speculations, but Cornwell went further by turning to the science of DNA identification to prove her case. The DNA samples came from letters, both those written by the killer and those written by Sickert. However, the results of the DNA tests did not conclusively single out Sickert. They only indicated that the DNA residue *could* have belonged to Sickert—and thousands of other people. For the time being, Cornwell's assertion will be definitive only until the publication of the next book that purports to solve the ultimate true-crime riddle for once and for all.

Recommended Reading

Paul Begg, *The Jack the Ripper A–Z* (1996)
Stewart Evans and Keith Skinner, *The Ultimate Jack the Ripper Sourcebook* (2000)
Miriam Rivett and Mark Whitehead, *The Pocket Essential Jack the Ripper* (2001)
Donald Rumbelow, *The Complete Jack the Ripper* (1988)
Philip Sugden, *The Complete History of Jack the Ripper* (1995)

The Twentieth Century

No sooner had the new century dawned than America was stunned by the disclosure that a genial, highly respected New England nurse named Jane Toppan was one of the most depraved multiple murderers in the country's history, a sadistic psychopath (or "moral imbecile," as such beings were called back then) who had poisoned thirty-one people, many of them close friends, because homicide gave her a sexual thrill.

Each succeeding decade of the century produced new and ever more sensational cases of serial murder both here and abroad.

The World War I Era

Around the time of the First World War, a Hungarian tinsmith named Bela Kiss used lonely hearts ads to lure at least two dozen women to his home in the village of Czinkota, then strangled them and sealed their corpses in alcohol-filled metal drums. By the time his atrocities were discovered in 1916, Kiss had presumably been killed in action after being drafted and sent to the front. In truth, however, he appears to have switched papers with a battlefield casualty, assumed the latter's identity, and gotten away. To this day, his fate remains a mystery.

A perennial mystery surrounds another serial murder case from roughly the same time. On the night of May 23, 1918, a New Orleans couple named Maggio were butchered in bed by an intruder who shattered their skulls with an ax blade, then slashed their throats with a razor, nearly decapitating the woman. For the next two and a half years, New Orleans would be periodically terrorized by the night-prowling "Ax Man," who followed the same MO in each case, chiseling out a back-door panel of the targeted house, then slipping inside and attacking the occupants while they slept. Altogether, he murdered seven people—including a two-year-old girl—and savagely wounded another eight. An alleged Mafia hit man named Joseph Mumfre is regarded as a prime

Hungarian police discover the metal drums containing the victims of Bela Kiss

suspect by some historians of crime, and it is true that the murders came to an abrupt halt when Mumfre was shot and killed by the widow of the Ax Man's last victim. Still, there is a good deal of uncertainty about Mumfre's role in the case, and it seems likely that the Ax Man's identity will never be conclusively established.

1920s–1930s

The single most sensational crime of Jazz Age America was the slaying of a fourteen-year-old Chicago boy named Bobby Franks by the wealthy young "thrill killers" Nathan Leopold, Jr. and Richard Loeb. That murder—senseless and shocking though it was—pales by comparison to the countless outrages perpetrated during the 1920s by Earle Leonard Nelson and Carl Panzram—two of the most ferocious serial killers in US history. A Bible-quoting sex maniac whose squat physique and enormous hands earned him the nickname the "Gorilla Murderer," Nelson made his way across the country, killing as he went. During a sixteen-month period that began in February 1926, he strangled nearly two dozen women, most of them middle-aged landladies. He then raped their bodies after death. Captured in Canada after murdering his final two victims in Winnipeg, he was hanged in 1928.

Panzram—arguably the most incorrigible killer ever produced on these shores—blamed his vicious nature on the brutal treatment he received as an inmate of various penal institutions, which—in striving to reform him—only filled him with an implacable hatred of all mankind. Making good on his lifelong credo—"Rob 'em all! Rape 'em all! Kill 'em all!"—he led a life of spectacular brutality, leaving countless corpses in his wake as he traveled around the world—from the US to South America, Europe, Africa, and back. Arrested in 1928 for a string of burglaries, he was sent to Leavenworth, where he earned a long-overdue death sentence for smashing in the head of a fellow inmate who looked at him the wrong way. His last words as the hangman fit the noose around his neck were typical of the unrepentant Panzram: "Hurry it up, you Hoosier bastard—I could hang a dozen men while you're fooling around!"

Overseas in Germany, the period between the two world wars produced some of the most appalling sex-killers of modern times. Indeed, the German term *lustmord* ("lust-murder")—extreme sexual homicide involving mutilation, disembowelment, etc.—was coined to describe the atrocities of a handful of hideously depraved psychopaths who were active during the turbulent years of the Weimar Republic: Georg Grossmann, the "Berlin Butcher," charged with murdering and cannibalizing fourteen young women; Karl Denke, the "Mass-Murderer of Münsterberg," another cannibal who butchered at least thirty people and stored their pickled flesh in the basement of his inn; Peter Kürten, the "Monster of Düsseldorf," who murdered, raped, and mutilated a minimum of thirty-five victims, mostly women and children; and Fritz Haarmann, the "Vampire of Hanover," responsible for the slaughter of as many as fifty young men.

Haarmann's American admirer, Albert Fish—who saved every newspaper clipping he could find about the German lust-murderer—committed most of his own atrocities during the 1920s. It wasn't until 1934, however, that the appalling truth about the old man's enormities came to light. Fish's confession to the murder, dismemberment, and cannibalizing of a lovely twelve-year-old girl—along with a string of earlier pedophiliac torture-slayings—instantly turned him into the most horrifying American monster of the Great Depression.

Fish's arrest in late 1934 coincided with the start of a four-year serial murder spree by one of the most mysterious figures in the annals of American crime. This was the so-called Cleveland Torso Killer (aka the "Mad Butcher of Kingsbury Run"). This blood-crazed maniac chopped up more than a dozen people—most of them prostitutes, hoboes, and other social castoffs—and left their body parts strewn around the city. The killer eluded arrest, despite the all-out efforts of law officials (led by the legendary Eliot Ness, the former "Untouchable" who was then serving as Cleveland's Director of Public Safety). Though theories about his identity abound, the "Mad Butcher" case remains one of the great unsolved serial murder stories in the chronicles of American crime.

The 1940s

Wartime London was the scene of a short but unusually savage serial murder spree by a young Royal Air Force cadet named Gordon Cummins. On the night of February 9, 1942—while the city was living through the terrors of the Blitz—the twenty-eight-year-old fighter-pilot-in-training accosted a female pharmacist named Evelyn Hamilton as she walked home from a restaurant. In the darkness of the blacked-out city, he strangled her with her scarf and left her corpse sprawled in the entrance of an air-raid shelter.

The following night in Piccadilly Circus, he picked up a prostitute named Evelyn Oatley. She took him back to her Soho apartment, where he slit her throat, then mutilated her genitals with a can opener. Two more mutilation-murders occurred on the next two successive nights, leading police to conclude that a Jack-the-Ripper-style killer was at large in their embattled city.

Cummins undoubtedly would have gone on killing if he hadn't been stopped. However, he was caught after two abortive murder attempts on the night of February 13. First, he tried to strangle a woman named Greta Haywood in the doorway of an air-raid shelter. He fled when the noise of the struggle attracted the notice of a passerby. He then immediately picked up another woman, who invited him home. This time, Cummins was scared off by her violent screams when he attacked her. Not only did Cummins leave two living witnesses who could identify him, he had also dropped his gas mask, which was tagged with his name, rank, and serial number. Promptly arrested, he was hanged in June 1942 during an air raid.

Just a few years after Cummins's execution, another member of the Royal Air Force went to the gallows after committing a pair of gruesome sex-murders. Dashingly handsome and irresistible to women, Neville Heath was a con man, thief, and compulsive Don Juan who did several stints in the RAF even while pursuing his life of petty criminality. In June 1946, he crossed the line from small-time crook and impostor to sadistic killer when he flogged and suffocated a thirty-two-year-old film extra named Margery Gardner in a London hotel room. He then chewed off her nipples and rammed a poker up her vagina.

(Novelty trading card courtesy of Roger Worsham)

Police immediately began searching for Heath, who had registered at the hotel under his own name. By then, however, he had headed South to Bournemouth, where, on July 3, he slit the throat of another young woman. Mutilating her body, he inflicted a massive gash that ran from the inside of her thigh up to her breast. He left her savaged corpse in the woods, where it would not be discovered for several days.

While the search was on for the missing girl, Heath—displaying either an unconscious death wish or the kind of reckless bravado typical of psychopaths—showed up at the police station to offer his help. He was immediately identified as the fugitive in the London murder and placed under arrest. He was hanged in October 1946.

Of the US serial killers active during the 1940s, two of the most notorious were African-American: Jarvis Catoe and Jake Bird. In 1943, Catoe was electrocuted for the rape-murder of a twenty-five-year-old Washington, DC newlywed—one of three women he had murdered during a serial murder spree two years earlier. His death toll was far exceeded, however, by Louisiana-born Jake Bird. In October 1947, while drifting through Tacoma, Washington, Bird entered the home of fifty-three-year-old Bertha Kludt and her teenage daughter, Beverly. He slaughtered them both with an ax he had found in their backyard. Taken into custody after a ferocious fight—during which he badly wounded two policemen with his knife—he eventually confessed to numerous slayings in at least eight different states. His victims were all white women, bludgeoned with axes or hatchets. Police were able to confirm Bird's involvement in eleven unsolved homicides, though he was suspected in as many as forty-four. He was hanged in Walla Walla in July 1949.

The single most infamous American serial killer of the 1940s was William Heirens, whose case continues to generate controversy to this day. Raised by sexually repressive parents who imbued him with the belief that "all sex is dirty," Heirens grew up to be a fetishist who achieved orgasmic release from breaking into women's homes and stealing their underwear (which he sometimes wore at home while reading books on Nazi war crimes). Like other serial killers, he was also turned on by fire-starting. An inveterate housebreaker, he began burglarizing apartments around Chicago while still in grade school. A pair of arrests during his adolescence earned him two extended stints in reform schools. In 1945, at the age of sixteen, the intellectually gifted Heirens won admission to the University of Chicago, where he enrolled as an electrical engineering major. Even while leading a stereotypical collegiate existence—dating, hanging out with buddies, cutting classes—he continued to pursue his clandestine life as a cat burglar and panty fetishist.

On June 5, 1945, a forty-three-year-old Chicago woman, Josephine Ross, surprised an intruder looting her bedroom. She was found that afternoon, sprawled across her bed, her throat slashed, her dress wrapped around her head.

Six months later, on December 10, the naked corpse of a petite, thirty-three-year-old brunette named Frances Brown was found in the bathroom of her Chicago apartment not far from the scene of the earlier crime. She had been shot in the head, a butcher knife protruded from her neck, and her housecoat was draped over her head. Scrawled in lipstick on the living room wall was a cry for help that would become the single most famous serial killer message of the century: "For heavens sake catch me before I kill more. I cannot control myself."

The "Lipstick Killer" (as he was instantly dubbed by the press) committed his last—and most heinous—crime in early January when he abducted six-year-old Suzanne Degnan from her bedroom, strangled her, dismembered her body with a hunting knife, and dumped the pieces into the sewer.

The shocking murder of the little girl set off the largest manhunt in Chicago's history. It did not end until the following June, when police—responding to a report of a prowler in a North Side apartment building—cornered Heirens. Drawing a gun, Heirens took aim at the officers, but his weapon misfired. After a fierce struggle, he was subdued when an off-duty cop who had joined in the fight brained him with a flowerpot.

In custody and drugged up with sodium pentothal—"truth serum"—Heirens initially claimed that the killings had been committed by an evil alter ego named "George Murman" (short for "Murder Man"). To avoid the chair, he agreed to confess to all three slayings in exchange for life in prison. On the day of his formal sentencing, he tried to commit suicide by hanging himself with a bedsheet but was saved by a quick-acting guard. Since the day he entered prison, Heirens—who has recanted his confession and stoutly maintains his innocence—has been a model prisoner, earning a college degree in 1972. He continues to have supporters who believe that he was railroaded, and who point to another suspect—a drifter named Richard Russell Thomas, with a long record of brutal crimes—as the likelier culprit.

The 1950s

Bathed in the rosy glow of nostalgia, the 1950s are generally regarded as a uniquely placid era in the life of America. Despite its aura of "Happy Days" innocence, however, the Eisenhower decade witnessed some of the most shocking serial murders of the modern age.

(Corbis)

Harvey Glatman's victim Judy Dull, photographed in his apartment moments before she was killed

Harvey Glatman, for example—the nerdy-looking sadist who snapped pictures of bound and terrified women before raping and garroting them—epitomized the sleazy underbelly of 1950s, finding his prey in the tawdry "camera clubs" that flourished in those sexually repressive times. The photographic souvenirs he kept of his tormented victims were chilling enough to cause even case-hardened LA cops to feel sick at the sight of them.

Even more ghastly were the anatomical trophies investigators turned up in the ramshackle farmhouse of the Wisconsin ghoul, Ed Gein, whose crimes—partly inspired by the lurid men's magazines of the period and their obsession with Nazi atrocities—also reflected the dark side of 1950s culture.

In 1957—the same year that Glatman embarked on his murder spree and the Gein horrors were uncovered—another American serial killer appeared on the scene.

That June, a woman named Margaret Harold and her army sergeant boyfriend were parked in a lover's lane near Annapolis, Maryland, when a green Chrysler pulled up beside them. A tall, thin-faced man emerged from the Chrysler and, after identifying himself as the owner of the property, drew a gun, climbed into the backseat of the couple's car, and demanded their money. When Margaret Harold refused, she was shot in the back of the skull. Leaping from the car, her boyfriend ran to the nearest house and called for help. When the police arrived at the crime scene, they found Margaret's body still in the car. Her clothes had been stripped from her body, and she had been raped after death.

Searching the area, police found a cinder-block shack, its walls plastered with pornographic pictures, morgue shots of murdered women, and—incongruously—the yearbook photo of a coed who had graduated from the University of Maryland in 1955.

A year and a half later, in January 1959, a family of four out for a drive near Apple Grove, Virginia, was run off the road by a man in a blue Chevrolet, who forced them into the trunk of his car at gunpoint. Two months later, the body of the husband, Carroll Jackson, was found in a roadside ditch, lying atop the corpse of his infant daughter, Janet. Mr. Jackson had been bound and shot in the back of the head; the baby had been tossed alive into the ditch, where she had smothered under the weight of her dead father.

The other two members of the family—mother Mildred and her five-year-old daughter, Susan—were discovered in the woods by some young squirrel hunters a few weeks afterward. Both victims had been raped and beaten to death with a blunt instrument. Evidence suggested that the killer had tortured Mrs. Jackson to force her to perform fellatio upon him.

The investigation into both cases had run into a dead end when police received an anonymous letter in May, pointing a finger at a young jazz musician named Melvin Rees, who—according to the tipster—had been making suspicious comments while hopped up on Benzedrine at the time of the Jackson killings. Checking into Rees's background, detectives discovered that he had once dated the University of Maryland coed whose yearbook picture had been taped to the wall of the cinder-block structure near the first crime scene. It wasn't until FBI agents searched Rees's home, however, and found a saxophone case full of incriminating evidence—including handwritten notes describing his murder of the Jackson family—that officials knew they had their man.

(Novelty trading card courtesy of Roger Worsham)

Eventually, Rees—or the "Sex Beast," as the newspapers dubbed him—was linked to the unsolved rape-murders of four adolescent girls in Maryland. He was condemned to death, but the sentence was later commuted, and he died of natural causes in prison.

One of the most infamous multiple murderers of the 1950s was not, strictly speaking, a serial killer. A sociopathic punk who liked to think of himself as romantic young rebel à la his idol, James Dean, Charlie "Little Red" Starkweather was responsible for murdering ten people during a twenty-six-day period in early 1958. Starkweather and his fourteen-year-old girlfriend Caril Ann Fugate, however, fall into the category of "spree killers." Their rampage through Nebraska and Wyoming was not a series of distinct events motivated by recurrent need for sadistic gratification but rather a single, if protracted, massacre.

CASE STUDY

Reg Christie, the Monster of Rillington Place

America wasn't the only place to produce serial killers in the 1950s. In England, the decade began with one of the most notorious sex-murder cases of modern times.

The full story began to come to light in March 1953, when the new residents at 10 Rillington Place in London's Notting Hill section began to remodel their kitchen. One section of the wallpapering seemed to have nothing but air behind it. Tearing away the wallpaper, they discovered that it had been concealing a cupboard. In the cupboard were three dead women wrapped in blankets. The police arrived to investigate and found that the three corpses were just the tip of the iceberg. Under the floorboards in the dining room they found another dead woman and outside buried in the garden they found two more.

The previous resident was a man named John Reginald Christie—Reg to his friends. A quiet, balding, bespectacled man, he had been in the public eye three years earlier during a notorious murder trial. A dim-witted young man named Timothy Evans had confessed to killing his wife and baby, then retracted his admission. He eventually claimed that the real killer was his downstairs neighbor, Christie. At the trial, the respectable-looking Christie testified to Evans's guilt and the jury concurred. Evans was hanged. Now, after uncovering six more bodies, the police were beginning, a bit belatedly, to rethink the case. Christie himself filled in the details for them when they arrested him eleven days later.

Christie came from a working-class family and supported himself over the years with a series of menial and clerical jobs. But there were disturbing undercurrents coursing just beneath the surface of his seemingly unexceptional life. One was a chronic hypochondria that began in childhood and culminated when he was a young man in a case of hysterical muteness that went on for over three years. Christie also had an inability to resist other people's property. He stole frequently from his various employers.

He and his wife Ethel moved into the flat on Rillington Place in 1938. Two years later, when he was forty-two, he began to murder women.

He pursued his secret homicidal life when his wife was away visiting relatives. He brought Ruth Fuerst to his apartment in 1940 and offered to help ease her respiratory condition by administering an herbal steam concoction. Instead, he gassed her, then strangled and raped her. He waited three years before he killed his second victim, Muriel Eddy—a friend of his wife. Both Fuerst and Eddy ended up in his garden.

In 1949, he got the wife of Timothy Evans alone under the pretext of offering another service. He claimed to be able to perform an abortion for her. He strangled and raped her and murdered her baby as well. The police found the bodies in the building's toolshed. Christie may have somehow tricked the feebleminded Evans into confessing.

Once again he let three years go by without any further murders; then he set his sights closer to home, strangling his wife and stashing her beneath the floorboards. No more would he have to wait to have the house to himself. In less than three months, he killed three more women. They would be the ones he halfheartedly concealed in the kitchen cupboard before moving out at the end of March 1953.

After the police caught up with Christie, the tabloids dubbed the mild-mannered maniac the "Monster of Rillington Place." The judicial system was no less appalled by his crimes than the public was. Christie went to the gallows just three and a half months after his arrest.

The 1960s

The serial killers of sixties America were as emblematic of that socially turbulent era as race riots, political assassinations, and the British Invasion. If we remember the decade as the time of JFK, Martin Luther King, the Beatles, and Woodstock, we also associate it with the sensational crimes of the Boston Strangler, the Zodiac killer, and—most notoriously—the demon-hippie, Charles Manson.

More than forty years after the Boston Strangler committed his first atrocity, the case remains one of the most controversial in the annals of modern crime. The first five of the Strangler's eleven confirmed murders occurred during the summer of 1962. The initial victims were all older women, ranging in age from fifty-five to seventy-five. Each had willingly let her killer into her apartment, taken in by his story that he was a repairman sent by the landlord. Besides raping and strangling the women, he desecrated their corpses, sometimes by shoving bottles or other objects up their vaginas. In most cases, he left a grotesque "signature," knotting his makeshift garrote (often a nylon stocking, though sometimes a bathrobe sash) into an ornamental bow beneath the dead woman's chin.

Toward the end of 1962, his MO changed. He began targeting younger women, most in their twenties. And his killings became even more vicious: in one instance, he stabbed a victim twenty-two times, savaging her throat and leaving eighteen wounds in a bull's-eye pattern on her left breast. Another young woman was left propped up against the headboard of her bed, a pink bow tied around her neck, a broomstick jutting from her vagina, and a "Happy New Year's" card resting at her feet.

With the women of Boston in a panic, a special task force was set up to track down the killer. With no solid leads, however, investigators were reduced to calling in psychics whose paranormal assistance—unsurprisingly—proved worthless. The big break in the case did not come until 1965 when a rape victim led the police to Albert DeSalvo.

DeSalvo had the kind of nightmarish childhood that is a prescription for future psychopathology. His father was the type of man who liked to bring whores home with him, have sex with them in front of the family, then beat his wife when she complained. One of DeSalvo's most vivid childhood memories was of watching his father knock out all his mother's teeth, then break her fingers one by one as she lay sprawled beneath the kitchen sink. The children were also subjected to savage abuse. On one typical occasion, Albert was clubbed with a lead pipe for not moving fast enough when his father asked for something.

Like other budding psychopaths, Albert displayed a sadistic streak from an early age. One of his favorite childhood pastimes was sticking a dog inside an orange crate with a starving cat so he could watch the cat scratch out the dog's eyes.

By the time he was a teenager, DeSalvo had accumulated a long rap sheet for breaking and entering. Joining the army at seventeen, he was shipped to Europe, where he married a German girl and brought her back home to the States. In 1955, while stationed in Fort Dix, New Jersey, he was charged with molesting a nine-year-old girl. He escaped prosecution when her mother decided not to press charges.

Afflicted with a volcanic sex drive, DeSalvo routinely demanded sex a half dozen times a day from his long-suffering wife, accusing her of being "frigid" whenever she rebuffed him. Back in Boston after his discharge from the army, he struggled to support his growing family with blue-collar jobs, supplementing his meager income with occasional petty burglaries.

He also began to assault women. His earliest technique was to go door to door, posing as a scout for a modeling agency. If a woman fell for this line and invited him in, he would pull out a tape measure and proceed to check out her vital statistics, a ploy that allowed him to indulge in crude sexual fondling. Before long, the women of Boston were warned to beware of the smooth-talking pervert known as the "Measuring Man."

In March 1961, the thirty-year-old DeSalvo was caught while attempting to burglarize a house. Under arrest, he confessed to being the "Measuring Man" and was given a two-year sentence. Back on the streets after just eleven months, he embarked on a new, more violent spree of sexual assault. Posing as a repairman in green work clothes, he managed to talk his way into the homes of countless women throughout New England. Over a two-year span, the "Green Man"—as he came to be dubbed—raped as many as three hundred victims in Massachusetts, New Hampshire, Connecticut, and Rhode Island.

During this same period, eleven Boston women were strangled and defiled by a smooth-talking sex maniac posing as a workman.

In November 1964—ten months after the Strangler killed his last victim—a victim of the "Green Man" rapes gave police a description that led them to DeSalvo. Confessing to those crimes, he was committed for psychiatric observation to Bridgewater State Hospital, where he befriended a hardened killer named George Nassar, whose attorney was a young hotshot named F. Lee Bailey. Before very long, Bailey became DeSalvo's lawyer, too. That's when DeSalvo confessed to being the Boston Strangler.

In the end, DeSalvo was never punished for the Boston Strangler crimes. Under an unusual deal engineered by Bailey, he was spared the chair and given a life sentence for the "Green Man" rapes instead. In November 1973, at the age of forty-two, he was stabbed to death by a fellow inmate.

DeSalvo's death, however, was not the end of the story. From the time of his confession, doubts about his guilt have been raised both by his own family members and relatives of his victims. Some believe that DeSalvo—knowing that he was already facing life imprisonment for the "Green Man" crimes—claimed to be the Strangler in order to cash in on the book and movie rights he assumed would be coming his way. Others believe that there was more than one Strangler. Support for the doubters came in 2001, when the remains of both DeSalvo and the Strangler's final victim, Mary Sullivan, were exhumed and examined by forensic experts. DNA evidence taken from Mary Sullivan did not provide a match with DeSalvo. It seems unlikely that there will ever be definitive answers to the questions that still swirl around the case.

Another famous serial murder case also remains shrouded in mystery, though at least one writer claims to have come up with the long-sought solution.

During a nine-month span that began in late 1968, the citizens of San Francisco were terrorized by a night-prowling gunman who, in the years to follow, would assume near-mythic proportions in the popular mind. His notoriety stemmed from several sources: his seemingly preternatural ability to elude capture, the viciously taunting messages he sent to the press, and, perhaps most importantly, his chilling nickname, which has become almost as infamous as that of Jack of the Ripper—the Zodiac.

His first victims were a teenage couple shot to death in a remote lover's lane about twenty miles northeast of San Francisco on the night of December 20, 1968. Six months later, at midnight on July 5, 1969, he struck again, shooting another young couple in the parking lot of a public golf course. Forty minutes after that attack—which left the girl dead and her boyfriend severely wounded—police received an anonymous phone call from a gruff-voiced man, who directed them to the scene of the shooting and claimed credit for the earlier double murder.

The matter-of-fact tone in which this message was delivered made it clear that a homicidal maniac was on the loose. The full extent of his madness, however, didn't become apparent until six weeks later, when he sent three separate letters to local newspapers. Each contained a cryptogram. Deciphered by a high school teacher and his wife, the three coded passages formed a single, wildly deranged message:

> I LIKE KILLING PEOPLE BECAUSE IT IS SO MUCH FUN IT IS MORE FUN THAN KILLING WILD GAME IN THE FORREST BECAUSE MAN IS THE MOST DANGEROUE ANIMAL OF ALL TO KILL SOMETIMES GIVES ME THE MOST THRILLING EXPERENCE IT IS EVEN BETTER THAN GETTING YOUR ROCKS OFF WITH A GIRL THE BEST PART IS THAE WHEN I DIE I WILL BE REBORN IN PARADICE AND ALL THE I HAVE KILLED WILL BECOME MY SLAVES I WILL NOT GIVE YOU MY NAME BECAUSE YOU WILL TRY TO SLOI DOWN OR STOP MY COLLECTING OF SLAVES FOR MY AFTERLIFE

The letter was signed with a peculiar symbol that resembled the sight of a rifle scope—a circle intersected by a cross.

Just a few days later, the killer sent another letter to the *San Francisco Examiner.* True to his previous message, he did not provide his name. Instead, he used a pseudonym that immediately entered the mythology of modern-day serial murder.

"This is the Zodiac speaking," the letter began. From that point on, he would start each of his communications with the same ominous greeting.

(Courtesy of Tom Voight)

The Zodiac in full regalia

Two months passed. On September 27, 1969, two twenty-year-old college students, Bryan Hartnell and Cecilia Shepard, were picnicking at a lake near Vallejo when a frightening figure emerged from behind some trees. His face was hidden beneath an oversized black hood embroidered with the Zodiac's crossed circle device, a large, wood-sheathed knife—possibly a bayonet—hung from his belt, and he had a semiautomatic pistol in his hand. Tying up the couple at gunpoint, he savaged them with his knife, then walked to their car and, with a black Magic Marker, inscribed his crossed circle logo on the door, along with the dates of all three of his Bay Area attacks. An hour later, he put in a call to the police, announcing that he had just committed a "double murder." As it happened, he was wrong. Stabbed ten times, Cecelia Shepard would die a few days later. Her boyfriend would survive his half dozen wounds.

His last known victim was a San Francisco cab driver named Paul Stine who was killed with a point-blank shot to the head. Before fleeing the crime scene, Zodiac cut off a large piece of the victim's shirt, soaked it in the dead man's blood, and carried it away with him. Shortly afterward, the editor of the *San Francisco Chronicle* received an envelope. Inside was a swatch of the cab driver's shirt and a letter from Zodiac in which he promised to "wipe out a school bus some morning." Fortunately, he never made good on his threat. Nor—as far as anyone knows—did Zodiac ever kill again.

He did, however, keep up his bizarre correspondence, sending sporadic greeting cards and letters to the papers for the next several years. As for his identity, it remains a mystery, though one expert on the case has named Arthur Leigh Allen—a gun buff and convicted child molester who died in 1993—as the likeliest suspect.

> School children make nice targets, I think I shall wipe out a school bus some morning. Just shoot out the front tire + then pick off the kiddies as they come bouncing out.
>
> —from one of the Zodiac letters

The Dark Prince of the decade was Charles Manson, the evil incarnation of all that was most insidious about the 1960s counterculture, a social movement that began with dreams of free love and flower power and ended with the violent chaos of Altamont. Manson is unique among serial killers: a legendary monster whose most infamous crime was committed by proxy. Profoundly manipulative, he was able to transform his "family" of fanatical worshipers into a troop of hippie-assassins only too eager to do his homicidal bidding.

He was born in 1934, the illegitimate son of a bisexual teenage prostitute, Kathleen Maddox, who routinely brought her tricks home for sex, left him alone for weeks at a time, and reportedly once traded him to a waitress for a pitcher of beer. Sent to jail in 1939 after knocking over a gas station with her brother, Kathleen shipped little Charlie off to live with her aunt and uncle—the former a religious fanatic, the latter a sadist who constantly derided the boy as a "sissy" and forced him to wear girl's clothes to school. By twelve, Manson was living on the streets and surviving by theft. His adolescence was a continuous cycle of petty crime, arrest, incarceration, and escape. At eighteen—while doing time in Utah for stealing cars—he sodomized another boy at knifepoint, earning a stint in a federal reformatory, where he racked up eight major disciplinary infractions, including three for homosexual rape. Paroled in 1954, he spent the next dozen years in and out of various prisons for crimes ranging from check forgery to pimping. In 1967, at the age of thirty-two, Manson—who had taught himself guitar and dabbled in Scientology and Buddhism while in jail—came up for parole. He himself expressed doubts about the wisdom of being set free. "Oh, no, I can't go outside there. I couldn't adjust to that world, not after all my life had been spent locked up." In spite of his protests, he was unleashed on the world.

Making his way to San Francisco during the so-called Summer of Love, this charismatic con man quickly mastered the psychedelic gobbledygook of the counterculture, attracting a band of drug-addled dropouts—many of them naive and emotionally unstable young women—who revered him as a guru.

Eventually, Charlie and his ragtag commune settled in a dusty, disused ranch outside LA, where they enjoyed a squalid, orgiastic existence overseen by their increasingly crazed messiah. Manson developed a bizarre obsession with the song "Helter Skelter" from the Beatles' "White Album." In his flourishing madness, Manson interpreted the song (which refers to an amusement park thrill ride) as a prophecy about an impending race war in which blacks would rise up and destroy all white people, except for Manson and his followers, who would find refuge in a cave beneath Death Valley. Eventually, Charlie and his family would emerge from hiding and—thanks to their innate superiority over "blackie" (as the racist Manson called African-Americans)—take over the world.

To expedite things, Manson dispatched a band of followers on an insane mission, commanding them to slay some prominent white people in a way that would implicate black revolutionaries and spark an apocalyptic race war. On the night of August 9, 1969—in one of the most shocking atrocities of modern times—five of Manson's demented disciples invaded the home of film director Roman Polanski (who was away on a shoot) and savagely butchered his eight-months-pregnant wife, Sharon Tate, along with four other people. Before leaving, they used the victims' blood to scrawl incendiary graffiti on the walls. The following night, Manson himself led a party of his "creepy crawlers" to the home of a couple named LaBianca. They murdered both husband and wife, leaving Mr. LaBianca with a carving fork jutting from his chest and the word "WAR" carved into his flesh. Once again, the victims' blood was used to inscribe pseudorevolutionary messages on the walls: "DEATH TO PIGS," "RISE," and "HEALTER SKELTER."

Later, one of the participants in the Tate horrors explained that the Manson gang "wanted to do a crime that would shock the world, that the world would have to stand up and take notice." If that was their plan, they succeeded. The massacre at the Polanski residence set off a panic in Los Angeles and sent shock waves throughout the nation. Ultimately, Manson was arrested when one of his brain-fried groupies—Susan Atkins, who was behind bars on an unrelated charge—blithely confessed to a jail mate.

After a lengthy trial, which Manson did his best to turn into a circus, he and four followers were condemned to the gas chamber. In 1972, however, their sentences were commuted to life when the California Supreme Court abolished the death penalty. Still immured behind prison walls, as he has been for the bulk of his lamentably misspent life, Manson is now an old man. Still, it is hard to picture him as anything but the wild-eyed, scraggly-haired demon-hippie of the Woodstock era, an icon every bit as symbolic of that turbulent time as Timothy Leary and the Four Moptops.

(Bill Lignante—ABC News)

Charles Manson at his trial

I am what you have made me and the mad-dog devil killer fiend leper is a reflection of your society.

—Charles Manson

The 1970s to Now

The 1970s witnessed such a sharp increase in the number of psychopathic sex murders that it seemed—in the words of a pioneering paper presented by members of the FBI's Behavioral Science Unit—as if "a new phenomenom in homicide" had suddenly appeared on the scene. To describe the perpetrators of these supposedly unprecedented crimes, Robert Ressler and his colleagues at the Bureau adopted a term that had been coined a decade earlier and that quickly entered the popular lexicon: "serial killers."

As the foregoing historical survey shows, however, there is nothing new about sadistic lust-murder beyond the name we now apply to it. Still, it is clearly the case that—particularly in the United States—there was a definite spike in such crimes during the 1970s.

Why did this happen? Various reasons suggest themselves, most having to do with the upheaval in sexual mores precipitated by the social revolution of the 1960s. In reaction to the inhibited 1950s, the hippie counterculture preached the joys of "letting it all hang out"—of shedding all repressions and indulging in the Dionysian pleasures of sex, drugs, and rock 'n' roll. But the unconscious mind is a Pandora's box, and when you open the lid on the id, all kinds of forces—some exhilarating and creative, others scary and destructive—come gushing out. The counterculture started out with the utopian, all-you-need-is-love daydreams epitomized by the Beatles' "Let It Be." But it ended up steeped in the nightmarish darkness of the Stones' "Let It Bleed."

The permissive ethos that sprang up in the sixties and spread throughout the culture in the 1970s did more than liberate the libidos of middle-class Americans; it gave permission to some extraordinarily aberrant people to act out their sickest fantasies. The countercultural slogan—"If it feels good, do it!"—was intended to encourage a healthy sense of sexual freedom in people. But it's a dangerous philosophy when adopted by madmen who feel best when they are raping, torturing, and butchering helpless victims. The breaking down of long-standing sexual prohibitions also made it easier for serial killers to find potential victims in the singles bars, gay bathhouses, and other pickup places of the era.

It is important, however, to put the recent rise in sex-murders in perspective. The surge in such crimes has led to a lot of alarmist talk about an "epidemic" of serial killing. This makes for good news copy but—like more recent scares about shark attacks and child abductions—is mostly hyperbole. To be sure, the last few decades have produced a striking number of world-class lust-murderers in America: John Wayne Gacy, Ted Bundy, the Hillside Stranglers, Edmund Kemper, etc. But even during the heyday of these sickos, the number of serial killers at large in our country was infinitesimal. Ordinary Americans who fear that there is a psycho-killer lurking around every corner are far less likely to die at the hands of a knife-wielding slasher than in a car accident on their way to the local video store to rent *The Silence of the Lambs.*

The serial killer who best exemplifies the shadow side of the sexually freewheeling 1970s was undoubtedly Bundy, the living incarnation of one of that decade's darkest anxieties: the fear of meeting a seductive stranger whose charm conceals the vicious soul of a psychopath.

Surviving family photographs from Bundy's early years suggest a *Leave It to Beaver* childhood of wiener roasts, fishing trips, and warm Christmas holidays. Still, there were striking abnormalities in his background. An illegitimate child, he was forced to pretend that his mother was his sister and his grandparents—Sam and Eleanor Cowell—were his father and mother. There are also indications that—despite Bundy's avowed adoration of his grandfather—Sam Cowell was a virulent racist and petty tyrant who freely dispensed abuse to every member of the household, from the family pets to his long-suffering wife (who was eventually driven into electroshock therapy).

Even so, there is little in Bundy's background to account fully for the sheer malevolence of his adult behavior. Perhaps, as he himself suggested, there were unknown genetic factors that contributed to his monstrous makeup.

Whatever the case, his disturbing tendencies manifested themselves at a young age. He was only three when he slipped some butcher knives under the bedclothes of his sleeping aunt. In elementary school—despite his obvious intelligence and superior grades—his recurrent temper tantrums were violent enough to worry his teachers. By high school, he had become a chronic Peeping Tom and petty thief.

By that point, even Bundy was becoming aware that he lacked certain basic human qualities: a conscience, a capacity to see people as anything more than objects to be manipulated for his own gratification. By studying others, he learned to mimic normal behavior so skillfully that, for the rest of his life, even those closest to him failed to perceive his monstrous nature.

While attending the University of Washington, Bundy became involved with a lovely, cultivated young woman named Stephanie Brooks who—insofar as he was capable of such an emotion—would become the love of his life. He was presumably devastated when she broke up with him. Much has been made of the fact that his subsequent victims bore a vague resemblance to Stephanie. The implication is that Bundy's homicidal career was provoked by this traumatizing incident, that he was taking revenge on the woman who rejected him. The more probable explanation is that Bundy, like many psycho-killers, was simply turned on by a certain kind of woman. Indeed, he took pride in choosing only "quality" victims—pretty, intelligent, college-age women—to abduct, torture, mutilate, and kill.

His first attack occurred in January 1974, when he broke into the basement bedroom of an eighteen-year-old coed, bludgeoned her skull with a metal rod yanked from her bedframe, then rammed it into her vagina. If the word can be applied to a young woman who has suffered such appalling injuries, she was lucky: she survived. At least three dozen other young women whose lives intersected with Ted Bundy's would not.

He was a genuine Jekyll-and-Hyde. He led an outwardly exemplary life: making a name for himself as a rising young star of the local Republican party, helping to man a suicide hotline, even winning a police commendation for saving the life of a drowning toddler. Simultaneously, however, the bright, personable Bundy was pursuing his secret career of unspeakable crime. In 1974, while still living in Washington state, he slaughtered at least seven young women in as many months. Two were lured from a crowded beach in broad daylight on the same afternoon.

(Pin button courtesy of Roger Worsham)

Ted Bundy

That September, he moved to Salt Lake City and enrolled at the University of Utah. Two months later, the bestial second self he described as "the entity" came roaring to the surface. Young women began to vanish, including the teenage daughter of a local police chief. Her nude, hideously mutilated remains were later found in a canyon. During this period, Bundy also made occasional forays into Colorado, where at least five other young women died at his hands.

For authorities, the turning point in the case came after midnight on August 16, 1975. A Utah Highway Patrolman pulled over Bundy for erratic driving. Inside the Volkswagen the officer found a cache of suspicious items, including an ice pick, a mask made of panty hose, and handcuffs. Before long, Bundy was picked out of a lineup by a young woman he had attempted to abduct the year before. Found guilty of aggravated kidnapping, he was sentenced to one to fifteen years at the Utah State Penitentiary. He was then transferred to Colorado to stand trial for murder.

It appeared to be the end of the line for Bundy, but authorities had underestimated his psychopathic cunning. Taking control of his own defense, he was a given access to the courthouse law library. On June 7, 1977, while his guard stepped into the hallway for a smoke, Bundy jumped from the library's second-story window and escaped.

He was recaptured eight days later but escaped again in December, squeezing through a trapdoor in the ceiling of his cell that he had painstakingly made with a smuggled hacksaw. This time, he headed to Tallahassee, Florida, where he committed a series of attacks so inhumanly savage that even he would later refuse to discuss them. On February 15, 1978—one week after he slaughtered a twelve-year-old girl and dumped her ravaged remains in a pig shed—his luck finally ran out. He was arrested for driving a stolen car and quickly identified as the homicidal fugitive.

Eventually, he was sentenced to death, though he managed to delay his execution for a decade. When the day finally arrived, a huge, festive crowd gathered outside the prison walls to celebrate the event, while a local radio station diverted its listeners with the sound of frying bacon and a parody of "On Top of Old Smokey":

On top of Old Sparkey
All loaded with juice,
Good-bye to old Bundy
No more on the loose.

In surveying the serial killers of the past quarter century, there is a kind of hierarchy of evil, with such big-name psychos as Bundy, Gacy, Dahmer, Ramirez, Berkowitz, and Lucas topping the list. Just below them in the ranks of infamy are some well-known lust-killers who, for whatever reason, have never achieved the same near-mythic status.

Joel Rifkin, for example, stands as the most prolific serial killer in the history of New York State. That he has never achieved the notoriety of Gacy et al is undoubtedly due to his choice of victims: drug-addicted streetwalkers, the type of social outcasts whose deaths don't generate the kind of media hoopla that attends the serial slaughter of middle-class marrieds and clean-scrubbed coeds.

(Corbis)

Portrait of a serial killer, Joel Rifkin

Adopted at three weeks, Rifkin grew up to be a quintessential nerd—physically gawky, hopeless at sports, socially inept, and afflicted with a stutter and assorted learning disabilities. His school years were an endless ordeal of humiliation and harassment by bullying peers. Plenty of geeky young men, of course, suffer such torment and end up taking refuge in *X-Men* comics or *Star Trek* fandom or *The Lord of the Rings.* For whatever reason, Rifkin developed a different form of imaginative escape. From an early age, according to his own testimony, he indulged in vivid fantasies involving sex slaves, torture, and female gladiators battling each other to bloody deaths. His favorite movie was Alfred Hitchcock's 1972 *Frenzy,* about an English sex-killer who can only perform sexually while strangling women.

An utter failure in his academic pursuits as in every other area of his life, the virginal Rifkin began to cruise for hookers shortly before his twentieth birthday. Before long, he was deeply immersed in his sordid secret life, spending whatever small earnings he made from various odd jobs on trysts with junkie prostitutes. By the time he committed his first murder, he had, by his own estimate, engaged in three hundred such squalid encounters.

In March 1989, the thirty-year-old Rifkin was still living at home with his widowed mother, who was away on vacation. Cruising Manhattan's East Village, he picked up a crack-addicted prostitute whose name he never bothered to learn. He drove her back to his house on suburban Long Island and, after some perfunctory sex, bludgeoned her to death with an old howitzer shell he had bought at a military flea market. Then he cleaned up the blood, straightened up the living room, and took a nap.

Waking up refreshed a few hours later, he dragged the corpse down to the basement, draped it over his mother's washer and dryer, and—using an X-Acto knife—dismembered it as though he were carving up a roast chicken. To foil identification, he sliced off the fingertips and yanked the teeth out with pliers. Then he shoved the severed head into an empty paint can, stuffed her body parts into plastic trash bags, loaded the remains into his pickup, and headed for New Jersey, depositing the parts in various locations.

Throughout this atrocity, Rifkin proceeded with the cool deliberation of a Mafia hit man, as though he'd been murdering and disposing of victims his whole life. Finally, he had found something he had an aptitude for: sexual homicide.

Eighteen months would pass before he claimed his second victim. He brought home another young prostitute while his mother was out of town, then bludgeoned, strangled, and dismembered her. Before long, however, he plunged into what he would later describe as his "acceleration period," strangling hookers at a frenzied rate, sometimes at home, sometimes while they performed fellatio on him in his car. Seventeen women would die at his hands during his four-year spree.

He was caught in June 1993, when a pair of New York State Troopers spotted him driving his pickup without a rear license plate. When they tried to pull him over, Rifkin sped away, leading the cops on a high-speed chase that only ended when he smacked his vehicle into a telephone pole. Under a tarp in the pickup's bed, the troopers found the decomposing corpse of Rifkin's final victim.

He was given a 203-year sentence in prison. He now spends his time working on his pet project, a proposed rehabilitation center for prostitutes, where they would get free medical and psychological care, receive job training, and learn home, parenting, and financial skills. Rifkin calls his brainchild the Oholah House Foundation—supposedly named after two biblical prostitutes in the Book of Ezekiel murdered by their clientele.

Another notorious New York serial killer of this period, Arthur Shawcross, committed atrocities even more unspeakable than those of Rifkin. Like the latter, however, he preyed primarily on hard-luck prostitutes—a fact that has undoubtedly contributed to the public's relative lack of interest in his crimes.

If Shawcross's account of his childhood is to be fully believed, he suffered the sort of torture almost guaranteed to produce a violent psychopath. According to his story, he was molested by an aunt, sodomized by his mother, and raped by a pedophile while still in grade school. He also insists that he regularly engaged in incest with his sister and cousin, was forced to perform fellatio on his girlfriend's brother, and practiced bestiality with a variety of creatures, including chickens, sheep, and a horse.

Whatever the truth of these claims, there is no doubt that he was a deeply disturbed child, so bizarre in his behavior that his schoolmates nicknamed him "Oddie." He also manifested classic early warning signs of future psychopathology, including unnaturally protracted bed-wetting (which continued well into his teens) and a fondness for fire-starting.

In 1968, this profoundly unstable young man—then twenty-three years old—was drafted into the army and sent to Vietnam. During one jungle mission, he supposedly raped, slaughtered, and cannibalized two peasant women who were collaborating with the Vietcong. Like the tales of his childhood torture, it is hard to know how much of this story is true, how much the rabid imaginings of a sick mind. He also bragged of having murdered a string of preadolescent prostitutes in Saigon, a claim that—in light of his later behavior—seems more plausible. In any event, there is little doubt that, as a forensic psychiatrist would later testify, Shawcross left the army suffering from a serious case of posttraumatic stress disorder.

Discharged in 1969, he returned to his hometown in upstate New York, where he soon began to suffer from such violent flashbacks that an army psychiatrist recommended a stay at a mental hospital. Shawcross's Christian Scientist wife, however, refused to sign the commitment papers. Not long afterward, his pyromaniac compulsions began to reassert themselves. After setting a string of fires—including a blaze that did $280,000 worth of damage to the paper factory where he worked—he was arrested and sentenced to five years in prison.

Two years later, however, he was given an early release after saving the life of a prison guard during a riot. Returning to Watertown, he found a job as a handyman and spent his spare time fishing the local creeks and rivers. On June 4, 1972—less than a year after his parole—he was walking across some open lots near his home when he heard someone call his name. Turning, he saw a ten-year-old neighbor boy, Jack Blake, stuck waist deep in a mudhole. Pulling the boy free, Shawcross, according to his story, told him to go home and clean up. When the boy refused and insisted on following the older man across a swamp and into the woods, something in Shawcross snapped. Hitting the boy across the throat with a savage chopping blow, he raped and strangled him. Then, as he subsequently confessed to police, he "cut parts of him out and ate them. I took his penis, his balls, his heart and ate them. Why I did this, I don't know." Later, Shawcross would tell psychiatrists that, sometime after sticking the body in a shallow grave, he had dug it up and had sex with it.

Three months later, while fishing in a river, Shawcross spotted eight-year-old Karen Ann Hill playing nearby. After raping the little girl, he buried her, still alive, in a shallow grave beneath a bridge, packing leaves and wet mud into her mouth and nostrils until she suffocated. Later that same day, Shawcross returned to the crime scene to enjoy an ice-cream cone. He was spotted by a witness and quickly identified as a prime suspect. Cutting a deal with prosecutors, he confessed to the murder of Karen Hill and led investigators to Jack Blake's body. In exchange he was given a maximum sentence of twenty-five years with a possibility of parole in fifteen.

Astonishingly—and over the vehement objections of various prison psychiatrists—he won parole in March 1987, after doing his minimum sentence. At the time of his release, his parole officer penned a prescient memo: "At the risk of being melodramatic, the writer considers this man to be possibly the most dangerous individual to have been released to the community in many years." This warning went unheeded. As a result, eleven more people would die at Arthur Shawcross's hands.

In January 1988, after moving to Rochester, he picked up a twenty-seven-year-old prostitute, strangled her to death in his car, then tossed her body into the Genesee River. For the next year and a half, his MO would remain much the same. Sometimes, after killing a victim and dumping her body along the riverbanks or in the nearby woods, he would sneak back to have sex with the decomposing corpse. Occasionally, he carved out the sex organs and ate them.

Most of his victims were local hookers, but a few were acquaintances like thirty-year-old June Stotts, a mildly retarded family friend. Offering to drive her to the beach one unseasonably warm November day, Shawcross suffocated her, raped her corpse, then—as he later described it—"cut her wide open in a straight line from neck to asshole. Cut out her pussy and ate it. I was one sick person."

Shawcross's habit of visiting the bodies of his victims to practice necrophilia and cannibalism proved to be his undoing. In June 1990, a police surveillance helicopter—on the lookout for the "Genesee River Killer" (as the media had dubbed him)—spotted him masturbating on a bridge over the area where one of the bodies had been recently recovered. Brought in for questioning, he quickly confessed to his crimes, though he showed no signs of repentance. On the contrary, he insisted that his victims were responsible for their own deaths since they had provoked him by ridiculing his sexual inadequacies.

In the end, despite expert witnesses who testified that Shawcross was profoundly psychotic, he was found guilty and sentenced to ten consecutive twenty-five-year terms in prison.

Besides Rifkin and Shawcross, there have been other, no less despicable killers who have achieved notoriety in recent annals of serial murder. Among them are:

Harvey Carignan

While stationed in Alaska during an army stint in 1949, the sociopathic Carignan was sentenced to hang for rape-murder, but escaped the gallows because of a legal technicality. Paroled after just nine more years, he embarked on a string of burglaries and assaults and soon landed back behind bars, where he remained until 1969.

Four years later, while managing a gas station in Seattle, he murdered a teenage job applicant who had answered his "Help Wanted" classified—a crime that would earn him his homicidal nickname, the "Want-Ad Killer." Shortly afterward—with detectives making things hot for him in Seattle—he decamped for Minneapolis, where, over the next two years, he perpetrated a series of shockingly brutal crimes, sexually assaulting his victims before bludgeoning their skulls with a hammer.

Despite the savagery of these attacks, several women survived to identify Carignan, who was taken into custody by the Minneapolis police. Inside his car, investigators discovered road maps marked with dozens of incriminating, red-penciled circles that corresponded to the sites of various crimes linked to the "Want-Ad Killer." Under questioning, Carignan tried paving the way for an insanity defense by claiming that he had killed under direct orders from God (whom he described somewhat vaguely as a mysterious figure "who has a large hood on and you can't see His face"). The jury at his 1975 trial was unconvinced, and Carignan received the maximum sentence of forty years in prison.

Patrick Kearney

The psychopathic counterparts of the immaculately tidy gay men in the TV hit *Queer Eye for the Straight Guy,* Patrick Kearney and his live-in lover were fastidious in their habits. Inside their meticulously clean Redondo Beach apartment, more than a dozen murder victims were neatly dismembered with a hacksaw, then carefully arranged in identical trash bags for disposal along the Southern California freeways.

The "Trash Bag Murders," as the killings came to be known, began in April 1975, when the mutilated remains of a naked twenty-one-year-old male were discovered off a highway near San Juan Capistrano. Over the next two years, eight more male corpses turned up in various Southern California counties. All of them were shot in the head, sawed into pieces, and methodically packaged for dumping. Police finally got their break in March 1977, when friends of the final victim, seventeen-year-old John LaMay, supplied them with the name and address of the acquaintance LaMay had gone to visit on the day of his disappearance: David Hill. Warrants were immediately issued for Hill and Kearney, who remained at large until the first day of July, when they suddenly appeared at the Riverside County Sheriff's Office, pointed to their wanted posters hanging on the wall, and cheerfully announced, "That's us."

Shouldering full responsibility for the slayings, Kearney claimed that he killed because "it excited him and gave him a feeling of dominance." He eventually confessed to twenty-eight homicides. He received a life sentence; Hill was released for lack of evidence.

Paul John Knowles

A frequently reprinted news photo of Paul John Knowles shows him with a mane of tousled dark hair, cigarette dangling insouciantly from his lips—a brooding, darkly handsome man with a striking resemblance to the young Kris Kristoferson. His craggy good looks, combined with his easy charm and an indefinable air of danger, made him catnip to women and eventually earned him his homicidal nickname, the "Casanova Killer." That psychonym, however, is somewhat misleading, since it suggests that Knowles was a Ted Bundy-like lady killer, a predatory sadist who preyed on the opposite sex. In truth, Knowles—for all the romantic-outlaw fantasy that women projected onto him—was nothing but a nihilistic lowlife who degenerated from a petty criminal into a homicidal drifter, randomly killing anyone unlucky enough to get in his way—male or female, young or old. At least eighteen people—and possibly as many as thirty-five—would die at his hands.

His murderous spree began in July 1974. Escaping from a jail in Jacksonville, Florida—where he'd been locked up after a bar fight—he broke into

From *The Final Days of John Knowles* by Joe Coleman

the home of sixty-five-year-old Alice Curtis, who suffocated on her gag while Knowles ransacked the place. Though that killing was inadvertent, his next homicides were perpetrated with a frightening premeditation. While driving Mrs. Curtis's stolen car, he spotted two little girls who knew his family—seven-year-old Mylette Anderson and her eleven-year-old sister, Lillian. Afraid that the girls had seen him and might serve as potential witnesses to his whereabouts, Knowles strangled both and dumped their corpses in a swamp.

From that point on, Knowles became a one-man crime wave, drifting northward to Georgia, then across the country and back, leaving corpses wherever he went. He killed indiscriminately—hitchhikers and campers, stranded female motorists and businessmen befriended in bars. He broke into houses and murdered their owners. He picked up women in bars and killed them when they brought him home for sex. In Macon, Georgia, he stabbed to death a woman named Carswell Carr, then strangled her fifteen-year-old daughter and molested the teenager's corpse.

In November 1974—four months into his cross-country killing spree—Knowles met a British journalist named Sandy Fawkes at a Holiday Inn bar in Atlanta. They embarked on a six-day fling, marred only by Knowles's pathological inability to achieve an erection with a willing sex partner. Though sufficiently fond of Fawkes not to kill her, Knowles took out his frustration by attempting to rape one of Fawkes's friends, Susan Mackenzie, at gunpoint. She managed to escape and notified the police.

Like other spree killers, Knowles now acted with a suicidal abandon. Brandishing a sawed-off shotgun, he hijacked two vehicles in succession—first a police car, then a car belonging to a passing motorist—taking both drivers as prisoners. Heading to a remote spot in Pulaski County, Georgia, he handcuffed both men to a tree and executed each with a shot to the head. Not long afterward, he tried to crash through a police roadblock and was finally captured after a chaotic foot chase, bringing his four-month rampage to an end. The following day, while being escorted to a maximum security prison by a sheriff and an FBI agent, he lunged for the former's revolver and was shot dead by the latter.

Robert Hansen

In Richard Connell's famous 1924 short story, "The Most Dangerous Game," a crazed Russian general named Zaroff—bored with shooting lions, tigers, and other conventional species of big game—stocks his private island with shipwrecked sailors and begins hunting humans. During a ten-year period beginning in 1973, a Jekyll/Hyde sex-killer named Robert Hansen acted out a true-life version of this fantasy, turning lurid make-believe into nightmarish reality for more than a dozen unfortunate women.

In many respects, Hansen's life conformed to the familiar, if not stereotypical, pattern seen in the backgrounds of so many serial killers. Afflicted in his boyhood with a severe stutter, a disabling shyness, and a disfiguring case of acne, he grew up feeling shunned by the world, and especially by members of the opposite sex, for whom he developed a profound lifelong hatred.

In his late twenties, he relocated from Idaho to Alaska—a haven for misfits seeking to remake their lives. Settling in Anchorage, he established himself as a successful entrepreneur, the owner of a thriving bakery business. Securing a pilot's license, he purchased his own plane and became an expert wilderness hunter, stalking mountain goats, grizzlies, and wolves with bow and arrow and rifle. To his neighbors, he appeared to be a paragon: a prosperous self-made family man and community booster.

By his early thirties, however, cracks were beginning to show in his exemplary facade. He was caught shoplifting a chain saw and arrested twice for attempted rape. These crimes were just a prologue for the enormities to come.

Starting in 1973, when he was thirty-three years old, Hansen brought dozens of prostitutes and topless dancers to his wilderness retreat, flying them into the mountains in his private plane. Those who provided sex for free—"who came across with what I wanted," as Hansen later put it—were taken back to Anchorage unharmed. The ones who demanded money for their favors met a terrible fate. After keeping them tied up in his cabin for several days of rape and torture, he would release them naked into the wilderness. Then, after giving them a head start, he would stalk them with a .223-caliber hunting rifle. Altogether, seventeen women were slain in this hideously depraved "sport."

The end came for Hansen in 1983, when one of his intended victims managed to break free as he was attempting to force her into his plane. Picking up Hansen for questioning, police quickly punctured his alibi. Before long, they had found incriminating evidence in his possession, including the hunting rifle and a map marked with the burial sites of his prey. The hunter was caged for life in 1984.

Christopher Wilder

Born and raised in Australia, Wilder began his life of sex crime at an early age. Before he was out of his teens he had been arrested for gang rape and given mandatory electroshock therapy, which proved to be totally useless. A few years later, he was back in trouble with the law after extorting sex from a student nurse. Emigrating to America, he prospered in the construction business and was soon leading the glamorous life of a swinging, 1970s-era playboy, complete with swanky seaside home in Boynton Beach, a speedboat, and a high-powered sports car that he raced in professional competitions.

Beneath the glitzy exterior, however, Wilder was the same compulsive sex criminal he had been since his early adolescence. Time and again, his depraved behavior nearly landed him in prison. In 1971, not long after moving to Florida, he was arrested on a charge of soliciting women to pose for nude photos. A few years later, he was jailed after using physical force to coerce oral sex from an underage girl. Another arrest followed in 1980, when he lured a teenage girl into his car with the promise of a modeling job, drove her to a remote area, and raped her. For various reasons—through plea bargaining or the complainant's refusal to testify or the inadmissibility of vital evidence—Wilder managed to evade long-term imprisonment in each of these cases.

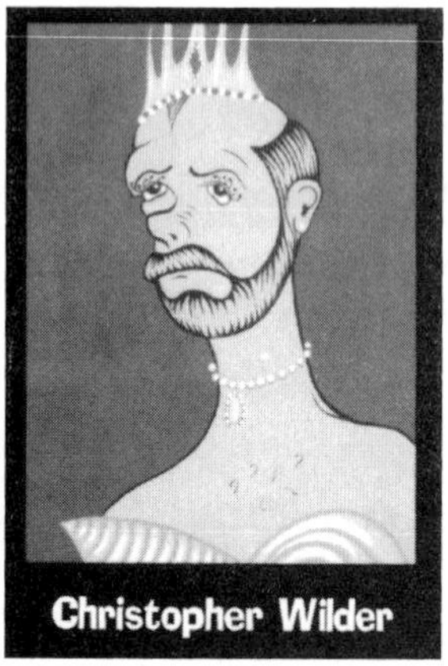

(Novelty trading card courtesy of Roger Worsham)

His luck appeared to run out in 1983. During a trip back home to Australia, he abducted two fifteen-year-old girls and forced them to pose for pornographic pictures. Charged with kidnapping and indecent assault, he was slated for a trial that seemed certain to end with a long-deferred and richly deserved prison term. Once again, however, he managed to wriggle free, returning to the United States when his family posted the $350,000 bail.

Not long afterward, Wilder's demons finally took full possession of him. In February 1984, a twenty-year-old aspiring model named Rosario Gonzalez—hired to hand out aspirin samples at the Miami Grand Prix, where Wilder was competing in his 310-horsepower Porsche—vanished without a trace. One month later, a former girlfriend of Wilder's—a twenty-three-year-old part-time model named Elizabeth Kenyon—also disappeared. When the local newspaper reported that a Boynton Beach race driver was wanted for questioning in connection with the two cases, Wilder packed his car, kenneled his three pedigreed setters, and embarked on his final insane spree: an eight-thousand-mile cross-country odyssey of torture, rape, and murder that left a half dozen victims dead.

Shopping malls were his preferred hunting ground. Approaching attractive young women, he would introduce himself as a professional photographer and offer them modeling opportunities. Some went with him willingly, others were forced into his car. Once alone with Wilder, the young women were subjected to prolonged torment. Several were hooked up to live electrical wires and tortured for hours. At least one had her eyelids sealed with superglue. When Wilder was done with them, he generally savaged their bodies with a knife and dumped the remains in some out-of-the-way spot, often in a canal or reservoir.

On April 4—one day after being added to the FBI's "Ten Most Wanted" list—Wilder abducted a sixteen-year-old girl named Tina Risico in Torrance, California. After repeatedly raping her, he forced her to become his accomplice in luring other young women into his clutches. Whatever shreds of humanity he retained seemed to manifest themselves a week later when—after having perpetrated several final atrocities—he drove Risico to Boston's Logan Airport, bought her a ticket home to California, and saw her off at the gate.

The following day, April 13, 1984, Wilder's car was spotted at a New Hampshire gas station by two state troopers. As the lawmen approached, Wilder lunged for the .357 Magnum in his glove compartment. One of the troopers threw himself on Wilder, and in the ensuing struggle, the gun went off twice. Wilder was killed—perhaps in an intentional act of suicide—with a bullet to the heart.

Danny Rolling, the Gainesville Ripper

CASE STUDY

The crimes committed by Danny Rolling sound like the stuff of a low-budget slasher film: five college students—four female, one male—brutally murdered by a madman over a weekend of terror. These ghastly killings occurred in Gainesville, Florida—an idyllic college town that had only recently been rated as one of America's most livable places. Within a week of the murders, however, the media had bestowed a new and chilling nickname on the community: "Grisly Gainesville."

The first victims died August 24, 1990. Christina Powell and Sonja Larson, eighteen-year-old roommates at the University of Florida, were found butchered in their student apartment. The killer had broken in while they slept, bound and gagged them with duct tape, then raped and savaged them with a KA-BAR knife. Afterward, he had mutilated the corpses and arranged them in obscene poses as a final insult to the victims and an affront to the people who would discover them.

The next night he struck again. This time the victim was eighteen-year-old Christa Hoyt, a sophomore at Santa Fe Community College. The killer broke into her home, then waited for her to return. When she did, he duct-taped her mouth and raped her. In a frenzy of violence reminiscent of the atrocities of the original Jack the Ripper, he then stabbed her to death, sliced off her nipples, cut her open from breastbone to groin, and decapitated the corpse, placing the head on a shelf before fleeing the scene. The savagery of this crime would earn him his tabloid nickname, the "Gainesville Ripper."

Hysteria gripped the community. Hundreds of students fled the state. Many who remained traveled in groups and avoided being alone.

Though twenty-three-year-old Tracey Paules shared in the general unease, she was not overly concerned. Her roommate, also twenty-three, was an old high school pal; Manuel Taboada, a strapping six-foot-three-inch senior who weighed over two hundred pounds. With Manny around, no harm would befall her, she believed.

She was wrong.

In the early-morning hours of August 27, the Ripper crept into their apartment while they slept. Manny awoke to find himself under attack by the knife-wielding maniac. Though the young man put up a ferocious struggle, he was no match for the Ripper's blade. Hearing the commotion, Tracey hurried to Manny's bedroom door, where she was set upon by the killer. He subdued her with duct tape, raped, then killed her.

With the city in a panic, police intensified their search for the sex-killer. Suspicion fell heavily on a local man named Edward Humphrey—a chronic troublemaker with a history of violently erratic behavior. But as the authorities focused their attentions on Humphrey, the real killer was miles away.

His name was Daniel Harold Rolling. Born in Shreveport, Louisiana, in 1954, he seems never to have had a chance at a normal life. His policeman father was a brutal martinet who terrorized the family, subjecting his children—and especially young Danny—to unrelenting physical and verbal abuse. By his early adolescence, the boy was heavily into alcohol and drugs and had made several failed suicide attempts. He had also become a Peeping Tom, a compulsion that would later evolve into housebreaking, rape, and, ultimately, sex-murder.

At seventeen, he joined the Air Force, but was discharged two years later after being caught with marijuana. By 1979, he had turned to armed robbery—an offense that earned him several stints in the penitentiary. Paroled in 1989, Rolling returned to Shreveport and tried living with his parents. This ill-advised move culminated in an explosion of gun violence between father and son. After putting two bullets into the old man, Danny fled to Kansas City, then made his way down to Florida. August 1990 found him in Gainesville, camping in the woods not far from the homes of the women who would become his first victims.

After the slaughter in Gainesville, Rolling headed for Ocala, where, on September 8, he was captured after robbing a supermarket at gunpoint. At first, the police didn't realize that they had bagged the Ripper. Rolling seemed like nothing more than a petty thief, short on talent and luck. Further investigation into his background, however, uncovered some disturbing facts. Officials learned that Rolling was wanted in Shreveport for the attempted murder of his father. Moreover, there had been a horrific triple homicide in Shreveport during the time that Rolling resided there with his parents—a crime that bore marked similarities to the Gainesville horrors.

An examination of evidence gathered from the campsite where Rolling had stayed after arriving in Gainesville produced overwhelming physical evidence linking him to the murders, including a pubic hair that—thanks to DNA analysis—was matched with one of the victims. Before long, Rolling had confessed to the crimes, though he tried to pin the blame on an evil alter ego named "Gemini"—a ploy that fell apart when investigators discovered that he had gotten the idea from watching the movie *Exorcist III.*

At his 1994 trial, his lawyer tried to persuade the jury that Rolling deserved sympathy because of his brutalized upbringing. Whatever sympathy they might have felt for the mistreatment he had suffered as a child, however, failed to mitigate their outrage over the atrocities he had committed as an adult. For five counts of murder, Danny Rolling was sentenced to die in the electric chair.

Recommended Reading

Colin Wilson and Damon Wilson, *The Killers Among Us,* Book II (1995)
Time-Life Books, *Serial Killers* (1992)

GALLERY OF EVIL: TEN AMERICAN MONSTERS

LYDIA SHERMAN
1825–1879

Every era is haunted by its own particular monsters—dark, unsettling figures who incarnate the dominant fears of the time. In the late 1800s, when American women first organized to demand social and political equality, triggering powerful anxieties in men, that figure was the female serial poisoner. This nightmarish being became a stock feature of late-nineteenth-century popular culture, which spawned a whole genre of fictional crime stories about the unspeakable doings of assorted "domestic fiends"—homicidal maniacs in the guise of loving housewives, mothers, and caretakers. Far more unnerving, of course, were the real-life cases of women who gleefully wiped out large numbers of their nearest and dearest. Among the most infamous of these was the woman who has gone down in the annals of crime under the name of Lydia Sherman.

Her original name was Lydia Danbury. Born in New Brunswick, New Jersey, in 1825, she was just seventeen when she married her first husband, Edward Struck, a forty-year-old widower with six children. Within a year of

Lydia Sherman encourages her elderly husband to drink a glass of doctored wine

their wedding, Lydia had given birth to a healthy girl. Six more babies followed in rapid succession.

With a wife and thirteen children to support, Struck—by then living with his family in Manhattan—took a job as a police officer. In 1863, however, he was fired in disgrace after failing to respond quickly enough when a knife-wielding drunkard attacked a hotel bartender.

By then, Struck's children from his first marriage had grown up and left home, and one of Lydia's babies had died of an intestinal ailment. That left six children in the household. With not a penny coming in to feed them, Struck plunged into a state of extreme despondency. Eventually, he refused to leave his bed. Deciding that he had become more trouble than he was worth, Lydia killed him with arsenic-laced porridge. The attending physician diagnosed the cause of death as "consumption."

Lydia was a forty-two-year-old widow with no income. Just a month after disposing of her husband, she began to feel disheartened by the difficulty of supporting six children on her own. In the first week of July, she poisoned the three youngest with arsenic.

Freed of these burdens, Lydia's situation improved, particularly since her fourteen-year-old son George had gotten a job as a painter's assistant. Unfortunately, George soon developed a condition known as "painter's colic" and was forced to quit work. His mother gave him a week to recuperate. When he showed no signs of improvement, she killed him with arsenic-spiked tea.

Only two of Lydia's children still remained above ground: her eighteen-year-old daughter, also named Lydia, and little Ann Eliza, aged twelve. Ann Eliza was a frail child, frequently sick with fever and chills. Lydia began to feel oppressed by the burden of caring for her. In March 1864, she killed the little girl by mixing a few grains of arsenic into a spoonful of patent medicine. The cause of death was given as "typhoid fever."

For the next six or seven weeks, the two Lydias—mother and daughter—lived together in a small apartment on upper Broadway. In early May, after paying an overnight visit to her half sister in lower Manhattan, young Lydia returned home with a fever and took to bed. Her mother did not feel like caring for her. On May 16, 1866, after dutifully taking the foul-tasting medicine her mother had fed her, the eighteen-year-old girl died in convulsive agony and was laid to rest beside the bodies of her father and five siblings.

Shortly afterward, Lydia moved to Stratford, Connecticut, where she met and married an old man named Dennis Hurlburt, a local farmer of considerable means. Slightly more than one year later, Hurlburt fell violently ill and died after eating a bowl of his wife's special clam chowder. His death was attributed to "cholera."

The forty-six-year-old widow came into a considerable inheritance. If her motives had been entirely mercenary, she could then have tossed away her arsenic and never killed again. But—though Lydia was happy to profit from her crimes—money was not, in the end, what drove her. Like others of her breed, she was a confirmed predator, addicted to cruelty and death.

Within months of Hurlburt's death, Lydia married Horatio N. Sherman, a hard-drinking widower with four children. In mid-November 1870—just two months after the wedding—Lydia murdered Sherman's youngest child, a four-month-old baby named Frankie. The following month, she poisoned his fourteen-year-old daughter, Ada.

The sudden death of his two children devastated Sherman. He began to hit the bottle harder than ever. After returning from one weeklong bender, he took to bed for several days before returning to work on Monday, May 8, 1871. When he came home from the factory that evening, Lydia was waiting with a nice cup of poisoned hot chocolate. Two days later, he was dead.

The sudden, shocking death of the seemingly healthy Sherman aroused the suspicions of his physician, Dr. Beardsley. Securing permission to conduct a postmortem, Beardsley removed the stomach and liver and shipped them to a toxicology professor at Yale for analysis. Three weeks later, he received the results. Sherman's liver was saturated with arsenic. A warrant was promptly issued for the arrest of Lydia Sherman.

On June 7, 1871, she was picked up in New York City and transported back to New Haven, where she was charged with the murder of Horatio Sherman. Her trial was a nationwide sensation. In the end, Lydia was found guilty of second-degree murder and sentenced to life imprisonment in the state prison at Wethersfield, where she died of cancer in 1879.

BELLE GUNNESS
1859–?

She was that rarest of all psychopaths: a woman who engaged in wholesale slaughter, partly out of greed but mostly for the sheer joy of it. Even more unusual was the extreme savagery of her crimes. There had been other female "murder fiends" in the late nineteenth century—Lydia Sherman, Sarah Jane Robinson, Jane Toppan. But they had all shared the traditional MO of female serial killers: poisoning their victims, then pretending that the deaths were due to natural causes.

Belle Gunness was frighteningly different. True, she was not averse to eliminating an expendable spouse or superfluous child with a dose of strychnine when it suited her purposes. But the corpses that were dug up on her Indiana "murder farm" hadn't been poisoned. They had been butchered.

A forty-two-year-old Norwegian emigrant, Belle had purchased the farm in 1902 with the $8,500 insurance money she came into when her first husband, Mads Sorenson, died suddenly in convulsive agony. Her first two babies—also heavily insured—had perished the same way. Though the symptoms were characteristic of strychnine poisoning, the doctors who examined the corpses saw nothing suspicious.

Moving to the small town of La Porte, she set herself up on what she liked to call "the prettiest and happiest country home in northern Indiana." Shortly thereafter, she married a young widower, Peter Gunness. Just nine months after the nuptials, he was killed when a cast-iron sausage grinder fell from the stove top and struck him directly between the eyes while he was reaching for a shoe. At least that was Belle's explanation. So bizarre was this story that neighbors talked openly of murder. The insurance company, however, declared her husband's death an accident, and Belle collected another hefty payment.

That was when her homicidal career began in earnest. Over the course of the next six years, a succession of men found their way to Belle Gunness's happy country home. Some were hired hands brought in to help with the farm work. Others were well-to-do bachelors lured to the farm by the classified matrimonial ads that Belle regularly took out in Norwegian newspapers throughout the Midwest. All of them vanished without a trace.

Then, in the early-morning hours of April 27, 1908, the Gunness farmhouse burned to the ground. When the blaze was finally extinguished, firemen were aghast to discover the remains of four people—three children and an adult woman—stacked like cordwood in the cellar of the incinerated house. Though badly charred, the murdered children were recognizable as the youngest of Belle's six offspring. The fourth corpse was assumed to be that of Belle herself. Positive identification was impossible, however. The woman had been decapitated, and her head was nowhere to be found.

(Corbis)

Belle Gunness

Suspicion immediately fell on a disgruntled farmhand named Ray Lamphere, who was charged with murder. In the meantime, searchers sifted through the ashes in a search for the missing head. They never found it. What they *did* unearth sent shock waves throughout the nation—and earned Belle Gunness everlasting infamy as one of the most terrifying sociopaths in the annals of American crime.

A dozen butchered corpses lay buried around the property: in a rubbish pit, a privy vault, a chicken yard. Each of the bodies had been carved up like a Thanksgiving turkey—head hacked off, arms removed from the shoulder sockets, legs sawed off at midthigh. The various pieces of each body—limbs, head, trunk—had been stuffed into separate grain sacks, sprinkled with lime, then buried.

The discovery of these atrocities turned the Gunness farmstead into an instant, macabre tourist attraction. On the following Sunday, ten thousand curiosity seekers descended on the property, some from as far away as Chicago. Whole families strolled about the place like vacationing sightseers, while hawkers did a booming business in hot dogs, lemonade, and souvenir postcards of the "murder farm." Inset was a photograph of Belle: "America's Female Bluebeard," as the newspapers quickly dubbed her.

Under arrest, Lamphere—who had served not only as Belle's hired hand but her lover as well—told a gruesome tale. Each of the victims had been murdered for money. But greed wasn't Belle's only motive. Judging from Lamphere's testimony (and from the grisly evidence unearthed in the Gunness farmyard), it was clear that she was a sexual psychopath. Despite her 250-pound bulk and mannish features, she wielded a seductive charm. Her victims had been lured into a secret bedchamber, where they were chloroformed, then slaughtered with an ax by the monstrous Belle.

As to her fate, questions linger to this day. Did Lamphere—her suspected accomplice—kill her and her children for unknown reasons, then set fire to the farmhouse in an attempt to cover up his crimes? Many people believed so.

Others, however, had doubts that the charred, decapitated woman in the cellar was Belle. For one thing, the body weighed just seventy-three pounds—inordinately small, even allowing for the shrinkage that results when meat is roasted at high temperatures. Lamphere himself claimed that Belle had staged her own death, then absconded with $100,000 in ill-gotten gains. In the end, she was officially declared dead. For many years, however, sightings of the infamous "Lady Bluebeard" were reported in places across America. In the popular mind, she continued to live on, a legendary monster immortalized in story and song:

Belle Gunness was a lady fair,
In Indiana State.
She weighed about three hundred pounds,
And that is quite some weight.

That she was stronger than a man
Her neighbors all did own;
She butchered hogs right easily,
And did it all alone.

But hogs were just a sideline
She indulged in now and then;

Her favorite occupation
Was a-butchering of men.

To keep her cleaver busy
Belle would run an ad,
And men would come a-scurrying
With all the cash they had.

Now some say Belle killed only ten,
And some say forty-two;
It was hard to tell exactly,
But there were quite a few.

And where Belle is now no one knows,
But my advice is fair:
If a widow advertises
For a man with cash—beware!

H. H. HOLMES
1860–1896

Herman Mudgett was a native of Gilmanton Academy, a tiny hamlet nestled among the Suncook hills at the southern end of New Hampshire's Lake District. Born in 1860, Herman was a delicately built boy, blue-eyed and brown-haired, with a reputation as "the brightest lad in town." Among his schoolmates he was also known to be slightly odd. His father devoutly believed in the Bible, especially Proverbs 13:24: "he that spareth his rod, hateth his son." Herman's father loved his son and displayed his devotion by beating the boy with savage regularity.

Throughout his childhood, Herman kept mostly to himself, shunning other children. He did have one friend, a slightly older boy named Tom. But Tom died under tragic circumstances, plunging to his death from the upstairs landing of a deserted house he was exploring with Herman. Herman saw the accident clearly. He was standing right behind Tom at the time, so close that he could put out his hand and touch his friend's back without even reaching at all.

Partly because of his delicate stature and partly because of his peculiar personality, Herman was often persecuted by the village bullies. One episode in particular left a lasting impression. One morning, two of Herman's older schoolmates waited until the village doctor was away from his office on a house call, then waylaid Herman. Dragging him kicking and screaming inside, they wrestled him over to the human skeleton that the doctor had mounted on a metal stand in a shadowy corner of the office. They forced the

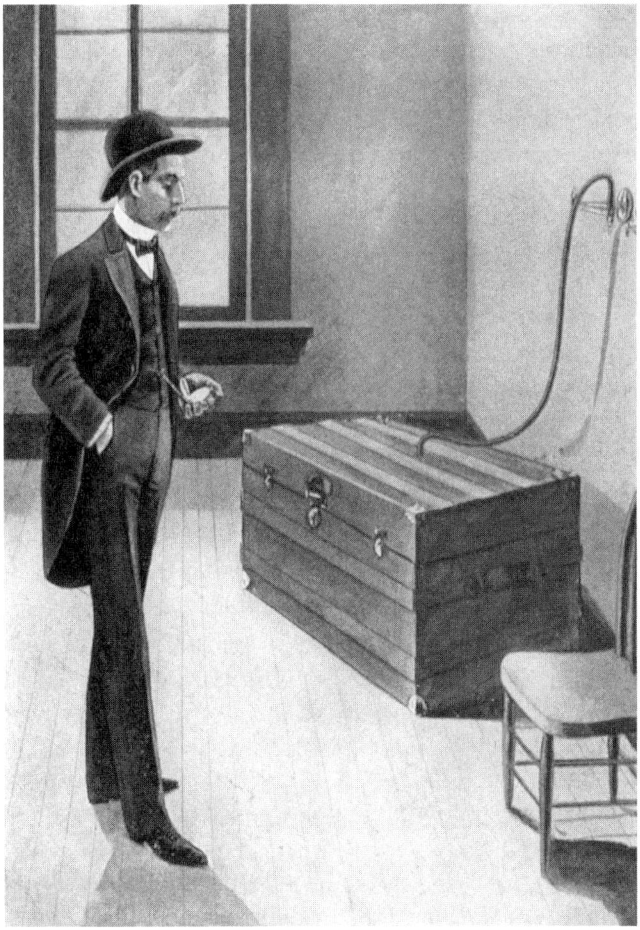

H. H. Holmes asphyxiates two child victims inside a steamer trunk

bony fingers of the skeleton against the hysterical boy's face, then let Herman go and left him shrieking on the floor.

Ironically, it was to this traumatic experience that Herman later attributed his lifelong interest in anatomy. By the time he was eleven, he was already conducting secret medical experiments—first on frogs and salamanders, then on rabbits, kittens, and stray dogs.

New England was not large enough to contain Herman Mudgett's ambitions. After a year of college in Vermont, he transferred to the University of Michigan at Ann Arbor, graduating with a medical degree in 1884. By then, Mudgett was an accomplished con artist who had learned how to bilk insurance companies of thousands of dollars. His method was simple: he would take out a life insurance policy for a fictitious person, acquire a corpse, claim that the corpse was the insured individual, and cash in the policy. Of course, the success of the scheme depended on Mudgett's ability to acquire dead bodies. But at that activity, too, he had already become quite proficient.

In 1886, Herman Mudgett showed up in Chicago. By this time, he had assumed the pseudonym by which the whole world would eventually know him: Dr. Henry Howard Holmes.

Within a few months, the debonair Dr. Holmes had taken a job as a druggist's assistant in the fashionable suburb of Englewood. The drugstore was owned by an elderly widow named Holton. Before the year was out, Mrs. Holton had abruptly disappeared. "Gone to California to visit relatives," the handsome young assistant told inquiring customers. Only by then, he was no longer an assistant. The 1887 city directory listed a new proprietor of the pharmacy at Sixty-third and Wallace Streets in Englewood: Dr. H. H. Holmes.

Before long, the profits from his store—combined with proceeds from assorted scams—allowed Holmes to construct a magnificent new residence for himself on a vacant lot across the street from his drugstore. In one respect, the building bore a striking similarity to its owner. Its exterior spoke of nothing but affluence and good taste. But behind the handsome facade it presented to the world, there existed a labyrinthine realm of madness and horror.

Holmes called his new building the Castle. It contained over one hundred rooms linked by secret passageways, fake walls, concealed shafts, and trapdoors. Some rooms were soundproofed and padded with asbestos; peepholes in the doors allowed Holmes to see into them. Many were equipped with gas pipes connected to a large tank in the cellar. From a control panel in his office, Holmes could fill any of the chambers with poison gas. Chutes ran from the second and third floors of the building to the basement, where Holmes kept a laboratory, complete with dissection table, surgical instruments, and an oven large enough to accommodate a human body.

Shortly after moving into the Castle, Holmes invited a watchmaker named Conner—who was blessed with a statuesque wife, Julia, and a lovely infant daughter named Pearl—to set up shop in a section of the pharmacy. Before long, the seductive Dr. Holmes had made Julia his mistress. When she became pregnant by Holmes, the outraged Mr. Conner packed up his belongings and left for good. Holmes, however, was not prepared for the responsibilities of fatherhood. He performed a crude abortion on Julia, killing her in the process, then dispatched little Pearl with chloroform.

When the Chicago World's Fair opened in 1893, decent lodgings were hard to find in the city. Holmes began renting rooms to tourists. Few were ever seen alive again. Throughout this period, local medical schools received a regular supply of human skeletons from Dr. Holmes. Since the schools were in desperate need of high-grade anatomical specimens, no questions were asked.

Holmes was finally arrested after killing his confederate, Ben Pitezel. Holmes used Pitezel's corpse to pull off his favorite life insurance fraud, but was caught by clever investigators. The discovery of the horrors inside his

(Courtesy of Rick Geary)
Police discover human remains in the basement of Holmes' "Murder Castle"

Chicago "Murder Castle"—along with the revelation that he had killed three of Pitezel's children to cover up his scam—sent shock waves throughout the country. The trial of the "Arch-Fiend" (as Holmes was quickly dubbed) became the century's greatest criminal sensation. Following his conviction, he confessed to twenty-seven murders, though authorities believed that the death count was closer to fifty—ten times the number racked up by Jack the Ripper.

Because the careers of these two serial killers coincided, some crime buffs regard them as transatlantic counterparts. But others—in recognition of the handsome young doctor's appalling double life—have seen Holmes as the American version of a different Victorian monster. If ever there was a real-life Dr. Jekyll and Mr. Hyde, these people say, then surely Henry H. Holmes was the man.

ALBERT FISH
1870–1936

Edward Budd was an able-bodied, energetic young man, the eldest child of a poor, working-class family scraping by in a New York City tenement. In late May 1928, hoping to find summer work as a farmhand, he placed a classified ad in a newspaper: "Youth, 18, wishes position in country."

Albert Fish by Joe Coleman

Several days later, a frail-looking old man with gentle eyes and a drooping mustache showed up at the Budds' apartment. Introducing himself as Frank Howard, the little man explained that he was hiring help for his truck farm on Long Island. He had spotted Edward's ad in the paper and had come to interview the young man for a job.

Mr. Howard gave Edward the once-over and seemed satisfied by what he saw. He made a generous offer and arranged to return in a few days to pick Edward up and drive him to the farm.

A few days later, on Sunday, June 3, the old man returned. Edward was out on an errand. Mrs. Budd invited her son's new employer to have lunch with the family while they awaited the young man's return.

Shortly afterward, while Mr. Howard sat at the Budds' kitchen table, the youngest member of the family—a glowing little girl named Grace—wandered into the room. She instantly caught the old man's eye. He called her over, sat her on his knee, and exclaimed over her beauty. She reminded him, he said as he caressed her silky brown hair, of his own ten-year-old granddaughter.

Suddenly, he turned to her parents as though an idea had just struck him. His niece, who lived in upper Manhattan, was having a birthday party that afternoon. He had decided to attend the party for a few hours, then pick Edward up afterward. Perhaps Grace would like to come along with him? It was going to be quite a party—with lots of children and games and ice cream. He would take good care of her and bring her home before dark.

Mrs. Budd felt a little uncertain about letting her child go off with a virtual stranger. Still, Mr. Howard seemed so utterly harmless that her qualms seemed foolish. And besides, the old gentleman had offered her son a desperately needed job.

She allowed herself to be persuaded. "Let her go," Grace's father urged. "She doesn't see much good times." Grace was gotten up in her prettiest outfit. Then, the creature known as Frank Howard—whose name was really Albert Fish and whose kindly demeanor concealed a mind of unimaginable depravity—took the child by the hand and led her away from home toward a subway station.

Before boarding the train, the old man stopped to retrieve a canvas bundle he had stashed behind a corner newsstand on his way to the Budds' apartment. Wrapped inside were a butcher's knife, a cleaver, and a saw.

To describe Albert Fish as the black sheep of his family is almost a laughable understatement. No eminent American family has ever been cursed with any sheep blacker. Though his ancestors fought in the Revolutionary War and his namesake had served as secretary of state in the Grant administration, Albert Fish—whose given name was actually Hamilton Fish—came from a branch of the family characterized by poverty and psychosis. When he was five, his parents, unable to afford his upbringing, placed him in a public orphanage. There, Fish had a teacher whose preferred form of discipline was to strip her young charges naked and beat their bare bodies while the other boys and girls watched. Fish came away from this experience with a singular education. What he learned, as he later put it, was to "enjoy everything that hurt."

At twenty-eight, Fish was making an irregular living as a housepainter and handyman. He married a nineteen-year-old woman who would eventually abandon him for another man, leaving Fish to care for their six children. He was an affectionate father and grandfather. At the same time, he admitted to other feelings toward children. As he grew older, he became increasingly possessed by what he described as a "lust for their blood."

Obsessed throughout his life with religion, Fish began to have searing visions of Christ and His angels and to hear the voice of God addressing him in dark, quasi-biblical terms. "Blessed is the man who correcteth his son in whom he delighteth with stripes." "Happy is he that taketh Thy little ones and dasheth their head against their stones." He saw himself as Abraham and each of his little victims as a young Isaac. "It seemed to me," he later explained, "that I had to offer a child for sacrifice, to purge myself of sins, iniquities, and abominations in the sight of God."

His compulsion to kill grew overpowering.

Even today, no one knows the precise number of Fish's victims, though it seems certain that he molested several hundred and slew at least fifteen. Most were children of the slums. Many of his victims were black, and authorities—after a cursory investigation—simply gave up the search. Eventually, authorities would learn some of the horrifying details from Albert Fish himself.

But that wouldn't happen until six years after Grace Budd's disappearance. And on June 3, 1928, Grace Budd's parents had no way of knowing any of these facts about the monster who called himself Frank Howard—the friendly old man who led their little daughter onto the New York Central Railroad, while, tucked under one arm, he carried the canvas bundle containing the tools he liked to think of as his "implements of hell."

Over the course of the next six years, the New York City police—led by Detective William King of the Missing Persons Bureau—conducted a massive manhunt for the Budd girl and her kidnapper. Hopes were raised and dashed with dismaying regularity.

Then, in November 1934, a letter addressed to Grace's mother arrived at the Budds' apartment. Its contents were unspeakably demented. The anonymous writer began by recounting a story he had heard about "a famine in China," during which boys and girls under the age of twelve were seized and cut up and their meat sold. The writer explained that he had been told this story by an acquaintance, a sea captain who had lived in Hong Kong. "On Sunday June the 3 1928," the letter continued, "I called on you at 406 W. 15 St. . . . We had lunch. Grace sat in my lap and kissed me. I made up my mind to eat her. On the pretense of taking her to a party. . . . I took her to an empty house in Westchester. . . . I choked her to death, then cut her in small pieces so I could take her meat to my rooms. Cook and eat it. How sweet and tender her little ass was roasted in the oven."

By dint of old-fashioned sleuthing, Detective King managed to trace the letter to its source. A trap was laid, and Fish was arrested. His confession stunned even the most hardened officers.

Fish revealed that Grace was not his intended victim at all. He had originally planned to kill her brother. His intent was to lure Edward up to an abandoned house in suburban Westchester, overpower him, bind him with stout cords—and slice off his penis. Afterward, he planned to take the train back to the city, leaving the trussed and mutilated boy to bleed to death on the floor of the cottage.

The moment he saw little Grace, however, he changed his plan. It was *she* he wanted to sacrifice, not her brother. And so he made up the birthday party story on the spot.

After leading her out of the city to a place known locally as Wisteria Cottage, he left her out in the empty house's front yard picking wildflowers. He then had made his way to an upstairs bedroom and stripped completely naked. Concealing himself behind a door, he called to Grace to come upstairs. When she reached the landing, he leapt out at her and strangled her, kneeling on her chest and climaxing twice as she expired.

Then he cut her body into pieces and disposed of them in various places around the property. All except for a few pounds of her flesh, which he had carried back into the city with him, wrapped in newspaper. Fish's trial in 1935 held the nation riveted with its steady stream of shocking revelations—including Fish's incredible disclosure that he had used the butchered chunks of the little girl's body to make a human stew, cooking her flesh in a pot with carrots, onions, and strips of bacon, devouring the infernal concoction over a period of about a week.

Meanwhile, Fish took a liking to Dr. Fredric Wertham, senior psychiatrist at Bellevue Hospital, who had been retained by the defense to examine the madman. For the first time, Fish opened himself up to another human being, revealing the incredible story of his life and crimes—a history so appalling that, years later, after a long career of dealing with the criminally insane, Wertham would continue to regard Fish as the most wildly deranged human being he had ever encountered.

Among other incredible admissions, Fish explained that one of his favorite forms of sexual gratification consisted of shoving sewing needles up into his crotch, just behind the scrotum. Wertham had difficulty believing this claim until X-rays were taken which revealed twenty-seven sewing needles lodged around Fish's pelvic region.

In the end, Fish was found guilty and sentenced to death. Even the jurors believed he was insane. But as one of them later explained, they felt he should be electrocuted anyway.

On Thursday, January 16, 1936, Albert Fish went to the chair—the oldest man ever to be electrocuted at Sing Sing.

EARLE LEONARD NELSON
1897–1928

Even as a baby, Earle Nelson had the ability to unsettle those who encountered him. According to one crime writer, the earliest surviving photograph of little Earle showed "a loose-mouthed degenerate infant with a vacant expression." The picture was taken shortly after Earle was left an orphan, both his parents having died of syphilis. Less than a year old, he was taken into the home of his maternal grandmother, a Bible-thumping widow who instilled in him a lifelong fascination with Scripture.

In spite of her efforts to provide him with a stable home life, Earle's behavior grew increasingly erratic as he matured. At the dinner table, he seemed barely socialized, devouring food with the ferocity of a caged beast. He rou-

Earle Leonard Nelson in custody

tinely managed to lose his clothing whenever he left the house. When he wasn't sunk into profound self-pitying depressions, he was gripped by uncontrollable rages. By the age of seven, he had already been expelled from grade school and earned a neighborhood reputation as a petty thief and shoplifter.

In 1907, shortly after his tenth birthday, Earle suffered a serious head injury when he bicycled in front of an oncoming trolley car and was sent flying into the cobblestones. He remained in a coma for nearly a week before regaining consciousness. It is possible that the brain damage he sustained in this accident contributed to his future psychopathology. Or perhaps—given his family inheritance of instability and the bizarre behavioral symptoms he had manifested from infancy—his life would have turned out the same even if he hadn't been hit by the trolley.

In any event, his formal education ended when he was fourteen. Dropping out of school, he took a succession of menial jobs, supplementing his meager earnings (most of which he spent in the brothels of the Barbary Coast) with burglary. By then he was residing with his aunt Lillian, his grandmother having died a few years earlier. Despite Earle's increasingly erratic behavior—his Tourette's-like tendency to spew obscenities at the dinner table, his brooding obsession with the Book of Revelation, his freakish habit of walking around on his hands whenever a guest dropped by for coffee—Lillian remained staunchly supportive of her bizarre nephew. When he was arrested for housebreaking in 1915, she made a tearful appeal on his behalf at his trial. Her plea was ignored, however, and Earle was sentenced to two years in San Quentin.

Released from prison during the height of the Great War, Earle enlisted in the military but spent a good part of his stint in a naval mental hospital, where he was diagnosed as a constitutional psychopath. Discharged in 1919, the twenty-two-year-old Nelson took a job as a hospital janitor and soon fell in love with a grizzled fifty-eight-year-old spinster named Mary Martin. Before long, this very odd couple had married. The new Mrs. Nelson found herself living with a madman who continuously accused her of infidelity when he wasn't ranting about the Great Beast of the Book of Revelation and proclaiming that he himself was Jesus Christ. Not long after Earle raped her in a hospital bed while she was recuperating from a serious illness, Mary decided to leave him. A year later, he attacked a twelve-year-old girl in the basement of an apartment building and landed back in a mental hospital.

He was discharged in June 1925. Less than one year later, he embarked on the rampage that would make him the most feared and prolific serial killer of his era.

On February 20, 1926, he showed up at the doorstep of Mrs. Clara Newman, a sixty-year-old spinster who ran a boardinghouse in San Francisco. There was a vacancy sign in her front window. Nelson, explaining that he was looking for a place to stay, asked to see the available room. Once he had the landlady alone, he strangled her with his bare hands, then raped her corpse.

During the next few months, Nelson ranged along the West Coast—from San Francisco to Seattle and back—on a monstrous spree of murder and sexual mayhem. Ten more women died at his hands between February and November 1926. All his victims were landladies. All were strangled, then raped after death. A number of the corpses were left stuffed in small spaces—inside a trunk, behind the basement furnace. By now, the press had dubbed the unknown maniac the "Dark Strangler." A massive manhunt was launched all along the West Coast.

Nelson moved inland. On December 2, he murdered Mrs. John Brerard, forty-nine, of Council Bluffs, Iowa. On December 27, he strangled twenty-three-year-old Bonnie Pace of Kansas City, Missouri. The following day, he killed another Kansas City woman, twenty-eight-year-old Germania Harpin. He also choked to death Mrs. Harpin's eight-month-old son by stuffing a rag down the infant's throat.

A nationwide alert was now on for the monster. Witnesses had provided the police with a description of the suspect: dark hair, stocky build, sloping forehead, protruding lips, and grotesquely oversized hands. There was something apelike about his appearance. The press hung a new tag on the phantom killer: the "Gorilla Murderer."

Nelson headed eastward. Between April and June he murdered four more women in Philadelphia, Buffalo, Detroit, and Chicago. Then he turned north into Canada, where he was finally captured after murdering two final victims in Winnipeg, a sixteen-year-old flower girl named Lola Cowan and a housewife named Emily Patterson, whose violated corpse he stuffed under a bed.

Tried and convicted in November 1927, Nelson was hanged the following January in Winnipeg. He went to his death clutching his Bible and proclaiming his innocence. His blood rampage had lasted for slightly more than a year, from February 1926 until June 1927. During that brief span of time, twenty-two victims met their death at the beastlike hands of the Gorilla Murderer.

EDWARD GEIN
1906–1984

A beautiful blonde slides out of her bathrobe, steps into the shower, and turns on the water. She pulls the plastic curtain closed. The water gushes down. She soaps herself, smiling. Suddenly, over her shoulder, a shadow appears on the other side of the curtain. It draws nearer. The curtain rips back. The shadow, shaped like an old woman, clutches a butcher knife. The big blade slashes downward, then slashes again. And again. Screeching chords on the sound track match the dying shrieks of the victim. Her streaming blood whirlpools down the drain.

The sequence, of course, is the famous shower scene from Alfred Hitchcock's *Psycho*—the most frightening moment from the most influential horror movie of modern times. After *Psycho,* a new kind of monster began stalking the movie screens of America: the psychotic "slasher." And showering was never the same again.

Ed Gein

The brilliance of Hitchcock's film derives from his genius for drawing us into a world of total insanity—a nightmare realm where a bathroom becomes a chamber of horrors, a shy young man turns into a crazed transvestite, and a sweet little old lady turns out to be a mummified corpse. By the time the film is over, the shaken audience steps away from the screen saying, "Thank God it was only a movie."

Perhaps the scariest thing about *Psycho,* then, is this—

It was based on the truth. There really was a maniac whose unspeakable deeds served as the inspiration for *Psycho.* His name wasn't Norman Bates, however. It was Edward Gein.

Gein grew up on a hardscrabble farmstead a few miles outside of Plainfield, Wisconsin, a small, featureless town situated in an area that has been called the "Great Dead Heart" of the state. His father, George, was a hard-luck type with a weakness for alcohol. Though George could be brutal when drunk, he was no match for his domineering wife, Augusta.

But then, it's hard to imagine how *anyone* could have matched Augusta's ferocious willpower. Or her all-consuming madness.

Raised in a fiercely religious atmosphere, she had gradually developed into a ranting fanatic who harped on a single theme: the loathsomeness of sex. Looking around the world, all she perceived was rottenness and filth. She had fled the city of LaCrosse—the place of Eddie's birth—because she regarded it as modern-day Sodom, reeking of sin and perversion. But Plainfield, in her warped view, had turned out to be no better. The small, God-fearing town was, in her eyes, a hellhole of depravity. She kept her two boys—Ed and his older brother Henry—tightly bound to her apron strings and imbued them with her own twisted sense of universal wickedness, the whorish ways of women, and the vileness of carnal love.

When George Gein dropped dead of a heart attack in 1940, no one—not even his family—was sorry to see him go. Left alone with their mother, the two boys fell even more powerfully under her poisonous spell. Henry, at least, seems to have had some sense of Augusta's destructive influence and tried to help his brother break away. But Eddie wouldn't listen. He worshiped Augusta and did not take kindly to his brother's criticisms.

In 1944, Henry was found dead on the Geins' property—presumably from a heart attack while putting out a brush fire. No one ever came up with a convincing explanation for the strange bruises on the back of his head.

Now Eddie had his mother all to himself. But not for long. In 1945, Augusta suffered a stroke. Eddie tended to her day and night, though nothing he did ever seemed to be good enough. Sometimes—her voice slurred but still dripping with contempt—she would call him a weakling and a failure, just like his father. At other times, she would beckon him to her side and pat the mattress beside her. Eddie would crawl into her bed and cling to her, while she cooed in his ear: he was her own little man, her baby. At night, he wept himself to sleep, praying to God to spare his mother's life. Eddie could never manage life without her; she had told him so herself.

But his prayers went unheeded.

A few months later, Augusta was stricken with another, even more devastating stroke. She died in December 1945. Eddie Gein, thirty-nine years old, was left all alone in his dark, empty, shut-off world.

It was then that he began his descent into the chaos of unutterable madness. For a long time, no one seemed to notice. A loner all his life, Ed started keeping more to himself—locked up behind the weather-beaten walls of his gloomy, ramshackle farmhouse. And even when he did venture out in public—to run an errand in town or perform some handyman chores or drink an occasional beer at Mary Hogan's roadside tavern—he didn't seem that much stranger than he had before. A little dirtier maybe, more in need of a bath. But he had always been a queer one, ever since childhood. Folks just accepted Eddie's peculiarities.

True, he seemed to talk more and more about the magazine articles he was fascinated by: stories of Nazi atrocities, South Sea headhunters, and sex-change operations. And then there were the "jokes" he told. When Mary Hogan, the big, foul-mouthed tavern keeper, suddenly disappeared from her place one afternoon, leaving nothing but a puddle of blood, Eddie began kidding that she was staying over at his house. But that kind of sick humor was just something you'd expect from a weirdo like Eddie Gein.

Even the stories about the creepy things at his farmhouse didn't faze most folks. Some neighborhood kids who had visited his home claimed that they had seen shrunken heads hanging on the walls of Eddie's bedroom. Eventually the rumors got back to Eddie, who had a plausible explanation. The heads, he said, were World War II souvenirs, sent to him by a cousin who had served in the South Seas. His neighbors shrugged. Trust Eddie to have weird souvenirs like that.

They never imagined that Eddie was capable of hurting anyone. Hell, the meek little man with the lopsided grin couldn't stand the sight of blood. He wouldn't even go deer hunting, like every other man in town.

That's what folks said. Then Bernice Worden disappeared.

It happened on November 16, 1957—the first day of deer-hunting season. Late that afternoon, Frank Worden returned home from a fruitless day in the woods and proceeded directly to the corner hardware store owned and managed by his mother, Bernice. To his surprise, she wasn't there. Searching the premises, Worden discovered a trail of dried blood leading from the storefront out the back door. He also discovered a sales receipt for a half gallon of antifreeze made out to Worden's last customer: Eddie Gein.

When the police arrived at Eddie's farmhouse to question him about Mrs. Worden's whereabouts, they came upon the body of the fifty-eight-year-old grandmother in the summer kitchen behind the house. Hanging by her heels from a pulley, she had been beheaded and disemboweled—strung up and dressed like a butchered deer.

The stunned and sickened officers called for reinforcements. Before long, a dozen or more lawmen showed up at the farm and began exploring the unspeakable contents of Ed Gein's house of horrors. What they found during that long, hellish night was appalling beyond belief.

Soup bowls made from the sawed-off tops of human heads. Chairs upholstered in human flesh. Lampshades fashioned of skin. A boxful of noses. A shade pull decorated with a pair of women's lips. A belt made of female nipples. A shoe box containing a collection of preserved female genitalia. The faces of nine women, carefully dried, stuffed with paper and mounted, like hunting trophies, on a wall. A skin vest, complete with breasts, which had been fashioned from the tanned upper torso of a middle-aged woman.

Later, Eddie confessed that, at night, he would lace the skin around himself and go mincing around the farmhouse, pretending to be his mother.

At around 4:30 A.M., after much searching through the ghastly clutter of Gein's home, an investigator discovered a bloody burlap sack shoved under a fetid mattress. Inside was a freshly severed head. Two tenpenny nails, each with a loop of twine tied to the end of it, had been inserted in the ears. The head was Bernice Worden's. Eddie Gein was going to hang it on the wall as a decoration.

At first, everyone assumed that Eddie Gein had been running a murder factory. But during his confessions he made a claim that seemed, at first, almost too incredible to accept. He wasn't a mass murderer at all, he insisted. Yes, he had killed two women—Bernice Worden and the tavern keeper Mary Hogan, whose preserved, peeled-off face had been found among Ed's gruesome collection. But as for the rest of the body parts, Eddie revealed that he had gotten them from local cemeteries. For the past twelve years, ever since his mother's death, he had been a grave robber, turning to the dead for the companionship he could not find among the living.

In the strict definition of the term, Eddie Gein was not a serial killer. He was a ghoul.

Gein spent the remainder of his days locked away in mental institutions. Long before his death from cancer at the age of seventy-eight, he had been immortalized in Alfred Hitchcock's *Psycho,* based on a novel whose author—Robert Bloch—had been inspired by the Gein affair. When Eddie died on July 26, 1984, they took his body back to Plainfield and buried it next to his mother. Eddie Gein was back where he belonged.

HARVEY MURRAY GLATMAN
1928–1959

Born in the Bronx in 1927, Harvey Glatman moved to Denver with his parents, Albert and Ophelia, while in grade school. With his big nose, Dumbo ears, and horn-rimmed glasses, he grew up to resemble a flesh-and-blood version of the nerdy Milhouse from TV's *The Simpsons.* His lifelong terror of the opposite sex was clear from the beginning. A socially maladroit loner, he couldn't speak to a girl without turning beet red.

(Novelty trading card courtesy of Roger Worsham)

He was also a precocious sex pervert, indulging in bizarre erotic practices at a shockingly early age. Glatman was no older than four when his mother walked into his bedroom and found him naked, one end of a taut string tied around his penis, the other attached to a dresser drawer. It was the first manifestation of the rope fetish that would dominate Glatman's life and ultimately lead to the terrible deaths of three women.

By the time Harvey was eleven, he was heavily into the perilous activity known as autoerotic asphyxiation: putting his head in a noose, throwing the rope over a rafter, and choking himself while he masturbated with his free hand. When his parents discovered him at this "game," they consulted a doctor, who attributed it to "growing pains." He assured the Glatmans that their boy would outgrow it.

Far from subsiding, Glatman's perverse compulsions only grew worse. In high school, he began breaking into homes, coming away from one these forays with a stolen .26-caliber handgun. Soon he had progressed from thievery to sexual assault. Sneaking into the houses of attractive young women, he would tie them up at gunpoint and caress them while he masturbated.

In June 1945, while awaiting trial on a burglary charge, the seventeen-year-old Glatman abducted a Denver woman and subjected her to the usual molestation before driving her home. She immediately informed the police, and, before long, the teenager was behind bars in Colorado State Prison.

Paroled after less than a year, Glatman—at the urging of his parents, who hoped he could put his checkered past behind him—moved to Yonkers, New York, where he found a job as a TV repairman—a trade he had learned in prison. In the grip of his growing pathology, however, he managed to stay out of trouble for less than a month. In August 1946, brandishing a toy pistol, he accosted a pair of strolling young lovers at midnight, bound the man with a length of rope, then began fondling the woman. Wriggling free of his bonds, the boyfriend attacked Glatman, who drew a pocketknife, slashed at the man's shoulders, then fled into the shadows.

Boarding a train that night, he headed for Albany, where, a few days later, he made a botched assault on a nurse, then mugged two middle-aged women. The police—by then on the lookout for someone who was targeting women—spotted Glatman just two days later as he followed a potential victim along a darkened street. Searching him, they found his toy pistol, a pocketknife, and a length of stout rope. Two months later, Glatman—just nineteen years old—found himself back in prison, this time with a sentence of five to ten years.

During his incarceration, Glatman was evaluated by a prison psychiatrist who diagnosed him as a "psychopathic personality—schizophrenic type" with "sexually perverted impulses as the basis for his criminality." Despite this grim assessment, Glatman won parole after less than three years.

Released into parental custody, he returned to Denver, moved in with his mother, and spent the next four and a half years working at various odd jobs and checking in with his parole officer. Finally, in early 1957, having earned his full liberty, he moved to Los Angeles, where his dormant psychopathic cravings burst into full, deadly bloom.

Finding work as a TV repairman, Glatman began to frequent the seedy photography clubs where sex-starved creeps could shoot "art pictures" of naked young models. Many of these women were aspiring starlets, eking out a living any way they could. They also accepted jobs on the side. Glatman, using the pseudonym "Johnny Glenn," approached a baby-faced nineteen-year-old named Judy Dull. He explained that he worked as a freelance photographer for a true detective magazine and asked if she would be interested in posing for him. The pay was twenty dollars an hour.

Judy Dull agreed.

Taking her to his apartment, Glatman explained that she would have to be bound and gagged and look convincingly frightened, as though she were about to be raped. Whatever apprehensions Judy Dull might have had, they were allayed by the innocuous appearance of the goofy-looking Glatman. Trussed up and placed in an armchair, the young woman threw herself into her part—assuming a terrified expression and twisting in her seat—while Glatman snapped away. All at once, the game turned terribly real. Pulling out a gun, he undid her bonds, forced her to strip, and repeatedly raped her. When darkness fell, he drove her out to the desert, strangled her with a length of sash cord, took some photographs of her corpse, and left her there for the buzzards and coyotes.

Two more victims followed: a twenty-four-year-old divorcee he met at a lonely hearts club and a former striptease dancer who, like Judy Dull, posed for a seedy "modeling agency." Both were killed in Glatman's signature style: trussed, photographed, raped at gunpoint, garroted, then posed after death and photographed again before being dumped in the desert.

In the summer of 1958, a state patrolman cruising the Santa Ana freeway happened upon a man and a woman struggling beside a car parked on the shoulder. Stopping to investigate, the officer found Glatman grappling with a twenty-eight-year-old model named Lorraine Vigil, who had managed to wrestle the killer's gun away from him as he was attempting to abduct her.

In custody, Glatman confessed to everything. Searching his apartment, police discovered a toolbox containing his horrifying photo collection. In some of the pictures, the women were fully clothed. In others, they were partly or completely nude. Bound and gagged, they wore terrified expressions. The most appalling photographs of all, however, were the ones he took of each victim after her death, the limbs carefully arranged, the corpses posed just so for his camera.

After pleading guilty, Glatman was sentenced to death. "It's better this way," he said when the judgment was handed down. He died in San Quentin's gas chamber on September 18, 1959.

> To understand Harvey Glatman is to understand the basic psychology of the serial killer.
>
> —Colin Wilson

JOHN WAYNE GACY
1942–1994

The cops had already paid one visit to John Wayne Gacy in 1978. Awakened in the middle of the night by shrill, continuous shrieks coming from the house behind her own, a neighbor had called the police. A squad car was dispatched to Gacy's brick ranch house in the Chicago suburb of Norwood Park. But the officers who questioned the owner came away convinced that nothing was wrong.

Then a fifteen-year-old boy named Robert Piest disappeared.

Piest was a bright, ambitious student who worked after school as a stockboy in a pharmacy. On the day of his disappearance—December 11, 1978—he told his mother that he was leaving the drugstore early to see a man about a summer job. The man was a local building contractor. His name was John Wayne Gacy.

When Piest's parents reported that their son was missing, the cops put a tracer on Gacy and discovered that he'd done time in jail ten years earlier. The charge was sodomy. The victim had been a fifteen-year-old boy.

Before long, Gacy was under arrest and a team of investigators was headed for his house with a search warrant. As they combed the rooms for clues, they turned up suspicious and increasingly ominous bits of evidence—pornographic magazines featuring sex between older men and young boys. A vibrating dildo encrusted with fecal matter. And—stashed throughout the house and garage—personal items that clearly belonged to a number of teenage boys: jewelry, clothes, wallets.

They also found something else—a trapdoor in a living room closet that opened into a flooded crawl space.

(Novelty trading card courtesy of Roger Worsham)

After draining the crawl space, the inspectors lowered themselves into the putrid muck. There they uncovered the sickening evidence of horrendous crimes: lardlike globs of decomposed human flesh and an assortment of human bones, some of them blackened with rot, others covered with dried, mummified flesh.

Confronted with these discoveries, Gacy immediately confessed to the atrocities that would mark him as one of America's most monstrous serial killers: the torture-murder over a period of half dozen years of thirty-three young men.

The news seemed unbelievable at first, not only because of the enormity of the crimes—which set a new, nightmarish record—but also because of Gacy's public persona. As far as the outside world was concerned, John Wayne Gacy was a pillar of the community—a successful, hard-driving businessman who still found time to devote himself to community affairs and charitable causes. One of his favorite activities was dressing himself up as "Pogo the Clown" and performing for sick children at the local hospital. He was also active in local politics and was a valued member of the Junior Chamber of Commerce. Hanging on the wall of his home office were photographs of him shaking hands with the mayor of Chicago and First Lady Rosalynn Carter.

But a very different picture emerged in the course of Gacy's examination by court-appointed psychiatrists.

Raised by an abusive, alcoholic father—who spent much of his time deriding his son as a "sissy"—Gacy grew up to be a pudgy hypochondriac whose homosexual drives were a source of profound self-loathing. In an attempt to appear "normal," he married early and settled down in Waterloo, Iowa, where he ran a Kentucky Fried Chicken franchise. Even while cultivating this unimpeachable persona, however, he was leading a secret life as a seducer and molester of underage males. Arrested in 1968 for sodomy, he was hit with a ten-year jail term. His wife filed for divorce on the day of the sentencing.

Gacy proved to be such a model prisoner that he was paroled after less than two years. Relocating to Chicago, he married again and started his contracting business. Before long, however, his darkest impulses reasserted themselves—in even ghastlier form. He became a human predator, a cunning, remorseless sadist who tortured and murdered for his own depraved pleasure.

Though some of his victims were acquaintances or employees, most were street hustlers and runaways. Gacy—sometimes posing as a cop—would snare his prey at the bus station or the local gay district, "Bughouse Square." Back in his house, he would lock the young man in handcuffs, then spend hours sodomizing and torturing him before committing the final outrage—the "rope trick." Looping a length of nylon rope around the victim's neck, Gacy would insert a wooden hammer handle through the cord, then twist the handle slowly, reaching his own sexual climax as the victim strangled to death.

Once the boy was dead, Gacy buried the remains in the crawl space. Twenty-nine decomposed corpses were recovered from the muck beneath his house. Eventually, Gacy ran out of room in the crawl space and began dumping bodies in a nearby river.

Gacy tried to convince the court that he suffered from a split personality and should not be punished for his crimes since they were committed by an evil alter ego named "Jack." The jury did not accept his insanity plea and, in March 1980, sentenced him to death.

Fourteen years passed before the sentence was carried out. During that time, he turned out scores of grotesquely cheery paintings—many of circus clowns and Disney characters. These became coveted collectibles among connoisseurs of such things. He also took pride in his sinister celebrity, bragging that he had been the subject of "eleven hardback books, thirty-one paperbacks, two screenplays, one movie, one off-Broadway play, five songs, and over 5,000 articles."

Just after midnight on May 10, 1994, he was executed by lethal injection. His last words were: "Kiss my ass."

GARY HEIDNIK
1943–1999

Vincent Nelson hadn't seen his girlfriend, Josefina Rivera, since Thanksgiving Day 1987, when she'd stormed out of his apartment after a bitter fight. So he was amazed when she suddenly showed up at his front door four months later, close to midnight on March 24. But it wasn't just her unexpected reappearance that stunned him. It was Josephine's physical condition. She looked like hell; as haggard and ghastly as a concentration camp victim.

Most shocking of all was the incredible story that Josefina had to tell. Barely keeping her hysteria under control, she poured out an unbelievable tale of horror to Nelson—how she and several other women had been kept chained in a basement by a madman who had subjected them to four months of rape, beatings, and torture. And there was even worse. Two of the girls had died. The madman—whose name was Gary Heidnik—had chopped up the body of the first murder victim and forced Josefina and the other captives to eat the dead woman's flesh.

In short, Josefina Rivera looked like hell for a good reason. She had been living there for the past four months.

Nelson's first impulse was to go after Heidnik himself but, after reconsidering, he called 911 instead. At first, the cops were dubious. But their skepticism gave way to horror after they obtained a search warrant and broke into Heidnik's North Philadelphia slum house early the next morning. Josefina Rivera had been telling the truth. Gary Heidnik's basement was a torture dungeon. Inside the dank, filthy cellar, the cops found two half-naked black women chained to the pipes. A third, completely naked, was imprisoned in a shallow, plank-covered pit.

Upstairs, they found grisly support for Rivera's most incredible accusation. Carefully stored inside Heidnik's kitchen freezer was a woman's chopped-off forearm, while a roasting pan inside the oven contained a charred human rib bone. Rivera's claim was evidently true: Gary Heidnik had force-fed human flesh to his captives. He had turned them into cannibals.

By then, Heidnik was under arrest. Across the country, headlines blared the news about the "Philadelphia Torture Dungeon" and "Heidnik's House of Horrors." Staggered by the story, Americans shook their heads and asked themselves one question: What kind of creature could commit such atrocities?

Gary Heidnik had been born with real potential. He possessed a superior, 130-point IQ and the kind of stock market savvy that makes for Wall Street success. But Heidnik was not destined for a career on Wall Street. His parents made sure of that.

His father was a savage disciplinarian—the kind of man who dealt with his son's bed-wetting problem by hanging the stained bedsheets out the front window for the whole world to see. His mother was a drunkard who left the family when Gary was two. She ultimately committed suicide.

By the time Heidnik entered the army in 1962, he was beginning to manifest the severe psychological problems that would afflict him for the rest of his life. Between the time the army discharged him for mental disability in 1963 and the day of his arrest nearly a quarter century later, Heidnik would be in and out of psychiatric institutions twenty-one times. He also made more than a dozen suicide attempts through hanging, drug overdose, and reckless driving. One time, he smashed up a lightbulb and forced himself to swallow the pulverized glass.

During more lucid periods, Heidnik applied himself to a variety of pursuits. He trained as a practical nurse. With the savings from his army pension, he purchased a run-down three-story house and became a landlord. He also found Jesus. In 1971, he incorporated the United Church of the Ministers of God, elected himself bishop, and attracted a handful of followers, who contributed $1,500 to the operation. Heidnik invested the funds in the stock market and, within ten years, built up a half-million-dollar portfolio.

Heidnik's sexual tastes ran to mentally retarded black women. One of his many girlfriends bore him a daughter in 1978. In May of that year, Heidnik and his girlfriend drove up to a mental institution in Harrisburg, Pennsylvania, where the woman's sister, Alberta—a thirty-four-year-old with the IQ of a toddler—had resided for the past twenty years. Heidnik and his girlfriend got permission to take Alberta for a day's outing. When they failed to bring her back, the cops were alerted. They found Alberta cowering in Heidnik's basement. Medical tests revealed that she had been raped and sodomized, her throat infected with gonorrhea from forced oral sex.

Heidnik was arrested, convicted, and sentenced to three to seven years in the penitentiary. He ended up serving only four years of the time, most of it in various mental institutions. One day, halfway through his sentence, Heidnik scribbled a message and passed it along to his guards. He couldn't talk anymore, the message read, because the devil had shoved a cookie down his throat. For the next two and a half years, Gary Heidnik was a mute.

Following his discharge, he married a Filipino mail-order bride who bore him a son. She abandoned him after tiring of being forced to watch him have sex with assorted black prostitutes. Shortly after her departure, Heidnik became obsessed with a plan to create a baby factory in the basement of his house. His intention was to kidnap, imprison, and impregnate ten women. Josefina Rivera, a twenty-six-year-old part-time prostitute, became the first. Heidnik picked her up on Thanksgiving Day and took her to his apartment. When they finished having sex, he performed the "Heidnik Maneuver" on her, throttling her into submission. Then he forced her down to the basement and chained her to a pipe.

Two days later, he added another victim to his horror harem—a mildly retarded African-American acquaintance named Sandra Lindsay. The women were subjected to torture, beatings, and daily rape. Their diet consisted of bread and oatmeal, with an occasional dog biscuit treat. Before long, other victims followed—five women in all.

Heidnik's punishments became more insane. He subjected them to electrical shocks and shoved screwdrivers into their ears. When Sandra Lindsay died after dangling by her wrists from a pipe for a week, Heidnik dragged her body upstairs, dismembered it with a power saw, cooked her head in a saucepan, roasted her rib cage in the oven, and ground up her flesh in a food processor.

Then he mixed the ground meat with dog food and fed it to the surviving captives.

When twenty-three-year-old Deborah Dudley started giving him trouble, Heidnik decided to treat her to some electric shock therapy. He threw her in a water-filled pit and stuck a live electric wire in after her. The wire touched her chains and killed her. Heidnik stored her body in his freezer for a few days, then drove it out to Wharton State Forest in New Jersey and dumped it in the woods.

Two days later, Rivera managed to escape and made a beeline for her boyfriend's apartment.

On July 1, 1988, Gary Heidnik was found guilty on eighteen counts, including two of first-degree murder. When his father was informed that his son had been sentenced to die, the old man replied, "I'm not interested." After the usual delays, Heidnik was executed by lethal injection on July 6, 1999.

JEFFREY DAHMER
1960–1994

Perhaps the horror could have been avoided. Certainly, warning signs appeared along the way—signs that there was something wrong with Jeffrey Dahmer. Something very wrong.

But then, millions of people suffer from emotional disturbances during their early years, and they do not grow up to be like Jeffrey Dahmer. They do not grow up to be monsters.

He was born in Milwaukee but raised in Bath, Ohio—a comfortable middle-class community. His parents detested each other and were—as

(Courtesy of Hart D. Fisher)

Jeffrey Dahmer comic book

Dahmer later recalled—"constantly at each other's throats." Their endless squabbling left them little time for their eldest son. Friendless and neglected, Dahmer retreated deeper and deeper into his own little world of fantasy.

He took up a unique hobby: killing small animals, skinning them, and scraping off their meat with acid. In a backyard shed, he displayed his collection of squirrel and chipmunk skeletons. He also created his own, private pet cemetery at the side of his house. Sometimes, however, he didn't bury the bodies. Sometimes, he staked them into trees.

Starved for attention, he resorted to desperate acts. Though he did well in high school, his behavior was often bizarre. He would emit sheeplike bleats during class and collapse in the hallways in mock-epileptic fits. When the high school honor roll society assembled for its yearbook portrait, Dahmer sneaked into the picture. The prank was not discovered until the photograph was developed. The editor was so outraged that he took a Magic Marker and blotted out Dahmer's face. In the published picture, Dahmer stands surrounded by other students, his features veiled in blackness.

It was an appropriate image. By that time, a deadly darkness had already begun to envelop Dahmer's life. He had started to drink heavily. His fantasies of torture, mutilation, and death had become even more intense—more obsessive.

One day in 1975, several neighborhood boys, strolling through the woods behind the Dahmer house, came upon a shocking sight—a decapitated dog's head impaled on a stick. Nearby, they found its skinned and gutted body nailed to a tree.

In 1978, during Dahmer's senior year, his parents' poisonous marriage finally came to an end. The couple split up, going their separate ways. Dahmer was left alone in the house with nothing but his increasingly deranged fantasies.

A few weeks after his mother abandoned him, he picked up a nineteen-year-old hitchhiker named Steven Hicks and invited him home. The two shared some beers, chatted, had sex. When Hicks announced that he had to be moving on, Dahmer smashed him in the back of the skull with a barbell and strangled him. Then he dragged the body into the crawl space under the house, dismembered it, and stored the pieces in plastic bags. Later, he buried the bones—only to dig them up, pulverize them with a sledgehammer, and scatter the fragments in a wooded ravine behind the house.

Jeffrey Dahmer's career of carnage had begun. He was eighteen years old.

He tried college for a while, but dropped out of the Ohio State University after only a few months and enlisted in the army. To his buddies, he seemed like a "regular guy" until he began to drink. Then a very different Jeffrey Dahmer emerged: moody, aggressive, defiant. Though he had enlisted for six years, the army discharged him after two.

He went to live with his grandmother in West Allis, near Milwaukee, getting a job in a blood bank. In 1985, he went to work at the Ambrosia Chocolate Company as a general laborer. That same year, something else happened to Jeffrey Dahmer. Something far more significant—and far more appalling. His terrifying pathology, dormant for nearly six years, came raging back to life.

He began hanging out at a local gay bar. One night, he and a pickup took a room at the Ambassador Hotel. The two men got drunk, had sex, passed out. When Dahmer awoke the next morning, the other man was dead, blood dripping from his mouth. Dahmer went to a nearby shopping mall and purchased a suitcase, which he took back to the hotel room. After stuffing the corpse inside, he called a cab and transported the body back to his grandmother's house, where he dismembered and disposed of it.

A year later, Dahmer killed his next victim: another gay man he had picked up at the club and taken to his grandmother's house. Dahmer kept the victim's skull as a ghoulish souvenir after scraping it clean of flesh. Another victim followed soon afterward.

Dahmer had several brushes with the law during the next few years. In 1986, he was arrested for lewd and lascivious behavior after urinating in front of some children. Two years later, he lured a thirteen-year-old Laotian boy to his apartment in Milwaukee, drugged him with a sedated drink, and fondled him. Arrested on a charge of second-degree sexual assault and enticement of a child for immoral purposes, he spent ten months in jail before being released in March 1990.

During the next year, Dahmer butchered three more men. At some point, neighbors noticed a putrid odor leaking from his apartment. But when they knocked on Dahmer's door to complain, he explained that his freezer had broken and the meat gone rotten. His apologetic manner was so convincing that the neighbors bought the story.

In May 1991, he came even closer to being caught. Shortly after midnight on the twenty-seventh, two women spotted Dahmer chasing a naked and bleeding teenage boy down an alley. The cops were called. But when they arrived to question Dahmer, his powers of persuasion saved his skin once again. He managed to convince the cops that he and the boy were gay lovers engaged in a harmless spat. The police left the dazed fourteen-year-old boy in Dahmer's clutches.

Later, the teenager's butchered remains were found amid the other human debris in Jeffrey Dahmer's charnel house.

During the next two months, Dahmer claimed five more victims. Then, on a muggy night in late July 1991, two Milwaukee patrolmen saw a dazed man stumbling toward them, a pair of handcuffs dangling from one wrist. Flagging down their squad car, he gestured wildly toward Dahmer's apartment building and stammered out a tale of attempted murder. The police went to investigate. What they found left them reeling with disbelief. They found Jeffrey Dahmer's chamber of horrors.

The drawers of the bedroom highboy were crammed with Polaroids of body parts and mutilated corpses—including one shot of a torso eaten away from the nipples down by acid. That was just the beginning of the nightmare. Inside a freezer, police found three human heads plus an assortment of organs: intestines, lungs, livers, kidneys, and a heart. Dahmer told the police that he was saving the heart to "eat later."

Another head was stored in the refrigerator next to an open box of baking soda. Seven skulls and five complete skeletons were stashed in various places around the apartment, along with miscellaneous remains: bone fragments, decomposed hands, sexual organs in a lobster pot. The police also found bottles of acid, chloroform, and formaldehyde, and three electric saws.

Altogether, these ghastly trophies represented the remains of eleven victims. Dahmer would later confess to seventeen murders in all.

The revelation of Dahmer's unspeakable deeds sent shock waves across America. At his 1992 trial, his attorney argued that the very nature of Dahmer's atrocities—"skulls in a locker, cannibalism, making zombies, necrophilia, lobotomies, defleshing"—was proof of his madness. The jury, however, rejected the insanity defense and found Dahmer guilty. During his own final statement, Dahmer expressed a desire to die—a wish that was fulfilled in November 1994, when he was bludgeoned to death by another prisoner.

Dahmer was cremated, though not before his brain was removed, setting off one last bitter dispute between his parents. Arguing that her son "always said that if he could be of any help, he wanted to do whatever he could," Dahmer's mother petitioned to have the brain donated to science for research into the neurological roots of antisocial behavior. His father, on the other hand—claiming that he wanted "to put the whole thing behind him"—was eager to have the organ destroyed. The matter was settled in December 1995, when a judge, citing Dahmer's own wishes as conveyed in his last will and testament, ordered the brain cremated.

SEX AND THE SERIAL KILLER

It goes without saying that serial killers tend to have extraordinarily aberrant sex lives. Their brutalized upbringings render them incapable of experiencing anything resembling real love. Many of them are impotent under normal conditions. They can only get aroused when they have another human being in their absolute power—a helpless, terrified object to be tortured, debased, slaughtered, and perhaps violated after death.

Lacking any capacity for empathy or guilt, serial killers are unconstrained by the inhibitions that keep other people from acting out their darkest fantasies. To these psychopaths, there is nothing forbidden, nothing taboo. They exist in a realm beyond the bounds not only of civilized behavior but even of ordinary criminal behavior. As a result, they indulge in activities that most people would find not just incomprehensible but inconceivable.

PERVERSIONS

The technical term for a sexual perversion is "paraphilia," which literally means "abnormal love." In our own anything-goes age, of course, it's seriously unhip to suggest that there is something "abnormal" about any form of sex play between consensual adults, whether it's smearing baked beans all over each other or watching videos in which scantily clad females squish earthworms beneath their feet. Still, even the most diehard erotic libertarian would be hard put to defend the kinds of practices routinely engaged in by serial killers.

The average panty fetishist, for example, might purchase some lingerie from Victoria's Secret under the pretense of buying a sexy gift for his girlfriend—or, in more extreme cases, acquire a used pair of female underpants from a sleazy adult-oriented Web site. A serial killer like William Heirens, however, is more likely to break into the bedroom of a sleeping woman, rifle through her bureau, have an orgasm while slipping into her undies, then murder and mutilate her when she wakes up and discovers him in the act.

Clipping and saving pubic hair from their sexual conquests is another common fetish among men. The serial killer's version of this practice is to remove the entire vulva of a victim, as exemplified by the Wisconsin ghoul, Ed Gein, who collected a whole shoe box full of preserved female genitalia.

Sexual voyeurism—which the average Peeping Tom satisfies by peering into his neighbors' bedroom windows—is another aberration that serial killers practice in a particularly malevolent way. They may masturbate while watching an accomplice rape and kill a captive. In the case of Charles Ng and Leonard Lake, they produced their own pornographic videos by abducting victims and subjecting them to horrendous sexual torture before the camera.

In short, anyone delving into the sex lives of serial killers will find that these psychopaths often take common paraphilias to the most hideous extremes. Others indulge in the kind of unspeakable acts described by Krafft-Ebing in *Psychopathia Sexualis:* cannibalism, vampirism, necrophilia. And a few serial killers have engaged in practices so outrageously sick, so grotesquely depraved, that it is impossible to find parallels to them, even in the pages of Krafft-Ebing's massive survey of sexual deviancy.

SADISM

The standard psychiatric reference book known as the *DSM*—the *Diagnostic and Statistical Manual of Mental Disorders*—distinguishes between two forms of sadism. The first is "Sadistic Personality Disorder," a condition in which someone "is amused by or takes pleasure in the psychological or physical suffering of others."

It's safe to say that all serial killers fit this diagnosis. Whatever other rewards they may derive from their crimes—a warped sense of omnipotence, media celebrity, even, at times, money—the fundamental fact is that they enjoy what they do. Making other people suffer and die is their idea of fun. Their credo is summed up by one of the scariest characters in American fiction, the psychopathic killer in Flannery O'Connor's famous story "A Good Man Is Hard to Find," who declares: "No pleasure but meanness."

The second type of sadism identified by the *DSM* is "Sexual Sadism." This is one of the major paraphilias—a perversion of the erotic instinct in which the suffering of a victim is not just generally enjoyable but intensely arousing, often to the point of orgasm.

While not every serial murderer suffers from this perversion, a great many do. Indeed, the figures most closely associated in the popular mind with the term "serial killer"—from Jack the Ripper to John Wayne Gacy—were all, to one extent or another, sexual sadists.

The Man Who Invented Sadism

No single person "invented" sadism, of course. The love of cruelty is a component of human psychology as old as the species itself. From the enormities of Caligula to the unspeakable crimes of Vlad the Impaler and Gilles de Rais, there have always been people who revel in inflicting torture and death on their fellow beings.

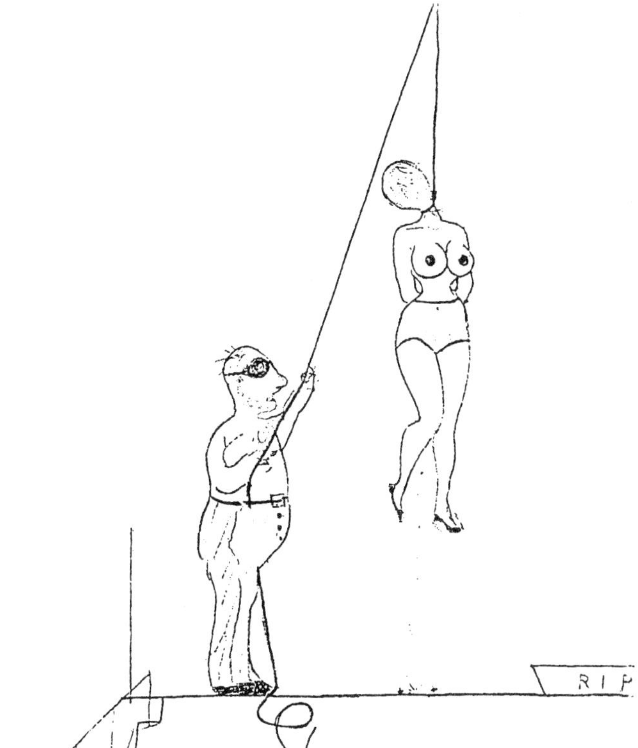

(Courtesy of Adam Parfrey)

Sadistic sketch by Gerard Schaefer

Until relatively recently, however, there was no technical term to describe such behavior. In the English language, the word "sadism" only goes back a hundred years or so. (It wasn't until 1897 that it first appeared in print, according to the *Oxford English Dictionary.*) In that sense, "sadism" is like "serial killer": a modern expression for an age-old phenomenon.

The man we have to thank for this useful addition to our vocabulary was Comte Donatien Alphonse François de Sade, commonly known as the Marquis de Sade (1740–1814). Possessed of a "volcanic" sex drive coupled with a taste for extreme depravity, de Sade was tossed into the Bastille in 1778 for various perverse activities. (Knifing prostitutes and pouring hot wax into their wounds and masturbating on a crucifix were just a few of the "excesses" he was accused of.) During his many years in prison, he passed the time dreaming up the most violently pornographic fantasies imaginable and turning them into books like *Justine, Philosophy of the Boudoir,* and *The 120 Days of Sodom.*

Anyone who has seen the movie *Quills* might get the impression that de Sade was a champion of sexual and artistic liberation, unjustly persecuted by a repressive, hypocritical regime threatened by his lust for life. In fact, he was a fantastically depraved aristocrat with a nihilistic contempt for everything that ordinary people value as decent, moral, and virtuous. To say that his notorious work, *The 120 Days of Sodom,* is a catalogue of every conceivable perversion is not quite accurate, since the activities it describes are so sheerly monstrous as to go well beyond what most of us are capable of conceiving.

> Formerly he loved to fuck very youthful mouths and asses; his later improvement consists in snatching out the heart of a living girl, widening the space that organ occupied, fucking the warm hole, replacing the heart in that pool of blood and come, sewing up the wound, and leaving the girl to her fate, without help of any kind.
>
> —from *The 120 Days of Sodom*

Science Looks at Sadism

The first psychiatrist to look closely at the more extreme forms of sadistic behavior was the eminent German physician Richard von Krafft-Ebing. Besides coining the term "masochism" (named after the Austrian writer Leopold von Sacher-Masoch, whose famous novel, *Venus in Furs,* deals with a man who craves humiliation), Krafft-Ebing made a major contribution to the literature of morbid psychology with his classic book, *Psychopathia Sexualis*—a massive compendium of every known perversion, illustrated with hundreds of detailed case histories. At the time of its initial publication in 1886, the book was considered so shocking that its author was nearly expelled from the prestigious British Medico-Psychological Association. Even today, it makes for deeply disturbing reading. Still, it is a significant work, one that clearly demonstrates there's nothing new about serial murder.

Of course, Krafft-Ebing doesn't use the term "serial murder," which wouldn't enter the language for another hundred years. The term he uses is the German word *lustmord* or "lust-murder." The essence of this crime is extreme sadistic violence against the victim. The lust-murderer doesn't just kill his victims. His ultimate pleasure comes from savaging their bodies: disemboweling them, cutting out their genitals, etc. For such blood-crazed sadists, violence is a substitute for sex. In a later edition of his book Krafft-Ebing cites Jack the Ripper as a classic example, noting that the killer did "not seem to have had sexual intercourse with his victims, but very likely the murderous act and subsequent mutilation of the corpse were equivalents for the sexual act."

Besides Jack the Ripper, Krafft-Ebing included case studies of other equally deranged, but far less famous, lust-murderers of the day. There was a man named Gruyo, who strangled six prostitutes in the course of ten years. After each murder he "tore out their intestines and kidneys through the vagina." There was an English clerk named Frederick Baker, who abducted and butchered a little girl, then went home and wrote in his diary: "Killed today a young girl; it was fine and hot." There was a young Frenchman named Leger who, while wandering through a forest, "caught a girl twelve years old, violated her, mutilated her genitals, tore out her heart, ate of it, drank the blood, and buried the remains." There was a Hungarian hospital worker named Tirsch, who waylaid an old woman in the woods, strangled her, then "cut off the dead woman's breasts and genitalia with a knife, cooked them at home, and in the course of the next few days, ate them."

Verzeni the Lust-Killer

CASE STUDY

One of the cases to which Krafft-Ebing devotes particular attention was that of an Italian man, Vincenz Verzeni. Though infinitely more obscure than his contemporary Jack the Ripper, Verzeni committed a series of crimes so appalling that Krafft-Ebing regarded him as the "prototypical" lust-murderer for whom "sadistic crime was a substitute for coitus."

Verzeni was born in a small Italian village in 1849. As is often the case with serial killers, his perverted predilections began to manifest themselves in childhood, when he discovered that strangling chickens gave him "a peculiar feeling of pleasure." From the age of twelve, he killed large numbers of hens, then covered up the act by claiming that a weasel had gotten into the coop.

By the time he reached adulthood, he had begun to crave human victims. He assaulted several women, including a twenty-seven-year-old named Gala, attempting to strangle her while kneeling on her abdomen. For unexplained reasons, he was not arrested for these attacks. In the meantime, his blood mania was growing more intense by the day.

In December 1871, a fourteen-year-old servant girl named Johanna Motta set out for a neighboring village at around seven in the morning. When she failed to return by evening, her master set out to look for her. He found her naked corpse lying by a path near some fields not far from the village. The girl had been horribly mutilated. Her intestines had been torn from her body and were lying nearby. Her mouth had been stuffed with dirt. A chunk of her right calf had been ripped from her leg and was hidden under a pile of straw, along with scraps of her clothing. There were strange abrasions on her thighs.

Nine months later, early on the morning of August 28, 1871, a twenty-eight-year-old woman named Frigeni set out into the same fields. Several hours later, her naked body was found by her husband. She had been strangled with a leather thong. As with the previous victim, her abdomen had been ripped open and her intestines yanked out.

The following day, as nineteen-year-old Maria Previtali was walking through a field, she became aware that someone was following her. It was her cousin, Vincenz Verzeni. All at once, the twenty-two-year-old Verzeni sprang at the girl and began to strangle her. As he loosened his grip for an instant to see if anyone was near, the girl scrambled to her knees and begged for mercy. Verzeni relented and let her go. He was quickly arrested.

In custody, Verzeni readily confessed to his crimes. Strangling women gave "indescribable feelings" of pleasure. As soon as he wrapped his fingers around their throats, he got an erection. It didn't matter if the victims were "old, young, ugly, or beautiful." Choking them, he said, was better than masturbation.

He was also a vampire. The abrasions on young Johanna Motta's thighs were from his teeth. After strangling her, he had sucked her blood in a frenzy of "lustful pleasure." He had then torn out a piece of her calf, intending to roast it at home, though he had abandoned this plan, fearing that his mother would be suspicious if she saw him cooking a strange piece of meat.

The texture and odor of his victims' intestines were another source of pleasure. After disemboweling the women, he carried pieces of their entrails away with him, so he could smell and touch them. He possessed no normal sexual interest of any kind; it had never occurred to him to touch or even look at his victims' genitals. "To this very day, I am ignorant of how a woman is formed," he declared. He never felt the slightest pang of guilt or remorse for his crimes.

Verzeni advised the authorities that "it would be a good thing if he were kept in prison, because with freedom he could not resist his impulses." The judges agreed, and he spent the remainder of his life behind bars.

Wilhelm Stekel

Next to Krafft-Ebing, the psychiatrist who made the most detailed study of sadistic behavior was one of Freud's former colleagues, Dr. Wilhelm Stekel. Stekel's two-volume, 1929 work, *Sadism and Masochism,* contains dozens of extraordinary case histories: men and women in thrall to the most extreme, and often appalling, sexual aberrations.

> I should like most of all to kiss her breasts . . . and then tear them or bite them off . . . and then eat them. I would tear out the vagina, the uterus . . . and the rectum. I would eat all of them and with them the inner portions of the thigh which border on the sexual parts. I would then tear her open and fondle the viscera—take them out and put them back. I should like to feel their warmth. Finally, I should want to suck the blood from the side of her neck.
>
> —One of Wilhelm Stekel's patients, describing a favorite fantasy

Some of the individuals described by Stekel might well have become serial killers if they hadn't found ways to sublimate their violence—to vent their violent impulses on substitute objects. There was, for example, a man Stekel identifies only as "Mr. K. H.," who "always has a fowl with him when he goes to a brothel. This fowl he has to strangle before the eyes of the prostitute; then he throws himself upon her and performs coitus with a great orgasm. Without the bird, he is completely impotent. In this case, the fowl plays the role of the prostitute. He must strangle a living being, wring its neck."

Another patient examined by Stekel was "a fifty-three-year-old very elegant man known as the 'sofa-stabber.' He goes only to those prostitutes who know his mania and are not afraid of him. He undresses himself, murmurs all sorts of wild but completely unintelligible words, throws himself upon the sofa, and stabs it through ever so many times with a knife. Then brief coitus, after which he lies for some time as if unconscious."

However bizarre, these activities—which allowed these two men to act out their murderous impulses without actually killing a woman—seem relatively benign. Other sadists mentioned by Stekel were genuine monsters, including the notorious Fritz Haarmann—one of the most ghastly of all twentieth-century serial killers.

Fritz Haarmann, the Vampire of Hanover

CASE STUDY

Born in 1879, Haarmann was a mama's boy who liked to play with dolls and dress in girl's clothes—activities that didn't sit well with his surly, alcoholic father. Like many incipient serial killers, he began displaying bizarre behavior at an early age. One of his favorite pastimes was trussing up his sisters and terrorizing them by banging at their window and pretending to be a demon.

As he grew into adolescence he became a habitual child molester. Shortly after his eighteenth birthday, he was sent to an asylum after being diagnosed as "mentally deficient." Six months later, he managed to escape and, after a stint in

Switzerland, made his way back home. In what his biographers generally refer to as the only sexually "normal" period of his life, he seduced and impregnated a young woman and even got engaged. Before long, however, he deserted her and their unborn child and joined the military.

For a while, he did well as a soldier but eventually suffered a mental collapse and was discharged as unfit.

Back in Hanover, he launched a life of petty crimes that ran the gamut from small-time swindling to house burglary to grave-robbing. Throughout his twenties, he was in and out of jail for various offenses. He spent World War I behind bars.

Released in 1918, he returned to his native city and joined a postwar smuggling ring that trafficked, among other things, in old clothes and black-market beef. He also served as a police stool pigeon—a sideline that afforded him protection for his illicit activities. In 1919, however, after being caught in bed with a young boy, he was shipped back to prison.

It was after his release nine months later that Haarmann embarked on his career of unparalleled depravity. Living in Hanover's seedy Old Quarter with a young lover named Hans Grans, he set about preying on the young male refugees pouring into the city. Picking up one of these penniless boys at the railway station, he would invite him back home, feed him a meal, then demand sexual favors in return. As Haarmann approached his climax, he would suddenly clamp his teeth around the boy's throat and tear at the flesh, reaching his orgasm as he chewed through the Adam's apple. He would later describe his method of disposal to the police:

> I'd make two cuts in the abdomen and put the intestines in a bucket, then soak up the blood and crush the bones until the shoulders broke. Now I could get the heart, lungs, and kidneys and chop them up and put them in my bucket. I'd take the flesh off the bones and put it in my waxcloth bag. It would take me five or six trips to take everything and throw it down the toilet or into the river.

When human remains began washing up on the riverbank in the spring of 1924, it became clear that a monster was on the loose in the city. Haarmann, like every other known sex offender, fell under suspicion. He was arrested when the mother of one missing boy noticed another young man wearing her son's jacket. The young man turned out to be the son of Haarmann's landlady. He had been given the garment by Haarmann.

Haarmann was charged with twenty-seven counts of murder, though he intimated that the total was closer to forty. Hans Grans—whose role in the atrocities is still a matter of dispute—was charged with "instigating" two murders. After a two-week trial in December 1924, Haarmann was found guilty of twenty-four murders and sentenced to death. When the verdict was announced, he proclaimed: "I want to be executed in the marketplace. On the tombstone must be put this inscription: 'Here Lies Mass-Murderer Haarmann.' "

While awaiting execution, he produced a written confession in which he described, with undisguised relish, the sensual pleasure he had derived from his atrocities. His request for a public execution was ignored. He was decapitated behind the walls of the Hanover Prison in April 1925, at the age of forty-six.

de River and Reinhardt

Two psychiatrists with close ties to law enforcement published important studies of sadistic crime in the post–World War II era. In 1949, Dr. J. Paul de River, head of the Sex Offense Bureau for the LAPD, came out with the first edition of his book, *The Sexual Criminal* (a work recommended only for those with a high tolerance for stomach-churning gore, since de River chose to illustrate it with photographs of hideously mangled victims). And in 1957, James Melvin Reinhardt, a criminology professor at the University of Nebraska, published *Sex Perversions and Sex Crimes,* which contained an important chapter on lust-murder—or, as Reinhardt called it, "mutilation madness."

Among the cases cited by Reinhardt was that of a seventeen-year-old boy who, in 1947, lured an eight-year-old boy into a barn, then "seized the boy around the throat from behind, dragged him across the barn floor, took a beer can opener from his coat pocket, stripped off the unconscious child's pants, threw the shirt over the child's face, and with the beer can opener tore open the rectum and slashed the testicles of the victim. He then sat down beside this small mutilated body and engaged in an act of onanism."

> I likes to see blood. Then I feel great—I feel like I could tear up anything. I once was in a place where there was a shooting and there was blood all over the place. I wanted to go and wet my shoes and walk in the blood. I likes blood.
>
> —Sadistic lust-murderer quoted by Dr. J. Paul de River

One sobering lesson taught by these works is that—though a relative rarity in regard to other kinds of crime—sadistic lust-murder is more common than most people suppose. Fortunately, the vast majority of deviants who commit such outrages are caught after their first murder and so never have a chance to turn into serial killers.

Those who *do* manage to get away with their crime are almost certain to repeat it, since the very essence of this perversion is—as Reinhardt puts it—"uncontrollable lust urges to mutilate and kill."

Disciples of De Sade

Some notorious serial killers are known to have been fans of the Marquis de Sade. Ian Brady, for example—the male half of the infamous British couple known as the "Moors Murderers"—praised de Sade as a "good writer" and endorsed the Sadean belief that murder is "necessary, never criminal."

Ted Bundy was also familiar with de Sade's fiction. During a jailhouse interview conducted shortly before his execution, Bundy—speaking of himself in the third person—referred to de Sade when describing his own malevolent desire to dominate and possess his victims:

> "Uh, with respect to the idea of possession. I think that with this kind of person, control and mastery is what we see here. . . . In other words, I think we could read about the Marquis de Sade and other people who take their victims in one form or another out of a desire to possess and would torture, humiliate, and terrorize them elaborately—something that would give them a more powerful impression that they were in control."

Of course, to say that people like Brady and Bundy enjoyed de Sade's writings does not mean that they were directly inspired by him, or that they wouldn't have committed their atrocities if they hadn't read him. It is probably more accurate to say that, in the case of these particular psychopaths, de Sade provided them with a philosophical justification for their crimes. Serial killers, after all, don't need books to give them hideous ideas. Jeffrey Dahmer, for example, is said to have perpetrated an atrocity very much like the one described in the above quotation from *120 Days of Sodom.* Turned on by the sight of human viscera, Dahmer reportedly slit open the bellies of his victims and—there's no other way to put this—fucked the entrails. And there's no indication that Dahmer ever read de Sade. He dreamed it up all by himself.

CASE STUDY

Robert Berdella, Torture-Slayer

His business card alone should have been a giveaway. Underneath the name of his shop—"Bob's Bizarre Bazaar"—was a quotation that could only make sense to a madman:

> "I rise from death. I kill death, and death kills me—although I carry poison in my head. The antidote can be found in my tail, which I bite with rage."

Still—in a way that so often seems true with serial killers—none of his neighbors or acquaintances in Kansas City, Missouri, thought there was anything particularly wrong with Robert Berdella. He seemed friendly enough, a quiet man who belonged to the neighborhood "Crime Watch" and had turned his modest home—so he claimed—into a kind of halfway house for troubled young men.

His store, located in the section of town known as "Olde Westport," was one of those supposedly hip "head shops" that—along with pot paraphernalia like bongs and roach clips—specialize in macabre curios beloved by adolescent "Goths": plaster-of-Paris skulls, statuettes of capering skeletons, and the like.

These pseudo-Satanic gewgaws paled beside the actual horrors in Berdella's home. But until the spring of 1988, only a few people had discovered that terrifying fact. And they didn't live to reveal it.

The beginning of the end for Berdella occurred on the morning of Saturday, April 2, 1988, when one of his neighbors heard a frantic pounding on the front door. Opening it, he was startled to discover a terrified young man, naked except for a dog collar around his neck. There was something wrong with his eyes. The young man, whose name was Chris Bryson, explained that he had just escaped from the house next door, where he'd been held captive for several days.

The neighbor summoned the police. Bryson told them that he'd been picked up a few days earlier by Berdella, who took him home, led him upstairs, then knocked him unconscious with a blow to the back of the head. When Bryson awoke, he was naked and tied spread-eagle to a bed.

Over the next four days, he was subjected to a horrendous range of torture—sodomized with various objects, beaten with an iron club, shocked with electrodes attached to his testicles. His throat had been injected with animal tranquilizer, his eyes jabbed with chemical-soaked Q-Tips. Eventually, he had managed to escape when Berdella went off on an errand. Getting hold of a matchbook left on a bed table, he had burned the rope binding one wrist, freed himself from his other restraints, and jumped from the second-floor window.

Berdella was immediately arrested on charges of forced sodomy, felonious restraint, and first-degree assault. A search warrant was obtained. Amid the squalid clutter of his house, investigators turned up a weird assortment of artifacts: skulls, devil masks, a hooded red robe. There were also books on voodoo and novels by the Marquis de Sade. However disturbing, none of these items proved anything more than Berdella's interest in the bizarre and occult.

The photographs were a different story.

Police found them in a box: about two hundred Polaroids of naked young men being raped and tortured. There was also a diary, written in crude shorthand, meticulously detailing the type of abuse each victim had been subjected to.

The police still hadn't found any hard evidence of murder, however. There were two human skulls in Berdella's bedroom, but it wasn't immediately clear if they were the real thing or the kind of replicas Berdella sold in his store. In fairly short order, however, a forensic anthropologist determined that one of the skulls was authentic. It belonged to a young man who had evidently died sometime within the previous two years. Another skull—this one with hair and some tissue still intact—was unearthed in Berdella's backyard. Through dental charts, both skulls were eventually identified. Berdella was charged with first-degree murder.

At his arraignment, he shocked the court by pleading guilty—a tactic that spared him the death sentence. Eventually, he offered a full confession. Between 1984 and 1987, he had tortured and killed six young captives. Like other sadists, he derived his highest pleasure from asserting complete control over his bound and terrified victims. He injected them with animal tranquilizer to turn them into "playtoys." When they died, he dismembered their bodies in his bathtub, stuffed them into trash bags, and left them at the curb for the garbagemen.

In spite of his atrocities, Berdella—displaying the utter lack of moral awareness that is typical of psychopaths—saw himself as a basically decent human being. To prove the point, he set up a trust fund for the families of his victims. On October 8, 1992—just four years after the start of his life sentence—he died of a heart attack at the age of 43.

DOMINANCE

Sadistic pleasure isn't just about the infliction of pain. It also has to do with the assertion of power—the lust to dominate, to reduce a victim to a state of total submission.

The psychological reasons for this behavior aren't hard to understand. According to experts, the vast majority of serial killers were subjected to extreme forms of psychological abuse as children. They were made to feel utterly helpless and humiliated. As a result, they grew up with a malevolent need to inflict the same condition on others. The only way to overcome their deep-rooted feelings of impotence is by asserting total control over another human being.

> It was the power and domination and seeing the fear. That was more exciting than actually causing the harm.
>
> —Serial killer John Joubert, explaining why he slaughtered three boys

In its most extreme form, the serial killer's need for control involves turning another human being into a completely passive object, a kind of doll that belongs entirely to him. Incapable of normal human relationships with willing partners, he seeks gratification with inanimate bodies that offer no resistance.

Edmund Kemper—the "Coed Killer," who committed a range of atrocities on the corpses of his female victims—was quite explicit about this aspect of his crimes. "I couldn't follow through with the male end of the responsibility," he told police, "so my fantasies became . . . if I killed them, you know, they couldn't reject me as a man. It was more or less making a doll out of a human being and carrying out my fantasies with a doll, a living human doll."

Edward Gein—the notorious Wisconsin ghoul of the 1950s, whose crimes served as the inspiration for *Psycho, The Texas Chainsaw Massacre,* and *The Silence of the Lambs*—sought to slake his terrible loneliness by digging up the corpses of middle-aged women and taking them home to his desolate farmhouse. Interviewed by psychiatrists after his arrest, he spoke of the bodies "as being like dolls" and described the "comfort he received from their presence."

Jeffrey Dahmer—whose greatest urge was to have a person who was "totally compliant, willing to do whatever I wanted"—made an abortive attempt at Gein's necrophiliac method. After reading the obituary of an eighteen-year-old, he went to the funeral home to view the young man's body (which he found so attractive that he immediately hurried to the bathroom and masturbated). After the funeral, Dahmer sneaked into the cemetery late one night with a shovel and wheelbarrow, intending to take the corpse back home, but gave up because the ground was frozen.

Later, Dahmer tried to satisfy his need for a completely inert sex object with a mannequin, but that proved unsatisfactory. Ultimately, he devised the staggeringly sick plan of trying to turn a living victim into a "sex zombie." After bringing a young man back to his apartment, Dahmer would slip him a mickey, then make a hole in the victim's skull with a power drill and inject muriatic acid into his brain with a turkey baster. Needless to say, these hideous experiments only ended up killing the victims. Robert Berdella tried something similar, injecting his victims with animal tranquilizers in an effort to turn them into "sex toys."

Dennis Nilsen—the so-called British Jeffrey Dahmer—was similarly driven by a monstrous need to dominate. Nilsen once told an interviewer that the most exciting part of his fifteen murders "was the moment when he lifted the dead victim and saw the dangling limbs, which represented his power and control over the victim, and the victim's passivity."

Recommended Reading

J. Paul de River, *The Sexual Criminal* (1949)
Richard von Krafft-Ebing, *Psychopathia Sexualis* (1886)
James Melvin Reinhardt, *Sex Perversions and Sex Crimes* (1967)
Robert K. Ressler, Ann W. Burgess, and John E. Douglas, *Sexual Homicide* (1988)
Wilhelm Stekel, *Sadism and Masochism* (1929)

FETISHISM

In the strict, psychoanalytic sense of the term, fetishism is a disorder in which a person, usually a man, can only be turned on by an object associated with the opposite sex, generally either an intimate article of clothing—shoes, bras, panties, nylon stockings, etc.—or a specific body part, most commonly the feet. The fetishist is so fixated on the object itself that the actual sex partner becomes secondary. That is to say, a male shoe fetishist will be more aroused by his girlfriend's spike-heeled footwear than by the woman herself. According to the American Psychiatric Association, "The person with fetishism frequently masturbates while holding, rubbing, or smelling the fetish object, or may ask his sexual partner to wear the object during their sexual encounters."

There's nothing inherently harmful about fetishism. It is, after all, just an exaggerated form of an interest shared by most red-blooded males. (As John Douglas points out in his book *The Anatomy of Motive,* "It's safe to say that a significantly large percentage of the normal American male population is turned on by black lace panties.")

The fetishes of psychopaths, however, are often unspeakably extreme. The average fingernail fetishist, for example, might be aroused by the sight of a woman with unusually long, sharp, clawlike nails. By contrast, one of the deviants described by R. E. L. Masters in his study *Sex Crimes in History* could only get sexually aroused by eating the fingernail clippings of female corpses.

According to John Douglas, fully 72 percent of serial killers are "preoccupied with fetishism during their formative years." The fetishistic impulses of serial killers account for their tendency to take "trophies" from their murder victims—anything from wallets to underpants to body parts. These items—which the killers use to relive their crimes in fantasy, often while masturbating—are essentially fetish objects, providing them with intense, perverted pleasure.

CASE STUDY

Jerry Brudos, Fetishist from Hell

Exactly how or why Jerome Brudos became a foot fetishist is a mystery. One thing is certain, however: he began to manifest his obsession at a startlingly early age. Born in 1939, Jerry was only five when he found a pair of woman's shoes in the local dump and brought them home. When his mother found him clumping around his bedroom in the patent leather high heels, she confiscated them, tossed them into the furnace, and gave little Jerry a lively beating.

The punishment did nothing to curb his footwear fixation. In first grade, he was severely reprimanded after swiping his teacher's spare pair of high heels. By his early teens, he was breaking into homes to steal women's shoes, along with various items of female underwear, which he had developed a taste for wearing beneath his street clothes.

At sixteen, Brudos—his mind full of fantasies about abducting a sex slave—went so far as to dig a tunnel in a hillside near his home, where he planned to keep his captive. The following year, he assaulted a young girl at knifepoint and tried to make her strip. Arrested, he was sent to Oregon State Hospital for psychiatric observation. Despite the hair-raising thoughts he revealed to his doctors—one recurrent fantasy, for example, involved putting women into freezers so that he could arrange their stiffened bodies into pornographic poses—he was judged sane enough to be released after only nine months.

Brudos tried the army but was discharged before long because of his bizarre and increasingly frequent delusions.

In 1961, twenty-three-year-old Brudos, making good money by then as an electrician, impregnated and married a seventeen-year-old girl. Brudos demanded that she do her housework in the nude while he photographed her. He also liked to parade around in high heels, bra, and panties. His young wife displayed a high degree of tolerance for her husband's peculiarities. Of course, she had no idea that he was also much engaged in much darker pursuits. On the night she was in the hospital giving birth to their child, Brudos broke into the home of a young woman, choked her unconscious, then raped her before fleeing with her shoes.

His escalating violence evolved into murder in 1968. In January of that year, a nineteen-year-old girl named Linda Slawson—who was going door-to-door selling encyclopedias—had the misfortune of approaching Brudos as he stood in his backyard. Inviting her into his garage-workshop, he bludgeoned her with a two-by-four, then strangled her to death. After playing with her corpse for a while—removing her clothes and dressing her up in items from his own underwear collection, as though she were an oversized Barbie doll—he carried his foot fetishism to a new and unparalleled level of monstrosity. He severed the dead woman's left foot, slipped a stolen spike-heeled shoe on it, and stored it away in his freezer. Then he tied an engine block to the corpse and sank her in the nearby Willamette River.

Eleven months later, he killed his second victim, twenty-three-year-old Jan Whitney. Offering her a lift when her car broke down, he drove her to his garage, where he strangled her to death, anally raped her corpse, then spent some time dressing up the dead body in different articles of lingerie and photographing the results. Brudos had so much fun with her that he suspended her corpse from a ceiling hook and kept it in the garage for two days before disposing of it in the river. Even then, he couldn't entirely let her go. Before getting rid of the remains, he sliced off one of her breasts, which he later made into a paperweight by treating it with epoxy.

He performed a similar mutilation on the corpse of his next victim, a nineteen-year-old girl named Karen Sprinker, whom he abducted at gunpoint the following March. After choking her to death and subjecting her to the usual postmortem violation, he amputated both her breasts. Then he stuffed the cups of one of his own bras with brown paper and put it on the mutilated body before dumping the remains in the Willamette.

His last known victim, killed just four weeks later, was twenty-two-year-old Linda Salee. After strangling and raping her in his garage, he suspended her body from the ceiling, rigged up wires to a pair of hypodermic needles, stuck them in her chest, and jolted her with electricity to see if he could make her "dance." This time, he did not slice off her breasts because he was turned off by her pink nipples. ("They should be brown," he later explained to police.)

Not long after the corpses of two of his victims were recovered from the river, Brudos was nabbed when police got a tip from some coeds he had been pestering. Searching his garage, they found overwhelming evidence of his guilt, including photographs of his victims. Charged with three counts of first-degree murder at his trial in July 1969, he pleaded guilty and drew three consecutive life sentences.

TRANSVESTISM

In horror films, guys who like to wear female clothing tend to be psychotic, woman-hating slashers, a tradition that began with *Psycho*'s Norman Bates, was carried on by Michael Caine's razor-wielding psycho in Brian De Palma's *Dressed to Kill,* and continued with the mincing "Buffalo Bill" in *The Silence of the Lambs.* Even Leatherface added a touch of transvestism by putting on a female wig in *The Texas Chainsaw Massacre.*

Real life, of course, is a different matter. For the most part, guys who enjoy strutting their stuff in high heels and Angora sweaters are about as dangerous as Nathan Lane's character in *The Birdcage.* Still, there have been several instances of serial killers who have engaged in cross-dressing.

During their boyhoods, both Charles Manson and Henry Lee Lucas were forced to wear girl's clothing—Manson by a sadistic uncle who sent him off to school in a dress, Lucas by the insanely vicious mother he would ultimately murder. The same was true of the so-called Barfly Strangler, Carroll Cole, who—according to crimewriter Michael Newton—"was forced to dress in frilly skirts and petticoats for the amusement of his mother's friends, dispensing tea and coffee at sadistic 'parties' where the women gathered to make sport of 'mama's little girl.' "

These cases, however, have less to do with transvestism than with child abuse. They are examples of the kind of extreme humiliation to which future psychopaths are often subjected and which fills them with a lifelong hatred of themselves and the world.

The legendary Wisconsin psycho, Ed Gein (the real-life model for Norman Bates, Leatherface, and Buffalo Bill) was less a transvestite than a frustrated transsexual, whose desire to turn himself into a woman led him to create a grotesque female skin suit in which he would sashay around the house. Gein, however, was not a sadistic lust-killer. Though he executed two women, he acquired his raw material largely from the graveyard, exhuming and flaying the corpses of elderly women who resembled his mother.

CASE STUDY

Hadden Clark, Cross-Dressing Cannibal Killer

Though regarded as the prototype of the modern-day slasher, the necrophiliac Ed Gein doesn't quite match the image of the deranged, cross-dressing psycho-killer so familiar from "splatter" movies. There is, however, one serial killer who really does seem to have stepped from the gender-bending nightmare of *Psycho* or *Dressed to Kill.* His name was Hadden Clark.

Unlike many serial killers who come from sordid, hardscrabble backgrounds, Clark was a child of money and privilege. His mother traced her ancestry back to the *Mayflower* Pilgrims, while his father was a chemical engineer with several advanced degrees who, among his other accomplishments, helped invent Saran Wrap. Despite their pedigree and wealth, the elder Clarks were bitterly mismated alcoholics. Constantly at each other's throats, they created a pernicious and profoundly unstable atmosphere at home, as evidenced by the fate of three of their four children. Their youngest daughter, Alison, would run away in her teens and permanently renounce her parents. Their oldest son, Bradfield, would end up in prison after murdering a girlfriend, roasting chunks of her breasts on a barbecue grill, and eating them.

And then there was Hadden.

Derided by his father as a "retard" and treated as a female plaything by his mother—who liked to put him in girl's clothing and address him as "Kristen"—Hadden, perhaps unsurprisingly, grew up to be a severely disturbed youth. He enjoyed running down other children with his bike and leaving the decapitated heads of house pets on the doorsteps of schoolmates who annoyed him.

Unable to succeed academically, he eventually decided to become a chef. Despite his malicious temperament (he retaliated for real or imagined slights, for example, by pissing into the mashed potatoes of people he disliked), he managed to graduate from the prestigious Culinary Institute of America. With degree in hand, he landed a job in the tony Cape Cod town of Provincetown—a community with a high tolerance for alternative lifestyles. Even there, however, Clark's behavior—guzzling beef's blood in the kitchen, for example—was regarded as extreme. He was constantly moving from job to job.

In the meantime—so he claimed—he was using the cutlery skills he had acquired as a chef for far more sinister purposes than cooking. According to his later admissions, he murdered a number of victims while residing on Cape Cod, burying one naked woman in the sand dunes of Wellfleet after cutting off her hands.

Having worn out his welcome among the restaurateurs of Cape Cod, Clark drifted from job to job during the next few years, working in the kitchen of a cruise ship, at banquet halls on Long Island, and in Lake Placid, New York, at the 1980 Olympics. He enlisted as a cook in the navy. His shipmates, however, did not take well either to his increasingly erratic behavior or his fondness for frilly panties, and Clark was subjected to frequent savage beatings at their hands.

Diagnosed as a paranoid schizophrenic and given a medical discharge, Clark went to live with his older brother, Geoffrey, in Silver Spring, Maryland. Less than a year later, he committed his first confirmed atrocity. It happened on the sweltering afternoon of May 31, 1986. Clark—who had been kicked out of the house after masturbating in front of his young niece, Eliza—was packing up his belongings when six-year-old Michelle Dorr, dressed in a pink, ruffled swimsuit, drifted over from her backyard wading pool, looking for Eliza. Luring her into the house, Clark butchered the girl with one of his chef's knives, made an abortive attempt to have sex with her corpse, then stuffed the body into a duffel bag, drove it to a nearby park, and buried it in a shallow grave after devouring some of her flesh.

While police focused their attention on the wrong suspect—Michelle's distraught father—Clark embarked on a rootless existence, living in his pickup truck and working at odd jobs. His mental condition continued to deteriorate at an alarming pace. By 1989, he had been arrested on various charges: assaulting his mother, shoplifting women's apparel, destroying a rented home with black dye, rotting fish heads, and dead cats. He had also begun conversing with squirrels and birds.

In 1992, while working as a gardener in Bethesda, Maryland, for a woman named Penny Houghteling, he committed his final atrocity. Around midnight on October 17, he sneaked into the bedroom of Mrs. Houghteling's daughter, Laura, a recent college graduate. He was got up in full female regalia—wig, purse, blouse, and slacks—and carried a .22-caliber rifle. Nudging the girl from her sleep, he demanded to know what she was doing in his bed. He then forced the terrified young woman to admit that *he* was Laura.

It was a scene straight out of a horror movie: a beautiful young woman being awakened by a deranged transvestite who claims her identity and accuses her of being an impostor.

After forcing her at gunpoint to undress and bathe, Clark asphyxiated her by covering her face with duct tape. He then removed her earlobes with a scissor, smuggled her body, along with the bloody bed linens, into his pickup, drove her to a deserted spot, and buried her in a shallow grave.

Quickly identified as a suspect, Clark was arrested when his fingerprint was found on one of the bloody pillowcases he had saved as a souvenir. In 1993, he pleaded guilty to second-degree murder and was given a thirty-year sentence. While in prison, he began bragging about the Michelle Dorr murder and eventually led police to her remains. Tried again, he received another thirty years.

The world hadn't heard the last of Clark. Following his second conviction, he became convinced that a long-haired fellow inmate was actually Jesus Christ and confessed to this supposed Messiah that he had killed as many as a dozen women throughout the Northeast during the 1970s and 1980s. In early 2000, Clark agreed to show investigators the murder sites on the condition that they purchase a female wardrobe for him at Kmart. Decked out in his new wig, panties, bra, and skirt, he then led detectives to various spots in Connecticut, New Jersey, Pennsylvania, and Massachusetts. On a piece of Cape Cod property that had once belonged to Clark's grandfather, police dug up a bucket containing two hundred pieces of jewelry, including items belonging to Laura Houghteling. Clark claimed that these were articles he had taken as trophies from his many victims. Beyond the remains of the Houghteling girl and little Michelle Dorr, no additional bodies have been found to date.

VAMPIRISM

In folklore, myth, and Gothic literature, the word "vampire" conjures up images of the evil "undead"—supernatural, seductively creepy beings who spend their days snoozing in coffins, emerge after dark to batten on the blood of the living, and are highly susceptible to garlic, crucifixes, and sharp wooden stakes. Happily, such creatures do not exist outside of Bram Stoker's *Dracula,* the novels of Anne Rice, and about a zillion grade-Z horror movies, many of them starring Christopher Lee.

In the realm of abnormal psychology, however, "vampirism" refers to a different and all-too-real phenomenon: a perversion (or paraphilia) in which people derive intense sexual pleasure from the drinking of human blood. It should be stressed that—as repellent as such a practice might seem to most people—not all, or even most, real-life "vampires" are criminal psychopaths. Indeed, nowadays—when even the most *outré* sexual activities have their advocates—there are socially responsible Web sites like *Sanguinarius.org* which advise vampirically inclined individuals on medical precautions ("Make sure your victims get blood tests done!"), legal matters ("Have them sign some form of consent!"), and etiquette ("When feeding, it is impolite to lap blood like an animal!").

Needless to say, serial killers with a yen for drinking blood do not observe such niceties. They are not politically correct paraphiliacs who ask permission from their victims and take care not to slurp while they feed. Rather, they are blood-crazed maniacs who resort to the most hideous acts to satisfy their monstrous cravings.

A classic example of a vampiric lust-killer is Vincenz Verzeni, one of the many cases included in Krafft-Ebing's classic study of extreme aberration, *Psychopathia Sexualis.* In 1871, in a frenzy of blood mania, this Italian madman savaged two young women, ripping open their bodies, chewing on their flesh, and gorging on their blood.

Verzeni wasn't the only vampiric lust-killer at large in late-nineteenth-century Europe. His countryman, Eusebius Pieydagnelle, got so turned on whenever he passed a butcher's shop and caught a whiff of fresh blood that he was impelled to go out and commit some butchery of his own, slaughtering six women in 1878. Nineteen years later, the "French Ripper," Joseph Vacher, admitted that blood-drinking was one of the many atrocities he committed on the bodies of nearly a dozen male and female victims.

Some of the most notorious serial killers of the twentieth century engaged in vampirism, along with other abominations. During his uniquely depraved childhood, for example, Peter Kürten managed to perform several deviant acts at once—sadism, vampirism, bestiality, and necrophilia—by cutting off the heads of swans and drinking their spurting blood while sexually violating their dying bodies. In adulthood, the so-called "Monster of Düsseldorf" gratified his unspeakable lusts on human victims, mutilating—and often drinking the blood of—more than two dozen men, women, and children. Equally horrific was Kürten's Weimar-era contemporary, Fritz Haarmann, known as the "Vampire of Hanover" for his habit of of chewing through the throats of his young male victims.

The extravagantly perverted Albert Fish—a big fan of Haarmann's, who saved newspaper stories about the German lust-killer the way teenage girls collect clippings of their favorite pop stars—sampled the blood of at least one of his juvenile victims. Fish, however, did not find the reeking fluid especially palatable. The same was true of another all-American cannibal, Jeffrey Dahmer, who told FBI profiler Robert Ressler that he had drunk some human blood out of "curiosity" but "hadn't liked the experience nor found it stimulating."

By contrast, the Russian "Mad Beast," Andrei Chikatilo—a twentieth-century monster every bit as appalling as Kürten or Fish or Dahmer—eagerly consumed the blood of his many victims, along with other parts of their anatomy, including their genitals.

A recent case of alleged vampiric serial murder involved a young African-American named Marc Sappington. Raised in a slum district of Kansas City, Kansas, by a hardworking, churchgoing mother, Sappington was, by all accounts, a model child: bright, fun-loving, and well behaved. During his adolescence, however, his personality underwent a radical change when, succumbing to the temptations of the streets, he got hooked on angel dust and "danks"—cigarettes soaked in embalming fluid. In March 2001, the onetime choirboy gunned down a young man during a robbery for no other reason than sheer malice.

His vampiric spree began a month later. By then—possibly because of the effects of the drugs—he had begun hearing voices commanding him to taste human flesh and blood. On April 7, he lured a longtime friend, twenty-five-year-old Terry Green, into the basement of his home, savaged Green with a hunting knife, then knelt by the mangled carcass and lapped up some blood from the cement floor.

Just three days later, he committed a nearly identical atrocity, luring another old friend—twenty-two-year-old Michael Weaver—into an alley, stabbing him to death, then drinking his blood. The sound of approaching footsteps, however, caused Sappington to cut short his vampiric feast and flee.

On his way home from the murder, Sappington—his bloodlust unsated—spotted a neighborhood teenager named Alton "Freddie" Brown. Inviting the boy into his basement, Sappington quickly dispatched him with a shotgun, then leisurely drank some blood and cannibalized the body. He then stuffed the remains in a trash bag and went out for a postprandial stroll.

When his mother returned a few hours later, she quickly discovered the scene of carnage in her basement and notified the police. Sappington was arrested a short time later. In custody, he maintained a stubborn silence before spilling out his grisly tale—a confession that earned him his media nickname, the "Kansas City Vampire."

Richard Chase, the Vampire of Sacramento

CASE STUDY

Dr. John Seward runs an "immense lunatic asylum" in Bram Stoker's 1897 Gothic masterpiece *Dracula.* Under his care is a patient named Renfield who has caught Seward's attention as a new kind of lunatic:

> My homicidal maniac is of a peculiar kind. I shall have to invent a new classification for him, and call him a *zoophagous* (life-eating) maniac; what he desires is to absorb as many lives as he can, and he has laid himself out to achieve it in a cumulative way. He gave many flies to one spider and many spiders to one bird, and then wanted a cat to eat the many birds. What would have been his later steps?

Bloodlust powers Renfield's madness—a bloodlust spawned and controlled by his Transylvanian master, Count Dracula. It is a famous fiction. It is the novel that gave us the most popular image of the vampire.

In late-twentieth-century America that fiction turned into nightmarish fact.

His name was Richard Chase. Early in his life, he tortured and killed small animals—birds, rabbits, cats, dogs—and drank their blood. He also gorged upon the intestines of his animal victims. He believed their blood would prevent his own from turning to dust. Sometimes, he injected the blood of rabbits into his veins. At other times, he used kitchen blenders to mix together the blood and entrails of animals for hideous gore shakes.

He spent two prolonged stays in mental institutions, where he puzzled fellow patients and health-care professionals with his obsession with blood. They called him "Dracula" but thought he was as harmless as Renfield, that his obsession was limited to animal blood.

They were horribly wrong.

By 1977, he progressed from rabbits to larger mammals. That year, police spotted him stumbling naked across the Nevada desert covered in blood. In his car, they found a bucket of coagulated blood and two rifles that had been used to stir the horrid concoction. Tests revealed the blood to be that of cows, and Chase was released. But this blood collecting soon turned even more monstrous.

Chase's first human victim was a middle-aged man whom he shot dead on the street for no apparent reason. Then he began breaking into houses. In late January 1978, he barged into a Sacramento home and shot a twenty-two-year-old woman to death. He disemboweled her body and covered himself in her blood. He used an empty yogurt cup to collect and drink her blood. His victim had been three months pregnant.

Four days later, he broke into the home of thirty-eight-year-old Evelyn Miroth and shot her to death along with her six-year-old son and a visiting male friend.

He eviscerated Miroth, mutilated her face, and sodomized her. He also collected her blood and drank it. Chase committed a final outrage upon the dead woman by stuffing her mouth with animal feces. But the worst atrocity was still to come.

Miroth had been babysitting her twenty-two-month-old nephew. When the crime scene was discovered the baby was missing. The vampire had taken the little boy back to his lair. The decapitated child was eventually found in a box dumped in a vacant lot.

A classic "disorganized killer," Chase had left footprints and fingerprints all over the crime scenes and had used a car of one of the victims. He was soon apprehended. Inside his apartment, police discovered a vampire's inner sanctum. Blood covered everything, including the blenders Chase used to mix his horrid zoophagous shakes.

Remarkably, given how wildly deranged he clearly was, Chase was declared sane. He was quickly convicted of six murders and condemned to die in California's gas chamber. FBI profilers interviewed him in prison and learned about several of his obsessions: his blood was turning to powder because he found a gooey substance underneath his soap dish; Nazis with ties to UFOs were following him; and somebody was trying to poison him in jail. In the end, he escaped execution. In 1980, he died of of an overdose of antidepressants that he had been hoarding in his death row cell.

Recommended Reading

Sondra London, *True Vampires* (2003)

CANNIBALISM

Cannibalistic urges are deeply rooted in our instinctual makeup. Indeed, they appear to be part of our evolutionary heritage.

Recent scientific research makes it very clear that our closest primate relatives routinely engage in cannibalism. While studying rain forest apes in the wild, for example, Harvard anthropologist Richard Wrangham observed two adult males—whom he nicknamed "Figan" and "Humphrey"—capture a pair of juvenile monkeys: "With small screams of excitement, Figan raced to where Humphrey sat and, clutching his own prey, seized hold of Humphrey's also. He did not try to wrest it away from the older male, but bit open the head and consumed it, together with the brain, while Humphrey disemboweled the infant and ate the viscera. After this, Figan ate the brain of his own monkey, and Humphrey moved off with the headless body of his!"

That our earliest ancestors dined on the bodies of their own kind has been firmly established by archaeologists, who have found ample evidence of cannibalistic activity in the cave dwellings of Stone Age people: human bones split to provide access to the savory marrow, skulls cracked open at their

(from "Very Interesting News," 1911 broadsheet with white-line illustration by Posada, Amon Carter Museum, 1978.123.)

Cannibal killer by José Guadalupe Posada

bases for easy removal of the brains. Cannibalism has been practiced by aboriginal peoples all over the globe, from Africa to New Zealand. Recent studies have shown that even the Chaco Anasazi of what is now the American Southwest—a tribe long thought to be peace-loving tenders of the land—engaged in systematic cannibalism.

According to current theories, the Anasazi used cannibalism as an instrument of terror, but people have consumed human flesh for all kinds of reasons, from the dietary to the ceremonial. Some aborigines ate the bodies of their dead relatives out of love and respect ("When you die, wouldn't you rather be eaten by your kinsmen than by maggots?" one Mayoruna cannibal asked a European visitor). Others ate the flesh of their defeated enemies as a sign of contempt. The devouring of sacrificial victims was a central feature of Aztec religion. Fijians, on the other hand, practiced cannibalism simply because they liked the taste, preferring the flavor of "long pig" (as they called human flesh) to that of actual pork.

In the Judeo-Christian tradition, however, cannibalism is looked upon as an ultimate taboo, which may be broken only under the most dire imaginable circumstances—by the dying sailors on a drifting lifeboat, say, who are forced to draw straws to see which of them will be sacrificed to supply sustenance for the rest. Even then, it is regarded with such abhorrence that some people would rather starve than eat human flesh. This was the case, for example, with several survivors of the 1972 plane crash that stranded a party of Uruguyans in the high Andes. Though they were all devout Catholics who routinely partook of the body and blood of Christ during Communion, some of them were so repelled by the thought of cannibalism that they chose to die instead.

Because most civilized people regard cannibalism with such horrified fascination, it is often regarded as the worst possible atrocity a serial killer can commit. It's for this very reason that—when Thomas Harris set out to create the ultimate psychopathic monster in *Red Dragon* and its sequels—he came up with "Hannibal the Cannibal," a man-eating gourmet who wouldn't dream of taking a transatlantic flight without bringing along a snack of human brains.

In point of fact, however, cannibalism is a relative rarity among serial killers. Those who practice it are motivated as much by deviant sexual impulses as anything else. Unlike Hannibal Lecter—whose fondness for human flesh seems to be a warped feature of his epicurean lifestyle—the most notorious cannibal killers have derived intense erotic pleasure from eating their victims.

A prime example is the pedophiliac lust-killer Albert Fish. Having tried every perversion in the book (plus a few that no one had ever heard of before), the wildly deranged old man developed a growing obsession with tasting the flesh of a child. Luring a twelve-year-old girl away from her parents and bringing her to an abandoned house in Westchester County, he strangled and beheaded her, then sliced about four pounds of flesh from her breast, buttocks, and abdomen. Wrapping the "meat" (as he referred to it) in a piece of old newspaper, he carried it back to his Manhattan boardinghouse, where he cut it into small pieces and made it into a stew with carrots, onions, and strips of bacon. Over the course of nine days, he consumed the stew a little at a time, so aroused by the taste of the child's flesh—which he likened to veal—that he masturbated constantly.

> First I stripped her naked. How she did kick—bite and scratch. I choked her to death, then cut her in small pieces so I could take my meat to my rooms, Cook and eat it. How sweet and tender her little ass was roasted in the oven. It took me 9 days to eat her entire body.
>
> —Albert Fish

The "Milwaukee Cannibal" Jeffrey Dahmer was also turned on by the act of feasting on the flesh of his victims. During his final interview, Dahmer told pioneering profiler Robert Ressler that eating his victims "made it feel like they were more part of me," a sensation he found "sexually stimulating."

Though reluctant to divulge all the grisly details of his atrocities, Dahmer admitted to having eaten the flesh of at least three of his victims, turning some of it into human hamburger patties and experimenting with various seasonings to enhance the flavor. He froze a heart for future consumption, devoured part of another victim's thigh, and fried and ate the pumped-up biceps of twenty-four-year-old Ernest Miller because it looked so big and juicy.

Every bit as monstrous as Dahmer and Fish—and arguably even more so—was the Russian psycho Andrei Chikatilo. Aptly dubbed the "Mad Beast," Chikatilo was the kind of killer that the FBI now labels "disorganized." People in the Middle Ages would have called him a werewolf: a blood-crazed monster who, in a frenzy of sadistic lust, committed the most unimaginable atrocities on his victims, ripping them open with his bare hands, wallowing in their blood, devouring their tongues, breasts, and sex organs.

Germany has produced an unusually large number of twentieth-century man-eaters. During the social chaos of the post–World War I era, the homosexual lust-murderer Fritz Haarmann slaughtered as many as fifty young men, battened on their flesh, then sold the leftovers as black market beef. His abhorrent countryman Georg Grossmann also trafficked in human meat, turning his fellow Berliners into unwitting cannibals by selling them the flesh of butchered prostitutes, which he passed off as pork. Yet another postwar German cannibal was Karl Denke, an innkeeper who killed and consumed at least thirty of his lodgers.

More recently, Germany was transfixed by the first recorded case of Internet-era cannibalism. In the spring of 2001, a forty-one-year-old software technician identified in news reports as "Armin M." placed the following notice on the Web: "Wanted: Well-built man for slaughter."

Though arguably the least enticing come-on in the history of advertising, this classified ad actually worked. A forty-three-year-old microchip designer, identified only as "Bernd Jürgen B.," showed up at M.'s front door.

What happened next staggers belief. As the *New York Times* reported on December 18, 2002: "M. removed the victim's genitals. The two men then ate them. Later, M. stabbed B. to death as a video camera recorded the event. He carved up the victim and stored parts in a freezer for occasional consumption, burying other parts in his garden."

The experience worked out so nicely for M. that he posted another advertisement, seeking more volunteers. Police quickly arrested him, aborting his incipient career as a serial killer. His case became a nationwide sensation. One German pundit immediately put the blame on Hollywood for glamorizing cannibalism in movies like *The Silence of the Lambs* and *Hannibal.* "One thinks such a case would only happen in the movies, in America, but not in Germany" this commentator declared—a remarkable statement in light of his country's rich heritage of horror, psychopathology, and lust-murder.

Recommended Reading

Moira Martingale, *Cannibal Killers* (1993)
Reay Tannahil, *Flesh and Blood: A History of the Cannibal Complex* (1975)
Christy Turner II and Jacqueline Turner, *Man Corn: Cannibalism and Violence in the Prehistoric American Southwest* (1999)

CASE STUDY

Andrei Chikatilo: The Mad Beast

In its efforts to explain the behavior of serial killers, modern psychiatry has applied various clinical labels to these murderers: sociopaths, psychopaths, antisocial personalities. But only one label seems appropriate for Andrei Chikatilo: *monster.* Indeed, had Chikatilo lived a few centuries earlier, he would have been regarded as a very specific type of monster: a lycanthrope, a seemingly ordinary man who, when overcome by bloodlust, would transform into a ravening creature, clawing and biting his victims to pieces, tearing open their bodies, devouring their flesh, and exulting in the gore.

Chikatilo lived two lives. One was that of a middle-aged grandfather and committed Communist Party member. He held a university degree in Russian literature and engineering and—following a ten-year teaching career—worked as a trusted supply clerk for an industrial conglomerate. Shy and soft-spoken, he was considered by his wife of twenty-five years to be an attentive, if somewhat mousy, man who always provided for his family.

He was also one of the most terrifying serial killers in history.

After indulging himself in torture, rape, cannibalism, and mutilation-murder for more than a decade, Chikatilo was finally caught. At his 1992 trial he offered a self-diagnosis that few would dispute: "I am a freak of nature, a mad beast." The Mad Beast confessed to the unimaginably brutal murder of fifty-three victims—most of them children—though he acknowledged that the real body count could be higher.

Chikatilo was born in 1936 in the Ukraine. Stalin's harsh collectivization of rural land during the thirties made his childhood one of dire poverty and constant hunger. One incident from this period haunted Chikatilo throughout his life and is sometimes cited as a source of his own monstrous obsessions: an older brother was allegedly killed and eaten by starving peasants.

An introverted and painfully shy boy whose somewhat effeminate mannerisms made him the target of incessant teasing by his schoolmates, Chikatilo matured into a confused and obsessive adolescent. Early attempts at sex with women proved difficult, and he became convinced that he was impotent. He married in 1963 but was unable to consummate the marriage for some time. The Russian Ripper never thought of himself as sexually normal: "I never had sexual relations with a woman, and I had no concept of a sex life. I always preferred listening to the radio."

It would take many years before his sexual self came fully to life. When it did, it would take the shape of something more animal than human.

After working for a time as a telephone engineer while earning his college degree through a correspondence course, Chikatilo embarked on his life as a vocational school teacher, a job for which he was painfully unsuited. His pathological shyness made it impossible for him to exert discipline upon his students, who treated him with unconcealed derision. Colleagues, too, found him odd and withdrawn. But the future "Butcher of Rostov" had his own reasons for pursuing his pedagogical career. By then, he had discovered his perverted attraction to children. It wasn't long before he began molesting them. Eventually, he was driven from his job as a school dormitory supervisor after attempting to perform fellatio on a sleeping boy.

He progressed—or degenerated—from pedophilia to murder in 1978.

By then, he was already forty-two—a late bloomer in the ranks of lust-killers, who generally begin their ghastly work in their teens or twenties. Luring a nine-year-old girl named Lena Zakotnova from a streetcar stop with the promise of imported chewing gum, he led her to a run-down shack, where, after attempting unsuccessfully to rape her, he stabbed her repeatedly with a knife. He then dumped her body in the river. Despite strong evidence linking him to the crime, the police remained stubbornly convinced that the killer was a young man with a prior conviction for rape and murder, who was ultimately convicted and executed for the Zakotnova slaying. It was the first of many official blunders that would allow Chikatilo to remain at large for another dozen years and lead to untold horror and suffering.

Following the loss of his teaching job, Chikatilo moved his family to the industrial town of Rostov-on-Don, where he found work as a factory supply clerk. It was at this point that his inner beast was truly unleashed. For the next twelve years, he prowled bus stops and train stations in Rostov and farther afield. His method was simple: he would approach his victim—girls or boys or young women—and offer food or money or a car ride. Then—like some dark creature from a fairy tale—he would lead his unwary prey into the woods, where a terrifying metamorphosis would take place. Overpowering his victims, he would bind them with rope, then—in an ecstatic frenzy—savage them with knife, teeth, and bare hands, ripping open their bellies, chewing off their noses, gouging out their eyes, slicing off and eating their tongues, nipples, genitals—sometimes while they were still alive. He wallowed in their internal organs and would later confess to having a particular fondness for the taste and texture of the uterus.

Because Soviet dogma insisted that serial murder was a product of capitalist decadence—something that could never exist in a communist state—the gruesome murders were never reported in the press, leaving the unalerted public even more vulnerable to the depredations of the monster. On several occasions, Chikatilo fell under suspicion, but was let go each time for lack of solid evidence. In 1984, he was arrested on a theft charge but released after just three months in jail. Within weeks, he butchered eight more victims.

Despite a massive (if unpublicized) manhunt, it was not until 1990 that Chikatilo was finally nabbed. At his 1992 trial, he was kept inside a cage for his own protection. Jamming the courtroom, relatives of his victims howled for his blood, while—behind the steel bars—the Mad Beast ranted, raved, tore off his clothes, waved his penis at the crowd, and spewed obscenities at the judge.

As the trial progressed, his behavior grew increasingly outrageous. At one point, he claimed that he was pregnant and lactating, and accused his guards of hitting him in the stomach to deliberately damage his baby.

If his wildly bizarre behavior was—as some people thought—a calculated attempt to prove he was insane, the tactic failed. On February 14, 1994—after his appeal for clemency was rejected by President Boris Yeltsin—he was led into a prison courtyard and executed with a bullet to the base of his skull.

NECROPHILIA

The suffix "phile" is used to denote a person who is especially enamored of something. There are bibliophiles (book lovers), oenophiles (wine lovers), Anglophiles (lovers of English culture). And then there are necrophiles—lovers of the dead, people who get sexually aroused by the thought, sight, smell, and feel of corpses.

So revolting is this aberration that even Richard von Krafft-Ebing—who adopts a tone of scientific detachment in his classic text, *Psychopathia Sexualis*—can't discuss it without using words like "horrible," "repugnant," and "monstrous." Still, there are degrees of evil even in regard to necrophiliacs. Some are far more monstrous than others—with serial killers, unsurprisingly, representing the most appalling end of the spectrum.

Bizarre as it may sound, some necrophiliac acts have been motivated by overpowering love. According to his own journal entry, Ralph Waldo Emerson, one of the most revered figures in American literary history, was so devastated by the death of his young wife, Ellen, that, shortly after her burial, he went out to the cemetery one night and dug up her corpse. (What he did with it once he raised it from the grave is anybody's guess.) This grief-stricken variety of necrophilia has even been commemorated in literature. In the famous ballad, "The Unquiet Grave," for example, an anguished young man visits the burial place of his beloved in the hope of getting one last kiss from her "clay-cold lips."

As awful as it may be to contemplate, this sort of necrophilia—in which a profoundly bereft individual, driven wild by sorrow, digs up his lover for a final embrace—is at least comprehensible. Significantly creepier was the case of Carl von Cosel, a middle-aged radiologist working at a sanitarium in Key West, Florida. In 1931, Cosel became so obsessed with a beautiful, twenty-two-year-old patient named Maria Elena de Hoyos that, when she died of tuberculosis, he smuggled her body back to his home. Despite being treated with formaldehyde, the dead woman's corpse gradually decomposed. As it did, Cosel tried various desperate measures to preserve it, using piano wire to string the bones together, sticking glass eyes in the sockets, replacing the rotting skin with wax and silk. Most ghastly of all, he inserted a tube between her legs to serve as a makeshift "vagina," so that he could continue having sex with the remains. This nightmarish travesty of true love went on for a full seven years before it came to light. But nothing could dim Cosel's obsession. He died in 1952, clutching a doll wearing a death mask of his beloved.

However horrific, Cosel's ghoulish activities were at least confined to a single corpse. Other notorious necrophiles have been far more promiscuous. Perhaps the most infamous case on record is that of a young French soldier, Sergeant François Bertrand, whose hideous career began in the late 1840s. Possessed of an overwhelming compulsion to violate the dead, Bertrand would dig up freshly buried female bodies in Parisian cemeteries—sometimes with his bare hands. Then—"with a madman's frenzy" (as he himself described it)—he would rape, dismember, disembowel, and occasionally chew on the corpses. Compared to the pleasure he derived from his "mad embrace" of the dead, he confessed, "all the joy procured by possession of a living woman was as nothing."

Another nineteenth-century French necrophile, twenty-six-year-old Henri Blot, was in the habit of dozing off contentedly after digging up and performing coitus on female cadavers in the cemetery of Saint-Ouen. On one of these occasions, Blot passed out so completely that, the next morning, cemetery workers found him sound asleep beside the ravished corpse of a young ballerina. Brought to trial, Blot earned a certain immortality in the annals of psychopathology when—after being rebuked by the judge for the "depravity of his offense"—he indignantly replied: "How would you have it? Every man to his own tastes. Mine is for corpses."

And then there was Viktor Ardisson, a feebleminded gravedigger who reportedly had sex with over one hundred dead bodies. Ardisson was finally captured when police—who had received reports of a terrible stench emanating from his rooms—found the decaying corpse of a three-year-old girl that he had brought back from the cemetery and performed cunnilingus on every night for a week.

America's best-known necrophile was the Midwestern ghoul Ed Gein. In the years following his mother's death in 1947, this lonely, demented little bachelor made dozens of nocturnal forays into local cemeteries, where he dug up the bodies of middle-aged women and brought them back to the squalor of his decrepit farmhouse on the outskirts of Plainfield, Wisconsin.

Gein, however, differed from his European counterparts like Bertrand and Blot in several significant ways. For one thing, though there was clearly a sexual component to his acts (he performed gynecological examinations on the corpses and carefully removed and preserved the vulvas), he appears not have engaged in coitus. Instead, he used the bodies as raw material to make various macabre artifacts, from human-skin lampshades, to cranium soup bowls, to a "mammary vest" that he wore in his deranged efforts to turn himself into a woman.

Moreover, Gein was not just a grave robber and violator of the dead. He was a multiple murderer. When the supply of middle-aged female cadavers ran dry in the Plainfield cemetery, he resorted to murder, coolly dispatching two middle-aged women and carrying his booty home, where he butchered their carcasses like deer and put their body parts to various unimaginable uses.

This, of course, is what makes necrophiliac serial killers especially evil. Abhorrent as it may be to violate graves and sexually defile corpses, deviants like Sergeant Bertrand and Henri Blot limited their abominations to victims that were already dead. Serial killers who perform necrophilia, on the other hand, don't dig up corpses: they create their own.

The best that can be said about Gein is that he was not a sadist. Uninterested in living women, he dispatched his victims swiftly, with a bullet to the back of the head, so that he could take their corpses home and play with them at leisure in the privacy of his hellish homestead. The same cannot be said about other serial killers who have practiced necrophilia, like Ted Bundy and Andrei Chikatilo. For lust-murderers like these, raping a corpse is part of their unspeakably vicious sadism, an expression of their need to dominate, humiliate, and annihilate other human beings.

> I should like to wallow in corpses. I want to be stronger and stronger. I know that the dead bodies cannot defend themselves. I should like to torture people, even after they are dead.
>
> —from the fantasies of a necrophile, as recorded by Dr. Wilhelm Stekel

The abominations which serial killers have perpetrated on the dead are beyond the lurid. Edmund Kemper not only raped the corpses of his coed victims before dismembering them, but—on at least one occasion—had sex with a victim's body *after* cutting off her head. Conversely, the "Sunset Slayer," Douglas Clark, used the decapitated head of a murdered prostitute for necrophiliac fellatio.

According to one of his apparently autobiographical short stories, Gerard Schaefer—aka the "Butcher of Blind Creek"—dug up the body of one female victim several days after burying it in a swamp and masturbated on the rotting remains. And Jeffrey Dahmer performed oral sex on corpses of his male victims (who would often die with an erection, a common physiological reaction to strangulation). He also took pleasure from cutting open their bellies and having sex with their viscera.

CASE STUDY

Dennis Nilsen, Lover of the Dead

Along with Jeffrey Dahmer—the killer he most closely resembles in terms of aberrant behavior and ghastly MO—Dennis Nilsen is the most infamous necrophile of the late twentieth century.

Exactly where his grotesque psychopathology sprang from is difficult to say. Certainly he showed none of the classic warning signs associated with budding serial killers—childhood sadism, for example. On the contrary, as a young boy he recoiled from cruelty to animals. Some experts who have studied his case attribute his lifelong fascination with cadavers to the sudden, shocking death of his beloved grandfather—the sight of whose laid-out corpse left a profound mark on young Nilsen's psyche. Equally important in terms of his emotional development was the terrible isolation, the crushing sense of loneliness, that he experienced as a child and suffered throughout his life. And then there were his own powerfully conflicted feelings about his homosexuality.

Whatever the sources of his unspeakable perversions, they manifested themselves at an early age. In his teens, he liked to stretch out before a mirror and masturbate while pretending that the body reflected in the glass was a corpse.

In 1961, the sixteen-year-old Nilsen enlisted in the army. He became a cook and learned how to butcher meat—a skill later put to horrific use. It was during this period that he fell in love with an eighteen-year-old private, who indulged his friend's peculiarities by stripping naked and pretending he was dead while Nilsen shot home movies of him. Leaving the army after eleven years, he tried his hand at police work. Though he enjoyed his occasional trips to the morgue, the work wasn't for him, and he soon took a civil service job for the Manpower Commission Services.

After the breakup of a two-year live-in relationship with another young man, Nilsen—cut off from all meaningful human contact—began to revert to his bizarre autoerotic rituals, applying cadaverous paint to his naked body, then masturbating in front of a mirror. By 1978, his simmering sickness—his utter inability to connect with another human being, his sadistic need for control, the grotesque attraction he felt for lifeless male flesh—reached a boiling point.

His first atrocity set the pattern for all the others to follow. In late December 1978, the thirty-three-year-old Nilsen picked up a teenage boy at a local pub and brought him home for a one-night stand. The next morning—unable to bear the thought of being alone for New Year's Eve—Nilsen garroted the sleeping boy with a necktie, then finished him off by submerging his head in a bucket of water. After enjoying a cup of coffee and a cigarette, he stripped the body, bathed it, then laid it out in his bed. Over the next few days, he treated the stiffening corpse like a new lover, dressing it in fresh underwear, caressing it, masturbating over it. Eventually, he stashed it under the floorboards, though he would remove it from time to time for a bath and a bit of necrophiliac sex. He kept it around for seven months until he disposed of it in a backyard bonfire.

For Nilsen, it was the end of one kind of life and the beginning of another. "I had started down the avenue of death," he would later say, "and possession of a new kind of flatmate."

Over the next five years, he would find and acquire fourteen more such "flatmates"—young pickups he turned into corpses, then kept around for companionship, sleeping with them, bathing them, having sex with them. Sometimes, he would prop a corpse beside him on the sofa and watch TV in an unspeakable travesty of domestic coziness. At times, there were as many as a half dozen cadavers stashed in his apartment at once—some in the cupboard, some under the floorboards, a few in the garden shed. When it finally came time to dispose of them, he would call on his old butchering skills, dismembering the bodies with a kitchen knife, putting the viscera in a plastic bag, boiling the flesh off the skulls in a soup pot, stuffing the torsos in suitcases, then cremating the remains in his backyard.

The problem of disposal became trickier when he moved to an attic apartment in 1983. Without access to a secluded garden, Nilsen resorted to the ill-advised method of chopping up his victims and flushing the pieces down the toilet. His horrors were uncovered when the building pipes became clogged and the horrified plumber discovered that the problem was caused by a nauseating sludge composed of human bones and decomposing flesh.

Under arrest, Nilsen freely confessed to his atrocities. Indeed, he seemed eager to fathom his own motives, cooperating with writer Brian Masters on the 1985 book, *Killing for Company.* In the end, however, such evil remains beyond comprehension. Nilsen himself put his finger on the frighteningly fundamental motive that drives all psychopathic sex criminals when—asked what made him commit such horrors—he replied: "Well, enjoying it is as good a reason as any."

PEDOPHILIA

To a certain kind of psycho, children are just targets of opportunity, no different from any other vulnerable people unlucky enough to cross his path. In 1920, for example, while residing in Luanda, Angola, Carl Panzram found himself relaxing in a park not far from the US consulate. As he sat there, an African boy, eleven or twelve years old, came wandering by.

"He was looking for something," Panzram writes in his chilling jailhouse memoir. "He found it, too. I took him out to a gravel pit about ¼ mile from the main camp of the Sinclair Oil Company at Luanda. I left him there, but first I committed sodomy on him and then killed him. His brains were coming out of his ears when I left him and he will never be any deader. He is still there."

Despite this and other outrages perpetrated against juveniles, Panzram did not specifically target children. Totally undiscriminating when it came to mayhem, he would happily kill anyone, regardless of age or gender. There *are* some serial predators, however, whose taste runs exclusively to children: pedophiliac monsters who derive intense sadistic pleasure from raping and slaughtering the young.

Albert Fish was arguably the most terrifying of this abhorrent breed. From adolescence through old age, his entire life was consecrated to the sexual torture of children, primarily boys. Constantly on the move, he raped at least a hundred little victims and murdered a minimum of fifteen in twenty-three states from New York to Montana.

What made Fish particularly appalling was that, in the words of one court-appointed psychiatrist, "his interest was not so much to have sexual relations with these children as to inflict pain on them." Many of his victims were African-American slum children, targeted "because the authorities didn't pay much attention when they were hurt or missing." Fish would lure them into basements with offers of candy or pocket change, then pounce on them, tie them up, rape and torture them. Sometimes he would gag them, though, as he explained, "he preferred not to gag them, circumstances permitting, for he liked to hear their cries." In contrast to some psychopaths, whose violent tendencies subside somewhat as their sex drives diminish with age, Fish's atrocities only grew more extreme as the years passed. His ultimate outrage—the abduction, dismemberment, and cannibalizing of twelve-year-old Grace Budd in 1928—was not committed until he was in his sixties.

Other infamous American child-killers of the twentieth century include:

Westley Allan Dodd

Like Albert Fish, Westley Dodd spent much of his time daydreaming about the most unspeakable acts. "The more I thought about it, the more exciting the idea of murder sounded," he confessed in a letter. "I planned many ways to kill a boy. Then I started thinking of torture, castration, and even cannibalism. . . . I was mainly interested in eating the genitals while kids watched. I was going to do this as a form of torture more than anything else." Though his odious career was brought to an end before he had a chance to act on the most deranged of his fantasies, he still managed to commit an appalling number of crimes, including three horrendous child murders and an estimated 175 molestations.

Dodd's pedophiliac compulsions first took hold of him at the age of thirteen, when he began exposing himself to passing children from his bedroom window. He soon progressed to more active forms of abuse, playing sexual "games" with younger cousins, neighborhood kids, and the children at the Midwestern summer camps where he sought work as a counselor specifically to gain sexual access to little victims. By his late teens, he had become an accomplished predator. Though repeatedly apprehended for accosting children, Dodd never received more than a slap on the wrist—generally a brief stint behind bars plus counseling. In 1987, after being arrested for attempting to lure an eight-year-old boy into a vacant building, he was convicted of a "gross misdemeanor" and spent less than four months in jail. The psychologist who treated him at that time accurately predicted that the lifelong pederast was "an extremely high risk for future offense." But he tragically underestimated Dodd's potential for violence, concluding that, though driven by deviant sexual desires for children, Dodd "didn't want to hurt them."

In September 1989, having selected a park in Vancouver, Washington, as a "good hunting ground," Dodd snared, molested, and savagely murdered eleven-year-old Cole Neer and his ten-year-old brother, William. Slightly more than a month later, he abducted four-year-old Lee Iseli from a playground in Portland, Oregon, took the child home with him, then molested and tortured him for nearly twenty-four hours before strangling him and hanging the corpse in his bedroom closet. Dodd documented these outrages with a series of Polaroid photographs later discovered by police—along with other appalling evidence—in a suitcase under his bed.

Not long afterward, Dodd was captured in the act of abducting a six-year-old boy from a movie theater in Camas, Washington. Pleading guilty to the three murders and attempted kidnapping, he was sentenced to death and was hanged on January 5, 1991, at the age of thirty-one.

The thoughts of killing children are exciting to me.

—Westley Allan Dodd

Arthur Gary Bishop

Born in 1951, Arthur Bishop was raised by devout Mormon parents, excelled at school, and earned promotion to the exalted rank of Eagle Scout. Following his graduation from high school, he served as a teenage missionary in the Philippines. Exactly what forces in this seemingly exemplary early life turned him into a psychopathic monster are unknown.

What *is* certain is that, by the time he reached his midtwenties, he was addicted to kiddie porn. Excommunicated in 1978 after embezzling nearly $10,000 from an employer, he took on a new identity—"Roger Downs"—and moved to an apartment complex in Salt Lake City. Before long, he had joined the Big Brother Program so that he could get access to the little boys he craved.

He progressed from molestation to murder in October 1979, when he lured a four-year-old neighbor named Alonzo Daniels to his apartment and began to fondle the boy. When the child burst into sobs and threatened to tell, Bishop clubbed him with a hammer, drowned him in his tub, stuffed the body into a large cardboard box, and carried it out to his car, right past the boy's mother, who was frantically searching for her missing son. Driving the corpse twenty miles outside the city, he buried it in the desert.

Like Jeffrey Dahmer—who made a futile effort to satisfy his necrophiliac cravings with manikins—Bishop tried to find a safer outlet for increasingly homicidal urges. In the year following the murder of Alonzo Daniels, he killed nearly two dozen puppies, adopting them from animal shelters, then taking them home and strangling, drowning, or bludgeoning them to death. In the end, these canine surrogates worked no better than Dahmer's dummies.

In November 1980, Bishop killed eleven-year-old Kim Peterson after luring the boy to his apartment with the promise to buy his old roller skates. Peterson's body ended up in the desert beside Alonzo Daniels. Other victims followed: four-year-old Danny Davis, snatched from a supermarket in October 1981, and six-year-old Troy Ward, abducted from a local playground in June 1983.

Bishop was finally caught in July 1983, after killing a thirteen-year-old acquaintance he was scheduled to chaperone on a camping trip. After a six-week trial in 1984, he was convicted of five counts of capital murder and put to death by lethal injection.

Robert Black

Pedophiliac sex-killers aren't just an American phenomenon. These monsters exist throughout the world. Nor do they only prey on little boys, as the case of British serial murderer Robert Black illustrates.

Born out of wedlock in 1947, Black was placed in foster care at six months of age and raised in the Scottish Highlands. During his early school years, he gained a reputation as a vile-tempered bully who preyed on weaker children (one of his victims was a younger boy with an artificial leg). He also displayed a precocious fascination with perverse sexuality. From childhood on, he enjoyed inserting objects into his anus, a practice he continued throughout his life. (After his arrest, police were stunned to find photographs he had taken of himself with all sorts of bizarre items protruding from his rectum, including a wine bottle, a telephone handset, and a table leg.)

Black's foster mother died when he was eleven. A year later—along with a schoolmate—he attempted to rape a little girl. Shipped off to a home for troubled boys, he was the target of regular sexual abuse by a male staffer.

In 1962, at the age of fifteen, Black was released from the home and took a job as a delivery boy in a town outside Glasgow. During the next two years, by his own later admission, he molested as many as forty little girls while making his rounds, including a seven-year-old he lured into a derelict building, strangled to unconsciousness, then stripped and molested. After masturbating over the inert body, he fled the scene but was later arrested. Inexplicably, his punishment consisted of nothing more than a stern admonishment. Black was soon back to his deviant ways.

Continuing to prey on little girls—including the nine-year-old granddaughter of his landlord—he was incarcerated for a year in 1967 after being found guilty of three charges of indecent assault. Upon his release, he sought fresh hunting grounds in London, where he found work as a swimming pool attendant—a job that permitted him to spy on little girls as they frolicked in the water. His own preferred form of exercise at this time was to break into the pool after closing time and swim laps with a broomstick lodged in his anus.

Exactly when Black began to kill is a matter of dispute, though some experts believe he claimed his first underage victim as early as 1969. There is no question, however, that between July 1982, and March 1986, he abducted and murdered three little girls along the England-Scotland border. He was caught red-handed while abducting a fourth intended victim in July 1990, and ultimately imprisoned for life. In addition to the trio of children he is known to have snatched, raped, and smothered, he is suspected in as many as ten other child murders, though he has staunchly refused to confess.

GERONTOPHILIA

However repugnant, pedophilia is an all-too-familiar perversion. Hardly a week goes by without some news account of a respected authority figure—schoolteacher, scoutmaster, man of the cloth—being arrested for abusing children or downloading kiddie porn.

Far less common is another aberration involving abnormal love between the generations. Gerontophilia—the polar opposite of pedophila in regard to age—is the technical term for a morbid sexual fixation on the elderly.

Some serial killers prey on old people for the same reason that they murder children: because defenseless seniors make easy targets. Others, however, are sadistic gerontophiles—deviants who derive perverted pleasure from attacking and killing the old.

John Wayne Glover

Even more than most of his duplicitous breed, John Glover was the last person you'd suspect of being a psycho-killer. A big, jovial family man in his late fifties, he lived a life of impeccable middle-class respectability in a fashionable suburb of Sydney, Australia. He had a solid marriage, two beloved daughters, a comfortable house, good friends, admiring neighbors, and a solid job as a salesman for the Four 'n' Twenty Pie Company. He was drinking pals with the former mayor of his community and devoted his spare time to doing charity work for the local Senior Citizens Society.

But Glover had another and far more sinister connection to senior citizens. Unbeknownst to the world, the affable middle-age suburbanite was a vicious serial murderer whose homicidal impulses were triggered by little old ladies.

A native of England, Glover emigrated to Australia in 1956 at the age of twenty-four and within a few years was convicted of two counts of indecent assaults on female victims. Punished with nothing more than three years' probation, he promptly ran afoul of the law again, getting arrested on a Peeping Tom charge in 1965. After a brief stint in jail, he married, settled down, and appeared to reform. But, as with all psychopaths, it was only a matter of time before his darkest nature showed itself again.

In March 1989, he began the series of atrocities that would earn him lasting infamy as the so-called Granny Killer—one of the most savage and twisted serial murderers in Australia's history. Glover's signature method—his homicidal "calling card"—was to bash in his victim's skull with a hammer, strangle her with her own panty hose, and make off with her money. His victims were frail, often sickly women in advanced old age—most in their eighties, one in her nineties, none younger than seventy-seven. Several could only walk with the help of canes, one was partially deaf and blind, another suffered from cancer.

Though Glover did not rape them, there was a clear sexual motive to his crimes, since he took pleasure from stripping off their hosiery and undergarments. During the period of his killing spree, he also began molesting infirm old women in their beds while making the rounds of nursing homes in his capacity as a pie salesman.

By the time he committed his fifth murder, the biggest task force in Australia's history had been assembled to catch him. Their big break came in January 1990, when—while visiting a hospital on business—he attempted to sexually molest an elderly cancer patient in her bed. Realizing he had been identified, Glover went home and attempted suicide, leaving a note that read, in part, "No more grannies, no more grannies." Recovering from this attempt, he managed to commit one final murder, even while under police surveillance. Tried in November 1991, he was found guilty on six counts of murder and received a life sentence for each.

> I just see these ladies and it triggers something. I just have to be violent towards them.
>
> —John Wayne Glover

Daniel Ray Troyer

Suspected of as many as thirteen homicides, Troyer committed his first known attack on an elderly woman in 1978, when he beat, choked, and attempted to rape a seventy-one-year-old quadriplegic in Salt Lake City, Utah.

Sent to prison for the crime, he was paroled after seven years. One month later, on July 17, 1985, he murdered eighty-three-year-old Drucilla Ovard, who was found beaten and strangled in her bathroom. Though she had not been raped, her killer had stripped her naked, arranged her in an obscene position, and masturbated over her body, leaving behind a semen-stained towel.

Two weeks after this outrage, Troyer invaded the home of seventy-year-old Carol Nelson, just a few blocks away from the Ovard apartment. Luckily for Mrs. Nelson, she was not at home. Alerted by a neighbor who had witnessed the break-in, police promptly arrived and arrested Troyer, who received a sentence of one to fifteen years for burglary.

He was paroled three years later. On August 17, 1988—just two weeks after his release—he left his halfway house to apply for a job at a nearby barber's college. That same day, he beat and strangled eighty-eight-year-old

Ethel Luckau in her home, three blocks away from the barber's school. Once again, a semen-stained towel was found beside the nude body of the victim.

Thanks to DNA technology, which matched him to the semen left at both crime scenes, Troyer eventually received consecutive life sentences for the Ovard and Luckau murders. Authorities in Utah, however, believe that he may be responsible for killing up to thirteen elderly women, including sixty-nine-year-old Thelma Blodgett, murdered less than a week before Drucilla Ovard, and seventy-three-year-old Lucille Westermann, slain just six days after Ethel Luckau.

Thierry Paulin

Alternately dubbed the "Monster of Montmartre" and the "Little Old Lady Killer," Thierry Paulin stood out as an anomaly not only within "normal" society but among serial killers. The victims of most sadistic psychopaths generally mirror the murderer's own sexual orientation and race: whites tend to prey on whites, blacks on blacks, straight males on women, gay males on other men, etc. Paulin violated all these expectations. A bleached blond black drag queen, he savagely murdered nearly two dozen old white women in the Montmartre neighborhood of Paris in the mid-1980s, creating a panic among the city's elderly female population.

Paulin's crime wave began in 1984, when he was twenty-one. Accompanied on occasion by his nineteen-year-old lover, Jean-Thierry Maturin, Paulin would trail old ladies home as they returned from the market, then pounce when they unlocked the front door. He and his accomplice killed with unusual ferocity. One victim, eighty-year-old Marie Choy, was bound with steel wire and forced to drink bleach before she was beaten to death. Another, seventy-five-year-old Maria Mico-Diaz, was so savagely hacked with a knife that she was nearly cut in two.

The "Monster of Montmartre" celebrated his twenty-fourth birthday in November 1997, by attacking three victims during a single weekend. One survived to describe him to police, who had little trouble in tracking down a black transvestite with platinum blond hair. In custody, Paulin confessed to the murder of twenty-one female victims between the ages of sixty and ninety-five. He died of AIDS in April 1989, while awaiting trial.

THE WORLD'S WORST PERVERT

On the face of it, it might seem like a quixotic effort to identify the most sexually aberrant serial killer of all time. Who, after all, was sicker: Jeffrey Dahmer, who admitted that cutting open his victims and seeing their internal organs got him aroused? Fritz Haarmann, who had orgasms while tearing open the throats of his victims with his teeth? Arthur Shawcross, who derived sexual pleasure from digging up the decaying corpse of a murdered prostitute, cutting out her vulva, and eating it? Douglas Clark, who liked to perform fellatio on the decapitated heads of his victims? The Hillside Stranglers, who got off on raping their victims while forcing Drano down their throats?

Even in this field of unspeakable psychos, however, one figure stands out above the rest: Albert Fish. Several things made this Depression-era lust-killer uniquely monstrous.

To begin with, he was a lifelong pedophile who preyed exclusively on children. Moreover, he was an unbridled sadist, who not only raped and murdered his little victims but subjected them to the most hideous tortures. (On at least one occasion, he tied up a young boy, cut off his penis with scissors, and left him alone to bleed to death.)

Fish's need to inflict pain extended to himself. Not only a sadist, he was an ardent masochist. He hired women to bind and whip him. When no one was available for the job, he flagellated himself with a specially designed, nail-studded paddle.

But sadism and masochism were only two of Fish's paraphilias. He routinely engaged in both *urophilia* (a perverted fascination with urine, which in Fish's case involved forcing little boys to piss on him and drinking their urine) and *coprophagy* (eating feces). He was also a cannibalistic monster straight out of "Hansel and Gretel." On two separate occasions, he dismembered his young victims and turned parts of their bodies into a stew, which he devoured over the course of several days.

A compulsive writer of obscene notes, Fish loved to regale his correspondents with graphic descriptions of his atrocities. In one letter, he recounted the horrors he had perpetrated on a four-year-old boy named Billy Gaffney after snatching him from home and leading him to a city dump:

> I took the G boy there. Stripped him naked and tied his hands and feet and gagged him with a piece of dirty rag I picked out of the dump. Then I burned his clothes. Threw his shoes in the dump. Then I walked back and took the trolley to 59 St. at 2 A.M. and walked from there home.
>
> Next day about 2 P.M. I took tools, a good heavy cat-o-nine tails. Home made. Short handle. Cut one of my belts in half, slit these half in six strips about 8 in. long.
>
> I whipped his bare behind till the blood ran from his legs. I cut off his ears—nose—slit his mouth from ear to ear. Gouged out his eyes. He was dead then. I stuck the knife in his belly and held my mouth to his body and drank his blood.
>
> I picked up four old potato sacks and gathered a pile of stones. Then I cut him up. I had a grip with me. I put his nose, ears and a few slices of his belly in grip. Then I cut him thru the middle of his body. Just below his belly button. Then thru his legs about 2 in. below his behind. I put this in my grip

> with a lot of paper. I cut off the head—feet—arms—hands and the legs below the knee.
>
> This I put in sacks weighed with stones, tied the ends and threw them into the pools of slimy water you will see all along road going to North Beach. Water is 3 to 4 ft. deep. They sank at once.
>
> I came home with my meat. I had the front of his body I liked the best. His monkey and pee wees [i.e., penis and testicles] and a nice little fat behind to roast in the oven and eat. I made a stew out of his ears—nose—pieces of his face and belly. I put onions, carrots, turnips, celery, salt and pepper. It was good.

While in prison, Fish underwent an intensive examination by a prominent New York City psychiatrist, Dr. Fredric Wertham, who concluded that Fish's life had been one of "unparalleled perversity"—that the old man had routinely practiced "every known sexual perversion and some perversions never heard of before." He arrived at this assessment after Fish described some of his favorite activities: shoving alcohol-soaked cotton up his rectum and setting it on fire, for example, or inserting a long-stemmed rose into his penis, looking at himself in the mirror, then pulling out the rose and eating the petals. When his jailers noticed that he had trouble sitting down, Fish explained that he liked to stick sewing needles up into his groin and leave them there. No one believed him until an X-ray revealed the presence of more than two dozen needles inside his pelvic region.

Altogether, Wertham concluded that Fish was afflicted with no fewer than seventeen paraphilias. In a futile attempt to save his client from the electric chair, Fish's attorney cited all seventeen of these perversions to prove that the old man was insane.

"It is noteworthy," he wrote to the Court of Appeals, "that no single case-history report, either in legal or medical annals, contains a record of one individual who possessed all of these sexual abnormalities."

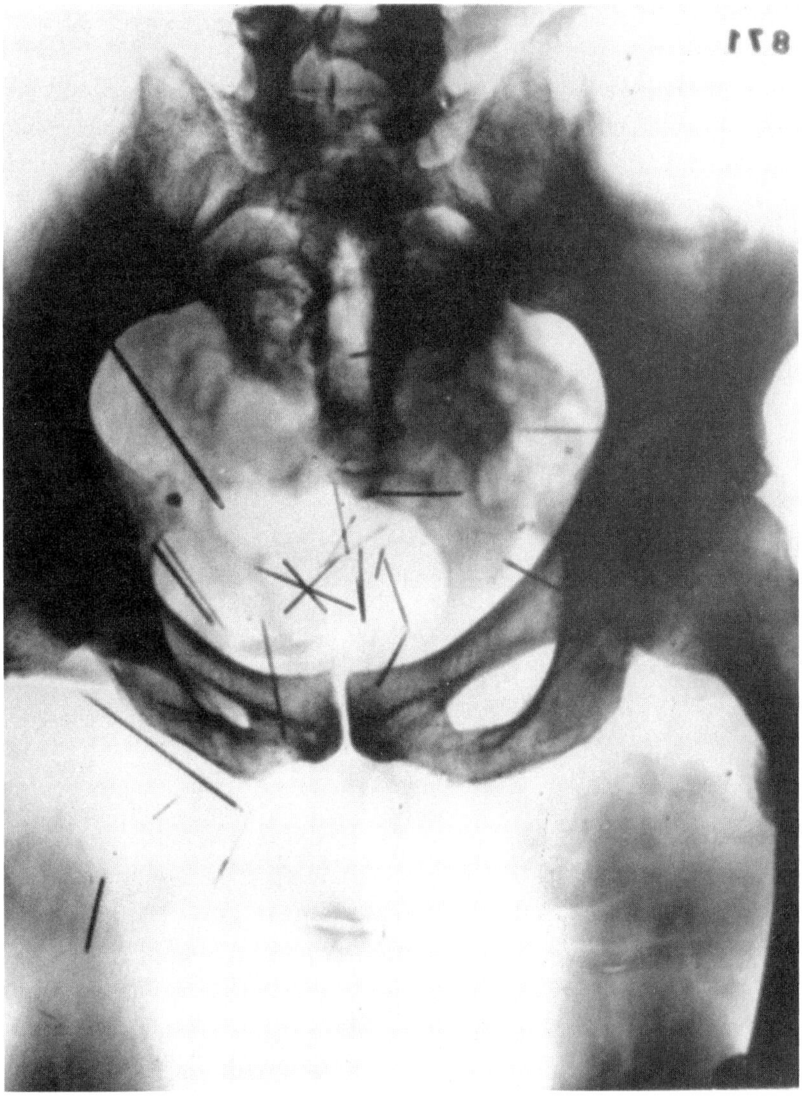

(New York Daily News)

X-ray showing needles in Albert Fish's pelvic region

WHY THEY KILL

It's natural to crave a simple explanation for the sources of serial murder. To the normal mind, the crimes of creatures like Jeffrey Dahmer and Ted Bundy seem so inconceivable that we desperately seek rational explanations for them. If we could only pinpoint a specific cause for such enormities—child abuse, media violence, biochemical imbalance, anything—the horror would at least seem comprehensible. Just being able to make sense of it would offer a degree of comfort. Perhaps we might even be able to prevent it in the future.

Unfortunately, some mysteries can never be fully resolved. Even a genius like Sigmund Freud admitted defeat when it came to answering certain questions about human psychology. Exactly why a person "should have turned out the way he did and in no other way" was, he insisted, impossible to say. There are too many random, unknowable factors that go into the development of an individual life to allow for any sort of definitive explanation.

Freud was talking about creative geniuses like Leonardo da Vinci when he made this observation. But his point holds true for serial killers as well. A prodigy of evil like Jeffrey Dahmer is, on some level, every bit as unfathomable as a prodigy of artistic or mathematical creativity, like Picasso or Einstein.

Philosophers, poets, great thinkers, and writers have wrestled with the question of evil throughout the millennia. In our own country, one of the most profound minds ever to grapple with this issue was the nineteenth-century novelist Herman Melville. In his final masterwork, *Billy Budd,* Melville ponders the depravity of the psychopathic villain John Claggart, who sets out to destroy the innocent title character for no apparent reason. What, Melville wonders, could possibly have created a being like Claggart? Melville considers several possibilities. Perhaps Claggart was the product of "vicious training." Or maybe he had read too many "corrupting books." Or possibly he had overindulged in "licentious living."

In the end, none of these explanations seems adequate, and Melville is forced to throw up his hands and conclude that evil on the scale of Claggart's can never be fully accounted for, that it is—in the words of Scripture—a "mystery of iniquity."

Still, to admit that we may never know the ultimate sources of serial murder shouldn't stop us from considering some of the contributing causes. Various theories have been advanced over the years. Some of these have been discredited, others are questionable, while still others have a good deal of validity, even if they don't offer a full and final explanation.

ATAVISM

The word "atavism" refers to an ancient, ancestral trait that reappears in modern life. And there's no question that there is something atavistic about certain serial killers, who—in their unbridled savagery—seem like creatures from a primitive age when cannibalism, human sacrifice, and similar barbaric practices were rife in the world.

Indeed, it is precisely this atavistic quality that accounts for the terrible fascination some of these psychos exert. It is both appalling and weirdly compelling to think of someone like Eddie Gein—a meek, Midwestern farmer who dressed in the flayed skin of corpses—as though he were an ancient Aztec priest performing a ritual to propitiate the gods of death. Or Jeffrey Dahmer, constructing a pagan altar of skulls, bones, and body parts in his Milwaukee apartment as a way of magically absorbing the "essence" of his victims. Or Ted Bundy, the clean-cut young law student, reverting to a state of werewolflike ferocity when his bloodlust overcame him.

These and other examples have led some psychologists to argue that sadistic lust-killers are individuals who have suffered a complete breakdown of the normal socialization process. The kind of childhood training that instills morals, empathy, and conscience in the rest of us has totally failed. As a result, they become susceptible to dark, barbaric urges that well up from the most primitive levels of the mind. It is as if, under the right circumstances, a savage, subhuman creature breaks through the surface of their modern-day selves and takes temporary possession of them, much as the apelike Mr. Hyde

Illustration of an atavistic "born criminal" from Cesare Lombroso's *Criminal Man*

does in Robert Louis Stevenson's classic fable, *The Strange Case of Dr. Jekyll and Mr. Hyde.*

There is something to be said for this atavistic view of serial murder. At the very least, it's a useful metaphor for the kind of monstrous transformations that killers like Bundy undergo. One scientist, however, took the theory to ludicrous extremes. His name was Cesare Lombroso. Nowadays, he is regarded as something of a crackpot whose theories have been completely discredited. In his own time, however, he was admired as the foremost criminologist of his age and the father of something called "criminal anthropology."

In his 1876 book *L'Uomo Delinquente* (*Criminal Man*), Lombroso (who was heavily influenced by Darwin's theories) argued that violent criminals were not merely barbaric in their behavior. They were literal atavisms—savage, Neanderthal-like beings born, by some unexplained evolutionary glitch, into the modern world. Because they were throwbacks to the prehistoric past, they could be identified by certain physical characteristics which made them resemble a lower, more apelike species. According to Lombroso, natural-born criminals were distinguished by small skulls, sloping foreheads, jutting brows, protruding ears, bad teeth, barrel chests, disproportionately long arms, and various other traits. They also often had tattoos, which he associated with members of aboriginal tribes, or as he put it, "primitive humanity."

> I seemed to see all of a sudden, lighted up as a vast plain under a flaming sky, the problem of the nature of the criminal—an atavistic being who reproduces in his person the ferocious instincts of primitive humanity and the inferior animals. Thus were explained anatomically the enormous jaws, high cheek-bones, prominent superciliary arches, solitary lines in the palms, extreme size of the orbits, handle-shaped ears found in criminals, savages, apes, insensibility to pain, extremely acute sight, tattooing, excessive idleness, love of orgies, and the irresponsible craving of evil for its own sake, the desire not only to extinguish life in the victim, but to mutilate the corpse, tear its flesh and drink its blood."
>
> —Cesare Lombroso

Needless to say, Lombroso's theory holds as much water as the nineteenth-century pseudoscience of phrenology (the belief that you can analyze someone's personality by feeling the bumps on his head). Nowadays, we know all too well that ultraviolent criminals come in all shapes and sizes. If—as Lombroso suggested—you could tell that someone was a savage killer just by looking at him, then the women who fell victim to dapper H. H. Holmes, or dashing Ted Bundy, or dorky Harvey Glatman might still be alive today.

And if tattoos were a sign of someone's innate criminality, a significant part of the US population—including, at this point, a fair number of suburban soccer moms—would be behind bars.

Recommended Reading

Robert Eisler, *Man into Wolf* (1951)
Stephen Jay Gould, *The Mismeasure of Man* (1981)

BRAIN DAMAGE

Serial killers are such spectacular cases of mental aberration that it is natural to wonder if they suffer, not merely from severe psychological problems, but from physiological ones as well—specifically, if their brains are actually different from those of normal people. In order to test this theory, scientists have, on occasion, performed postmortem dissections on notorious psychopaths. After his execution in 1924, the brain of the infamous German lust-killer Fritz Haarmann was removed from his skull and shipped off to Göttingen University for study.

Nothing came of this effort. And in the decades since, no one has been able to identify a specific neurological defect that would account for monstrous criminal behavior.

One intriguing fact has emerged in recent years, however: severe head injuries are surprisingly common in the early lives of serial killers.

At the age of ten, for example, Earle Leonard Nelson—the notorious "Gorilla Murderer" who strangled nearly two dozen victims in the 1920s—collided with a trolley car while riding his bike in San Francisco, crashed headfirst into the cobblestones, and lay comatose for nearly a week. At his 1927 murder trial, his attorney argued (unsuccessfully) that Nelson's homicidal behavior was a direct result of this dire childhood accident.

Arthur Shawcross—who slaughtered a string of prostitutes in upstate New York and occasionally consumed parts of their bodies—suffered at least four major head injuries in his youth that left him with scars on his brain and a cyst on the temporal lobe. Even more accident-prone was Bobby Joe Long, convicted killer of nine women, who was hospitalized four times in his childhood for various head injuries, plus once in his early twenties after he crashed his motorcycle into a car and slammed his skull into the vehicle with such force that his helmet was crushed.

At seventeen, the British psychopath Fred West—half of the notorious killer couple whose victims included their own teenage daughter—also had a nasty motorcycle accident, which left him with a metal plate in his head. John Wayne Gacy developed a blood clot on the brain after being hit by a swing as a child. And young Gary Heidnik sustained such a severe injury when he plunged from a tree that his skull was permanently deformed, earning him the cruel playground nickname, "Football Head."

These and many other cases of ultraviolent criminals who have sustained severe head traumas in their youth have convinced some researchers that brain damage is a key element in the development of serial killers. Even proponents of this theory, however, admit that brain damage alone isn't the ultimate explanation for serial murder. After all, countless children take headlong spills from the bikes or swing sets or Jungle Gyms each year without growing up to be cannibalistic lust-killers. Moreover, a close look at the backgrounds of serial killers reveals other factors that clearly contribute to their psychopathology.

Earle Leonard Nelson, for example, had a severely dysfunctional family background. Orphaned as an infant when both his parents died of syphilis, he was taken into the home of a fanatical grandmother and displayed signs of extreme emotional disturbance long before his bicycle accident. Arthur Shawcross was repeatedly molested by a pedophiliac neighbor and sodomized with a broom handle at the age of ten. Fred West was the product of a household in which incest was rife, while Bobby Joe Long's mother allegedly forced him (by his account, which she denies) to share her bed throughout his childhood and witness her lovemaking with her boyfriends.

John Wayne Gacy was raised by a viciously demeaning father, whose unrelenting ridicule of his son's effeminate mannerisms created a bottomless well of self-loathing in the boy. Gary Heidnik's father also subjected his son to systematic humiliation, publicly displaying the urine-stained sheets whenever the boy wet his bed.

Indeed, the head injuries suffered by serial killers are often the direct result of childhood maltreatment. Henry Lee Lucas's mother once beat him so severely with a piece of lumber that he lay in a coma for three days. Of a group of death row inmates described in a study by Dr. Jonathan Pincus, one had been "beaten almost to death" by his father at age three, another had repeatedly been "beaten in the head with two-by-fours by his parents," and the third had received a severe wound to his cranium when a family member "deliberately dropped a glass bottle on his head."

In short, while brain damage is often present in the case histories of serial killers, other kinds of damage play a central role, too—especially the emotional and psychological damage inflicted by a shockingly abusive upbringing.

Recommended Reading

Dorothy Otnow Lewis, *Guilty By Reason of Insanity* (1998)
Jonathan H. Pincus, *Base Instincts: What Makes Killers Kill?* (2003)

CHILD ABUSE

Though often gussied up in technical jargon, a great deal of psychiatric theory is just plain common sense. It makes perfect sense, for example, that if human beings are raised in warm, loving households—if they are brought up to believe that the world is a secure and decent place—then they will grow up with a healthy relationship to themselves and other people, able to give love freely and receive it in return.

Conversely, if a person is severely maltreated from his earliest years—subjected to constant psychological and physical abuse—he or she will grow up with a malignant view of life. To such a person, the world is a hateful place, where all human relationships are based, not on love and respect, but on power, suffering, and humiliation. Having been tortured by his earliest caretakers, he will, in later life, seek to inflict torture on others, partly as a way of taking revenge, partly because he has been so psychologically warped by his experiences that he can only feel pleasure by inflicting pain—and, in the most extreme cases, only feel alive when he is causing death.

In short, while neurological problems—either from brain damage or hereditary defects—often play a role in the making of serial killers, severely abusive upbringings are more or less universal in their family backgrounds.

To be sure, not every abused child grows up to be a psychopathic killer. But virtually every psychopathic killer has suffered extreme, often grotesque, mistreatment at the hands of his or her parents or guardians. In the language of logic, severe child abuse may not be a sufficient cause in the creation of serial murderers, but it appears to be a necessary one.

Based on their pioneering prison interviews with the likes of David Berkowitz and Edmund Kemper, John Douglas and his fellow "mindhunters" in the FBI's Behavioral Science Unit concluded that all serial killers come from dysfunctional backgrounds: "unstable, abusive, or deprived family situations." Dr. Dorothy Otnow Lewis—who has also conducted jailhouse interviews with notorious psychopaths, including Ted Bundy—flatly declares that, in addition to whatever neurological problems they may suffer, serial killers have invariably experienced a "violent abusive upbringing." Other theorists on the origins of homicidal behavior have confirmed this view. In his highly publicized 1999 book, *Why They Kill,* for example, Pulitzer Prize–winning author Richard Rhodes describes the discoveries of a sociologist named Lonnie Athens, who, after many years of research, concluded that children who grow up to be cold-blooded killers undergo a four-stage process, beginning with what Athens calls "brutalization"—i.e., "coarse and cruel treatment at the hands of an aggressive authority figure," generally one or another (or both) of the parents.

Recent scientific research has reinforced the findings of people like Otnow and Athens by demonstrating that a traumatic upbringing can actually alter the anatomy of a person's brain. Brain scans performed on severely abused children have found that specific areas of the cortex—related not just to the intelligence but to the emotions—never develop properly, leaving them incapable of feeling empathy for other human beings.

Given the kind of abuse suffered by some serial killers, it's no surprise that they turn out to be homicidal sadists; indeed, it would be more surprising if they *didn't.* Mary Bell—the juvenile serial killer who murdered two little boys in Newcastle, England, in 1968—was raised by a mother who, on at least four occasions, tried to get rid of her unwanted child by feeding her drugs. After turning to prostitution, Mary's mother participated in the sexual torture of the little girl, holding her daughter down while her tricks orally raped the child and ejaculated in her mouth. Henry Lee Lucas was also raised by an alcoholic prostitute, who forced him to watch her have sex with her clients, beat him so severely that she once put him into a coma, and—when his brother accidentally gashed him in the eye—waited so long to get him medical attention that the eye had to be removed.

"Negative parenting"—the phrase used by sociologists to describe the kind of dysfunctional upbringings that serial killers are subjected to—doesn't begin to suggest the monstrous behavior of beings like Charlie Manson's teenage mother, who once traded him to a barmaid in exchange for a bottle of beer. Or Jesse Pomeroy's brutish father, who liked to strip his son naked and flog him half to death for the slightest infraction. Or Joseph Kallinger's pathological stepparents, who disciplined the boy with hammers, cat-o'-nine tails, and the threat of castration, and, on at least one occasion, forced him to hold his palm over an open flame until the skin began to smolder. Or Hugh Morse's grandmother, who butchered his pet mice before his eyes as punishment for his sneaking off to the movies.

Sometimes, the childhood horrors experienced by future serial killers occur, not at home, but in various institutions. Shipped off to a Dickensian orphanage at the age of five, Albert Fish acquired his lifelong taste for sadomasochistic torture from one of the matrons, who liked to strip the little boys naked and savagely flog one of them while the others stood in a circle and watched. After stealing some license plates when he was eight, William Bonin was sent to reform school, where he was regularly raped by the older boys. Carl Panzram's implacable character was forged in a series of brutal "training schools," where juvenile inmates were subjected to unimaginable punishment, often for such minor offenses as failing to fold their dinner napkins properly.

> They used to have a large wooden block which we were bent over and tied face downward after first being stripped naked. Then a large towel was soaked in salt water and spread on our backs from the shoulders to the knees. Then the man who was to do the whipping took a large strap about ¼ of an inch thick by 4 inches and about two feet long. This strap had a lot of little round holes punched through it. Every time that whip came down on

> the body the skin would come up through these little holes in the strap and after 25 or 30 times of this, little blisters would form and then burst, and right there and then hell began. The salt water would do the rest. About a week or two later a boy might be able to sit down.
>
> —Carl Panzram, describing the punishment he regularly received as a twelve-year-old inmate of the Minnesota Training School

Some people question the findings of researchers like Dorothy Otnow Lewis and Jonathan Pincus, who insist that all serial killers have severe abuse in their backgrounds. After all, they argue, there have been homicidal monsters like Jeffrey Dahmer and Ted Bundy who don't appear to have experienced such childhood torture.

There are problems with this argument, however. For one thing, even in the cases of such notorious figures, whose lives have been studied by all manner of experts, there is a great deal that we simply don't know. Dahmer, for example, may well have been sexually molested by a neighbor. And—despite family snapshots showing little Ted Bundy enjoying an all-American boyhood of fishing, camping, and roasting hot dogs in a fireplace—there were very weird things going on in his childhood home. He was born to a young, unwed mother who pretended to be his older sister as he grew up, and was co-raised by a viciously racist, wife-beating grandfather who got a kick out of tormenting house pets.

It is clear, moreover, that psychological abuse can be every bit as devastating to the emotional development of a child as physical maltreatment. According to psychoanalyst Carl Goldberg, a child who is systematically shamed and humiliated—who is made to feel that he is utterly worthless and undeserving of love—is almost bound to develop into a malevolent personality. His feeling of self-contempt becomes so profound "that the only way to survive is to become indifferent to other people, too." In effect, such a person grows up to believe that "I may not be worthy, but neither is anyone else." Convinced of his own badness, he bitterly lashes out at the world.

Certainly—in addition to regular beatings—John Wayne Gacy received nothing but humiliation from his father, who constantly belittled his son's masculinity. Ed Kemper's mother ridiculed him relentlessly during his youth, mocking his physical appearance and telling him that no woman would ever love him. Henry Louis Wallace's mother not only thrashed him regularly with a switch but liked to shame him by dressing him up as a girl and parading him around in public—a form of mortification also endured by Charles Manson, Henry Lee Lucas, and Carroll Cole. According to Goldberg, Jeffrey Dahmer, too, experienced intense feelings of "shame and betrayal" in relation to his parents, feelings that afflicted him with a profound, lifelong sense of "loneliness and self-hatred."

In short, whatever other factors enter into the making of a serial killer, one element stands out above the rest—what best-selling novelist and child psychologist Jonathan Kellerman calls "overall rotten families." Indeed, in looking at the nightmarish childhoods of these psychopaths, it is hard not to feel sorry for them—at least until you recall the kinds of horrors they commit as adults. In the end, they elicit a twofold response—pity for the hideously abused children they were, outrage at the monsters they ended up becoming.

Recommended Reading

John Douglas and Mark Olshaker, *The Anatomy of Motive* (1999)
Carl Goldberg, *Speaking with the Devil* (1996)
Jonathan Kellerman, *Savage Spawn* (1999)
Richard Rhodes, *Why They Kill* (1999)

MOTHER HATE

In world mythology, there is a figure known as the Terrible Mother: a nightmarish female who, instead of offering nurture and comfort, dominates and destroys her own offspring. Unfortunately, this type of female isn't limited to myths, fairy tales, and horror fantasies like *Carrie* and *Psycho.* She sometimes appears in real life. Her effect on the vulnerable young males unlucky enough to be her sons can be devastating, causing them to grow up with a virulent hatred, not just of the maternal monsters who raised them, but of womankind in general.

Blaming your problems on mommy, of course, is the oldest excuse in the psychoanalytic book. Still, if you have the kind of mother who sodomized you with a broomstick—or forced you to hold your open palm over a flame—or punished you by slaughtering your favorite pets—or made you watch her have sex with strangers—or subjected you to incessant mockery because of the way you looked—chances are pretty good that you will end up with a profound animosity toward members of the opposite sex.

Indeed, some criminologists have claimed that serial killers who target women are driven largely by mother hate. Dr. David Abrahamsen, who has written extensively about the "murdering mind" (to use the title of one of his books), maintains that the crimes of psychopathic killers are invariably rooted in their unconscious need to "take revenge" upon their rejecting mothers.

Whatever the truth of this assertion, there is no doubt that some serial killers grow up with a murderous rage against their monstrously abusive mothers. Though it is impossible to tell how many victims actually died at the hands of the spectacularly unreliable Henry Lee Lucas, we know for certain that one of them was his appallingly vicious mother, Viola, whom he stabbed to death during an argument in 1960. Edmund Kemper, too, spent his teenage years indulging in homicidal fantasies about his relentlessly demeaning mother—fantasies that he finally put into action in 1974, when he killed her in her sleep, cut off her head, and (in one of the more symbolically resonant acts in the annals of serial murder) shoved her larynx down the garbage disposal. "It seemed appropriate," he later told the police, "as much as she'd bitched and screamed and yelled at me over so many years."

Even serial killers who haven't acted out their matricidal fury have openly acknowledged it. Joe Fischer, for example—responsible for an indeterminate number of killings during the 1970s—bore a murderous hate for his prostitute mother long after she died of natural causes. "I would have killed her ten times over," he told investigators, "but I really believe it would have broken my father's heart."

According to psychiatrists, the loathing such killers feel for their mothers becomes projected onto all females, resulting in what crime writer Stephen Michaud calls "malignant misogyny." Women come to be seen as noxious, disgusting creatures that deserve whatever horrors are inflicted on them—a sentiment chillingly expressed by "Hillside Strangler" Kenneth Bianchi, who steadfastly defended his atrocities.

"It wasn't fuckin' wrong," he blithely told his interrogators. "Why is it wrong to get rid of some fuckin' cunts?"

> If I could dig up my mother's grave, I'd take out her bones and kill her again.
>
> —Joe Fischer

BAD SEED

The term "bad seed" was popularized by the 1956 movie of that title, which was based on a successful Broadway play by Maxwell Anderson (which in turn was adapted from a 1954 novel by William March). In the film, an adorable, pigtailed moppet (played by the child actor Patty McCormack) turns out to be a frighteningly cold-blooded serial killer who dispatches her victims with all the childlike exuberance of Lisa Simpson tootling away on her saxophone.

The phrase "bad seed," however, does not relate to killer-kids in general, but specifically to the notion that a profoundly psychopathic child can grow up in a normal, stable, loving household—in other words, that some people are just born evil. Here's how one of the characters, a writer named Reginald Trasker, puts it in the play when the little girl's mother asks him if "criminal children are always the product of environment":

> Some doctor friends of mine assure me that we've all been putting too much emphasis on environment and too little on heredity lately. They say there's a

> type of criminal born with no capacity for remorse or guilt . . . They can't prove it, but they think there are such people. They say there are children born into the best families with every advantage of education and discipline—that never acquire any moral scruples. It's as if they were born blind—you couldn't expect to teach them to see.

While this theory makes for effective drama—and is certainly reassuring to parents who don't want to accept responsibility for raising severely screwed-up kids—it does not conform to real life. There are simply no serial killers who have been "born into the best families"—if by the phrase "best families" one means households where children are given real love, a deep sense of security, and solid moral values.

True, the precise degree to which *bad* families contribute to the creation of criminal psychopaths is still a matter of debate. The range of mistreatment that serial killers have suffered as children varies widely, from outright physical and sexual torture to extreme humiliation and other forms of emotional abuse. But one thing is certain: there is no such thing as a serial killer who has come from a healthy, happy home. All of them are the products of distinctly dysfunctional backgrounds.

Listening to Reginald Trasker speak, another character in the play, a writer name Richard Bravo, replies: "If you encounter a human without compassion or pity or morals, he grew up where these things weren't encouraged. That's final and absolute." Bravo calls Trasker's "bad seed" theory "tommyrot."

And he's right.

MEAN GENES

To say that there are no such things as "bad seeds"—children who are born evil—is not to claim that inherited factors play no role at all in the creation of serial killers.

In his indispensable book *The Blank Slate,* MIT professor Steven Pinker sets out to counter the currently fashionable notion that there is nothing innate in human nature and that people are purely the products of their environment. Pinker begins his book with an intriguing example. "Many policies on parenting," he writes, "are inspired by research that finds a correlation between the behavior of parents and the behavior of children. Loving parents have confident children, authoritative parents (neither too permissive nor too punitive) have well-behaved children, parents who talk to their children have children with better language skills, and so on. Everyone concludes that to grow the best children parents must be loving, authoritative, and talkative, and if children don't turn out well, it must be the parents' fault." This conclusion, as Pinker points out, "depends on the belief that children are blank slates"—that their minds, characters, and behavioral patterns are entirely shaped by their upbringing.

But there is another possibility, too: "The correlations between parents and children may be telling us only that the same genes that make parents loving, authoritative, and talkative make their children self-confident, well-behaved, and articulate." In other words, heredity also plays a role in producing good children.

The same principle applies to serial killers. Most experts believe that certain children grow up to be violent psychopaths because they are treated so monstrously by their parents. And there is no doubt that, almost without exception, serial killers grow up in wretchedly dysfunctional households. But it is possible that—to paraphrase Pinker—the same genes that make some adults miserable excuses for parents make their children warped and pernicious human beings.

Recent scientific discoveries seem to confirm that severely antisocial personalities are at least partly the product of genetic factors. Experiments have shown that when people born with a certain "low-active" gene (specifically, something called the "monoamine oxidase A gene") are subjected to severe childhood maltreatment, they grow up to be criminally violent at a far higher rate than people born with a "high-active" gene.

In short, it seems likely that both nurture *and* nature play a part in producing serial killers.

Recommended Reading

Steven Pinker, *The Blank Slate: The Modern Denial of Human Nature* (2002)

Matt Ridley, "What Makes You Who You Are?" *Time Magazine* (June 2, 2003)

ADOPTION

Obviously there are millions of adopted children who grow up to be perfectly happy and well-adjusted adults (or at least as happy and well-adjusted as any nonadopted person). Still, a surprisingly high percentage of serial killers have been raised in adoptive or foster homes.

There shouldn't be anything surprising about this fact, since it reflects, among other things, the kinds of extremely unstable backgrounds—the "overall rotten families"—as Jonathan Kellerman calls them—that psychopaths invariably spring from. Jane Toppan's father, for example, was an illiterate, abusive drunk who stuck both his daughters in an orphanage after the death of his wife and never saw them again. Earle Leonard Nelson was born to a dissolute couple who died of syphilis within a few months of each other when their son was an infant. A fair number of notorious serial killers have been children of prostitutes who couldn't wait to get rid of their kids. From the moment of her birth, Mary Bell was spurned by her mother, Betty, who—when the midwife tried to put the newborn in her arms—shouted: "Get that thing away from me!" Throughout Mary's early years, her mother made every effort to dispose of her unwanted child, once even taking her to an adoption agency and leaving her there with a stranger.

The belief (usually fully justified) that they have been rejected by their birth parents contributes to the sense of worthlessness and shame that typically afflicts budding psychopaths. Throughout his life, for example, David Berkowitz was told by his adoptive parents that his mother had died while giving birth to him—a story that burdened him with a heavy load of guilt. When Berkowitz later discovered that his mother was actually alive, he tracked her down, only to discover that she wasn't especially interested in having a relationship with him.

The adoptive or foster homes that some children find themselves in can also have a deeply pernicious effect on their developing personalities. Joseph Kallinger's adoptive parents scourged him with a cat-o'-nine tails and assured him that his penis would remain permanently stunted from a childhood hernia operation. Though Jane Toppan (born Honora Kelley) was given the name of her foster family, she was never formally adopted and was made to feel like a perennial outsider in the only home she ever knew. Described by a social worker as "deeply disturbed," Kenneth Bianchi's adoptive mother treated him with pathological overprotectiveness, smothering the little boy with bizarre medical attention (once, when he accidentally wet his pants, she rushed him to the doctor to have his genitals examined). And after the death of his parents, Earle Nelson was raised by a Bible-crazed grandmother who was the source of his own lifelong obsession with the Whore of Babylon from Revelation—an obsession that helped fuel his homicidal rage against women.

To be sure, the correlation between serial murder and adoption can be easily overstated. Some experts dismiss it entirely and scoff at defense attorneys who argue that their clients should not be held responsible for their crimes because they were abandoned at birth (a tactic tried—unsuccessfully—in the case of the Long Island serial killer Joel Rifkin, who murdered seventeen prostitutes in the home of his adoptive parents supposedly, so he claimed, to alleviate the pain of having been rejected by his birth mother). Certainly the vast majority of adopted Americans grow up to be productive, law-abiding citizens. It is also the case that being raised by a birth parent is no guarantee that a child will turn out to be normal.

Mary Bell's mother, after all, never managed to rid herself of her unwanted daughter. Instead, the little girl was kept at home and subjected to such unimaginable torture that it would have been better if she *had* been given up for adoption.

FANTASY

In his landmark 1899 book, *The Interpretation of Dreams,* Sigmund Freud quotes Plato on the difference between ordinary citizens and criminals: "The virtuous man is content to dream what the wicked man really does." Freud's point is that, in the depths of the unconscious mind, even the most morally upright person harbors fantasies of forbidden behavior—of savage lust and primal violence. But the quote implies something else, too: that what differentiates "wicked men" (and women) from the rest of us is their willingness to *act* on their darkest desires.

After a long day at the office, for example—where he was passed over yet again for promotion, then embarrassed by the attraction he felt for a cute summer intern no older than his own daughter—a law-abiding, happily married husband and father might fall asleep and dream of butchering his boss and forcing himself sexually on the girl. Chances are, he'll wake up feeling so shaken and guilty that he will erase all memory of this disturbing dream from his mind.

For a serial killer, on the other hand, mental images of mayhem and rape aren't the stuff of nightmare; on the contrary, they form the basis of his favorite daydreams. Far from trying to put such unwholesome thoughts out of his mind, he will cultivate them—wallow in them. The recollection of a real or perceived slight inspires him to envision the most sadistic forms of revenge. The sight of a pretty girl arouses thoughts of abduction, sexual torture, and dismemberment-murder. For days, weeks, months, he will dwell on—and masturbate to—such imagined atrocities.

Then—when his perverted fantasies have reached an unbearable pitch of intensity—he will go out and attempt to commit them.

> I knew long before I started killing that I was going to be killing, that it was going to end up like that. The fantasies were too strong. They were going on for too long and were too elaborate.
>
> —Edmund Kemper

The twisted fantasies of serial killers begin at a young age. While other little boys are daydreaming about scoring the winning run in a Little League game or becoming a member of the X-Men, these budding psychopaths are already lost in all-consuming reveries of sadism and mass murder. In their groundbreaking 1988 study *Sexual Homicide,* Robert Ressler, John Douglas, and their collaborator Ann Burgess discuss one serial murderer who, as a schoolboy, drove his teachers crazy by spending so much time woolgathering in class. When psychiatrists later asked him what he had been thinking about, he replied: "Wiping out the whole school." At the tender age of twelve, another future sex-killer was so obsessed with masochistic fantasies of slow, agonizing death that he regularly forced his little sister to tie him up in a chair and pretend that she was executing him in a gas chamber.

As psychopaths reach puberty, their fantasies become increasingly sexual and more alarmingly aberrant. Normal adolescent daydreams of wild sex with an enthusiastic partner are replaced, in the psychopathic mind, with sadistic thoughts of dominance and degradation, perversion and pain. While jailed for double murder in 1874, Jesse Pomeroy, the so-called Boy Fiend, begged his friend Willie Baxter, who was occupying an adjacent cell, to provide him with detailed written descriptions of every flogging Willie had ever received, urging him to "tell me of the hardest licking you ever got. Tell me all the particulars of it!" The sadistic Pomeroy then used these lurid accounts of punishment and humiliation to enhance his own autoerotic pleasures. Jeffrey Dahmer told his examiners that he began masturbating at the age of fourteen to conventional homosexual fantasies of sex with well-built young males. A few years later, however, he was getting off while imagining that he was rendering his partners unconscious and exposing their viscera.

It's not just extreme deviance that distinguishes the fantasy life of psychopaths but their overpowering urge to translate their sickest fantasies into fact. The most extravagant erotic daydreams of normal people always run up against what Freud called "the reality principle." However much fun it might be to lie in bed and masturbate while imagining that you are making love to your favorite movie star or pop singer, the average person understands that such erotic pipe dreams are never going to come true.

Serial killers, on the other hand, have only a tenuous hold on reality. They live inside their heads, locked within their own bizarre, pathological dreamworlds. Isolated from most social contacts—unconstrained by the scruples of conscience—possessed of an infantile narcissism that places their own sordid needs above all other concerns—they eventually cross the threshold that separates imagination from actuality and carry out the horrors they have been brooding over for so long. According to the testimony of many serial killers, the experience of stepping over that line fills them with an intoxicating sense of power, even invincibility. Once they have taken that fateful step, they cannot—and have no wish to—go back. Far from satisfying their degenerate desires, each new act of violence only supplies more fuel for their fantasies. In the "cooling-off" periods between their crimes, they masturbate to the memories of the horrors they have already perpetrated and fantasize of the outrages still to come.

Because of the prominent role that such vicious daydreams play as a preliminary to the act of serial murder, Robert Ressler and his colleagues reached the conclusion that fantasy is the mainspring of sexual homicide. "My research convinced me that the key was not the early trauma but the development of perverse thought patterns," Ressler has written. "These men were motivated to murder by their fantasies."

Recommended Reading

Robert K. Ressler, Ann W. Burgess, John E. Douglas, *Sexual Homicide* (1988)
Robert I. Simon, *Bad Men Do What Good Men Dream,* (1996)

Killer Fantasy

Since fantasies are, by definition, private, imaginary scenarios that are played out in the secrecy of the mind, it's hard to get a direct firsthand sense of the unspeakably fetid inner worlds inhabited by serial killers.Thanks to one notorious psychopath, however, that distinctly unpleasant experience is not entirely impossible.

A reasonably skilled writer who studied with Southern Gothic novelist Harry Crews, Gerard J. Schaefer—the onetime Florida deputy sheriff who committed an indeterminate number of horrendous torture-slayings in the early 1970s—churned out a series of hair-raising short stories collected by former girlfriend Sondra London and published under the title *Killer Fiction.* Exactly how much of this appalling stuff is make-believe and how much memoir is unclear, though that very ambiguity is in itself an accurate reflection of the twisted mentality of serial killers, whose depraved fantasies eventually spill out into the real world, wiping out the barrier between fantasy and fact. Schaefer himself was deliberately coy about this question. In the typical way of psychopaths, he was also utterly hypocritical and self-serving about his intent in composing his stories. Though they undoubtedly served as a form of masturbatory pornography for him, he claimed that they were written with a serious sociological purpose—to give readers an unvarnished view of the "horrible malignancies" perpetrated by serial killers.

To give the devil his due, his stories do, in fact, offer unparalleled insight into the obscene workings of a psycho-killer's mind. Since the experience of reading them is a bit like opening the cover of a septic tank and sticking your head inside for a better look, his book can only be recommended with an asterisk. The selection reprinted here, from a story with the straightforward and typically Schaeferian title "Whores," is one of the milder passages to be found in his work. The narrator—having read a magazine article about an Old West prostitute named Cattle Kate who was hanged for her sins—picks up a young woman and offers her thirty dollars if she will "model like Cattle Kate for me." When she agrees, he drives her to an abandoned garage:

> We got out of the car and I fetched a rope from the carry-all section of the station wagon. I leaned against the bumper and fashioned the line into a hangman's noose while she watched. She'd picked a wild daisy and was twirling it in her fingers, picking it apart petal by petal and chanting as she dropped each piece, "He loves me loves me not." She finished up on "he loves me not" and shot me a crooked smile. "Bad luck in love."

"Ah, you don't believe in bad luck, do you? Come on over here, Kate!"

I tossed the noose over the heavy beam at the front of the garage where at one time engines were raised from the bodies of cars. I widened the loop and placed it over her head. She fiddled with her long ponytail while I adjusted the coil around her neck. I set the knot behind her ear just like the picture in the magazine. I asked her if it was too tight. She said it wasn't tight at all. Then I tied her wrists behind her with green nylon twine, and arranged her ankles the same way: took a few turns around them and made a nice tight knot. I moved a few steps back, put my hands on my hips, and told her that she made a perfect Cattle Kate.

She smiled, stuck out her tongue, and crossed her eyes. I told her to hold the pose, and I'd take a picture of her and mail it to Otto Preminger in Hollywood with a movie suggestion. She thought that was a great idea. I told her I'd get the camera from the glove compartment, turned and picked up the loose end of the rope and tied it to the car bumper. I slid behind the wheel, cranked up the ignition, put the car in reverse and backed up.

The whore rose right up in the air and once again stuck out her tongue. It was comical the way it popped right out of her mouth, all wet and pink. Her eyes were wide open and staring straight at me. Her expression was fascinating. Her face turned pink, then red, then blue—a pleasant lavender-blue. Her body quivered and shimmied; as she turned blue she wet her pants. A dark stain materialized at the juncture of her thighs, then quickly slid down the legs of her pedal pushers. The pee streamed down over her calves and dribbled from her toes making a puddle on the concrete floor under her. The pretty face turned purple, her body shivered violently; then she went limp. It was interesting to watch.

BAD BOOKS, MALIGNANT MOVIES, VILE VIDEOS

Ever since cheap, mass-produced popular art first appeared in the eighteenth century, critics have blamed it for debasing public taste, corrupting the morals of minors, and providing potential psychopaths with helpful hints on how to commit crimes. When thirteen-year-old Jesse Harding Pomeroy was arrested for the mutilation-murder of two younger children in 1872, for example, critics immediately pointed an accusing finger at the action-packed "dime novels" beloved by juvenile readers in post–Civil War America. The fact that there was not a single shred of evidence to show that Pomeroy had ever read such literature made no difference to these moralists, who insisted that the frontier bloodshed depicted in books like *Raiders of the Rawhide Range* and *Rattlesnake Ned's Revenge* had inspired the "Boy Fiend" to perpetrate his atrocities.

As soon as movies were invented, attention shifted to the new medium. Shortly after the release of the first cinematic Western, Edwin S. Porter's 1903 *The Great Train Robbery,* a train was held up near Scranton, Pennsylvania, and one passenger murdered. Critics immediately blamed the film, despite the fact that (as it later turned out) none of the culprits had seen it.

The story has been the same ever since. Whenever a new mass medium comes along, it is immediately accused of undermining moral values and instigating crime. During the "Golden Age" of radio, one critic claimed that children were being "rendered psychopathic" by popular on-air melodramas like *Lights Out* and *The Shadow,* which glorified "every form of crime known to man." In the 1950s, self-proclaimed child-rearing experts declared that comic books caused everything from juvenile delinquency to homosexuality (a type of behavior that, at the time, was regarded as only slightly less heinous than mass murder).

By the early 1960s, the culprit of choice had become television—particularly violent cop and cowboy shows. Nowadays, it is gangsta rap and Grand Theft Auto. In another fifty years, it will undoubtedly be virtual reality shooter games in which players actually feel the blood-spray from the blown-off head of a cannibal zombie (at which point, of course, today's media scapegoats will be looked at in the same way we now regard radio shows and television Westerns—as the quaint relics of a more innocent past).

Though media violence makes a convenient whipping boy (particularly for people who would rather blame their child's behavioral problems on *The Matrix* and PlayStation 2 than on their own parental shortcomings), there is—despite the countless scientific studies devoted to the question—no definitive proof of a direct relationship between watching make-believe violence and committing real-life murder. In his exceptionally well informed and level-headed book, *Savage Spawn: Reflections on Violent Children,* Jonathan Kellerman is so insistent on this point that he puts it in italics: "*Not a single causal link between media violence and criminality has ever been produced.*"

To be sure, the occasional serial killer might be incited by a movie, book, or piece of music. The problem with psychopaths, however, is that there's no telling *what* will set them off. In 1959, German lust-killer Heinrich Pommerencke—aka the "Beast of the Black Forest"—felt compelled to commit four savage murders after watching Cecil B. DeMille's *The Ten Commandments.* And the atrocities perpetrated by the Manson family were at least partly inspired by their leader's obsession with the Beatles' "White Album," one of the most benign works of pop art ever produced.

Moreover, when a person commits an appalling crime after watching a movie or reading a book or hearing a rock song, it's invariably because he was severely disturbed to begin with. In his 1999 study, *Serial Killers: The Insatiable Passion,* for example, David Lester describes a case in which psychiatrists initially tried to pin the crimes of one serial killer on his addiction to lurid detective magazines. As they probed into his background, however, they discovered that, throughout his childhood and early adolescence, his mother had relentlessly subjected him to public ridicule for bed-wetting, while his stepfather had routinely tortured him with lighted cigarettes and forced him to drink his own urine. Moreover, on two separate occasions during his boyhood, he had suffered head injuries severe enough to put him into a coma.

In short, it became clear that this man's sadistic compulsions were rooted in his severely abused upbringing (as is so often the case), and that his psychopathology was firmly established long before he became such an obsessive reader of true-crime magazines. His insatiable appetite for sleazy entertainment, in other words, was a *symptom* of his sickness, not its cause.

One particularly twisted individual—a serial killer named David Harker, who strangled a thirty-two-year-old woman during sex, then cut up her body and ate chunks of her thigh with pasta and cheese—put the matter in perspective. Known to be a fan of *The Silence of the Lambs,* he was questioned after his arrest about the possible influence of the film on his own cannibalistic crime. "People like me don't come from films," he replied. "Films come from people like me."

Nowadays, of course, whenever a horrific murder occurs, the reading, listening, and viewing habits of the perpetrator are immediately scrutinized for evidence that his crimes were somehow triggered by today's supposedly debased popular entertainment. When mass murderer Michael McDermott slaughtered seven employees of a Boston high-tech company in December 2000, reports quickly surfaced that his home video library was heavily weighted with action films like *Lethal Weapon* and *Die Hard*—as though his enjoyment of these Hollywood blockbusters explained his appallingly violent act. Only later did the press reveal that his video collection also included the Steve Martin comedy, *The Jerk;* the Academy Award–winning drama *One Flew Over the Cuckoo's Nest;* the Grade-Z sci-fi flick, *Plan 9 from Outer Space;* and *Pee Wee's Big Adventure.* As one criminologist wisely advised, "I would caution against looking at this list as any indicator of violent tendencies."

Indeed, anyone inclined to blame psychopathic violence on a killer's favorite books or movies must deal with the discomfiting fact that a significant number of serial murderers have been devoted students of the Bible, capable of committing the most horrendous crimes even while reciting Scripture.

Several years before metamorphosing into the crazed, woman-hating gunman known as "Son of Sam," David Berkowitz underwent a religious awakening, becoming a convert to evangelical Christianity during an army stint in Fort Knox, Kentucky. Embracing his new faith with a near-obsessive zeal, he became a fixture at the Beth Haven Church, listening raptly to the hellfire sermons, undergoing the ritual of full-immersion baptism, and taking to the sidewalks to preach about sin and salvation. Even in his ardent religiosity, however, Berkowitz's pathology shone through. The only souls he was interested in saving were those of men. As he later explained to a prison psychiatrist, "I just wanted to see the men get into heaven. Who the hell needed those sluts, those go-go dancers? Too many women in heaven would spoil it."

John George Haigh was raised in a hyperreligious household, his parents being devout members of a puritanic sect, the Plymouth Brethren. Throughout his life—even during the years when he was busily dispatching victims and dissolving their bodies in drums of hydrochloric acid—he loved to take part in theological discussions, impressing his listeners with his intimate knowledge of the Bible.

Earle Leonard Nelson, too, was highly conversant with Scripture, having been brought up by a fanatically religious grandmother. Obsessed with the Book of Revelation, he could quote his favorite passage by heart:

> So he carried me away in the spirit into the wilderness: and I saw a woman sit upon a scarlet-colored beast, full of names of blasphemy, having seven heads and ten horns. And the woman was arrayed in purple and scarlet color, and decked with gold and precious stones and pearls, having a gold cup in her hand full of abominations and filthiness of her fornication: and upon her forehead was a name written, MYSTERY, BABYLON THE GREAT, THE MOTHER OF HARLOTS AND ABOMINATIONS OF THE EARTH. And I saw the woman drunken with the blood of the saints, and with the blood of the martyrs of Jesus.

Nelson used his religious training to win the confidence of his potential victims, who never suspected—until it was too late—that the well-spoken, seemingly devout young man was really the notorious "Gorilla Murderer" wanted from coast to coast for the savage slaying of nearly two dozen women.

Another Scripture-spouting serial strangler was the still-anonymous psychopath known only as "Bible John," who murdered three women in Glasgow, Scotland, in the late 1960s. The killer's nickname derived from his habit of reciting scraps of the Old Testament, particularly bits relating to Moses. The identity of the Bible-quoting psycho-killer remains one of the great unsolved mysteries in the annals of Scottish crime.

Of all Bible-crazed serial killers, however, the most terrifying was undoubtedly Albert Fish, whose obsession with the story of Abraham and Isaac drove him to act out hideous sacrificial rituals on a string of child victims. The cannibalistic Fish—who described the eating of one twelve-year-old girl as an act of "Holy Communion"—spent years poring over Scripture, searching for the most disturbing passages, which he would then commit to memory. His favorite was Jeremiah 19:9: "And I will cause them to eat the flesh of their sons and the flesh of their daughters, and they shall eat every one the flesh of his friend in the siege and straitness, wherewith their enemies, and they that seek their lives, shall straiten them."

Recommended Reading

Jib Fowles, *The Case For Television Violence* (1999)

Gerard Jones, *Killing Monsters: Why Children Need Fantasy, Super Heroes, and Make-Believe Violence* (2002)

PORNOGRAPHY

It's a common occurrence. A serial killer is captured, and the police—while searching his living quarters—turn up a stash of violent sadomasochistic porn. Immediately, the proponents of censorship trumpet this discovery as proof of the evils of pornography in general, its insidious power to corrupt morality and inspire crimes against women.

Clearly, there are problems with this argument. For one thing, the vast majority of porn consumers are law-abiding citizens who use XXX-rated material to excite their libidos, not their aggressions. There's no solid evidence that pornography has anything other than an aphrodisiacal effect on such viewers.

For another thing, it makes perfect sense that serial killers seek out sadomasochistic porn. Criminal psychopaths, after all, are predisposed to violent fantasy. It would be far more surprising if the cops broke into the home of a sadistic lust-killer and discovered that his entire video library consisted of the collected episodes of *SpongeBob Squarepants.*

Still, the arguments of the antipornography crusaders received a powerful boost from a source who certainly seemed to know as much about the subject as any man alive (however temporarily). On the night of January 23, 1989, just hours before his execution, Ted Bundy gave an interview to Christian psychologist Dr. James Dobson, an antiporn crusader and former member of President Reagan's Commission on Pornography.

Hailed by some as compelling testimony of the dangers of pornography—and dismissed by others as the self-serving rationalizations of a pathological liar—Bundy's responses are fairly thoughtful, if not consistent or especially convincing. At one point he states that his atrocities cannot be blamed on pornography; at another, he describes himself as someone who was perfectly normal until he fell under the evil sway of dirty magazines. He denies that he is trying to evade responsibility for his behavior, even while insisting that he would never have committed his outrages if it hadn't been for his exposure to images of "sexualized violence."

In the end, it is hard to know what to make of the interview. Was Bundy—a quintessential psychopath who had gone through life masquerading as normal—simply playing one final role, that of the repentant sinner? Or was he really struggling to comprehend his own evil nature and grasping at an easy explanation for that ultimately unknowable mystery?

Here are the relevant parts of the interview:

> *Bundy:* As a young boy of twelve or thirteen, I encountered, outside the home, in the local grocery and drug stores, soft-core pornography. Young boys explore the sideways and byways of their neighborhoods, and in our neighborhood, people would dump the garbage. From time to time, we would come across books of a harder nature—more graphic. This also in-

cluded detective magazines, etc., and I want to emphasize this. The most damaging kind of pornography—and I'm talking from hard, real, personal experience—is that that involves violence and sexual violence. The wedding of those two forces—as I know only too well—brings about behavior that is too terrible to describe.

Dobson: Walk me through that. What was going on in your mind at that time?

Bundy: Before we go any further, it is important to me that people believe what I'm saying. I'm not blaming pornography. I'm not saying it caused me to go out and do certain things. I take full responsibility for all the things that I've done. That's not the question here. The issue is how this kind of literature contributed and helped mold and shape the kinds of violent behavior.

Dobson: It fueled your fantasies.

Bundy: In the beginning, it fuels this kind of thought process. Then, at a certain time, it is instrumental in crystallizing it, making it into something that is almost a separate entity inside.

Dobson: You had gone about as far as you could go in your own fantasy life, with printed material, photos, videos, etc., and then there was the urge to take that step over to a physical event.

Bundy: Once you become addicted to it, and I look at this as a kind of addiction, you look for more potent, more explicit, more graphic kinds of material. Like an addiction, you keep craving something which is harder and gives you a greater sense of excitement, until you reach the point where the pornography only goes so far—that jumping-off point where you begin to think maybe actually doing it will give you that which is just beyond reading about it and looking at it.

Dobson: How long did you stay at that point before you actually assaulted someone?

Bundy: A couple of years. I was dealing with very strong inhibitions against criminal and violent behavior. That had been conditioned and bred into me from my neighborhood, environment, church, and schools. I knew it was wrong to think about it, and certainly, to do it was wrong. I was on the edge, and the last vestiges of restraint were being tested constantly, and assailed through the kind of fantasy life that was fueled, largely, by pornography.

Dobson: Do you remember what pushed you over that edge? Do you remember the decision to "go for it"? Do you remember where you decided to throw caution to the wind?

Bundy: It's a very difficult thing to describe—the sensation of reaching that point where I knew I couldn't control it anymore. The barriers I had learned as a child were not enough to hold me back from seeking out and harming somebody.

Dobson: You hadn't known you were capable of that before?

Bundy: There is no way to describe the brutal urge to do that, and once it has been satisfied, or spent, and that energy level recedes, I became myself again. Basically, I was a normal person. I wasn't some guy hanging out in bars, or a bum. I wasn't a pervert in the sense that people look at somebody and say, "I know there's something wrong with him." I was a normal person. I had good friends. I led a normal life, except for this one, small but very potent and destructive segment that I kept very secret and close to myself. Those of us who have been so influenced by violence in the media, particularly pornographic violence, are not some kind of inherent monsters. We are your sons and husbands. We grew up in regular families. Pornography can reach in and snatch a kid out of any house today. It snatched me out of my home twenty or thirty years ago. As diligent as my parents were, and they were diligent in protecting their children, and as good a Christian home as we had, there is no protection against the kinds of influences that are loose in a society that tolerates.

PROFIT

When the term "serial killer" exploded into public consciousness in the early 1980s, it was applied to madmen like Ted Bundy, John Wayne Gacy, Richard Ramirez et al. These were classic sexual predators—lust-killers, as they used to be called—who could only get aroused and reach climax when they were perpetrating unspeakable acts on the bodies of helpless victims.

Though most serial killers fall into this category, not all of them are motivated primarily by sexual sadism. Some commit their crimes not only for pleasure but also for monetary gain.

Such profit-driven killers are no less psychopathic than their sexually perverted brethren. In conceiving and carrying out their atrocities, they proceed in a rational, cunning, often highly intelligent manner. They are also utterly without conscience, remorse, or the capacity to empathize. To them, other human beings are simply objects to be manipulated, destroyed, and disposed of for their own narcissistic ends.

A classic example of this breed is Dr. H. H. Holmes, the notorious nineteenth-century "Torture Doctor" who killed an indeterminate number of victims around the time of the 1893 Chicago World's Fair. Though this suave lady killer and bigamist was certainly interested in sex, his crimes were fueled largely by an insatiable greed, characteristic of the money-crazed ethos of the post–Civil War "Gilded Age." One of Holmes's many scams required the use of dead bodies to defraud insurance companies. In his published autobiography, he repeatedly refers to these corpses as "material"—a term that says a great deal about his psychopathic personality. To Holmes, the decomposing remains of a fellow human being meant nothing more than a piece of lumber does to a carpenter—and if no dead bodies were available when required, he was only too happy to create his own.

The same was true of the entrepreneurial eighteenth-century ghouls, Burke and Hare, who began by supplying dead bodies to British anatomists desperate for human specimens and quickly progressed to serial murder as a way of maintaining their inventory.

In our own century, another medical monster, Dr. Marcel Petiot, disposed of dozens of trusting victims—desperate Jews hoping to flee Nazi-occupied France who were killed, incinerated, and relieved of their earthly possessions by the homicidal physician.

The kinds of serial killers known as Bluebeards and Black Widows—respectively, male and female psychopaths who murder a succession of spouses—also fall into this motivational category, since greed, as much as the gratification of malevolent impulses, underlies their crimes.

There is a tendency to see mercenary serial killers as less horrific than lust-murderers. And it is true that, as a general rule, such psychopaths tend not to indulge in the most appalling atrocities: torture, dismemberment, evisceration, cannibalism, etc. Even so, murder isn't just a matter of business to them. It's a distinct and very twisted pleasure.

Holmes, for example, may have killed his victims primarily for money, but he also liked to see them suffer, reportedly outfitting some of the rooms in his "Murder Castle" with peepholes that permitted him to watch the death agonies of his victims. Marcel Petiot also had a peephole installed in the door of his basement death chamber for similarly sadistic reasons. The nineteenth-century "Angel of Death," Jane Toppan stole sizable sums from her victims. But she also derived exquisite pleasure from climbing into bed with them during their dying moments and holding them tight as they suffered their final convulsions. And greed alone can't account for the actions of John George Haigh, who supported himself for years by murdering some of his closest acquaintances, then dissolving their bodies in metal drums filled with acid and pouring the resulting unspeakable muck into the sewers. As Haigh himself put it, "There are easier ways of making money."

John George Haigh, The Acid Bath Killer

CASE STUDY

People who believe that posting the Ten Commandments in public schools is the cure for today's social problems would surely be confounded by the case of John George Haigh. Born in 1909, Haigh was raised in a strict religious sect known as the Plymouth Brethren, whose members not only abjured the usual puritanical bugaboos—alcohol, tobacco, gambling, theatergoing, and the reading of novels—but refused to socialize with people of any other persuasion, all whom they derided as "gentiles." Despite (or possibly because of) this godly upbringing, Haigh grew up to be an inveterate hedonist with a taste for fast cars, fine food, and expensive clothing. He was also a lifelong criminal, who spent much of his young manhood behind bars and ended up becoming one of the most notorious figures in the history of modern British crime.

To be sure, his upstanding background did endow him with some attractive features: a keen intelligence, fastidious personal habits, and a polite and charming manner. More than one constable and prison official who came to know him near the end of his life attested that he was the "nicest murderer they ever met."

After leaving school in his late teens, Haigh worked at a succession of jobs: government clerk, insurance salesman, apprentice engineer. The knowledge he gained from each of these occupations—coupled with a gift for calligraphy that made him an excellent forger—would prove useful in his future life of crime.

At twenty-four, Haigh married a vivacious young woman named Betty Hamer, who had no idea that her suave, well-spoken husband was supporting himself by swindling. She discovered the truth four months later when he was arrested for fraud. While Haigh was serving his fifteen-month sentence, his wife gave birth and immediately put the child up for adoption. Apart from one brief meeting after his release, Haigh would never see her again.

Nor would he ever remarry. Despite his easy charm and dapper appearance—the Brylcreemed hair, pencil mustache, handsome suits, and lemon yellow gloves he wore indoors and out—he was not a ladies' man. Unlike other serial killers, his crimes were not motivated by depraved sexual compulsions. His madness took a more mercenary form. Like other serial killer con men—H. H. Holmes, for example—Haigh was blessed with many admirable qualities: industriousness, intelligence, ingenuity. Had he put those traits to legitimate uses, he would undoubtedly have done very well in the world. But he was undermined by his psychopathology. Making money by killing acquaintances wasn't necessarily easier than earning an honest living—indeed, Haigh devoted a great deal of time and energy to his terrible crimes—but it was more gratifying. It fulfilled his darkest, most twisted needs.

Released from prison in 1935, Haigh, the prodigal son, returned to his parents' home. He worked for a while at the dry-cleaning business, then moved to London, where he befriended a young man named William McSwan, owner of a pinball arcade business, who offered him a job as secretary/chauffeur. Haigh stayed on the job for just a year before striking out on his own. Setting up a phony solicitor's office, he contrived an elaborate stock scam which eventually landed him behind bars again, this time for four years.

He put his time in prison to productive use, studying law books to learn how to commit the perfect crime. It was during this period that he acquired the notion that a murder could not be legally proved without a dead body, a misconception based on his flawed understanding of the term *corpus delecti* (which does not refer to a corpse but rather to the body of evidence that proves a crime has been committed). Within a year of his release, he found himself back in jail for scamming money from a female acquaintance. While there, he managed to steal some sulfuric acid from a tinsmith's shop and experimented on field mice to see how long it took for their bodies to dissolve.

Released in 1943, the thirty-four-year-old Haigh got a legitimate job as a bookkeeper, saved up his money, and, after about a year, moved to London, where he set himself up in a basement workshop, passing himself off in public as a company director with an engineering degree.

In September 1944, after he and his old pal, William McSwan, ran into each other at a pub and renewed their friendship, Haigh invited the young man down to his basement workshop, bludgeoned him to death with a lead pipe, then dissolved his body in a forty-gallon oil drum filled with hydrochloric acid. When nothing was left of "Mac," Haigh poured the stinking, porridgelike fluid down the drain. After persuading McSwan's parents that their son had gone to Scotland to avoid the draft, Haigh—using his skills as a forger—managed to get power of attorney over his old friend's property. Later, when the parents began asking too many questions about their son's abrupt departure, Haigh dispatched them in the same way, luring them to his workshop, smashing in their skulls, turning them into sludge, and dumping them into the sewers.

More victims followed, including a well-to-do couple named Henderson. Haigh killed each with a pistol shot to the head before liquefying them in his acid-filled oil drum. Afterward, he managed to get hold of the Hendersons' substantial estate, though he soon squandered the money at the track.

His final victim was a sixty-nine-year-old widow named Mrs. Olivia Durand-Deacon. When the well-to-do widow failed to return from a visit to Haigh's workshop, her friends notified the police, who soon turned up incriminating evidence in Haigh's possession, including some of the missing woman's jewelry. Realizing that the jig was up, the audacious con man made a startling admission, confessing not only to the murders of Mrs. Durand-Deacon, the Hendersons, and all three McSwans, but to three other killings as well. With the arrogance typical of psychopaths, he then challenged the police to convict him, declaring that—since "every trace" of the victims had been dissolved in acid—he couldn't possibly be found guilty. "How can you prove murder without a body?" he asked with a smile.

His smug belief that he had left no physical evidence of his atrocities was quickly shattered. Searching Haigh's premises, investigators turned up twenty-eight pounds of human fat, three gallstones, eighteen fragments of human bone, part of a foot, and Mrs. Durand-Deacon's undissolved dentures.

As if the case weren't already gruesome enough, Haigh began to lay the groundwork for an insanity plea by claiming that the real motive for his crimes was a lifelong vampiric compulsion. For many years, he claimed, he had been tormented by the same recurring nightmare of driving through a forest of crucifixes while blood rained from the sky. He would awaken each time with an overwhelming thirst for human blood. In each of his murders, he had slit the victim's carotid artery with a penknife, drained off a glass of blood, and drunk it.

Needless to say, these ghastly revelations turned the trial of Haigh—alternately dubbed the "Acid Bath Killer" and the "Vampire Killer"—into a media sensation. Unsurprisingly, psychiatric witnesses disagreed about the defendant's mental condition, even after Haigh—as though to prove just how disturbed he really was—drank a cup of his own urine in prison. In the end, the jury found him guilty, agreeing with the prosecution's argument that the inveterate con artist had committed his atrocities out of greed, not vampiric need. He was hanged on August 6, 1949.

CELEBRITY

When the so-called Beltway Snipers were at large in the fall of 2002, many people were outraged over the nonstop saturation coverage of the case. Television and radio talk shows were deluged with callers, complaining that such unrelenting media attention only glamorized the gunmen and encouraged other potential psycho-killers to seek their own fifteen minutes of notoriety.

Though understandable, such reactions aren't especially valid. For one thing, it's hypocritical for people to stay glued to their TV sets, eagerly lapping up every morsel of information about a grisly murder case, while simultaneously clucking their tongues over the crass and insensitive behavior of the media. After all, when cable news networks devote twenty-four/seven coverage to a particularly ghastly crime, they are only giving the public what it wants—and what it has *always* wanted.

The fascination with gruesome murders existed long before there was such a thing as "the media." In preliterate times, people learned about sensational crimes through orally transmitted ballads. Every time a dissatisfied wife poisoned her abusive husband, or a jealous young man hacked to death his unfaithful lover, or a desperate mother smothered her sleeping children, or a band of brigands slaughtered a party of travelers—the details were turned into a song and transmitted from person to person, village to village, until everyone had heard the news.

When movable type was invented, these so-called murder ballads were printed on cheap sheets of paper and sold for a penny apiece. Many of these "broadsides" still exist, and their titles make it abundantly clear that people have always had an insatiable appetite for news about the latest horrific crimes: "Horrible and Atrocious Murder of a Woman at Wednesbury," "Frightful Murder of the Rev. Mr Huelin and His Housekeeper at Chelsea," "Shocking Murder of a Wife at Oving, Near Aylesbury," "Horrid Murder Committed by Mary Wilson Upon the Body of George Benson, Through Disappointment in Marriage."

Serial murder was big news back in the Victorian era, as the frenzied tabloid coverage of the Jack the Ripper case attests. There is no question that, had cable TV existed back then, Geraldo Rivera would have been on the scene, interviewing the residents of Whitechapel about their reactions to the latest disemboweling. When the atrocities of Dr. H. H. Holmes were uncovered a few years after the Ripper horrors, the American public couldn't get enough of them. Publishers churned out instant true-crime books on the case, newspapers printed every trivial detail they could dig up, and one entrepreneur even opened an H. H. Holmes museum, complete with replicas of his victims' remains.

Indeed, popular nineteenth-century museums often appealed to the public's interest in macabre crime. From the moment Madame Tussaud's first opened its doors for business in 1835, the exhibition hall known as the "Chamber of Horrors"—featuring wax effigies of world-famous murderers, along with torture tableaux and other macabre dioramas—has always been the biggest attraction, far outdrawing the high-minded displays of politicians, philosophers, and artists. The character played by Vincent Price in the 1953 movie *House of Wax* understood this. Planning to open his own Madame Tussaud-like museum, he announces: "I'm going to give the people what they want: sensation, horror, shocks!"

There is no doubt that the possibility of being immortalized—if not in Madame Tussaud's wax museum then in a made-for-TV movie or best-selling true-crime book—is an appealing prospect to many serial killers, who revel in the celebrity that their crimes confer on them. There's nothing surprising about this. Most serial killers are complete nonentities: total losers who have failed in every important area of life. Even those who have managed to forge respectable careers—John Wayne Gacy, for example, who ran a successful contracting business—feel like nothing inside. Having been subjected, almost without exception, to brutalized upbringings, they are instilled with a sense of utter worthlessness. Seeing their names in the papers or their faces on TV fills their hollow souls with an intoxicating sense of power and importance. Murder is their only means of making a mark on the world, of proving (to themselves as much as to anyone else) that they *exist.* As Pete Hamill said of David "Son of Sam" Berkowitz: "He was a nobody who became somebody by killing people."

Berkowitz, in fact, is an interesting case, a perfect illustration of the slogan used in the ads for the movie *Chicago:* "If you can't be famous, be infamous." As noted by Dr. David Abrahamsen, who got to know him through extensive interviews, Berkowitz had a desperate lifelong need "to be noticed, attract attention, create a sensation." His transformation from obscurity to notoriety—from being an unknown postal clerk to the world-famous "Son of Sam"—openly thrilled him.

Certainly, in the twenty-five years since his chubby face was first plastered on the front pages, Berkowitz has remained addicted to his infamy, periodically finding ways to get his name in the papers. In 1997, he made

(Button pin courtesy of Roger Worsham)

David Berkowitz

headlines when he announced that he had found God, changed his nickname from "Son of Sam" to "Son of Hope," and begun preaching the Gospel on public access TV. Two years later, the *New York Times* ran a page-one story, describing how distressed he was over the release of Spike Lee's movie *Summer of Sam,* which was reawakening painful memories of his 1977 reign of terror. And when the Beltway Snipers were at large, Berkowitz insinuated himself back in the papers by releasing a letter to the press in which he declared that the current serial shooter rampage was causing him to "relive a nightmare."

Clearly, media notoriety is an important fringe benefit for many serial killers, another sick gratification they derive from their crimes. Whether it is also the *cause* of their behavior is another question. To be sure, at least one homicidal maniac—not a serial killer but a mass murderer named Robert Benjamin Smith—is on record as saying that he committed his crime because "I wanted to get known, to get myself a name. I knew I had to kill a lot of people to get my name in the newspapers all over the world."

Even in this case, however, it is legitimate to wonder if the desire for media attention was really what made Smith walk into a Mesa, Arizona, beauty parlor in 1966 and execute four victims, including a three-year-old girl. After all, anyone who thinks that cold-blooded mass murder is a good way to become well-known has to be deeply psychopathic to begin with.

In short, while many serial killers certainly enjoy being the center of the media attention, they are motivated by far darker compulsions. The sinister celebrity they achieve from their atrocities may afford them a twisted satisfaction—what psychoanalysts call a *secondary gain.* But the root causes of their monstrous behavior lie elsewhere.

Recommended Reading

David Abrahamsen, *Confessions of Son of Sam* (1985)

Joseph C. Fisher, *Killer Among Us: Public Reactions to Serial Murder* (1997)

COPYCATS

Whenever a sensational crime occurs—one that receives lots of media coverage and rivets the attention of the public—chances are good that it will inspire some desperately disturbed individual to commit a similar—or "copycat"—crime as a way of making himself feel important. The

Columbine massacre, for example, was followed by a spate of high school shootings perpetrated by juvenile copycats looking to make their own bloody mark on society. And in the midst of the post–9/11 anthrax scare, various anonymous crackpots crawled out of the woodwork, adding to the general panic by sending powder-filled envelopes through the mails.

Despite the premise of the 1995 movie *Copycat,* however—in which the villain duplicates the precise MO of such notorious psycho-killers as the Hillside Stranglers, Son of Sam, and Jeffrey Dahmer—serial murder cases do not usually incite copycat crimes. In real life, the discovery of Dahmer's atrocities did not encourage anyone else to run out and cannibalize young gay males. To commit such horrors, a person has to be in the grip of the most grotesque and aberrant compulsions. No one is going to start dismembering prostitutes or burying dead bodies in his crawl space just because he read about it in the newspaper.

Nevertheless—while serial murder may not be *caused* by copycat motives—there have certainly been psychopaths who have looked up to earlier homicidal maniacs as role models and even wished to emulate their depravities. This phenomenon extends all the way back to the Middle Ages. Gilles de Rais—the monstrously depraved, fifteenth-century French aristocrat who supposedly served as the model for the fairy-tale figure, Bluebeard—claimed that his favorite author was Suetonius, the Roman historian who chronicled the degenerate doings of Imperial madmen like Nero and Caligula.

In our own century, there have been several notable examples of frighteningly sadistic lust-killers who openly admired others of their breed. Peter Kürten—the so-called Monster of Düsseldorf—was a big fan of Jack the Ripper's, reading every book on the Whitechapel Horrors that he could get his hands on. And Albert Fish, the cannibalistic pedophile who perpetrated some of the most appalling murders in the annals of American crime, idolized the German madman Fritz Haarmann, saving news clippings about the "Vampire of Hanover" the way teenage girls keep scrapbooks of their favorite pop stars.

There have also been some severely disturbed individuals who can only be described as serial killer "wannabes." Such psychos don't identify with, or seek to emulate, specific murderers from the past. They aren't trying to be the new Jack the Ripper or Jeffrey Dahmer. Their great ambition is simply to be known as a "serial killer," as if that in itself were a badge of distinction.

In the spring of 1993, for example, a British psychopath named Colin Ireland perpetrated a string of savage murders for the express purpose of being labeled a serial killer. On March 9 of that year, the thirty-eight-year-old Ireland showed up at a gay pub in London, secretly equipped with a "murder kit," consisting of cord, knife, and gloves. After flirting with a forty-five-year-old choreographer named Peter Walker, Ireland and his pickup went back to Walker's flat. There, Ireland proceeded to bind, beat, torture, and finally suffocate Walker with a plastic bag. Afterward, he burned his victim's pubic hair—to see, he later told police, "how it would smell"—stuffed condoms in the dead man's mouth and up his nostrils, and placed two teddy bears on his chest in the "69" position.

Two months later, on May 29, Ireland returned to the same pub, met another gay man who was into S&M sex—a thirty-seven-year-old librarian named Christopher Dunn. After returning to Dunn's flat, Ireland handcuffed him to the bed, beat him with a belt, and held a cigarette lighter to his testicles before suffocating him by shoving pieces of cloth down his throat.

Ireland claimed his third victim just six days later, when he strangled a thirty-five-year-old American expatriate named Perry Bradley III. Having committed three, virtually identical murders within such a short span of time, Ireland eagerly scanned the news each day, expecting to find stories about the killing spree. The police, however, had not yet linked the three deaths. Frustrated at this lack of recognition, Ireland struck again just three days later, torturing and murdering a thirty-three-year-old gay man named Andrew Collier after picking him up at the same pub. For spite, he also strangled Collier's cat and left it lying atop the corpse with its gaping mouth around the dead man's penis.

On June 12, exactly a week after killing Collier, Ireland put in an anonymous phone call to the police and—after announcing that he had already committed four murders and intended to do one more—scolded them for failing to recognize that a serial killer was on the loose. "Doesn't the death of a homosexual man mean anything?" he demanded.

The day after the phone call, Ireland killed his final victim, a forty-one-year-old chef named Emanuel Spiteri. He was arrested after police found a security video showing him walking with Spiteri at a subway station. In custody, he quickly confessed.

Unlike most serial killers who target gay men, Ireland wasn't gay himself. Nor did he have any particular animosity toward homosexuals. ("It might just as well have been women," he insisted.) He had chosen S&M types, he said, because they were easy targets who would go home with a total stranger and let themselves be tied up.

Ireland steadfastly insisted that he had savagely murdered five men for one simple reason: he aspired to be a serial killer and had read in a book that, to be so classified, a person had to slay a minimum of four. The last homicide was committed just for good measure.

In December 1993, an Old Bailey judge told Ireland: "You expressed the desire to be regarded as a serial killer. That must be matched by your detention for life." He was given five consecutive life sentences and told that he would never be released from prison.

> I have read a lot of books on serial killers. I think it is from four people that the FBI class as serial, so I may stop now I have done five.
>
> —Colin Ireland in an anonymous call to police

Heriberto Seda, Zodiac Copycat

CASE STUDY

People—especially New Yorkers—often react with surprise when told that the infamous Zodiac killer was never caught. After all, they can clearly remember the newspaper headlines from 1998 trumpeting the arrest and conviction of the Zodiac shooter. The man referred to in those stories, however, was not the famously elusive gunman who terrorized San Francisco in the late 1960s, but rather a young psychopathic New Yorker named Heriberto Seda—a classic copycat killer whose warped admiration for the original Zodiac inspired him to conduct an astrologically themed murder spree of his own.

Twenty-two at the time he embarked on his homicidal campaign, Seda was a high school dropout who lived with his mother and sister, had neither friends nor romantic relationships, and picked up pocket money by stealing coins from pay phones and vending machines. With no job or social life, he appears to have spent much of his time shut up in his room reading *Soldier of Fortune* magazine and books about serial killers. A gun nut whose schooling came to an end when he was suspended for carrying a concealed weapon, Seda was particularly obsessed with the Bay Area Zodiac, partly because the latter was one of the rare serial killers who relied on firearms. Seda was also something of a religious fanatic and was fascinated by the Zodiac's bizarre quasi-mystical letters in which he spoke of collecting slaves to serve him in the afterlife.

Taking a leaf from his role model's book, Seda sent a letter to the "Anti-Crime" unit of his local police precinct in November 1989:

This is the Zodiac.
The First Sign is dead.
The Zodiac will Kill the twelve signs in the
Belt when the Zodiacal light is seen.
The Zodiac will spread fear
I have seen a lot of police in Jamaica Ave and
Elden Lane but you are no good and will not get
the Zodiac.
Orion is the one that can stop Zodiac and the
Seven Sister.

Given the number of bizarre communications they receive on a regular basis, the cops saw no reason to pay particular attention to this apparent crank letter and filed it away.

Despite the second line of this letter—which suggests that Seda had already committed a murder at the time he sent it—his first two shootings appear to have occurred the following March, when, wielding a homemade 9mm zip gun, he ambushed two people several weeks apart in Brooklyn. Both men survived.

At the time, the police didn't connect the attacks, assuming that they were simply two more of the many gun-related incidents afflicting New York City in that era of rampant crime.

When Seda struck again on May 31, however—mortally wounding an elderly Brooklynite out for a late-night stroll—he left one of his bizarre notes beside the body. Soon, more communications from the self-styled Zodiac began arriving at the offices of the *New York Post,* which broke the story on June 19. *Riddle of the Zodiac Shooter,* read the headline. Suddenly, the police and the public were faced with the unnerving realization that—twenty years after the city was terrorized by the "Son of Sam"—New York had another phantom shooter in its midst.

After consulting astrologers who predicted that the killer would strike again in the early-morning hours of June 21, officials put scores of policemen on the streets of Brooklyn to watch for the shooter. Seda outwitted them, however, by shifting his hunting grounds to Manhattan, shooting a homeless man in Central Park. The following day, he sent another letter to the *Post,* insisting that he and the San Francisco Zodiac were one and the same. Few believed, however, that the legendary West Coast psycho-killer had suddenly surfaced in New York City, particularly since several witnesses to the Brooklyn shootings described a figure far too young to be the Woodstock-era madman. It was clear that the new spree was the work of a deranged copycat.

With the whole city focused on his capture, Seda—who had lovingly compiled a scrapbook of clippings about his crimes—decided to take a break. When the next astrologically significant date came and went without another shooting, the public began to relax. Before long, Zodiac had been largely forgotten.

He returned with a vengeance the following year, attacking four people—two fatally—in a Brooklyn park between June 4 and October 2, 1992. In June 1994, after another prolonged hiatus, he shot a fifth victim in the same park. A month after the latter incident, he mailed the final—and in many ways most bizarre—of his Zodiac letters to the *New York Post.* "Sleep my little dead," he wrote after listing his latest victims. "How we lothe them."

Two more years would pass before Seda attacked another person. This time, it would be his own sister. Seda shot her in the back with one of his zip guns during a violent argument. Wounded, she made it to the apartment of a neighbor, who dialed 911.

Taken to the station house, Seda was asked to describe the incident in writing. He complied, signing the statement with the same arcane symbols—a cross and three sevens—he had used on his Zodiac letters. Suddenly, the detectives realized that the young man in their custody was the long-sought shooter. Before long, they obtained a full confession from him.

In June 1998, Heriberto Seda was convicted and sentenced to a minimum term of eighty-plus years behind bars. He reportedly spends much of his time in prison poring over the Bible and quoting Scripture to his fellow inmates.

THE DEVIL MADE ME DO IT

While supernatural explanations for homicidal mania have not been in vogue since the Middle Ages, some serial killers continue to insist that they were the victims of demonic possession. David Berkowitz, for example, stoutly maintained that "a demon has been living in me since birth." And Herbert Mullin—the California psycho who believed that he could stave off a cataclysmic earthquake by slaughtering eight people—once accounted for his actions by explaining that "Satan gets into people and makes them do things they don't want to."

Still, it's been a long time since anyone tried the "devil made me do it" defense in a courtroom—at least in the United States. As recently as the 1950s, however, one South African serial murderer gave it a shot.

His name was Elifasi Msomi. During a span of twenty-one months in the early fifties, this part-time witch doctor, a native of Natal, butchered fifteen people. Most of his victims were young children. Posing as a "labor agent," Msomi lured the little ones away from home by promising to get them well-paying jobs as servants. Once he had them safely in his clutches, he hacked them to death with an ax.

He was arrested in 1955 and confessed to his crimes, though he claimed that he was under the sway of an invisible demon known as a "tokoloshe" that supposedly perched on his shoulder and commanded him to kill. Court-appointed psychiatrists dismissed this story as so much mumbo jumbo and offered a more plausible explanation.

Msomi, they said, derived sadistic sexual pleasure from his atrocities. He was hanged in Pretoria prison in February 1956.

EVIL IN ACTION

For months, even years, his fantasies have become more obsessive, dominating his waking life. His imagined scenarios of torture and death have grown so intense that he thinks of little else. Finally, he can no longer stand the pressure from within. Lying in bed and masturbating as he thinks about strangling a coed or disemboweling a male hustler isn't enough anymore. It is time to make his dreams come true—to appease his monstrous hunger with living flesh and blood.

But how?

TRIGGERS

At the end of Alfred Hitchcock's *Psycho,* a psychiatrist named Dr. Richmond describes the circumstances that caused mild-mannered Norman Bates to transform into a crazed, cross-dressing killer. Whenever the profoundly schizoid Norman "felt a strong attraction to any other woman," Dr. Richmond explains, the evil "mother side of him would go wild." That's exactly what happened with Marion Crane (the character played by Janet Leigh). When Norman met her, says Richmond, "He was touched by her—aroused by her. He *wanted* her. That set off the jealous mother." Next thing you know, poor Marion was slashed to death in a scene that caused an entire generation of moviegoers to feel a twinge of anxiety every time they stepped into the shower.

Though some film critics see the psychiatrist as a ludicrous figure—a deliberate caricature of a smug Freudian know-it-all—he actually does a pretty good job of describing the phenomenon that criminologists call a "triggering factor." This is the thing that (in Dr. Richmond's words) "sets off" a serial killer and causes him—after a prolonged period during which his fantasies have been lying dormant—to "go wild."

In real life, as in *Psycho,* the triggering factor is often a specific type of victim, one who has the kinds of qualities that turn the killer on. For psychopaths, as for normally constituted human beings, these features vary widely. In contrast to the movie, the homicidal impulses of Ed Gein—the real-life prototype of Norman Bates—were provoked not by young, attractive females but by stout, middle-aged women with a physical resemblance to his mother. Ted Bundy, on the other hand, was drawn to pretty college-age brunettes with their hair parted down the middle. Other serial killers have been excited to a murderous frenzy by muscular adolescent boys, drug-addicted hookers, or defenseless little girls. A powerful portrayal of a "triggering" episode can be seen in the classic 1931 movie *M,* when the pedophiliac lust-killer, Franz Becker (brilliantly played by Peter Lorre) spots a pretty prepubescent girl as he strolls along a Berlin street. The look that passes over Beckert's face chillingly conveys the hideous lust that is suddenly aroused in him by the sight of the unwary child.

As in *Psycho*—where a beautiful, unescorted blonde unexpectedly shows up at the Bates Motel—an unforeseen opportunity can also serve as a triggering factor. In 1874, a ten-year-old girl named Katie Curran, looking to buy a new notebook for school, wandered into the newspaper shop where Jesse Pomeroy was working by himself. Though Pomeroy preferred boy victims, the circumstance of suddenly finding himself alone with the trusting child incited his homicidal mania. Luring the little girl into the cellar, he set upon her with a pocketknife, then concealed her mutilated corpse in an ash heap. In a similar way, during the spring of 1928, the cannibalistic monster Albert Fish presented himself at the home of a couple named Budd, having been drawn there by a classified newspaper ad placed by their adolescent son—Fish's intended target. During the visit, however, the Budds' lovely twelve-year-old daughter, Grace, suddenly showed up. Something about the little girl's appearance triggered Fish's bloodlust. On the spot, he determined to abduct, kill, and eat her instead.

Clearly, it would be useful for law enforcement officials to know exactly what "triggering factors" lead to serial murder. The trouble is that—precisely because psychopathic killers are so profoundly disturbed—there is no telling *what* may set any one of them off. The German lust-killer Heinrich Pommerencke—aka the "Beast of the Black Forest"—progressed from serial rape to serial slaughter after seeing Cecil B. DeMille's biblical epic, *The Ten Commandments* in 1959. The Manson family's atrocities were triggered by, of all things, the Beatles' "White Album." Some psycho-killers grow enraged when their captives try to run away, others when their victims are overly cooperative. The frighteningly psychotic serial killer Joseph Kallinger abandoned his plans to assault several women when he discovered that they were menstruating. In the late 1960s, on the other hand, a still-unknown serial killer nicknamed "Bible John" picked up three women at a Glasgow dance hall called the Barrowland Ballroom. Their fully or partially unclothed corpses were subsequently found with "sanitary napkins they had been using discarded beside them." It appeared, as crime writer Martin Fido has put it, that the Scripture-citing psycho was "somehow provoked by menstruation."

> I saw women dancing around the Golden Calf and I thought they were a fickle lot. I knew I would have to kill.
>
> —Heinrich Pommerencke

HUNTING GROUNDS

From coyotes and wolves to bobcats and lions, creatures who prey on other, weaker animals tend to be highly territorial, confining their kills to a specific hunting ground. The same holds true for most serial killers. Like their four-legged counterparts, these human predators generally commit their atrocities within a particular area.

These places vary widely in size. Some killers restrict themselves to a single neighborhood. Jack the Ripper, for example, committed all his butcheries within the Whitechapel slum district of East London. Others range around an entire city, like David "Son of Sam" Berkowitz—whose victims were shot in different boroughs of New York. Still others might cover one or more counties, like the so-called Green River Killer, who prowled the area between Seattle and Tacoma. In each case, however, the killer sticks to a distinct territory. Depending on the extent of this area, he might stalk his quarry on foot (like Jack the Ripper) or rely on a vehicle. The Southern California psycho-killers Lawrence Bittaker and Roy Norris, for example, purchased a 1977 GMC cargo van—which they christened "Murder Mack"—specifically for the purpose of cruising for victims along the Pacific Coast Highway.

Serial killers select particular areas for their crimes partly because of the availability of their preferred form of prey. If you are stalking prostitutes, for example, you will obviously focus on red-light districts where streetwalkers flaunt their wares. As crime writer Michael Newton says, "Hunters go where there is game."

> I love to hunt. Prowling the streets looking for fair game—tasty meat. . . . I live for the hunt—my life.
>
> —David "Son of Sam" Berkowitz

Another factor is what criminologists refer to as the killer's "comfort zone." Most serial killers commit their crimes relatively close to home because they prefer to hunt in places they are familiar with, where they feel confident and in control. They like to know the lay of the land—the best spots to snare victims, the quickest escape routes.

Some serial killers actually feel most comfortable committing their outrages right *inside* their own homes. Even this kind of psycho is territorial, however, in the sense that he will haunt particular locales in search of prey. Jeffrey Dahmer, for example, favored a gay bar in Milwaukee, which kept him stocked with the young male victims he slaughtered inside his squalid apartment. John Wayne Gacy, who turned his suburban split-level into a private torture dungeon and charnel house, cruised the Greyhound bus station in central Chicago and other seamy areas where street hustlers congregated. David and Catherine Birnie trolled the highways of Perth for their victims, who were then raped and tortured in the couple's white brick bungalow, a ramshackle dwelling that became known as "Australia's House of Horrors."

At the opposite extreme from such home-based sadists are the *nomads*. The least territorial of all serial killers, these itinerant psychos—who depend on modern modes of transportation, from planes to trains to automobiles—travel across states, countries, and sometimes entire continents, killing as they go. Because this type of serial killer is so mobile, he is often able to stay several steps ahead of the law. Indeed, he is generally long gone by the time his latest atrocity is even discovered. As a result, such vagabonds are particularly hard to catch. Often, authorities aren't even aware that one of these killers is on the loose, since they fail to recognize that, say, two middle-aged women—one found strangled and raped in San Francisco, the other in Seattle—were actually the victims of the same psycho, a phenomenon that criminologist Stephen Egger has called "linkage blindness."

Earle Leonard Nelson, who actually did strangle landladies in San Francisco and Seattle (as well as in San Jose, Santa Barbara, Oakland, Portland, Kansas City, Philadelphia, Buffalo, Detroit, Chicago, and Winnipeg) was the first of this breed, at least in twentieth-century America. A compulsive drifter from adolescence on, he made his way back and forth across the country, generally by car, leaving nearly two dozen corpses in his wake.

Nelson's contemporary Carl Panzram was even more peripatetic. In the course of his extraordinarily brutal life, he traveled around the world, committing, by his own estimate, twenty-one murders, along with countless assault and homosexual rapes. In the mid-1920s, after shipping out to West

Africa as a merchant seaman, he hired eight native bearers to help him hunt crocodiles, then ended up killing and raping the Africans and feeding their bodies to the crocs.

More recently, Angel Maturino Resendez—aka the "Railway Killer"—slaughtered a minimum of nine known victims as he aimlessly rode the rails from place to place. A Mexican national, Resendez crossed the Texas border at will, hitching rides on freight cars that carried him as far north as Kentucky and Illinois. With no specific destination in mind, he would hop off at random locales and commit an atrocity in close proximity to the tracks. His usual MO was to invade a residence, club the inhabitants to death with whatever implement was at hand (a tire iron, a sledgehammer, a gardening tool), burglarize the place, then hop on the next passing train and vanish before the crime was even discovered.

Because he traveled in such a haphazard way, without knowing where he was heading or who his next victim would be, authorities were slow to see a pattern in the string of savage murders committed along the railroad tracks between August 1997 and June 1999. Eventually, however, Resendez was placed on the FBI's Top Ten Most Wanted List. In July 1999, he surrendered himself peacefully at the behest of his beloved older sister. He was later found guilty of capital murder.

His traveling days over, the infamous "Railway Killer" now sits on death row in Livingston, Texas.

CASE STUDY

John Eric Armstrong, Psycho Sailor

There's an old saying about the "sailor with a girl in every port." If the claims of John Eric Armstrong are true, he was a frighteningly psychopathic variation of that stereotype: a sailor who *murdered* girls in every port.

In 1992, at the age of eighteen, Armstrong enlisted in the US Navy and served the next seven years aboard the aircraft carrier *Nimitz.* At no time during this period did his shipmates or superiors detect signs of mental instability. On the contrary, he earned four promotions and two Good Conduct Medals. After leaving the navy in 1999, he and his wife settled in Dearborn Heights, Michigan, a working-class suburb of Detroit. Neighbors regarded him as a solid citizen: a good family man devoted to his wife and infant son, a reliable worker at the Detroit Metropolitan Airport, and a generally decent guy, the kind who sometimes ran errands for the blind woman across the street.

What no one around him knew, of course, was that—beneath his respectable veneer—the baby-faced, three hundred-pound Armstrong was a classic "harlot-killer," a psycho whose virulent hatred of prostitutes was directly proportional to his irresistible compulsion to have sex with them. Cruising the seedy Michigan Avenue strip in southwest Detroit after dark, he would pick up a hooker in his black Jeep Wrangler, then—as soon as their tryst was over—

undergo a frightening metamorphosis, yelling "I hate whores" while trying to strangle the woman to death.

On January 2, 2000, Detroit police received a call from a man who told them of a female body floating in the Rouge River. The man explained that—while crossing the bridge on foot—he suddenly felt ill and leaned over the railing to vomit. That's when he spotted the corpse.

The dead woman turned out to be Wendy Jordan, a drug addict and prostitute whose family had reported her missing several days earlier. A postmortem exam determined that she had been strangled to death, then tossed from the bridge.

The man who called the police to report the discovery was John Eric Armstrong.

Whether Armstrong's call was prompted by an unconscious desire to confess or the twisted need—common among serial killers—to play head games with the cops is unknown. In any event, the police found his story deeply suspicious and put him under surveillance. After collecting physical evidence from the victim—DNA from her killer's sperm, plus fibers on her clothes that apparently came from vehicle she'd been killed in—they visited Armstrong at home and, with his consent, took fibers from his Jeep, along with a blood sample.

When the preliminary test results came back in March, they showed definite matches between the evidence gathered from the victim and the samples taken from Armstrong. But prosecutors elected not to issue an arrest warrant until the final, official report arrived from the lab.

In the meantime—even knowing he was under police scrutiny—Armstrong was unable to resist his deadly compulsion.

On the morning of April 10, the bodies of three prostitutes in varying stages of decomposition were found beside the tracks in an isolated rail yard—clearly the work of a serial killer. By that evening, a task force had been assembled. Questioned by investigators, streetwalkers along Michigan Avenue described their terrifying encounters with a beefy, baby-faced john who would go berserk and try to strangle them after sex in his Jeep Wrangler. The police immediately made the connection to Armstrong. He was arrested on April 12—the same day the official report arrived, confirming his links to the Jordan murder.

No sooner was he in custody than Armstrong broke down and spewed out a tearful confession that stunned his interrogators. During his years in the navy, he said, he had strangled at least eleven prostitutes throughout the world—Seattle, Honolulu, Hong Kong, Singapore, Bangkok, and Newport News, Virginia. "Basically," one police official told reporters, "he said he either killed or tried to kill every prostitute he'd ever had sex with."

In March 2001—while international investigators tried to confirm Armstrong's claims—he was put on trial for the murder of Wendy Jordan. His lawyers tried an insanity defense, arguing that Armstrong had been sexually abused by his father as a child. The tactic failed to persuade the jury, who convicted him of first-degree murder. He was sentenced to life in a state maximum-security prison.

PREY

A report on the six o'clock news that an unknown serial killer has just claimed his fifth victim is enough to send a city of two million people into a panic. Why—given the astronomically high odds that any one resident will end up as number six—should this be so?

According to one thinker, the answer has to do with evolutionary biology. In her thought-provoking 1997 book *Blood Rites,* Barbara Ehrenreich argues that, for millions of years in the early development of our species, human beings were not just predators but *prey,* hunted down, slain, and devoured by other, stronger carnivores. As a result, our brains are hardwired with a built-in fear of bloodthirsty creatures. This age-old instinct expresses itself, among other ways, in our lifelong fascination with stories about vulnerable people being chased by predatory monsters, from rampaging *T. rexes* to chain-saw-wielding psychos. Such scary tales not only tap in to our primitive anxieties; they also offer a reassuring sense of control. As Ehrenreich puts it:

> In our own time, the spectacle of anti-human violence is replayed endlessly by a commercial entertainment industry which thrives on people's willingness to pay for the *frisson* inspired by images of their fellow humans being stalked by killers, sucked dry by vampires, or devoured by multi-mouthed beasts from outer space. There is even a vogue of what could be called "predation porn": depictions (on the Discovery Channel, for example) of actual predators in the act of actual predation . . . All such spectacles offer a "safe" version of the trauma of predation, one in which we approach the nightmare—and survive.

Whatever validity there may or may not be to this theory, there's no question that the mere thought of serial killers stirs up powerful, irrational terrors in us, far out of proportion to the actual threat posed by these criminals. The best estimate of experts like James Alan Fox of the College of Criminal Justice at Northeastern University is that, at any given time, there are two to three dozen serial killers at large in the country, responsible for the deaths of between one and two hundred victims. Compare that to the nearly forty-three thousand fatalities that resulted from traffic accidents in 2002, and it's clear that the average American runs a substantially greater risk of getting killed by a drunk driver than by a criminal psychopath.

Recommended Reading

Barbara Ehrenreich, *Blood Rites* (1997)

Eric Edgar Cooke

CASE STUDY

The vast majority of serial killers have a signature style of murder, selecting specific types of victims and destroying them in a preferred manner: strangling, shooting, stabbing, etc. Eric Cooke was different. He killed young and old, male and female; and he murdered his victims in a variety of ways. As a result, it took the police a while just to realize that the string of random homicides that terrorized the Australian city of Perth in 1963 was the work of a single psychopath.

Born with a harelip and cleft palate, Cooke had the classic background of a serial killer: an agonizing childhood of abuse and humiliation, most of it inflicted by his alcoholic father, who not only thrashed his son regularly but relentlessly mocked his looks. It's no surprise that Eric grew up with a seething rage against the world. ("I just wanted to hurt somebody," was the only explanation he ever gave for his crimes.) By his late adolescence, he was already leading a Jekyll-Hyde existence: an apparent life of bland normality and a secret one of compulsive criminality.

He was only eighteen when he was arrested for the first time on burglary and arson charges. Supposedly rehabilitated after a brief stint in jail, he joined a church, got married, found a job as a truck driver, and settled down in a suburb of Perth. But even while passing as a hardworking husband and father, he was continuing his nocturnal life as a cat burglar, car thief, Peeping Tom, and sexual fetishist.

His first known murder occurred in January 1959, when he crept into the apartment of a sleeping, thirty-three-year-old divorcee, startled her awake, then stabbed her to death with a diver's knife. Four years later, almost to the day, he embarked on a spree of serial murder that would throw the entire city into a panic. At 2:00 A.M. on Sunday, January 27, 1963, he approached a parked car, then opened fire at its occupants with a .22 rifle, wounding the couple inside. When the car sped away, he went prowling for other victims. That same night, he shot two young men while they slept in their beds, killing one outright and mortally wounding the other. He also murdered a middle-aged businessman, rousing him from his sleep, then firing a bullet between his eyes when he came to the front door.

While the police searched for a deranged shooter, Cooke switched his MO. In the early-morning hours of February 16, while looting another apartment, he inadvertently awoke its occupant, a twenty-four-year-old woman. Knocking her unconscious, he strangled her to death with a light cord, then raped her corpse, dragged it outside to a nearby backyard, and arranged it in an obscene pose for the neighbors to find. Six months later, he killed another young woman, an eighteen-year-old female babysitter who was shot through the head as she sat in an easy chair doing her homework.

Cooke was captured when an elderly couple chanced upon his rifle, which he had stashed beneath some bushes. The police mounted a stakeout, and when Cooke came to retrieve the weapon, they nabbed him. He was tried in November 1963 and hanged slightly less than one year later.

TARGETS OF OPPORTUNITY

Though the odds are infinitesimal, dying at the hands of a serial killer is, theoretically at least, something that could happen to anyone—like winning the lottery or being struck by lightning. Still, some people run a much greater risk than others. A crack-addicted streetwalker in an inner-city slum, for example, is far more likely to end up strangled, dismembered, and left in a Dumpster than a white suburban soccer mom (though the public is far more likely to *hear* about the savage sex-murder of a white middle-class woman than of a black hooker).

Prostitutes (especially when they come from the underclass)—along with street hustlers, teenage runaways, vagrants, junkies, and other social outcasts—are what criminologists call "targets of opportunity": people who are especially vulnerable to serial homicide because they are easy to snare and overpower and are so marginalized that no one, including members of the police and the press, pays much attention when they go missing. When Gary Heidnik, for example, set out to fulfill his insane plan to trap sex slaves for his personal "baby farm," he chose the perfect targets of opportunity: mentally retarded black women from Philadelphia's worst slum, the kind of person he knew he could trap with ease and keep in prolonged captivity without attracting anyone's notice.

The term "target of opportunity" is also used to describe victims who are randomly slain by a serial murderer simply because they are in the wrong place at the wrong time. The people murdered by the Beltway Snipers, died for no other reason than that they were within convenient shooting range when those sociopaths took aim. Similarly, Bertha and Beverly Kludt—a mother-daughter pair butchered in Tacoma, Washington, in 1947—met their awful end merely because they had the misfortune of being at home when a psychopathic drifter named Jake Bird passed by the house and spotted an ax in their backyard.

If some serial killers will murder any easy target that crosses their path, others have distinct preferences when it comes to their victims. When "Son of Sam" was on the loose in the summer of 1976, for example, newspapers reported that his victims tended to be young women with long brown hair—a fact that led countless brunettes throughout the city to cut, dye, or conceal their tresses under hats.

Following his arrest, psychologists theorized that there was a symbolic dimension to his choice of victim. One expert posited that the young women shot by Berkowitz represented his hated birth mother, who had given him up for adoption. Others claimed that they were surrogates for the girls who had snubbed him in high school. Whatever validity there may be to such speculations, there's no doubt that Berkowitz himself took perverse pride in the appearance of his victims. Like some sick travesty of a Don Juan boasting of his conquests, Berkowitz bragged: "I only shoot pretty girls."

Ted Bundy, too, prided himself not only on the "quality" of his victims—bright, attractive, generally middle-class young women—but on the skill with which he snared them. On Sunday, July 14, 1974, within the space of a few hours, he managed to abduct two young women in broad daylight amid thousands of people sunbathing and picnicking at a state park in Seattle.

Even killers like Berkowitz and Bundy, however—who derive a warped sense of superiority not from dating desirable women but from slaughtering them—tend to kill targets of opportunity. Berkowitz may have set his sights on "pretty girls" in general. But the ones who actually died were the unlucky few he accidentally happened upon when he went out prowling for blood.

Indeed, except for the rare psycho who targets specific individuals (H. H. Holmes, for example, who eliminated his wives, mistresses, business associates, and potential witnesses), all of these killers are opportunistic. A serial murderer may set out to slaughter a particular *type* of person. But the specific individuals who end up dead at his hands are the ones who present him with the best opportunity to work evil.

Robert Lee Yates, Jr., Prostitute Slayer

CASE STUDY

Once a thriving working-class neighborhood, the East Sprague area of Spokane had, by the early 1990s, degenerated into a wasteland—a blighted stretch of porn shops, strip joints, and hot-sheet motels where drug-addicted hookers plied their desperate trade, and where the long-elusive psycho known as the "Spokane Serial Killer" harvested most of his victims.

The first to die was a twenty-six-year-old African-American prostitute named Yolanda Sapp, whose naked corpse was found sprawled on a highway embankment near the Spokane River on February 22, 1990. The killings would continue for the better part of a decade, interrupted by intervals of wildly varying lengths. On two occasions, several years would elapse between murders. Later—in the pattern of escalation typical of sex-killers—victims would be slain within months, weeks, or even days of each other.

Almost all the victims were women in their thirties or forties, though the youngest was only sixteen, the oldest sixty. All were shot repeatedly with a small-caliber handgun and their nude corpses dumped in various locations around the city.

It was not until 1997 that a task force was established to hunt for the killer.

An FBI profile solicited by the police department proved so general as to be useless. The culprit was most likely a "white man between twenty and forty years old who might be a loner"—a description that, as one local sheriff wryly noted, applied to "most of the male residents of the state, including all the investigating officers."

Assiduous police work, as it often does, finally provided the break in the case. In November 1998, an officer on stakeout in an area frequented by prostitutes spotted a car pull up to the curb and admit a young woman. The driver turned out to be forty-seven-year-old Robert Lee Yates, Jr., who had previously been ticketed for a minor traffic violation while cruising around the East Sprague red-light neighborhood. When the officer questioned him about the streetwalker in his passenger seat, Yates managed to talk his way out of trouble. A short time later, however, another prostitute—who had barely escaped with her life after being attacked by her "date"—reported the incident to police, providing them with a description of her assailant that matched certain known facts about Yates's background. Police moved in on the suspect.

To all outward appearances, Yates had led not merely a respectable but an exemplary life. A middle-aged family man with five children, he was a highly decorated ex-army helicopter pilot who had participated in Desert Storm, served with distinction in Somalia, and flown rescue missions in Florida following the devastation wrought by Hurricane Andrew.

He was also a remorseless and frighteningly prolific sex-killer. Faced with overwhelming physical evidence—including DNA tests linking him to several victims—Yates eventually struck a deal that spared him the death penalty. In exchange for pleading guilty to thirteen counts of first-degree murder—and leading investigators to the corpse of one of his victims—he was sentenced to 408 years behind bars.

SNARES

The methods by which a serial killer snares his victims vary according to his particular pathological needs. Some prefer the simplest, most direct approach. Often referred to as a "blitz" attack, this may involve ambushing an unwary pedestrian, for example, as she hurries home at night down a darkened street. Or striding up to a parked car in a lovers' lane and blasting away at the embracing couple through the windshield. Or following an old lady to her apartment and shattering her skull with a clawhammer as she fiddles with her door keys. Or slashing a prostitute's throat from behind.

Another sort of "blitz" attack is the kind committed by household invaders like Richard the "Night Stalker" Ramirez or the still-unknown "Ax man of New Orleans": blood-crazed prowlers who break into unguarded homes and savage the sleeping inhabitants in their beds.

Some killers "troll" for victims, cruising hunting grounds where they can be sure of finding an abundant supply of game. To snag a prostitute, a psychopathic "harlot-killer" has to do nothing more than drive to a red-light area, conduct a brief transaction from behind the wheel, open the passenger door, and speed away.

Children, of course, can be enticed with the simplest of promises—candy or coins or ice cream—or easily coerced with violent threats to themselves or their families.

Other serial killers rely on more elaborate ruses. Indeed, for some of these psychos, the cunning they exert to snare their victims is half the fun. Ted Bundy prided himself on having lured several young women to horrible deaths by wearing one arm in a sling and pretending that he needed help with a task. To Dr. Marcel Petiot, the intricate scheme he devised to murder dozens of desperate Jews seeking to flee France during the Nazi occupation was proof of his superior intelligence.

Others, like the Boston Strangler, have gained access to their unwary victims by posing as repairmen. Or pretending to be police officers, like the Hillside Stranglers. Or presenting themselves as professional photographers, like Harvey Murray Glatman. Or passing themselves off as hospital workers, like Australian "Granny Killer" John Wayne Glover.

In several notorious cases, sadistic killers have employed willing accomplices to supply them with victims. The homosexual sadist Dean Corll, for example, relied on Elmer Wayne Henley, who lured his own teenage acquaintances into Corll's clutches with promises of liquor and drugs. Similarly, Charlene Gallego—the distaff half of one of the most notorious killer couples of the twentieth century—used the bait of free marijuana to snag nubile victims for her depraved husband, Gerald.

Arguably the most complex—and certainly grandiose—approach to acquiring victims was the one devised by the infamous Gilded Age "Torture Doctor," H. H. Holmes, who constructed a sprawling building in the Englewood suburb of Chicago during the time of the Chicago World's Fair—a structure erected, among other reasons, to keep himself supplied with corpses.

Given the growing pervasiveness of computers in our lives, it's no surprise that some serial killers have recently turned to the Internet to locate victims.

John E. Robinson already had a long criminal record before his story burst into the headlines in the summer of 2000. A con artist since his twenties, he had committed a variety of white-collar crimes—from embezzlement to securities fraud—and spent seven years behind bars both in Kansas and Missouri.

Paroled in 1993 at the age of forty-nine, he seemed to put his checkered past behind him, marrying a woman who managed a mobile home park, fathering four children who regarded him as a loving dad, getting named Man of the Year for his charitable work on behalf of the homeless, and hosting neighborhood cookouts at his home in Olathe, Kansas.

Like others of his ilk, however, Robinson led a frighteningly dual, Jekyll-Hyde existence. Posing as a philanthropist interested in helping unwed mothers, he befriended several young women who disappeared soon after making his acquaintance. He was also a frequent visitor to Internet S&M chat rooms, where—using the Web name "Slavemaster"—he arranged to meet willing partners for bouts of kinky sex.

In early June 2000, two of these women complained to police that, after hooking up with Robinson at a Kansas City hotel, he had assaulted and robbed them. By then, Robinson was already under suspicion by the Kansas City police. They had become aware of his connection to the missing unwed mothers.

During the first weekend of June 2000, police searched a farm Robinson owned in La Cygne, Kansas, fifty-seven miles south of Kansas City. There, at the edge of the woods, they discovered two eighty-five-gallon drums, each containing the corpse of a woman. Three more bodies were found in identical drums in three separate storage units Robinson rented at a facility in Raymore, Missouri, fifty-four miles northeast. All the victims had gaping wounds in their skulls.

In the fall of 2002, the fifty-eight-year-old Robinson—by then dubbed the "Cyber Sex Slayer"—was tried in Kansas, convicted of three counts of capital murder, and sentenced to death by lethal injection.

"WANTED: WELL-BUILT MAN FOR SLAUGHTER"

As anyone knows who has ever answered an ad in the Personals (only to discover that the Ruggedly Handsome DWM is thirty pounds overweight and sports a really bad toupee) people who place these notices don't always tell the truth about themselves. Normally, this situation results in nothing worse than a disappointing date. But some unwary people who have responded to such come-ons have met with far worse fates.

Luring victims through the classifieds has been the favored technique of certain psycho-killers since the dawn of the twentieth century—especially the types known as Bluebeards and Black Widows, who combine the sadistic lust of the serial predator with the ravenous greed of the con artist.

Beginning in 1902, for example, a middle-aged Norwegian widow named Belle Gunness lured a succession of men to her Indiana "murder farm" with a matrimonial ad placed in the Midwestern newspaper *Skandinaven:*

> WANTED—A WOMAN WHO owns a beautifully located and valuable farm in first class condition, wants

> a good and reliable man as partner in same. Some little cash is required for which will be furnished first class security.

The eager bachelors who responded to this ad vanished without a trace. Their fate remained a mystery until April 1908, when a fire razed the Gunness farmhouse, and more than a dozen dismembered corpses were uncovered on the property.

Around the time of the Great War, Europe produced a pair of notorious Bluebeard killers who relied on lonely hearts ads to supply themselves with victims. Seven women ended up strangled and stuffed into alcohol-filled oil drums after answering the matrimonial advertisements placed in a Budapest newspaper by a young tinsmith named Bela Kiss. A typical ad, which Kiss ran at least ten times, read as follows:

> Bachelor: aged 40: lonely; good income from commercial enterprises averaging £3000 per annum, is desirous of corresponding with educated lady with a view to matrimony. Address: De Koller, Post Restante, Granatos, Budapest.

Kiss's contemporary, Henri Landru—the so-called Bluebeard of Paris—resorted to the same ploy to lure ten lonely women to their destruction. Exactly how he killed them is unknown, though the charred human bones discovered in his oversized stove left no doubt as to their ultimate fate.

Widower with two children, aged forty-three, with comfortable income, affectionate, serious and moving in good society, desires to meet widow with a view to matrimony.

—ad placed by Henri Landru

Some serial killers have found their victims, not by placing classified ads but by *answering* them. In May 1928, for example, the hideously deranged Albert Fish came upon a "Situation Wanted" ad placed in the classified section of the *New York World* by eighteen-year-old Edward Budd, who was looking for a summer job away from the sweltering heat of the city: "Young man, 18, wishes position in the country." Assuming the identity of a Long Island farmer named "Frank Howard," the monstrous Fish—who had been dreaming about castrating a young man, then letting him to bleed to death—soon showed up at the Budd home in Manhattan, shifting his sights to Edward's twelve-year-old sister Grace the moment his eyes fell on the lovely little girl.

A more recent example was Bobby Joe Long. Before turning to serial murder, Long became known as the "Classified Rapist" for his signature MO. Scanning newspapers in the Miami area for classifieds offering furniture and other household items, he would call the numbers and—if a woman answered—arrange to see the articles during the weekday, when her husband was at work and the kids were in school. Once inside the house, he would pull a knife on the woman, tie her up, and rape her, then make off with whatever loot he could carry. Long committed more than fifty of these crimes, terrorizing the communities around Fort Lauderdale, Ocala, Miami, and Dade County for more than two years.

Perhaps the most bizarre use of advertising in the annals of sexual psychopathology occurred in late 2002, when a forty-one-year-old German software technician identified in newspapers only as "Armin M." posted an ad on the Internet that read: "Wanted: Well-built man for slaughter." Remarkably, someone actually found this offer appealing. After selling his car, a forty-three-year-old microchip designer identified as "Bernd Jürgen B." presented himself at the dilapidated home of Armin M. in the river town of Rotenburg an der Fulda.

What happened next so defies belief that it is best to simply quote from the account that appeared in the December 18, 2002, edition of the *New York Times:*

> M. surgically removed the victim's genitals, according to a prosecutor's statement, which said the two men then ate them. Later, M. stabbed B. to death as a video camera recorded the event. He carved up the victim and stored parts of the body in a freezer for occasional consumption, burying other parts in his garden.

Only quick action by the German police—who arrested the cannibal killer after he posted another advertisement seeking more volunteers—prevented Armin M. from committing additional atrocities and becoming a bona fide serial killer.

If there is any mitigating circumstance to Armin M.'s outrage it is that his victim volunteered to be slaughtered and eagerly participated in his own butchery. Compared to other psychos who have lured victims to horrible deaths under false pretenses, the German man-eater at least deserves credit for truth in advertising.

SIGNATURE, RITUAL, MO

At the height of the hysteria provoked by the shooting spree in the Washington, DC area in the fall of 2002, police found a tantalizing item at one crime scene: a tarot card featuring the figure of death on one side and, on the other, an ominous inscription: "Dear Policeman, I am God." The media jumped all over this discovery, labeling the unknown perpetrator the "Tarot Card Killer."

Even at the time, there seemed to be something a little pat, even hokey, about this clue—as though the killer had decided that, to fit the role he was playing, he'd better come up with a sinister trademark. And in fact, as it turned out, there really wasn't any significance to the tarot death card. Evidently, it was just something that the sniper suspects figured would be kind of cool—the sort of thing real serial killers are supposed to leave behind.

It's easy to understand why the sniper team thought this way. In the popular imagination, serial killers invariably have their own sinister, often highly creative "signatures." They may leave a symbolic object like a moth cocoon stuffed down a corpse's throat. Or carve bizarre messages into the flesh of their victims. Or scrawl blood-lettered biblical passages on the bedroom walls.

In truth, however, this sort of behavior is more likely to be found in a Hollywood thriller than in real life. To be sure, there have been some notorious serial killers who were closely associated with particular symbols. The original Zodiac, for example, signed his letters with a distinctive crossed-circle mark. The Boston Strangler identified his grisly handiwork by tying his lethal ligatures into grotesquely cheerful, birthday-ribbon bows. Richard the "Night Stalker" Ramirez used lipstick to draw Satanic pentagrams in the homes—and occasionally on the bodies—of his victims. And several of the victims of the "Green River Killer" were found with weird, pyramid-shaped stones inserted in their vaginas.

Generally speaking, however, this type of ostentatious "signature" is used only by those psycho-killers who derive particularly intense gratification from taunting the police and generating as much media publicity as possible (both of these motives figured prominently in the case of the Beltway Snipers). But not every serial killer fits this pattern; indeed, most of the really notorious lust-murderers of the latter part of the twentieth century don't conform to it—Gacy, Dahmer, Dean Corll, Fred and Rosemary West, Leonard Lake and Charles Ng, and many others. These world-class psychos had no interest in drawing attention to their crimes. On the contrary, they wanted to be left alone to pursue their atrocities in secret. Far from trumpeting their existence to the world by leaving colorful clues like lipstick-inscribed pentagrams or smiley face symbols (the "logo" of the so-called Happy Face Killer, Keith Hunter Jesperson), they did everything possible to keep the world from knowing that horrible crimes were even taking place.

There is, however, another, more subtle and specialized sense in which criminologists use the term "signature"—and in this case it applies to most serial killers, even those who take great pains to keep a low profile. In this more technical meaning, the term doesn't refer to a literal message or symbol left behind by the killer—the psychopathic equivalent of the mark of Zorro—but to a feature of the murder that reflects some deep-seated psychological quirk. Driven by his lifelong rope fetish, for example, Harvey Murray Glatman left his victims trussed up like Thanksgiving turkeys. Savage bite marks on his victims' breasts were the grisly "calling card" of Canadian "Vampire Rapist" Wayne Boden. The corpses of the six London prostitutes killed in 1964 by the still-unidentified lust-murderer dubbed "Jack the Stripper" were all found nude, asphyxiated, and—in four cases—with their front teeth either missing or forced down their throats.

In these and countless other cases, the killer is driven to commit specific acts of violence or desecration on the victim's body. These distinctive, often highly grotesque, actions—mutilating the corpses in particular ways or arranging them in obscene poses—constitute the serial killer's unique "signature." Because there is a ritualistic quality to such behavior—a compulsion to perform it over and over again in fulfillment of some twisted psychosexual need—criminologists sometimes use the term "signature" and "ritual" interchangeably.

A good (if fictitious) example of this kind of behavior appears in Thomas Harris's *Red Dragon,* whose main villain—the facially disfigured psycho, Francis Dolarhyde, aka the "Tooth Fairy"—inserts mirror shards into the eyes and orifices of his dead female victims. This outrage—performed out of bizarre unconscious drives related to his own appearance—is what experts mean by a ritualistic "signature."

In attempting to create a psychological profile of an unknown serial killer, investigators try to distinguish between the perpetrator's "signature"—the seemingly gratuitous acts of excessive violence or sadistic cruelty he commits for his own depraved pleasure—and his MO or *modus operandi.* Technically speaking, the latter term refers to the killer's preferred method of committing his crimes without getting caught: how he selects, snares, subdues, and dispatches his victims, then makes his getaway.

Several problems, however, often confront investigators. For one thing, a serial killer's MO often evolves over time as he grows more comfortable with his killings, tries to throw the police off his scent, or just gets bored with one kind of homicide and looks for a little variety. Former criminal profiler Pat Brown talks about one serial killer, Gary Taylor, who "began his career by whacking women over the head at bus stops. Then he started shooting them with a rifle through their bedroom windows. He got caught and put away in a mental institution at this point. But when he was out on pass . . . he bought some machetes and attacked women on the street." Later, after his release, he "invited a couple of prostitutes to his house, where they ended up buried in his backyard." Clearly, it would be hard, if not impossible, to identify a single MO for a psycho as eclectic in his murder methods as Taylor.

Another problem is that it's not always easy to distinguish between a killer's MO and his signature. Supposedly, a signature act is something the killer needs to do to satisfy his sickest urges—"whatever he gets his rocks off on," as Ted Bundy so bluntly put it—whereas the MO relates to the purely practical aspects of pulling off and getting away with the crime. But it's often hard to make such hard-and-fast distinctions.

Again, Brown provides a useful example, citing the case of a serial rapist who breaks into the bedroom of a sleeping couple, subdues the husband, then makes him lie in the next room with a cup and saucer on his back. "If I hear that cup move or hit the floor," he tells the husband, "your wife dies." Supposedly, this cup-and-saucer gambit is part of the killer's MO, since it is designed for purely pragmatic reasons—to keep the husband under control while the rapist assaults the wife.

But as Brown observes, it could also be a "signature" element. After all, "who's to say [the rapist] didn't get a sick kick out of thinking of the husband lying helpless and looking like an idiot with a cup and saucer on his back listening to his wife's screaming in the next room?"

Recommended Reading

Pat Brown, *Killing for Sport* (2003)
Robert D. Keppel, *Signature Killers* (1997)

METHODS

In attempting to get a handle on the complex phenomenon of serial homicide, experts have come up with various ways of classifying these killers. Crime historian Philip Jenkins, for example, proposes two major categories: the *predictable* type (criminals with a long history of brutal fantasy and behavior whose progression to serial murder seems unsurprising) versus the *respectable* type (petty felons with no prior history of violent crime whose sudden turn to serial murder is unexpected). Forensic psychiatrist Park Dietz identifies three major kinds of serial murderers: psychopaths who kill for sadistic sexual pleasure, psychotics who act under the influence of hallucinations, and custodial killers like doctors, nurses, and other caretakers who usually poison or smother their victims. R. M. Holmes and J. DeBurger divide serial killers into four varieties, based on their underlying motivations: *visionary* types (psychotics who hear voices or see visions commanding them to kill); *mission-oriented* types (generally prostitute killers who believe they are on a crusade to rid the world of scum); *hedonistic* types (lust-killers who murder for perverted pleasure); and *control-oriented* types (who derive their sick gratification less from sex than from the assertion of power and dominance over the victim).

There is, however, another, and in certain respects more useful, way of categorizing serial killers—namely, according to their preferred methods of murder, their favorite ways of dispensing death. How a homicidal maniac *kills*—the weapons he uses, the kinds of injuries he enjoys inflicting—reveals as much about his underlying psychology, his twisted needs and fantasies, as any other feature of his behavior.

To be sure, there are some psychos who don't limit themselves to any one specific type of weapon or killing method. According to the FBI's classification system, "disorganized" killers—whose crimes are often committed in a frenzied, spontaneous outburst—will dispatch their victims with whatever weapons are at hand. Other serial murderers have been known to enjoy some variety in the way they kill. Profiler Pat Brown, for example, discusses the case of Gary Taylor, who shot some victims with a rifle, strangled others, and hacked up a few with a machete.

For the most part, however, serial killers display definite homicidal preferences, so much so that their characteristic techniques often become part of their tabloid monikers: the "Boston Strangler," the "Yorkshire Ripper," the "Ax Man of New Orleans," the "Sunday Morning Slasher," the "Poison Fiend," etc.

If Hollywood movies and literary thrillers are to be believed, serial killers spend much of their time contriving ingenious and colorful ways to commit their atrocities—binding a victim to a kitchen table and forcing him to gorge himself to death, surgically removing the top of someone's skull and feeding him parts of his own brain before putting him out of his misery. And it is true that the occasional psychopath may resort to elaborate means of dispatching his prey. H. H. Holmes, for example, constructed specially rigged chambers in his Gothic "Horror Castle," evidently for the express purpose of asphyxiating unwanted girlfriends and unwary lodgers.

For the most part, real-life psychos are more conventional in their homicidal approaches. What distinguishes them from run-of-the-mill murderers is their distinct preference for *manual* means of killing. Most homicides in the United States—68%, according to the FBI—are committed with firearms, and only 26% by "hands-on" methods like strangulation, bludgeoning, and stabbing. For serial killers, the percentages are almost the exact reverse: 55% rely exclusively on manual means, 22% on guns, and 14% alternate between the two.

The reason for this disparity is frighteningly simple. Driven by depraved sadistic needs, most serial killers derive their deepest pleasure from getting up close and personal with their victims—from feeling their flesh tear, their blood spurt, their bodies convulse, from looking deep into their eyes as the life drains out of them.

Rippers

The most spectacularly gruesome of all homicides are the ones perpetrated by this type of maniac. As Richard von Krafft-Ebing writes in his classic text, *Psychopathia Sexualis,* police are always justified in classifying a murder as the work of a ripper when the victim's corpse has been subjected to horrific mutilation, particularly "when the body has been opened and parts

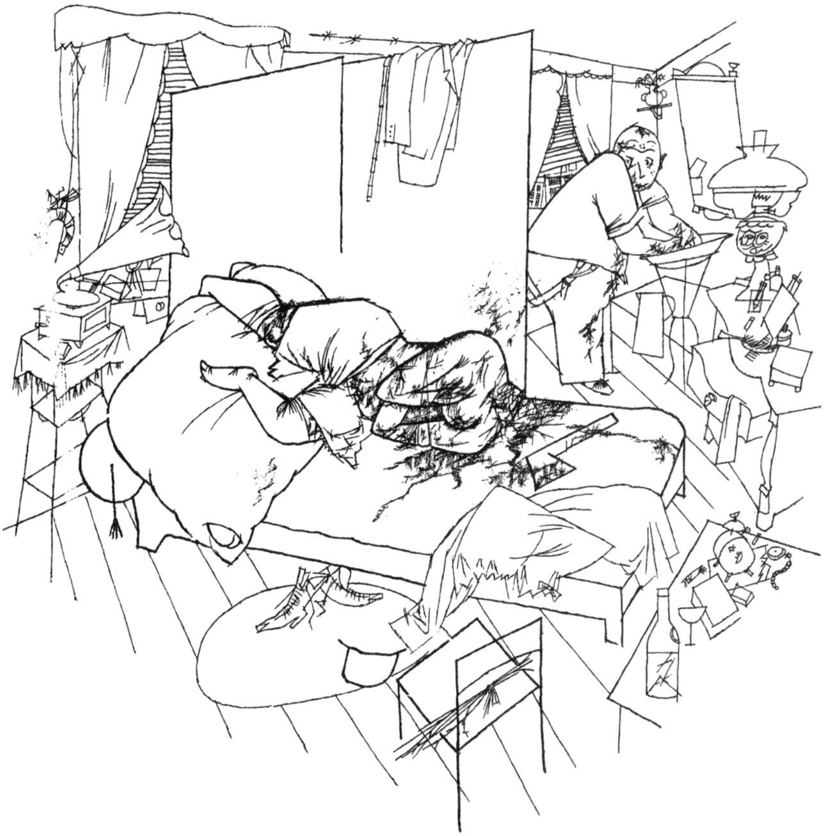

Sex Murder on Acker Street by George Grosz (1916)

(intestines, genitals) torn out." So savage are these crimes that, in earlier times, they were attributed to the actions of lycanthropes—men who literally transformed into wolves. The modern designation for such lust-killers—"rippers"—derives, obviously, from the legendary monster of Whitechapel. The unspeakable butcheries that Saucy Jack perpetrated on a twenty-five-year-old prostitute named Mary Kelly typify the kinds of mutilations these madmen are driven to inflict on the bodies of their victims. As an 1888 newspaper reported:

> The throat had been cut right across with a knife, nearly severing the head from the body. The abdomen had been partially ripped open, and both of the breasts had been cut from the body. . . . The nose had been cut off, the forehead skinned, and the thighs, down to the feet, stripped of the flesh. . . . The entrails and other portions of the frame were missing, but the liver, etc., were found placed between the feet of this poor victim.

> The flesh from the thighs and legs, together with the breasts and nose, had been placed by the murderer on the table, and one of the hands of the dead woman had been pushed into her stomach.

Krafft-Ebing's book includes case histories of other such monsters, among them the "French Ripper," Joseph Vacher, who roamed the countryside in the 1890s armed with scissors, cleaver, and knife, strangling, stabbing, disemboweling, and sexually mutilating victims of both sexes; a German psycho-killer named Leger, who "caught a girl twelve years old, violated her, mutilated her genitals, tore out her heart, ate it, drank the blood, and buried the remains"; and "a certain Gruyo" who strangled six women, then "tore out their intestines and kidneys through their vaginas." Krafft-Ebing also discusses the Boston "Boy Fiend," Jesse Pomeroy, a juvenile ripper who—after luring a four-year-old boy to a remote stretch of beach—gashed his throat with a pocketknife, stabbed him a dozen times in the chest and abdomen, punctured one of his eyeballs, and ripped open his scrotum, leaving his testicles hanging out.

I opened her breast and with a knife cut through the fleshy part of the body. Then I arranged the body as a butcher does beef and hacked it with an axe into pieces of a size to fit the hole which I had dug in the mountain for burying it. I may say that while opening the body I was so greedy that I trembled, and could have cut out a piece and eaten it.

—Andreas Bichel

More recent examples include the "Yorkshire Ripper," Peter Sutcliffe, who preferred to bludgeon his victims to death with a hammer before savaging their bodies, and the Russian "Mad Beast" Andrei Chikatilo, who performed such hideous atrocities on his victims—slicing off their faces, gouging out their eyes, ripping out their tongues, tearing out their entrails, devouring their genitals—that investigating officers who worked on the case had to be treated for psychological trauma.

CASE STUDY

Peter Sutcliffe, the Yorkshire Ripper

Three-quarters of a century after Jack the Ripper stalked the shadowed streets of London, a new killer appeared who seemed to be a reincarnation of the infamous Victorian harlot-killer. Preying largely on streetwalkers, he murdered with a ferocity that equaled that of his notorious namesake. Indeed, he outdid the original Ripper in terms of sheer deadliness, claiming more than twice as many victims during his reign of terror.

His name was Peter Sutcliffe, though it would take five years and the largest manhunt in British history before police discovered his identity. He appeared to be a perfectly ordinary man, a hardworking truck driver and devoted husband. Behind his unremarkable mask, however, he harbored a monstrous pathology: a sexual hatred so extreme that he felt utterly justified in committing the most fearful barbarities on women. When asked to account for the motives behind his atrocities, he calmly replied: "I were just cleaning the streets."

The sources of his sickness are hard to trace, though he appears to have been raised in a household charged with psychosexual tension. A classic "momma's boy," he grew up worshiping his mother, even while his overbearing father constantly accused her of sexual infidelity. This situation was bound to exacerbate the normal Oedipal conflicts of adolescence and produce a being who (even more so than is common) divided all womankind into virgins and whores—one deserving of slavish devotion, the other of nothing but death.

A misfit and loner throughout his boyhood, Sutcliffe developed into a young man with morbid preoccupations. After dropping out of school at fifteen, he found employment in a mortuary, where he enjoyed toying with the corpses—arranging them in grotesque poses and using them as ventriloquist dummies. When he wasn't engaged in these quasi-necrophiliac activities, he liked to visit a local wax museum and ogle the displays that showed the devastating symptoms of advanced venereal disease.

Married at twenty-eight to the first woman he ever dated, he eventually became a truck driver and seemed to settle into the comforting routines of a solid working-class life. If there was any outward indication that all was not right with Sutcliffe, it was the bizarre handwritten sign he kept in his vehicle: "In this truck is a man whose latent genius, if unleashed, would rock the nation, whose dynamic energy would overpower those around him. Better let him sleep?" Though no one recognized it as such, the message reflected the extreme narcissism of the typical psychopath, whose underlying feelings of inadequacy and worthlessness are often offset by delusions of grandeur.

Sutcliffe's first assault occurred in July 1975 when he sneaked up on a woman from behind, bludgeoned her with a hammer, then lifted up her skirt and went to work on her with a knife. This victim survived, as did seven more of the twenty-one women he would attack over the next five years. His MO was always the same: he would beat them unconscious with a ball peen hammer, then savage their torsos and genitalia with a knife or sharpened screwdriver. In all, thirteen people died at his hands. Though most were streetwalkers, others were housewives or students or civil servants. All, however, had one thing in common: they were women and, therefore, targets of Sutcliffe's virulently misogynistic rage.

During their search for the "Yorkshire Ripper," detectives interviewed more than two hundred thousand people. Sutcliffe himself was questioned on no fewer than nine separate occasions. Each time, however, police accepted his alibi and let him go. The very size of the manhunt hampered the investigation. The police were overwhelmed with thousands of useless leads and thrown off track by tape-recorded messages ostensibly from the Ripper that turned out to be hoaxes perpetrated by a very sick mind.

In the end, routine police work led to Sutcliffe's capture. In January 1981, Sergeant Robert Ring, an officer on a stakeout, spotted the killer in a car with a prostitute. Before being hauled into the station for questioning, Sutcliffe asked for permission to go behind some shrubbery to urinate. As soon as he was out of sight of the officer, he emptied his pockets of their incriminating contents: his ball peen hammer and knife.

The next morning, while Sutcliffe was still being interrogated, Ring had a realization. Recalling Sutcliffe's request to relieve himself, the policeman hurried back to the spot, where he discovered the discarded implements. Confronted with the evidence, Sutcliffe broke down. His full confession extended over sixteen hours.

At his trial, he pleaded insanity, claiming that he had committed his murders in obedience to a divine commandment. The jury was unconvinced, and he was sentenced to life. Shortly thereafter, however, he was found insane by prison psychiatrists and transferred to Broadmoor Hospital, where—in March 1997—he received a taste of his own medicine when a fellow inmate stabbed him in both eyes. Emergency surgery saved the right one. Half-blind, he remains incarcerated as of this writing.

Stranglers

Though a ripper-style killer might choke the life out a victim, his real pleasure comes from the frenzied mutilations he performs *afterward*—hacking up the body, tearing out the genitals, wallowing in the entrails, etc. By contrast, serial killers classified as stranglers do not engage in these postmortem atrocities. Their sadistic satisfaction comes from the act of strangulation itself. Indeed, some of these psychos become so aroused while throttling a victim that they reach a sexual climax during the murder. (A chilling cinematic portrayal of such a moment appears in Alfred Hitchcock's 1972 movie, *Frenzy,* when the so-called Necktie Killer has an orgasm while garroting a woman.)

The first American serial killer of the twentieth century was a strangler—Earle Leonard Nelson, aka the "Gorilla Murderer," a Bible-quoting psycho who traveled from coast to coast, choking women to death before raping their corpses (Alfred Hitchcock also made a movie loosely inspired by this notorious case: his 1943 masterpiece, *Shadow of a Doubt*).

Whereas Nelson (who was also known as the "Dark Strangler") enjoyed throttling his victims with his bare hands, Harvey Murray Glatman—the nerdy-looking sex maniac who liked to take pictures of his bound and terrorized victims before taking their lives—employed his favorite fetish object: a length of stout rope. The Boston Strangler, by contrast, preferred articles belonging to his victim, garroting them with scarves or bathrobe sashes or nylon stockings. He was also known for his grotesque "signature," tying the ligatures into extravagant, gift-wrap bows as a taunt to the police. African-

American sex-killer Carlton Gary—aka the "Stocking Strangler"—also used hosiery as a murder weapon, leaving all seven of his elderly victims with their nylons tightly knotted around their necks.

Arguably the most vile of all modern stranglers were the psychopathic cousins Kenneth Bianchi and Angelo Buono. These women-hating sadists took pleasure not only from the murder method that earned them their infamous nickname—the "Hillside Stranglers"—but from subjecting their young victims to various, and often prolonged, forms of torture—injecting them with cleaning solution, attaching live electric wires to their palms, raping them with soda bottles, asphyxiating them with slow, voluptuous cruelty. Then they would add to their unspeakable fun by dumping the young women's violated corpses out in the open, as a final indignity to the victim and a taunt to the police.

> I am fond of women, but it is sport for me to strangle them after having enjoyed them.
>
> —Serial strangler quoted by Krafft-Ebing

Carroll Edward Cole, the Barfly Strangler

CASE STUDY

Everybody failed Carroll Cole: his mother, teachers, psychiatrists, and police detectives. His entire life was one downward spiral of mental illness, alcoholism, and murder. It was also one of the most blatant examples of how the health-care and legal systems can completely fail to treat and capture an out-of-control serial killer. Near the end of the ordeal that was his existence, someone finally came to his aid. This person was the Nevada judge who handed down a death sentence. For this help—for this much needed relief—Cole had a laconic reply: "Thanks, Judge."

Cole's life, like that of so many criminal psychopaths, began with parental abuse. His sadistic mother forced him to accompany her on her adulterous liaisons and enjoyed dressing him up as a girl to entertain her friends at parties. As with Ed Gein, Edmund Kemper, and Henry Lee Lucas, the hatred he developed for his monstrous mom figured prominently in his crimes. Cole himself made this perfectly clear. "I think I kill her through them," he would later remark of his victims.

Murderous rage ran through Cole's head; to drown it out he used copious amounts of alcohol. By late adolescence he could not control himself. In 1960, he attacked a couple in a car with a hammer. Concerned about the demon inside of him, Cole turned himself in to police. He spent the next three years in several mental institutions where he was deemed "antisocial" but harmless. In 1963 he left treatment and married an alcoholic topless dancer who occasionally worked for Jack Ruby. The marriage was predictably rocky. Cole left her in 1965 after burning down the fleabag hotel where they lived because he was convinced she was sleeping with other tenants.

Cole again surrendered himself to police in 1970, but this time with a specific fear: he was having uncontrollable fantasies about raping and strangling women. This happened in Nevada. Taken in for a psychiatric evaluation, the report on his mental condition typified the quality of treatment he received throughout his life: "Prognosis: Poor. Condition on Release: Same as on admittance. Treatment: Express Bus ticket to San Diego."

With a human time bomb on their hands, the authorities just shipped him out of town.

Over the next decade Cole went on a rampage of drinking and murder across the states of Nevada, Texas, California, Wyoming, and Oklahoma. His victims were classic "targets of opportunity"—female barflies easily lured to their deaths by the good-looking, charismatic psychopath. As crime writer Cliff Linedecker puts it, "Cole didn't prey on healthy, sober women who could wage a fair fight. He was a scavenger who looked for lonely alcoholics who were so weakened as a result of their dissolute living that they had no chance to defend themselves . . . They were broken, bruised, and defeated. And most had either lost contact with their families or had no close friends who would create a fuss over their deaths."

Once Cole had a woman alone, he strangled her and often raped the corpse. Alcohol clouded his mind, and he later had trouble recounting all the details of his atrocities. One of his most horrific crimes occurred in Oklahoma City, where Cole emerged from a stupor to find a mutilated body in a bathtub, slices of the woman's buttocks in a pan on the stove and the sweet taste of blood in his mouth.

As in the case of so many serial killers, Cole's murders escalated in frequency as his homicidal mania spun out of control. In November 1980, he strangled two women to death within twenty-four hours. Less than three weeks later, he picked up a forty-three-year-old woman at a Dallas honky-tonk, accompanied her back to her apartment, and killed her with his bare hands during a violent struggle. When neighbors showed up to investigate the ruckus, they discovered the victim's corpse stretched out on the floor. Under questioning by police, Cole claimed that the woman had simply dropped dead—a story that did not seem entirely implausible given the exceptionally high concentration of alcohol discovered in her blood by the medical examiner. Cole was allowed to go free.

By that point, he had tired of his life. When the cops returned to question him again several days later, he greeted them with a startling admission. "I need some help," he declared. "I see a woman with a drink in her hand and I have to kill her. I am tired of killing."

Cole then proceeded to pour out a confession to all the murders he could remember. He was eventually convicted of thirteen homicides, though he maintained that the body count might have reached as high as thirty-five. He was executed in the early-morning hours of December 6, 1985,—the first person put to death in Nevada by lethal injection.

Ax Murderers

Back in the nineteenth century—when many Americans still lived on farms, butchered their own chickens, and relied on cordwood to heat their homes—hatchets and axes were standard equipment in most households, as common as corkscrews and can openers are today. It's not surprising, therefore, that—when someone flew into a homicidal rage—he or she often grabbed one of these readily available chopping implements to do the job. Search through the archives of any small-town newspaper from the 1800s and you're likely to come across a case of gruesome ax murder, like the slaughter of two sisters, Maren and Anethe Hontvet, in a remote New Hampshire fishing village in 1873 ("Terrible Tragedy on the Isle of Shoals! Two Women Killed with an Axe!"). Or the massacre of the Vacelet family of Knox County, Indiana, in 1878 ("Brutal Butchery! A Whole Family Brained in Bed with a Blunt-Edged Axe!"). Or the 1894 murder of Missouri farmer Gus Meeks and his family, memorialized in a ballad supposedly sung by a surviving daughter ("They murdered my mamma and pappa, too/And knocked baby in the head/They murdered my brothers and sisters four/And left me there for dead").

While these and most other nineteenth-century ax murders stirred up intense local interest in the places they occurred, they quickly faded from the news. A few, however, became bona fide national sensations. In 1836, a young man named Richard Robinson—the spoiled scion of a wealthy Connecticut family—murdered a beautiful New York City prostitute named Helen Jewett by smashing in her skull with a hatchet. Thanks to its irresistibly juicy combination of sex, violence, and scandal, the Jewett ax murder case became one of the most highly publicized crimes of its era. Even more notorious, of course, was the 1892 case of Lizzie Borden who, as the famous nursery rhyme put it, "gave her mother forty whacks/And when she saw what she had done/She gave her father forty-one."

Even assuming she committed this double murder (which, despite her acquittal, seems probable), Lizzie Borden was not a serial killer but rather an emotionally unstable Victorian spinster who went berserk one sweltering summer day and committed a singular act of parricide. Likewise, the ax slayings of the Hontvet sisters, the Meeks family, and the Vacelets were cases of multiple murder, not serial homicide. Indeed—contrary to countless slasher movies which routinely portray psycho-killers as ax-wielding maniacs (such as the 2001 thriller, *Frailty*)—axes are rarely the weapon of choice for serial killers, being hard to conceal and awkward to wield, especially indoors.

There have been notable exceptions. Though a good deal of uncertainty surrounds the 1901 case of Belle Gunness—whose farmstead outside La Porte, Indiana, became a mass grave for more than a dozen victims—it is generally believed that she dispatched most of them with a hatchet. (A pop ballad written about the case describes the notorious Lady Bluebeard as a "Hatchet-hackin' Mama"). During the World War I era, New Orleans was haunted by a night-prowling intruder known as the Ax Man who attacked a dozen people in their homes. In the late 1940s, African-American serial killer Jake Bird was captured after breaking into the Tacoma, Washington, home of fifty-three-year-old Bertha Kludt and butchering Mrs. Kludt and her teenage daughter with an ax he had found in their backyard. Under arrest, the hard-bitten drifter confessed to numerous slayings in at least eight different states, all involving white women bludgeoned with axes or hatchets.

There have also been some international cases, such as that of the South African ax-murderer Elifasi Msomi, a self-styled witch doctor who, in the mid-1950s hacked to death fifteen people (most of them young children), then tried to pin the blame on demonic possession.

Poisoners

Partly, no doubt, because it was the favorite murder method of Victorian women, most people tend to think of poisoning as a comparatively genteel way to commit serial homicide, not nearly as savage as, say, slitting a victim's throat and tearing out his entrails. And it is certainly true that mutilation-murder is far more sensationally grisly. Whether it is also *crueler* than poisoning is an open question. Though a significant number of male serial killers engage in hideous torture, many others—including some of the most notorious ones—have dispatched their victims in a fairly quick manner. This is true, for example, of most rippers. The atrocities perpetrated by Jack the Ripper seem nearly inhuman in their ferocity. But at least they were inflicted on his victims after death, which came with merciful swiftness.

By contrast, poisoners often subject the people closest to them—friends, family members, and coworkers—to excruciatingly slow and painful deaths, and derive considerable pleasure from observing the torments of their victims.

During the Victorian era, for example, arsenic was a popular, over-the-counter item, sold in various forms and used as everything from a pesticide to a cosmetic. Generously mixed into someone's food, however, it had devastating results.

In most cases of arsenic ingestion, the commencement of symptoms occurs within the hour. The first sign is an acrid sensation in the throat. Nausea sets in, growing more unbearable by the moment. Then the vomiting begins. It continues long after the stomach is empty, until the victim is heaving up a foul whitish fluid streaked with blood. The mouth is parched, the tongue thickly coated, the throat constricted. The victim is seized with a terrible thirst. Anything he drinks, however—even a few sips of icy water—only makes the vomiting worse.

Uncontrollable diarrhea—often bloody, and invariably accompanied by racking abdominal pain—follows the vomiting. Some victims experience a violent burning from mouth to anus. Urine is scanty and red in color. As the hours pass, the victim's face—deathly pale to begin with—takes on a bluish tint. The eyes grow hollow. The skin is slick with perspiration that gives off an unusually thick, fetid odor. The victim's breathing becomes harsh and irregular, his extremities cold, his heartbeat feeble. There may be convulsions of the limbs and excruciating cramps in the muscles of the legs. Depending on the amount of poison consumed, this torment may last anywhere from five or six hours to several days. Death, when it finally comes, is a mercy.

Female poisoners, in short, are capable of being every bit as sadistic as the sickest male torture-killer. They have also been among the most prolific serial killers in history. Mary Ann Cotton—a British serial murderer so infamous that she was immortalized in a popular nursery rhyme—killed an estimated twenty-three people, including three husbands, ten children, five stepchildren, a sister-in-law, and an unwanted suitor. Her American counterpart, the Massachusetts "Borgia" Jane Toppan—who liked to crawl into bed with her victims and feel their dying convulsions—admitted to thirty-one homicides after her trial in 1902. Another lethal New England caretaker, Amy Archer-Gilligan—proprietor of the Archer Home for Elderly and Indigent Patients in Windsor, Connecticut—dispatched as many as forty of her clients between 1911 and 1916. However impressive, these tallies were surpassed by the collective killings of the so-called Angel-makers of Nagyrev," a group of peasant women from a remote Hungarian village who—supplied with arsenic by their leader, a midwife named Julia Fazekas—murdered as many as one hundred victims in the decades after World War I.

This is not to say that only female psychopaths have resorted to poison. Victorian England was home to a trio of notorious male poisoners: Dr. William Palmer (who favored strychnine as a way of eliminating persistent creditors, professional rivals, and burdensome children); George Chapman (who poisoned a series of lovers with antimony tartrate); and Dr. Thomas Neill Cream (who slipped strychnine pills to several London prostitutes and went to his death claiming to be Jack the Ripper). And at the same time that Jane Toppan was committing her ghastly crimes, America was riveted by another sensational poisoning case, that of a dashing New York City playboy named Roland Molineux, accused of murdering several acquaintances with cyanide-spiked Bromo-Seltzer.

One of the deadliest American poisoners of recent years was Dr. Michael Swango, suspected of killing as many as sixty victims. Though his usual method was to inject them with fatal medications, Swango—who confessed that he loved nothing better than "the sweet, husky, close smell of indoor homicide"—resorted to other methods during those periods when he was banished from the hospital wards. In 1984, after leaving Ohio State University Medical Center under a cloud of suspicion, he returned to his hometown, Quincy, Illinois, where he joined an ambulance corps. Before long, he was secretly doctoring the donuts and soft drinks of his fellow paramedics with ant poison. After he was arrested and charged, police searched his apartment where they found a minilab, designed for the production of some of the most virulent poisons known, including botulism toxin and supersaturated cyanide.

CASE STUDY

Graham Young, Poisoner

Though poisoning has long been the preferred murder method for female serial killers, it is not the exclusive domain of women. Particularly in Britain there have been some notorious male serial poisoners, including Dr. Thomas Neill Cream, who dispatched a string of prostitutes with strychnine in the late 1800s. His Victorian compatriot, Dr. William Palmer, used the same substance to murder his mother-in-law, his brother, four children, an uncle, various creditors, and a close friend.

The most notorious serial poisoner in recent British history was, in many ways, the most remarkable: a precociously brilliant, remorseless psychopath who began his homicidal career while still in his boyhood.

Just three months after his birth in 1947, Graham Young's mother died. Initially, the infant was cared for by his aunt. At two, he was sent to live with his father, who had since remarried. Later, psychiatrists would trace Young's extreme psychopathology—his utter inability to feel human warmth or empathy—to the loss of his mother at such a critical moment in his emotional development.

His lifelong obsession with poison manifested itself from an early age. While his schoolmates idolized athletes and pop stars, Young's boyhood heroes were notorious English poisoners like Palmer and Dr. Hawley Crippen (whose case became an international sensation in 1910 after he murdered his wife, buried her in the coal cellar, and ran off with his secretary). Young was especially fascinated with another Victorian poisoner, Dr. Edward Pritchard, who was hanged in Glasgow in 1855 for murdering his wife and mother-in-law with antimony. He also developed an intense admiration for Adolf Hitler, whose malignant power he envied.

Obtaining a vial of antimony tartrate from a local pharmacist under the pretense of needing it for a school science project, Young began carrying it around with him. He referred to it as his "little friend."

Before long, Young began experimenting on his schoolmates, lacing their sandwiches with just enough of the poison to make them sick. He then shifted his attentions to his own family, beginning with his sister. Graham would observe with interest the effects that different doses of the toxin had on his loved ones—the vomiting, the agonizing stomach pains, the violent diarrhea. In 1962, after a prolonged siege of poison-induced suffering, his stepmother died.

After Young's chemistry teacher discovered alarming evidence in Young's desk—drawings of people dying in agony with poison bottles at their side, charts detailing the effects and lethal dosages of various toxins—the boy was questioned by police, who found his beloved vial of antimony in his pocket. He quickly confessed to having used it on his own family members. Put in jail to await trial, he tried to commit suicide—not because he felt shame or remorse but because he couldn't bear the thought of living without his poisons. At his 1962 trial, he was found guilty but insane, and committed to Broadmoor mental institution.

After nine years in the asylum, Young was released, presumably having made a "full recovery," according to a psychiatrist's report. He moved to the village of Bovingdon and found work in the storeroom of a company that manufactured optical equipment, telling his employers that he had spent time in an institution after suffering a nervous breakdown brought on by the death of his beloved stepmother.

The day after he started his new job, he went out and purchased enough poison to kill several hundred people.

It wasn't long before his coworkers began to suffer from a serious ailment whose symptoms included diarrhea, cramps, backaches, nausea, and numbness. As many as seventy workers were stricken with the illness, which was nicknamed the "Bovingdon bug." Several were hospitalized, and two of them—fifty-nine-year-old Bob Egle and sixty-year-old Fred Biggs—died after protracted suffering.

At first, no one seemed to notice that the victims were hit with the sickness after drinking the coffee and tea served to them by the ever-helpful Young. Eventually, however, suspicion grew that someone in the factory was poisoning his coworkers. An investigation was launched. When it was Young's turn to be questioned, he could not resist flaunting his superior knowledge of chemistry, setting off alarm bells when he remarked that the mysterious illness seemed consistent with the signs of thallium poisoning.

A check of Young's background revealed the chilling truth about his past. The police quickly arrested him on suspicion of murder. Searching his apartment, they found shelves of bottled poisons—thallium, antimony, aconitine—beneath framed photographs of Hitler and his henchmen. They also found a diary in which he detailed, with a monstrous detachment, the effects of the different toxins on his victims. "I have administered a fatal dose of the special compound to F," he had written after poisoning Fred Biggs, "and anticipate a report on his progress on Monday. I gave him three separate doses."

At first, Young claimed that the diary entries were simply notes for a novel. Later, he confessed. His sole motive was the power he exerted over others' lives. Human beings were nothing more to him than lab animals. "I could have killed them all if I wished," he boasted to detectives, "but I let them live."

His June 1972 trial lasted ten days. The jury needed less than an hour to convict him. He was sentenced to jail for the rest of his life, which turned out to be extremely abbreviated. In August 1990, he was found dead on the floor of his cell—killed by a heart attack at the age of forty-two.

Shooters

When people hear the term "serial killer," they tend to picture a creature like Jack the Ripper or Ted Bundy or Richard Ramirez: a blood-crazed madman, butchering or bludgeoning his victims with his favorite implement—hunting knife, hammer, meat cleaver, machete—or possibly dispatching them with his bare hands. And statistics confirm that most serial killers do, in fact, enjoy the sensations that come from direct physical contact with their victims.

Still, there have been a number of notorious serial murderers who preferred to do their killing with firearms. Shooting, after all—even at a long distance—can supply the kinds of sick thrills that psychopaths crave, including sexual gratification. As we know from Freud, guns can feel like erotic objects in the hands of their users. There is direct testimony to this effect from one of the most notorious serial shooters of modern times, David "Son of Sam" Berkowitz. As John Douglas reports in his book *The Anatomy of Motive,* Berkowitz admitted during an interview that "on nights when he could not find the appropriate victims of opportunity, he would return to the locations of his previous crimes and masturbate, recalling the sexual charge and feeling of supreme power he'd had as he pulled the trigger of his large Charter Arms Bulldog." Berkowitz's choice of victims—attractive young women, some of them parked in cars with their boyfriends—also reflects the sexual dimension of his crimes.

Even for those serial shooters who do not derive a specifically sexual kick from their crimes, guns can satisfy their psychopathic urges by giving them (as Berkowitz's statement also indicates) a godlike sense of power. Surely, this was true of the original San Francisco Zodiac, whose twisted megalomania was evident in the written taunts he sent to the press, as well as in his apparent belief that his victims would become his slaves in the afterlife.

Sheer viciousness seemed to underlie the crimes of Gary and Thaddeus Lewingdon, a pair of sociopathic siblings who randomly murdered ten residents of Columbus, Ohio, in the late 1970s. The ".22-Caliber Killings," as the newspapers dubbed them, began in December 1977 when two women were gunned down as they left a cafe late at night. Two months later, fifty-two-year-old Robert McCann, along with his mother and live-in girlfriend were savagely murdered at home, each shot multiple times in the face and head. The same savage "overkill" characterized the murder of the next victim, a seventy-seven-year-old named Jenkin Jones, whose four dogs were also shot dead. Three more victims followed in the next few months—a reverend named Gerald Fields and a middle-aged couple named Martin. After a six-month hiatus, the phantom shooter killed his tenth and final victim, fifty-six-year-old Joseph Annick, shot five times while working in his garage. The case finally broke when one of the brothers, Gary, tried to use Annick's stolen credit card at a local department store. Arrested on the spot, Lewingdon was placed in an interrogation room, where he immediately confessed to all ten murders and implicated his brother, Thaddeus, who proved equally forthcoming. Both brothers were convicted and received multiple terms of life imprisonment. Following the trial, however, Gary had a psychotic breakdown and was committed to a state hospital for the criminally insane. After an unsuccessful breakout attempt, he petitioned the court for permission to commit suicide, a request that was denied. Eventually, he was transferred back to the Southern Ohio Correctional Facility, where he remains incarcerated. In April 1989, his fifty-two-year-old brother, Thaddeus, died of lung cancer.

Ohio was the home of another serial shooter, Thomas Dillon. Though less well known than "Son of Sam" or Zodiac, Dillon was in many ways an equally chilling figure: a classic psychopath who killed for pure sadistic pleasure.

Born in 1950 and raised by a widowed mother who, according to reliable accounts, never displayed the slightest warmth or affection for her child, Dillon loved to shoot animals from an early age, keeping a running record of his kills on a wall calendar in his bedroom. Besides deer and other small game, he enjoyed shooting dogs, cats, and cows—generally with his large collection of firearms, though occasionally with a crossbow. He was also, like so many budding psycho-killers, an inveterate pyromaniac.

Dillon progressed to murder in April 1989, when he shot a thirty-five-year-old jogger through the heart from a distance of about ten feet on a remote stretch of highway in rural Ohio. In November 1990, he committed two cold-blooded murders within the space of a few weeks. First to die was a twenty-one-year-old bow hunter named Jamie Paxton, shot to death on a hillside. Eighteen days later, thirty-year-old Kevin Loring was killed with a bullet to the face, also while out hunting deer.

When police made no headway in the Paxton investigation, the young man's mother, Jean, took matters into her own hands, publishing a direct plea to her son's killer in a local newspaper, the *Ferry Times Leader:*

> To the murderer(s) of my son, Jamie,
> Would it be easier for you if I wrote words of hate? I can't because I don't feel hate. I feel deep sorrow at losing my son. You took a light from my life November 10 and left me with many days of darkness. Have you thought of your own death? Unless you confess your sin and ask for God's forgiveness, you will face the fire and fury of hell. When you are caught, I will be sorry for your family. They will have the burden of your guilt all their lives.

Though this letter produced no results, a second plea, published eleven months later, brought a remarkable reply—an anonymous typewritten note that revealed the utterly callous, sadistic sensibility of a classic psychopathic killer:

> I am the murderer of Jamie Paxton. Jamie Paxton was a complete stranger to me. I never saw him before in my life, and he never said a word to me that Saturday.
>
> Paxton was killed because of an irresistible compulsion that has taken over my life. I knew when I left my house that day that someone would die by my hand. I just didn't know who or where. Technically, I meet the definition of a serial killer, but I'm an average-looking person with a family, job, and home just like yourself.
>
> Something in my head causes me to turn into a merciless killer with no conscience. To the Paxtons, you deserve to know the details.
>
> I was very drunk and a voice inside my head said "do it." I stopped my car behind Jamie's and got out. Jamie started walking very slowly down the hill toward the road. He appeared to be looking past me at something in the distance.
>
> I raised my rifle to my shoulder and lined him up in the sights. It took at least five seconds to take careful aim. My first shot was off a little bit and hit him in the right chest. He groaned and went down. I wanted to make sure

> he was finished so I fired a second shot aimed half way between his hip and shoulder. He was crawling around on the ground. I jerked the shot and hit him in the knee. He raised his head and groaned again. My third shot also missed and hit him in the butt. He never moved again.
>
> Five minutes after I shot Paxton, I was drinking a beer and had blocked out all thoughts of what I had just done out of my mind. I thought no more of shooting Paxton than I thought of shooting a bottle at the dump.
>
> I know you hate my guts, and rightfully so. I think about Jamie every hour of the day, as I am sure you do.
>
> Don't feel bad about not solving this case. You could interview till doomsday everyone that Jamie Paxton ever met in his life and you wouldn't have a clue to my identity. With no motive, no weapon, and no witnesses, you could not possibly solve this crime.

When a forty-nine-year-old fisherman was shot in March 1992 on federal land, the FBI got involved. Less than a month later, another man was shot in the back while fishing. At that point, investigators issued a press release, revealing that a serial sniper was stalking outdoorsmen in rural eastern Ohio.

Shortly after the publication of the press release—which included an FBI profile of the suspect—investigators were contacted by a man named Roger Fry. He told him the published description of the killer sounded a good deal like his old buddy, Thomas Dillon—a lifelong gun fanatic who enjoyed shooting animals and openly admired Ted Bundy. Dillon was put under surveillance. Eventually, he was tied to one of the murder weapons, a Mauser rifle he had sold off at a gun show. Shortly after his arrest, he confessed to three murders. "I have a major problem," he declared. "I'm crazy. I want to kill." Under a plea agreement, he was spared the death penalty and received a life sentence in prison with no chance of parole for 165 years.

The Beltway Snipers

CASE STUDY

For three weeks in the fall of 2002, the citizens of Washington, DC and surrounding communities—still recovering from the trauma of the 9/11 attacks a year earlier—found themselves once again in the grip of terror. This time, the enemy was an unseen sniper who killed at whim, then vanished without a trace. The sheer randomness of the murders—which struck down men, women, and children as they went about their daily business—stirred up the public's most primal anxieties, creating a sense that anyone was vulnerable to sudden violent death anywhere, at any time.

As the killings proceeded, the sniper began to leave taunting messages, as if daring the police to capture him. In the meantime, the nation watched in grim fascination, as the twenty-four/seven news coverage turned the tragedy into a macabre reality show: a true-life police melodrama that pitted the full resources of federal and local law enforcement agencies against a cunning and implacable psycho-killer.

The first shot missed its target—barely. At 5:20 P.M. on Wednesday, October 2, a bullet from a high-powered rifle blew a hole through the window of a hobby shop in a run-down strip mall in Aspen Hill, Maryland, passing so close to the head of the cashier, Ann Chapman, that it grazed her hair. Just thirty-two minutes later, the sniper struck again. This time, he took closer aim. The victim was James Martin, a fifty-five-year-old family man, Civil War buff, and program analyst for the National Oceanic and Atmospheric Administration. At 6:04 P.M., as he walked across the parking lot toward a Wheaton Hills supermarket where he'd come to buy snacks for his son's church group, Martin was killed with a .223-caliber slug to the back, becoming the sniper's first fatality.

It wasn't until the following morning—Thursday, October 3—that the police realized they had a full-blown crisis on their hands. In the span of slightly more than two hours, four people were shot dead by the sniper in different areas of suburban Maryland. James Buchanan, a thirty-nine-year-old landscaper, was killed at 7:41 A.M. as he mowed a strip of grass outside a car dealership in Rockville. Premkumar Walekar, a fifty-four-year-old Indian émigré, was gunned down at 8:12 A.M. as he filled up his taxicab at a Mobil station in Aspen Hill. Sarah Ramos, a thirty-four-year-old housecleaner, got shot at 8:37 A.M. as she sat on a bench near a retirement community in Silver Spring. And Lori Ann Lewis-Rivera, a twenty-five-year-old professional nanny, was murdered at 9:58 A.M. as she vacuumed her minivan at a Shell station in Kensington. All the victims had been murdered close to major roadways. In each case, the faceless marksman had killed with a single shot before vanishing into the rush of the morning traffic.

That night, he claimed another life. At 9:15 P.M., seventy-two-year-old Pascal Charlot, a father of five who spent much of his time caring for his Alzheimer's-afflicted wife, was shot dead as he crossed the street near his home in northwest Washington, DC.

The shooter waited until the following afternoon before striking again. This time, he fired at a forty-three-year-old mother of two as she loaded packages into her minivan outside a crafts store in Fredericksburg, Virginia. The bullet hit her in the back and came out under her left breast. The woman—whose identity has never been made public—was one of the lucky few who survived.

Panic spread through the region. The simplest of tasks—shopping for groceries, gassing up a car, mowing a lawn—suddenly seemed fraught with peril. The job of reassuring the public—as well as coordinating the massive manhunt, while simultaneously dealing with the media, which had begun to set up a tent city outside headquarters—fell to Montgomery County police chief, Charles Moose. Moose reassured the parents of Maryland that there was no reason to keep their children home from school. "We have no information that this has anything to do with schools," he announced at a press conference. "None of the victims has been anything close to school age. None of the locations are close to the schools. . . . I think the schoolkids are safe."

At 8:09 A.M. on Monday, October 7—as if in spiteful response to Chief Moose's calming words—the sniper shot thirteen-year-old honors student Iran Brown in front of his middle school in Bowie, Maryland. If this heinous deed left any doubts that the sniper was a desperately sick individual, the item found by the police as they searched the schoolgrounds for clues dispelled them. The item was a tarot card depicting the figure of Death and inscribed with the handwritten message: "I am God."

For another two weeks—despite the unprecedented efforts to identify the diabolical killer now dubbed the "Tarot Card Killer"—the sniper continued to strike with an impunity that endowed him with an aura of almost supernatural evil, and that undoubtedly reinforced his own megalomaniacal sense of power and superiority. Between October 9 and October 22, five more victims were shot. Dean Harold Myers, fifty-three-year-old design engineer and Vietnam vet, killed at the Battlefield Sunoco gas station in Manassas, Virginia. Kenneth Bridges, fifty-three-year-old father of six, killed at an Exxon station in Fredericksburg, Virginia. Linda Franklin, forty-seven-year-old mother of two and FBI analyst, killed in a Home Depot parking garage in Falls Church, Virginia. Jeffrey Hopper, thirty-seven-year-old Florida man, wounded outside a Ponderosa Steak House in Ashland, Virginia. Conrad Johnson, thirty-five-year-old bus driver, killed while standing on the top step of his idling bus near Silver Spring, Maryland.

During this period, the sniper left more taunting catch-me-if-you-can messages, as well as a blackmail demand for $10 million to be deposited in the account of a Visa bank card. The writer warned of more "body bags" if the demand wasn't met and added a chilling P.S.: "Your children aren't safe anywhere at any time."

In the meantime, the airwaves were full of pundits, profilers, and self-professed experts offering highly conjectural characterizations of the killer, nearly all of which proved wildly inaccurate. Some believed that the sniper was a deranged teenage gamer who, after honing his skills on Doom, had progressed from virtual victims to flesh-and-blood targets. Others proposed that he was a Special Forces sniper gone bad. Some even speculated that he might be an al-Qaeda terrorist.

How exactly to classify the shooter was also a subject of debate. Was he a serial killer like Zodiac, driven by a sadistic need for power and the sheer pleasure of inflicting death? Or a spree killer like Versace-slayer Andrew Cunanan, a man at the end of his tether who had finally snapped and embarked on a rampage that was almost certain to end in his own death?

When the answer finally came, it caught everyone by surprise.

For one thing the sniper turned out to be—not the "well-organized white male" predicted by FBI profilers—but a team of two African-Americans: forty-one-year-old John Allen Muhammad and his juvenile sidekick, seventeen-year-old John Lee Malvo. For another, they were not driving the white box truck or van that investigators had been searching for since the start of the rampage, but rather a battered, blue Chevy Caprice.

The penniless pair were living in the car, whose trunk had been equipped with a small hole and converted into a mobile sniper's nest. It later emerged that, during the shooters' three-week reign of terror, the Caprice had been repeatedly stopped by police, generally for minor traffic infractions. On no fewer than ten separate occasions, authorities had run its license plate through the national police database, only to let the car and its drivers go on their way when the computerized check turned up nothing. Harsh criticism would eventually be leveled at the police for having allowed the killers to slip from their grasp so often during the manhunt.

Still, it was solid police work—along with the alleged killers' own overweening egos—that led to the break in the case. Constantly needing to prove what big bad men they were, the shooters couldn't resist bragging about their past criminal exploits, placing a phone call to Chief Moose's office in which they revealed their involvement in an earlier robbery-murder at a Montgomery, Alabama, liquor store. After a second such call to a priest in Ashland, Virginia, the FBI contacted Alabama authorities, who immediately turned over a package of evidence from that crime. Among the items was a gun magazine dropped near the liquor store by one of the perpetrators. When fingerprints lifted from the magazine were run through a national database, they matched those of young Lee Malvo, who was linked to Muhammad.

Probing into the backgrounds of the oddly matched duo, investigators quickly placed them at the top of their suspect list, launching a hunt for the car they were now known to be driving. The end came just after 3:00 A.M. on October 24, after the Caprice was spotted in a McDonald's parking lot near a highway rest stop in Frederick, Maryland. Swooping down on the car, a small army of lawmen—local police SWAT teams, the FBI's elite Hostage Rescue Team, and other state and federal paramilitary units—found the suspects dozing inside. Muhammad and Malvo surrendered so peacefully that, according to one official, "They practically slept through the takedown."

In the aftermath of the ordeal, a picture emerged of the senior sniper suspect as a classic sociopath. Effectively orphaned at three when his mother died of cancer and his father disappeared, Muhammad—born John Williams—was raised by an abusive grandfather who dealt out regular thrashings to the little boy. He grew up to be a lone wolf with a volatile temper and a powerful streak of arrogance. During a stint in the Louisiana National Guard after high school he was court-martialed twice, once for disobeying an order, the second time for striking a noncommissioned officer.

An inveterate ladies' man, he moved from woman to woman, impregnating one girlfriend, who gave birth to a son, marrying another, who bore him a second son in 1982. When the marriage fell apart three years later, he joined the army and converted to Islam, taking the surname Muhammad. During his nine-year stint, he served in the first Gulf War, qualifying as a hand grenade expert and an M-16 marksmanship expert.

After leaving the service, nothing in his life went right. Every business scheme he tried fell apart, as did his second marriage. In late 1999—with failure piled upon failure and Muhammad becoming increasingly unstable and abusive—his wife filed for divorce and got a restraining order against him. Shortly thereafter, he absconded with their three children to Antigua.

He remained there for slightly more than a year, supporting himself in various shady ways, including the sale of forged US travel documents. During this time, he struck up an intense mentoring relationship with Lee Malvo, a young man who had been raised by his divorced mother and was desperate for attention from a strong father figure. When Muhammad—unable to support his kids—returned them to the United States in May 2001, he brought Malvo with him.

Just three months after their return, Muhammad's three children were taken away from him and put into protective custody. In September, his wife was granted full custody. She lost no time in moving them across the country to suburban Washington, DC.

Not long afterward, Muhammad seems to have snapped. An inordinately arrogant man whose life had come to nothing, he blamed everyone but himself for his failures. Seething with resentment at the society he could not manage to succeed in—and at the contented middle-class world that seemed to make a mockery of his own botched life—he was ready to use his army-honed skills to take his revenge. Abetting him was the worshipful acolyte who, in a classic instance of a *folie à deux,* came to share in his pathology.

The Beltway Snipers weren't the first homicidal maniacs to leave a tarot-related "calling card" at a crime scene. In 1970, after slaughtering five people, a psychotic hippie named John Linley Frazier left a bizarre typewritten note at the victims' home that ended by invoking four of the figures from the deck:

> halloween. . . . 1970
>
> today world war 3 will begin as brought to you by the people of the free universe.
>
> From this day forward any one and?/or company of persons who missuses the environment or destroys same will suffer the penalty of death by the people of the free universe.
>
> I and my comrades from this day forth will fight until death or freedom, against anything or anyone who dose not support natural life on this planet, materialisum must die or man-kind will.
>
> KNIGHT OF WANDS
> KNIGHT OF CUPS
> KNIGHT OF PENTICLES
> KNIGHT OF SWORD

TAUNTS

There is a widespread notion—reinforced by countless movies in which the hero receives a steady stream of sneering messages from the psychopathic creep he's chasing—that serial killers typically engage in taunting communications with authorities. Like many stereotypes, this one is mostly false. However much satisfaction they may derive from outwitting the police, most serial killers have no desire to draw undue attention to themselves. Every time they get away with murder, they may exult in their sense of supposed superiority—their distorted idea of how much smarter and more cunning they are than other mere mortals. For the most part, however, they prefer to keep those feelings to themselves, without sending gloating letters or making boastful phone calls that sometimes offer an inadvertent clue to their whereabouts and might lead to their arrest.

Stereotypes, however, often contain an element of truth. In fact, there have been a number of notorious serial killers who took delight in thumbing their noses at authorities. For these psychopaths, taunting their pursuers and manipulating the media are an integral part of the criminal experience, adding to their sadistic fun and reinforcing their delusions of omnipotence.

Though serial murder is at least as old as the human species, psychos who get a kick out of playing such games did not appear until the nineteenth century. There is a good reason for this. Before there could be criminals who enjoyed jeering at the police and generating frenzied news coverage, two things were required: police departments and a popular press. These institutions didn't come into being until the Victorian era. The modern London police force was not established until 1839, and sensationalistic tabloids didn't appear until the late 1800s. So it's not surprising that the first serial killer who fits this pattern was Jack the Ripper.

Ironically, the most famous of the written taunts received by the police during the height of the Whitechapel horrors—indeed the one that gave this shadowy madman his legendary pseudonym—was probably not written by the killer at all. Inscribed in red ink, it read:

> 25 Sept: 1888
>
> Dear Boss
> I keep on hearing the police have caught me but they won't fix me just yet. I have laughed when they look so clever and talk about being on the right track. That joke about Leather Apron gave me real fits. I am down on whores and I shant quit ripping them till I do get buckled. Grand work the last job was. I gave the lady no time to squeal. How can they catch me now. I love my work and want to start again. You will soon hear of me with

> my funny little games. I saved some of the proper red stuff in a ginger beer bottle over the last job to write with but it went thick like glue and I cant use it. Red ink is fit enough I hope ha ha. The next job I do I shall clip the ladys ears off and send to the police officers just for jolly wouldnt you. Keep this letter back till I do a bit more work, then give it out straight. My knife's so nice and sharp I want to go to work right away if I get a chance. Good luck.
>
> Yours truly
> Jack the Ripper

In the view of most students of the case—Ripperologists, as they call themselves—this message was most likely a hoax. A few weeks later, however, a letter was received that is generally regarded as the only authentic communication sent by the Whitechapel monster. On October 16, 1888—two weeks after the Ripper savaged a streetwalker named Catherine Eddowes and removed her left kidney—a parcel arrived at the home of George Lusk, head of the Mile End Vigilance Committee, a group of local tradesman who had organized to assist in the hunt for the killer. Inside the package was a rotting chunk of human kidney, accompanied by a jeering letter addressed to Lusk. Printed on the upper left-hand corner of the letter was the sender's return address (which, a century later, would supply the title for an acclaimed graphic novel and movie on the Ripper case): "From hell."

The letter itself read as follows:

> Sor
> I send you half the Kidne I took from one woman prasarved it for you tother piece I fried and ate it was very nise I may send you the bloody knif that took it out if you only wate a whil longer
> signed
>
> Catch me when
> you can
> Mishter Lusk

The practice of mailing taunting letters to their pursuers, first established by the monster of Whitechapel, has been carried on by other serial killers, whose infamy partly derives from the correspondence they have entered into with authorities and/or members of the press. In April 1977, for example, police investigating the latest double murder committed by the phantom shooter who had begun terrorizing New York City the previous summer found a letter that—like the first message from the self-styled "Jack the Ripper"—would provide this notorious figure with his homicidal nickname. The letter was addressed to Captain Joseph Borrelli, a key member of the police task force that had been established to track down the shadowy gunman known, until then, as the ".44-Caliber Killer":

> Dear Captain Joseph Borrelli,
> I am deeply hurt by your calling me a wemon hater. I am not. But I am a monster. I am the "Son of Sam." I am a little brat.
> When father Sam gets drunk he gets mean. He beats his family. Sometimes he ties me up to the back of the house. Other times he locks me in the garage. Sam loves to drink blood.
> "Go out and kill," commands father Sam.
> Behind our house some rest. Mostly young—raped and slaughtered—their blood drained—just bones now.
> Papa Sam keeps me locked in the attic too. I can't get out but I look out the attic window and watch the world go by.
> I feel like an outsider. I am on a different wavelength then everybody else—programmed to kill.
> However, to stop me you must kill me. Attention all police: Shoot me first—shoot to kill or else keep out of my way or you will die!
> Papa Sam is old now. He needs some blood to preserve his youth. He has had too many heart attacks. "Ugh, me hoot, it hurts, sonny boy."
> I miss my pretty princess most of all. She's resting in our ladies house. But I'll see her soon.
> I am the "Monster"—"Beelzebub"—the chubby behemouth.
> I love to hunt. Prowling the streets looking for fair game—tasty meat. The wemon of Queens are prettyist of all. It must be the water they drink. I live for the hunt—my life. Blood for papa.
> Mr. Borrelli, sir, I don't want to kill anymore. No sur, no more but I must, "honour thy father."
> I want to make love to the world. I love people. I don't belong on earth. Return me to yahoos.
> To the people of Queens, I love you. And I want to wish all of you a happy Easter. May God bless you in this life and in the next. And for now I say goodbye and goodnight.
> POLICE: Let me haunt you with these words:
> I'll be back! I'll be back!
> To be interrpreted as—bang, bang, bang, bang—ugh!!
> Yours in murder
> Mr. Monster

Son of Sam's West Coast counterpart, the elusive psycho-killer known as Zodiac, was an even more inveterate writer of sadistically gloating letters. Typical of his epistolary style, which combined sneering references to police incompetence with promises of future atrocities, was a letter he mailed to the editor of the *San Francisco Chronicle* in October 1969, shortly after he shot San Francisco cab driver Paul Stine to death. Enclosed with the letter was a bloody swatch of fabric he had removed from the victim's shirt:

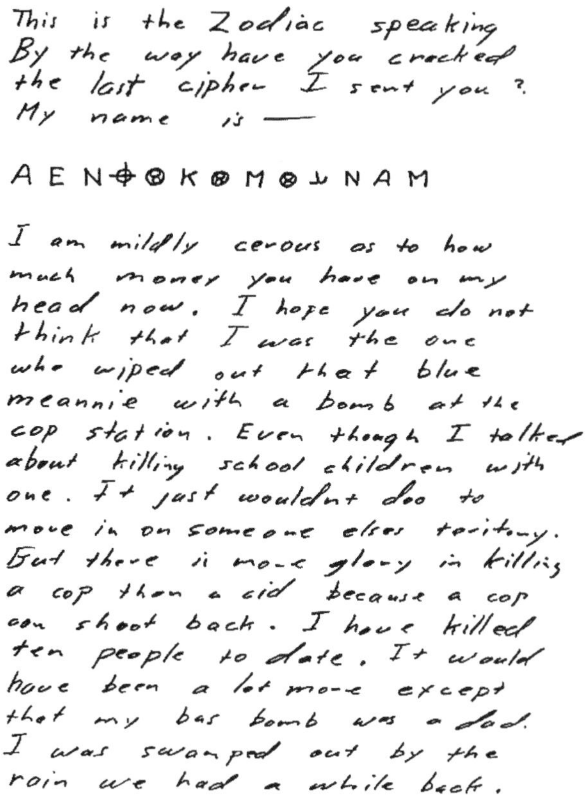
This is the Zodiac speaking
By the way have you cracked
the last cipher I sent you ?
My name is —

AEN⊕⊗K⊗M⊗⊥NAM

I am mildly cerous as to how
much money you have on my
head now. I hope you do not
think that I was the one
who wiped out that blue
meannie with a bomb at the
cop station. Even though I talked
about killing school children with
one. It just wouldnt doo to
move in on someone elses teritory.
But there is more glory in killing
a cop than a cid because a cop
can shoot back. I have killed
ten people to date. It would
have been a lot more except
that my bus bomb was a dud.
I was swamped out by the
rain we had a while back.

(Courtesy of Tom Voight)

Zodiac letter

This is the Zodiac speaking. I am the murderer of the taxi driver over by Washington St + Maple St last night, to prove this here is a blood stained piece of his shirt. I am the same man who did in the people in the north bay area. The S.F. Police could have caught me last night if they had searched the park properly instead of holding road races with their motorcicles seeing who could make the most noise. The car drivers should have just parked their cars and sat there quietly waiting for me to come out of cover. School children make nice targets, I think I shall wipe out a school bus some morning. Just shoot out the frunt tire + then pick off the kiddies as they come bouncing out.

Heriberto "Eddie" Seda—the New York City Zodiac copycat who shot four people in 1990—also sent several written taunts to local papers, vowing to kill one person born under each of the twelve astrological signs.

If the Jack the Ripper case represented the first time that a psycho-killer played mind games with his pursuers by mailing them taunting letters, it also established another pattern that would be repeated in future instances of serial murder: the tendency of some sick individuals to get in on the fun by sending hoax messages to the police. A century after the Whitechapel horrors, for example, Great Britain was shocked by the murder spree of another savage harlot-killer dubbed the "Yorkshire Ripper." During the manhunt for this vicious psycho (who would ultimately turn out to be a seemingly stable and contentedly married truck driver named Peter Sutcliffe), George Oldfield, the chief investigator, received a taunting tape-recorded message, presumably from the killer, outlining his plans to slay another victim and challenging the authorities to find him:

"I'm Jack. I see you are still having no luck catching me. I reckon your boys are letting you down, George. Can't be much good, can you? I'm not sure when I will strike again, but it will definitely be sometime this year, maybe September or October—even sooner if I get the chance."

As it turned out, this and other communications from the same source were not from the actual perpetrator but were rather the twisted handiwork of a hoaxer—a "criminal joke," in the words of writer Jane Caputi, "that disastrously diverted the police from the track of the actual killer as they assiduously searched for someone who matched the voice and accent of the wrong man."

The arrogance that underlies the act of sending taunting messages—the killer's deluded belief that his superior intellect and cunning make him invincible—can sometimes lead to his undoing. Theodore Kaczynski, for example—the so-called Unabomber whose mad crusade against modern technology left three people dead and twenty-nine injured—was finally captured after the *New York Times* agreed to publish his thirty-five-thousand-word manifesto, "Industrial Society and Its Fate." Recognizing its writing style—to say nothing of its fanatical views—Kaczynski's brother notified authorities, and the Unabomber was soon in custody.

Overweening arrogance also led to the arrest of the men believed to be the Beltway Snipers in the fall of 2002. In mid-October, an anonymous caller contacted a police hotline, claiming to be the sniper and bragging about a murder-robbery he had committed in Montgomery, Alabama. Pursuing the lead, investigators ran a fingerprint found at the Alabama crime scene through the FBI database and found a match with the prints of seventeen-year-old Jamaican-born John Lee Malvo which were on file with the Immigration and Naturalization Service. Before long, both Malvo and his sociopathic mentor, John Allen Muhammad—who allegedly had placed the boastful call—were under arrest, bringing to an end one of the most sensational and highly publicized homicide cases of recent times.

A Maniac's Twisted Taunt

Undoubtedly, the most viciously taunting letter ever written by a serial killer was not sent to the police (though it quickly found its way into their hands). It was mailed to the mother of one of the killer's young victims. In 1934, six years after committing one of the most heinous acts in the history of American crime—the murder, dismemberment, and cannibalization of twelve-year-old Grace Budd—the insanely perverted Albert Fish, who had gotten away scot-free with the atrocity, felt impelled to compose a letter to little Grace's mother, detailing the outrages he had perpetrated on the child. Fortunately, Fish's sadistic intention in composing this message—i.e., to rub the poor woman's nose in the horror—was thwarted by the fact that she was functionally illiterate. When her adult son read the letter, he immediately passed it along to the lead detective on the case, who used it (or more precisely, the envelope it came in) to track down the monster.

Here is the content of this appalling communication:

> My dear Mrs. Budd,
>
> In 1894 a friend of mine shipped as a deck hand on the steamer Tacoma, Capt. John Davis. They sailed from San Francisco for Hong Kong China. On arriving there he and two others went ashore and got drunk. When they returned the boat was gone. At that time there was a famine in China. Meat of any kind was from $1–3 Dollars a pound. So great was the suffering among the poor that all children under 12 were sold to the Butchers to be cut up and sold for food in order to keep others from starving. A boy or girl under 14 was not safe in the street. You could go to any shop and ask for steak—chops—or stew meat. Part of the naked body of a boy or a girl would be brought out and just what you wanted cut from it. A boy or girls behind which is the sweetest part of the body and sold as veal cutlet brought the highest price. John staid [sic] there so long he acquired a taste for human flesh. On his return to N.Y. he stole two boys one 7 and one 11. Took them to his home stripped them naked tied them in a closet. Then burned everything they had on. Several times every day and night he spanked them—tortured them—to make their meat good and tender. First he killed the 11 yr old boy, because he had the fattest ass and of course the most meat on it. Every part of his body was Cooked and eaten except head—bones and guts. He was Roasted in the oven (all of his ass), boiled, broiled, fried, stewed. The little boy was next, went the same way. At that time, I was living at 409 E. 100 St. near—right side. He told me so often how good Human flesh was I made up my mind to taste it. On Sunday June the 3—1928 I called on you at 406 W. 15 St. Brought you pot cheese—strawberries. We had lunch. Grace sat in my lap and kissed me. I made up my mind to eat her. On the pretense of taking her to a party. You said Yes

> she could go. I took her to an empty house in Westchester I had already picked out. When we got there, I told her to remain outside. She picked wildflowers. I went upstairs and stripped all my clothes off. I knew if I did not I would get her blood on them. When all was ready I went to the window and Called her. Then I hid in a closet until she was in the room. When she saw me all naked she began to cry and tried to run downstairs. I grabbed her and she said she would tell her mamma. First I stripped her naked. How she did kick—bite and scratch. I choked her to death, then cut her in small pieces so I could take my meat to my rooms, Cook and eat it. How sweet and tender her little ass was roasted in the oven. It took me 9 days to eat her entire body. I did not fuck her tho I could have had I wished. She died a *virgin.*

ESCALATION

Nine years elapsed between Jeffrey Dahmer's first and second murders. In June 1978, while his parents were away on vacation, the eighteen-year-old Dahmer picked up a hitchhiker named Steven Hicks and brought him home for beers. A few hours later, when the handsome young man got ready to leave, Dahmer smashed his skull with a barbell, choked him to death, dismembered the body, and buried it in the backyard. He did not kill again until September 1987, when he met twenty-eight-year-old Steven Tuomi at a gay bar in Milwaukee, took him to a nearby hotel, and murdered him during the night.

By contrast, in the two months between May 24 and July 22, 1991, when he was finally arrested, Dahmer committed no less than six homicides, killing at the approximate rate of one young man per week. Not only had the pace of his murders accelerated dramatically; the horrors he perpetrated on his victims had also grown increasingly grotesque. By the end, he was having anal sex with the corpses, saving the heads, torsos, and genitalia in his refrigerator, and cutting out the hearts for consumption.

When Dahmer was later interviewed by Robert Ressler, the famed FBI profiler asked him why he had begun indulging in such extreme practices. "It was just another step," said Dahmer. "An escalation. Trying something new to satisfy." The answer was revealing. As uniquely depraved as Dahmer was, his crimes were typical in one regard. It is often true of serial murderers that their bloodlust becomes more urgent and irresistible the longer they continue to kill—as if (to quote Hamlet) "increase of appetite had grown by what it fed on." Each new atrocity only makes them hungrier for more. The intervals between their killings—the so-called cooling-off periods—grow shorter and shorter. Eventually, they may lose control altogether and give way to a frenzy of sadism.

The cross-country serial murder spree of Earle Leonard Nelson, for example—the so-called Gorilla Murderer of the 1920s—began with three stranglings committed over a four-month period. By contrast, his last three homicides were not only perpetrated over a span of just five days but were characterized by exceptional brutality. (The ravaged corpse of one victim, a Winnipeg housewife named Emily Patterson, was left shoved under the bed of her three-year-old son.) Homicidal nurse Jane Toppan was so out of control by the end of her murderous career that she wiped out an entire family of four adults within a few weeks of each other, the last two killings occurring only four days apart. (During the final murder, she also committed an unspeakable perversion, taking her victim's ten-year-old son to bed with her while the mother lay dying in the next room.) The first two murders committed by Michigan sex-killer John Norman Collins were separated by almost a year; the third and fourth by only three days. When Ted Bundy began his one-man crime wave in 1974, his homicides occurred roughly a month apart. Four years later, in January 1978, he savaged four sorority girls in Tallahassee, Florida, all within the space of an hour.

There are different explanations for this phenomenon. Sometimes this sort of unbridled escalation is a symptom of the killer's spiraling mental disintegration, the utter breakdown of his impulse control. At other times, it springs from his megalomaniacal belief that he is invulnerable, that he can get away with murder as often as he likes. In rare instances, such growing recklessness may even reflect the killer's unconscious desire to get caught.

The main reason for this behavior, however, was the one suggested by Dahmer, when he remarked that he began cannibalizing his victims as a way of "trying something new to satisfy." For homicidal psychopaths, lust-killing often becomes an addiction. Like heroin users, they not only become dependent on the thrilling sensation—the *rush*—of torture, rape, and murder; they come to require ever greater and more frequent fixes. After a while, merely stabbing a coed to death every few months isn't enough. They have to kill every few weeks, then every few days. And to achieve the highest pitch of arousal, they have to torture the victim before putting her to death.

This kind of escalation can easily lead to the killer's own destruction. Like a junkie who ODs in his urgent quest to satisfy his cravings, serial killers are often undone by their increasingly unbridled sadism, which drives them to such reckless extremes that they are finally caught.

> Monsters tend to be sadists, deriving sexual gratification from imposing pain on others. Their secret perversions, at first sporadic, often trap them in a pattern as the intervals between indulgences become briefer: it is a pattern whose repetitions develop into an hysterical crescendo, as if from one outrage to another the monster were seeking as a climax his own annihilation.
>
> —John Brophy, *The Meaning of Murder*

TORTURE

Who was the worst serial killer of all time? That's a question frequently asked of experts on the subject. If somebody you know has fallen victim to one of these psychos, the answer is easy: the worst serial killer is the monster who murdered your friend or family member. Otherwise—given the range of atrocities these deviants have committed—it's impossible to say.

Still—even among a group of criminals as universally vile as psychopathic killers—there are degrees of monstrosity. Though Jeffrey Dahmer would rank high on anyone's list of the most appalling psycho-killers of modern times, he insisted that he never wanted his victims to suffer. He may have drugged them, drilled holes in their skulls, injected their brains with acid, then strangled, eviscerated, and eaten them. But as he told one interviewer, "I wanted to make it as painless as possible."

Though Dahmer, like all psychopaths, was incapable of comprehending the full horror of his behavior, his statement reflects a sense that, however dreadful his deeds, at least he wasn't the kind of killer who subjected his victims to extreme torment. And indeed, it can be argued that, of all psycho-killers, the most unspeakably evil are those who do not merely engage in serial slaughter or even in such postmortem atrocities as necrophiliac rape and cannibalism but who derive sadistic sexual pleasure from inflicting unbearable agony on their helpless victims—who indulge in deliberate, protracted torture.

In the long, gruesome history of sadistic lust-murder, there have been a number of infamous torture-killers, such as Gilles de Rais, the fifteenth-century French aristocrat who luxuriated in the hideous cruelties he perpetrated on countless children. Another, more recent—though no less monstrous—child-torturer was Albert Fish, who spent a lifetime committing the most hideous atrocities imaginable. On more than one occasion, he abducted little boys, took them to remote locations, bound them, castrated them, then left them there to bleed to death.

> I always had a desire to inflict pain on others and to have them inflict pain on me. I always seemed to enjoy everything that hurt.
>
> —Albert Fish

The Hillside Stranglers, Kenneth Bianchi and Angelo Buono, became increasingly sadistic as their murder spree progressed, burning one victim with an electrical cord, injecting another with cleaning solution and asphyxiating her with a gas hose, an agonizing ordeal that lasted at least thirty minutes. The Australian-born playboy-psycho, Christopher Wilder, also favored electrical torture, attaching a fifteen-foot cord to the toes of one victim and jolting her for several hours after sealing her eyelids shut with superglue. Electrocution also figured in the crimes of Gary Heidnik, the sex-slave psycho who kept a half dozen women chained to a pipe in his "Philadelphia Torture Dungeon." To punish one captive who seemed insufficiently subservient, he tossed her in a water-filled pit, then dropped in a live electric wire, killing her when the wire came in contact with her chains.

Gerard Schaefer—who, like the Hillside Stranglers, regarded all sexually attractive young women as "whores"—not only committed an untold number of horrifically sadistic murders (often involving his preferred mode of torture, slow hanging), but left written accounts of his enormities that rank among the most appalling documents ever written. Other serial killers have also left documented evidence of their tortures. Ian Brady and Myra Hindley, the infamous Moors Murderers, tape-recorded the piteous pleas and heart-wrenching screams of one little victim. Harvey Glatman shot photographs of the bound and terrorized women he was about to kill. Leonard Lake and Charles Ng videotaped the sex-and-torture sessions they conducted in their California horror bunker. Not every homicidal sadist, however, has left a detailed record of his atrocities. Ted Bundy, for example, was relatively forthcoming in his confessions. Some of the things he did to his victims were so unspeakable, however, that he refused to discuss them with authorities.

In her book *Killing for Sport: Inside the Minds of Serial Killers,* profiler Pat Brown offers this description of the typical serial torture-killer:

> While a "normal" serial killer might brutally beat, rape, strangle, and shove a tree limb into his victim, this is not the same type of behavior exhibited by the sexually sadistic serial killer. The latter keeps his victim alive for hours or days while he tortures her with all variety of sexually sadistic acts. He likes to see her pain, hear her screams, and make her beg and plead. He may have all manner of implements in his rape kit to accomplish the level of torture he wishes to achieve: whips, nipple clamps, X-Acto blades, dildos, hot wax, enemas, garrotes, gags, and various bondage material.

The only flaw in this passage is Brown's exclusive use of the feminine pronoun to refer to the victim. In point of fact, the victim of one of these psychos is just as likely to be a "he," since sadistic torture-slaying is a common feature of gay serial murder. John Wayne Gacy anally raped his adolescent male victims with various objects, shoved their heads into water-filled bathtubs until they lost consciousness, and subjected them to other torments before slowly garroting them. Dean Corll inserted glass pipettes into the urethras of his teenage victims before castrating them with a knife or his teeth. Bob Berdella kept his male victims captive for days, injecting Drano into their throats, jabbing alcohol-soaked Q-Tips into their eyes, beating them with iron clubs, clamping electrodes to their testicles.

Though women rarely engage in brutal sex-torture, except as part of a killer couple, female poisoners can be extremely sadistic, taking voluptuous pleasure in the torments that their victims undergo. Sometimes they even dole out their lethal doses over a period of days or weeks in order to prolong their own sick enjoyment. Considering the agonizing symptoms of, say, arsenic poisoning—the terrible thirst, the uncontrollable vomiting and diarrhea, the excruciating muscle cramps and violent convulsions—there is no doubt that this typical form of female serial murder qualifies as genuine torture.

Recommended Reading

Rose G. Mandelsberg, *Torture Killers* (1993)

TROPHIES

Even as a middle-aged man, the psychologically stunted Eddie Gein related better to youngsters than to grown-ups. In the early 1950s, a few juvenile visitors to his decrepit farmhouse were startled to see several preserved human heads hanging on his bedroom walls. When the boys asked where these ghastly items had come from, Eddie explained that they were shrunken South Seas heads, sent by a cousin who had fought in the Philippines in the Second World War. Only later did the appalling truth come to light—that the supposed war artifacts were actually stuffed and mounted "face masks" that the Plainfield ghoul had flayed from female corpses, crudely preserved, and mounted on his wall like hunting trophies.

Gein's practice of saving human body parts and displaying them at home is an extreme example of a common tendency among serial killers, who often keep mementos of their crimes. But the fact that his neighbors believed his original story—that the heads were war souvenirs—is also significant. Gein's explanation was, in fact, fairly plausible. The grisly trophies of South Seas headhunters have always been popular collectibles. American soldiers who fought in the Pacific *did* sometimes bring home, not just old shrunken heads, but other kinds of human keepsakes—some of them quite recently stripped from the enemy.

Indeed, throughout human history, victors in battle have routinely taken trophies from the corpses of their fallen foes—not only valuables like rings or amulets or articles of clothing but parts of their anatomy: scalps, ears, teeth, fingers, and even genitalia. Warriors engage in this savage practice for various reasons: it serves as proof of their prowess, it is a way of inflicting an ultimate humiliation on their enemy, and it permits them to recall their moment of triumph at a later time.

All of these factors operate in the cases of serial killers, whose behavior reflects the very worst, most bestial aspects of human nature—barbarities that

At Home with Ed Gein in the Trophy Room
DOROTHY DALE

Ed Gein with his Trophies by Michael Rose

civilization has largely outgrown (though they occasionally surface in the chaos of war).

According to the FBI, there are two categories of serial killer keepsakes: the "souvenir" and the "trophy." The first presumably serves the same function that a statuette of the Eiffel Tower does for a tourist who has just vacationed in Paris—it reminds the killer of how much fun he had and allows him to relive the experience in fantasy until he can do it again. Trophies, on the other hand, are analogous to the mounted moose head or stag antlers that a hunter might proudly display over the fireplace—prideful evidence of the killer's lethal skill.

In practice, it's difficult to make such hard-and-fast distinctions, and most criminologists use the two terms interchangeably to describe the items that serial killers take from their victims.

Occasionally, this stuff is actual booty that the killer can convert into cash—an expensive watch, a wedding ring, a gold necklace. Generally, however, the things most cherished by serial killers have no inherent value. Searching the bedroom of the Florida sex-killer Gerard Schaefer, for example, police found a stash of sinister keepsakes that had belonged to his victims, including a cheap shamrock pin, an address book, a passport, a diary, a driver's license, a poetry book, and two gold-filled teeth. Hadden Clark, the cross-dressing cannibal killer who murdered an indeterminate number of women, not only accumulated a bucketful of costume jewelry but kept the bloody pillowcase of a coed he had slain in bed.

However intrinsically worthless, these macabre souvenirs possess an almost magical power for the killer, who clearly runs a great risk by holding on to such incriminating evidence. (Clark, for example, was arrested after police retrieved his victim's pillowcase and found his bloody fingerprint on it). But—like the pederast who cannot stop himself from downloading illegal child porn—serial killers derive such profound, perverted pleasure from their creepy treasures that they cannot give them up. Indeed, in many cases, trophies aren't just a way for them to commemorate their deeds; they are a masturbatory turn-on.

That some serial killers use their sick mementos for specifically sexual purposes is evinced by the kinds of things they hoard: fetish objects like underwear, shoes, or nylon stockings; tufts of their victims' pubic hair; or erogenous body parts. Among the unspeakable artifacts uncovered in Eddie Gein's horror house was a shoe box full of preserved vulvas. Robin Gecht and his team of "Chicago Rippers" sliced off and saved their victims' breasts. And the fetishistic maniac Jerry Brudos kept the sliced-off left foot of one female victim in his freezer, so that he could deck it out in shoes from his collection of stolen high heels.

Sometimes, instead of souvenirs, the killer might shoot pictures of his atrocities or document them in some other way, like a traveler eager to preserve his memories of a thrilling experience. Indeed, every new advance in recording technology has been applied in this way. In the 1950s, Harvey Murray Glatman photographed his bound and terrified victims with a Rolleicord camera. In the 1960s, Ian Brady and Myra Hindley tape-recorded the desperate pleas of one little girl before killing her. In the 1980s, Leonard Lake and Charles Ng videotaped their captives.

Next to Ed Gein—whose farmhouse full of body part artifacts stands as the sickest such assemblage in the annals of crime—Jeffrey Dahmer was probably the most obsessive collector of unspeakable trophies. Police who searched his nightmarish Milwaukee apartment were aghast to discover Polaroid snapshots of mutilated victims, refrigerated heads, and frozen packages of human viscera, male genitalia in a lobster pot, painted skulls on a shelf, and more. Dahmer was a supremely sick version of one of those out-of-control collectors whose hobby begins to take over his living space. Every victim who fell into his hands ended up as another grisly relic, so precious to the "Milwaukee Cannibal" that he couldn't bear to part with it.

Because it wouldn't be a remembrance—it would have been a stranger.

—Jeffrey Dahmer, when asked why—instead of attempting to construct a skeleton from the bones of his victims—he didn't just buy one from a medical supply store.

A sex-killer dismembers his victim in this engraving from an 1834 crime pamphlet

DISPOSAL

What a serial murderer does with the remains of his victims is as much a part of his MO as his preferred method of killing them. Indeed, for some psychos, getting rid of the corpse is the high point of the crime. In their groundbreaking study, *Sexual Homicide,* for example, John Douglas and his collaborators talk about one serial killer who got his biggest thrill, not from the murder itself, but from "the successful dismemberment and disposal of the body without detection"—an act that provided him with an exhilarating sense of power, of having committed an ultimate transgression and gotten away with it.

For most serial killers, however, body disposal is less a source of pleasure than a purely practical concern—a problem to be solved. Because of their aberrant psychological makeup—their inability to feel guilt or empathy or moral revulsion—they are able to go about this nerve-wracking, often horrendously gruesome, task with a bizarre emotional detachment.

After strangling his first victim to death, for example, Joel Rifkin—the Long Island serial prostitute killer responsible for seventeen grisly homicides during the early 1990s—dragged the corpse to the basement, draped it across the washer and dryer, and coolly dismembered it with an X-Acto knife. After the young woman was in pieces, he sliced off her fingertips to foil identification, yanked out her teeth with a pliers, shoved her decapitated head into an empty paint can, stuffed the limbs and torso into separate thirty-three-gallon trash bags, loaded the parts into his mother's car, and drove the ghastly cargo out to New Jersey, disposing of it in different locations, some in the woods, the rest in the river.

Years later, after his arrest, Rifkin was asked how he felt while performing this horrific operation—the first time he had ever committed such an enormity. "I reduced it to biology class," he said with a shrug. "It was just a straight dissection, done as fast as you can. I made very small, controlled cuts over the joints and popped the bones out of the sockets. As a kid you learn how to carve a turkey. You just go to the bone on the wing and the bone on the leg. You can't cut the bone with a knife, you find it and pop it." It would be hard to find a more chilling example of the way serial killers dehumanize their victims, treating them as objects to be used for their own pleasure, then tossed away without a second thought.

Rifkin *did* experience a moment of panic when—less than a week after the murder—a golfer at a New Jersey course sliced his ball into the woods and stumbled upon the paint can containing the prostitute's head. Thereafter, Rifkin tried different means of disposing of his victims. He placed the dismembered parts of one woman in separate buckets, filled them with concrete, and threw them in the river. Others were stuffed into fifty-five-gallon oil drums and left in recycling plants or tossed into creeks. Still others were discarded in garbage dumps, pine barrens, or along freeways.

Rifkin drove considerable distances to get rid of the bodies. He was, in fact, arrested while transporting the remains of his last tarp-wrapped victim in the bed of his pickup truck. Rifkin is an example of a serial killer who perpetrates his atrocities at home, then smuggles the gory evidence off the premises—a sensible precaution when you live with your mother, as he did. Remarkably, not all psycho-killers go to such trouble. When, in September 1998, police in Poughkeepsie, New York—who had been investigating a string of mysterious disappearances—finally searched the home of the leading suspect, a twenty-seven-year-old African-American named Kendall Francois, they were stunned to discover the decomposing bodies of eight young women stashed in the attic of the two-story colonial he shared with his mother, father, and younger sister. Given the stench given off by the putrefying remains, many people assumed that Kendall's parents must have known about his crimes. Evidently, however, they had accepted their son's explanation that a family of raccoons had died in the attic crawl space, suffusing it with a rank, stubborn smell.

The overpowering stink of death led to the arrest of another serial strangler, a hulking twenty-eight-year-old named Harrison Graham who kept seven female cadavers in his squalid North Philadelphia apartment. His crimes were discovered when his neighbors finally complained about the smell. In custody, the mentally retarded, drug-addicted Graham explained that he kept the corpses at home because he "didn't know where else to put them."

Other serial killers have also stored the rotting remains of their victims right on their premises, turning their nondescript living quarters into secret charnel houses. Besides burying one victim in his garden, two others in a shed, and his wife under the floorboards, John Reginald Christie—the British psycho known as the "Monster of Rillington Place"—stuck three female corpses into his kitchen cupboard, then plastered it over with wallpaper before vacating the house. Needless to say, the new tenants came in for a nasty surprise when they began making renovations.

John Wayne Gacy did a more effective job of stashing his victims at home, interring the bodies of twenty-eight young men in the crawl space beneath his house in suburban Chicago. Like Gacy, who ran a successful contracting business, the British sex-slayer Frederick West was a builder by trade, a vocation that made it easier for him to conceal his atrocities by carrying out his own at-home renovations. The corpses of some of his victims ended up in the cellar, which—grotesquely—he later converted to a nursery bedroom for his children. Another body was buried underneath a bathroom that West had constructed where an attached garage had previously stood. Other young women—including his own teenage daughter, Heather—were planted in the rear garden. It was, in fact, West's repeated threat—that if his other children misbehaved they would "end up under the patio like Heather"—which led to his arrest when it was reported to the police.

In contrast to Gacy and West, Dean Corll—another horrifically sadistic sex-killer who turned his home into a torture chamber—took care to remove the corpses from the premises, renting a boat storage shed several miles south of Houston, which became the burying place for seventeen of his mutilated male victims.

Serial killers who commit their atrocities at home (or at a secret location specifically designed for that purpose, like the remote murder bunker constructed by the homicidal team of Charles Ng and Leonard Lake) can generally take their time to dispose of their victims in a carefully planned and organized way. Like Gacy or the nineteenth-century "Lady Bluebeard," Belle Gunness—whose Indiana "murder farm" eventually yielded the remains of at least a dozen dismembered people—such killers can often accumulate a sizable collection of corpses on their property.

Obviously, the case is different for serial killers who do their killing outside the house. How such psychos dispose of their victims depends on various factors, some calculated, others having to do with the warped psychology of the killer. Some serial killers might snatch a victim, drive her to a secluded spot—a remote woodland area, say—then rape her, kill her, and make a quick getaway, leaving the corpse exposed to the elements or possibly concealed in a shallow, hastily dug grave with a pile of dead leaves scooped over it. This was the MO, for example, of the Florida sex-slayer Gerard Schaefer, some of whose victims were taken to a swampy island, where—after being tortured and killed—they were simply left to rot.

In other cases a psycho-killer who has, say, murdered a hitchhiker or snatched a victim from a shopping mall parking lot might dump the body along the roadside, or at an abandoned industrial area, or into a ravine. Depending on how "organized" he is, the killer may devote a fair amount of time to checking out potential dumping sites in advance before selecting the one that seems to offer the best opportunities for disposal.

By contrast, other killers deliberately leave their victims' corpses in conspicuous places—a decision that generally has as much to do with their perverted need to taunt the police and terrorize the public as with anything else. Several of the hideously butchered women slain by Jack the Ripper, for example, were simply left sprawled in the street. Besides the obvious reason for this—his desire to flee the crime scene as quickly as possible—the consternation he created by flaunting his atrocities undoubtedly added to his sick, sadistic fun. Similarly, the Hillside Stranglers expressed their contempt for authority, for society, and for the entire female sex in general by leaving the naked bodies of their victims exposed to public view in obscenely flagrant poses.

If the Hillside Stranglers seemed intent on advertising their atrocities, other serial killers have done the opposite, going to great lengths to obliterate every trace of their victims' existence. Henri Landru, the Parisian "Bluebeard" who murdered ten wives in the decade following World War I, got rid of their corpses so efficiently that, even today, no one knows for certain how they died. Apparently, he disposed of the remains by incinerating them in a large stove he had specifically purchased for that purpose. Incineration was also the preferred disposal method of another French psychopath, Dr. Marcel Petiot, who turned his basement furnace into a private crematorium where the bodies of his Jewish victims were reduced to ash during the Nazi occupation of Paris. Another medical monster, Dr. H. H. Holmes, installed a kiln in the cellar of his "Horror Castle," where an indeterminate number of people vanished forever during the time of the Chicago World's Fair of 1893.

In other cases, Holmes—never one to miss an opportunity to make an extra buck—sold the skeletal remains of his victims to local medical schools. Burke and Hare—the notorious British body snatchers—also disposed of their victims by selling them as anatomical specimens. (Indeed, supplying dead bodies to a London doctor was the explicit motive for their crimes.)

Other serial killers have found diabolical ways to profit from the disposal of their victims. Most ghastly of all was undoubtedly the German lust-killer, Georg Grossmann, who capitalized on the severe meat shortage that afflicted Germany during World War I by selling the butchered flesh of his female victims as beef and pork.

Another serial killer who went to extraordinary trouble to make his victims disappear was John George Haigh, the British "Acid-Bath Killer," who dissolved a half dozen acquaintances in a forty-gallon oil drum filled with sulfuric acid. Unfortunately for Haigh, even this extreme method was not sufficient to eliminate every vestige of his victims. Police searching his workshop were ultimately able to recover twenty-eight pounds of human body fat, three gallstones, part of a left foot, eighteen bone fragments, and a set of dentures.

The Hungarian serial killer Bela Kiss took the opposite tack in dealing with the remains of his victims. Instead of attempting to dissolve them with acid, he preserved them in wood alcohol. It wasn't until Kiss had vanished from his village that authorities discovered the bodies of seven strangled women sealed inside large metal drums in his house.

Arguably the most frightening variety of serial killer—the type that touches our deepest sense of vulnerability—is the household invader, the psycho who slaughters total strangers in the sanctity of their own home. Occasionally, this kind of killer will make a perfunctory effort to conceal his victims. Earle Leonard Nelson, for example—the "Gorilla Murderer" of the 1920s—hid one body in a trunk, another behind a furnace, a third underneath a bed. More frequently, such monsters will leave the bodies where they are, sometimes after committing some appalling desecration on them. The night after the infamous massacre at the Sharon Tate–Roman Polanski mansion, for example, Charles Manson and his "creepy crawlers" broke into the home of a couple named Rosemary and Leno LaBianca. After hacking the pair to death, the hippie killers carved the word *war* into the husband's chest and left a serving fork sticking from his stomach. By contrast, other murderers actually display a perverse concern for the condition of the corpses they have created. The "Lipstick Killer" William Heirens took time to wash the blood from several of his victims and drape bathrobes over their naked bodies.

Sometimes, a killer's attempt to get rid of remains will backfire. In the 1980s, homicidal caretaker Dorothea Puente murdered seven of her elderly tenants, buried their corpses in her backyard, and sprinkled quicklime over the bodies to expedite their decomposition. Puente, however, did not realize that, unless quicklime is treated with water, it actually acts as a preservative, preventing decay by desiccating the tissue. As a result, when the bodies were ultimately uncovered, they were in surprisingly good shape, allowing medical examiners easily to ascertain that the cause of death was poisoning.

Both Dennis Nilsen—the so-called British Jeffrey Dahmer—and the cannibalistic German lust-murderer Joachim Kroll (responsible for fourteen between 1959 and 1976) made the mistake of flushing human body parts down the toilet, a method of disposal that led to their arrest when the plumbing in their respective apartment buildings became clogged with flesh and viscera, bringing their atrocities to light.

Were it not for the unfortunate tendency of corpses to rot, the necrophiliac Nilsen would undoubtedly have saved the dead bodies of his victims forever, since he enjoyed keeping them around the house for companionship. The same was true of Jeffrey Dahmer, who did, in fact, preserve various parts of the young men he killed. Another notorious Wisconsin necrophile, the ghoul Ed Gein, was the ultimate example of a madman who—instead of getting rid of his cadavers as quickly as possible—took them home to play with.

A few serial killers have resorted to such bizarre methods of disposal that they have become infamous less for the murders they committed than for the way they got rid of the bodies. One of the most outlandish of these psychopaths was Joe Ball.

A sullen, beer-bellied reprobate rumored to have sprung from a family of respectable ranchers, Ball took to bootlegging in the 1920s, earning enough money to open his own drinking establishment once Prohibition was repealed. His tavern—a rowdy, roadside joint called the Sociable Inn, situated on US Highway 181 south of San Antonio—became locally famous for an offbeat feature Ball installed out back: a large cement pond stocked with five, fully grown alligators whose frenzied feedings became a nightly attraction for Joe's hard-bitten regulars, particularly when he tossed in a live cat or dog.

Besides the reptile shows, Ball's place was known for its high turnover of waitresses, who seemed to come and go with surprising regularity. In 1937, rumors began to circulate that Joe was keeping his gators fat and happy with more than horsemeat and stray animals. One local laborer claimed that, while passing the property on horseback one moonlit night, he had seen Ball dumping what appeared to be human limbs into the pond. Relatives of several young women who had worked for Ball—and subsequently disappeared

Disposal by fire: an 1842 engraving showing the incineration of a victim's dismembered remains

without a trace—began pressuring authorities to launch an investigation. Checking into the case, Texas Rangers discovered that at least a dozen of his former waitresses, along with two of his ex-wives, had gone missing. When a pair of Rangers showed up at the Sociable Inn on the night of September 24, 1938, the proprietor—realizing that the jig was up—casually stepped to the cash register, rang up "No Sale," then, when the register drawer sprang open, pulled out an automatic pistol and shot himself in the head.

The horrific truth was confirmed when his janitor, Clifford Wheeler, confessed that he had been coerced into helping Ball dispose of dismembered women—some in the desert, others in the alligator pond. Wheeler was sent to jail as an accomplice; the gators ended up in the San Antonio zoo.

A more recent case of a serial sex-murderer who reportedly relied on voracious creatures to dispose of his victims is that of Robert Pickton, alleged to be the most savage psycho-killer in Canadian history. In November 2002, authorities announced that the remains of eighteen missing women—drug-addicted prostitutes from the skid row section of Vancouver—had been uncovered on a pig farm owned by Pickton. He is suspected of as many as sixty-three murders.

"The sufferings of the women can only be imagined," the *New York Times* reported shortly after Pickton's arrest. "Not one body has been found intact, and a wood chipper and Mr. Pickton's pigs are believed to have devoured much of the evidence, leaving behind mostly microscopic traces of DNA."

Recommended Reading

Brian Lane, *The Butchers: A Casebook of Macabre Crimes and Forensic Detection* (1998)

HOW IT ENDS

In popular culture, even the most fiendishly cunning serial killer can't elude the forces of law and order forever. Heroic profilers create uncannily accurate psychological portraits of their quarry that lead straight to the killer's lair. Crime scene investigators employ a dazzling array of high-tech tools to identify a perpetrator from the merest, microscopic traces of evidence. FBI field agents defeat their diabolical foes by solving elaborate puzzles that would tax the deductive genius of Sherlock Holmes.

Of course, the reason people turn to movies, TV shows, and best-selling thrillers is precisely because these works depict a world far tidier and more reassuring than the one we actually inhabit. In reality, stopping serial killers is a grueling and distinctly unglamorous business, owing more to sheer accident, dumb luck, criminal incompetence, and old-fashioned dogged detective work than to the kind of forensic razzle-dazzle that makes for an exciting movie or suspense novel. And then, of course, there is another sobering difference between make-believe and fact.

In real life, the bad guy sometimes gets away with murder.

PROFILING

In the world of pop entertainment, criminal profilers are generally portrayed as the modern-day descendants of Sherlock Holmes: investigative prodigies whose uncanny powers of observation, deduction, and intuition inevitably lead to the killer's arrest. This glamorized view of profiling has been encouraged by some of its more celebrated practitioners. In a pioneering 1986 article on the subject, "Criminal Profiling from Crime Scene Analysis," John Douglas and Robert Ressler—two of the founding members of the FBI's Behavioral Science Unit—liken the profiler to Agatha Christie's famed fictional detective, Hercule Poirot. "The ability of Hercule Poirot to solve a crime by describing the perpetrator is a skill shared by the expert investigative profiler," they proclaim. "Evidence speaks its own language of patterns and sequences that can reveal the offender's behavioral characteristics. Like Poirot, the profiler can say, 'I know who he must be.' "

Such boasts have created an inevitable backlash among other law enforcement types, who scoff at the notion that the profiler is some kind of forensic genius—part scientist, part psychic—who can deduce the identity of an "unsub" (police slang for "unknown subject") by analyzing the evidence gathered from a crime scene. Some skeptics dismiss the usefulness of profiling altogether, claiming that, by itself, it has never led to the solution of a crime and that it has actively hampered some investigations.

Certainly, the record of profilers has been spotty. Between September 2001 and May 2003—to cite just one example—five women, all of them white, were raped and killed in and around Baton Rouge by a sex-slayer dubbed the "Louisiana Slasher." Because statistics show that the majority of serial killers choose victims of their own race, profilers initially described the "unsub" as a white male, a description that in retrospect seemed totally wrong when the prime suspect—linked to the murders by DNA evidence—turned out to be Derrick Todd Lee, a thirty-four-year-old African-American.

Even Douglas and Ressler have backtracked from some of their more extravagant claims. In the very same article in which they compare themselves to real-life Poirots, they subsequently modify the claim, offering a more modest assessment of what profiling can accomplish: "Profiling does *not* provide the specific identity of the offender. Rather, it indicates the *kind* of individual most likely to have committed a crime."

In this more limited sense—as a tool for narrowing the field of suspects, for helping police focus on certain avenues of investigation—profiling has often proved useful. And occasionally it has produced startlingly accurate results.

Origins

Experts agree that the earliest documented instance of the practice we now know as profiling occurred during the Jack the Ripper case. Following the

Ripper's final and most appalling murder—the butchery of twenty-five-year-old Mary Jane Kelly on November 9, 1888—a postmortem was carried out by several physicians, including police surgeon Dr. Thomas Bond. Afterward, Bond assembled his findings into a report that (as crime writer Martin Fido puts it) took "the form of primitive deductive offender profile"—one that can be favorably compared to any "drawn up by the best and most experienced criminal profilers in the world today":

> The murderer must have been a man of physical strength and of great coolness and daring. There is no evidence that he had an accomplice. He must in my opinion be a man subject to periodic attacks of Homicidal and erotic mania. The character of the mutilations indicate that the man may be in a condition, sexually, that may be called satyriasis. It is of course possible that the Homicidal impulse may have developed from a revengeful or brooding condition of the mind, or that Religious Mania may have been the original disease, but I do not think either hypothesis is likely. The murderer in external appearance is quite likely to be a quiet inoffensive looking man probably middle-aged and neatly and respectably dressed. I think he must be in the habit of wearing a cloak or overcoat or he could hardly have escaped notice in the streets if the blood on his hands or clothes were visible.
>
> Assuming the murderer to be such a person as I have just described he would probably be solitary or eccentric in his habits, also he is most likely to be a man without regular occupation, but with some small income or pension. He is possibly living among respectable people who have some knowledge of his character and habits and who may have grounds for suspicion that he is not quite right in his mind at times. Such persons would probably be unwilling to communicate suspicions to the Police for fear or trouble or notoriety; whereas if there were a prospect of reward it might overcome their scruples.

Fifty years later, Dr. J. Paul de River of Los Angeles created another early criminal profile. On Saturday June 26, 1937, three little girls from Inglewood—six-year-old Madeline Everett, her nine-year-old sister Melba Marie, and their neighbor, eight-year-old Jeanette Stephens—went off to play in a local park and never came home. Two days later, their bodies—raped, strangled, and horribly mutilated—were found in a nearby ravine.

The crimes—dubbed the "Babes of Inglewood Murders" by the press—sent shock waves through the city and set off a massive police manhunt. When the investigation hit a dead end, Captain James Doyle of the LAPD decided to consult Dr. de River, a psychiatrist he had previously worked with. After viewing the corpses of the children and the physical evidence at the crime scene, de River wrote up this report for the district attorney's office:

> Look for one man, probably in his twenties, a pedophile who might have been arrested before for annoying children. He is a sadist with a superabun-

> dance of curiosity. He is very meticulous and probably now remorseful, as most sadists are very apt to be masochistic after expressing sadism. The slayer may have a religious streak and even become prayerful. Moreover, he is a spectacular type and has done this thing, not on a sudden impulse, but as a deliberately planned affair. I am of the opinion that he had obtained the confidence of these little girls. I believe they knew the man and trusted him.

There is some question as to how much this protoprofile actually contributed to the arrest of the perpetrator, a school crossing guard named Albert Dyer who was eventually hanged for the atrocities. De River got a few things wrong: Dyer was in his thirties, not his twenties, and had been previously arrested only for vagrancy, not child molestation. Still, de River's speculations were remarkably astute. In his confession, Dyer revealed that the crime was carefully planned, that he had used his position as a crossing guard to win the trust of the girls, and that he was overcome with remorse after killing them and had prayed over their dead bodies.

Another pioneering profiler was Harvard psychiatrist Walter Langer. In 1943, Dr. Langer was asked by the OSS (the forerunner of the CIA) to construct a psychological portrait of Adolf Hitler. Langer's report not only offered a number of intriguing speculations about the Führer's sexuality and overall psychopathology but correctly predicted that he would become increasingly unstable as Germany suffered more and more defeats and would commit suicide rather than face capture.

It was a New York psychiatrist named James A. Brussel, however, who is universally regarded as the direct forerunner of the modern profiler.

Between 1940 and 1956 (with a temporary "truce" during the war years, declared as an act of personal "patriotism"), an unknown madman planted several dozen pipe bombs around Manhattan: in public buildings, movie theaters, railway stations, and the facilities of the Con Edison utilities company. Most of these devices failed to detonate, though a few went off, severely injuring several people. The bombs were accompanied by anonymous notes, composed of cut-and-pasted letters from various publications, in which the writer—who identified himself only by the initials "F. P."—ranted at and swore vengeance on Con Ed.

After years of fruitless search for the "Mad Bomber"—as the tabloids dubbed him—investigators decided to consult Dr. Brussel, Assistant Commissioner of Mental Hygiene for the State of New York. After reviewing all the evidence, Brussel suggested that police focus their search on a paranoid, middle-aged, Roman Catholic bachelor of medium build and Eastern European descent who lived with a brother or sister in a Connecticut city, hated his father, and bore a grudge against Con Ed. He was also likely to be meticulous in his personal habits.

"When you find him," the report famously concluded, "chances are he'll be wearing a double-breasted suit. Buttoned."

(Corbis)

George "The Mad Bomber" Metesky—complete with buttoned double-breasted suit—under arrest

Not long afterward, thanks partly to Brussel's profile, police tracked down the bomber, a disgruntled former Con Ed employee named George Metesky, who had suffered a minor on-the-job injury in 1931 and whose claim for permanent disability payment had been rejected. Just as Brussel had predicted, Metesky (whose cryptic signature, "F. P." stood for "Fair Play"), was a fifty-four-year-old bachelor of Polish descent who lived with two older sisters in Waterbury, Connecticut. He was a regular churchgoer, had not gotten along with his father, and suffered from acute paranoia. Before being led away by police, he changed into a carefully pressed pinstriped, double-breasted suit, which he made sure to button before leaving the house.

The Mind Hunters

Though their contributions are regarded as landmarks in the history of profiling, Langer, de River, and Brussel were not criminologists but psychiatrists whose opinions were occasionally sought by frustrated law officials. It was not until the 1960s that efforts were made to place the profiling process on a more professional and scientific footing—to add it to the repertoire of forensic techniques used to track down serial killers.

The acknowledged father of this effort was Howard Teten, who began his career as an investigator with the San Leandro Police Department in California. During the 1960s, Teten started working with instructors at the School of Criminology at the University of California to develop a more systematic approach to profiling. After joining the FBI, he teamed up with fellow agent Pat Mullany—a specialist in abnormal psychology—to create the Bureau's first profiling program.

Teten—who was often consulted by police officers from across the country—had a reputation for being able to come up with amazingly detailed suspect descriptions based on the scantiest data. In an article in the April 1983 issue of *Psychology Today,* writer Bruce Porter describes one memorable incident:

> On one occasion, a California policeman telephoned about a baffling case involving the multiple stabbing of a young woman. After hearing just a quick description of the murder, Teten told him he should be looking for a teenager who lived nearby. He would be a skinny kid with acne, a social isolate, who had killed the girl as an impulsive act, had never killed before, and felt tremendous guilt. "If you walk around the neighborhood knocking on doors, you'll probably run into him," Teten said. "And when you do, just stand there looking at him and say, 'You know why I'm here.' Two days later, the policeman called back to say that he had found the teenager as Teten had said he would. But before the officer could open his mouth, the boy blurted out: "You got me."

Teten was succeeded at the Bureau's Behavioral Science Unit by a younger generation of agents who refined and improved upon his groundbreaking techniques. The most prominent of these individuals were John Douglas, Robert Ressler, and Roy Hazelwood. Along with a half dozen others—Richard Ault, Roger Depue, Jim Reese, Swanson Carter, Robert Schaeffer, Ken Lanning—these agents constituted the now-celebrated team of "Mind Hunters" whose pioneering interviews with notorious serial murderers like David Berkowitz, John Wayne Gacy, and Edmund Kemper would shed vital new light on the mental and behavioral patterns of psychopathic sex-killers.

Besides making key innovations in the still-evolving science of profiling (for example, by introducing the basic distinction between "organized" and "disorganized" offenders), Douglas and Ressler were also instrumental in bringing the once-obscure figure of the psychological profiler to the forefront of public awareness. Their work (especially as popularized by Thomas Harris in *The Silence of the Lambs*) transformed the profiler into a modern-day media icon, the glamorous hero of countless fictional and cinematic thrillers.

In more recent years—while Douglas and Ressler, now retired from the Bureau, have become best-selling authors and media celebrities in their own right—sophisticated new techniques have been developed by other criminologists. These include the "Behavioral Evidence Analysis" method of Brent E. Turvey, a California-based private criminal profiler who has made extensive studies of sex offenders, and the "Investigative Psychology" approach of British criminologist David Canter, whose profile of England's notorious "railway rapist" in the 1980s led directly to the perpetrator's arrest.

How It Works

By now, the FBI's criminal profiling program has been going on for more than thirty years. In its efforts to help local law enforcement agencies identify and track down psychopathic killers, the Bureau's behavioral specialists are far better equipped than their predecessors. One of the most powerful tools at their disposal is the high-tech system known as the Violent Criminal Apprehension Program, established in 1985. The brainchild of a former Los Angeles homicide detective named Pierce Brooks, VICAP is a computerized database that collects, collates, and analyzes information on solved and unsolved serial homicide cases across the nation.

For all the advances made in the field, however, criminal profiling still remains essentially what it has always been: a painstaking procedure of deducing certain facts about an elusive, unknown killer, based on statistical probabilities, years of investigative experience, psychological training, plus a healthy dose of intuition and educated guesswork.

However astonishing it may sometimes seem to a layman, there is nothing magical about the profiler's art. For example, when James Brussel correctly predicted that the "Mad Bomber" would turn out to be a severely paranoid middle-aged Catholic of Eastern European background and medium build who lived with a sibling in Connecticut and would be dressed in a neatly buttoned, double-breasted suit when arrested, the psychologist was basing his conjecture on both fairly obvious assumptions and solid probabilities.

The ranting letters that accompanied the bombs were clearly the work of a paranoiac, and since the writer had been sending them out for so many years, it was a pretty safe bet that he had reached middle age by 1956. From the work of a German psychiatrist named Ernst Kretschmer—who correlated body types with different kinds of psychoses—Brussel concluded that the suspect would be neither fat nor skinny but of medium build. He deduced that the bomber was not native-born from the stiffly formal style of his writing and guessed that he was part of the large wave of Eastern Europeans who had emigrated to America in the 1930s. Slavs, Brussel believed, were particularly prone to using bombs as weapons, and—if the bomber were in fact Slavic—he would obviously be Catholic and very likely living in Connecticut, which had a large population of such immigrants. Anyone as crazy as the Mad Bomber, Brussel assumed, would not be married and would probably be living with relatives, as was often the case in immigrant families.

As for the bit about the buttoned, double-breasted suit—which struck so many people as nothing short of supernatural—that prediction was, in a sense, the most obvious of all. From the care he had taken in constructing his devices and cutting and pasting his communications, it was clear that the bomber was a finicky fellow, the kind who would likely be meticulous in other areas of his life, including the way he dressed. Double-breasted suits were a popular style in the 1950s, and—unlike the single-breasted variety—the jackets couldn't be worn unbuttoned without appearing extremely slovenly.

The same kind of reasoning employed by Brussel is still used by current-day profilers. When local police officers, stymied in their search for a serial killer, seek help from the FBI, they will send all available information of the case—from crime scene photos to autopsy reports to the victims' background—to the Bureau's Behavioral Analysis Unit, part of the National Center for the Analysis of Violent Crime (NCVAC). There, agents will study the material and draw up a profile intended to help the police focus their search on a particular type of victim.

When twenty-two-year-old, three-month pregnant Terry Wallin was found hideously butchered in her Sacramento home in January 1978, for example, Robert Ressler drew up the following preliminary profile, based on information about the crime sent to him via teletype:

> White male, aged 25–27 years thin, undernourished appearance. Residence will be extremely slovenly and unkempt and evidence of the crime will be found at the residence. History of mental illness, and will have been involved in use of drugs. Will be a loner who does not associate with either males or females, and will probably spend a great deal of time in his own home, where he lives alone. Unemployed. Probably receives some form of disability money. If residing with anyone, it would be with his parents; however this is unlikely. No prior military record; high school or college dropout. Probably suffering from one or more forms of paranoid psychosis.

In his 1992 book, *Whoever Fights Monsters,* Ressler explains the reasoning that lay behind this description. He assumed that the killer, like the victim, was white because serial homicide is usually *intra*racial—that is, a crime involving members of the same race. He also knew that savage lust-murders—of which the Wallin killing was a particularly appalling example—are virtually always committed by males in their twenties or thirties.

Ressler narrowed the suspect's presumed age to between 25 and 27 because the murder was so unusually violent as to suggest that the perpetrator was in the grip of a full-blown psychosis. (Mrs. Wallin had been partly eviscerated, animal feces had been stuffed in her mouth, and a yogurt cup found near the corpse clearly indicated that her attacker had used it to drink some of her blood.) "To become as crazy as the man who ripped up the body of Terry Wallin is not something that happens overnight," Ressler explains in his book. "It takes eight to ten years to develop the depth of psychosis that surfaces in such an area of apparently senseless killing. Paranoid schizophrenia is usually first manifested in the teenage years. Adding ten years to an inception-of-illness age of about fifteen would put the slayer in the mid-twenties age group."

The rest of Ressler's profile had followed logically from the inference that the killer was suffering from a raging psychosis:

> That was why I thought this killer was bound to be a thin and scrawny guy. Introverted schizophrenics don't eat well, don't think in terms of nourishment and skip meals. They similarly disregard their appearance, not caring at all about cleanliness or neatness. No one would want to live with such a person, so the killer would have to be single. This line of reasoning led me to postulate that his domicile would be a mess, and also to guess that he would not have been in the military, because he would have been too disordered for the military to have accepted him as a recruit in the first place. Similarly, he would not have been able to stay in college, though he might well have completed high school before he disintegrated. If he had a job at all, it would be a menial one, a janitor perhaps, or someone who picked up papers in a park; he'd be too introverted even to handle the task of a delivery man. Most likely he'd be a recluse living on a disability check.

Ressler's profile was instrumental in helping the police track down the madman, Richard Trenton Chase, aka the "Vampire of Sacramento" (though not before the blood-crazed young man butchered several other victims). In his book, Ressler takes justifiable pride in his contributions, though he is careful not to overstate the role of profiling in the solution of such crimes: "Some people later said that the profile caught the killer. That, of course, is not true. It's *never* true. Profiles don't catch killers, cops on the beat do, often through dogged persistence and with the help of ordinary citizens, and certainly with the aid of a little bit of luck. My profile was an investigative tool, one that in this instance markedly narrowed the search for a dangerous killer."

There have been times, of course, when profiles have been, not just wrong, but wildly off base. Roy Hazelwood was known among his colleagues for having produced one of the most inaccurate profiles on record. As Bruce Porter describes it:

> He did it in a Georgia case in which a stranger showed up at a woman's door one day and for no apparent reason punched her in the face and shot her little girl in the stomach. Hazelwood told local police to look for a man who came from a broken home, had dropped out of high school, held a low-skilled job, hung out in honky-tonk bars, and lived far from the crime scene. When the culprit was finally caught, he turned out to have been raised by

> both his parents who had stayed married for 40 years. He had a college degree and had earned above-average grades. He held an executive job at a large bank, taught Sunday school and regularly attended church, never touched a drop of alcohol, and lived in a neighborhood close to the crime scene.

Even when profiles aren't this wide of the mark, some law enforcement professionals remain deeply skeptical about their effectiveness. At the height of the Hillside Strangler murders, for example, a forensic psychiatrist offered this suspect profile:

> The Strangler is white, in his late twenties or early thirties, separated or divorced—in any case not living with a woman. He is of average intelligence, unemployed or existing on odd jobs, not one to stay with a job too long. He has probably been in trouble with the law before. He is passive, cold, and manipulative—all at once. He is the product of a broken family whose childhood was marked by cruelty and brutality, particularly at the hands of women.

The disdain of profiling felt by many cops was summed up by one investigator on the case—Bob Grogan of the LAPD—who, after hearing this description, dryly remarked: "Gee, all we got to do now is find a white male who hates his mother."

Recommended Reading

D. Canter, *Criminal Shadows: Inside the Mind of the Serial Killer* (1994)
John Douglas and Mark Olshaker, *The Anatomy of Motive* (1999)
Ronald M. Holmes and Stephen T. Holmes, *Profiling Violent Crimes* (1996)
H. Paul Jeffers, *Who Killed Precious?* (1992)
Robert Ressler and Tom Shachtman, *Whoever Fights Monsters* (1992)
B. E. Turvey, *Criminal Profiling: An Introduction to Behavioural Evidence Analysis* (1999)

CAPTURE

Mass murderers—"human time bombs," as they're often described—cause enormous damage when they go off without warning. But once the explosion is over, there's not much for the police to do in terms of solving the crime. These killers don't conceal their identities or commit their atrocities in secret. Their massacres are carried out in full public view, as though they were seeking to inflict the greatest possible trauma not just on their immediate targets but on society at large. They will stride brazenly into a populated place—a bustling office, a packed high school cafeteria, a busy fast-food restaurant—and open fire. Once they have finished slaughtering everyone within range, their own fate is a foregone conclusion. If they don't commit suicide or contrive to be killed in a shoot-out, they will often surrender without a fight, allowing the state to dispense the inevitable punishment that, one way or another, puts an end to their intolerable existence.

The situation is different with serial killers, who are driven—not by a slow-burning rage that erupts one day in a single, cataclysmic act of gun-crazed vengeance—but by a profound sadistic lust, a terrible joy in inflicting suffering and death on helpless victims. Because they derive such intense satisfaction from their enormities, serial killers generally try everything in their power to escape detection and capture. As a result, they present significant challenges to the police—so much so that, according to one expert on the subject, "nearly one in five escape completely and are never brought to justice for their crimes."

Though it's easy to overestimate the intelligence level of serial killers—particularly since they are typically portrayed in pop entertainment as criminal masterminds—most of them *do* possess a sinister cunning that allows them to get away with their outrages, often for considerable stretches of time. Some limit themselves to "low-priority" victims, knowing that such socially despised individuals can be preyed upon without attracting undue official notice. The small-town sex-killer who specializes in teenage male hustlers understands that if a few of these "undesirables" vanish from the streets, the police will shrug off the matter, assuming that the young men have simply taken off for the more congenial environment of San Francisco or New York City.

Other serial killers keep on the move, committing their atrocities in different jurisdictions so that the police do not even realize that the various murders are the work of one madman (a phenomenon known as "linkage blindness"). Still others strike in such sudden, random ways that investigators are unable to discover any clues that might point to a suspect.

There's no question that investigative techniques have become infinitely more advanced than they were in the days of Jack the Ripper, when several crime scenes were immediately scrubbed clean of evidence (like a chalked anti-Semitic message possibly left by the killer) because authorities were afraid of offending the sensibilities of the public. Even so, there's only so much that modern forensic procedures can accomplish.

While there have been exceptions—instances where masterful police work or brilliant psychological deduction or sophisticated scientific analysis has led to the capture of a serial killer—many cases are resolved as a result of other factors. The thirty-six serial killers interviewed by John Douglas and his collaborators for their landmark 1988 book, *Sexual Homicide,* had been apprehended for various reasons. Police investigation had played a key role in half the cases, but other killers had been betrayed by accomplices or identified by spouses or had turned themselves in. And some serial killers end up being caught because—after getting away with a string of audacious murders—they start to feel invulnerable and grow increasingly careless.

A case that demonstrates the variety of factors involved in catching an elusive serial killer is that of Albert Fish. After a lifetime of preying on children, Fish committed his ultimate atrocity in 1928, when he abducted, strangled, butchered, and cannibalized twelve-year-old Grace Budd of Manhattan. Despite a massive manhunt—led by a fiercely determined New York City police detective named William King—the diabolical old man managed to escape scot-free.

Six years later, however, his sadistic compulsions led him to send Grace's mother an appalling letter in which he detailed the horrors he had perpetrated on the little girl. He wrote this obscenity on the stationery of an organization called the New York Private Chaffeur's Benevolent Association. Fish had found several sheets of this letterhead, along with some envelopes, on a shelf in his boardinghouse room when he noticed a cockroach crawling on the wall and rose to kill it.

As soon as the Budd family received this deranged communication, they turned it over to Detective King. Because Fish did such a sloppy job of crossing out the embossed return address on the envelope, King was ultimately able to track Fish down to the boardinghouse and bring the sick old man to long-deferred justice.

Albert Fish might well have gotten away with one of the most shocking murders in New York City history had it not been for a combination of three things: the unwavering resolve of a New York City police detective who never gave up his search to find the monster; Fish's own twisted need to send the awful letter and his inexplicable failure to obscure the return address; and the pure happenstance that led him to find the telltale stationery in the first place, something that would never have occurred if a passing cockroach hadn't caught his eye.

The following ten representative examples illustrate how often the apprehension of a serial killer depends on a combination of factors, from police persistence to the killer's own blundering behavior to sheer chance.

Bob Berdella

After spending several days in his Kansas City horror house raping and torturing a young male prostitute named Chris Bryson, sadistic sex-killer Bob Berdella left home to run some errands, leaving the still-living Bryson tied to the headboard. Seizing the opportunity, Bryson worked one hand free of his bonds, grabbed a matchbook that Berdella had carelessly left near the bed, burned the rope binding his other hand, then escaped through the window and ran to the nearest neighbor, who alerted the cops.

Lawrence Bittaker and Roy Norris

This pair of vicious psychopaths was stopped when Norris couldn't keep from bragging about his role in the 1978 murder spree to an old prison pal, who promptly transmitted the information to his lawyer who, in turn, reported the news to the Los Angeles police.

David Berkowitz

Son of Sam's reign of terror came to an end when a woman out walking her dog on the night of his final murder recalled that, just before the shooting, she had noticed a policeman ticketing an illegally parked car. A check of tickets handed out in the neighborhood revealed that a summons had been left on the windshield of a Ford Galaxie sedan registered to Berkowitz.

Ian Brady and Myra Hindley

The infamous Moors Murderers were arrested after the megalomaniacal Brady decided that it would be a good idea to involve a new recruit in his sadistic undertakings and invited seventeen-year-old David Smith (Hindley's brother-in-law) to participate in a horrendous ax murder. The next morning, the sickened Smith contacted the police who soon uncovered the appalling evidence of Brady and Hindley's atrocities.

John Reginald Christie

After committing a series of grisly rape-murders, the so-called Monster of Rillington Place grew so incautious that he disposed of his final three victims in the most perfunctory way imaginable, sticking the corpses in a kitchen cupboard, then covering it over with a sheet of wallpaper before vacating the house. When the new tenants moved in and began to renovate the kitchen, they came in for a nasty surprise and the meek-looking psycho was soon under arrest.

John Wayne Gacy

The "Killer Clown" was caught after luring teenager Rob Piest to a grisly death with the offer of a job. Before leaving for his "interview" with Gacy, Piest told his mother where he was going. When her son didn't return, the frantic mother notified the police.

Randy Kraft

Guilty of at least sixteen murders, the so-called Scorecard Killer was arrested after driving around drunk with a strangled corpse on his passenger seat, forty-seven Polaroids of his victims beneath the floor mat, and a briefcase in the trunk containing a legal pad filled with notes about his various murders.

Dennis Nilsen

The end came for the "British Jeffrey Dahmer" when he began disposing of his victims by the ill-advised method of flushing their dismembered bodies down the toilet of his North London flat. When the building pipes became clogged, neighbors called a plumber who was understandably staggered to discover that the blockage was caused by a thick porridge of putrefying human flesh.

Joel Rifkin

After committing seventeen murders, the Long Island prostitute-slayer was caught when police officers spotted him driving a pickup truck with no rear license plate. When they pulled him over after a high-speed chase, they discovered the nude decomposing corpse of a woman in the back of his vehicle.

Jane Toppan

After a decade of serial poisoning, Nurse Toppan grew so reckless that she blithely wiped out an entire family of four adults in a matter of weeks: a father, mother, and two grown daughters, none of whom seemed in especially poor health before Jane showed up to care for them. Needless to say, their shockingly abrupt extinction set off alarms in relatives and friends, and Jane was soon in custody.

PSYCHICS

The fear of monsters is deeply rooted in the human psyche. Huddled in our beds as little children, we imagine terrifying creatures lurking in the closet, ready to spring out and devour us as soon as our parents turn out the lights. This primitive anxiety remains alive in the recesses of the adult mind and is stirred up whenever a serial killer is on the loose. We are all too prone to view these desperately sick individuals as larger-than-life demons—a perception reinforced by the tendency of the media to christen them with horror-movie nicknames: the "Night Stalker," the "Vampire of Sacramento," the "Sunday Morning Slasher." The longer a serial killer remains at large—committing his atrocities, even with an entire police force on the hunt for him—the more supernatural he seems, a malevolent phantom haunting the shadows just outside our living room windows.

Because serial killers arouse such primal, irrational feelings in us, people have sometimes turned to the occult in the form of self-professed psychics in a desperate attempt to identify these psychos.

Ostensibly possessed of extrasensory perception that allows them to visualize the location of missing victims and sense the identity of the killer, so-called psychic detectives have an extremely spotty record when it comes to solving crimes, though occasionally (whether through sheer luck or the kind of gut instinct that all good detectives rely on) they have produced startling results. A representative instance of psychic detective work applied to the pursuit of a serial murderer occurred during the frustrating hunt for the Michigan sex-killer John Norman Collins.

Over a two-year period, beginning in August 1967, seven young women—a number of them students at either Eastern Michigan University in Ypsilanti or the University of Michigan at Ann Arbor—were murdered in especially brutal ways. Like many serial sex-killers, the perpetrator had particular tastes in victims. Ranging in age from thirteen to twenty-three, they were all petite, long-haired brunettes with pierced ears. That his crimes were fueled by extreme sadistic rage was clear from the inordinately savage injuries he inflicted. All the victims were subjected to frenzied "overkill": raped, tortured, slashed, mutilated, garroted, and bludgeoned. In several cases, their faces had been pulped with a hammer. One thirteen-year-old girl had a three-inch nail driven into her skull.

Despite intensive efforts by local police agencies, the investigation went nowhere. The late 1960s, of course, were the era of *The Exorcist* and *Rosemary's Baby*—a time when belief in the occult flourished in the United States. All manner of soothsayers, mind readers, and astrologers began coming out of the woodwork to offer solutions to the crime. In mid-1969, a group of local hippies calling themselves the "Psychedelic Rangers" decided to take action by calling in the most famous, self-professed clairvoyant of the time, Peter Hurkos.

Hurkos had presumably acquired his powers in 1941 after falling off a ladder while painting a house and surviving a four-story plunge. He had come to the United States in 1956 under the sponsorship of a research society and gained national celebrity for his work on the Boston Strangler case, despite the fact that he ended up identifying the wrong suspect.

Arriving in Michigan, Hurkos—a master showman if nothing else—began a highly publicized quest for the killer that he presented as a titanic struggle between his own mysterious God-given powers and the Satanic genius of his adversary. He performed feats worthy of the most skilled "mentalist," holding sealed envelopes containing crime scene photos to his brow, then reciting amazingly detailed reconstructions of the murders. To those inclined to believe in his powers, he achieved what seemed like miracles—though other, less starry-eyed observers were far more skeptical of his results. (At one point, he predicted that a body would be found "beside a short ladder." When the remains of one victim turned up near a derelict barn with broken cellar steps, Hurkos's supporters hailed this as a vindication of his extraordinary psychic abilities.)

In the end, despite a steady stream of announcements that he was on the brink of identifying the killer, Hurkos never managed to come up with a name, let alone a consistent description. At various times, he characterized the perpetrator as a self-taught genius, a depraved homosexual, a homicidal transvestite, a member of a Satanic hippie cult, a traveling salesman, and a scavenger who hung around garbage dumps. He was certain that the killer was a baby-faced blond of medium height who went to night school and possibly lived in a trailer.

Insisting that he would return the following week to wrap up the case, Hurkos flew back to his home in Los Angeles in late July. Within days of his departure, the killer was finally caught.

A handsome, dark-haired student preparing for a career as an elementary school teacher, John Norman Collins bore no resemblance to the suspect visualized by Hurkos. Typically described as the quintessential "all-American boy," he had been an honors student and star athlete in high school. His affable, well-groomed exterior, however, was just a mask that sometimes slipped, revealing the true face beneath. With his good looks and easy charm he had no trouble attracting women. But a number of his girlfriends quickly realized that their handsome catch was a deeply troubled young man—moody, sullen, prone to violent tirades against women. And a few of his professors at EMU were surprised by some of the ideas expressed in John's papers: that a man is bound by no laws but those of his own making. That he who is smart enough can get away with anything. That the Ten Commandments do not hold—particularly the fifth, "Thou shalt not kill." Collins was apprehended when the manager of a wig shop was able to identify him as the person she had seen with the killer's final victim on the day of the latter's disappearance. Despite his protestations of innocence, he was eventually convicted of murder.

In the end—as is virtually always the case—it was not ESP but dogged police fieldwork that solved the mystery.

SUICIDE

Though lacking a political motivation, mass murderers are akin to suicide bombers: men and women determined to go out with a literal bang and take as many people as possible with them. By contrast, suicide is relatively rare among serial killers. They derive such intense, twisted pleasure from their atrocities that they keep committing them until forced to stop.

There have been exceptions to this rule. Some serial killers seem to reach a point where they can no longer stand the unremitting horror their lives have become. They may begin to behave in such self-destructive ways that they are certain to get caught. Toward the end of his rampage, for example, playboy killer Christopher Wilder not only let one of his captives go free but drove her to the airport, bought her a plane ticket, and saw her off at the gate. And Jeffrey Dahmer seemed genuinely eager to put his nightmarish existence to an end. In contrast to other monsters like John Wayne Gacy and Ted Bundy—who did everything in their power to delay their executions—Dahmer made no efforts to avoid death. On the contrary, he refused protective custody in prison, though he surely knew that—given his notoriety—he made a particularly tempting target for other inmates. When he was murdered by another prisoner in November 1994, the act seemed almost self-ordained.

> It is now over. This has never been a case of trying to get free. I didn't ever want freedom. Frankly, I wanted death for myself.
>
> —Jeffrey Dahmer in his final statement to the court

For the most part, however, serial killers only commit suicide when—realizing that the jig is up—they choose a quick death at their own hands (or those of the police) over public disgrace and imprisonment. When two Texas Rangers showed up to arrest him at his roadhouse, for example, Joe Ball—the homicidal tavern keeper who disposed of some of his victims by feeding them to his pet alligators—stepped behind the bar, rang up "No Sale" on his cash register, then pulled a gun from the drawer and shot himself in the head. When police began to dig up human remains on his Indiana estate, Herb Baumeister—the seemingly stable family man who led a secret existence as a gay sex-slayer—took off for Canada, where he ended his life with large-caliber bullet to the brain. Taken into custody on a shoplifting charge, Leonard Lake—who, along with his equally psychopathic partner Charles Ng, committed assorted horrors in his northern California torture bunker—downed a concealed cyanide pill. The British sex maniac Fred West hanged himself in his jail cell before his trial. "Casanova Killer" Paul John Knowles committed "suicide by cop": the day after his arrest, while flanked by a sheriff and an FBI agent who were escorting him to prison, Knowles made a mad grab for the sheriff's gun and was swiftly shot dead by the FBI agent.

Of course, it's likely that some serial killers have committed suicide before they were identified or caught. Experts theorize that certain notorious murder sprees have come to abrupt, inexplicable ends precisely for this reason. Over the span of a year beginning in February 1964, for example, a still-unknown maniac killed a half dozen hookers and dumped their naked bodies around London, a feature of his crimes that earned him the tabloid moniker, "Jack the Stripper." One of the prime suspects in the case—a security guard who worked near the site of the final murder—committed suicide in February 1965, leaving a note that said he could no longer "stand the strain." Since his death coincided with the sudden cessation of the crimes, some people are convinced that the guard (whose identity has never been made public) was, indeed, the perpetrator.

It is even possible that Jack the Stripper's legendary Victorian forebear—Jack the Ripper himself—took his own life. In the view of some experts, the inhuman ferocity with which the Ripper carried out his final act of butchery shows that he was in the throes of a complete mental disintegration, a spiraling madness that may well have culminated in suicide. This would account for the fact that the Whitechapel Horrors—the single most notorious killing spree in the annals of serial murder—stopped as suddenly as they began, and why the identity of their perpetrator may never be definitively established.

PUNISHMENT

Some atrocities committed by serial killers are so unspeakable—torturing children while tape-recording their agonized pleas, slitting the mouths and slicing off the noses of still-living victims, castrating boys and forcing them to eat their own genitals—that just hearing about them is enough to convert the most committed pacificist into an ardent supporter of capital punishment. And a fair number of serial killers have, in fact, been executed. This was especially true in the past.

For all the denunciations of capital punishment as a barbaric relic of the past, modern methods of execution are positively humane compared to those of the premodern era. From an old woodcut pamphlet, for example, we know the fate of the sixteenth-century "lycanthrope," Peter Stubbe. Bound to the spokes of a wheel, chunks of his body were ripped off with red-hot pincers, his limbs were pulverized with an iron rod, his head was cut off, and his torso was tied to a stake and incinerated.

(Courtesy of Rick Geary)

The execution of H. H. Holmes

In the nineteenth century, hanging was the preferred way of dealing with convicted sex-killers, at least in America. Thomas Piper—the so-called Boston Belfry Murderer—dangled for his atrocities, as did his West Coast counterpart, Theo the "Demon of the Belfry" Durrant (who was regarded as so loathsome by the citizens of San Francisco that no cemetery would accept him, and his parents were forced to transport his corpse to Los Angeles for cremation). The Chicago "Arch-Fiend," Dr. H. H. Holmes, was also sent to the gallows, after which, by his own request, his body was interred under several tons of concrete to ensure that it would not be exhumed by grave robbers. Jesse Pomeroy, the "Boston Boy Fiend," was initially condemned to be hanged, but—because of his extreme youth—the sentence was commuted to life in solitary confinement, a form of living entombment that he endured for over forty years before being released into the general prison population.

In Europe, a number of the most notorious serial killers of the late nineteenth and early twentieth centuries were beheaded. Both Joseph Vacher, the "French Ripper," and Henri Landru, the "Bluebeard of Paris," were guillotined. So was the German lust-killer Peter Kürten, the so-called Monster of Düsseldorf, who announced that he would die a happy man if he could only have the pleasure of hearing the blood spurt from his neck stump. Kürten's equally depraved contemporary, Fritz Haarmann, was beheaded by sword in the Hanover public square, after which his brain was removed and sent to Göttingen University for study.

All sorts of legends sprang up around the execution of Haarmann's American admirer, Albert Fish, who, upon receiving the death sentence, reportedly declared: "What a thrill it will be to die in the electric chair! It will be the supreme thrill—the only one I haven't tried!" Following his execution in January 1936, rumors circulated that the twenty-nine needles lodged in the bizarre old man's groin had produced a burst of blue sparks when the switch was thrown and short-circuited the chair.

Nowadays, the death penalty is meted out much more sparingly. Ted Bundy and John Wayne Gacy were put to long-deferred (and, in the view of many people, richly deserved) deaths. Both of them did everything possible to delay the inevitable for as long as possible. Bundy in particular—like virtually all psychopaths, capable of feeling pity for no one but himself—was so weak-kneed at the end that he virtually had to be carried to the death chamber.

> He lived too long, if you ask me. If they'd have asked me, I probably would have pulled the switch myself.
>
> —Carol DaRonch, one of the lucky few who escaped Ted Bundy's clutches

By contrast, other serial killers have gone willingly to their deaths. When Harvey Murray Glatman received the death sentence, his only comment was,

"It's better this way." He refused to appeal and did everything possible to expedite his execution. Aileen Wuornos—whose disgust at the world was such that she could not wait to depart from it—similarly put an end to her appeals process after firing her lawyers. And Jeffrey Dahmer—who declared his eagerness to die at his trial—refused to accept protective custody in prison, fully aware that (as happened) he would most likely be killed by another inmate.

G. J. Schaefer was another monstrous sex-slayer who escaped the death penalty only to be murdered in prison. Others have been killed off by various ailments while serving out their terms. A combination of cirrhosis of the liver and AIDS took care of the odious Ottis Toole; his equally repellent partner, Henry Lee Lucas (one of the very few condemned prisoners whose death sentence was actually commuted by then–Texas governor George W. Bush) ended up expiring of heart disease.

Given the primordial human urge for vengeance, the fact that some psychopathic killers escape execution because of legislative bans on capital punishment can seem like a gross injustice, particularly to friends and family members of their victims. Such survivors often grow especially outraged when they see the butcher of their loved ones exploiting his notoriety (by selling his "artwork" to collectors, for example) or otherwise enjoying himself in prison.

(Courtesy of Dan Spiegle)

Aileen Wuornos on death row

A particularly egregious case was that of Richard Speck, perpetrator of one of the most heinous American crimes of the twentieth century—the rape and murder of eight student nurses in Chicago in 1966. Speck was originally condemned to death, but when the US Supreme Court abolished the death penalty, he was resentenced to consecutive life terms amounting to four hundred years. He ended up serving fewer than twenty, however, dying of a massive heart attack in 1991.

Five years later, a bizarre videotape—sent to a CBS News anchor in Chicago—set off of a tidal wave of revulsion when it was aired on national TV. Shot in Statesville Correctional Institute, it showed an unspeakably grotesque Speck sporting hormone-induced breasts, wearing blue panties, performing fellatio on a cellmate, and bragging about all the fun he was having in prison. Questioned by the off-screen cameraman about why he had slaughtered the eight young women, Speck merely shrugged, and said: "It just wasn't their night."

It was enough to make a person long for the age of Peter Stubbe, when criminals who indulged in acts of barbaric violence were punished with commensurate cruelty.

A Bluebeard Beheaded

In his 1936 book, *I Found No Peace,* foreign correspondent Webb Pierce—who was present at the execution of the French Bluebeard, Henri Landru in the early hours of February 25, 1922—vividly describes the scene:

> Nearly 100 officials and newspaper men gathered in a circle around the guillotine; I stood 15 feet away. News arrived from the prison that Landru, whose long black beard had been cut off previously, asked that he be shaved. "It will please the ladies," he said. He wore a shirt from which the neck had been cut away, and cheap dark trousers—no shoes or socks.
>
> Just as the first streaks of chilly dawn appeared, a large horse-drawn van arrived and backed up within a few feet of the guillotine. The executioner's assistants pulled two wicker baskets from it; placed the small round one in front of the machine where the head would fall, and the large coffin-shaped one close behind the guillotine.
>
> Suddenly the great wooden gates of the prison swing open. Three figures appeared walking rapidly. On each side a jailer held Landru by his arms, which were strapped behind him, supporting him and pulling him forward as fast as they could walk. His bare feet pattered on the cold cobblestones and his knees seemed not to be functioning. His face was waxen and as he caught sight of the ghastly machine, he went livid.
>
> The jailers hastily pushed Landru face downward under the lunette, a half-moon-shaped wooden block which clamped his neck beneath the suspended knife. In a split second the knife flicked down, and the head fell with a thud in the basket. As an assistant lifted the hinged board and rolled the headless body into the big wicker basket, a hideous spurt of blood gushed out. . . .
>
> Since Landru had first appeared in the prison courtyard, only 26 seconds had elapsed.

NGRI (NOT GUILTY BY REASON OF INSANITY)

Common sense suggests that a person who rapes dead bodies or cannibalizes children or drills holes in his lovers' skulls to turn them into sex-zombies qualifies as insane. Common sense and the law, however, don't always coincide.

In the strict legal sense of the term—based on a 160-year-old precedent known as the M'Naghten Rule—insanity is defined as the inability to distinguish right from wrong. Since the majority of serial killers are psychopaths—beings who, however devoid of moral faculties, behave in rational, often highly calculating, ways—it is hard to argue that they meet the legal criterion for insanity. The mere fact that most serial killers go to such lengths to elude capture suggests that they know they're engaged in wrongdoing.

As psychiatrist Donald Lunde puts it in his classic book *Murder and Madness,* the purpose of an insanity trial is to "separate the mad from the bad." American juries, however, as Lunde also points out, are often reluctant "to believe that someone who kills is mad rather than bad. In fact, many people suspect that the insanity defense is a ruse employed by clever lawyers in collaboration with naive psychiatrists to win an acquittal of an obviously guilty client." The case of Albert Fish is instructive. Possessor of one of the most extravagantly bizarre psychologies in the annals of crime, Fish was convicted and sentenced to death by a jury that—though acknowledging his extreme mental derangement—found his crimes so appalling that they could not bring themselves to acquit him.

Even judges can be hard to convince. Despite testimony from a team of psychiatrists that David "Son of Sam" Berkowitz was mentally "incapacitated" and therefore legally insane (a reasonable diagnosis of someone who believed he was taking orders from a demon-possessed dog), the presiding judge sided with the lone prosecution expert, who declared that "while the defendant shows paranoid traits, they do not interfere with his fitness to stand trial."

To be sure, some infamous serial killers have been found mentally incompetent and committed to asylums. Though convicted of first-degree murder, the Wisconsin ghoul Ed Gein was simultaneously judged insane and spent the rest of his days in mental institutions. So did Jane Toppan, the female serial poisoner who confessed to thirty-one murders following her trial in 1901. (In Toppan's case, there is reason to believe that she was spared the death penalty, not because she was truly insane, but because a jury of Victorian gentlemen couldn't bring themselves to sentence a "respectable" woman to the gallows.)

For the most part, winning an acquittal with an insanity plea is so difficult that few defense lawyers attempt it. In the last hundred years, barely one percent of all felons brought to trial in this country have resorted to this tactic. And of that tiny minority, only one in three has been found NGRI ("not guilty by reason of insanity").

As for serial killers, "Only 3.6 percent have been declared incompetent for trial or cleared by reason of insanity," according to one expert. Even a severely delusional psychotic like Herbert Mullin—who believed he could ward off an apocalyptic earthquake by slaughtering strangers—was deemed "sane by legal standards" and convicted of murder.

Of course, the long odds against prevailing with an insanity plea haven't stopped some serial killers from trying. In England, John George Haigh, the infamous "Acid-Bath Killer" of the 1940s, made a futile attempt to convince the jury that his murders were motivated, not by pathological greed, but by a vampiric lust for body fluids. To prove that he was possessed of unnatural thirsts, he even drank a cup of his own urine in prison—all to no avail. Thirty years later, Haigh's psychopathic countryman Peter Sutcliffe, aka the "Yorkshire Ripper," made an equally fruitless attempt to depict himself as insane, claiming that he had been commanded to kill prostitutes by the voice of God, issuing from a grave in a local cemetery.

Perhaps the most popular ploy has been the "multiple personality" gambit, which has been attempted—with a stunning lack of success—by a number of infamous serial killers. These include William the "Lipstick Killer" Heirens, Kenneth "Hillside Strangler" Bianchi, and John Wayne Gacy—each of whom tried to pin his crimes on a murderous alter ego named, respectively, "George Murman," "Steve," and "Jack." Ted Bundy, though he did not attempt an insanity defense, also claimed that he was occasionally possessed by a malevolent being he referred to as "the entity."

Indeed—partly no doubt because of Alfred Hitchcock's *Psycho* (which popularized the concept of the "split personality"), it has become almost commonplace for serial killers to shift responsibility for their acts onto the evil second selves that supposedly dwell inside them. When Australian serial killer William MacDonald was asked why he butchered a half dozen men, he breezily declared, "I didn't murder those men. It is the other person who lives inside me that actually killed them." As is typically the case, the jury declined to believe this glib explanation, sentencing the "Mutilator" to life for his atrocities.

UNSOLVED

In the realm of serial homicide, as in all other areas of human activity, some individuals achieve far greater renown than others. Because their crimes were so sensationally horrific, psychopaths like Charles Manson, Ted Bundy, John Wayne Gacy, Jeffrey Dahmer, and a handful of others have achieved something close to legendary status. In the popular imagination, they have assumed the role of real-life, flesh-and-blood bogeyman—all-American personifications of absolute evil.

Most serial killers, however, never rate such dark celebrity. How many people have ever heard of Michael Ross, a forty-year-old serial killer sentenced to death for slaying four teenage girls in Connecticut in the 1980s? Or Tommy Lynn Sells, a thirty-five-year-old drifter who—following his arrest in Del Rio, Texas, for slitting the throats of two girls with a boning knife—confessed to ten other slayings in six states? Or Corey Morris, a twenty-four-year-old Phoenix man charged with the murder of six prostitutes in 2003? There is nothing about such degenerates that seizes the imagination of the public. They don't exert the grim fascination of Jekyll-Hyde types like Bundy and Gacy: the handsome law student whose charming personality conceals the soul of a monster; the roly-poly clown who entertains hospitalized children by day and spends his nights torturing and murdering teenagers. Ross,

Sells, Morris, and others of their ilk don't seem mythically evil—just sick, vicious, and repellent.

The same principle applies to *unsolved* serial homicides. A surprising number of these never make the national headlines. Many are barely noted in the communities where they are taking place. This is largely because they so often involve male or female street prostitutes—socially despised victims whose death and disappearance arouse little interest or concern among the public. Even the police sometimes pay little attention to such crimes, making only the most perfunctory efforts to solve them.

By contrast, there are a number of unsolved serial killer cases that have become legendary in the annals of crime. Foremost among these, of course, is that of Jack the Ripper. By now, there is an entire cottage industry devoted to the solution of this century-old mystery. Every few years, a new "expert" comes forward with a book purporting to provide definitive proof of the Whitechapel monster's identity. The most recent (as of this writing, at least) is *Portrait of a Killer,* the 2002 best seller by mystery writer Patricia Cornwell, who—with much ballyhoo—announced that she had finally identified the legendary harlot-slayer. The culprit, she claimed, was Walter Sickert, a renowned post-Impressionist painter with an intense fascination with the macabre and a supposed sexual pathology allegedly brought about by a bungled penile operation.

Not everyone, however, has been convinced by Cornwell's "proof." Savaging the book in the *New York Times,* for example, Caleb Carr—author of the 1995 blockbuster, *The Alienist*—not only denounced it as an "exercise in calumny" but demanded that Cornwell apologize for having written it. It might be added that Sickert was long ago identified—and dismissed—as a possible suspect by other Ripperologists.

In short, it seems likely that—despite her claims (and the sizable amount of her personal fortune that she invested in the project)—Cornwell's book will not be the last word on this subject.

Though less well-known than the Ripper murders, there are several celebrated cases that continue to tantalize armchair detectives. They include:

The Ax Man of New Orleans

One of the great unsolved mysteries in the annals of American serial murder began in the waning days of the World War I era. In the predawn hours of May 23, 1918, an unknown madman broke into the home of Mr. and Mrs. Joseph Maggio, battered in their skulls with an ax, then put a razor to their throats and delivered the coup de grace.

He struck again in the dead of night on June 28, invading the home of a grocer named Louis Besumer, who escaped the attack with a nasty gash to the head. His wife, however, was mortally wounded. She lingered until August 5 before succumbing to her injuries.

On the same night that she died, the pregnant wife of a man named Schneider was attacked in her bed by the ax-wielding maniac. Though Mrs. Schneider (and her unborn infant) survived, she was unable to provide police with anything more than a vague description of the shadowy intruder.

Five days later, two young sisters, Pauline and Mary Bruno, were awakened by the sounds of a commotion from the adjoining bedroom. Hurrying to investigate, they caught a glimpse of a sinister figure—"dark, tall, heavyset, wearing a dark suit and black slouch hat," as they would describe him—making his escape. In the bed lay their uncle, Joseph Romano, bleeding copiously from a savage head wound that would prove fatal.

By this point, New Orleans was experiencing the kind of panic that, a half century later, would grip New York City when the phantom shooter known as "Son of Sam" was on the loose. People began sleeping with loaded pistols at their sides and inundating the police with reports of attempted nighttime break-ins, discarded murder weapons found on their front lawns, and countless hysteria-induced sightings of the killer.

After a seven-month hiatus, he committed another attack, this time in the town of Gretna, just across the river from New Orleans. His victims were the three members of the Cortimiglia family. The parents, Charles and Rose, survived with fractured skulls but their two-year-old daughter was murdered.

Four days later, on March 14, 1919, a letter arrived at the offices of the *New Orleans Times-Picayune.* It was undoubtedly a hoax, much like the fraudulent letter that gave the Whitechapel monster his immortal nickname. Describing himself as a "demon from the hottest hell," the writer declared his

(© 2003 Nathan MacDicken)

The Ax Man of New Orleans awakens the Bruno sisters

intention to terrorize the city on the night of March 19, sparing only those houses where jazz was playing. He signed the note, "The Ax Man."

In an early instance of a now commonplace phenomenon—the kind of coping mechanism that causes people to indulge in sick jokes whenever a catastrophe occurs—the citizens of New Orleans resorted to macabre humor to relieve their tensions, throwing "Ax Man parties" on the designated night and playing a popular new piano tune, "The Mysterious Ax Man's Jazz."

Despite the arrest and conviction of several suspects (who were later released when their accuser confessed to perjury), the killings continued. Between August 10 and October 27, three more attacks occurred, bringing the Ax Man's toll to six dead and six wounded.

Then, as abruptly as they had started, the murders came to a halt. Some scholars of American crime have identified a likely suspect, a Mafia hit man named Joseph Mumfre who was shot dead by the widow of the Ax Man's last victim, and whose murder would account for the sudden cessation of the ax killer's spree. Others, however, have called this theory into question. In any event, the Ax Man killings remain officially unsolved.

The Toledo Clubber

In a two-week spasm of violence that terrorized the city of Toledo, Ohio, and drew nationwide attention in the press, a "murderous maniac" (as the papers described him) savagely attacked a dozen women in the fall of 1925, leaving five dead and the rest severely wounded. Wielding a heavy bludgeoning object, he clubbed his victims from behind, then continued to smash their faces and skulls as they lay unconscious from the initial blow.

The first to encounter the "Clubber" was Mrs. Frank Hall, who was set upon outside her home on the night of November 10, 1925. One of the luckier victims, she survived the attack, though her injuries were severe enough for her never to regain her full health.

Mrs. Emma Hatfield and Lydia Baumgartner were the next to fall victim to the madman. Both were attacked as they made their way down deserted streets after dark. Both would ultimately die of their injuries, though not before giving deathbed statements to the police. Unfortunately, neither woman could provide a precise description of the assailant.

The following week brought additional attacks—seven more in as many days. By then, the city was in an uproar. The American Legion put a thousand men on the streets to help in the search for the killer while the city's Medical Service Bureau offered escorts for the scores of women suddenly afraid to walk alone after nightfall. The police conducted a sweeping roundup of the usual suspects—mostly "mental defectives" and any swarthy-skinned stranger unlucky enough to find himself in Toledo at the time. They also had to deal with the usual deluge of hysterical "tips," including sightings of bizarre creatures with green-rimmed eyes and hulking figures who haunted the rooftops, issuing weird cries.

In the meantime, the authorities circulated a profile of the Clubber as "a beastlike man, more than six feet tall, of dark hue, with long woolly hair, protruding front teeth, fiery eyes, and almost superhuman strength." Given the hackneyed nature of this description—which sounds like a composite of every monster cliché in the book—it seems likely that it says less about the killer than about the feverish fantasies of the panic-stricken public. Indeed, by issuing this description, the police probably made it easier for the killer to avoid capture. With the entire city on the lookout for a supernatural ogre, the Clubber (who, like many other serial killers, probably looked perfectly ordinary, if not totally unprepossessing) could move about without attracting suspicion.

Following the savage double murder on a single day of a twenty-six-year-old schoolteacher and a forty-seven-year-old housewife (both of whom were also sexually assaulted), the Toledo Clubber's reign of terror came to an abrupt halt. Exactly who he was and what became of him remains a mystery to this day.

The Mad Butcher of Kingsbury Run

A decade after the end of the Toledo Clubber affair, Ohio was the site of another unsolved serial murder case, perhaps the most famous in the annals of twentieth-century American crime. What made this case so notable was not only the unusual savagery of the killings but the involvement of Eliot Ness, the legendary lawman of *Untouchables* fame.

It happened in Cleveland during the height of the Great Depression. In September 1934, the lower half of a woman's torso, the legs severed at the knees, washed up on the shore of Lake Erie near the Euclid Beach amusement park. The victim—dubbed "the Lady of the Lake" by the local press—was never identified, and the story quickly vanished from the news. Only later did people come to see this incident, not as an isolated atrocity, but as a harbinger of the horrors to come.

One year later, while roaming through Kingsbury Run—a weed-choked, garbage-strewn ravine on the east side of Cleveland that served as a hobo jungle—two young boys stumbled upon a pair of headless, decomposing male corpses, both with their genitals severed. Postmortem examinations suggested that they had been decapitated—and probably castrated—while still alive. Though the older victim was never identified, fingerprints showed the younger man to be Edward Andrassy, a "snotty punk" (as one cop described him) with a long rap sheet of petty arrests. Given his reputation for unsavory behavior—which included an affair with a married woman whose husband had threatened Andrassy's life—police concluded that the two killings were crimes of passion.

They were obliged to reassess that opinion when other bodies began to

ALL FEATURE SECTION

CLEVELAND PLAIN DEALER

ALL FEATURE SECTION

SUNDAY, APRIL 2, 1939

Does "TORSO SLAYER" Resemble "BLUEBEARDS" OF PAST?

Police Draw Parallel Between Cleveland's Killer and Notorious Landru and George Smith of Britain

By Harold F. Tarbox

A newspaper artist's conception of "The Mad Butcher of Kingsbury Run" from the Cleveland *Plain Dealer,* April 2, 1939

turn up. In January 1936, the hacked-up remains of a forty-one-year-old prostitute—stuffed inside in a half bushel basket and a few burlap sacks—were found behind a Central Avenue butcher shop. Four months later—in a virtual replay of the September 1935, incident—two boys cutting through Kingsbury Run on their way to go fishing—stumbled upon a man's decapitated head. The next day, searchers found the naked corpse, which was adorned with a half dozen distinctive tattoos. Despite all efforts, however—which included displaying the victim's death mask at the Great Lakes Exposition in the hope that one of the seven million visitors would recognize him—the identity of the "Tattooed Man" was never established.

On July 22, another headless corpse was discovered—this one across town from Kingsbury Run. The killer returned to his favorite dumping ground a few months later, in September 1936. Waiting to hop one of the eastbound freight trains that passed through Kingsbury Run, a hobo spotted the bisected halves of a human torso floating in a stagnant pond. The missing parts—which included the head, arms, and genitals—were never found.

By this point, the newspapers were having a field day with the case, running daily, sensationalistic front-page stories written in the purplest prose.

"Of all horrible nightmares come to life," ran one typical lead, "the most shuddering is the fiend who decapitates his victims in the dark, dank recesses of Kingsbury Run. That a man of this nature should be permitted to work his crazed vengeance upon six people in a city the size of Cleveland should be the city's shame. No Edgar Allan Poe in his deepest, opium-induced dream could conceive horror so painstakingly worked out."

Having been recently hired as Cleveland's safety director, Eliot Ness—whose energies had been largely devoted to rooting out corruption in the police department while overseeing security measures for the Republican National Convention—found himself under enormous pressure to track down the maniac, alternately dubbed the "Cleveland Torso Killer" and the "Mad Butcher of Kingsbury Run." Nothing, however—neither the sizable reward offered by the *Cleveland News* nor the full-time efforts of two dozen detectives, including a tireless pair named Merylo and Zalewski, who interrogated hundreds of suspects and pursued numberless leads—made a difference. For two more years, the dismembered corpses continued to pile up—twelve in all, a "Butcher's dozen," in crime writer Max Allan Collins's phrase.

The remains of Butcher's last two victims turned up in August 1938. What became of him after that has remained a matter of speculation ever since. A Cleveland physician named Frank Sweeney—reputedly a bisexual alcoholic with a hair-trigger temper—fell briefly under suspicion. So did a Slavic immigrant named Frank Dolezal, who initially confessed to several of the "Torso" murders, though he later recanted, claiming that the police had beaten the confession out of him. A month after his arrest, he was found hanged in his cell, an apparent suicide.

While some crime mavens believe that Mad Butcher migrated to Los Angeles, others agree with Eliot Ness's biographer Oscar Fraley, who claimed that the real culprit was a mentally unstable premed student. The scion of a prominent Cleveland family, it is said, the killer eluded arrest by having himself committed to a mental institution, where he died of natural causes in the early 1940s.

The Green River Killer: Case Closed

It is a truism in law enforcement that, with every passing day, the chances of cracking an unsolved case grow progressively slimmer. So it seems highly improbable that we could ever learn the true identities of long-vanished phantoms like the New Orleans "Ax Man" or Cleveland's "Mad Butcher." Thanks to recent advances in forensic science, however—specifically the development of DNA analysis—a number of infamous serial murder cases, which have frustrated investigators for decades, appear to have been solved at last.

Police in Glasgow, Scotland, for example, believe that they have finally solved the quarter-century-old case of the Scripture-quoting sex-killer nicknamed "Bible John." A DNA sample taken from semen stains on the tights of one of his victims was found to match a sample from one of the suspects, a married former Scots Guard with three children who committed suicide in 1980. Though the man's identity has not been made public, authorities appear confident that the mystery has been solved.

In our own country, one of the most notorious and baffling serial murder cases of the past quarter century took an unexpectedly auspicious turn in the fall of 2001, more than ten years after most people had given up on it. Between 1982 and 1984, no fewer than forty-nine young women were stabbed to death or strangled and their bodies dumped at various woodland sites. Some were runaways and transients, though most of them were prostitutes working a sleazy strip along the Seattle-Tacoma highway. Despite a massive investigation that lasted nearly a decade, cost $15 million, accumulated four thousand pieces of physical evidence, and enlisted the help of everyone from FBI profiler John Douglas to Ted Bundy (who offered his own unique insights into the operations of the psychopathic mind), the "Green River Killer" managed to elude capture. When the task force that had been assembled to track him finally disbanded in 1990, there was little hope that he would ever be captured.

All that changed suddenly and dramatically in November 2001, when Gary Leon Ridgway was arrested for the relatively minor offense of "loitering for the purposes of soliciting prostitution." A married fifty-two-year-old father who lived in the Seattle suburb of Austin and worked as a painter for a local trucking company, Ridgway had had a number of previous run-ins with the law, all involving prostitutes. In 1980, a hooker he had picked up on the "Sea-Tac" strip accused him of driving her out to the woods and trying to strangle her. Charges were dropped when Ridgway told authorities that the woman had started to bite him while performing oral sex, and he only choked her to make her stop.

Two years later, he was arrested after propositioning a police decoy during a prostitution sting. Admitting that his compulsion to pick up prostitutes was akin to an alcoholic's craving for drink, he pleaded guilty and was given a slap on the wrist. In 1984, he was a prime suspect in the disappearance of one of the Green River Killer's victims, but was released from custody after passing a polygraph test. Jokingly, his coworkers at the Kenworth Truck Company began calling him "Green River Gary"—or "G. R." for short.

To police officers, however, there was nothing funny about the situation. By 1988, Ridgway was still regarded as a "person of interest" by investigators, who obtained a warrant to search his house (which yielded no evidence), as well as a court order that directed him to provide a saliva sample by chewing on a piece of gauze.

This latter piece of evidence ultimately led to the big break in the case. When Ridgway was arrested again in the fall of 2001 for soliciting prostitution, improved technology allowed forensic scientists to match the DNA in his saliva sample with semen found in three of the victims. His employment records were immediately subpoenaed, and a thorough check revealed that his absences from work coincided with the disappearances of many of the Green River victims.

On Wednesday, December 5, 2001, Gary Ridgway was formally charged with the deaths of four women. "What cracked this case, in a word, was science," one official declared. Due credit was also given to tenacious police work, particularly on the part King County sheriff Dave Reichert, who could barely contain his jubilation when he saw the results of the DNA tests. After pursuing his quarry for nearly twenty years, the hunt finally appeared to be at an end.

Ridgway's responsibility for the Green River Killings was confirmed in November 2003, when—as part of a plea agreement that spared him the death penalty—he stood in a Seattle courtroom and admitted to the murder of forty-eight women.

SERIAL KILLER CULTURE

Ever since the phrase "serial killer" gained currency in the early 1980s, the predatory psycho has become a standard (if not stereotypical) feature of our popular arts. To many finger-wagging critics, America's fixation on these blood-crazed beings is yet another deplorable sign of our supposed cultural decadence, proof that we have lost our moral bearings as a society.

In truth, however, there is nothing new or uniquely American about the "glorification" of criminals. Throughout history, people have been fascinated by what crime writer Jay Robert Nash calls "bloodletters and badmen." Back in eighteenth-century England, the public couldn't hear enough about the exploits of famous rogues like Jack Sheppard, Jonathan Wild, and Colonel Blood. A century later, British readers eagerly devoured every grisly tidbit printed about Jack the Ripper. In our own country, frontier psychopaths like Billy the Kid and John Wesley Hardin were transformed into folk heroes. The same thing happened during the Depression, when cold-blooded killers like Bonnie and Clyde, Pretty Boy Floyd, and John Dillinger were viewed by many people as modern-day Robin Hoods.

Why decent, upstanding citizens should be so intrigued by violent criminals is a complex psychological question, though surely it has something to do with the guilty pleasure we take from vicariously identifying with people who act out the dark, lawless impulses the rest of us repress. In any event, just as serial murder itself is an age-old phenomenon under a new and modern name, the kind of activities that seem so reprehensible to certain moralists—collecting serial-killer-related memorabilia, for example, or turning the sites of notorious murders into tourist attractions—have also existed for centuries.

FUN WITH SERIAL KILLERS

In the twenty years since its publication, Thomas Harris's groundbreaking pop novel *Red Dragon* has already been filmed twice, first by Michael Mann in the 1986 thriller *Manhunter,* then, under its original title, in Brett Ratner's 2002 version. Between those two versions, something interesting happened to Hannibal Lecter. He went from being a minor character who appeared for only a few minutes in the original movie to the star of the show. Why? Simply because audiences couldn't get enough of the suave, man-eating psychopath as portrayed so chillingly by Anthony Hopkins. They wanted to see him fix his prey with his creepy gaze, lick his chops, and devour the vitals of a few more deserving victims.

The audiences who flocked to their local multiplexes to watch "Hannibal the Cannibal" disembowel a pesky policeman and dine on the brains of an obnoxious bureaucrat weren't blood-crazed weirdos. To pretend that it's just perverts and potential Ted Bundys who are fascinated by serial murder and other sensational crime is the height of hypocrisy. There aren't enough sociopaths in the country to account for the 300-million-dollar domestic box office take of *The Silence of the Lambs.* Upstanding, law-abiding citizens are drawn to this gruesome stuff.

Purveyors of popular entertainment have always recognized this fact. "I'm going to give the people what they want," Vincent Price exclaims in the 1953 horror movie *House of Wax.* "Sensation, horror, shocks!" The great pioneer of the wax museum, the nineteenth-century entrepreneur Madame Tussaud, certainly would have approved of this sentiment. With its gruesome torture dioramas and lifelike effigies of infamous murderers, the "Chamber of Horrors" featured at her celebrated London establishment has always been its most popular attraction, far outdrawing the high-minded exhibits of statesmen, ecclesiastical figures, and world-famous writers.

For centuries, pop impresarios have found ways to exploit a truism noted as far back as 1757 by philosopher Edmund Burke that—given a choice between sitting through an opera or watching the public execution of a notorious criminal—the average crowd of people would flock to the latter. When mass murderer Albert Hicks was hanged in 1860, P. T. Barnum paid $25 and two boxes of cigars for the clothing Hicks wore to the gallows and promptly put it on display. One of Barnum's competitors went the "master showman" one better. Acquiring the amputated right arm of another infamous mass murderer—Philadelphia handyman Anton Probst who massacred all seven members of his employer's family in 1865—he exhibited the severed limb at his Bowery dime museum, where it drew enormous crowds.

Neither Barnum nor his rivals, moreover, had the slightest compunction about wringing every last nickel from such macabre "curiosities," selling souvenirs in the form of photographic "*cartes de visite*" and fully illustrated crime booklets. Indeed, in terms of sheer ghoulishness, many of the killer collectibles from the past far exceeded those of the present. During the Reign of Terror, for example, there was an enormous demand for guillotine-related mementos. Spectators who came to enjoy the daily beheadings could go home with a souvenir program adorned with an image of a severed head, while fashionable women wore guillotine earrings and children played with working toy replicas that could decapitate live mice and birds.

There's little doubt that some of the serial-killer-related stuff that has incurred the outrage of today's moral crusaders seriously violates the standards of conventional good taste—board games in which players compete to amass the highest body count, activity books featuring macabre connect-the-dot puzzles and "Help John Wayne Gacy Find an Empty Grave in His Crawl Space" mazes. Indeed, some of this material is deliberately created out of a distinctly juvenile impulse to offend middle-class sensibilities—*épater le bourgeois,* as they say in France. (The cover of Rich Hillen's *Serial Killer Coloring Book #4* bears the message: "For Immature Colorers Over 18.") Very little of it, however, actually depicts graphic scenes of hard-core violence.

The once-controversial (now out-of-print) serial killer trading cards published by Eclipse Enterprises, for example, featured handsomely rendered full-face portraits without a suggestion of gore. The card sets still available from Mother Productions of Atwood, California, likewise consist entirely of portraits (done in a playfully expressionistic style that often suggests, quite appropriately, the art of the insane).

And the oft-maligned genre of serial killer comic books has produced some highly literate and visually sophisticated works. Especially noteworthy are Rick Geary's elegant re-creations of sensational Victorian cases, including the Lizzie Borden murders, the Jack the Ripper crimes, and, most recently, the story of Dr. H. H. Holmes; Alan Moore and Eddie Campbell's celebrated graphic novel, *From Hell;* and the moody, noirish *Torso* by Brian Michael Bendis and Marc Andreyko, about the still-unsolved case of the 1930s Cleveland maniac known as the "Mad Butcher of Kingsbury Run."

Recommended Reading

Martha Grace Duncan, *Romantic Outlaws, Beloved Prisons* (1996)
Robert I. Simon, *Bad Men Do What Good Men Dream* (1996)

ART

Serial killer art is generally divided into two categories: works of art *about* serial killers and works created *by* serial killers. Both types have been known to spark firestorms of outrage, though for different reasons.

In 1997, for example, an exhibit called "Sensation"—featuring works by edgy young British artists—provoked heated controversy on both sides of the Atlantic. In New York City, the show (mounted at the Brooklyn Museum) became the target of a widely publicized attack by then-mayor Rudolph Giuliani, who was deeply offended by a painting by artist Chris Ofili: a portrait of the Virgin Mary that used, along with other materials, lumps of dried elephant dung. In England, however, the work that incited howls of protest was not Ofili's African-inspired icon but Marcus Harvey's *Myra:* an enormous black-and-white mug shot of Myra Hindley—the female half of the infamous "Moors Murderers"—created in a kind of pointillist style out of hundreds of children's handprints.

The accusations leveled against Harvey's work—that it trafficked in cheap sensationalism, that it was an obscene exploitation of an unspeakable atrocity, that it profaned the memories of the child victims while glorifying a monster—are typical of the kinds of charges aimed at artists who treat such disturbing subject matter. Since most of us have been educated to think of art as something spiritually elevated, even sacred, the mere notion of hanging a picture of a sadistic lust-murderer on the walls of a museum strikes many people as blasphemous—a symptom of the debased, anything-for-a-shock, sex-and-violence-obsessed culture we live in.

It is helpful to remember, however, that—since they deal with every aspect of human behavior, including the most painful and grotesque—serious artists have never shied away from portraying our proclivity for cruelty and violence. Medieval art is full of pictures showing religious martyrs being subjected to every variety of unspeakable torture, from flaying to slow evisceration. Goya's astonishing suite of etchings, *The Disasters of War*—with its appalling images of castration, impalement, beheading, and dismemberment—makes the most graphically gory "splatter" movie seem almost laughably tame. Art scholar Robert Simon has shown that, between 1859 and 1872, the great post-Impressionist painter Paul Cézanne—associated in the public mind with ravishing landscapes and still lifes—turned out a string of paintings and drawings depicting exceptionally grisly sex crimes: "bizarre, violent, aggressive images in which women are raped, strangled, and stabbed." Another late-nineteenth-century artist, the Victorian painter Walter Sickert, produced a series of dark, disturbing works inspired by the savage slaying of a prostitute. (Indeed, crime writer Patricia Cornwell found Sickert's paintings so brutal and morbid that she became convinced he was the real Jack the Ripper—an accusation that has been greeted with hoots of derision by both serious art critics and responsible Ripperologists.)

In the twentieth century, serial killers have been a frequent subject of serious art, from the Expressionistic works of Weimar-era painters like Otto Dix and George Grosz (who were both obsessed with the subject of sex-murder) to the cartoon-inspired creations of Pop surrealist Peter Saul, whose *oeuvre* includes the 1984 painting *Sex Deviate Being Executed,* which depicts John Wayne Gacy molesting one final victim while seated in the electric chair. Though it doesn't deal with serial killers *per se, In the Realms of the Unreal*—the epic masterwork of "Outsider" genius Henry Darger—contains scenes that would have warmed the heart of Albert Fish: graphic depictions of little girls being mutilated, disemboweled, and slaughtered. Another important American artist affiliated with the "Outsider" movement, Joe Coleman—whose paintings seem like some fantastical hybrid of Byzantine icons and carnival freak show banners—has produced astonishing portraits of some of our country's most notable serial killers, including Fish, Ed Gein, Carl Panzram, and Charles Manson.

When discussing the second category—works created *by* serial killers—it's necessary to place quotation marks around the word "art," since the paintings and sketches produced by these homicidal maniacs are generally devoid of anything approaching aesthetic value. There are a few exceptions: the ingenious, if predictably bizarre, pop-up greeting cards of Lawrence Bittaker, the surprisingly delicate watercolors of "Lipstick Killer" William Heirens, and some of the charcoal studies of Elmer Wayne Henley. The erotic fantasy-drawings of Bobby Beausoleil—an associate of the Manson "family" convicted of one count of murder—display the draftsmanship of a professional illustrator, while Nicolas Claux, a Parisian mortician and self-confessed cannibal, has provided powerfully unsettling portraits for Sondra London's 2003 book, *True Vampires* (in which he is also featured as a subject). For the most part, however, the average piece of serial killer artwork has all the technical skill and aesthetic interest of a badly applied prison tattoo or a paint-by-numbers picture done by an especially clumsy grade-schooler.

The seminal figure in the brief history of this unsavory genre was John Wayne Gacy, who took up painting in prison and began turning out crude, if creepy, oils of a range of subjects. These included Disney characters to Renaissance *Pietàs* to portraits of himself in the guise of Pogo the Clown—the role he assumed in his prearrest days, when he would entertain children at local hospitals. The growing popularity and monetary value of Gacy's work among collectors of the macabre led a Louisiana funeral director and horror enthusiast named Rick Staton to contact other imprisoned psycho-killers and encourage them to create works of their own. Before long, Staton was staging "Death Row Art Shows" featuring everything from Charlie Manson sock

(Courtesy of Adam Parfrey)

Torture illustration by John Wayne Gacy

puppets to Elmer Wayne Henley sunflowers to New Testament scenes painted by Henry Lee Lucas. These public exhibitions never failed to attract intense media attention and arouse outrage.

What people have found so reprehensible about art produced by serial killers is not the subject matter itself. With some exceptions (like the demon-obsessed doodles of Richard the "Night Stalker" Ramirez or some of the degenerate scratchings of Ottis Toole), most of the imagery is utterly banal, often highly sentimental: sunsets and seascapes, angels and koala bears. What inspires such widespread disgust is the mere notion that convicted lust-

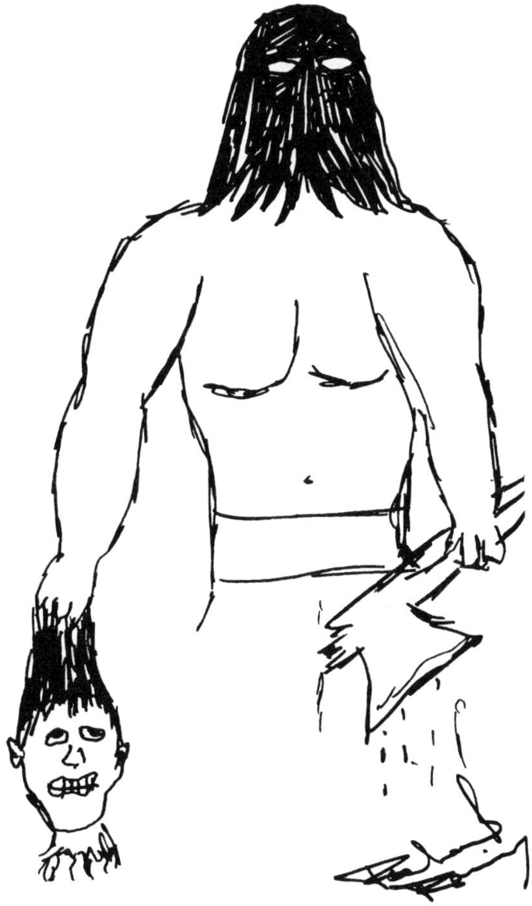

(Courtesy of Adam Parfrey)

"Art" by Richard Ramirez

killers are allowed to be treated like minor celebrities and enjoy the ego gratification of having their work put on public display.

> Those boys died in agony. This guy up here gets an art show. That's not right.
>
> —Brother of a teenage boy tortured and killed by Dean Corll and Elmer Wayne Henley, protesting a show of Henley's work at a Houston art gallery.

There is also the issue of money. Though "Son of Sam" laws bar criminals from profiting from their crimes by writing books, doing interviews, or selling film rights, current legislation doesn't ban the sale of art. This situation led to a highly publicized uproar in April 2001, when the *New York Daily News* reported in a page-one story that a state-sponsored art show for inmates included a pencil portrait of Princess Diana done by cannibal killer Arthur

(Courtesy of Julian Hobbs. Art by Andrew Brooks and Chris Trent)

Poster for Julian Hobbs' documentary "Collectors"

Shawcross, who stood to make 50 percent of the five-hundred-dollar asking price from its sale. This disclosure caused such a flap that, within a month, the state Senate passed legislation prohibiting inmates from pocketing any of the proceeds of the sales.

For a fascinating look at the world of serial killer art, its creators, devotees, and detractors, see Julian Hobbs's compelling 1999 documentary *Collectors.*

Recommended Reading

Lionello Puppi, *Torment in Art: Pain, Violence, and Martyrdom* (1991)
Robert Simon, "Cézanne and the Subject of Violence," *Art in America* (May, 1991)
Maria Tatar, *Lustmord: Sexual Murder in Weimer Germany* (1995)

Joe Coleman, Delineator of America's Dark Soul

A cult figure since the 1970s when he burst (quite literally) onto the underground scene as the self-exploding, rodent-chomping Professor Mombooze-o,

Joe Coleman

Joe Coleman possesses a genius for generating controversy that has shown no signs of abating in more than a quarter century. It's a testimony to the profoundly unsettling power of his work that it still manages to shock and offend everyone from mainstream critics to the self-appointed arbiters of "Outsider" art. With his shattering portrayals of American pathology, he is the anti–Norman Rockwell—a painter who renders with visceral force the nightmare realities behind the sugar-coated delusions that are generally referred to as the American Dream.

Though Coleman's subjects are international in scope, ranging from the depravities of ancient Rome to infamous British criminals like the juvenile psychopath Mary Bell, the majority of his paintings explore our country's anarchic shadow side as embodied by our indigenous outlaws and madmen, fanatics, and freaks. His portraits of legendary psycho-killers like Ed Gein, Albert Fish, Carl Panzram, and Charles Manson (a self-proclaimed admirer of Coleman's art) present these figures as all-American icons, no less representative of our violence-drenched culture than the mythicized heroes we are taught to worship in grade school. To study his riveting depictions of Devil Anse Hatfield (of the notorious Hatfield-McCoy feud) or Boston Corbett (killer of John Wilkes Booth) or Outsider artist Henry Darger (creator of the epically bizarre *In the Realms of the Unreal*) is to gain unparalleled insight into poet William Carlos Williams's famous dictum, "The pure products of America go crazy."

In his life no less than his art, Coleman immerses himself in the lurid underside of our history. Crammed with countless bizarre artifacts, his home—the "odditorium," as he calls it—resembles a nineteenth-century dime museum, where a visitor can view everything from P. T. Barnum's original Feejee mermaid to the actual letter that Albert Fish sent to his child-victim's mother (a document that Coleman proudly describes as the Magna Carta of serial killer collectibles).

Though he has been compared to everyone from Hieronymus Bosch to Otto Dix, his dense, obsessively detailed paintings are inimitably his own—a wholly unique and original body of work that has been reproduced in three volumes to date: *Cosmic Retribution* (1992), *Original Sin* (1997), and *The Book of Joe* (2003).

Coleman's Life of Panzram

Though the sheer body count he tallied in his ferocious life of wide-ranging destruction puts Carl Panzram high on the list of America's worst serial murderers, he was not a sexual psychopath like most of the deviants in this book. True, by his own proud estimate, he committed more than one thousand acts of forced sodomy, along with nearly two dozen murders and more felonies than he could keep track of. But his homosexual rapes—like his countless other outrages—were motivated less by sexual sadism than by his savage will to power.

Having been brutalized in various institutions from his childhood on, Panzram grew up to believe that—beneath its sanctimonious veneer of God-fearing righteousness—American society, like every other human culture throughout history, operated according to only one primal rule: the exploitation of the weak by the strong, "might makes right." Embracing this law of the jungle, he turned himself into an implacable predator, heaping murderous contempt on everyone from lawmen to well-meaning reformers whose kindness he dreamed of repaying by wrapping his hands around their throats and squeezing until their eyeballs popped from their skulls.

However appalling their crimes, America's other infamous serial killers were no match for Panzram in terms of sheer hard-bitten fury. Locked in a jail cell with Panzram, Ted Bundy, John Wayne Gacy, or Jeffrey Dahmer would have ended up becoming his bitch.

Here is his story, as told in pictures by today's premiere artist of American pathology, Joe Coleman.

CARL PANZRAM, #31614

A True Tale Adapted & Drawn by Joe Coleman

In my lifetime I have murdered 21 human beings, I have committed thousands of burglaries, robberies, larcenies, arsons and last but not least I have committed sodomy on more than 1,000 male human beings. For all of these things I am not the least bit sorry. I have no conscience so that does not worry me. I don't believe in man, God or Devil. I hate the whole damned human race, including myself. If you or anyone else will take the trouble and have the intelligence or patience to follow and examine every one of my crimes, you will find that I have consistently followed one idea through all of my life. I preyed upon the weak, the harmless and the unsuspecting. This lesson I was taught by others: might makes right.

I was born June 28, 1891, on a small farm in Minnesota. My mother and father split up when I was seven. This left my mother with a family of six on a worked-out farm. I decided I wanted to leave my miserable home. I was caught on a freight train with some things I stole and sent to the Minnesota State Training School. They trained me all right. These good Christians had a method of training—it was to beat goodness into me and all the badness out. Their beatings were meant to teach me to love Jesus and be a good boy. Naturally I love Jesus very much now. I love him so damn much I'd like to crucify him all over again.

Oh yes, I had plenty of abuse. They had various methods of punishing us for doing wrong and for teaching us to do right. First I began to think I was being unjustly imposed upon. Then I began to hate those who abused me. Then I began to think I would have my revenge just as soon as I could injure someone else. Anyone at all would do. If I couldn't injure those who injured me I would injure someone else. The only thing I could think up at the time was to burn down the "Paint Shop," where they used to paint our bodies black and blue. That night I burned the place down at a cost of over $100,000. Nice, eh?

After serving about two years there, I was pronounced by the parole board to be a nice, clean boy of good morals, as pure as a lily and a credit to those in authority where I had been reformed. Yes, I was reformed all right, damn good and reformed too.

When I left the Minnesota State Training School I knew all about Jesus and the Bible. I knew it was all a lot of hot air. And I learned from Christians how to be a hypocrite—how to steal, lie, hate, burn and kill. In later years I have met thousands of graduates of these kinds of institutions, and they were either in, going into, or just leaving jails, prisons, madhouses—or the rope and the electric chair were yawning for them as for me.

At 13 I was a hobo, and soon learned to ride freight trains. One experience I had during that time I never forgot. I was riding a box car with four big burly bums who got real interested in me. They began to tell me what a nice boy I was and promised me everything in the whole world. But first they wanted me to do a little something for them. What they couldn't get by moral persuasion, they proceeded to get by force. I cried, begged, pleaded for mercy, pity, sympathy, but nothing I could say would sway them from their purpose. I did not want to learn this lesson, but I found out that it isn't what one wants in this world that one gets. Force and might make right.

At 16, I joined the army. But I was only in the army a month or two when I got three years in the U.S. Military Prison at Fort Leavenworth, Kansas. While there, I was shackled to a 50 lb. iron ball which I wore day and night. I had to load my iron ball, 18 lb. hammer, a pick and shovel, and a six-foot iron crow bar into a wheel barrow and march back and forth to the rock quarry, three miles from the prison. But the harder they worked me, the stronger I got. I was a pretty rotten egg before I went there, but when I left, all the good that may have been in me had been kicked and beaten out of me long before.

In every joint I was ever in, there is always some form of torture that was on tap. I had them all, at one time or another. One ingenious little device was the Humming Bird. The Bird is not a bird and yet the Bird is a bird. This bird is a bird that was conceived in the mind of another kind of bird—a human bird. He must have been a buzzard of the human species to figure out a device that would inflict the maximum punishment with the minimum harm to himself and the most exquisite anguish on the victim. The agony is so *intense*, that after two or three minutes you're ready for the grave or the mad house.

When I was discharged from prison, I was the spirit of meanness personified. I hated everyone. I made up my mind that I would rob, rape, burn, destroy, and kill *everywhere* and *anywhere* I went. I got a job with the Illinois Central Railroad as a guard and a strike breaker. I was told if I saw anyone who had no business there, to knock their blocks off and run 'em ragged, and I did. I started in to lick every union striker I saw. I didn't see many, so I licked the scabs and guards too. A copper tried to stop me, so I licked him too. He stopped fighting long enough to blow his whistle for help. So I figured it was time for me to blow this whole town.

I got pinched and held for the grand jury under charges of aggravated assault and inciting to riot. I got out on bail and immediately jumped it.

I sat down to think things over a bit. While I was sitting there, a little kid about 11 or 12 years came bumming around. He was looking for something. He found it too. I took him out to a gravel pit about one-quarter mile away. I left him there, but first committed sodomy on him and then killed him. His brains were coming out of his ears when I left him, and he will never be any deader. He is still there.

I bought a yacht with some money from a couple of robberies. Every day or two I'd go to New York and hang out on 25 South Street and size up the sailors. Whenever I saw a couple who seemed to have money, I'd hire them to work my yacht. I would always promise big pay and easy work. What they got was something else. We would wine and dine, and when they were drunk enough they would go to bed. When they were asleep I would get my 45 Colt army automatic and blow their brains out. Then I would take a rope and tie a rock on them and put them into my rowboat, row out to the main channel about one mile and drop 'em overboard. They are there yet, ten of 'em.

My whole mind was bent on figuring out ways to punish my enemies, and everybody was my enemy. My intention was to rob, rape and kill everyone and anyone I could. I would commit enough burglaries to get together a few hundred dollars. With that, I'd go to a railroad tunnel, where I would wait for an all steel pullman train to come along. I would have a large contact bomb which would explode and wreck the engine and block up the tunnel. The explosion would burst open containers of poison gas which, in the closed tunnel, would kill every living thing. I would be stationed in the rear of the tunnel with a gas mask, ready to shoot anything that moved.

I went around doin' my job of robbing, raping and killing everything I came across. When the bulls picked me up for a minor house-breaking charge, they asked me what my occupation was. I told them "thief" and said the charge was a big joke. "I've killed too many people to worry about a house-breaking charge." They didn't know I was telling the truth. "I have put a lot of people out of their misery, and now I am looking for someone to put me out of mine." They paid me no mind, of course, and put me in the Washington District Jail, the south wing, under the providence of Henry Lesser, the one man I would come to respect, and the one man in the world I don't want to kill.

The captain of the guard discovered a loose bar I was working on and brought me to the basement of the jail. With a Dr. Harris and a couple of guards who I don't know by name—but I'll know them in hell when we meet—I was tied naked to a post for two days, tortured and beaten, while the doc checked my ticker to make sure I wouldn't leave this world and miss all the fun. I cursed them all, the whole human race, to eternal damnation, and told them how much I enjoyed killing people, giving them every single detail. They finally started to believe me and looked up my story.

I was dumped back in my cell burning with hate and pain, when a dollar was sent to me from a guard who had been making known his disapproval of my treatment. His name was Henry Lesser. At first I thought it was a joke or some new torture. When I finally realized it was sincere, I was in shock. No screw ever done me a favor. I thanked him and told him, "I'm going to see that you get the story of my life. I may leave here anytime for some big house, mad house or death house. I want to write it out before I kick off so I can explain my side of it. Even though nobody hears or reads it except one man."

To Judge Hopkins: You've acted without my consent. I do not want a lawyer. Regardless of the outcome and sentence of this trial, I refuse to appear for a new trial—Carl Panzram.

"I take the stand now, do I? I have a few words to say. While you were trying me here, I was trying all of you. I've found you guilty. Some of you I've executed. If I live, I'll execute more of you. I hate the whole human race. You think I'm crazy, don't you? I'm not. I know right from wrong. My conscience doesn't bother me. I have no conscience. I believe the whole human race should be exterminated. I'll do my best to do it every chance I get. Now I've done my duty, you do yours."

I told you all while in my cell, again in the open court, and again when I came here. I told everyone I came in contact with that I would sure knock off the first guy who bothered me. I even told that to the deputy warden here and the man I killed. They didn't leave me alone. I killed one and tried to kill a dozen others. The way I figure things out is this way: if it's all right for the law to do the things to me it has, then it's all right for me to do the same thing to the law. That makes 21 that I have to my credit. You can put that down in your little storybook, and if I keep on living much longer, I may have some more to put in my graveyard.

Society for the Abolishment of Capital Punishment 5/23/30
National Headquarters, Washington, D.C.

The only thanks you or your kind will get from me for your efforts on my behalf is that I wish you all had one neck and that I had my hands on it. I'd sure put you out of your misery, just the same as I have done with numbers of other people.

I have no desire whatever to reform myself. My only desire is to reform people who try to reform me, and I believe the only way to reform people is to kill 'em. My motto is "Rob 'em all, Rape 'em all, and Kill 'em all."

Very Truly Yours—COPPER JOHN II

"Are there any Bible-backed cocksuckers in here?" screamed Panzram. "Get 'em out! I don't mind being hanged, but I don't need any hypocrites around me! Run 'em out, warden, or you're going to have a hell of a time getting me out of this cell." The clergymen were escorted out. Panzram bolted out the door into the courtyard and bellowed "Boo," as the crowd jerked back in fear. Suddenly he whipped around, spitting full into the face of the captain of the guard...

"Anything you want to say?" asked the hangman. "Yes," snapped Panzram. "Hurry it up you Hoosier bastard! I could hang a dozen men while you're fooling around."

I would like to have it known just why I do this. I had no choice about coming into this world, and nearly all my 38 years in it I have had very little to say and do about how I should live my life. People have driven me into doing everything I have ever done. Now the time has come when I refuse to be driven any farther.

Today I live. Tomorrow I go to the grave. Farther than that no man can drive me. I am sure glad to leave this lousy world and the lousier people in this world. But of all the lousy people in this world, I believe I am the lousiest of 'em all. Today I am dirty, but tomorrow I'll be just DIRT. •

MUSIC

Contrary to popular belief, songs about criminal violence existed long before rap artists started celebrating the thug life. Back in the premodern era, when literacy was largely confined to the clergy and aristocracy, accounts of sensational crimes were circulated among the peasantry by means of grim little ditties known as "murder ballads." Whenever a particularly ghastly homicide occurred, it was immediately translated into a song that could be transmitted orally from person to person, village to village.

In later centuries, as reading became more widespread among the common folk, these graphic true-crime lyrics were printed up on cheap sheets of paper and peddled to the hardworking masses eager to brighten their overburdened lives with a little morbid titillation. Throat slittings, stranglings, bludgeoning, and ax murder were among the most popular topics of these crudely composed verses. One surviving ballad describes a ghastly case of child murder, perpetrated by a woman named Emma Pitt. Typically, the anonymous author omits no detail of the grisly killing:

> This Emma Pitt was a schoolmistress,
> Her child she killed we see,
> Oh mothers, did you ever hear,
> Of such barbarity.
>
> With a large flint stone she beat its head
> When such cruelty she'd done,
> From the tender roof of the infant's mouth
> She cut away its tongue.

The tradition of the murder ballad continued well into the twentieth century. Indeed, one of the most popular songs of the 1950s, the Kingston Trio's early hit "Tom Dooley," was a somewhat sanitized version of a traditional murder ballad about a man about to hang for slaughtering his girlfriend ("Met her on the mountain/ There I took her life/ Met her on the mountain/ Stabbed her with my knife").

Naturally enough, mass murderers and serial killers—though they were called by other names back then—were immortalized in ballads, like this one about Lydia Sherman, America's "Queen Poisoner" who dispatched three husbands, six children, and two stepchildren in the late 1800s:

> Lydia Sherman is plagued with rats.
> Lydia has no faith in cats.
> So Lydia buys some arsenic,

And then her husband gets sick;
And then her husband, he does die,
And Lydia's neighbors wonder why.

Lydia moves, but still has rats;
And still she puts no faith in cats;
So again she buys some arsenic,
This time her children, they get sick,
This time her children, they do die,
And Lydia's neighbors wonder why.

Lydia lies in Wethersfield jail,
And loudly does she moan and wail.
She blames her fate on a plague of rats;
She blames the laziness of cats.
But her neighbors questions she can't deny—
So Lydia now in prison must lie.

Belle Gunness, the so-called Lady Bluebeard, was likewise commemorated in a ballad whose first few verses went like this:

Belle Gunness was a lady fair,
In Indiana State.
She weighed about three hundred pounds,
And that is quite some weight.

That she was stronger than a man
Her neighbors all did own;
She butchered hogs right easily,
And did it all alone.

But hogs were just a sideline
She indulged in now and then;
Her favorite occupation
Was a-butchering of men.

Ever since the late 1960s—when the dark id of the counterculture came roaring forth in the form of everything from the Manson murders to Altamont—rock, like every other medium of popular art, has dealt with the figure of the serial killer. Among the classics of this genre are: The Rolling Stones' "Midnight Rambler" (about the Boston Strangler), Warren Zevon's creepily sardonic "Excitable Boy," and Talking Heads' "Psycho-Killer." Even the ultrabenign Beatles recorded "Maxwell's Silver Hammer," an infectious tune about a homicidal maniac whose MO bears a resemblance to that of Peter "Yorkshire Ripper" Sutcliffe. More recent examples include the Bundy-inspired "Ted, Just Admit It" by Jane's Addiction, "Killer on the Loose" by Thin Lizzy, and The Blues Traveler's "Psycho Joe." Special mention must also be made of Nick Cave's 1996 *Murder Ballads,* a powerful updating of the traditional genre.

Some of the more aggressively hard-edged "death metal" bands of recent years have made a career out of singing about serial killers. Foremost among these are Slayer (whose "Dead Skin Mask" is a tribute to Ed Gein) and Macabre, whose discography includes such songs as "Nightstalker," "The Ted Bundy Song," "Gacy's Lot," and "Edmund Kemper Had a Terrible Temper," as well as an entire concept album about Jeffrey Dahmer (featuring titles like "Drill Bit Lobotomy" and "Temple of Bones"). Paeans to serial murder can also be found in the *oeuvre* of 9 Inch Nails and Marilyn Manson (each of whose band members has adopted the surname of a notorious psycho-killer: Twiggy Ramirez, Madonna Wayne Gacy, Ginger Fish, Gidget Gein, Daisy Berkowitz, and of course the front man himself).

A couple of actual serial killers have tried their hand at songwriting. The most notable is Charles Manson, who actually possesses a certain musical flair. Manson's best known number, "Look at Your Game, Girl," set off an uproar when it was included as an unlisted cut on Guns N' Roses' 1993 album *The Spaghetti Incident?* The original version, sung by Charlie himself, appears in the best-known of his several albums, *LIE,* recorded in August 1968. Another serial-killer-penned song is "Strangler in the Night" by Albert DeSalvo, which appears on the rarity *Joe Coleman's Infernal Machine,* an entire album of mayhem-related music that also features such obscure treasures as Red River Dave's country-western yodel, "California Hippie Murders."

(Courtesy of Timothy Carroll. Art by Scott Weiss.)

Poster for the 1980s punk-rock band Ed Gein's Car

On the opposite end of the cultural spectrum are those highbrow works that deal with serial killers. One of the most celebrated is Stephen Sondheim's *Sweeney Todd,* the operatic Grand Guignol musical about the Victorian "Demon Barber of Fleet Street" (who may or may not have been a real person).

FILM

Violence has been a crowd-pleasing feature of the motion picture since the medium was invented at the tail end of the nineteenth century. The very first special effect created for the movies was the graphic beheading of an actor (done by means of primitive stop-motion photography) in Thomas Edison's 1895 peep show short *The Execution of Mary, Queen of Scots.*

Exactly when the psychopathic killer first entered cinematic history is a matter of debate, though one scholar points out that *The Cabinet of Dr. Caligari*—the 1920 classic of German Expressionist cinema—was partly inspired by a real-life case of a pedophiliac sex-murder. Another German silent classic, G. W. Pabst's 1929 *Pandora's Box,* features a heroine who ends up as a victim of Jack the Ripper. The Ripper case is also the focus of Alfred Hitchcock's 1927 *The Lodger* (remade in 1944).

In 1931, German filmmaker Fritz Lang came out with one of the greatest psycho-killer movies of all time: *M,* a riveting study of evil starring Peter Lorre as a serial child-killer modeled on the real-life lust-murderer Peter Kürten. The following decade saw the release of several classic movies featuring memorable psycho-killers, including Alfred Hitchcock's 1943 *Shadow of a Doubt* (reportedly inspired by serial strangler Earle Leonard Nelson), Edgar G. Ulmer's 1944 *Bluebeard,* starring ever-creepy John Carradine in the title role, and Henry Hathaway's 1947 *Kiss of Death.* Though not technically a serial killer, the villain of the latter film—a giggling hit man named Tommy Udo unforgettably played by Richard Widmark—is one of the most terrifying sociopaths in screen history. Another 1947 movie, Charlie Chaplin's *Monsieur Verdoux,* is a black comedy about a Parisian Bluebeard modeled on Henri Landru (who was also the subject of a 1963 film by French *auteur* Claude Chabrol).

The single most frightening cinematic psychopath of the 1950s was undoubtedly the Bible-spouting maniac in Charles Laughton's *Night of the Hunter* (1955), played by Robert Mitchum. (The actor would go on to turn in another unforgettably menacing performance as the implacable Max Cady in the original 1962 version of *Cape Fear.*) Another important psycho-film from the 1950s is Edward Dmytryk's 1952 *The Sniper,* about a serial shooter who substitutes killing for sex. No fewer than three Jack the Ripper films appeared in the fifties: *Room to Let* (1950), *Man in the Attic* (1954), and *Jack the Ripper* (1959). Saucy Jack would remain the single most popular of all cinematic psychos, appearing in numerous films in succeeding decades, including the nifty little 1979 thriller, *Murder by Decree* (which pits the Ripper against Sherlock Holmes), the time-travel fantasy *Time after Time* (which also appeared in 1979 and in which H. G. Wells pursues Jack to modern-day America) and, most recently, the 2001 comic-based period piece, *From Hell.*

The decade of the 1960s opened with the release of two seminal serial killer films, one a triumph for its director, the other an unmitigated disaster. In America, the stunning commercial success of Hitchcock's *Psycho* paved the way for the "slasher" film craze of the 1970s. The story was different in England, where Michael Powell's now-acclaimed *Peeping Tom* (1960)—

about a sadistic voyeur who films his victims while impaling them with a lethal camera-tripod—sparked such outrage that it effectively ended the distinguished director's career. The first feature-length film devoted entirely to a sensational, true-life serial murder case appeared near the end of the decade: Richard Brooks's gritty *The Boston Strangler* (1968), starring one-time matinee idol Tony Curtis as Albert DeSalvo.

Two equally grim, black-and-white films about notorious serial killers were released at the very start of the 1970s: *10 Rillington Place* (1971), about the necrophiliac British psychopath John Reginald Christie, and *The Honeymoon Killers* (1970), about the ineffably creepy killer couple, Martha Beck and Raymond Fernandez, aka the "Lonely Hearts Killers." As the decade progressed, the psycho-killer became an increasingly familiar presence on screen. Notable films include Alfred Hitchcock's 1972 *Frenzy* (loosely based on the still-unidentified sex killer known as "Jack the Stripper"), Terrence Malick's 1973 *Badlands* (based on the murder spree of killer couple Charles Starkweather and Caril Ann Fugate, whose homicidal exploits also inspired Oliver Stone's 1994 *Natural Born Killers*), and Tobe Hooper's 1976 *Eaten Alive* (inspired by homicidal tavern keeper Joe Ball, who fed victims to his pet alligators). Special mention must also be made of Don Siegel's 1972 *Dirty Harry,* which—though a Clint Eastwood action film—contains an unforgettable performance by Andy Robinson as a sniveling psycho (based on the San Francisco Zodiac killer) so utterly detestable that it's hard not to leap up and cheer when Dirty Harry finally gets around to blasting him with his .44 Magnum.

It wasn't until the 1980s that the term "serial killer" became part of the common vocabulary and the serial killer film a distinct cinematic genre. Examples range from slick, big-budget Hollywood productions like *Kalifornia* (1993), *Copycat* (1995), *The Bone Collector* (1999), and *The Cell* (2000) to a recent spate of cheaply made mockumentaries about notorious psycho-killers like Ted Bundy, Jeffrey Dahmer, and John Wayne Gacy.

Psycho-cinema: A Deadly Dozen

Though critical judgments are highly subjective, here's a list of twelve recommended psycho-killer movies, each worthwhile in its own way.

1. *Citizen X* (1995). This riveting, made-for-cable thriller—about the hunt for the Russian "Mad Beast" Andrei Chikatilo—deals with a forensic scientist struggling to track down the most savage lust-murderer of modern times while dealing with all the obstacles that the Soviet bureaucracy can put in his way, beginning with the government's refusal to acknowledge the very existence of the killer.
2. *Fear City* (1984). A woefully neglected thriller about a psycho-killer stalking topless dancers in New York City. The director, Abel Ferrara,

does a highly effective job of capturing the sleazy soul of midtown Manhattan before it turned into a sanitized, Disneyfied tourist destination.

3. *Felicia's Journey* (1999). This artful, understated film from director Atom Egoyan—about a pregnant Irish runaway who crosses paths with a pudgy, food-obsessed, seemingly nurturing serial killer (played by Bob Hoskins)—manages to generate nail-biting tension without spilling a single drop of blood.
4. *Henry: Portrait of a Serial Killer* (1990). Loosely based on the purported depravities of Henry Lee Lucas and Ottis Toole, this small-scale, critically acclaimed movie stands as one of the most harrowing cinematic experiences of all time.
5. *Manhunter* (1986). Michael Mann's stylish version of Thomas Harris's *Red Dragon* (remade under its original title in 2002), with Brian Cox turning in a quietly chilling performance as Hannibal the Cannibal.
6. *Maniac* (1980). Watching it may be a brutalizing (if not degrading) experience, but this sickeningly gory, low-budget shocker—about a psychocreep who harvests the scalps of his victims—does a more effective job of evoking the repugnant reality of serial homicide than any slick Hollywood thriller.
7. *Rampage* (1988). Based on the atrocities of Richard the "Sacramento Vampire" Chase and directed by William Friedkin of *Exorcist* fame, this movie eventually degenerates into a talky polemic against capital punishment. The first half, though—which re-creates Chase's insanely gruesome crimes—is very powerful stuff.
8. *Se7en* (1995). Grueling, if artfully made, box office smash about the kind of highly creative serial killer only a Hollywood screenwriter could dream up: a deranged religious fanatic who kills his victims in accordance with the Seven Deadly Sins.
9. *The Silence of the Lambs* (1991). Jonathan Demme's blockbuster version of Thomas Harris's best seller not only generates edge-of-the-seat suspense but managed the startling feat of transforming a cannibalistic psychopath (marvelously incarnated by Anthony Hopkins) into a modern-day pop icon, so bizarrely appealing that audiences demanded to see more of him in two cinematic sequels, Ridley Scott's *Hannibal* (2001) and Brett Ratner's *Red Dragon* (2002).
10. *Summer of Sam* (1999). Though not entirely able to live up to its own ambitions, Spike Lee's 1999 movie deals with those sweltering, tension-charged months in 1976 when New York City was terrorized by David "Son of Sam" Berkowitz. The killings themselves are the backdrop to—not the center of—the action, but the glimpses we get of the ranting Berkowitz, holed up in his squalid lair, are deeply disturbing.
11. *The Vanishing* (1988). From Holland (of all places) comes this profoundly unsettling film about a young man obsessed with locating his girlfriend, who has been abducted by one of the creepiest psychos ever

put on film—a seemingly meek, soft-spoken family man with a taste for unspeakable torture. The ending is absolutely devastating. *Warning:* Do not confuse with the lame 1993 American remake, starring Kiefer Sutherland and Jeff Bridges.

12. *The Young Poisoner's Handbook* (1995). Real-life British killer-kid Graham Young was the inspiration for this gruesome black comedy about an adolescent psychopath who uses his family as guinea pigs for his lethal experiments.

LITERATURE

Serious writers have grappled with the problem of what we now call psychopathic behavior for many centuries. Iago, the cunning villain of Shakespeare's *Othello,* is a classic instance; a frighteningly cold and conscienceless being who cares about nothing but himself and whose malevolence is so well concealed behind a mask of normality that he strikes virtually everyone who knows him as the most honest and trustworthy fellow imaginable. Another example is Melville's John Claggart: the intelligent, seemingly normal petty officer of *Billy Budd* who delights in evil for its own sake. Homicidal madmen appear throughout the Gothic short stories of Edgar Allan Poe, though none is more unnerving than the nameless narrator of "The Tell-Tale Heart," who goes about committing an ultimate atrocity—the murder and dismemberment of his elderly housemate—while insisting on his own perfect sanity.

In more recent times, Flannery O'Connor's 1955 short story "A Good Man Is Hard to Find" offers one of the most chilling fictional portraits of a psycho-killer ever created, in the character called "The Misfit," a Bible-obsessed madman who travels around the Southern countryside conducting unspeakable massacres. Joyce Carol Oates's deeply unsettling 1966 short story "Where Are You Going, Where Have You Been?"—loosely based on the case of serial killer Charles Schmid, the so-called Pied Piper of Tucson—is another classic of contemporary Gothic fiction.

Psycho-killers have also appeared in the work of serious poets. The speaker of Robert Browning's 1842 "Porphyria's Lover," for example, seems rational enough—until he decides that the best way to express his love for his girlfriend is by strangling her with her own hair:

> That moment she was mine, mine, fair,
> Perfectly pure and good: I found
> A thing to do, and all her hair
> In one long yellow string I wound
> Three times her little throat around,
> And strangled her.

More recent poets have also explored the psychology of serial murderers in their work. Notable examples include Ai's "The Good Shepherd: Atlanta, 1981" (about the Atlanta Child Murders) from her 1986 book *Sin,* and the sequence of poems called "Troubadour: Songs for Jeffrey Dahmer" from Thom Gunn's 2000 book *Boss Cupid.*

Even before the term "serial killer" was invented, some outstandingly scary examples of the species had appeared in works of popular fiction. Now considered a classic, Jim Thompson's 1952 *The Killer Inside Me*—about a deputy sheriff in a small Texas town whose aw-shucks manner conceals the sick mind of a sadistic murderer—is one of the most unsettling portraits of a psychopath in print. The decade of the 1950s ended with the publication of Robert Bloch's pulp classic, *Psycho,* the granddaddy of serial killer novels and inspiration for Alfred Hitchcock's classic movie.

The enormous critical and commercial success of Thomas Harris's first two Hannibal Lecter books, *Red Dragon* (1981) and *The Silence of the Lambs* (1988) unleashed a flood of popular procedural thrillers focusing on investigative heroes and their struggles with assorted, highly colorful serial killers. Among the most popular works in this genre are James Patterson's Alex Cross books (*Along Came a Spider, Kiss the Girls, Jack and Jill,* etc.); Patricia Cornwell's Kay Scarpetta novels (including *Postmortem, Cruel & Unusual,* and *The Body Farm*), John Sandford's "Prey" series (*Rules of Prey, Shadow Prey, Night Prey,* and so on), and Jeffery Deaver's novels featuring quadriplegic criminologist Lincoln Rhymes (*The Coffin Dancer, The Bone Collector, The Vanished Man*).

A comprehensive list of contemporary serial killer fiction has been compiled by Martin Kich, professor of English at Wright State University—Lake Campus in Ohio, and can be found on his Web site, *www.wright.edu/~martin.kich.*

Recommended Reading

Philip L. Simpson, *Psycho Paths: Tracking the Serial Killer Through Contemporary Film and Fiction* (2000)

Killer Fiction

By dint of their superior literary qualities, a handful of novels dealing with psychopathic criminals stand out above the rest. These include:

1. Sherman Alexie, *Indian Killer* (1996). Set in Seattle, this thematically complex, racially charged thriller centers on a Native American serial killer who targets whites in retribution for the historical injustices suffered by his people.

2. Toni Cade Bambara, *Those Bones Are Not My Child* (2000). A hugely ambitious, posthumously published novel about the Atlanta Child Murders of the early 1980s, told from the point of view of an African-American mother whose eldest son disappears one afternoon on the way home from an outing.
3. Caleb Carr, *The Alienist* (1994). This mega-selling historical mystery is not only a highly suspenseful psychological thriller but a brilliant evocation of late-nineteenth-century New York City.
4. Bret Easton Ellis, *American Psycho* (1991). A savage satire of Yuppie consumerism that largely consists of detailed itemizations of upscale consumer goods alternating with scenes of dizzyingly baroque, stomach-churning violence, most of it directed against women.
5. John Fowles, *The Collector* (1963). Though the protagonist of this book is more serial kidnapper than serial killer, the fantasy he enacts—abducting a beautiful young woman and holding her captive in a dungeon—has made this story a perennial favorite among actual psychopathic sex-killers.
6. Patricia Highsmith, *The Talented Mr. Ripley* (1955). The first of Highsmith's books to feature her sociopathic hero, Tom Ripley, this gripping novel sends him to Europe where he becomes entranced with the life of golden-boy acquaintance Dickie Greenleaf, with fatal consequences for the latter.
7. Gordon Lish, *Dear Mr. Capote* (1983). A deeply unsettling, unconventional novel that takes the form of a letter to Truman Capote (author of the true-crime classic *In Cold Blood*) written by a homicidal maniac who intends to murder forty-seven women, one for each year of his life.
8. Cormac McCarthy, *Child of God* (1974). A haunting, lyrical novel about an Eddie Gein-like outcast named Lester Ballard who holes up in a Tennessee cave with his necrophiliac trophies, emerging periodically to seek new victims.
9. Susanna Moore, *In the Cut* (1995). A brutally suspenseful erotic thriller about a New York City college professor who finds herself caught up in an intense sexual affair with a cop who may also be a serial killer.
10. Joyce Carol Oates, *Zombie* (1995). A profoundly disquieting book, inspired by the doings of Jeffrey Dahmer, about a young psycho obsessed with the idea of turning victims into mindless sex slaves by subjecting them to ice pick lobotomies.

HUMOR

There's nothing amusing about serial murder. By the same token, there's nothing intrinsically funny about dead babies, quadriplegics, and Princes Di's death in a car crash—all of which have been the subjects of widely circulated jokes.

Psychologists and other academic experts tell us that sick humor functions as a coping mechanism—a way to ventilate the fears stirred up in us by the overwhelming horrors and tragedies of existence. "Where there is anxiety, there will be jokes to express that anxiety," says folklorist Alan Dundes, adding: "The expression 'laughing to keep from crying' has a good deal of merit in it."

According to Professor Dundes in his 1987 book *Cracking Jokes,* the tradition of American sick humor dates back to the beginning of the twentieth century, when macabre rhymes about a character called "Little Willie" became popular throughout the United States. Though sometimes the victim of horrible accidents ("Little Willie, in bows and sashes/ Fell in the fire and got burned to ashes"), the incorrigible Willie was more often portrayed as a pint-sized psychopath—Dennis the Menace with a seriously homicidal streak:

> Willie poisoned his father's tea
> Father died in agony.
> Mother came, and looked quite vexed.
> "Really, Will," she said, "What next?"

> Little Willie hung his sister;
> She was dead before we missed her.
> Willie's always up to tricks.
> Ain't he cute? He's only six.

Willie, of course, was a fictional creation. The now-familiar custom of swapping sick jokes about real-life serial killers seems to have begun in the late 1950s, when crude little riddles about the Wisconsin ghoul Ed Gein became the rage throughout the Midwest. These so-called Geiners caught the attention of psychologist George D. Arndt, who wrote an article about the phenomenon, "Community Reaction to a Horrifying Event," in which he reprinted a number of examples:

Why did they let Ed Gein out of jail on New Year's Eve?
So he could dig up a date.

Why wouldn't anyone play poker with Ed Gein?
They were afraid he'd come up with a good hand.

Forty years later, the discovery of Jeffrey Dahmer's atrocities set off another wave of morbid rib ticklers:

What did Jeffrey Dahmer say when his mother told him she didn't like his friends?
"That's OK, Mom, just eat the noodles."

(Courtesy of Roger Worsham)

Jeffrey Dahmer novelty pin

What did Jeffrey Dahmer do when he finished his vegetables?
He threw away their wheelchairs.

More recently, serial killer humor has been a staple of the parody newspaper *The Onion,* which has run such classic stories as WHY MUST THE MEDIA CALL MY RITUAL KILLINGS "SENSELESS"? ("Is it that the media simply don't see the pride and craftsmanship I put into my work? What about the way I wrap the victims' own intestines around their necks not once, not twice, but three times, then tie them off in a sheepshank?) and NEIGHBORS REMEMBER SERIAL KILLER AS SERIAL KILLER (" 'He was kind of a murderous, insane, serial-killer type of fellow,' said Will Rowell, 57, who lived next door to the man arrested for the murder of 14 nurses in Florida and Georgia. 'He sort of kept to himself, killing nurses, having sex with their corpses and burying the bodies in his backyard.' ").

MURDERBILIA

Some people collect autographs of movie stars. Others invest in sporting equipment signed by their favorite athletes—a Wayne Gretzky hockey puck or Derek Jeter jersey. Still others have been known to bid thousands at auction for John Kennedy's golf clubs or a cocktail dress worn by Princess Di.

And a small but highly controversial subculture of hobbyists devote themselves to the acquisition of artifacts connected to serial killers.

Why anyone would seek out, let alone spend good money on, a lock of Charles Manson's hair or Ted Bundy's high school yearbook seems deeply perplexing, if not downright immoral, to many right-thinking people. Apart from changes in technology, however—the fact that such collecting is now typically conducted over the Internet—there is nothing new about this phenomenon.

From crucified criminals lining the Appian Way in ancient Rome, to medieval traitors left to rot in dangling gibbets, to the gunned-down outlaws exhibited in store windows and undertaking parlors in the Old West, the dead and decomposing bodies of murderers, thieves, and rapists (and sometimes of perfectly innocent victims of lynch mobs) have always been put on public display. And the law-abiding, God-fearing types who flock to see these gruesome spectacles have often felt a need to procure a little keepsake.

Exactly how long this practice has been going on is impossible to pin down, though—extrapolating from the known anthropological evidence (such as the habit of various aboriginal peoples to collect skulls, scalps, and other anatomical relics)—the most likely answer is forever. When King Charles I was executed in 1649, for example, his blood was mopped up with rags, which were torn to pieces and sold to eager bystanders. Even the sawdust that had been sprinkled on the scaffold to soak up the gore was swept up and offered for sale.

Describing the "grisly appetite of souvenir hunters" as a "timeless" phenomenon, historian Michael Hollingsworth cites the case of Maria Marten, a young Englishwoman who vanished after supposedly eloping with a man named William Corder in 1827. The following April—acting on pleas from her mother, who had dreamed that the girl was buried beneath the floor of a local barn—police discovered the young woman's body, just where her mother had said it would be. The crime became a nationwide sensation. When Corder was executed three months later, the crowd was so eager for souvenirs that the hangman's noose was cut into pieces and sold for a guinea per inch. Corder's skin was subsequently flayed from his body, tanned like cowhide, and sold piecemeal at auction. One of the larger sections ended up being made into a tobacco pouch. The barn itself was reduced to splinters by the owner, who made a small fortune by peddling them as individual souvenirs.

When actual relics of a murder weren't available, the public has happily settled for other sorts of mementos. In 1889, a Paris court bailiff named Gouffé was murdered, stuffed into a trunk, and transported to Lyons, where the horribly decomposed corpse was eventually discovered. When the killer was guillotined on February 2, 1891, a horde of spectators turned out for the beheading. To satisfy the demand for souvenirs, peddlers strolled among the crowd, selling miniature replicas of the trunk with a little lead corpse inside.

(Courtesy of Roger Worsham)

Serial killer novelty pins

The situation hasn't changed in the past hundred years. When the junkyard possessions of Wisconsin ghoul Ed Gein were auctioned in the spring of 1958, twenty thousand people showed up. One enterprising bidder drove away with Gein's battered Ford sedan, which he promptly put on display at county fairs and carnivals. Over the next few months, more than two thousand

Midwesterners—men, women, and children—eagerly forked out a quarter each for a peek at "the car that hauled the dead from their graves."

Forty years later, another proposed sale of serial killer belongings set off an uproar in Wisconsin, when a lawyer representing the families of Jeffrey Dahmer's victims announced plans to auction off a bunch of items owned by the Milwaukee Cannibal, including the drill he used to perform his makeshift lobotomies and the freezer in which he stored human body parts for future consumption. So frenzied was the interest in these macabre artifacts among serious collectors of psycho-memorabilia that the organizers of the event expected to reap a profit of one million dollars. In the end, however, the auction was canceled when a civic group—fearful that such a ghoulish event would tarnish Milwaukee's image—purchased the goods and destroyed them (much to the dismay of Dahmerphiles everywhere).

Owning a Gein, for some, is to own a Rembrandt for other collectors.

—Andy Kahan, commenting on the theft of Ed Gein's gravestone in June 2000

Beyond good old morbid fascination, the lure of such grisly items appears to have something to do with the kind of primitive thinking that humans

Ed Gein's "death car" on display at a county fair

never seem to outgrow. There is a demonic quality to these objects. They are the antithesis of saints' relics—artifacts that are infused, not with the sacred, but with the profane. To possess something owned by a serial killer offers some people titillating contact with the taboo—the *frisson* of the forbidden. It is also a way to ward off anxiety, as though having control of something belonging to a monster will magically keep evil at bay.

Of course, there are many people who have no use for psychological rationales for such behavior, which they simply view as inexcusably wrong. One of these is Andy Kahan, Director of the Mayor's Crime Victims Assistance Office in Houston, Texas. Acting on behalf of the families of those who have been preyed on by serial murders, Kahan has led a crusade against such material, which he has memorably labeled "murderbilia." To date, his efforts have been instrumental in the adoption of a Texas "Son of Sam" law—which prevents criminals from profiting from the sale of their goods—and in the banning of serial killer memorabilia from the online auction site eBay.

TOURIST SPOTS

On Sunday, July 28, 1895—following reports of the horrors that had presumably taken place in the Chicago "Murder Castle" of Dr. H. H. Holmes—five thousand people descended on the building, hoping for a glimpse of what the newspapers had described as its "torture dungeon," "suffocation vault," and "corpse chambers." Recognizing the money that could be made from such morbid fascination, an enterprising ex-policeman named A. M. Clark lost no time in securing the lease to the building. Two weeks later, newspapers announced that, under Clark's management, the Castle would be turned into a tourist attraction—a "murder museum" with an admission charge of fifteen cents per person and guided tours conducted by a Chicago detective named Norton. Unfortunately for Clark, nothing came of his get-rich-quick scheme. Just days before the renovated "Castle of Horrors" was set to open for business, a mysterious fire broke out, completely gutting the building.

Something similar happened sixty years later when the ramshackle farmhouse in which Ed Gein had practiced his necrophiliac abominations was reduced to ashes by a blaze apparently set by outraged townspeople, determined to prevent the unhallowed place from being turned into a "museum for the morbid." The obliteration of Gein's dwelling, however, could not stop countless curiosity seekers from making the pilgrimage to his hometown over succeeding decades, much to the chagrin of the residents of Plainfield, sick of having their community forever associated in the public mind with America's most notorious psycho.

The sites of notorious, highly publicized crimes have always exerted a mysterious, magnetic pull on the public. In 1908, the discovery of a dozen dismembered bodies on the Indiana farm of the "Lady Bluebeard" Belle Gunness, brought thousands of Midwesterners flocking to her property, where they could gape at the open graves and peer at the decaying corpses on display in the carriage house. Ninety years later, John D. Long Lake in Union, South Carolina—where, on the evening of October 25, 1994, Susan Smith rolled a car containing her two young sons down a boat ramp into the waters—became a tourist destination for sightseers from as far away as Alaska. In 1996, while visiting the site, one family became the victims of their morbid curiosity when—in a bizarre echo of the Smith crime—their truck accidentally rolled down the same ramp, drowning the mother, father, and three little children.

Not everyone, of course, thinks it's fun to take a day-trip to a place where children were murdered or teenagers tortured or female corpses exhumed and dismembered. Some people find the whole idea abhorrent. Ed Gein's house of horrors wasn't the only such place to be razed by an outraged citizenry. The suburban house in which John Wayne Gacy committed his abominations was leveled. So was Jeffrey Dahmer's apartment building, which a community group bought for the sole purpose of demolishing. In December 2002, Ted Bundy's onetime residence went the way of Gein's farmhouse and H. H. Holmes's Castle, when unknown arsonists torched the Tallahassee, Florida, house in which he was living at the time he committed his final string of atrocities.

For those interested in macabre sightseeing, writer Neal S. Yonover has put together *Crime Scene U.S.A.* (2000), a state-by-state traveler's guide that provides descriptions of, directions to, and other pertinent information about infamous murder locations throughout the country.

For those who feel sheer disgust at the whole notion of "psycho-tourism" (as he calls it), the following excerpt is reprinted from writer Peter Schuller's scathing satire on the phenomenon. (The entire essay can be found on Jeff Vogel's Web site *Ironycentral.com.*)

"Psycho-tourism"

> You've heard of Eco-tourism, where handfuls of broke-ass hippies go out to the boonies and "tread lightly on Mother Earth" as if this was some namby-pamby socialist state. Shit! More people would drive ten hours to see the face of the Virgin Mary weeping in an oil leak on some guy's driveway than would paddle a kayak for ten minutes to see the last breeding pair of Wood-crested Chirrups in the wild.
>
> Eco-Tourism, pshaw! Psycho-Tourism is where it's at. People don't want to see rare ferns or endangered predators. They want to see human predators! They want to see John Wayne Gacy's crawlspace, where Pogo the Clown buried thirty victims. They want to see the soup kitchen where Henry Lee Lucas and Ottis Toole struck up their highly successful necrophiliac-cannibal partnership. They want to sit in the V.W. van that Ted Bundy drove.

They want to open Jeffrey Dahmer's fridge. These are the kind of things that matter to people.

. . . Given America's obsession with crime, Psycho-tourism is an All-American, capitalist venture that can't miss. Property of killers is inexplicably cheap. The killer generates free publicity and a fan base to draw from. Tours can be arranged for next to nothing. All it would take are a few guides and some buses.

Let's use Dean Corll as an example. We could buy his home, the factory and the boathouse for a few 100 grand. Tour buses would deliver pilgrims from surrounding Motel Sixes and Holiday Inns. They'd tour the candy factory and get to purchase authentic Corll Candy. Maybe they'll offer some to kids in the playground next door.

Then it's back on the bus and over to Dean's. Here a Disney-esque diorama awaits. First, we walk through the living room where a Dean-robot gets the boy-robots high on glue and paint fumes. Then we move to the bedroom where the boys are handcuffed to the torture-bed. Be careful not to trip on the plastic floor-liner. In the next room, we see Dean's bloody, bullet ridden body lying on the floor. Turncoat Henley stands over him with a smoking gun. Dean's penis collection lies on a nearby table.

After that, it's off to the boathouse, where we're met with another scene. A couple of backhoes are there. The boathouse floor has been dug up, exposing replicas of the bodies. Henley is there too, leaning on the driver's side of the police car, talking to his mother on the police radio.

"Mama, I'm with the police . . . Mama, I killed Dean." The police recorded the actual conversation and it will be played on a tape loop for tourists as they pass by.

From there, they're funneled into the gift shop where various Corll-themed knickknacks are available. Items include: life preservers, handcuffs, glue, plastic tarpaulins and "I survived the Dean Corll Tour" T-shirts. Also for sale: toy boats with Skipper Dean and 1st Mate Henley, Dean's Bag O'Penises and a variation of the kiddie board game, Candymanland.

Pockets emptied and shopping bags filled, the tourists exit the giftshop, board a barge and serenely float down river. This symbolizes Candyman's victims drifting peacefully into the hereafter while taking our victims to the parking lot and their buses.

This is an example of what can be done with lesser known serial killers. Imagine what you could do with Jeffrey Dahmer's apartment or Leonard Lake and Charles Ng's mountain hideaway. At the very least, Psycho-tourism should surpass military air shows, Civil War battle recreations and tours of Graceland or the White House.

—Peter Schuller

GROUPIES

It's a striking fact of life that—in fantasy at least—women seem to go for bad boys. The standard formula of female-oriented romance, whether in fiction or film, involves a respectable, well-brought-up woman who is married or engaged to or just going steady with a perfectly nice, if somewhat bland, fellow of her own social station and breeding. Suddenly, a seductively dangerous, often "lower-class," stranger (or former lover) appears in her life and sweeps her away on a forbidden passionate adventure.

The vast majority of women are content to confine this thrillingly erotic scenario to the realm of daydream. Some, however, feel the need to go further, pursuing a relationship with the baddest men of all—serial killers.

It is this female proclivity for flirting with danger that undoubtedly accounts for the otherwise inexplicable appeal that even the most repugnant psychopaths have been known to exert over women. Men who, prior to their arrest, could never get a date—who sometimes turned to serial murder as a way of taking vengeance on all the women who rejected them—have suddenly found themselves the object of swooning attention from members of the opposite sex.

There's nothing new about this phenomenon. For more than a century, observers have been struck by both the number of female spectators who flock to the trials of notorious murderers and the unabashedly heart-smitten behavior of some of these women. During the 1895 trial of the San Francisco sex-killer Theo Durrant, for example, a young woman named Rosalind Bowers showed up in the courtroom each morning with a bouquet of sweet pea flowers, which she presented to the "Demon of the Belfry" as a token of her admiration. Before long, the papers had made the "Sweet Pea Girl" herself into a minor celebrity, foreshadowing the kind of media attention bestowed on today's serial killer groupies, whose strange infatuations are a favorite topic for supermarket tabloids and the sleazier TV talk shows.

Vile as he was, Durrant was at least a handsome (if profoundly psychopathic) young man. The same is true of other, more recent serial killers who have become homicidal heartthrobs—Ted Bundy, for example, and Paul Bernardo, the male half of Canada's infamous "Ken and Barbie" psycho-couple. But good looks are by no means a prerequisite for romantic success in the bizarre realm of serial killer groupiedom. Creatures as repulsive-looking as John Wayne Gacy and Henry Lee Lucas became the objects of female adoration once they were behind bars. Even Eddie Gein—a man who, prior to his arrest, had to dig up women from their graves in order to find companionship—was besieged by requests from gushing female admirers, begging for a lock of his hair.

Nor does the sheer atrocity of a killer's behavior discourage certain women from pursuing them. Edmund Kemper—whose sex life consisted of violating the corpses of butchered young women—had no trouble attracting girlfriends once he became infamous. Another psycho-killer with similarly abhorrent tastes, Douglas Clark—the "Sunset Strip Slayer" whose perversions included performing oral sex on the decapitated heads of his victims—became the love object of a woman who clearly viewed him as a soul mate, writing him a letter in which she wistfully asked: "I wonder why others don't see the necrophiliac aspects of existence as we do?"

While some groupies are content to remain pen pals with their idols, others pursue the relationship much further, even to the point of matrimony. Richard the "Night Stalker" Ramirez was wed in prison, as were both Hillside Stranglers. One of the most bizarre instances occurred during the penalty phase of Ted Bundy's 1980 trial for the murder of twelve-year-old Kimberly Leach. When his girlfriend, Carol Ann Boone, took the witness stand to plead for his life, Bundy—who had been serving as his own defense attorney—rose to his feet as though to question her. Instead—much to the astonishment of everyone present—he proposed marriage, taking advantage of an obscure Florida law that allowed a public declaration in open court to constitute a legal wedding. When Boone accepted with a delighted giggle, she immediately became Mrs. Ted Bundy. She later gave birth to a daughter she claimed was Bundy's, having become inseminated with sperm presumably smuggled from prison.

What lies behind the behavior of serial killer groupies? Perhaps these women are in the grip of a "Beauty and the Beast" fantasy, believing that their love is so powerful that it can transform a ferocious monster into a decent human being. Or perhaps the opposite is the case—that they are so devoid of any sense of self-worth that, on some level, they believe that only a monster could love *them.* Perhaps they just enjoy playing with fire—getting close to a source of tremendous physical peril while knowing that they are protected by the steel bars and unbreachable walls. Who knows? As novelist D. H. Lawrence said, the human soul is a dark forest.

In a looser sense, the phrase "serial killer groupie" is sometimes applied to anyone, male or female, who develops an obsessive fixation on serial murderers. Two interesting books written by people who found themselves caught up in intense correspondences with infamous, jailed psycho-killers are Jennifer Furio's *The Serial Killer Letters* (1998) and Jason Moss's *The Last Victim* (1999).

INTERNET RESOURCES

As with every other imaginable subject, there's plenty of information about serial murder on the Web, though it varies considerably in quality.

The single best site for biographies of individual figures—as well as for thoroughly researched articles on specific topics (like "Team Killers" and "Necrophilia")—is Court TV's Crime Library (*www.crimelibrary.com*). Also very useful is the Serial Killer Hit List (*www.mayhem.net*). Though its gleefully ghoulish tone flirts with the tasteless, this constantly updated site contains solid, concise biographies of hundreds of serial killers (organized according to body count), including many obscure murderers largely ignored by the mainstream media.

Serial Killer Central (*www.angelfire.com/oh/yodaspage*) features brief, nicely illustrated biographies, along with a selection of serial killer artwork and poetry, and even an online store where dedicated gorehounds can purchase everything from coffee mugs to baseball caps decorated with the Serial Killer Central logo. The Crime Web (*www.crimeweb.com*) supplements its biographical entries with features like "This Day in Serial Killer History" and up-to-the minute "Serial Killer News." Perhaps because it is a joint Australian-English venture, the Crime Web also pays particular attention to international serial killers, a nice change from the American-centric orientation of most of these Web sites. Good material can also be found on the Web site maintained by author Sondra London (*www.sondralondon.com*), whose relationships with sex-killers Gerard Schaefer and Danny the "Gainesville Ripper" Rolling have brought her a degree of personal notoriety.

Of the various Web sites devoted to individual serial killers like Charles Manson and Ted Bundy (easily found by typing their names onto any search engine), the best is undoubtedly Tom Voigt's Zodiac page (*www.zodiackiller.com*), a beautifully designed, exhaustive site devoted to this legendary, long-sought psycho.

Those with a particular interest in the most celebrated serial killer of all, Jack the Ripper, should check out the Web site called Casebook: Jack the Ripper (*www.casebook.org*). Advertising itself—justifiably—as "the world's largest public repository of Ripper-related information," this site is conveniently divided into extensive, well-researched chapters on victims, suspects, witnesses, Ripper letters, police officials, press reports, and other key topics. An indispensable site both for advanced and beginning Ripperologists.

LETHAL LIVES: A TRUE-CRIME BIBLIOGRAPHY

Ever since the 1970s, when the serial killer phenomenon exploded onto the cultural scene, there has been an avalanche of true-crime books on the subject. The following bibliography, which lists all available works on over one hundred individual cases, is meant for readers who'd like to learn more about the many infamous figures discussed throughout *The Serial Killer Files.*

Joe Ball

Radin, Edward D. *Crimes of Passion.* New York: Putnam Books (1953).

Elizabeth Bathory

McNally, Raymond. *Dracula Was a Woman.* New York: McGraw-Hill (1983).

Penrose, Valentine. *The Bloody Countess.* London: Calder & Boyars (1970).

Herb Baumeister

Weinstein, Fannie and Wilson, Melinda. *Where the Bodies Are Buried* (1998). New York: St. Martin's Press.

Mary Bell

Sereny, Gitta. *The Case of Mary Bell.* London: Methuen (1972).

Sereny, Gitta. *Cries Unheard: Why Children Kill—The Case of Mary Bell.* New York: Henry Holt/Owl Books (1998).

Bender Family

Adleman, Robert H. *The Bloody Benders.* New York: Stein & Day (1970).

James, John T. *The Benders in Kansas.* Wichita: Kan-Okla Publishing (1913).

Robert Berdella

Jackman, Tom and Cole, Troy. *Rites of Burial.* New York: Pinnacle (1998).

David Berkowitz

Abrahamsen, David. *Confessions of Son of Sam.* New York: Columbia University Press (1985).

Calohan, George H. *My Search for the Son of Sam.* New York: Universe.com (2001).

Carpozi, George. *Son of Sam: The .44-Caliber Killer* NY: Manor Books (1977).

Klausner, Lawrence D. and Klausner, Larry. *Son of Sam: Based on the Authorized Transcription of the Tapes, Official Documents, and Diaries of David Berkowitz.* New York: McGraw-Hill (1981).

Terry, Maury. *The Ultimate Evil.* New York: Doubleday (1987).

Paul Bernardo and Karla Homolka

Burnside, Scott and Cairns, Alan. *Deadly Innocence: The True Story of Paul Bernardo, Karla Homolka, and the Schoolgirl Murders.* New York: Warner Books (1995).

Davey, Frank. *Karla's Web.* Toronto: Penguin (1995).

Pron, Nick. *Lethal Marriage: The Unspeakable Crimes of Paul Bernardo and Karla Homolka.* New York: Bantam Books (1996).

Williams, Stephen. *Invisible Darkness: The Strange Case of Paul Bernardo and Karla Homolka.* New York: Bantam Books (1996).

"Bible John"

Crow, Alan and Damson, Peter. *Bible John: Hunt for a Killer.* New York: First Press Publishing (1997).

Stoddart, Charles. *Bible John: Search for a Sadist.* Edinburgh: Paul Harris (1980).

Lawrence Bittaker and Roy Norris

Markman, Ronald and Bosco, Dominic. *Alone with the Devil.* New York: Doubleday (1989).

Ian Brady and Myra Hindley

Goodman, Jonathan. *Trial of Ian Brady and Myra Hindley: The Moors Case.* London: David & Charles (1973).

Harrison, Fred. *Brady & Hindley: Genesis of the Moors Murders.* London: Ashgrove Press (1986).

Johnson, Pamela. *On Iniquity: Some Personal Reflections Arising Out of the Moors Murder Trial.* New York: Scribner (1967).

Potter, J. D. *The Monsters of the Moors.* New York: Ballantine (1966).

Sparrow, Gerald. *Satan's Children.* London: Odhams (1966).

Williams, Emelyn. *Beyond Belief.* New York: Random House (1968).

Wilson, Robert. *Devil's Disciples.* Poole, U.K.: Javelin Books (1986).

Jerome Brudos

Rule, Ann. *Lust Killer.* New York: Signet (1983).

Ted Bundy

Humphries, William. *Profile of a Psychopath.* Batavia, IL: Flinn (1999).

Kendall, Elizabeth. *The Phantom Prince: My Life with Ted Bundy.* Seattle: Madrona Publishers (1981).

Keppel, Robert. *The Riverman: Ted Bundy and I Hunt for the Green River Killer.* New York: Pocket Books (1995).

Larsen, Richard W. *The Deliberate Stranger.* Englewood Cliffs, NJ: Prentice Hall (1980).

Michaud, Stephen, Aynesworth, Hugh, and Hazelwood, Roy. *The Only Living Witness: The Story of Serial Killer Ted Bundy.* New York: Penguin Books (1989).

Michaud, Stephen and Aynesworth, Hugh. *Ted Bundy: Conversations with a Killer.* New York: New American Library (1989).

Nelson, Polly. *Defending the Devil: My Story as Ted Bundy's Last Lawyer.* New York: William Morrow (1994).

Rule, Ann. *The Stranger Beside Me.* New York: Norton (1996).

Winn, Steven and Merrill, David. *Ted Bundy: The Killer Next Door.* New York: Bantam (1980).

Angelo Buono and Kenneth Bianchi

O'Brien, Darcy. *Two of a Kind: The Hillside Stranglers.* New York: New American Library (1985).

Schwarz, Ted. *The Hillside Strangler.* Garden City, New York: Doubleday (1981).

Harvey Carignan

Rule, Ann. *The Want-Ad Killer.* New York: New American Library (1999).

David Carpenter

Graysmith, Robert. *The Sleeping Lady: The Trailside Murders Above the Golden Gate.* New York: Dutton (1990).

Richard Trenton Chase

Biondi, Lt. Ray and Hecox, Walt. *The Dracula Killer.* New York: Pocket Books (1992).

Markman, Ronald and Bosco, Dominic. *Alone with the Devil: Famous Cases of a Court Psychiatrist.* New York: Doubleday (1989).

Andrei Chikatilo

Conradi, Peter. *The Red Ripper.* New York: Dell (1992).

Cullen, Robert. *The Killer Department: Detective Viktor Burakov's Search for the Most Savage Se-*

rial Killer in Russian History. New York: Pantheon Books (1993).
Krivich, M. and Ol'gin, Ol'gert. *Comrade Chikatilo: The Psychopathology of Russia's Notorious Serial Killer.* New York: Barricade Books (1993).
Lourie, Richard. *Hunting the Devil: The Pursuit, Capture and Confession of the Most Savage Serial Killer in History.* New York: HarperCollins (1994).

John Christie
Eddowes, John. *The Two Killers of Rillington Place.* London: Little, Brown (1994).
Furneaux, Rupert. *The Two Stranglers of Rillington Place.* London: Panther (1961).
Kennedy, Ludovic. *10 Rillington Place.* London: Gollancz (1961).

Douglas Clark and Carol Bundy
Farr, Louise. *The Sunset Murders.* New York: Pocket (1992).

Hadden Clark
Havill, Adrian. *Born Evil: A True Story of Cannibalism and Sexual Murder.* New York: St. Martin's (2001).

Carrol Edward Cole
Newton, Michael. *Silent Rage: The 30-Year Odyssey of a Serial Killer.* New York: Dell (1994).

John Norman Collins
Keyes, Edward. *The Michigan Murders.* New York: Pocket Books (1978).

Dean Corll and Elmer Wayne Henley
Gurwell, John K. *Mass Murder in Houston.* Houston: Cordovan Press (1974).
Hanna, David. *Harvest of Horror: Mass Murder in Houston.* New York: Belmont Tower (1975).
Olsen, Jack. *The Man with the Candy: The Story of the Houston Mass Murders.* New York: Simon & Schuster (2001).

Mary Ann Cotton
Appleton, Arthur. *Mary Ann Cotton: Her Story and Trial.* London: Michael Joseph (1973).
Whitehead, Tony. *Mary Ann Cotton, Dead, but Not Forgotten.* London: Whitehead (2000).

Dr. Thomas Neill Cream
McLaren, Angus. *A Prescription for Murder: The Victorian Serial Killings of Dr. Thomas Neill Cream.* Chicago: University of Chicago Press (1993).

Jeffrey Dahmer
Baumann, Edward. *Step into My Parlor: The Chilling Story of Serial Killer Jeffrey Dahmer.* Chicago: Bonus Books (1991).
Dahmer, Lionel. *A Father's Story.* New York: William Morrow (1994).
Davis, Don. *The Milwaukee Murders: Nightmare in Apartment 213.* New York: St. Martin's (1993).
Dvorchak, Robert and Howlewa, Lisa. *Milwaukee Massacre: Jeffrey Dahmer and the Milwaukee Murders.* New York: Dell (1991).
Jaeger, Richard W. and Balousek, M. William. *Massacre in Milwaukee: The Macabre Case of Jeffrey Dahmer.* Oregon, WI: Waubesa Press (1991).
Masters, Brian. *The Shrine of Jeffrey Dahmer.* London: Hodder and Stoughton (1993).
Murphy, Dennis and Kennedy, Patrick. *Incident, Homicide: The Story of the Milwaukee Flesh-Eater.* Boston, MA: Quimby World Headquarters Publications (1992).
Norris, Joel. *Jeffrey Dahmer: A Bizarre Journey into the Mind of America's Most Tormented Serial Killer.* New York: Windsor (1992).
Schwartz, Anne E. *The Man Who Could not Kill Enough: The Secret Murders of Milwaukee's Jeffrey Dahmer.* Secaucus, NJ: Carol Publishing. (1992).
Tithecott, Richard. *Of Men and Monsters: Jeffrey Dahmer and the Construction of the Serial Killer.* Madison: University of Wisconsin Press (1997).

Gilles de Rais
Bataille, Georges. *The Trial of Gilles de Rais.* Translated by Richard Robinson. Paris: Jean-Jacques Pauvert (1965).
Benedetti, Jean. *The Real Bluebeard: The Life of Gilles de Rais.* New York: Stein & Day (1972).
Winwar, Frances. *The Saint and the Devil: The Story of Joan of Arc and Gilles de Rais.* New York: Harper (1948).
Wolf, Leonard. *Bluebeard: The Life and Crimes of Gilles de Rais.* New York: Clarkson N. Potter (1980).

Albert DeSalvo
Banks, Harold. *The Strangler!: The Story of Terror in Boston.* New York: Avon (1967).
Frank, Gerold. *Boston Strangler.* New York: New American Library (1966).

Kelly, Susan. *The Boston Stranglers: The Wrongful Conviction of Albert DeSalvo and the True Story of Eleven Shocking Murders.* New York: Birch Lane (1995).

Westley Alan Dodd

Dodd, Westley Alan, Steinhorst, Lori, and Rose, John. *When the Monster Comes out of the Closet: Westley Alan Dodd in His Own Words.* Salem, Oregon: Rose Publications (1994).

King, Gary. *Driven to Kill.* New York: Windsor (1993).

Larry Eyler

Kolarik, Gera-Lind. *Freed to Kill: The True Story of Serial Murderer Larry Eyler.* New York: Avon Books (1992).

Albert Fish

Angelella, Michael. *Trail of Blood: A True Story.* New York: Bobbs-Merrill (1979).

Heimer, Mel. *The Cannibal.* New York: Lyle Stuart (1971).

Schechter, Harold. *Deranged.* New York: Pocket Books (1990).

Wertham, Frederic. *The Show of Violence.* Garden City, New York: Doubleday (1949).

Kendall Francois

Rosen, Fred. *Body Dump.* New York: Pinnacle (2002).

John Wayne Gacy

Cahill, Tim. *Buried Dreams: Inside the Mind of a Serial Killer.* New York: Bantam Books (1986).

Gacy, J. W. *Question of Doubt: The John Wayne Gacy Story.* New York: Craig Bowley Consultants (1991).

Kozenczak, Joseph and Henrikson, Karen. *A Passing Acquaintance.* New York: Carlton Press (1992).

Linedecker, Clifford L. *The Man Who Killed Boys: A True Story of Mass Murder in a Chicago Suburb.* New York: St. Martin's Press (1980).

Nelson, Mark and Oswald, Gerald. *The 34th Victim.* Westmont, Illinois: Fortune Productions (1986).

Rignall, Jeff. *29 Below.* Chicago: Wellington Press (1979).

Sullivan, Terry and Maiken, Peter T. *Killer Clown: The John Wayne Gacy Murders.* New York: Pinnacle Books (1983).

Gerald Gallego

Biondi, Ray and Hecox, Walt. *All His Father's Sins.* New York: Pocket Books (1990).

Flowers, R. Barri. *The Sex Slave Murders.* New York: St. Martin's (1996).

Van Hoffman, Eric. *A Venom in the Blood.* New York: Pinnacle (1999).

Donald "Pee Wee" Gaskins

Gaskins, Donald and Earle, Wilton. *Final Truth: The Autobiography of Mass Murderer/Serial Killer Donald "Pee Wee" Gaskins.* New York: Pinnacle Books (1993).

Hall, Frances S. *Slaughter in Carolina.* Florence, South Carolina: Hummingbird Publishers (1990).

Robin Gecht

Fletcher, Jaye Slade. *Deadly Thrills.* New York: Onyx (1995).

Ed Gein

Gollmar, Robert H. *Edward Gein.* New York: Pinnacle (1984).

Schechter, Harold. *Deviant: The Shocking True Story of the Original "Psycho."* New York: Pocket Books (1989).

Harvey Glatman

Newton, Michael. *Rope: The Twisted Life and Crimes of Harvey Glatman.* New York: Pocket Books (1998).

Wolf, Marvin J. and Mader, Katherine. *Fallen Angels.* New York: Ballantine Books (1988).

Belle Gunness

de la Torre, Lillian. *The Truth about Belle Gunness.* New York: Gold Medal (1955).

Langlois, Janet. *Belle Gunness: The Lady Bluebeard.* Bloomington: Indiana University Press (1985).

John George Haigh

Bryne, Gerald. *John George Haigh, Acid Killer.* London: J. Hill (1954).

Briffett, David. *The Acid Bath Murders.* Sussex: Field Place Press (1988).

Dunboyne, Lord. *The Trial of John George Haigh: The Acid Bath Murderer.* London: William Hodge (1953).

La Bern, Arthur. *Haigh: The Mind of a Murderer.* London: W.H. Allen & Co., Ltd. (1973).

Robert Hansen

DuClos, Bernard. *Fair Game.* New York: St. Martin's (1993).

Gilmour, Walter and Hale, Leland E. *Butcher, Baker:*

A True Account of a Serial Murderer. New York: Onyx (1991).

Neville Heath

Selwyn, Francis. *Rotten to the Core: The Life and Death of Neville Heath.* London: Routledge (1988).

Gary Heidnik

Englade, Ken. *Cellar of Horror.* New York: St. Martin's (1989).

Apsche, Jack. *Probing the Mind of a Serial Killer.* Morrisville, Pennsylvania: International Information Associates (1993).

William Heirens

Downs, Thomas. *Murder Man.* New York: Dell (1984).

Freeman, Lucy. *Before I Kill More.* New York: Crown (1955).

Kallio, Lauri E. *Confess or Die: The Case of William Heirens.* New York: Minerva Press (1999).

Kennedy, Dolores. *William Heirens: His Day in Court.* Chicago: Bonus Books. (1991).

Lindberg, Richard. *Return to the Scene of the Crime.* Nashville: Cumberland House Publishers (1999).

Hillside Stranglers

O'Brien, Darcy. *Two of a Kind: The Hillside Stranglers.* New York: New American Library (1985).

Schwarz, Ted. *The Hillside Strangler.* Garden City, New York: Doubleday (1981).

H. H. Holmes

See HERMAN MUDGETT.

Joseph Kallinger

Downs, Thomas. *The Door-to-Door Killer.* New York: Dell (1984).

Schreiber, Flora R. *The Shoemaker: The Anatomy of a Psychotic.* New York: Signet (1983).

Ed Kemper

Cheney, Margaret. *The Co-Ed Killer.* New York: Walker and Co. (1976).

Damio, Ward. *Urge to Kill.* New York: Pinnacle (1974).

Paul John Knowles

Fawkes, Sandy. *Killing Time: Journey into Nightmare.* London: Peter Owen (1977).

Randy Kraft

McDougal, Dennis. *Angel of Darkness.* New York: Warner Books (1991).

Peter Kürten

Berg, Karl. *The Sadist.* London: Heinemann (1945).

Wagner, Margaret Seaton. *The Monster of Düsseldorf.* London: Faber and Faber (1932).

Leonard Lake and Charles Ng

Harrington, Joseph and Burger, Robert. *Eye of Evil.* New York: St. Martin's (1993).

Harrington, Joseph and Burger, Robert. *Justice Denied: The Ng Case, the Most Infamous and Expensive Murder Case in History.* New York: Plenum Press (1999).

Lasseter, Don. *Die for Me: The Terrifying True Story of the Charles Ng and Leonard Lake Torture Murders.* New York: Pinnacle Books (2000).

Owens, Greg and Henton, Darcy. *No Kill, No Thrill: The Shocking True Story of Charles Ng.* Calgary, Canada: Red Deer Press (2001).

Henri Landru

Bardens, Dennis. *The Lady Killer: The Life of Landru, the French Bluebeard.* London: P. Davies. (1972).

Papa, Juliet. *Lady Killer.* New York: St. Martin's (1995).

Wakefield, Russell. *Landru: The French Bluebeard.* London: Duckworth (1936).

Bobby Joe Long

Flowers, Anna. *Bound to Die: The Shocking True Story of Bobby Joe Long, America's Most Savage Serial Killer.* New York: Pinnacle Books (1995).

Ward, Bernie. *Bobby Joe: In the Mind of a Monster.* Boca Raton, Florida: Cool Hand Communications (1995).

Wellman, Joy, McVey, Lisa and Replogle, Susan. *Smoldering Embers: The True Story of a Serial Murderer and Three Courageous Women.* Far Hills, New Jersey: New Horizon Press (1997).

Henry Lee Lucas

Call, Max. *Hand of Death: The Henry Lee Lucas Story.* Lafayette, Louisiana: Prescott Press (1985).

Cox, Mike. *The Confessions of Henry Lee Lucas.* New York: Pocket Books (1991).

Norris, Joel. *Henry Lee Lucas: The Shocking True Story of America's Most Notorious Serial Killer.* New York: Zebra (1991).

Charles Manson

Baer, Rosemary. *Reflection on the Manson Trial: Journal of a Pseudo-Juror.* Waco, Texas: Word (1972).

Bishop, George. *Witness to Evil.* Los Angeles: Nash Publishing (1971).

Bugliosi, Vincent and Gentry, Curt. *Helter Skelter.* New York: Norton (1974).

George, Edward and Matera, Dary. *Taming the Beast: Charles Manson's Life Behind Bars.* New York: St. Martin's (1998).

Gilmore, John and Kenner, Ron. *Manson: The Unholy Trail of Charlie and the Family.* Los Angeles: Amok Books (2000).

Gilmore, John and Kenner, Ron. *The Garbage People: The Trip to Helter-Skelter and Beyond with Charlie Manson and the Family.* Los Angeles: Amok Books (1996).

Livsey, Clara. *The Manson Women.* New York: Marek (1980).

Manson, Charles and Emmons, Nuel. *Manson in His Own Words.* New York: Grove Press (1986).

Sanders, Ed. *The Family.* New York: Dutton (1971).

Schiller, Lawrence and Atkins, Susan. *The Killing of Sharon Tate.* New York: New American Library (1970).

Schreck, Nikolas. *The Manson File.* New York: Amok Press (1988).

Watkins, Paul and Soledad, Guillermo. *My Life with Charles Manson.* New York: Bantam (1979).

Herman Mudgett (Dr. H. H. Holmes)

Boswell, Charles and Thompson, Lewis. *The Girls in Nightmare House.* New York: Gold Medal (1955).

Eckert, Allan W. *The Scarlet Mansion.* New York: Little, Brown (1985).

Franke, David. *The Torture Doctor.* New York: Hawthorn Books (1975).

Schechter, Harold. *Depraved: The Shocking True Story of America's First Serial Killer.* New York: Pocket Books (1998).

Herbert Mullin

Lunde, Donald T. and Morgan, Jefferson. *The Die Song: A Journey Into the Mind of a Mass Murderer.* New York: W.W. Norton (1980).

Damio, Ward. *Urge to Kill.* New York: Pinnacle (1974).

West, Don. *Sacrifice Unto Me: The 21 Santa Cruz Murders.* New York: Pyramid (1974).

Earle Leonard Nelson

Anderson, Frank. *The Dark Strangler.* Calgary: Frontier (1974).

Schechter, Harold. *Bestial: The Savage Trail of a True American Monster.* New York: Pocket Books (1998).

Dennis Nilsen

Masters, Brian. *Killing for Company: The Story of a Man Addicted to Murder.* New York: Stein and Day (1986).

McConnell, Brian and Bence, Douglas. *The Nilsen File.* London: Futura (1983).

Carl Panzram

Gaddis, Thomas. *Panzram: A Journal of Murder.* Los Angeles: Amok Books (2002).

Marcel Petiot

Grombach, John. *The Great Liquidator.* New York: Doubleday (1980).

Maeder, Thomas. *The Unspeakable Crimes of Dr. Petiot.* Boston: Little, Brown (1980).

Jesse Pomeroy

Schechter, Harold. *Fiend: The Shocking True Story of America's Youngest Serial Killer.* New York: Simon & Schuster (2000).

Dorothea Puente

Blackburn, Daniel. *Human Harvest.* Los Angeles: Knightsbridge (1990).

Richard Ramirez

Carlo, Phillip. *The Night Stalker: The Life and Crimes of Richard Ramirez.* New York: Kensington Books (1996).

Linedecker, Clifford. *Night Stalker.* New York: St. Martin's (1991).

Angel Maturino Reséndez

Clarkson, Wensley. *The Railroad Killer: The Shocking True Story of Angel Maturino Resendez.* New York: St. Martin's (1999).

Joel Rifkin

Eftimiades, Maria. *Garden of Graves: The Shocking True Story of Long Island Serial Killer Joel Rifkin.* New York: St. Martin's (1993).

Mladinich, Robert. *The Joel Rifkin Story: From the Mouth of the Monster.* New York: Pocket Books (2001).

Pulitizer, Lisa Beth and Swirsky, Joan. *Crossing the Line.* New York: Berkley (1994).

Danny Rolling

Fox, James and Levin, Jack. *Killer on Campus: The Terrifying True Story of the Gainesville Ripper.* New York: Avon Books (1996).

Philpin, John and Donnelly, John. *Beyond Murder: The Inside Account of the Gainesville Murders.* New York: Onyx (1994).

Rolling, Danny and London, Sondra. *The Making of a Serial Killer: The Real Story of the Gainesville Student Murders in the Killer's Own Words.* Portland, Oregon: Feral House (1996).

Ryzuk, Mary S. *The Gainesville Ripper: A Summer's Madness, Five Young Victims, the Investigation, the Arrest, and the Trial.* New York: St. Martin's (1995).

Charles Schmid

Gilmore, John. *Cold-Blooded: The Saga of Charles Schmid, the Notorious Pied Piper of Tucson.* Portland, Oregon: Feral House (1996).

Moser, Don and Cohen, Jerry. *The Pied Piper of Tucson.* New York: New American Library (1967).

Arthur Shawcross

Norris, Joel. *Arthur Shawcross: The Genesee River Killer.* New York: Pinnacle Books (1992).

Olsen, Jack. *The Misbegotten Son: A Serial Killer and His Victims: The True Story of Arthur Shawcross.* New York: Delacorte (1993).

Dr. Harold Shipman

Clarkson, Wensley. *Good Doctor.* London: Blake Publishing (2001).

Sitford, Mikaela. *Addicted to Murder: The True Story of Dr. Harold Shipman.* London: Virgin Publishing (2000).

Whittle, Brian and Ritchie, Jean. *Prescription for Murder.* New York: Warner Books (2000).

Charles Starkweather

Allen, William. *Starkweather: The Story of a Mass Murderer.* Boston: Houghton Mifflin (1967).

Newton, Michael. *Waste Land: The Savage Odyssey of Charles Starkweather and Caril Ann Fugate.* New York: Pocket Books (1998).

O'Donnell, Jeff. *Starkweather: A Story of Mass Murder on the Great Plains.* Lincoln, Nebraska: J&L Lee Publishers (1993).

Reinhardt, Jim. *Murderous Trail of Charles Starkweather.* Springfield, Illinois: Charles C. Thomas (1960).

Peter Sutcliffe

Beattie, John. *The Yorkshire Ripper.* London: Quartet (1981).

Burn, Gordon. *Somebody's Husband, Somebody's Son.* New York: Penguin (1990).

Cross, Roger. *The Yorkshire Ripper.* New York: Dell (1981).

Jones, Barbara. *Evil Beyond Belief.* London: Blake Publishing (1992).

Jouve, Nicole. *The Street Cleaner: The Yorkshire Ripper Case on Trial.* London: Marion Boyars (1986).

Yallop, David. *Deliver us from Evil.* New York: Coward, McCann (1982).

Michael Swango

Stewart, James. *Blind Eye: How the Medical Establishment Let a Doctor Get Away with Murder.* New York: Simon & Schuster (2000).

Fred and Rosemary West

Burn, Gordon. *Happy like Murderers.* London: Faber & Faber (1999).

Masters, Brian. *She Must Have Known: The Trial of Rosemary West.* London: Transworld Publishers (1996).

Sounes, Howard. *Fred and Rose: The Full Story of Fred and Rose West and the Gloucester House of Horrors.* London: Warner (1995).

Wansell, Geoffrey. *An Evil Love: The Life of Frederick West.* London: Headline (1996).

West, Anne. *Out of the Shadows.* London: Pocket Books (1996).

Wilson, Colin. *The Corpse Garden: The Crimes of Fred and Rose West.* London: True Crime Library (1998).

Christopher Wilder

Gibney, Bruce. *The Beauty Queen Killer.* New York: Pinnacle (1990).

Wayne Williams

Baldwin, James. *The Evidence of Things Not Seen.* New York: Holt (1995).

Dettlinger, Chet. *The List.* Atlanta: Philmay Enterprises (1983).

Headley, Bernard. *The Atlanta Youth Murders and the Politics of Race.* Carbondale, Illinois: Southern Illinois University Press (1998).

Aileen Wuornos

Reynolds, Michael. *Dead Ends.* New York: Warner Books (1992).

Russell, Sue. *Lethal Intent.* New York: Pinnacle (2002).

INDEX

© Whitney Ward

Harold Schechter is a professor of American literature and culture at Queens College, the City University of New York. Renowned for his true-crime writing, he is the author of the nonfiction books *Fiend, Bestial, Deviant, Deranged, Depraved,* and, with David Everitt, *The A to Z Encyclopedia of Serial Killers.* He is also the author of the acclaimed Edgar Allan Poe series, including *Nevermore, The Hum Bug, The Mask of Red Death,* and *The Tell-Tale Corpse.* He lives in New York State.